The Mammoth Book of
Eyewitness Britain

The Mammoth Book of
Eyewitness Britain

Edited by
JON E. LEWIS

Carroll & Graf Publishers
NEW YORK

For Tristram, Freda and Penny

Carroll & Graf Publishers
161 William Street
New York
NY 10038–2607

First published in the UK by Robinson,
an imprint of Constable & Robinson Ltd, 2001

First Carroll & Graf edition 2001

ISBN 0–7867–0929–4

Printed and bound in the United Kingdom

CONTENTS

Part Three: The Tudors & The Stuarts, 1486–1688   147

Part Four: The Age of Empire 1689–1899   251

CONTENTS

Part Five: Modern Times, 1900–2001   437

THE BRITISH ISLES

ATLANTIC
OCEAN

SCOTLAND

NORTH
SEA

Antonine Wall
AD 140—142

Edinburgh

Dunbar
1650

Hadrians Wall
AD 122—127

R. Tees

Main area of
Danish settlement
865—1016

N.IRELAND
(Partitioned 1920)

Dublin

ANGELSEY

MERCIA

Naseby 1645

EIRE

WALES

Birmingham

EAST
ANGLIA

Cardiff

R. Thames

London

Canterbury

WESSEX

Edington 878

Hastings 1066

Key

⚔ Site of battle

ENGLISH CHANNEL

FRANCE

Scale

0   50   100 miles

INTRODUCTION

There's something about Britain. One doesn't have to be a red-white-and-blue patriot to see that. Britain was the first modern country to overthrow a monarchy and establish a parliamentary Republic (even if only temporarily, before settling for an constitutional monarchy). It was the first to undergo an Industrial Revolution. In the 19th Century, it built the biggest Empire the world has ever known. In the 20th Century, Britain played the pivotal role in the crucial event, the World War of 1939–45.

Not to put too fine a point on it, Britain was the matrix of the modern world. Why? There are no easy answers, athough climate and geography have something to do with it. An offshore island, washed by the warm waves of the Gulf Stream, Britain has tended to agricultural and mineral plenty. And political and cultural independence. Many of the great historical movements which have raged through the "Continent" have either passed Britain by or become transmogrified on crossing the Channel. In Britain, for instance, Protestant Reformation became less a matter of soul-searching principle than an expediency that allowed a king, Henry VIII, to continue a dynasty and many of his subjects to rob the Church of land. Few objected. Notoriously poor followers of abstract causes, the British thus tended to avoid the traumas of medieval religious bigotry, with its burnings and witch-hunts, which exercised the Continent. This, of course, was to Britain's advantage. Anyway given by Nature a definable, easily defended boundary (the last successful invasion of the isles was in 1066, by the Normans), Britain enjoyed a stability that encouraged trade and commerce. These, aided by the sort of vigorous navy an island nation should possess, prompted colonisation of foreign parts, which only produced more markets for British goods. The flourishing of trade, particularly during and after the Cromwellian Interregnum, stimulated capitalist credit expansion, "manufactories" and invention and the Industrial Revolution. On the back of the Industrial Revolution, Britain built an empire, one that covered a quarter of the globe's land mass.

Of course, there's more to the story of Great Britain than a fortuitous position in the Atlantic and a chain reaction of historical events that led to Empire. Many would ascribe a native wit, even a racial dynamic, to Albion's tale. Others would point to God's providence; indeed, the British have long believed themselves to be God's chosen people, even the direct beneficiaries of a visit from Christ himself (think of the words of Blake's messianic hymn "Jerusalem"). Certainly, the isles' people have long convinced themselves of certain national characteristics: a love of liberty ("the freeborn Englishman", Britain's long parliamentary history): a love of tradition (the British, even on their occasions of revolt, dress their actions in the clothes of the past); a love of "fair play" (of which the rules of cricket are emblematic); and grace under fire (battles galore). Whether these national characteristics are true is hardly the point. The British perceive them as valid, and thus act sometimes, at least, in accordance with them. The causes of World War II do not exonerate the British. Aside from the appeasement of Hitler practised by British political leaders, the British went to war at base because of imperialism, the preserving of Empire and commercial influence. But the nation also went off to war because many Britons sincerely detested Nazi tyranny and bullying. And for a whole year after the Fall of France in 1940, Britain stood alone against Hitler's blitzkrieg.

In other words, Britain is a worthwhile object of study, and not only for those that are its sons and daughters. The way of the world for the last half millennium is inexplicable without reference to Shakespeare's "sceptr'd isle". The history of Britain is also, dare say it, just plain interesting: Guy Fawkes' plot to blow up Parliament, Boudicca's revolt, the Black Hole of Calcutta, the Great Fire of London, England Winning the World Cup, the Execution of Mary Queen of Scots . . . events don't get more colourful than these.

All these happenings, plus three hundred others, are described on the following pages by those who saw them at first hand, eyewitnesses to the deed. The selection does not pretend to be exhaustive; this is not the complete and utter history of Britain in first person accounts. Most historical episodes – those which have influenced the course of national proceedings are "eyewitnessed", as are the Big Themes: the growth of empire (and its decline), the rise of parliament, the creation of Britain from the disparate nations of England, Wales, Scotland and Ireland. There are also eyewitness accounts illustrating the history of social improvement, the long march of Everyman and Everywoman. After all, the past is not just the doings of kings and queens, ministers and soldiers. To this end there are various vignettes of "how we lived" in days gone by, together with accounts of the struggles by which the people improved their lot. It may be unfashionable to say it, but the dignities and benefits enjoyed by 21st century British man, woman and child were won by mass protest over the previous hundreds of years. Nothing – the vote, old age pensions, free speech – has ever been given without the demanding of them.

If the peoples' lot has improved, the people of Britain have changed remarkably little in their habits and likes over two thousand years. You only have to look at the fifteenth century recipe for pork pie to see that, or William Clarke's account of a day at Brighton beach in 1736. Or to read that one of the glories of Norman London was the gardens of its inhabitants. Napoleon once jibed that the British were a nation of shopkeepers. He was wrong. They are a nation of peasant farmers, and even when removed from the land by urbanisation and industrialisation they created the facsimile of a farm complete with a lawn standing in for a meadow in their back gardens.

There remains the question of how valuable *is* eye-witness testimony? It is of course, the very building material of historical narratives, since all accounts of the past which are not pure guesswork ultimately derive from the pen of someone who "was there". More than that, eye-witness testimony has in the best hands (or optical fibres) the vividness which makes the past come alive and allows the modern day reader to enter the mind frame of an age. It allows the joys of experiencing eras gone by without enduring their hazards. A sort of written virtual reality tour. Of course, readers should be judiciously suspicious of the material on the following pages, because as everyone knows memories play tricks. But while there may be mistakes of detail in the extracts, the eyewitness will always be the most authentic communicant of what an event looked, sounded and felt like. As a rule, I have only included accounts of direct eye-witnesses, yet like most rules this rule was worth breaking several times. And I have done so in the opening sections, "Ancient and Dark Age Britain" and "The Medieval Era", where first hand sources are relatively scarce. So without much apology, I have included here commentators whose accounts are based on the eye-witness words of others. Tactitus, who surely founded his writings on Britain on discussion with his father-in-law Agricola, comes to mind. So too does Henry of Huntingdon, whose description of Canute defying the waves is the first putting to paper of a long oral tradition.

Exception aside, this is a book by those who can say "I was there". Captain Hardy saw what happened at the battle of Trafalgar, Edward Grim watched Thomas a Becket being murdered, Samuel Pepys gazed in trepidation at the Great Fire of London, Edward Jenner invented vaccination, Edmund Hillary climbed Everest, Guy Gibson flew a Lancaster on the "dambusters raid".

And you can, too.

CHRONOLOGY

KEY DATES	HISTORY, POLITICS, WAR	RELIGION, SCIENCE, CULTURE	SOCIAL LIFE
55–54 BC	Julius Caesar's expeditions to Britain		
AD 43	Claudian invasion; beginning of Roman occupation		
c50	Foundation of London		
61	Boudicca's revolt		
122	Hadrian's Wall begun		
166		First church built at Glastonbury	
383	"Magnus Maximus" declared Emperor in Britain		
410	End of Roman occupation		
449	Beginning of Saxon invasion		
c518	Battle of Mons Badonicus		
597		St. Augustine arrives in Kent	

KEY DATES	HISTORY, POLITICS, WAR	RELIGION, SCIENCE, CULTURE	SOCIAL LIFE
627		Conversion of Edwin of Northumbria to Christianity	
644		Synod of Whitby	
716	Aethelbald becomes King of Mercia	*Beowulf* composed	
731		Bede completes his *Ecclestiastical History*	Offa introduces silver penny in Mercia
793–5	Danish raids on Lindisfarne and Jarrow		
865	"Great Army" of the Danes lands in East Anglia		
878	Alfred defeats Danes at Edington/Dane law established	*The Anglo-Saxon Chronicle* begun	
1016	Canute becomes King of England		
1066	Duke William of Normandy defeats Harold at Hastings to become King of England		
1086	Domesday survey		
1100	Death of William Rufus;		
1110	accession of Henry I	First Miracle Play performed	
1139–53	Civil war between King Stephen and supporters of Empress Matilda		
1167		Foundation of Oxford University	

KEY DATES	HISTORY, POLITICS, WAR	RELIGION, SCIENCE, CULTURE	SOCIAL LIFE
1170		Murder of St. Thomas à Becket	glass windows in English houses
1189–1199	Reign of Richard I, "Lionheart"		
1215	Magna Carta		St. George's Day becomes national holiday in England
1282–3	Edward I's conquest of Wales		
1314	Scots victorious at Bannockburn		
1337	Hundred Years War begins		
1346	English longbow victorious at Crecy		
1348	"Black Death" appears in England		
1362		First version of Langland's *Piers Plowman*	
1381	Peasants' Revolt		
1390		Chaucer completes *The Canterbury Tales*	
1415	Battle of Agincourt		
1467			"Fute-ball" and golf prohibited in Scotland
c1471		William Caxton prints first books in English	
1485	Richard III defeated at Bosworth; Henry VII accedes to throne of England		
1509	Coronation of Henry VIII		
1516		Thomas More's *Utopia* published	

KEY DATES	HISTORY, POLITICS, WAR	RELIGION, SCIENCE, CULTURE	SOCIAL LIFE
1519			Hops introduced into England
1533	Henry VII marries Anne Boleyn; Princess Elizabeth born		
1536	Dissolution of Monasteries		First public records of cricket
1555	"Marian Reaction" against Protestants begins		
1558	Accession of Elizabeth I		
1562	Hawkins begins slave trade between Africa-West Indies		
1565			Tobacco introduced into England; First public lottery in England
1587	Execution of Mary, Queen of Scots		
1588	Defeat of Spanish Armada		
1590		Shakespeare publishes *Henry VI*	Water closets introduced at Queen's Palace, Richmond
1603	Accession of James I		
1605	Gunpowder Plot		
1607	Settlement of Virginia		
1611		Authorized Version of Bible published	
1625	Accession of Charles I		
1642–6	English Civil War		
1648	Second Civil War; Scots and King defeated		

KEY DATES	HISTORY, POLITICS, WAR	RELIGION, SCIENCE, CULTURE	SOCIAL LIFE
1649	Charles I executed		
1649–50	Cromwell conquers Ireland		
1652	Cromwell conquers Scotland		
1653	Cromwell becomes Lord Protector		
1658	Cromwell dies		
1660	Stuarts restored to throne in shape of Charles I		
1665		Newton discovers gravity	Great Plague
1666			Great Fire of London
1675		Wren begins build of St Paul's Cathedral, London	
1678		Publication of Bunyan's *Pilgrim's Progress*	
1688	"The Glorious Revolution"; William of Orange accedes to English throne		
1690	Irish Jacobites defeated at Battle of the Boyne		
1694	Bank of England founded		
1704	Marlborough wins Battle of Blenheim		
1707	Act of Union with Scotland		
1712		Last execution for witchcraft in England	
1720	South Sea Bubble		
1721	Walpole's first ministry		
1729		Wesley founds Methodism	

KEY DATES	HISTORY, POLITICS, WAR	RELIGION, SCIENCE, CULTURE	SOCIAL LIFE
1731		Tull's *Horse-Hoeing Husbandry* published	
1733		Kay invents flying-shuttle	
1740		*Rule Britannia* composed by Arne	
1745	Jacobite Rebellion of Bonnie Prince Charlie		
1752			Gregorian Calendar introduced
1756	British soldiers confined in "Black Hole of Calcutta"		
1757	Clive wins Battle of Plassey		
1759	British capture Quebec in Seven Years War		
1760	Accession of George III		
1761		*Tristram Shandy* by Sterne published	
1769		Watt's steam engine patented	
1770	Cook discovers Botany Bay, Australia		
1773	Boston Tea Party protest		
1775	American War of Independence (until 1783)	Adam Smith's *Wealth of Nations* published	
1780	Gordon Riots	First steam powered cotton mill, Manchester.	Epsom Derby founded
1791		Thomas Paine,	
1792		*The Rights of Man*	Gas lighting introduced
1793	Britain joins war against revolutionary France		

KEY DATES	HISTORY, POLITICS, WAR	RELIGION, SCIENCE, CULTURE	SOCIAL LIFE
1796		Vaccination against smallpox	
1801	Union with Ireland		
1803	Napoleonic War begins	Caledonian canal started	
1805	Nelson victorious over Franco-Spanish fleet at Trafalgar		
1806		Trevithick's railway at Coalbrookdale completed	
1811			Luddism at peak
1813		Jane Austen's *Pride and Prejudice* published	
1815	Battle of Waterloo ends Napoleonic Wars. Corn Law passed		
1819	Peterloo massacre of reform protestors		
1820	Coronation of George IV		
1825	Trade Unions legalized. Stockton & Darlington Railway opens		
1828	Wellington becomes Prime Minister		
1829	Metropolitan Police founded	Catholic emancipation	
1830	Death of George III		First major cholera epidemic
1834	Transportation of "Tolpuddle Martyrs"		
1837	Accession of Queen Victoria		

KEY DATES	HISTORY, POLITICS, WAR	RELIGION, SCIENCE, CULTURE	SOCIAL LIFE
1838	People's Charter drafted		
1844–5	Irish potato famine		
1846	Repeal of Corn Laws		
1847		Marx and Engels, Communist Manifesto	
1848			Cholera epidemic
1851		Great Exhibition	
1854–6	Crimean War		
1857–8	Indian Mutiny		
1859		Darwin, Origin of Species	
1866			Atlantic cable laid
1868	Disraeli becomes PM		
1871	Trades Union Act		Bank holidays introduced; first FA cup
1876			Agricultural depression
1879	Zulu War	Bell invents telephone	
1882	Britain occupies Egypt		
1886	Burma annexed		Rover manufacture safety bicycle
1888			Jack the Ripper active
1889	London Dock Strike		
1896		Daily Mail launched	
1897	Victoria's Diamond Jubilee		
1899–1902	Second Boer War		
1900	Labour Representation Committee formed	Premiere of Elgar's Dream of Gerontius	

KEY DATES	HISTORY, POLITICS, WAR	RELIGION, SCIENCE, CULTURE	SOCIAL LIFE
1901	Death of Victoria, accession of Edward VII		
1905			Motor buses in London;
1908–15	Asquith heads Liberal Government		Picadily and Bakerloo "tubes" opened
1909	Employment exchanges introduced	Bleriot flies Channel	Old age pension commences
1911	Parliament curtails power of House of Lords;		
1912	National Insurance Act	Scott reaches South pole	Women's suffrage movement at peak
1914–18	First World War; Irish Home Rule Act passed		
1916	Battles of the Somme and Jutland		Daylight Saving and conscription introduced
1918	Lloyd George coalition government returned; franchise extended to women over 30		Marie Stopes, *Married Love*
1919	Strike wave		Welwyn
1920			Garden City begun
1922		James Joyce, *Ulysses*	
1924	Labour Government returned		
1926	General Strike		
1927		BBC founded	
1928		DH Lawrence, *Lady Chatterley's Lover*	
1932	Mosley founds British Union of Fascists		
1935		First BBC TV broadcast	

KEY DATES	HISTORY, POLITICS, WAR	RELIGION, SCIENCE, CULTURE	SOCIAL LIFE
1936	Jarrow March against unemployment; Edward VIII abdicates		
1937	Chamberlain becomes PM		
1938	Munich Agreement		
1939–45	World War II		Conscription introduced
1940	Churchill becomes PM; Battle of Britain		Rationing; "Blitz" on London and South
1942	Singapore falls; British win at El Alamein		
1943	Invasion of Sicily		
1944	Invasion of Normandy; Butler Education Act		
1945	Landslide Labour government		
1946	National Health Service Act passed; coal industry nationalised		
1947	India becomes independent		Fuel crisis
1949	Eire independent	Geoerge Orwell, *1984*	
1950	Korean War (until 1953)		
1952	Accession of Elizabeth II		
1953	Hillary and Tenzing Norgay climb Everest		
1956	Anglo-French force invades Suez zone	John Osborne's *Look Back in Anger*	
1958	Race riots in Notting Hill		
1959			First motorway opens
1961	South Africa leaves Commonwealth		

KEY DATES	HISTORY, POLITICS, WAR	RELIGION, SCIENCE, CULTURE	SOCIAL LIFE
1962		Beatles sign recording contract	
1963	Profumo scandal; Beeching report on railways		
1965	Churchill dies		
1966			England win World Cup
1969	Troops sent to N. Ireland		Open University chartered
1971			Decimal currency introduced
1972	"Bloody Sunday" in N. Ireland		
1973	Britain joins EEC		Energy crisis; VAT introduced
1974	Miners' strike brings down Heath Government; Labour assumes power		
1976		Sex Pistol's perform "Anarchy in the UK";	
1978		Concorde makes first passenger flight	
1979	Conservatives under Margaret Thatcher form Government (until 1990)		
1980	SAS relieve siege of Princes Gate, London		
1981	Social Democratic Party formed (after split from Labour)		
1982	Falklands/Malvinas War		
1984–5	Miners' strike		

KEY DATES	HISTORY, POLITICS, WAR	RELIGION, SCIENCE, CULTURE	SOCIAL LIFE
1986	Channel Treaty signed Stock Exchange collapse		
1989	Poll Tax introduced		
1990	Thatcher resigns as PM; John Major becomes PM		
1991	Persian Gulf War		
1997	British cede Hong Kong to China; Diana, Princess of Wales, killed in car crash, Paris; Labour Government elected		
1999			Total eclipse of the sun
2000		Human genome mapped	
2001			Foot and mouth epidemic

Part One

Ancient & Dark Age Britain
55 BC–AD 1066

"Their sky is obscured by continual rain and cloud . . ."
>
> The Roman historian Tacitus
> on the weather of the Britons

INTRODUCTION

"This precious stone set in a silver sea" is how the Elizabethan playwright (and patriot) William Shakespeare described Britain. The local boy's exultation is forgiveable; the image of Britain surrounded by glorious waves is defining. It was Britain's island existence, its separateness from the rest of the world, that made the isles and the people distinct. Even superior. A difference only underlined by a naval prowess that saw off the Spanish Armada, defeated the perfidious French at Trafalgar and kept the nation supplied during the blitzkrieg of Corporal Hitler.

It is perhaps an irony for so proud an island race that their ancestors walked on landlubber's feet to Britannia. They did so about 40,000 years ago by the simple expedient of crossing over the isthmus that then connected the "peninsula" of Britain to France. Even after the Atlantic flooded through to create the Dover Straits 9000 years BC, Stone Age man could easily ford the waters. It was only with rising sea levels that salt water began to afford the sceptred isle a degree of God-given protection and isolation.

If salt water deterred tribal migration, it did not stop it. Among the later immigrants were blue-eyed Iron Age Celts who, from 300 BC, began arriving (by boat) in family and tribal bands and drove the earlier inhabitants into the mountains of the west and into legend as "the little people". The Celts were quarrelsome and endlessly warring (among themselves, if no one else could be found to fight), but they were agriculturalists too. Alongside their looming hill-forts, they established farms, villages, and made lanes for farm traffic, and cleared forests for arable crops. By 100 BC an advanced plough, and the hacking of thousands of iron axes, allowed, in addition to the farming of the uplands, the turning of the deep soils of lowland South East England. On the back of this agriculture and a native climate given to glorious green temperateness, the population rose to around 500,000 souls.

It was into this developing Celtic agrarian society that the Romans burst like a squall. Julius Caesar gave noble reasons (exploitation of mineral resources, prevention of Celtic arms-running to their blood cousins in Gaul) for his 55 BC invasion of the land he would name 'Britannia', but personal ambition lurked in the foreground. The conquest of Britain would have brought wealth and public prestige. Wealth and prestige would have brought high office. When his invasions of 55 BC and 54 BC were rebuffed, Caesar hit on the expedient of fabling his exploits to a credulous populace in Rome instead.

If Caesar's invasions failed, they put Britain on the Roman map. Once there, eventual conquest, which began in AD 43 (after the 40,000 shining-armoured legionnaires could be persuaded to get into the boats), was always inevitable. A number of British tribes resisted fiercely but superior Roman tactics and arms prevailed. The British also suffered from the curse of farmer-warriors everywhere; they had to stop fighting to tend their crops.

For four hundred years, Britain remained the far-flung outpost of the Roman empire. *Pax Romana* brought straight roads and trappings of civilization. But not many. Only Bath reached any real level of luxury and only Lincoln had sewers. A Romanized British aristocracy helped run the show in the South, but in the North and in Wales the Romans relied on their one true friend, the sword, and built garrisons at Chester, York and Caerleon. Scotland was never conquered, despite the best efforts of Agricola; instead the Romans put up Hadrian's Wall (AD 122) and the Antonine Wall (AD 142) and sheltered behind them from the Picts.

Roman civilization in Britain may have been a poor thing, but it was civilization – from the latin *civitas*, living in a city. The Roman occupation saw the development of tens of towns, five of which achieved municipal status. There was literacy. And, eventually, Christianity.

The relative splendour that was Roman Britain began to decline around AD 350. The empire was anyway sagging under the weight of fiscal crises and a parasitic upper-class, and had little interest its most far-flung colony. (Roman governors, conversely, tended to find Britannia a useful base to launch bids for the imperial crown.) More and more legions were withdrawn from the island to protect other, more valuable, possessions from the raids of Germanic barbarian nomads.

In 410 Britain ceased to be a Roman possession. Thereafter it slipped quickly into the Dark Ages, fought over by romanized Britons and Picts. And, from 430, the latest wave of invaders, Angles, Saxons and Jutes, who rowed to Britain in open boats from northern Germany and Denmark. It is to this shadowy, almost recordless age, that Arthur belongs, a semi-legendary war-leader associated with the British victory at *Mons Badonicus* in c. 500. Arthur and *Mons Badonicus* not withstanding, the Angles and Saxons pushed relentlessly westwards from their landings in the east and south. By the end of the seventh century, the Anglo-Saxon kingdoms of Kent, Sussex (South Saxons), Essex (East Saxons), Wessex (West Saxons), East Anglia, Mercia and Northumbria covered most of England.

What happened to the British? Some were pushed into the West (Cornwall held out until 838) and especially Wales, taking their Christianity with them to found hundreds of little monasteries in the mountains. Some were enslaved. More were killed, either by war or its faithful attendant, disease. Romano-British civilization was almost entirely wiped off the face of 'Angelcyn' (England) as the newcomers called the isles. A non-urban people, the Anglo-Saxons even turned up their noses at the land's towns.

The Anglo-Saxons were not only agriculturalists. They were pagans. Eventually they were Christianized by the missions sent by Rome (Saint Augustine landed in 597) and Saint Patrick's Irish Church, but not without several bouts of recidividism. These then were the English: a sea-faring people, inclined to fighting and farming and, up to a point, religion.

For three centuries thereafter, the Anglo-Saxons created a recognizably English language, culture and landscape. They even melded a national identity that transcended kith and tribe, for how else could the Venerable Bede title his master work of 731 *A History of the English Church and People*? People, not Peoples.

The work of national advance was rudely interrupted in the late eighth century by the Vikings. A pagan warrior people uncannily similar to the Angles and Saxons of yore, the Vikings did what every other hitherto unwelcome visitor to Albion had done. Raided a bit, liked what they saw, and decided on conquest. The Vikings penetrated most of the isles, with Scotland, Ireland, South Wales and the North West being settled by Norwegians (Norsemen) and East England by the Danes; the South, Midlands and West of England were saved for the English by the campaigns of Alfred the Great (849–99). A century later, however, England finally fell to the Danes, when Cnut was crowned king of England. Yet, rather than Cnut (Canute) imposing Danish Customs on the English, he became thoroughly Anglicized himself and ruled as a native monarch.

Something similar happened in 1066. In that year Duke William of Normandy defeated the Englishman Harold for the throne of England. William, a tough warrior (Normans being Christianized Norse settlers from France), won the battle of Hastings but the war was won by the English. For when William came to rule he left most of English society in place.

JULIUS CAESAR INVADES BRITAIN, 55 BC

Julius Caesar

Caesar's invasion was intended to prevent the Britons from aiding their subjugated kinsmen in Gaul. He writes in the third person.

. . . and so it was about 10 a.m. when Caesar arrived off Britain with the leading ships. Armed men could be seen stationed on all the heights, and the nature of the place was such, with the shore edged by sheer cliffs, that missiles could be hurled onto the beach from the top. Caesar considered this a totally unsuitable place for disembarkation, and waited at anchor till 3 p.m. for the rest of his invasion fleet to assemble. He then summoned a meeting of his brigade and battalion commanders, revealed the news he had from Volusenus, and outlined his orders. He wanted them to be ready to act immediately, on the slightest sign from him. For military practice demanded this, especially in a naval attack, which was liable to rapid, unexpected changes of circumstance. Dismissing his officers, he waited for a favourable combination of wind and tide, and then gave the signal to weigh anchor. Sailing on for about seven miles, he halted his line opposite an open, level beach.

The barbarians had discovered Caesar's plan by sending forward cavalry units and charioteers (a very common method of fighting with them). Their main force which had followed later was now in a position to prevent our men from disembarking. This caused considerable difficulty. The ships could only be drawn up in deep water because of their draught. The soldiers were faced with unknown ground and had their hands impeded, while they were burdened with a very heavy load of arms. And yet they had to leap down from the ships, keep their footing in the waves and fight the enemy. The latter, on the other hand, could either resist from dry land or by moving just a little forward into the shallows. So, completely unencumbered and with full knowledge of the ground, they boldly hurled their missiles, badly disturbing the horses which were totally unused to the conditions. Our men were shaken by these circumstances through lack of experience of this style of warfare, and failed to show the same dash and enthusiasm as they did in land battles.

As Caesar noticed this, he gave orders to the warships to row off slightly to the enemy's open flank away from the cargo ships. These ships were less well known to the barbarians and much more manoeuvrable. They were to halt, attack and move the enemy back by the use of slings, arrows and other missiles. All this helped our men considerably. The barbarians were affected by the strange shape of the ships, by the motion of the oars and the unusual type of catapult. Halting their advance, they slowly began to retire.

Our troops, however, were still hesitating, largely because of the depth of the sea, when the standard-bearer of the Tenth legion, with a prayer to the gods for a happy outcome for his legion, shouted, "Jump down, men, unless you want the enemy to get your standard. You will not find me failing in my duty to my country or my leader." This he yelled at the top of his voice, and then springing off the boat began to bear the eagle forward against the enemy. Our troops, with mutual words of encouragement not to commit a terrible wrong, all jumped down into the sea. Their fellows in the next boats saw what they were doing, followed suit and came to grips with the enemy . . .

Fighting was tough on both sides. My men could not keep in line, get a firm foothold or keep to their own standards. Each man joined the nearest unit irrespective of his ship and chaos reigned. The enemy knew the lie of the shoals and when they saw from the beach isolated groups disembarking they made a mounted charge

and attacked them in their difficulties. These they outnumbered
and surrounded, while their comrades raked the main party with
an enfilade. Caesar assessed the situation and had both the boats of
the warships and the sloops packed with soldiers to help wherever
he saw need. Our men reached the land and were there reinforced
by all those behind.

Then came the assault which routed the enemy, but we could
not follow up satisfactorily as the cavalry had failed to hold its
course and make the island. The enemy lost the day. As soon as
they could stop bolting they sent a peace delegation to Caesar.
Commius, the Atrebatian, came along with it. It was he whom
Caesar had sent to Britain to bring that general's instructions; but
they had seized him as soon as he stepped ashore and clapped him
in irons. The outcome of our victory was his release. In sueing for
peace they attributed this outrage to the lower classes and asked
him to let it pass as an act of their folly. Caesar protested at their
unprovoked aggression after they had taken it upon themselves to
send a delegation over to the continent to make peace with him.
Yet he forgave their folly and demanded hostages. Some they
delivered on the spot but promised to send for the others from up-
country in a few days. Meanwhile they demobilized the tribesmen,
and the chiefs came in from all quarters to surrender themselves
and their countries to Caesar. Thus peace was made within four
days of the landing in Britain.

The *pax* proved temporary and the British resumed campaigning.

A CHARIOT FIGHT, 55 BC

Julius Caesar

Meanwhile the Seventh legion was out on a routine foraging
mission without any thought of action as there were still people
on the farms and traffic in and out of the camp. Suddenly the
guards at the gate reported to Caesar an exceptional quantity of
dust where the legion had gone. Caesar rightly sensed a new native
stratagem. He told the two duty cohorts to follow him and the
other two to relieve them, and the rest to arm and follow at once.
After a short march he saw his troops pressed by the enemy almost
to breaking point with the legion undeployed and subject to cross-
fire. For the corn had been reaped in every district except one and
the enemy had guessed they would go there and had prepared an

ambush by night in the woods. Our men were scattered, busy reaping with arms piled, when the attack began. They killed some, put the others into confusion and surrounded them with both cavalry and chariots.

A chariot fight is like this: first they scour the field shooting and this often breaks the line just with the fear of the horses and the din of wheels. When they have infiltrated among the cavalry units they jump down and fight as infantry. Meanwhile the drivers withdraw a bit to wait where they can quickly escape to base if compelled by weight of numbers. Thus they show the dash of cavalry and the steadiness of infantry in action. Daily drill teaches them the habit of checking their steeds even in full career down a steep slope, of lightning turns and of running along the pole, standing on the yoke and getting back quickly into the chariot.

Caesar brought help in the nick of time to our men for they were dismayed by such novel tactics.

Caesar withdrew from Britain in 55 BC, only to reinvade in the following year.

THE BRITONS, 54 BC

Julius Caesar

The population is large with many buildings which follow practically the Gallic style. Cattle are numerous and they use brass or iron rings of fixed weights for currency. Tin occurs in the midlands, and a little iron near the coast. They import bronze. Varieties of timber are as in Gaul, except beech and fir. They have a taboo against eating hare, cock or goose, but rear them for sport. It is more temperate than Gaul and winter milder . . . The inhabitants of Kent are the most civilized as it is maritime and their customs are much like the Gallic. Inland, corn is little grown, but they live on milk and meat and wear skins. Most Britons are dyed with blue woad and this makes them look fiercer as warriors. They have long hair and shave everywhere except their heads and moustaches.

Troubles in Gaul forced Caesar to retreat from Britain again. It was not until AD 43, under Emperor Claudius, that the Romans successfully colonized England and Wales. Scotland remained unconquered.

THE ROMANS MASSACRE THE DRUIDS, AD 61

Cornelius Tacitus

The Druids were the priesthood of the Celts, whose main religious centre was the island of Anglesey off Wales. The historian Tacitus was the son-in-law of the Roman general Agricola, Governor of Britain, AD 78–87.

On the opposite shore stood the Britons, close embodied, and prepared for action. Women were seen running through the ranks in wild disorder; their apparel funeral; their hair loose to the wind, in their hands flaming torches, and their whole appearance resembling the frantic rage of the Furies. The Druids were ranged in order, with hands uplifted, invoking the gods, and pouring forth horrible imprecations. The novelty of the fight struck the Romans with awe and terror. They stood in stupid amazement, as if their limbs were benumbed, riveted to one spot, a mark for the enemy. The exhortations of the general diffused new vigour through the ranks, and the men, by mutual reproaches, inflamed each other to deeds of valour. They felt the disgrace of yielding to a troop of women, and a band of fanatic priests; they advanced their standards, and rushed on to the attack with impetuous fury.

The Britons perished in the flames, which they themselves had kindled. The island fell, and a garrison was established to retain it in subjection. The religious groves, dedicated to superstition and barbarous rites, were levelled to the ground. In those recesses, the natives [stained] their altars with the blood of their prisoners, and in the entrails of men explored the will of the gods.

BOUDICCA REVOLTS, AD 61

Cornelius Tacitus

The rapacity and callousness of Roman rule led to an uprising under Boudicca (Boadicea), Queen of the Iceni. Tacitus noted of the Britons that they could "bear to be ruled by others but not be their slaves".

Prasutagus, the late king of the Icenians, in the course of a long reign had amassed considerable wealth. By his will he left the whole to his two daughters and the emperor in equal shares, conceiving, by that stroke of policy, that he should provide at once for the tranquility of his kingdom and his family.

The event was otherwise. His dominions were ravaged by the centurions; the slaves pillaged his house, and his effects were seized as lawful plunder. His wife, Boudicca, was disgraced with cruel stripes; her daughters were ravished, and the most illustrious of the Icenians were, by force, deprived of the positions which had been transmitted to them by their ancestors. The whole country was considered as a legacy bequeathed to the plunderers. The relations of the deceased king were reduced to slavery.

Exasperated by their acts of violence, and dreading worse calamities, the Icenians had recourse to arms. The Trinobantians joined in the revolt. The neighboring states, not as yet taught to crouch in bondage, pledged themselves, in secret councils, to stand forth in the cause of liberty. What chiefly fired their indignation was the conduct of the veterans, lately planted as a colony at Camulodunum. These men treated the Britons with cruelty and oppression; they drove the natives from their habitations, and calling them by the (shameful) names of slaves and captives, added insult to their tyranny. In these acts of oppression, the veterans were supported by the common soldiers; a set of men, by their habits of life, trained to licentiousness, and, in their turn, expecting to reap the same advantages. The temple built in honour of Claudius was another cause of discontent. In the eye of the Britons it seemed the citadel of eternal slavery. The priests, appointed to officiate at the altars, with a pretended zeal for religion, devoured the whole substance of the country. To over-run a colony, which lay quite naked and exposed, without a single fortification to defend it, did not appear to the incensed and angry Britons an enterprise that threatened either danger or difficulty. The fact was, the Roman generals attended to improvements to taste and elegance, but neglected the useful. They embellished the province, and took no care to defend it.

While the Britons were preparing to throw off the yoke, the statue of victory, erected at Camulodunum, fell from its base, without any apparent cause, and lay extended on the ground with its face averted, as if the goddess yielded to the enemies of Rome. Women in restless ecstasy rushed among the people, and with frantic screams denounced impending ruin. In the council-chamber of the Romans hideous clamours were heard in a foreign accent; savage howlings filled the theatre, and near the mouth of the Thames the image of a colony in ruins was seen in the transparent water; the sea was purpled with blood, and, at the tide of ebb, the figures of human bodies were traced in the sand. By these appearances the Romans were sunk in despair, while the Britons anticipated a glorious victory. Suetonius, in the meantime, was detained in the isle of Mona. In this alarming crisis, the veterans sent to Catus Decianus, the procurator of the province, for a reinforcement. Two hundred men, and those not completely armed, were all that officer could spare. The colony had but a handful of soldiers. Their temple was strongly fortified, and there they hoped to make a stand. But even for the defense of that place no measures were concerted. Secret enemies mixed in all their deliberations. No fosse was made; no palisade thrown up; nor were the women, and such as were disabled by age or infirmity, sent out of the garrison. Unguarded and unprepared, they were taken by surprise, and, in the moment of profound peace, overpowered by the Barbarians in one general assault. The colony was laid waste with fire and sword.

The temple held out, but, after a siege of two days, was taken by storm. Petilius Cerealis, who commanded the ninth legion, marched to the relief of the place. The Britons, flushed with success, advanced to give him battle. The legion was put to the rout, and the infantry cut to pieces. Cerealis escaped with the cavalry to his entrenchments. Catus Decianus, the procurator of the province, alarmed at the scene of carnage which he beheld on every side, and further dreading the indignation of a people, whom by rapine and oppression he had driven to despair, betook himself to flight, and crossed over into Gaul.

Suetonius, undismayed by this disaster, marched through the heart of the country as far as London; a place not dignified with the name of a colony, but the chief residence of merchants, and the great mart of trade and commerce. At that place he meant to fix the feat of war; but reflecting on the scanty numbers of his little army, and the fatal rashness of Cerealis, he resolved to quit the station, and, by giving up one post, secure the rest of the province. Neither supplications, nor the tears of the inhabitants could induce him to change his plan. The signal for the march was given. All who chose to follow his banners were taken under his protection. Of all who, on account of their advanced age, the weakness of their sex, of the attractions of the situation, thought proper to remain behind, not one escaped the rage of the Barbarians. The inhabitants of Verulamium, a municipal town, were in like manner put to the sword. The genius of a savage people leads them always in quest of plunder; and, accordingly, the Britons left behind them all places of strength. Wherever they expected feeble resistance, and considerable booty, there they were sure to attack with the fiercest rage. Military skill was not the talent of Barbarians. The number massacred in the places which have been mentioned, amounted to no less than seventy thousand, all citizens or allies of Rome. To make prisoners, and reserve them for slavery, or to exchange them, was not in the idea of a people, who despised all the laws of war. The halter and the gibbet, slaughter and defoliation, fire and sword, were the marks of savage valour. Aware that vengeance would overtake them, they were resolved to make sure of their revenge, and glut themselves with the blood of their enemies.

The fourteenth legion, with the veterans of the twentieth, and the auxiliaries from the adjacent stations, having joined Suetonius, his army amounted to little less than ten thousand men. Thus reinforced, he resolved, without loss of time, to bring on a decisive action. For this purpose he chose a spot encircled with woods, narrow at the entrance, and sheltered in the rear by a thick forest. In that situation he had no fear of an ambush. The enemy, he knew, had no approach but in front. An open plain lay before him. He drew up his men in the following order: the legions in close array formed the center, the light armed troops were stationed at hand to serve as occasion might require: the cavalry took post in the wings. The Britons brought into the field an incredible multitude. They formed no regular line of battle. Detached parties and loose battalions displayed their numbers, in frantic transport bounding with exultation, and so sure of victory, that they placed their wives in wagons at the extremity of the plain, where they might survey the scene of action, and behold the wonders of British valour.

Boudicca, in a chariot, with her two daughters before her, drove through the ranks. She harangued the different nations in their turn: "This," she said, "is not the first time that the Britons have been led to battle by a woman." But now she did not come to boast the pride of a long line of ancestry, nor even to recover her kingdom and the plundered wealth of her family. She took the field, like the meanest among them, to assert the cause of public liberty, and to seek revenge for her body seamed with ignominious stripes, and her two daughters infamously ravished. "From the pride and arrogance of the Romans nothing is sacred; all are subject to violation; the old endure the scourge, and the virgins are deflowered. But the vindictive gods are now at hand. A Roman legion dared to face the warlike Britons: with their lives they paid for their rashness; those who survived the carnage of that day, lie poorly hid behind their entrenchments, meditating nothing but how to save themselves by an ignominious flight. From the din of preparation, and the shouts of the British army, the Romans, even now, shrink back with terror. What will be their case when the assault begins? Look round, and view your numbers. Behold the proud display of warlike spirits, and consider the motives for which we draw the avenging sword. On this spot we must either conquer, or die with glory. There is no alternative. Though a woman, my resolution is fixed: the men, if they please, may survive with infamy, and live in bondage."

Suetonius, in a moment of such importance, did not remain silent. He expected every thing from the valour of his men, and yet urged every topic that could inspire and animate them to the attack. "Despise," he said, "the savage uproar, the yells and shouts of undisciplined Barbarians. In that mixed multitude, the women out-number the men. Void of spirit, unprovided with arms, they are not soldiers who come to offer battle; they are bastards, runaways, the refuse of your swords, who have often fled before you, and will again betake themselves to flight when they see the conqueror flaming in the ranks of war. In all engagements it is the valour of a few that turns the fortune of the day. It will be your immortal glory, that with a scanty number you can equal the exploits of a great and powerful army. Keep your ranks; discharge your javelins; rush forward to a close attack; bear down all with your bucklers, and hew a passage with your swords. Pursue the vanquished, and never think of spoil and plunder. Conquer, and victory gives you everything."

This speech was received with warlike acclamations. The soldiers burned with impatience for the onset, the veterans brandished their javelins, and the ranks displayed such an intrepid countenance, that Suetonius, anticipating the victory, gave the signal for the charge.

The engagement began. The Roman legion presented a close embodied line. The narrow defile gave them the shelter of a rampart. The Britons advanced with ferocity, and discharged their darts at random. In that instant, the Romans rushed forward in the form of a wedge. The auxiliaries followed with equal ardour. The cavalry, at the same time, bore down upon the enemy, and, with their pikes, overpowered all who dared to make a stand. The Britons betook themselves to flight, but their waggons in the rear obstructed their passage. A dreadful slaughter followed. Neither sex nor age was spared. The cattle, falling in one promiscuous carnage, added to the heaps of slain. The glory of the day was equal to the most splendid victory of ancient times. According to some writers, not less than eighty thousand Britons were put to the sword. The Romans lost about four hundred men, and the wounded did not exceed that number. Boudicca, by a dose of poison, ended her life. Poenius Postumius, the Prefect in the camp of the second legion, as soon as he heard of the brave exploits of the fourteenth and twentieth legions, felt the disgrace of having, in disobedience to the orders of his general, robbed the soldiers under his command of their share in so complete a victory. Stung with remorse, he fell upon his sword, and expired on the spot.

GRAFFITI, c. AD 100–300

Anon

Romano-British inscriptions, from walls, tiles, stamps and potshards.

The Club of his fellow-slaves set this up to a well-deserving comrade. [A gravestone for Hardalio]

Enough!
[Found on a roof tile]

To the God Nodens. Silvianus has lost a ring, and dedicated half to Nodens. Among thosde who are called Senicianus, permit no health until he brings it to the temple of Nodens.
[Curse found at a temple in Gloucestershire]

For shame!
[Reply to a wall graffito]

Gaius Valerius Amandus' Drops for dim sight
[Proprietory stamp]

"THE RUIN OF BRITAIN": THE ANGLES AND SAXONS ARRIVE IN THE ISLES, c. AD 456

Saint Gildas

By the end of the fourth century, the Roman Empire was crumbling under barbarian attack. Legions were successively withdrawn from Britain for the defence of Rome itself. In 410 Britannia ceased to be a Roman colony. Over her body there developed a three cornered fight between Romanized Britons, Picts and Scots in the North, and Angles and Saxons from Germany. Gildas was a British monk. His *Concerning the Ruin of Britain (De Excidio Britanniae)* was written in the 540s.

Then all the councillors, together with that proud tyrant Gurthrigern (Vortigern), the British king, were so blinded, that, as a protection to their country, they sealed its doom by inviting in among them (like wolves into the sheep-fold), the fierce and impious Saxons, a race hateful both to God and men, to repel the invasions of the northern nations. Nothing was ever so pernicious to our country, nothing was ever so unlucky. What palpable darkness must have enveloped their minds – darkness desperate and cruel! Those very people whom, when absent, they dreaded more than death itself, were invited to reside, as one may say, under the selfsame roof. Foolish are the princes, as it is said, of Thafneos, giving counsel to unwise Pharaoh. A multitude of whelps came forth from the lair of this barbaric lioness, in three cyuls, as they call them, that is, in three ships of war, with their sails wafted by the wind and with omens and prophecies favourable, for it was foretold by a certain soothsayer among them, that they should occupy the country to which they were sailing three hundred years, and half of that time, a hundred and fifty years, should plunder and despoil the same. They first landed on the eastern side of the island, by the invitation of the unlucky king, and there fixed their sharp talons, apparently to fight in favour of the island, but alas! more truly against it. Their mother-land, finding her first brood thus successful, sends forth a larger company of her wolfish offspring, which sailing over, join themselves to their bastard-born comrades. From that time the germ of iniquity and the root of contention planted their poison amongst us, as we deserved, and shot forth into leaves and branches. The barbarians being thus introduced as soldiers into the island, to encounter, as they falsely said, any dangers in defence of their hospitable entertainers, obtain an allowance of provisions, which, for some time being plentifully bestowed, stopped their doggish mouths. Yet they complain that their monthly supplies are not furnished in sufficient abundance, and they industriously aggravate each occasion of quarrel, saying that unless more liberality is shown them, they will break the treaty and plunder the whole island. In a short time, they follow up their threats with deeds.

For the fire of vengeance, justly kindled by former crimes, spread from sea to sea, fed by the hands of our foes in the east, and did not cease, until, destroying the neighbouring towns and lands, it reached the other side of the island, and dipped its red and savage tongue in the western ocean. In these assaults, therefore, not unlike that of the Assyrian upon Judea, was fulfilled in our case what the prophet describes in words of lamentation: "They have burned with fire the sanctuary; they have polluted on earth the tabernacle of thy name." And again, "O God, the gentiles have come into thine inheritance; thy holy temple have they defiled," &c. So that all the columns were levelled with the ground by the frequent strokes of the battering-ram, all the husbandmen routed, together with their bishops, priests, and people, whilst the sword gleamed, and the flames crackled around them on every side. Lamentable to behold, in the midst of the streets lay the tops of lofty towers, tumbled to the ground, stones of high walls, holy altars, fragments of human bodies, covered with livid clots of coagulated blood, looking as if they had been squeezed together in a press; and with no chance of being buried, save in the ruins of the houses, or in the ravening bellies of wild beasts and birds; with reverence be it spoken for their blessed souls, if, indeed, there were many found who were carried, at that time, into the high heaven by the holy angels. So entirely had the vintage, once so fine, degenerated and become bitter, that, in the words of the prophet, there was hardly a grape or ear of corn to be seen where the husbandman had turned his back.

Some, therefore, of the miserable remnant, being taken in the mountains, were murdered in great numbers; others, constrained by famine, came and yielded themselves to be slaves for ever to their foes, running the risk of being instantly slain, which truly was the greatest favour that could be offered them: some others passed beyond the seas with loud lamentations instead of the voice of exhortation. "Thou hast given us as sheep to be slaughtered, and among the Gentiles hast thou dispersed us." Others, committing the safeguard of their lives, which were in continual jeopardy, to the mountains, precipices, thickly wooded forests, and to the rocks of the seas (albeit with trembling hearts), remained still in their country. But in the meanwhile, an opportunity happening, when these most cruel robbers were returned home, the poor remnants of our nation (to whom flocked from divers places round about our miserable countrymen as fast as bees to their hives, for fear of an ensuing storm), being strengthened by God, calling upon him with all their hearts, as the poet says, –

"With their unnumbered vows they burden heaven,"

that they might not be brought to utter destruction, took arms under the conduct of Ambrosius Aurelianus, a modest man, who of all the Roman nation was then alone in the confusion of this troubled period by chance left alive. His parents, who for their merit were adorned with the purple, had been slain in these same broils, and now his progeny in these our days, although shamefully degenerated from the worthiness of their ancestors, provoke to battle their cruel conquerors, and by the goodness of our Lord obtain the victory.

After this, sometimes our countrymen, sometimes the enemy, won the field, to the end that our Lord might in this land try after his accustomed manner these his Israelites, whether they loved him or not, until the year of the siege of Mount Badon (Literally "of Bath-hill"), when took place also the last almost, though not the least slaughter of our cruel foes, which was (as I am sure) forty-four years and one month after the landing of the Saxons, and also the time of my own nativity. And yet neither to this day are the cities of our country inhabited as before, but being forsaken and over-thrown, still lie desolate; our foreign wars having ceased, but our civil troubles still remaining. For as well the remembrance of such a terrible desolation of the island, as also of the unexpected recovery of the same, remained in the minds of those who were eyewitnesses of the wonderful events of both, and in regard thereof, kings, public magistrates, and private persons, with priests and clergymen, did all and every one of them live orderly according to their several vocations. But when these had departed out of this world, and a new race succeeded, who were ignorant of this troublesome time, and had only experience of the present prosper-ity, all the laws of truth and justice were so shaken and subverted, that not so much as a vestige or remembrance of these virtues remained among the above-named orders of men, except among a very few who, compared with the great multitude which were daily rushing headlong down to hell, are accounted so small a number, that our reverend mother, the church, scarcely beholds them, her only true children, reposing in her bosom; whose worthy lives, being a pattern to all men, and beloved of God, inasmuch as by their holy prayers, as by certain pillars and most profitable supporters, our infirmity is sustained up, that it may not utterly be broken down, I would have no one suppose I intended to reprove, if forced by the increasing multitude of offences, I have freely, aye, with anguish, not so much declared as bewailed the wickedness of those who are become servants, not only to their bellies, but also to the devil rather than to Christ, who is our blessed God, world without end.

INSTRUCTIONS ON CONVERTING THE PAGANS, AD 601

Gregory I

A letter from Pope Gregory to Bishop Mellitus, part of Augustine of Canterbury's mission to the English.

Tell Augustine that he should by no means destroy the temples of the gods but rather the idols within those temples. Let him, after he has purified them with holy water, place altars and relics of the saints in them. For, if those temples are well built, they should be converted from the worship of demons to the service of the true God. Thus, seeing that their places of worship are not destroyed, the people will banish error from their hearts and come to places familiar and dear to them in acknowledgement and worship of the true God. Further, since it has been their custom to slaughter oxen in sacrifice, they should receive some solemnity in exchange. Let them therefore, on the day of the dedication of their churches, or on the feast of the martyrs whose relics are preserved in them, build themselves huts around their one-time temples and celebrate the occasion with religious feasting. They will sacrifice and eat the animals not any more as an offering to the devil, but for the glory of God to whom, as the giver of all things, they will give thanks for having been satiated. Thus, if they are not deprived of all exterior joys, they will more easily taste the interior ones. For surely it is

impossible to efface all at once everything from their strong minds,
just as, when one wishes to reach the top of a mountain, he must
climb by stages and step by step, not by leaps and bounds . . .
Mention this to our brother the bishop, that he may dispose of the
matter as he sees fit according to the conditions of time and place.

KING EDWIN OF NORTHUMBRIA IS CONVERTED TO CHRISTIANITY, c. AD 625

Bede

The Venerable Bede was a monk at Jarrow, and author of *A History of the English Church and People*.

The king, hearing these words, answered, that he was both willing
and bound to receive the faith which he taught; but that he would
confer about it with his principal friends and counsellors, to the
end that if they also were of his opinion, they might all together be
cleansed in Christ the Fountain of Life. Paulinus consenting, the
king did as he said; for, holding a council with the wise men, he
asked of every one in particular what he thought of the new
doctrine, and the new worship that was preached? To which the
chief of his own priests, Coifi, immediately answered: "O king,
consider what this is which is now preached to us; for I verily
declare to you, that the religion which we have hitherto professed
has, as far as I can learn, no virtue in it. For none of your people
has applied himself more diligently to the worship of our gods than
I; and yet there are many who receive greater favours from you,
and are more preferred than I, and are more prosperous in all their
undertakings. Now if the gods were good for anything, they would
rather forward me, who have been more careful to serve them. It
remains, therefore, that if upon examination you find those new
doctrines, which are now preached to us, better and more efficacious, we immediately receive them without any delay."

Another of the king's chief men, approving of his words and
exhortations, presently added; "The present life of man, O king,
seems to me, in comparison of that time which is unknown to us,
like to the swift flight of a sparrow through the room wherein you
sit at supper in winter, with your commanders and ministers, and a
good fire in the midst, whilst the storms of rain and snow prevail
abroad; the sparrow, I say, flying in at one door, and immediately
out at another, whilst he is within, is safe from the wintry storm;

but after a short space of fair weather, he immediately vanishes out of your sight, into the dark winter from which he had emerged. So this life of man appears for a short space, but of what went before, or what is to follow, we are utterly ignorant. If, therefore, this new doctrine contains something more certain, it seems justly to deserve to be followed." The other elders and king's counsellors, by Divine inspiration, spoke to the same effect.

But Coifi added, that he wished more attentively to hear Paulinus discourse concerning the God whom he preached; which he having by the king's command performed, Coifi, hearing his words, cried out: "I have long since been sensible that there was nothing in that which we worshipped; because the more diligently I sought after truth in that worship, the less I found it. But now I freely confess, that such truth evidently appears in this preaching as can confer on us the gifts of life, of salvation, and of eternal happiness. For which reason I advise, O king, that we instantly abjure and set fire to those temples and altars which we have consecrated without reaping any benefit from them." In short, the king publicly gave his license to Paulinus to preach the Gospel, and renouncing idolatry, declared that he received the faith of Christ: and when he inquired of the high priest who should first profane the altars and temples of their idols, with the enclosures that were about them, he answered, "I; for who can more properly than myself destroy those things which I worshipped through ignorance, for an example to all others, through the wisdom which has been given me by the true God?" Then immediately, in contempt of his former superstitions, he desired the king to furnish him with arms and a stallion; and mounting the same, he set out to destroy the idols; for it was not lawful before for the high priest either to carry arms, or to ride on any but a mare. Having, therefore, girt a sword about him, with a spear in his hand, he mounted the king's stallion and proceeded to the idols. The multitude, beholding it, concluded he was distracted; but he lost no time, for as soon as he drew near the temple he profaned the same, casting into it the spear which he held; and rejoicing in the knowledge of the worship of the true God, he commanded his companions to destroy the temple, with all its enclosures, by fire. This place where the idols were is still shown, not far from York, to the eastward, beyond the river Derwent, and is now called Godmundingham, where the high priest, by the inspiration of the true God, profaned and destroyed the altars which he had himself consecrated.

THE SYNOD OF WHITBY, AD 664

Eddius Stephanus

At which it was decided that Britain should follow the customs of Rome, not the native Celtic Christian church.

On a certain occasion in the days of Colman, bishop of York and metropolitan, while Oswiu and Alhfrith his son were reigning, the abbots and priests and men of all ranks in the order of the Church gathered together in a monastery called Whitby, in the presence of the holy mother and most pious nun Hilda, as well as of the kings and two bishops, namely Colman and Agilbert, to consider the question of the proper date for the keeping of Easter – whether in accordance with the British and Scottish manner and that of the whole of the northern district, Easter should be kept on the Sunday between the fourteenth day of the moon and the twenty-second, or whether the plan of the apostolic see was better, namely to celebrate Easter Sunday between the fifteenth day of the moon and the twenty-first. The opportunity was granted first of all to Bishop Colman, as was proper, to state his case in the presence of all. He boldly spoke in reply as follows: "Our fathers and their predecessors, plainly inspired by the Holy Spirit as was Columba, ordained the celebration of Easter on the fourteenth day of the moon, if it was a Sunday, following the example of the Apostle and Evangelist John 'who leaned on the breast of the Lord at supper' and was called the friend of the Lord. He celebrated Easter on the fourteenth day of the moon and we, like his disciples Polycarp and others, celebrate it on his authority; we dare not change it, for our fathers' sake, nor do we wish to do so. I have expressed the opinion of our party, do you state yours."

Agilbert the foreign bishop and Agatho his priest bade St Wilfrid, priest and abbot, with his persuasive eloquence explain in his own tongue the system of the Roman Church and of the apostolic see. With his customary humility he answered in these words: "This question has already been admirably investigated by the three hundred and eighteen most holy and learned fathers gathered together in Nicaea, a city of Bithynia. They fixed amongst other decisions upon a lunar cycle which recurs every nineteen years. This cycle never shows that Easter is to be kept on the fourteenth day of the moon. This is the fixed rule of the apostolic see and of almost the whole world, and our fathers, after many decrees had been made, uttered these words: 'he who condemns any one of these let him be accursed.' "

Then, after St Wilfrid the priest had finished his speech, King Oswiu smilingly asked them all: "Tell me which is greater in the kingdom of heaven, Columba or the Apostle Peter?" The Lord whole synod answered with one voice and one consent: "The Lord settled this when he declared: 'Thou art Peter and upon this rock I will build my Church and the gates of hell shall not prevail against it. And I will give thee the keys of the kingdom of heaven; and whatsoever thou shalt bind on earth shall be bound in heaven; and whatsoever thou shalt loose on earth shall be loosed in heaven.' "

The king wisely replied: "He is the porter and keeps the keys. With him I will have no differences nor will I agree with those who have such, nor in any single particular will I gainsay his decisions so long as I live."

THE SINS OF KING AETHELBALD, AD 747

Saint Boniface

AEthebald was king of Mercia, and overlord ("bretwalda") of England. Boniface's letter urging him to desist from sinning was signed by seven other missionary bishops. AEthebald was murdered by his bodyguard in AD 757.

To the most dear lord, to be preferred in the love of Christ to all other kings, King Æthelbald, wielding the glorious sceptre of imperial rule over the English . . . there has reached our ears a report of an evil kind concerning your Excellency's way of life, and we were greatly grieved when we heard it. And we wish that it were not true. For it has been disclosed to us from the account of many persons that you have never taken in matrimony a lawful wife. This was ordained by the Lord God from the very beginning of the world, as is also enjoined and repeated by Paul, God's Apostle, who teaches and says: "But for fear of fornication, let every man have his own wife; and let every woman have her own husband." Now, if you desired to do this for the sake of chastity and abstinence, so that out of fear and love of God you abstained from union with a wife, and you prove it true and undertaken for God's sake, in this also we rejoice; for this is not reprehensible, but, on the contrary, laudable. If, however – which God forbid – you have, as many say, neither taken a lawful wife nor maintained chaste abstinence for God's sake, but governed by lust, have stained the fame of your glory before God and men by the sin of lasciviousness and adultery, we are extremely grieved by this; for it is regarded both as a disgrace in the sight of God and the ruin of your reputation among men.

And yet, what is worse, those who tell us this, add that this shameful crime is especially committed in the monasteries with holy nuns and virgins consecrated to God. For there is no doubt that this is doubly a sin. To give an illustration, to what punishment is a servant liable from his master if he violates his master's wife in adultery? How much more he who defiles with the filth of his lust the bride of Christ, the Creator of heaven and earth; as the blessed Apostle Paul says: "Know you not that your members are the temple of the Holy Ghost?"

And it should be noted, that under that crime there lurks another monstrous evil, namely homicide; because, when those harlots, whether nuns or laywomen, bring forth in sin offspring conceived in evil, they for the most part kill them; not filling the churches of Christ with adopted sons, but crowding graves with bodies and hell with unhappy souls.

Moreover, it has been told us that you have violated many privileges of churches and monasteries, and have stolen from them certain revenues. And this, if it is true, is regarded as a heavy sin, by the witness of Holy Scripture, which says: "He that stealeth any thing from his father, or from his mother, and saith: 'This is no sin', is the partner of a murderer.' Our Father without doubt is God, who created us, our Mother the Church which gave us spiritual regeneration in baptism. Therefore he who steals or plunders the possessions of Christ and the Church, will be adjudged to be a homicide in the sight of the just Judge. Concerning whom one of the wise said: "He who seizes the money of his neighbour, commits iniquity; but he who takes away the money of the Church, commits sacrilege."

And it is said that your ealdormen and companions offer greater violence and oppression to monks and priests, than other Christian kings have done before. Now, ever since the apostolic pope, St Gregory, sending preachers of the catholic faith from the apostolic see, converted the race of the English to the true God, the privileges of the churches in the kingdom of the English remained untouched and unviolated until the times of Ceolred, king of the Mercians, and Osred, king of the Deirans and Bernicians.

These two kings by the prompting of the devil showed by their wicked example an open display of these two greatest of sins in the provinces of the English, in defiance of the evangelical and apostolic commands of our Saviour. And lingering in these sins, that is, in debauchery and adultery with nuns and violation of monasteries, condemned by the just judgment of God, thrown down from the regal summit of this life and overtaken by an early and terrible death, they were deprived of the light eternal and plunged into the depths of hell and the abyss of Tartarus. For Ceolred, your venerable Highness's predecessor, feasting in splendour amid his companions, was – as those who were present have testified – suddenly in his sin sent mad by a malign spirit, who had enticed him by his persuasion to the audacity of breaking the law of God; so that without repentance and confession, raging and distracted, conversing with devils and cursing the priests of God, he departed from this light without a doubt to the torments of hell. Osred also was driven by the spirit of wantonness, fornicating, and in his frenzy debauching throughout the nunneries virgins consecrated to God; until with a contemptible and despicable death he lost his glorious kingdom, his young life and his lascivious soul.

Wherefore, most dear son, beware of the pit, into which you have seen others fall before you.

THE VIKINGS RAID BRITAIN, AD 787–93

The Anglo-Saxon Chronicle

AD 787 (789). In this year Beorhtric took to wife Eadburh, daughter of king Offa. And in his days came first three ships of Norwegians from Hörthaland (around Hardanger Fjord); and then the reeve rode thither and tried to compel them to go to the royal manor, for he did not know what they were: and then they slew him. These were the first ships of the danes to come to England.

AD 793. In this year terrible portents appeared over Northumbria, and miserably frightened the inhabitants: these were exceptional flashes of lightning, and fiery dragons were seen flying in the air. A great famine soon followed these signs; and a little after that in the same year on 8 January the harrying of the heathen miserably destroyed God's church in Lindisfarne by rapine and slaughter. In this year . . . Northumbria was ravaged by the heathen, and

Ecgfrith's monastery at *Donemup* (Jarrow) looted; and there one of their leaders was slain, and some of their ships besides were shattered by storms: and many of them were drowned there, and some came ashore alive and were at once slain at the river mouth.

The Vikings-Norwegians and Danes from Scandinavia-continued sporadic raiding until AD 865, when they began a campaign of conquest and settlement of Britain.

THE VIKING INVASION: ALFRED SAVES ENGLAND, AD 871–878

Asser

The King of Wessex, AD 871–899, Alfred led the Saxon resistance to the Viking invasions of the late ninth century. He also promoted learning; among the scholars attracted to Alfred's court was Asser, his eventual biographer.

The same year (AD 871), the aforesaid Alfred, who had been up to that time only of secondary rank, whilst his brothers were alive, now, by God's permission, undertook the government of the whole kingdom, amid the acclamations of all the people; and if he had chosen, he might have done so before, whilst his brother above-named was still alive; for in wisdom and other qualities he surpassed all his brothers, and, moreover, was warlike and victorious in all his wars. And when he had reigned one month, almost against his will, for he did not think he could alone sustain the multitude and ferocity of the pagans, though even during his brothers' lives, he had borne the woes of many, – he fought a battle with a few men, and on very unequal terms, against all the army of the pagans, at a hill called Wilton, on the south bank of the river, Wily, from which river the whole of that district is named, and after a long and fierce engagement, the pagans, seeing the danger they were in, and no longer able to bear the attack of their enemies, turned their backs and fled. But, oh, shame to say, they deceived their too audacious pursuers, and again rallying, gained the victory. Let no one be surprised that the Christians had but a small number of men, for the Saxons had been worn out by eight battles in one year, against the pagans (ie the Danes) of whom they had slain one king, nine dukes, and innumerable troops of soldiers, besides endless skirmishes, both by night and by day, in which the oft-named Alfred, and all his chieftains, with their men, and several of his ministers, were engaged without rest or cessation against the Pagans. How many thousand pagans fell in these numberless skirmishes God alone knows, over and above those who were slain in the eight battles above-mentioned. In the same year the Saxons made peace with the pagans, on condition that they should take their departure, and they did so . . .

In the year AD 879, the pagans, on the approach of autumn, partly settled in Exeter, and partly marched for plunder into Mercia. The number of that disorderly crew increased every day, so that, if thirty thousand of them were slain in one battle, others took their places to double the number. Then King Alfred commanded boats and galleys, (ie long ships), to be built throughout the kingdom, in order to offer battle by sea to the enemy as they were coming. On board of these he placed seamen, and appointed them to watch the seas. Meanwhile he went himself to Exeter, where the pagans were wintering, and having shut them up within the walls, laid siege to the town. He also gave orders to his sailors to prevent them from obtaining any supplies by sea; and his sailors were encountered by a fleet of a hundred and twenty ships full of armed soldiers, who were come to help their countrymen. As soon as the king's men knew that they were fitted with pagan soldiers, they leaped to their arms, and bravely attacked those barbaric tribes; but the pagans who had now for almost a month been tossed and almost wrecked among the waves of the sea, fought vainly against them; their bands were discomfited in a moment, and all were sunk and drowned in the sea, at a place called Suanewic (Swanwich) . . .

In the year of our Lord's incarnation AD 878, which was the thirtieth of king Alfred's life, the army above-mentioned left Exeter, and went to Chippenham, a royal villa, situated in the west of Wiltshire, and on the eastern bank of the river, which is called in British, the Avon. There they wintered, and drove many of the inhabitants of that country beyond the sea by the force of their arms, and by want of the necessaries of life. They reduced almost entirely to subjection all the people of that country . . .

The same year, after Easter, king Alfred, with a few followers, made for himself a stronghold in a place called Athelney, and from thence sallied with his vassals and the nobles of Somersetshire, to make frequent assaults upon the pagans. Also, in the seventh week after Easter, he rode to the stone of Egbert, which is in the eastern part of the wood which is called Selwood . . . Here he was met by all the neighbouring folk of Somersetshire, and Wiltshire, and Hampshire, who had not, for fear of the pagans, fled beyond the sea; and when they saw the king alive after such great tribulation, they received him, as he deserved, with joy and acclamations, and encamped there for one night. When the following day dawned, the king struck his camp, and went to Okely, where he encamped for one night. The next morning he removed to Edington, and there fought bravely and perseveringly against all the army of the pagans, whom, with the divine help he defeated with great slaughter, and pursued them flying to their fortification. Immediately he slew all the men, and carried off all the booty that he could find without the fortress, which he immediately laid siege to with all his army; and when he had been there fourteen days, the pagans, driven by famine, cold, fear, and last of all by despair, asked for peace, on the condition that they should give the king as many hostages as he pleased, but should receive none of him in return, in which form they had never before made a treaty with any one. The king, hearing that, took pity upon them, and received such hostages as he chose; after which the pagans swore, moreover, that they would immediately leave the kingdom; and their king, Gothrun, promised to embrace Christianity, and receive baptism at king Alfred's hands. All of which articles he and his men fulfilled as they had promised.

By the Peace of Wedmore between Alfred and Guthrum, a frontier was established between Alfred's Saxon England and the Danish held territories in north, central and east England, where "Danelaw" prevailed.

THE DOOMS OF ALFRED, c. AD 885–890

Alfred the Great

A selection of Alfred's famed laws or "dooms".

4. If anyone plots against the king's life, directly or by harbouring his exiles or his men, he is liable to forfeit his life and all that he owns.

   6. If anyone steals anything in church, he is to pay the simple compensation and the fine normally belonging to that simple

compensation, and the hand with which he did it is to be struck off.

6.1. And if he wishes to redeem the hand, and that is allowed to him, he is to pay in proportion to his wergild.*

10. If anyone lies with the wife of a man of a twelve-hundred wergild, he is to pay to the husband 120 shillings; to a man of a six-hundred wergild 100 shillings is to be paid; to a man of the *ceorl* class 40 shillings is to be paid.

12. If a man burns or fells the wood of another, without permission, he is to pay for each large tree with five shillings, and afterwards for each, no matter how many there are, with fivepence; and 30 shillings as a fine.

13. If at a common task a man unintentionally kills another (by letting a tree fall on him) the tree is to be given to the kinsmen, and they are to have it from that estate within 30 days.

16. If any one smite his neighbour with a stone or with his fist, and he nevertheless can go out with a staff; let him get him a leech, and work his work the while that himself may not.

18. If anyone in lewd fashion seizes a nun either by her clothes or her breast without her leave, the compensation is to be double that we have established for a lay person.

21. If an ox gore a man or a woman, so that they die, let it be stoned, and let not its flesh be eaten. The lord shall not be liable, if the ox were wont to push with its horns for two or three days before, and the lord knew it not; but if he knew it, and he would not shut it in, and it then shall have slain a man or a woman, let it be stoned; and let the lord be slain, or the man be paid for, as the "witan" decree to be right. If it gore a son or a daughter, let him be subject to the like judgment. But if it gore a "theow" or a "theow-mennen," let XXX shillings of silver be given to the lord, and let the ox be stoned.

25.1. If a slave rape a slave-woman, he is to pay by suffering castration.

32. If anyone is guilty of public slander, and it is proved against him, it is to be compensated for with no lighter penalty than the cutting off of his tongue, with the proviso that it be redeemed at no cheaper rate than it is valued in proportion to the wergild.

34. Injure ye not the widows and the step-children, nor hurt

---

* *Wergild* The price payable to the kin of a murdered or injured man.

them anywhere: for if ye do otherwise, they will cry unto me, and I will hear them, and I will then slay you with my sword; and I will so do that your wives shall be widows, and your children shall be step-children.

35. If thou give money in loan to thy fellow who willeth to dwell with thee, urge thou him not as a "niedling," and oppress him not with the increase.

36. If a man have only a single garment wherewith to cover himself, or to wear, and he give it (to thee) in pledge; let it be returned before sunset. If thou dost not so, then shall he call unto me, and I will hear him; for I am very merciful.

43. Judge thou very evenly: judge thou not one doom to the rich, another to the poor; nor one to thy friend, another to thy foe, judge thou.

THE FIRST CANDLE CLOCK, AD 887

Asser

An invention attributed by Asser to Alfred the Great; certainly promoted in England by him.

Alfred commanded his chaplains to procure a sufficient quantity of wax; when brought, he ordered them to place it in one scale and to weigh it against some pence placed in the other, and when a quantity had been weighed out which was found equal in weight to seventy-two pence, then he ordered his chaplains to make six candles, all of equal size, and each candle was to have twelve divisions marked by inches lengthways upon it. When this plan was adopted, these six candles were kept constantly burning night and day, without fail, before the sacred reliques of many of God's elect, which always accompanied him wherever he went. But sometimes these candles could not continue alight through a whole day and night, to the same hour on which they were lit on the preceding evening, in consequence of the violent gusts of wind which often blew without intermission day and night, through the doors and windows of the churches, and through the numerous chinks of the buildings, and planks, and walls, and also through the thin canvas of the tents. Thus they were compelled to finish their course before the same hour, by burning quicker than they ought. He reflected how he could prevent this draught of the winds, and by a plan cunningly and wisely invented, he ordered the construction of a beautiful lantern of wood and ox-horn; for white ox-horn, when thinly planed in single layers, becomes as translucent as a glass vessel. This lantern, then, as we said before, was wonderfully made of wood and horn, and the candle placed in it by night shines as clearly without as within, experiencing no hindrance from blasts of wind: for he also ordered a door to be made of horn to close up the opening. When this contrivance was used, the six candles, one after another, for twenty-four hours gave light without intermission, neither more nor less: and when these were burnt out, others were lighted.

A CHARM FOR STOMACH-ACHE, c. AD 900

Anon

Against stomach-ache and pain in the abdomen. When you see a dungbeetle throw up earth, catch it between your hands together with the heap. Wave it vigorously with your hands and say three times:

> *Remedium facio ad ventris dolorem.*

Then throw away the beetle over your back and take care that you do not look after it.

When a man's stomach or abdomen pains him, catch the belly between your hands.

He will soon be better.

For twelve months you may do so after catching the beetle.

THE VIKINGS MARTYR ARCHBISHOP AELFHEAH, 1012

The Anglo-Saxon Chronicle

1011 . . . And notwithstanding all this truce and peace and tribute, they went about everywhere in bands, and robbed and slew our unhappy people. Then, in this same year, between the nativity of St Mary (8 September) and Michaelmas (29 September) they besieged Canterbury, and made their way in through treachery, for Ælfmær, whose life archbishop Ælfheah had saved, betrayed Canterbury to them. And there they seized the archbishop Ælf-

heah: and Ælfweard, the king's reeve, and abbot Leofwine and
bishop of Godwine; and abbot Ælfmær they let go free. And they
seized all those in holy orders, both men and women, that were in
the borough, and it is impossible for any man to say how great a
part of the inhabitants that was.

And they remained in the borough as long as they wished; and
when they had searched it thoroughly, then they went to their
ships, taking the archbishop with them.

> Then was he a captive, he who had been
> The head of England and of Christendom.
> There might be seen wretchedness
> Where often bliss was seen before,
> In that unhappy city, whence came first to us
> Christendom, and both spiritual and earthly bliss.

And they kept the archbishop as their prisoner until the time when
they martyred him.

1012. In this year, before Easter, there came to London ealdor-
man Eadric and all the chief councillors of England, spiritual and
temporal. In this year Easter was on 13 April. And they remained
there until after Easter, until all the tribute was paid, amounting to
eight thousand pounds. Then on the Saturday the host became
greatly incensed against the bishop, because he was not willing to
offer them any money, and forbade any ransom to be given for him.
Moreover they were very drunk, for wine had been brought to them
from the south. Then they took the bishop, and led him to their
tribunal, on Saturday evening, within the octave of Easter, (19
April), and pelted him to death with bones and the heads of cattle;
and one of them smote him on the skull with the iron (head) of an
axe, so that with the blow he sank down and his holy blood fell upon
the earth, and his holy soul was sent forth to God's kingdom.

CANUTE AND THE WAVES, c. 1030
Henry of Huntingdon

The Danish monarch Canute seized control of England in 1017, reigning
thereafter as a native (and enlightened) king. Henry of Huntingdon was a
twelth century historian who seemingly preserved a long oral tradition
concerning Canute.

Canute reigned for twenty years. He died at Scaftesbirh (Shaftesbury) and was buried at Winchester in the old monastery. A few facts about his reign should be briefly told, for never before him was there a king in England of such greatness. For he was lord of all Denmark, all England, all Norway and at the same time of Scotland. Over and above the number of the wars in which he was so glorious, he did three handsome and magnificent acts. Firstly, he married his daughter (Gunhild) to the Roman emperor (Henry III) with indescribable riches. Secondly, on his path to Rome (1031) he paid money and reduced by as much as a half all those evil exactions called tolls and pontages on the road which leads to Rome through France. Thirdly, at the very summit of his power, he ordered his throne to be set on the seaside when the tide was rising. He addressed the mounting waters "You are under my sway as is the land on which is my throne and there has never been anyone who has resisted my rule without being punished. I therefore command you not to rise on to my land and you are not to dare to wet the clothes or limbs of your master." The sea rose in the usual way and wetted the feet and legs of the monarch without showing any respect. The king accordingly leapt up and said: "Know all inhabitants of earth, that vain and trivial is the power of kings nor is anyone worthy of the name of king save Him whose nod heaven and earth, and sea obey under laws eternal." King Canute therefore, never again set the golden crown upon his neck but set it for ever above an image of the Lord which is nailed to a cross, in honour of God the great king. By His mercy may the soul of King Canute rest in peace.

DEVILS TAKE THE WITCH OF BERKELEY'S SOUL, 1065

William of Malmesbury

At the same time something similar occurred in England, not by divine miracle, but by infernal craft; which when I shall have related, the credit of the narrative will not be shaken, though the minds of the hearers should be incredulous; for I have heard it from a man of such character, who swore he had seen it, that I should blush to disbelieve.

There resided at Berkeley a woman addicted to witchcraft, as it afterwards appeared, and skilled in ancient augury . . . and of bad character. On a certain day, as she was regaling, a jackdaw, which was a very great favourite, chattered a little more loudly than usual. On hearing which the woman's knife fell from her hand, her countenance grew pale, and deeply groaning, "This day," said she, "my plough has completed its last furrow; to-day I shall hear of, and suffer, some dreadful calamity." While yet speaking, the messenger of her misfortunes arrived; and being asked, "why he approached with so distressed an air", "I bring news," said he, "from that village," naming the place, "of the death of your son, and of the whole family, by a sudden accident." At this intelligence, the woman, sorely afflicted, immediately took to her bed, and perceiving the disorder rapidly approaching the vitals, she summoned her surviving children, a monk, and a nun, by hasty letters; and, when they arrived, with faltering voice, addressed them thus: "Formerly, my children, I constantly administered to my wretched circumstances by demoniacal arts: I have been the sink of every vice, the teacher of every allurement: yet, while practising these crimes, I was accustomed to soothe my hapless soul with the hope of your piety. Despairing of myself, I rested my expectations on you; I advanced you as my defenders against evil spirits, my safe guards against my strongest foes. Now, since I have approached the end of my life, and shall have those eager to punish, who lured me to sin, I entreat you by your mother's breasts, if you have any regard, any affection, at least to endeavour to alleviate my torments; and, although you cannot revoke the sentence already passed upon my soul, yet you may perhaps rescue my body, by these means: sew up my corpse in the skin of a stag; lay it on its back in a stone coffin; fasten down the lid with lead and iron; on this lay a stone, bound round with three iron chains of enormous weight; let there be psalms sung for fifty nights, and masses said for an equal number of days, to allay the ferocious attacks of my adversaries. If I lie thus secure for three nights, on the fourth day bury your mother in the ground; although I fear, lest the earth, which has been so often burdened with my crimes, should refuse to receive and cherish me in her bosom." They did their utmost to comply with her injunctions: but alas! vain were pious tears, vows, or entreaties; so great was the woman's guilt, so great the devil's violence. For on the first two nights, while the choir of priests was singing psalms around the body, the devils, one by one, with the utmost ease bursting open the door of the church, though closed with an immense bolt, broke asunder the two outer chains; the middle one being more laboriously wrought, remained entire. On the third night, about cockcrow, the whole monastery seemed to be overthrown from its very foundation, by the clamour of the approaching enemy. One devil, more terrible in appearance than the rest, and of loftier stature, broke the gates to shivers by the violence of his attack. The priests grew motionless with fear, their hair stood on end, and they became speechless. He proceeded, as it appeared, with haughty step towards the coffin, and calling on the woman by name, commanded her to rise. She replying that she could not on account of the chains: "You shall be loosed," said he, "and to your cost": and directly he broke the chain, which had mocked the ferocity of the others, with as little exertion as though it had been made of flax. He also beat down the cover of the coffin with his foot, and taking her by the hand, before them all, he dragged her out of the church. At the doors appeared a black horse, proudly neighing, with iron hooks projecting over his whole back; on which the wretched creature was placed, and, immediately, with the whole party, vanished from the eyes of the beholders; her pitiable cries, however, for assistance, were heard for nearly the space of four miles.

THE NORMAN INVASION, SEPTEMBER–OCTOBER 1066

William of Poitiers

With the death of Edward the Confessor, Harold II was chosen as king of England; however, his claim was disputed by Duke William of Normandy, who landed in England on 29 September 1066. William of Poitiers was the Duke's chaplain.

Rejoicing greatly at having secured a safe landing, the Normans seized and fortified first Pevensey and then Hastings, intending that these should serve as a stronghold for themselves and as a refuge for their ships. Marius and Pompey the Great, both of whom earned their victories by courage and ability (since the one brought Jugurtha in chains to Rome while the other forced Mithridates to take poison), were so cautious when they were in enemy territory that they feared to expose themselves to danger even by separating themselves with a legion from their main army: their custom was (like that of most generals) to direct patrols and not to lead them. But William, with twenty-five knights and no

more, himself went out to gain information about the neighbourhood and its inhabitants. Because of the roughness of the ground he
had to return on foot, a matter doubtless for laughter, but if the
episode is not devoid of humour it none the less deserves serious
praise. For the duke came back carrying on his shoulder, besides
his own hauberk, that of William fitz Osbern, one of his companions. This man was famed for his bodily strength and courage,
but it was the duke who relieved him in his necessity of the weight
of his armour.

A rich inhabitant of the country who was a Norman by race,
Robert, son of Wimarc, a noble lady, sent a messenger to Hastings
to the duke who was his relative and his lord. "King Harold," he
said, "has just given battle to his brother and to the king of
Norway, who is reputed to be the greatest warrior under heaven,
and he has killed both of them in one fight, and has destroyed their
mighty armies. Heartened by this success he now hastens towards
you at the head of innumerable troops all well equipped for war,
and against them your own warriors will prove of no more account
than a pack of curs. You are accounted a wise man, and at home
you have hitherto acted prudently both in peace and war. Now
therefore take care for your safety lest your boldness lead you into a
peril from which you will not escape. My advice to you is to remain
within your entrenchments and not at present to offer battle." But
the duke replied to the messenger thus: "Although it would have
been better for your master not to have mingled insults with his
message, nevertheless I thank him for his advice. But say this also
to him: I have no desire to protect myself behind any rampart, but
I intend to give battle to Harold as soon as possible. With the aid of
God I would not hesitate to oppose him with my own brave men
even if I had only ten thousand of these instead of the sixty
thousand I now command."

One day when the duke was visiting the guards of his fleet, and
was walking about near the ships, he was told that a monk had
arrived sent to him by Harold. He at once accosted him and
discreetly said: "I am the steward of William, duke of Normandy,
and very intimate with him. It is only through me you will have an
opportunity of delivering your message. Say therefore what you
have to say to me, and I will deliver a faithful report of your
message, for no one is dearer to him than I am. Afterwards through
my good offices you may in person say to him whatever you wish."
The monk then delivered his message without further delay, and

the duke at once caused him to be well housed and kindly entertained. At the same time he carefully considered with his followers what reply he should make to the message.

The next day, seated in the midst of his magnates, he summoned the monk to his presence and said: "I am William, by the grace of God, prince of the Normans. Repeat now therefore in the presence of these men what you said to me yesterday." The envoy then spoke: "This is what Harold bids you know. You have come into his land with he knows not what temerity. He recalls that King Edward at first appointed you as his heir to the kingdom of England, and he remembers that he was himself sent by the king to Normandy to give you an assurance of the succession. But he knows also that the same king, his lord, acting within his rights, bestowed on him the kingdom of England when dying. Moreover, ever since the time when blessed Augustine came to these shores it has been the unbroken custom of the English to treat death-bed bequests as inviolable. It is therefore with justice that he bids you return with your followers to your own country. Otherwise he will break the friendship and the pacts he made with you in Normandy. And he leaves the choice entirely to you."

When the duke had heard this message he asked the monk whether he would conduct his messenger safely into Harold's presence, and the monk promised that he would take as much care for his safety as for his own. Then the duke ordered a certain monk of Fécamp to carry this message forthwith to Harold: "It is not with temerity nor unjustly but after deliberation and in defence of right that I have crossed the sea into this country. My lord and kinsman, King Edward, made me the heir of this kingdom even as Harold himself has testified; and he did so because of the great honours and rich benefits conferred upon him and his brother and followers by me and my magnates. He acted thus because among all his acquaintance he held me to be the best capable of supporting him during his life and of giving just rule to the kingdom after his death. Moreover his choice was not made without the consent of his magnates since Archbishop Stigand, Earl Godwine, Earl Leo-fric and Earl Siward confirmed it, swearing in his hands that after King Edward's death they would serve me as lord, and that during his lifetime they would not seek to have the country in any way occupied so as to hinder my coming. He gave me the son and the nephew of Godwine as hostages. And finally he sent me Harold himself to Normandy that in my presence he might personally take the oath which his father and the others had sworn in my absence. While he was on his way to me Harold fell into a perilous captivity from which he was rescued by my firmness and prudence. He made himself my man by a solemn act of homage, and with his hands in mine he pledged to me the security of the English kingdom. I am ready to submit my case against his for judgment either by the law of Normandy or better still by the law of England, whichever he may choose; and if according to truth and equity either the Normans or the English decide that the kingdom is his by right, let him possess it in peace. But if it be decided that in justice the kingdom should be mine, let him yield it up. Moreover, if he refuses these conditions, I do not think it right that either my men or his should perish in conflict over a quarrel that is none of their making. I am therefore ready to risk my life against his in single combat to decide whether the kingdom of England should by right be his or mine."

We have been careful to record all this speech in the duke's own words rather than our own, for we wish posterity to regard him with favour. Anyone may easily judge that he showed himself wise and just, pious and brave. On reflection it will be considered that the strength of his argument was such that it could not have been shaken by Tully himself, the glory of Roman eloquence; and it brought to nought the claims of Harold. The duke (it will be seen) was ready to accept the judgment prescribed by the law of nations, since he did not desire that his enemies, the English, should perish because of his quarrel, but rather he wanted to decide the issue by means of a single combat and at the peril of his own life. When Harold advanced to meet the duke's envoy and heard this message he grew pale and for a long while remained as if dumb. And when the monk had asked more than once for a reply he first said: "We march at once," and then added, "We march to battle." The envoy besought him to reconsider this reply, urging that what the duke desired was a single combat and not the double slaughter of two armies. (For that good and brave man was willing to renounce something that was just and agreeable to him in order to prevent the death of many: he wished for Harold's head, knowing that it was defended by less fortitude than his own, and that it was not protected by justice.) Then Harold, lifting up his face to heaven, exclaimed: "May the Lord decide this day between William and me, and may he pronounce which of us has the right." Thus, blinded by his lust for dominion, and in his fear unmindful of the wrongs he had committed, Harold made his conscience his judge and that to his own ruin.

In the meantime trusty knights who had been sent out by the duke on patrol came back in haste to report the approach of the enemy. The king was the more furious because he had heard that the Normans had laid waste the neighbourhood of their camp, and he planned to take them unawares by a surprise or night attack. Further, in order to prevent their escape, he sent out a fleet of seven hundred armed vessels to block their passage home. Immediately the duke summoned to arms all those within the camp, for the greater part of his host had gone out foraging. He himself attended mass with the greatest devotion, and fortified both his body and soul by partaking of the Body and Blood of our Lord. With great humility he hung round his neck the relics on which Harold had sworn the oath he had now broken, and whose protection he had therefore lost. The duke had with him two bishops from Normandy, Odo, bishop of Bayeux, and Geoffrey, bishop of Coutances; and there were also with him many secular clergy and not a few monks. This company made ready to fight for him with their prayers. Anyone but the duke would have been alarmed at seeing his hauberk turn to the left when he put it on, but he merely laughed and did not allow the unlucky omen to disturb him.

Although no one has reported to us in detail the short harangue with which on this occasion he increased the courage of his troops, we doubt not it was excellent. He reminded the Normans that with him for their leader they had always proved victorious in many perilous battles. He reminded them also of their fatherland, of its noble history, and of its great renown. "Now is the time," he said, "for you to show your strength, and the courage that is yours." "You fight," he added, "not merely for victory but also for survival. If you bear yourselves valiantly you will obtain victory, honour and riches. If not you will be ruthlessly butchered, or else led ignominiously captive into the hands of pitiless enemies. Further, you will incur abiding disgrace. There is no road for retreat. In front, your advance is blocked by an army and a hostile countryside; behind you, there is the sea where an enemy fleet bars your flight. Men worthy of the name do not allow themselves to be dismayed by the number of their foes. The English have again and again fallen to the sword of an enemy; often, being vanquished, they have submitted to a foreign yoke; nor have they ever been famed as soldiers. The vigorous courage of a few men armed in a just cause and specially protected by heaven must prevail against a host of men unskilled in combat. Only be bold so that nothing shall make you yield, and victory will gladden your hearts."

He then advanced in good order with the papal banner which had been granted to him borne aloft at the head of his troops. In the van he placed foot-soldiers equipped with arrows and cross-bows; in the second rank came the more heavily armed infantry clad in hauberks; and finally came the squadrons of knights in the midst of whom he rode himself, showing invincible courage and in such a position that he could give his orders by hand or by voice. If any ancient writer had described the host of Harold, he would have said that at its passage the rivers became dry and the forests were turned into plains. From all the provinces of the English a vast host had gathered together. Some were moved by their zeal for Harold, but all were inspired by the love of their country which they desired, however unjustly, to defend against foreign-ers. The land of the Danes who were allied to them had also sent copious reinforcements. But fearing William more than the king of Norway and not daring to fight with him on equal terms, they took up their position on higher ground, on a hill abutting the forest through which they had just come. There, at once dis-mounting from their horses, they drew themselves up on foot and in very close order. The duke and his men in no way dismayed by the difficulty of the ground came slowly up the hill, and the terrible sound of trumpets on both sides signalled the beginning of the battle. The eager boldness of the Normans gave them the advantage of attack, even as in a trial for theft it is the prosecuting counsel who speaks first. In such wise the Norman foot drawing nearer provoked the English by raining death and wounds upon them with their missiles. But the English resisted valiantly, each man according to his strength, and they hurled back spears and javelins and weapons of all kinds together with axes and stones fastened to pieces of wood. You would have thought to see our men overwhelmed by this death-dealing weight of projectiles. The knights came after the chief, being in the rearmost rank, and all disdaining to fight at long range were eager to use their swords. The shouts both of the Normans and of the barbarians were drowned in the clash of arms and by the cries of the dying, and for a long time the battle raged with the utmost fury. The English, however, had the advantage of the ground and profited by remaining within their position in close order. They gained further superiority from their numbers, from the impregnable front which they preserved, and most of all from the manner in which their weapons found easy passage through the shields and armour of their enemies. Thus they bravely withstood and successfully repulsed those who were engaging them at close quarters, and inflicted losses upon the men who were shooting missiles at them from a distance. Then the foot-soldiers and the Breton knights, panic-stricken by the violence of the assault, broke in flight before the English and also the auxiliary troops on the left wing, and the whole army of the duke was in danger of retreat. This may be said without disparagement to the unconquerable Norman race. The army of the Roman emperor, containing the soldiers of kings accustomed to victory on sea and land, sometimes fled on the report, true or false, that their leader was dead. And in this case the Normans believed that their duke and lord was killed. Their flight was thus not so much shameful as sad, for their leader was their greatest solace.

Seeing a large part of the hostile host pursuing his own troops, the prince thrust himself in front of those in flight, shouting at them and threatening them with his spear. Staying their retreat, he took off his helmet, and standing before them bareheaded he cried: "Look at me well. I am still alive and by the grace of God I shall yet prove victor. What is this madness which makes you fly, and what way is open for your retreat? You are allowing yourselves to be pursued and killed by men whom you could slaughter like cattle. You are throwing away victory and lasting glory, rushing into ruin and incurring abiding disgrace. And all for naught since by flight none of you can escape destruction." With these words he restored their courage, and, leaping to the front and wielding his death-dealing sword, he defied the enemy who merited death for their disloyalty to him their prince. Inflamed by his ardour the Normans then surrounded several thousands of their pursuers and rapidly cut them down so that not one escaped. Heartened by this success, they then furiously carried their attack on to the main body of the English host, which even after their losses scarcely seemed diminished in number. The English fought confidently with all their strength, striving in particular to prevent the attackers from penetrating within their ranks, which indeed were so closely massed together that even the dead had not space in which to fall. The swords of the bravest warriors hewed a gap in some places, and there they were followed by the men of Maine, by the French, by the Bretons and the men of Aquitaine, and by the Normans who showed the greatest valour.

A certain Norman, Robert, son of Roger of Beaumont, being nephew and heir to Henry, count of Meulan, through Henry's sister, Adeline, found himself that day in battle for the first time: he was as yet but a young man and he performed feats of valour worthy of perpetual remembrance. At the head of the troop which he commanded on the right wing, he attacked with the utmost bravery and success. It is not, however, our purpose, or within our capacity, to describe as they deserve the exploits of individuals. Even a master of narrative who had actually been present that day would find it very difficult to narrate them all in detail. For our part we shall hasten to the point at which, having ended our praise of William the count, we shall begin to describe the glory of William the king.

Realising that they could not without severe loss overcome an army massed so strongly in close formation, the Normans and their allies feigned flight and simulated a retreat, for they recalled that only a short while ago their flight had given them an advantage. The barbarians thinking victory within their grasp shouted with triumph, and heaping insults upon our men, threatened utterly to destroy them. Several thousand of them, as before, gave rapid pursuit to those whom they thought to be in flight; but the Normans suddenly wheeling their horses surrounded them and cut down their pursuers so that not one was left alive. Twice was this ruse employed with the utmost success, and then they attacked those that remained with redoubled fury. This army was still formidable and very difficult to overwhelm. Indeed this was a battle of a new type: one side vigorously attacking; the other resisting as if rooted to the ground. At last the English began to weary, and as if confessing their crime in their defeat they submitted to their punishment. The Normans threw and struck and pierced. The movements of those who were cut down to death appeared greater than that of the living; and those who were lightly wounded could not escape because of the density of their formation but were crushed in the throng. Thus fortune crowned the triumph of William.

There were present in this battle: Eustace, count of Boulogne; William, son of Richard, count of Evreux; Geoffrey, son of Rotrou, count of Mortagne; William fitz Osbern; Haimo, *vicomte* of Thouars; Walter Giffard; Hughe of Montfort-sur-Risle; Rodulf of Tosny; Hugh of Grantmesnil; William of Warenne; and many other most renowned warriors whose names are worthy to be commemorated in histories among the bravest soldiers of all time. But Duke William excelled them all both in bravery and soldier-craft, so that one might esteem him as at least the equal of the most praised generals of ancient Greece and Rome. He dominated this battle, checking his own men in flight, strengthening their spirit, and sharing their dangers. He bade them come with him, more often than he ordered them to go in front of him. Thus it may be understood how he led them by his valour and gave them courage. At the mere sight of this wonderful and redoubtable knight, many of his enemies lost heart even before they received a scratch. Thrice his horse fell under him; thrice he leapt upon the ground; and thrice he quickly avenged the death of his steed. It was here that one could see his prowess, and mark at once the strength of his arm and the height of his spirit. His sharp sword pierced shields, helmets and armour, and not a few felt the weight of his shield. His knights seeing him thus fight on foot were filled with wonder, and although many were wounded they took new heart. Some weakened by loss of blood went on resisting, supported by their shields, and others unable themselves to carry on the struggle, urged on their comrades by voice and gesture to follow the duke. "Surely," they cried, "you will not let victory slip from your hands." William himself came to the rescue of many . . .

Evening was now falling, and the English saw that they could not hold out much longer against the Normans. They knew they had lost a great part of their army, and they knew also that their king with two of his brothers and many of their greatest men had fallen. Those who remained were almost exhausted, and they realised that they could expect no more help. They saw the Normans, whose numbers had not been much diminished, attack them with even greater fury than at the beginning of the battle, as if the day's fighting had actually increased their vigour. Dismayed at the implacable bearing of the duke who spared none who came against him and whose prowess could not rest until victory was won, they began to fly as swiftly as they could, some on horseback, some on foot, some along the roads, but most over the trackless country. Many lay on the ground bathed in blood, others who struggled to their feet found themselves too weak to escape, while a few, although disabled, were given strength to move by fear. Many left their corpses in the depths of the forest, and others were found by their pursuers lying by the roadside. Although ignorant of the countryside the Normans eagerly carried on the pursuit, and striking the rebels in the back brought a happy end to this famous victory. Many fallen to the ground were trampled to death under the hooves of runaway horses.

But some of those who retreated took courage to renew the struggle on more favourable ground. This was a steep valley intersected with ditches. These people, descended from the ancient Saxons (the fiercest of men), are always by nature eager for battle, and they could only be brought down by the greatest valour. Had they not recently defeated with ease the king of Norway at the head of a fine army?

The duke who was following the victorious standards did not turn from his course when he saw these enemy troops rallying. Although he thought that reinforcements had joined his foes he stood firm. Armed only with a broken lance he was more formidable than others who brandished long javelins. With a harsh voice he called to Eustace of Boulogne, who with fifty knights was turning in flight, and was about to give the signal for retreat. This man came up to the duke and said in his ear that he ought to retire since he would court death if he went forward. But at the very moment when he uttered the words Eustace was struck between the shoulders with such force that blood gushed out from his mouth and nose, and half dead he only made his escape with the aid of his followers. The duke, however, who was superior to all fear and dishonour, attacked and beat back his enemies. In this dangerous phase of the battle many Norman nobles were killed since the nature of the ground did not permit them to display their prowess to full advantage.

Having thus regained his superiority, the duke returned to the main battlefield, and he could not gaze without pity on the carnage, although the slain were evil men, and although it is good and glorious in a just war to kill a tyrant. The bloodstained battle-ground was covered with the flower of the youth and nobility of England. The two brothers of the king were found near him, and Harold himself stripped of all badges of honour could not be identified by his face, but only by certain marks on his body. His corpse was brought into the duke's camp, and William gave it for burial to William, surnamed Malet, and not to Harold's mother, who offered for the body of her beloved son its weight in gold. For the duke thought it unseemly to receive money for such merchandise, and equally he considered it wrong that Harold should be buried as his mother wished, since so many men lay unburied because of his avarice. They said in jest that he who had guarded the coast with such insensate zeal should be buried by the seashore . . .

Part Two

The Medieval Era
1067–1485

INTRODUCTION

On Christmas Day 1066 William of Normandy was acclaimed King of England. He held the crown, but not quite the country. The English rose in rebellion almost annually for the next five years, and had the dismaying habit of inviting the Vikings over to wreak havoc, such as the sack of Peterborough in 1070. To protect themselves from the two million English, Welsh and Scots, the ten thousand Normans who accompanied William built thick-walled castles and stuck it out. They persisted because like all victors they wanted the spoils, the reward for faithful service. The reward was land. To give land to his barons and knights, William took it from the English lords and thegns, and, almost at a stroke, destroyed the old English aristocracy.

The English peasants who came with this land were bound to the Norman overlord to provide labour in peace and footsoldiering in time of war. The Normans termed the system "feudalism", but it was not a new invention; most of Europe, Britain included, had been practising it for several centuries. Norman occupation or not, the peasants – who formed over 90 per cent of the population – got on with tilling the land and foddering their animals. The limited impact of the Norman invasion on English society is only proven by the continuation of English as the land's principal language; Norman French was restricted to the court, government, church, aristocracy – the apparatus of society.

William may have needed to reward his military helpers, but he also had a dynasty to build. To determine his potential economic wealth (and therefore his power), he ordered a survey of England's resources. So thorough was the job that it put the people in mind of the Last Day of Judgement, and they nicknamed the survey "Domesday" (Doom's Day').

The great advantage of the Domesday Book for William the Conqueror was that it allowed direct taxation by the king, rather than levies through feudal lords. The Norman knights might have put William on the throne but he had no intention of relying on them to stay there.

By the time of his death in 1087, William I had secured the new regime from within and without. True, he had failed to conquer Wales, but at least the Marcher Lords had made inroads. As for Scotland, he let sleeping Scots lie.

William's son Henry I continued in his father's footsteps, and dutifully strengthened centralized finances and administration. Henry's nephew Stephen ushered in anarchy, and without a whip hand over them the barons saw their chance to aggrandize power. Henry II, Henry I's grandson, restored order in 1153, razing illegally built baronial castles, and ensuring that the king's law – moderated and reformed – was obeyed throughout the land. But Henry's desire for greater temporal authority led directly to conflict with his archbishop, Thomas Becket, who (in the manner of Pope Gregory VII) denied that the crown had any power over the clergy. Becket's murder by some of Henry's more zealous followers put a blot on his reign that was never quite obscured. Becket aside, the English Church was notably given to a lack of fervour. When Richard the Lionheart went off to the Holy Land, the Church got on with making money at home.

Richard might have been the epitome of chivalry, but his reign was ruinous for the medieval British monarchy. Aside from his plain lack of interest in the island (he only visited twice, preferring the crown's possessions in France), his adventuring habits placed a groaning burden on the country's finances. More extortion by King John – through William's old centralized system – caused widespread discontent, which the barons utilized to their own ends, forcing King John at Runnymede in 1215 to seal the Magna Carta. If this essentially confirmed the nobles' own privileges, it also placed constitutional constraints on the monarch's power. When John reneged on the deal, the barons went to war, a strife against the crown which lasted on and off until 1267, when Edward I crushed the barons at Evesham. Conspicuously competent as a soldier, Edward extended English rule into Wales and subdued the Scots at Dunbar and Falkirk. A good king was then suceeded by a bad one, Edward II, who in turn was succeeded by a good one, Edward III. Edward III's reign, 1327–77, was notable for many things, not least beginning the Hundred Years' War with France. Originally waged to stop French interference in Scotland and protect the wool trade (England's principal money-earner during the Middle Ages) with Flanders, it rapidly turned into a war of conquest. Despite the resounding victories won by the English longbow at Creçy (1346), Poitiers (1356) and Agincourt (1415), the English quit the wars in 1453.

They were left with nothing but Calais, and recriminations which vortexed into the dynastic struggle for the throne known as the Wars of the Roses, which only ended with the victory of Henry Tudor at Bosworth in 1485.

There was one other result of the Hundred Year's War. A highly developed national consciousness, sharpened and honed in the long rivalry with France. (By the fifteenth century even the bastard Norman French of the court was on its way out.) Crucial to this national identity was an Englishman's belief in himself as a freeborn individual, a lover of liberty as well as country. It might have been vain, but it wasn't entirely self-delusion. By the fifteenth century England and Wales had a parliament, while feudalism was all but destroyed, with lords receiving money rents instead of feudal service. (Curiously enough, however, feudalism would not be destroyed as the law of the land until 1935.) England had become a land of tenant farmers and free labourers not serfs. Behind this change stood the ghost of the Black Death of 1348, when around two million of England's five million population were killed. Those who survived found their labour in demand, and were able to call the tune as well as whistle it. They did so many times, not least in the Peasants' Revolt of 1381.

FAMINE IN ENGLAND, 1068–70

Simeon of Durham

In consequence of the Normans having plundered England . . . almost the whole realm, yet principally Northumbria and the adjacent provinces – so great a famine prevailed that men, compelled by hunger, devoured human flesh, that of horses, dogs and cats, and whatever custom abhors; others sold themselves to perpetual slavery, so that they might in any way preserve their wretched existence; others, while about to go into exile from their country, fell down in the middle of the journey and gave up the ghost.

It was horrific to behold human corpses decaying in the houses, the streets, and the roads, swarming with worms, while they were consuming in corruption with an abominable stench. For no one was left to bury them in the earth, all being cut off either by the sword or by famine, or having left the country on account of the famine. Meanwhile, the land being thus deprived of any one to cultivate it for nine years, an extensive solitude prevailed all around. There was no village inhabited between York and Durham; they became lurking places to wild beasts and robbers, and were a great dread to travellers.

THE SACK OF PETERBOROUGH, 2 JUNE 1070
The Anglo-Saxon Chronicle

Viking raids on Britain continued after the Norman invasion

The same year king Sweyn came from Denmark into the Humber, and the people of those parts came to meet him and made an alliance with him, for they believed that he would conquer the land. Then the Danish bishop Christien, and Earl Osbern, and their Danish retainers, came into Ely, and all the people of the fens joined them, for they believed that they should conquer the whole country. Now the monks of Peterborough were told that some of their own men, namely, Hereward and his train, would pillage the monastery, because they had heard that the king had given the abbacy to a French abbot named Turold, and that he was a very stern man, and that he was come into Stamford with all his French followers. There was, at that time, a churchwarden named Ywar; who took all that he could by night, gospels, massrobes, cassocks, and other garments, and such other small things as he could carry away, and he came before day to the abbot Turold, and told him that he sought his protection, and told how the outlaws were coming to Peterborough, and he said that he had done this at the desire of the monks. Then early in the morning all the outlaws came with many ships, and they endeavoured to enter the monastery, but the monks withstood them, so that they were not able to get in. Then they set fire to it, and burned all the monks' houses, and all those in the town, save one: and they broke in through the fire at Bolhithe-gate (Bulldyke gate), and the monks came before them and desired peace. However they gave no heed to them, but went into the monastery, and climbed up to the holy crucifix, took the crown from our Lord's head, which was all of the purest gold, and the footstool of red gold from under his feet. And they climbed up to the steeple, and brought down the table (crozier or cope?) which was hidden there; it was all of gold and silver. They also seized two gilt shrines, and nine of silver, and they carried off fifteen great crosses of gold and silver. And they took so much gold and silver, and so much treasure in money, robes, and books, that no man can compute the amount; saying they did this because of their allegiance to the monastery: and afterwards they betook themselves to their ships and went to Ely, where they secured their treasures. The Danes believed that they should overcome the Frenchmen, and they drove away all the monks, leaving only one named Leofwin the Long, and he lay sick in the hospital. Then came the abbot Turold, and eight score Frenchmen with him, all well armed; and when he arrived he found all burnt both within and without, excepting the church itself; and all the outlaws were then embarked, knowing that he would come thither. This happened on the fourth day before the Nones of June (2 June). Then the two kings, William and Sweyn, made peace with each other, on which the Danes departed from Ely, carrying with them all the aforesaid treasure. When they were come into the midst of the sea, there arose a great storm, which dispersed all the ships in which the treasures were: some were driven to Norway, some to Ireland, and others to Denmark, and all the spoils that reached the latter country, being the table (crozier or cope?) and some of the shrines and crosses, and many of the other treasures, they brought to one of the king's towns called . . . and laid it all up in the church. But one night – through their carelessness and drunkenness the church was burned and all that was in it. Thus was the monastery of Peterborough burned and pillaged. May Almighty God have pity on it in his great mercy: and thus the abbot Turold came to Peterborough, and the monks returned thither and performed Christian worship in the church, which had stood a full week without service of any kind. When Bishop Egelric heard this, he excommunicated all the men who had done this evil.

THE DOMESDAY INQUISITION, 1086

Anon

AD 1086 William, king of the English, sent through all the provinces of England, and caused it to be inquired how many hides were held in the whole of England, and how much the king had in lands and cattle and livestock in each province, and what customary dues each year. This he caused to be done in respect of the lands and dues both of all churches and of all his barons. He inquired what these were worth, and how much they then rendered, and how much they were able to render in the time of King Edward. And so thoroughly was all this carried out that there did not remain in the whole of England a single hide or a virgate of land or an ox or a cow or a pig which was not written in that return. And all the writings of all these things were brought back to the king. And the king ordered that all should be written in one volume, and that that volume should be placed in his treasury at Winchester and kept there.

THE DOMESDAY BOOK: THE ASSESSMENT OF CANONS OF HEREFORDSHIRE, 1086

Anon

The national survey was arranged by holders of land, rather by area. Here are the some of the holdings of the Canons of Hereford.

THESE LANDS MENTIONED BELOW BELONG TO
THE CANONS OF HEREFORD

In STRETFORD Hundred
4 In LULHAM 8 hides which pay tax. In lordship 1 plough;
    11 villagers and 5 smallholders with 13 ploughs.
    1 female slave; meadow, 3 acres; 1 more plough would be
      possible in lordship . . .
    Of this land 2 clerks hold 2 hides and 3 virgates and 1 man-
      at-arms 1 hide. They have 2 ploughs in lordship;
    13 villagers and 2 smallholders with 8 ploughs.
  Before 1066 it was waste. Value now £10.

5 In PRESTON (on Wye) 6 hides which pay tax. In lordship 1
plough;
    9 villagers and 8 smallholders with 8½ ploughs.
    A mill at 2s; woodland 1 league long and ½ wide; 1 more
      plough would be possible in lordship.
    Of this land 2 clerks hold 2½ hides; 1 hide is waste. They
      have 7 villagers with 3 ploughs. The villagers have more
      ploughs than ploughable land.
Before 1066 it was waste. Value now 100s.

6 In TYBERTON 6 hides which pay tax. In lordship 1 plough;
    16 villagers and 6 smallholders with 9 ploughs; 1 more
      plough would be possible in lordship.
    Meadow, 3 acres; woodland 1 league long and ½ league
      wide.
Before 1066 it was waste. Value now £3.

7 In the same Hundred 1 rider holds 1 hide which is (part) of the
canons' barton; it pays tax. 1 plough in lordship.
Value 5s.

8 In EATON (Bishop) 5 hides. . . . In lordship 2 ploughs;
    12 villagers and 6 smallholders with 7 ploughs.
    2 slaves; a mill at 5s; meadow, 12 acres; woodland 1 league
      long and 2 furlongs wide.
Value £4.
    Earl Harold held this manor. Earl William gave it to Bishop
Walter for land in which the market is now and for 3 hides of
Lydney.

9 In MADLEY 3 hides . . .; they belong to the Bishop's barton.
In lordship 1 plough;
    6 villagers with 4 ploughs.
    Woodland ½ league long and 1 furlong wide. This wood-
      land is in the King's Enclosure.

10 In the same Hundred 2 free men hold 4 hides; they belong to
the Bishop's barton. They have 1½ ploughs in lordship;
    6 smallholders with 2 ploughs.
Value of the whole manor, 100s; of the men-at-arms' land, 15s
8d.

In DINEDOR Hundred
11 In "BARTON" 10 hides which pay tax. In lordship 1 plough;
    1 villager and 2 smallholders with 1 plough.
    1 female slave; meadow, 4 acres. The King has the woodland
        of this manor in his lordship.
    Of this land 4 clerks hold 4½ hides; 4 men-at-arms hold 5
        hides.
    They have 7½ ploughs in lordship and
    22 villagers and 12 smallholders with 10½ ploughs.
    ½ hide is waste. 2 more ploughs would be possible in
    lordship than there are.
    Before 1066 it was waste. Value now £7.

12 In HOLME (Lacy) 6 hides which pay tax. In lordship 2
    ploughs;
    16 villagers, a priest, a reeve, 1 Frenchman and 4 boors;
        between them they have 20½ ploughs.
    1 male and 2 female slaves; meadow, 10 acres; woodland ½
        league long and as wide.
    A church called LLANWARNE belongs to this manor. 3
    ploughs there, but the land of this church does not pay tax. A
    priest pays 2s from it. Roger of Lacy holds this land under
    the Bishop. Earl Harold held this manor wrongfully because
    it is for the canons' supplies. King William restored it to
    Bishop Walter.
    Value before 1066 £9; now £8.

In GREYTREE Hundred
13 In WOOLHOPE 16 hides which pay tax. In lordship 1
    plough; another would be possible;
    35 villagers and 7 smallholders with 35 ploughs.
    Meadow, 8 acres; woodland 3 furlongs long and 1 furlong
        wide.

A RECKONING OF WILLIAM THE CONQUEROR ON HIS DEATH, 1087

The Anglo-Saxon Chronicle

What can I say? That bitter death that spares neither high nor low
seized him. He died in Normandy on the day following the

Nativity of St Mary (9 September), and was buried at Caen in the abbey of St Stephen, which he had formerly built and afterwards endowed in various ways.

Alas! how deceitful and transitory is the prosperity of this world. He who was once a mighty king, and lord of many a land, was left of all the land with nothing save seven feet of ground: and he who was once decked with gold and jewels, lay then covered over with earth.

He left behind him three sons. The eldest was called Robert, who became duke of Normandy after him. The second was called William, who wore the royal crown in England after him. The third was called Henry, to whom his father bequeathed treasures innumerable.

If anyone desires to know what kind of man he was or in what honour he was held or how many lands he was lord over, then shall we write of him as we have known him, who have ourselves seen him and at one time dwelt in his court. King William, of whom we speak, was a man of great wisdom and power, and surpassed in honour and in strength all those who had gone before him. Though stern beyond measure to those who opposed his will, he was kind to those good men who loved God. On the very spot where God granted him the conquest of England he caused a great abbey to be built; and settled monks in it and richly endowed it. During his reign was built the great cathedral at Canterbury, and many another throughout all England. This land too was filled with monks living their lives after the rule of St Benedict. Such was the state of religion in his time that every man who wished to, whatever considerations there might be with regard to his rank, could follow the profession of a monk.

Moreover he kept a great state. He wore his royal crown three times a year as often as he was in England: at Easter at Winchester, at Whitsuntide at Westminster, at Christmas at Gloucester. On these occasions all the great men of England were assembled about him: archbishops, bishops, abbots, earls, thanes, and knights. He was so stern and relentless a man that no one dared do aught against his will. Earls who resisted his will he held in bondage. Bishops he deprived of their sees and abbots of their abbacies, while rebellious thanes he cast into prison, and finally his own brother he did not spare. His name was Odo. He was a powerful bishop in Normandy, and Bayeux was his episcopal see; he was the foremost man after the king. He had an earldom in England, and was master of the land when the king was in Normandy. William put him in prison. Among other things we must not forget the good order he kept in the land, so that a man of any substance could travel unmolested throughout the country with his bosom full of gold. No man dared to slay another, no matter what evil the other might have done him. If a man lay with a woman against her will, he was forthwith condemned to forfeit those members with which he had disported himself.

He ruled over England, and by his foresight it was surveyed so carefully that there was not a "hide" of land in England of which he did not know who held it and how much it was worth; and these particulars he set down in his survey. Wales was in his domain, in which country he built castles and so kept its people in subjection. Scotland also he reduced to subjection by his great strength. Normandy was his by right of birth, while he also ruled over the county called Maine. If he had lived only two years more he would have conquered Ireland by his astuteness and without any display of force. Assuredly in his time men suffered grievous oppression and manifold injuries.

He caused castles to be built
Which were a sore burden to the poor.
A hard man was the king
And took from his subjects many marks
In gold and many more hundreds of pounds in silver.
These sums he took by weight from his people,
Most unjustly and for little need.
He was sunk in greed
And utterly given up to avarice.
He set apart a vast deer preserve and imposed laws
    concerning it.
Whoever slew a hart or a hind
Was to be blinded.
He forbade the killing of boars
Even as the killing of harts.
For he loved the stags as dearly
As though he had been their father.
Hares, also, he decreed should go unmolested.
The rich complained and the poor lamented,
But he was too relentless to care though all might hate him,
And they were compelled, if they wanted

To keep their lives and their lands
And their goods and the favour of the king.
To submit themselves wholly to his will.
Alas! that any man should bear himself so proudly
And deem himself exalted above all other men!
May Almighty God shew mercy to his soul
And pardon him his sins.

We have set down these things about him, both the good and the evil, so that men may cherish the good and utterly eschew the evil, and follow the path that leads us to the Kingdom of Heaven.

THE DEATH OF WILLIAM RUFUS, 2 AUGUST 1100
William of Malmesbury

William Rufus was the son of William the Conqueror. Rufus ruled England from 1087 until his premature death.

The day before the king died, he dreamed that he was let blood by a surgeon; and that the stream, reaching to heaven, clouded the light, and intercepted the day. Calling on St. Mary for protection, he suddenly awoke, commanded a light to be brought, and forbade his attendants to leave him. They then watched with him several hours until daylight. Shortly after, just as the day began to dawn, a certain foreign monk told Robert Fitz Hamon, one of the principal nobility, that he had that night dreamed a strange and fearful dream about the king: "That he had come into a certain church, with menacing and insolent gesture, as was his custom, looking contemptuously on the standers by; then violently seizing the crucifix, he gnawed the arms, and almost tore away the legs: that the image endured this for a long time, but at length struck the king with its foot in such a manner that he fell backwards: from his mouth, as he lay prostrate, issued so copious a flame that the volumes of smoke touched the very stars." Robert, thinking that this dream ought not to be neglected, as he was intimate with him, immediately related it to the king. William, repeatedly laughing, exclaimed, "He is a monk, and dreams for money like a monk: give him a hundred shillings." Nevertheless, being greatly moved, he hesitated a long while whether he should go out to hunt, as he had designed: his friends persuading him not to suffer the truth of the dreams to be tried at his personal risk. In consequence, he abstained from the chase before dinner, dispelling the uneasiness of his unregulated mind by serious business. They relate, that, having plentifully regaled that day, he soothed his cares with a more than usual quantity of wine. After dinner he went into the forest, attended by a few persons; of whom the most intimate with him was Walter, surnamed Tirel, who had been induced to come from France by the liberality of the king. This man alone had remained with him, while the others, employed in the chase, were dispersed as chance directed. The sun was now declining, when the king, drawing his bow and letting fly an arrow, slightly wounded a stag which passed before him; and, keenly gazing, followed it still running, a long time with his eyes, holding up his hand to keep off the power of the sun's rays. At this instant Walter conceiving a noble exploit, which was while the king's attention was otherwise occupied to transfix another stag which by chance came near him, unknowingly, and without power to prevent it, Oh, gracious God! pierced his breast with a fatal arrow. On receiving the wound the king uttered not a word; but breaking off the shaft of the weapon where it projected from his body, fell upon the wound, by which he accelerated his death. Walter immediately ran up, but as he found him senseless and speechless, he leapt swiftly upon his horse, and escaped by spurring him to his utmost speed. Indeed there was none to pursue him: some connived at his flight; others pitied him; and all were intent on other matters. Some began to fortify their dwellings; others to plunder; and the rest to look out for a new king.

A few countrymen conveyed the body, placed on a cart, to the cathedral at Winchester; the blood dripping from it all the way. Here it was committed to the ground within the tower, attended by many of the nobility, though lamented by few. Next year (actually 1107), the tower fell; though I forbear to mention the different opinions on this subject, lest I should seem to assent too readily to unsupported trifles, more especially as the building might have fallen, through imperfect construction, even though he had never been buried there.

He died in the year of our Lord's incarnation 1100, of his reign the thirteenth, on the fourth of the nones of August, aged above forty years. . . . He was a man much to be pitied by the clergy, for throwing away a soul which they could not save; to be beloved by stipendiary soldiers, for the multitude of his gifts; but not to be lamented by the people, because he suffered their substance to be plundered.

THE CISTERCIANS, c. 1130

William of Malmesbury

The Cistercian monastic order founded its first house in England in 1128.

Certainly many of their regulations seem severe, and more particularly these: they wear nothing made with furs or linen, nor even that finely spun linen garment, which we call Staminium; neither breeches, unless when sent on a journey, which at their return they wash and restore. They have two tunics with cowls, but no additional garment in winter, though, if they think fit, in summer they may lighten their garb. They sleep clad and girded, and never after matins return to their beds: but they so order the time of matins that it shall be light ere the lauds begin; so intent are they on their rule, that they think no jot or tittle of it should be disregarded. Directly after these hymns they sing the prime, after which they go out to work for stated hours. They complete whatever labour of service they have to perform by day without any other light. No one is ever absent from the daily services, or from complines, except the sick. The cellarer and hospitaller, after complines, wait upon the guests, yet observing the strictest silence. The abbot allows himself no indulgence beyond the others – everywhere present – everywhere attending to his flock; except that he does not eat with the rest, because his table is with the strangers and the poor. Nevertheless, be he where he may, he is equally sparing of food and of speech; for never more than two dishes are served either to him or to his company; lard and meat never but to the sick. From the Ides of September till Easter, through regard for whatever festival, they do not take more than one meal a day, except on Sunday. They never leave the cloister but for the purpose of labour, nor do they ever speak, either there or elsewhere, save only to the abbot or prior. They pay unwearied attention to the canonical services, making no addition to them except the vigil for the defunct. They use in their divine service the Ambrosian chants and hymns, as far as they were able to learn them at Milan. While they bestow care on the stranger and the sick, they inflict intolerable mortifications on their own bodies, for the health of their souls . . .

THE ANARCHY OF THE BARONS, 1137–54

The Anglo-Saxon Chronicle

After the death of Henry I in 1135, a struggle developed over the English throne between King Stephen and the Empress Matilda (Henry I's daughter). The nobility took the opportunity of a weakened monarchy to aggrandize power.

When King Stephen landed in England he held his council at Oxford, and there he arrested Roger, bishop of Salisbury, and his "nephews", Alexander, bishop of Lincoln, and the chancellor Roger. He put them all in prison until they surrendered their castles. When the traitors saw that Stephen was a good-humoured, kindly, and easy-going man who inflicted no punishment, then they committed all manner of horrible crimes. They had done him homage and sworn oaths of fealty to him, but not one of their oaths was kept.

They were all forsworn and their oaths broken. For every great man built him castles and held them against the king; and they filled the whole land with these castles. They sorely burdened the unhappy people of the country with forced labour on the castles; and when the castles were built, they filled them with devils and wicked men. By night and by day they seized those whom they believed to have any wealth, whether they were men or women; and in order to get their gold and silver, they put them into prison and tortured them with unspeakable tortures for never were martyrs tortured as they were. They hung them up by the feet and smoked them with foul smoke. They strung them up by the thumbs, or by the head, and hung coats of mail on their feet. They tied knotted cords round their heads and twisted it till it entered the brain. They put them in dungeons wherein were adders and snakes and toads, and so destroyed them. Some they put into a "crucethus"; that is to say, into a short, narrow, shallow chest into which they put sharp stones; and they crushed the man in it until they had broken every bone in his body. In many of the castles were certain instruments of torture so heavy that two or three men had enough to do to carry one. It was made in this way: a weight was fastened to a beam which was attached to a sharp iron put round the man's throat and neck so that he could move in no direction, and could neither sit, nor lie, nor sleep, but had to bear the whole weight of the iron. Many thousands starved to death.

I know not how to, nor am I able to tell of, all the atrocities nor all the cruelties which they wrought upon the unhappy people of this country. It lasted throughout the nineteen years that Stephen was king, and always grew worse and worse. At regular intervals they levied a tax, known as "tenserie" (protection money) upon the villages. When the wretched people had no more to give, they plundered and burned all the villages, so that you could easily go a day's journey without ever finding a village inhabited or a field cultivated. Then was corn dear and flesh and cheese and butter, for there was none in the land. The wretched people perished with hunger; some, who had been great men, were driven to beggary, while others fled from the country.

Never did a country endure greater misery, and never did the heathen act more vilely than they did. Contrary to custom, they spared neither church nor churchyard, but seized everything of value that was in it, and afterwards burned the church and all it contained. They spared not the lands of bishops, nor of abbots, nor of priests, but plundered the monks and the clergy; and every man who could robbed his neighbour. If two or three men came riding towards a village, all the villagers fled for fear of them, believing that they were robbers. The bishops and the clergy were for ever cursing them, but that was nothing to them, for they were all excommunicated and forsworn and lost.

Wherever the ground was tilled the earth bore no corn, for the land was ruined by such doings; and men said openly that Christ and His saints slept. Such things and others more than we know how to relate we suffered nineteen years for our sins.

THE GREEN CHILDREN c. 1145

William of Newburgh

Nor does it seem right to pass over an unheard-of prodigy, which, as is well known, took place in England during the reign of King Stephen. Though it is asserted by many, yet I have long been in doubt concerning the matter, and deemed it ridiculous to give credit to a circumstance supported on no rational foundation, or at least one of a very mysterious character; yet, at length I was so overwhelmed by the weight of so many and such competent witnesses, that I have been compelled to believe, and wonder over a matter, which I was unable to comprehend, or unravel, by any powers of intellect.

In East Anglia there is a village, distant, as it is said, four or five miles from the noble monastery of the blessed king and martyr, Edmund; near this place are seen some very ancient cavities, called "Wolfpittes", that is, in English, "Pits for wolves", and which give their name to the adjacent village (Wulpet). During harvest, while the reapers were employed in gathering in the produce of the fields, two children, a boy and a girl, completely green in their persons, and clad in garments of a strange colour, and unknown materials, emerged from these excavations. While wandering through the fields in astonishment, they were seized by the reapers, and conducted to the village, and many persons coming to see so novel a sight, they were kept some days without food. But, when they were nearly exhausted with hunger, and yet could relish no species of support which was offered to them, it happened, that some beans were brought in from the field, which they immediately seized with avidity, and examined the stalk for the pulse, but not finding it in the hollow of the stalk, they wept bitterly. Upon this, one of the bystanders, taking the beans from the pods, offered them to the children, who seized them directly, and ate them with pleasure. By this food they were supported for many months, until they learned the use of bread. At length, by degrees, they changed their original colour, through the natural effect of our food, and became like ourselves, and also learned our language. It seemed fitting to certain discreet persons that they should receive the sacrament of baptism, which was administered accordingly. The boy, who appeared to be the younger, surviving the baptism but a little time, died prematurely; his sister, however, continued in good health, and differed not in the least from the women of our own country. Afterwards, as it is reported, she was married at Lynne, and was living a few years since, at least, so they say. Moreover, after they had acquired our language, on being asked who and whence they were, they are said to have replied, "We are inhabitants of the land of St Martin, who is regarded with peculiar veneration in the country which gave us birth." Being further asked where that land was, and how they came thence hither, they answered, "We are ignorant of both those circumstances; we only remember this, that on a certain day, when we were feeding our father's flocks in the fields, we heard a great sound, such as we are now accustomed to hear at St Edmund's, when the bells are chiming; and whilst listening to the sound in admiration, we became on a sudden, as it were, entranced, and found ourselves among you in the fields where you were reaping." Being questioned whether in that land they believed in Christ, or whether the sun arose, they replied that the country was Christian, and possessed churches; but said they, "The sun does not rise upon our countrymen; our land is little cheered by its beams; we are contented with that twilight, which, among you, precedes the sunrise, or follows the sunset. Moreover, a certain luminous country is seen, not far distant from ours, and divided from it by a very considerable river." These, and many other matters, too humerous to particularize, they are said to have recounted to curious inquirers. Let every one say as he pleases, and reason on such matters according to his abilities; I feel no regret at having recorded an event so prodigious and miraculous.

A PORTRAIT OF HENRY II, 1154–89

Peter of Blois

Born in 1133, Henry II was the first of the Angevin (Anjou descended) kings of England. He ruled an empire that stretched from Scotland to the Pyrenees. Peter of Blois was secretary to Henry II.

You ask me to send you an accurate description of the appearance and character of the king of England. That surpasses my powers, for the genius of a Vergil would hardly be equal to it. That which I know however I will ungrudgingly share with you. Concerning David we read that it was said of him, as evidence for his beauty that he was ruddy. You may know then that our king is still ruddy, except as old age and whitening hair have changed his colour a little. He is of medium stature so that among small men he does not seem large, nor yet among large men does he seem small. His head is spherical, as if the abode of great wisdom and the special sanctuary of lofty intelligence. The size of his head is in proportion to the neck and the whole body. His eyes are full, guileless and dove-like when he is at peace, gleaming like fire when his temper is aroused, and in bursts of passion they flash like lightning. As to his hair he is in no danger of baldness, but his head has been closely shaved. He has a broad, square, lion-like face. His feet are arched and he has the legs of a horseman. His broad chest and muscular arms show him to be a strong, bold, active man. His hands show by their coarseness that he is careless and pays little attention to his person, for he never wears gloves except when he goes hawking . . . Although his legs are bruised and livid from hard riding, he never sits down except when on horseback or at meals. On a single day, if necessary, he travels a journey of four or five days, and thus anticipating the plans of his enemies he baffles their devices by his sudden movements. . . . He is a passionate lover of the woods, and when not engaged in war he exercises with birds and dogs. . . . He does not loiter in his palace like other kings, but hurrying through the provinces he investigates what is being done everywhere, and is especially strict in his judgment of those whom he has appointed as judges of others. There is no one keener in counsel, of more fluent eloquence, no one who has less anxiety in danger or more in prosperity, or who is more courageous in adversity. If he has once loved any one, he rarely ceases to love him, while one for whom he has once taken a dislike he seldom admits to his favour. He always has his weapons in his hands when not engaged in consultation or at his books. When his cares and anxieties allow him to breathe he occupies himself with reading, or in a circle of clerks tries to solve some knotty question . . .

HERETICS BEATEN, OXFORD, 1166

William of Newburgh

There were, however, rather more than thirty persons, both men and women, who, dissimulating their errors, came hither as if in peace for the purpose of propagating their noxious teaching, their leader being a certain Gerard, whom they all looked up to as teacher and master; for he alone among them had a smattering of learning, but the others were ignorant folk, unlettered and wholly uncultivated, peasants of German race and tongue. Sojourning for some time in England they only deceived one wretched woman with their lying whispers, and, so it is said, having bewitched her with certain spells they joined her to their coterie. For they could not long lie hidden but were detected by certain men curious to explore to what strange sect they belonged, then seized and held in public custody. The king, however, being unwilling either to discharge them or to punish them without examination, ordered an episcopal synod to meet at Oxford. Here they were solemnly charged concerning their religion; the one among them who seemed literate, undertaking their common defence and speaking for them all, replied that they were Christians and reverenced the apostolic teaching. Interrogated successively concerning the articles of the Holy Faith, they answered rightly concerning the nature of Christ, the heavenly Physician; but concerning the saving remedies whereby he condescends to heal our human infirmity, that is, the Divine Sacraments, they answered perversely. Holy Baptism, the Eucharist, and Holy Matrimony they abhorred, and the Catholic unity sustained by these divine aids they wickedly dared to disparage. When they were pressed by texts taken from Holy Scripture, they answered they believed what they had been taught but were unwilling to dispute about their faith. Admonished that they should do penance and be united to the body of the Church, they spurned all sound advice. They laughed at the threats, with which in all piety they were confronted to induce them to recover their senses through fear; making wrongful use of the Lord's words: "Blessed are they which are persecuted for righteousness' sake, for theirs is the kingdom of heaven." Wherefore, lest the poison of heresy should be more widely dispersed, the bishops took the precaution of having the accused publicly proclaimed heretics and handed them over to the king to be subjected to corporal punishment. He commanded that the mark of heretical infamy should be branded upon their foreheads and in the sight of the people they should be beaten with rods and expelled from the city, sternly forbidding anyone to presume to offer them hospitality or supply any comfort. Sentence having been passed, they were led away rejoicing to suffer just punishment, their master marching in front with rapid strides and chanting, "Blessed are ye when men shall revile you." To such an extent did this deceiver mislead the minds of those seduced by him. The woman, however, whom they had perverted in England, deserted them through fear of punishment and on confession of her error obtained pardon and reconciliation. Next this hateful band were branded upon their foreheads and suffered stern justice. To mark his primacy of office their chief endured the shame of being twice branded, first on his forehead and then on his chin. Then with their clothes cut off to the waist they were publicly flogged and with resounding blows driven forth from the city into the intolerable cold, for it was winter-time. None shewed the slightest pity on them and they perished miserably. This pious severity not only purged the realm of England of this pest which had lately crept into it, but also prevented further inroads through the terror stricken into the heretics.

THE DUTY OF A KNIGHT, c. 1170

John of Salisbury

But what is the office of the duly ordained soldiery? To defend the Church, to assail infidelity, to venerate the priesthood, to protect the poor from injuries, to pacify the province, to pour out their blood for their brothers (as the formula of their oath instructs them), and, if need be, to lay down their lives. The high praises of God are in their throat, and two-edged swords are in their hands to execute punishment on the nations and rebuke upon the peoples, and to bind their kings in chains and their nobles in links of iron. But to what end? To the end that they may serve madness, vanity, avarice, or their own private self-will? By no means. Rather to the end that they may execute the judgment that is committed to them to execute; wherein each follows not his own will but the deliberate decision of God, the angels, and men, in accordance with equity and the public utility . . . For soldiers that do these things are "saints," and are the more loyal to their prince in proportion as they more zealously keep the faith of God; and they advance the more successfully the honour of their own valour as they seek the more faithfully in all things the glory of their God.

THE MURDER OF THOMAS À BECKET, CANTERBURY, 29 DECEMBER 1170

Edward Grim

Formerly Henry II's chancellor, Thomas à Becket was appointed archbishop of Canterbury in 1162; in this office he became an enthusiastic supporter of ecclesiastical claims against lay powers. Henry's expressed wish to be rid of "this turbulent priest", led to four knights – Hugh de Merville, Reginald Fitzurse, Richard le Breton and William de Tracy – murdering Becket in Canterbury cathedral.

When the monks had entered the church, already the four knights followed behind with rapid strides. With them was a certain subdeacon, armed with malice like their own, Hugh, fitly surnamed for his wickedness Mauclerc, who showed no reverence for God or the saint, as the result showed. When the holy archbishop entered the church, the monks stopped vespers which they had begun and ran to him, glorifying God that they saw their father, whom they had heard was dead, alive and safe. They hastened, by bolting the doors of the church, to protect their shepherd from the slaughter. But the champion, turning to them, ordered the church doors to be thrown open, saying, "It is not meet to make a fortress of the house of prayer, the church of Christ: though it be not shut up it is able to protect its own; and we shall triumph over the enemy rather in suffering than in fighting, for we came to suffer, not to resist." And straightway they entered the house of prayer and reconciliation with swords sacrilegiously drawn, causing horror to the beholders by their very looks and the clanging of their arms.

All who were present were in tumult and fright, for those who had been singing vespers now ran hither to the dreadful sight.

Inspired by fury the knights called out, "Where is Thomas Becket, traitor to the king and realm?" As he answered not, they cried out the more furiously, "Where is the archbishop?" At this, intrepid and fearless, as it is written, "The just, like a bold lion, shall be without fear," he descended from the stair where he had been dragged by the monks in fear of the knights, and in a clear voice answered "I am here, no traitor to the king, but a priest. Why do ye seek me?" And whereas he had already said that he feared them not, he added, "So I am ready to suffer in His name, Who redeemed me by His Blood: be it far from me to flee from your swords, or to depart from justice." Having thus said, he turned to the right, under a pillar, having on one side the altar of the blessed Mother of God and ever Virgin Mary, on the other that of S. Benedict the Confessor: by whose example and prayers, having crucified the world with its lusts, he bore all that the murderers could do with such constancy of soul as if he had been no longer in the flesh. The murderers followed him; "Absolve," they cried, "and restore to communion those whom you have excommunicated, and restore their powers to those whom you have suspended." He answered: "There has been no satisfaction, and I will not absolve them." "Then you shall die," they cried, "and receive what you deserve." "I am ready," he replied, "to die for my Lord, that in my blood the Church may obtain liberty and peace. But in the name of Almighty God, I forbid you to hurt my people whether clerk or lay." Thus piously and thoughtfully, did the noble martyr provide that no one near him should be hurt or the innocent be brought to death, whereby his glory should be dimmed as he hastened to Christ. Thus did it become the martyr-knight to follow in the footsteps of his Captain and Saviour Who when the wicked sought Him said: "If ye seek Me, let these go their way." Then they laid sacrilegious hands on him, pulling and dragging him that they might kill him outside the Church, or carry him away a prisoner, as they afterwards confessed. But when he could not be forced away from the pillar, one of them pressed on him and clung to him more closely. Him he pushed off calling him "pander", and saying, "Touch me not, Reginald; you owe me fealty and subjection; you and your accomplices act like madmen." The knight, fired with terrible rage at this severe repulse, waved his sword over the sacred head. "No faith", he cried, "nor subjection do I owe you against my fealty to my lord the king." Then the unconquered martyr seeing the hour at hand which should put an end to this miserable life and give him straightway the crown of immortality promised by the Lord, inclined his neck as one who prays and joining his hands he lifted them up, and commended his cause and that of the Church of God, to S. Mary, and to the blessed martyr Denys. Scarce had he said the words than the wicked knight fearing lest he should be rescued by the people and escape alive, leapt upon him suddenly and wounded this lamb, who was sacrificed to God, on the head, cutting off the top of the crown which the sacred unction of chrism had dedicated to God; and by the same blow he wounded the arm of him who tells this. For he, when the others, both monks and clerks, fled, stuck close to the sainted archbishop and held him in his arms till the one he interposed was almost severed . . .

Then he received a second blow on the head but still stood firm. At the third blow he fell on his knees and elbows, offering himself a living victim, and saying in a low voice, "For the Name of Jesus and the protection of the Church I am ready to embrace death." Then the third knight inflicted a terrible wound as he lay, by which the sword was broken against the pavement, and the crown which was large was separated from the head; so that the blood white with the brain and the brain red with blood, dyed the surface of the virgin mother Church with the life and death of the confessor and martyr in the colours of the lily and the rose. The fourth knight prevented any from interfering so that the others might freely perpetrate the murder. As to the fifth, no knight but that clerk who had entered with the knights, that a fifth blow might not be wanting to the martyr who was in other things like to Christ, he put his foot on the neck of the holy priest and precious martyr, and, horrible to say, scattered his brains and blood over the pavement, calling out to the others, "Let us away, knights; he will rise no more."

Becket was canonized in 1173, and Henry II did public penance at his tomb the following year. The shrine of St Thomas of Canterbury was a popular place of pilgrimage for several centuries.

A PICTURE OF LONDON, c. 1173

William Fitz-Stephen

London was seemingly founded by the Romans, who made Londinium their administrative centre. The city fell into disuse in the early Anglo-Saxon period, before being revived in the eleventh century as the capital of England. Cnut built a palace on the river and Edward the Confessor founded the abbey of Westminster. The Norman conquest made the city's pre-eminence permanent.

Of the Site thereof

Among the noble cities of the world that Fame celebrates the City of London of the Kingdom of the English, is the one seat that pours out its fame more widely, sends to farther lands its wealth and trade, lifts its head higher than the rest. It is happy in the healthiness of its air, in the Christian religion, in the strength of its defences, the nature of its site, the honour of its citizens, the modesty of its matrons; pleasant in sports; fruitful of noble men. Let us look into these things separately . . .

Of Religion

There is in the church there the Episcopal Seat of St. Paul; once it was Metropolitan, and it is thought will again become so if the citizens return into the island, unless perhaps the archiepiscopal title of Saint Thomas the Martyr, and his bodily presence, preserve to Canterbury where it is now, a perpetual dignity. But as Saint Thomas has made both cities illustrious, London by his rising, Canterbury by his setting, in regard of that saint, with admitted justice, each can claim advantage of the other. There are also, as regards the cultivation of the Christian faith, in London and the suburbs, thirteen larger conventual churches, besides lesser parish churches one hundred and twenty-six.

Of the Strength of the City
It has on the east the Palatine Castle, very great and strong, of which the ground plan and the walls rise from a very deep foundation, fixed with a mortar tempered by the blood of animals. On the west are two towers very strongly fortified, with the high and great wall of the city having seven double gates, and towered to the north at intervals. London was walled and towered in like manner on the south, but the great fish-bearing Thames river which there glides, with ebb and flow from the sea, by course of time has washed against, loosened, and thrown down those walls. Also upwards to the west the royal palace is conspicuous above the same river, an incomparable building with ramparts and bulwarks, two miles from the city, joined to it by a populous suburb.

Of Gardens
Everywhere outside the houses of those living in the suburbs are joined to them, planted with trees, the spacious and beautiful gardens of the citizens.

Of Pasture and Tilth
Also there are, on the north side, pastures and a pleasant meadow land, through which flow river streams, where the turning wheels of mills are put in motion with a cheerful sound. Very near lies a great forest, with woodland pastures, coverts of wild animals, stags, fallow deer, boars and wild bulls. The tilled lands of the city are not of barren gravel but fat plains of Asia, that make crops luxuriant, and fill their tillers' barns with Ceres' sheaves.

Of Springs
There are also about London, on the north side, excellent suburban springs, with sweet, wholesome, and clear water that flows

rippling over the bright stones; among which Holy Well, Clerken Well, and Saint Clements are frequented by greater numbers, and visited more by scholars and youth of the city when they go out for fresh air on summer evenings. It is a good city indeed when it has a good master.

Of Honour of the Citizens

That City is honoured by her men, adorned by her arms, populous with many inhabitants, so that in the time of slaughter of war under King Stephen, of those going out to muster twenty thousand horsemen and sixty thousand men on foot were estimated to be fit for war. Above all other citizens, everywhere, the citizens of London are regarded as conspicuous and noteworthy for handsomeness of manners and of dress, at table, and in way of speaking . . .

Of the ordering of the City

Those engaged in the several kinds of business, sellers of several things, contractors for several kinds of work, are distributed every morning into their several localities and shops. Besides, there is in London on the river bank, among the wines in ships and cellars sold by the vintners, a public cook shop; there eatables are to be found every day, according to the season, dishes of meat, roast, fried and boiled, great and small fish, coarser meats for the poor, more delicate for the rich, of game, fowls, and small birds. If there should come suddenly to any of the citizens friends, weary from a journey and too hungry to like waiting till fresh food is bought and cooked, with water to their hands comes bread, while one runs to the river bank, and there is all that can be wanted. However great the multitude of soldiers or travellers entering the city, or preparing to go out of it, at any hour of the day or night, – that these may not fast too long and those may not go supperless, – they turn hither, if they please, where every man can refresh himself in his own way. . . . Outside one of the gates there, immediately in the suburb, is a certain field, smooth (Smith) field in fact and name. Every Friday, unless it be a higher day of appointed solemnity, there is in it a famous show of noble horses for sale. Earls, barons, knights, and many citizens who are in town, come to see or buy . . . In another part of the field stand by themselves the goods proper to rustics, implements of husbandry, swine with long flanks, cows with full udders, oxen

of bulk immense, and woolly flocks. . . . To this city from every
nation under heaven merchants delight to bring their trade by sea
. . . This city . . . is divided into wards, has annual sheriffs for its
consuls, has senatorial and lower magistrates, sewers and aque-
ducts in its streets, its proper places and separate courts for cases
of each kind, deliberative, demonstrative, judicial; has assemblies
on appointed days. I do not think there is a city with more
commendable customs of church attendance, honour to God's
ordinances, keeping sacred festivals, almsgiving, hospitality, con-
firming betrothals, contracting marriages, celebration of nuptials,
preparing feasts, cheering the guests, and also in care for funerals
and the interment of the dead. The only pests of London are the
immoderate drinking of fools and the frequency of fires. To this
may be added that nearly all the bishops, abbots, and magnates
of England are, as it were, citizens and freemen of London;
having there their own splendid houses, to which they resort,
where they spend largely when summoned to great councils by
the king or by their metropolitan, or drawn thither by their own
private affairs.

Of Sports

Let us now come to the sports and pastimes, seeing it is fit that a
city should not only be commodious and serious, but also merry
and sportful; . . . But London . . . hath holy plays, representations
of miracles which holy confessors have wrought, or representations
of torments wherein the constancy of martyrs appeared. Every
year also at Shrove Tuesday, that we may begin with children's
sports, seeing we all have been children, the schoolboys do bring
cocks of the game to their master, and all the forenoon they delight
themselves in cock-fighting: after dinner, all the youths go into the
fields to play at the ball.

The scholars of every school have their ball, or baton, in their
hands; the ancient and wealthy men of the city come forth on
horseback to see the sport of the young men, and to take part of the
pleasure in beholding their agility. Every Friday in Lent a fresh
company of young men comes into the field on horseback, and the
best horseman conducteth the rest. Then march forth the citizens'
sons, and other young men, with disarmed lances and shields, and
there they practise feats of war. Many courtiers likewise, when the
king lieth near, and attendants of noblemen, do repair to these
exercises; and while the hope of victory doth inflame their minds,

do show good proof how serviceable they would be in martial affairs.

In Easter holidays they fight battles on the water; a shield is hung upon a pole, fixed in the midst of the stream, a boat is prepared without oars, to be carried by violence of the water, and in the fore part thereof standeth a young man, ready to give charge upon the shield with his lance; if so be he breaketh his lance against the shield, and doth not fall, he is thought to have performed a worthy deed; if so be, without breaking his lance, he runneth strongly against the shield, down he falleth into the water, for the boat is violently forced with the tide; but on each side of the shield ride two boats, furnished with young men, which recover him that falleth as soon as they may. Upon the bridge, wharfs, and houses, by the river's side, stand great numbers to see and laugh thereat.

In the holidays all the summer the youths are exercised in leaping, dancing, shooting, wrestling, casting the stone, and practising their shields; the maidens trip in their timbrels, and dance as long as they can well see. In winter, every holiday before dinner, the boars prepared for brawn are set to fight, or else bulls and bears are baited.

When the great fen, or moor, which watereth the walls of the city on the north side, is frozen, many young men play upon the ice; some, striding as wide as they may, do slide swiftly; others make themselves seats of ice, as great as millstones; one sits down, many hand in hand to draw him, and one slipping on a sudden, all fall together; some tie bones to their feet and under their heels; and shoving themselves by a little picked staff, do slide as swiftly as a bird flieth in the air, or an arrow out of a cross-bow. Sometime two run together with poles, and hitting one the other, either one or both do fall, not without hurt; some break their arms, some their legs, but youth desirous of glory in this sort exerciseth itself against the time of war. Many of the citizens do delight themselves in hawks and hounds; for they have liberty of hunting in Middlesex, Hertfordshire, all Chiltern, and in Kent to the water of Cray . . .

THE CHARACTER & CUSTOMS OF THE WELSH, c. 1188

Gerald of Wales

Gerald of Wales (Latinized name: Giraldus Cambrensis) was the son of a Welsh princess and a Norman baron.

Being particularly attached to family descent, they revenge with vehemence the injuries which may tend to the disgrace of their blood; and being naturally of a vindictive and passionate disposition, they are ever ready to avenge not only recent but ancient affronts; they neither inhabit towns, villages, nor castles, but lead a solitary life in the woods, on the borders of which they do not erect sumptuous palaces, nor lofty stone buildings, but content themselves with small huts made of the boughs of trees twisted together, constructed with little labour and expense, and sufficient to endure throughout the year. They have neither orchards nor gardens, but gladly eat the fruit of both when given to them. The greater part of their land is laid down to pasturage; little is cultivated, a very small quantity is ornamented with flowers, and a still smaller is sown . . .

No one of this nation ever begs, for the houses of all are common to all; and they consider liberality and hospitality amongst the first virtues. So much does hospitality here rejoice in communication, that it is neither offered nor requested by travellers, who, on entering a house, only deliver up their arms. When water is offered to them, if they suffer their feet to be washed, they are received as guests: for the offer of water to wash the feet is with this nation an hospitable invitation. But if they refuse the proffered service, they only wish for morning refreshment, not lodging. The young men move about in troops and families under the direction of a chosen leader. Attached only to arms and ease, and ever ready to stand forth in defence of their country, they have free admittance into every house as if it were their own.

Those who arrive in the morning are entertained till evening with the conversation of young women, and the music of the harp; for each house has its young women and harps allotted to this purpose . . . The kitchen does not supply many dishes, nor high-seasoned incitements to eating. The house is not furnished with tables, cloths or napkins . . . They place dishes before them (guests) all at once upon rushes and fresh grass, in large platters or trenchers. They also make use of a thin and broad cake of bread, baked every day . . . and they sometimes add chopped meat, with broth . . . While the family is engaged in waiting on the guests, the host and hostess stand up, paying unremitting attention to everything, and take no food till all the company are satisfied; that in case of any deficiency, it may fall upon them. A bed made of rushes, and covered with a coarse kind of cloth manufactured in the country, called *brychan* (blanket) is then placed along the side of the room, and they all in common lie down to sleep; nor is their dress at night different from that by day, for at all seasons they defend themselves from the cold only by a thin cloak and tunic. The fire continues to burn by night as well as by day, at their feet, and they receive much comfort from the natural heat of the persons lying near them; but when the under side begins to be tired with the hardness of the bed, or the upper one to suffer from cold, they immediately leap up, and go to the fire, which soon relieves them from both inconveniences; and then returning to their couch, they expose alternately their sides to the cold, and to the hardness of the bed.

BEAVERS ON THE RIVER TEIFI, WALES, 1188

Gerald of Wales

The Teifi has another remarkable peculiarity. Of all the rivers in Wales, and of those in England south of the Humber, it is the only one where you can find beavers. Beavers build their castle-like lodges in the middle of rivers. They have an extraordinary method of conveying and carting timber from the woods to the water, for they use other beavers as waggons. The beavers of one team gnaw down the branches, and then another group has the instinct to turn over on their backs and to hold this wood tightly against their bellies with their four feet. Each of these last grips a branch in its teeth which sticks out on either side. A third group holds tightly on to this cross-branch with its teeth and pulls the animal in question along backwards together with its load. Anyone who witnesses this manoeuvre cannot fail to be impressed. Badgers use a not dissimilar device when they are cleaning out their sets, which they arrange to their satisfaction by digging into the soil and scraping at it with their paws. It is remarkable that in both species of animal there are to be found slaves which are prepared to accept a debasement of their natural habits and to suffer at the same time a certain wear and tear of the skin on their backs.

There in some deep and tranquil bend of the river the beavers piece together with such skill the logs of wood which form their lodge that no drop of water can easily enter and no storm however violent do harm to it or loosen it. They have no reason to fear any attack, except that of us human beings, and even we must bring our weapons shod with iron. When they are building a lodge, they bind the logs together with willow-wands. The number of storeys placed one above the other varies according to the rise in the water-level which they foresee. They plan their construction so that it just protrudes from the water, with connecting door-ways inside to lead from one storey to another. Whenever they have decided that it is necessary, they can keep a lookout from the top and watch the rising waters when the river is in spate. As the years pass and the willow-wands keep on growing, the lodge is constantly in leaf and becomes, in fact, a grove of willow-trees, looking like a natural bush from the outside, however artificially constructed it may be within.

THE CORONATION OF RICHARD I, 5 JULY 1189

Anon

An absentee monarch – it is doubtful he could speak the king's English – the Angevin Richard I departed England within weeks of his coronation to join the Third Crusade; he spent the second half of his reign (1189–1199) in an obscure war in France against Phillip II Augustus. His military prowess, nonetheless, earned him the sobriquet 'Coeur de Lion' and an enduring place in Medieval legend.

Therefore in the same year, after the death of his father, Richard, Count of Poitou, having arranged his affairs in Normandy, in about two months crossed over to England, and on St. Giles's Day he was received at Westminster, with a ceremonious procession; and three days afterwards, viz., on the 3rd of September, the day of the ordination of St. Gregory the Pope, which was a Sunday, he was solemnly anointed king by the imposition of hands, by Archbishop Baldwin, in virtue of his office, who performed the service, assisted by many of his suffragans. At his coronation were present his brother John, and his mother Eleanor (of Aquitaine), who, after the death of King Henry, had been, by the command of her son Richard, the new king, released from prison, where she had been ten years; and there were also present counts and barons, and an immense crowd of men and soldiers; and the kingdom was confirmed to the hands of King Richard. On the 3rd day of September, in the year of our Lord 1189, Richard was anointed king, on a Sunday, with the dominical letter A., viz., in the year after leap year. Many were the conjectures made, because the day above that was marked unlucky in the calendar; and in truth it was unlucky, and very much so to the Jews in London, who were destroyed that day, and likewise the Jews settled in other parts of England endured many hardships. Having celebrated the occasion by a festival of three days, and entertained his guests in the royal palace of Westminster, King Richard gratified all, by distributing money, without count or number, to all according to their ranks, thus manifesting his liberality and his great excellence. His generosity, and his virtuous endowments, the ruler of the world should have given to the ancient times; for in this period of the world, as it waxes old, such feelings rarely exhibit themselves, and when they do they are subjects of wonder and astonishment. He had the valour of Hector, the magnanimity of Achilles, and was equal to Alexander, and not inferior to Roland in valour; nay, he outshone many illustrious characters of our own times. The liberality of a Titus was his, and, which is so rarely found in a soldier, he was gifted with the eloquence of Nestor and the prudence of Ulysses; and he shewed himself pre-eminent in the conclusion and transaction of business, as one whose knowledge was not without active goodwill to aid it, nor his goodwill wanting in knowledge. Who, if Richard were accused of presumption, would not readily excuse him, knowing him for a man who never knew defeat, impatient of an injury, and impelled irresistibly to vindicate his rights, though all he did was char-acterized by innate nobleness of mind? Success made him better fitted for action; fortune ever favours the bold, and though she works her pleasure on whom she will, Richard was never to be overwhelmed with adversity. He was tall of stature, graceful in figure; his hair between red and auburn; his limbs were straight and flexible; his arms rather long, and not to be matched for wielding the sword or for striking with it; and his long legs suited the rest of his frame; while his appearance was commanding, and his manners and habits suitable; and he gained the greatest celebrity, not more from his high birth than from the virtues that adorned him. But why need we take much labour in extolling the fame of so great a man? He needs no superfluous commendation, for he has a sufficient meed of praise, which is the sure companion of great actions. He was far superior to all others both in moral goodness and in strength, and memorable for prowess in battles, and his mighty deeds outshone the most brilliant description we could give of them. Happy, in truth, might he have been deemed had he been without rivals who envied his glorious actions, and whose only cause of enmity was his magnificence, and his being the searcher after virtue rather than the slave of vice.

THE LAWS OF RICHARD I CONCERNING CRUSADERS WHO WERE TO GO BY SEA, 1189

Roger of Hoveden

The fall of Jerusalem to Saladin in 1187 inspired a Third Crusade to deliver the Holy Land from Islam.

Richard by the grace of God king of England, and duke of Normandy and Aquitaine, and count of Anjou, to all his subjects who are about to go by sea to Jerusalem, greeting. Know that we, by the common counsel of upright men, have made the laws here given. Whoever slays a man on shipboard shall be bound to the dead man and thrown into the sea. But if he shall slay him on land, he shall be bound to the dead man and buried in the earth. If any one, moreover, shall be convicted through lawful witnesses of having drawn a knife to strike another, or of having struck him so as to draw blood, he shall lose his hand. But if he shall strike him with his fist without drawing blood, he shall be dipped three times in the sea. But if any one shall taunt or insult a comrade or charge him with hatred of God: as many times as he shall have insulted him, so many ounces of silver shall he pay. A robber, moreover, convicted of theft, shall be shorn like a hired fighter, and boiling tar shall be poured over his head, and feathers from a cushion shall be shaken out over his head, – so that he may be publicly known; and at the first land where the ships put in he shall be cast on shore. Under my own witness at Chinon.

THE THIRD CRUSADE; RICHARD I MASSACRES MUSSULMAN PRISONERS, ACRE, 2–20 AUGUST 1191

Beha-ed-Din

Richard I retook Acre (modern day Akka in Israel) from Saladin in July 1191.

The same day Hossam ad-Din Ibn Barîc, an interpreter working with the English, issued from Acre accompanied by two officers of the King of England. He brought news that the King of France had set out for Tyre, and that they had come to talk over the matter of a possible exchange of prisoners and to see the true cross of the Crucifixion if it were still in the Mussulman camp, or to ascertain if it really had been sent to Baghdad. The True Cross was shown to them, and on beholding it they showed the profoundest reverence, throwing themselves on the ground till they were covered with dust, and humbling themselves in token of devotion. These envoys told us that the European princes had accepted the Sultan's (Saladin's) proposition, viz., to deliver all that was specified in the treaty by three instalments at intervals of a month. The Sultan then sent an envoy to Tyre with rich presents, quantities of perfumes, and fine raiment – all of which were for the King of the French.

In the morning of the tenth day of Rajab, (3 August) Ibn Barîc and his comrades returned to the King of England while the Sultan went off with his bodyguard and his closest friends to the hill that abuts on Shefa'Amr . . . Envoys did not cease to pass from one side to the other in the hope of laying the foundation of a firm peace. These negotiations continued till our men had procured the money and the number of prisoners that they were to deliver to the Christians at the end of the first period in accordance with the treaty. The first instalment was to consist of the Holy Cross, 100,000 dinars and 1,600 prisoners. Trustworthy men sent by the Christians to conduct the examination found it all complete saving only the prisoners who had been demanded by name, all of whom had not yet been gathered together. And thus the negotiations continued to drag on till the end of the first term. On this day, the 18th of Rajab (11 August), the enemy sent demanding what was due.

The Sultan replied as follows: "Choose one of two things. Either send us back our comrades and receive the payment fixed for this term, in which case we will give hostages to ensure the full execution of all that is left. Or accept what we are going to send you today, and in your turn give us hostages to keep until those of our comrades whom you hold prisoners are restored." To this the envoys made answer: "Not so. Send us what is due for this term and in return we will give our solemn oath that your people shall be restored you."

This proposition the Sultan rejected, knowing full well that if he were to deliver the money, the Cross, and the prisoners, while our men were still kept captive by the Christians, he would have no security against treachery on the part of the enemy, and this would be a great disaster to Islam.

Then the King of England, seeing all the delays interposed by the Sultan to the execution of the treaty, acted perfidiously as regards his Mussulman prisoners. On their yielding the town of Acre he had engaged to grant them life, adding that if the Sultan carried out the bargain he would give them freedom and suffer them to carry off their children and wives; if the Sultan did not fulfil his engagements they were to be made slaves. Now the King broke his promises to them and made open display of what he had till now kept hidden in his heart, by carrying out what he had intended to do after he had received the money and the Christian prisoners. It is thus that people in his nation ultimately admitted.

In the afternoon of Tuesday, 27 Rajab (20 August), about four o'clock, he came out on horseback with all the Christian army, knights, footmen, Turcopoles and advanced to the pits at the foot of the hill of Al 'Ayâdîyeh, to which place he had already sent on his tents. The Christians, on reaching the middle of the plain that stretches between this hill and that of Keisân, close to which place the Sultan's advanced guard had drawn back, ordered all the Mussulman prisoners, whose martyrdom God had decreed for this day, to be brought before him. They numbered more than three thousand and were all bound with ropes. The Christians then flung themselves upon them all at once and massacred them with sword and lance in cold blood. Our advanced guard had already told the Sultan of the enemy's movements and he sent it some reinforcements, but only after the massacre. The Mussulmans, seeing what was being done to the prisoners, rushed against the Christians and in the combat, which lasted till nightfall, several were slain and wounded on either side. On the morrow morning our people gathered at the spot and found the Mussulmans stretched out upon the ground as martyrs for the faith. They even recognized some of the dead, and the sight was a great affliction to them. The enemy had only spared the prisoners of note and such as were strong enough to work.

The motives of this massacre are differently told; according to some, the captives were slain by way of reprisal for the death of those Christians whom the Mussulmans had slain. Others again say that the King of England, on deciding to attempt the conquest of Ascalon, thought it unwise to leave so many prisoners in the town after his departure. God alone knows what the real reason was.

LONDONERS RIOT AGAINST THE TALLIAGE TAX, 1194

Roger of Wendover

About this time there arose a dispute in the city of London between the poor and the rich on account of the talliage, which was exacted by the king's agents for the benefit of the exchequer: for the principal men of the city, whom we call mayors and aldermen, having held a deliberation at their hustings, wished to preserve themselves free from the burden, and to oppress the poorer classes. Wherefore William Fitz-Robert, surnamed "with the beard," because his ancestors in anger against the Normans never shaved, made opposition to the same, and called the mayors of the city traitors to our lord the king for the cause above-named; and the disturbances were so great in the city that recourse was had to arms. William stirred up a large number of the middle and lower classes against the mayors and aldermen, but by their pusillanimity and cowardice the plans of William's confederates in resisting the injury done them were dissipated and defeated: the middle and lower classes were repressed, and the king, his ministers, and the chief men of the city charged the whole crime on William. As the king's party were about to arrest him, he, being a distinguished character in the city, tall of stature and of great personal strength, escaped, notwithstanding their exertions, defending himself with nothing but a knife, and flying into the church of St. Mary of the Arches, demanded the protection of our Lord, St. Mary, and her church, saying that he had resisted an unjust decree for no other purpose than that all might bear an equal share of the public burden, and contribute according to their means. His expostulations, however, were not listened to, the majority prevailed, and the archbishop, to the surprise of many, ordered that he should be dragged from the church to take his trial, because he had created a sedition and made such a disturbance among the people of the city. When this was told to William, he took refuge in the tower of the church, for he knew that the mayors, whom he had contradicted, sought to take away his life. In their obstinacy they applied fire, and sacrilegiously burnt down a great part of the church. Thus William was forced to leave the tower, almost suffocated with the heat and smoke. He was then seized, dragged out of the church, stripped, and, with his hands tied behind his back, conveyed away to the Tower of London. Soon after, at the instigation of the archbishop, the principal citizens, and the king's ministers, he was taken from the Tower, and dragged, tied to a horse's tail, through the middle of London to Ulmet, a pitiable sight to the citizens and to his own respectable relations in the city: after which he was hung in chains on a gallows. Thus William of the Beard was shamefully put to death by his fellow citizens for asserting the truth and defending the cause of the poor: and if the justice of one's cause constitutes a martyr, we may surely set him down as one. With him also were hanged nine of his neighbours or of his family, who espoused his cause.

A BOXING DAY AFFRAY, 1197

Jocelin of Brakelond

Jocelin of Brakelond was a monk in the abbey of Bury St Edmunds.

On the day after Christmas Day, there were gatherings in the cemetery, with contests and competitions between the abbot's servants and the townspeople, but matters escalated from words to blows, and then from punches to wounds and bloodshed. When the abbot heard about it, he asked some of those who had gone to the show, but had stood on the sidelines, to come and see him privately, and he commanded the names of the miscreants to be written down. He had all these summoned to appear before him in St Denis's chapel on the day after St Thomas Becket's Day (i.e. 30 December). In the interim he did not invite any of the townspeople to his table as in previous years he had normally done on the first five days of Christmas. On the appointed day, after the evidence on oath of sixteen sworn men had been heard, the abbot said, "These wicked men obviously fall within the canon *sentenciae latae*, but because they are laymen from here and roundabout, and do not appreciate how outrageous it is to commit such sacrilege, I shall publicly excommunicate them by name, so that others may be more fearful. I shall begin with my own household and servants to ensure that justice is done impartially." This was carried out as soon as we had put on stoles and candles were lit. Then they all left the church, and after some discussion they undressed and, naked except for their pants, prostrated themselves in front of the church door. When the abbot's assistants, monks and clerks, came and told him tearfully that over a hundred naked men were lying there, the abbot also wept. But in his words and in his face he displayed the severity of the law, hiding his inner compassion, for he wished to be urged by his advisers to absolve the penitents, knowing that mercy is exalted above judgement, and that the church receives all those who repent. Therefore, when they had all been severely beaten and absolved, they took an oath that they would accept the church's judgement regarding the sacrilege they had committed. The following day they were given penances according to canon law, and the abbot took them all back into complete unity. But he uttered terrible threats against anyone who, by word or deed, should create discord, and he publicly prohibited assemblies and shows in the cemetery. So, when everyone had been restored to the blessing of peace, it was with great rejoicing that on the following days the townspeople feasted with their lord the abbot.

THE WINNING OF THE MAGNA CARTA, 1215
Roger of Wendover

A landmark in the struggle for English constitutional liberty, prised from King John by an uppity baronage opposed to his arbitrary rule and ruinous foreign policy.

Of a Conference held by the Barons Against King John
About this time (Summer 1214) the earls and barons of England assembled at St. Edmund's, as if for religious duties, although it was for some other reason; for after they had discoursed together

secretly for a time, there was placed before them the charter of king Henry the First, which they had received, as mentioned before, in the city of London from Stephen archbishop of Canterbury. This charter contained certain liberties and laws granted to the holy church as well as to the nobles of the kingdom besides some liberties which the king added of his own accord. All therefore assembled in the church of St. Edmund, the king and martyr, and, commencing from those of the highest rank, they all swore on the great altar that, if the king refused to grant these liberties and laws, they themselves would withdraw from their allegiance to him, and make war on him, till he should, by a charter under his own seal, confirm to them every thing they required; and finally it was unanimously agreed that, after Christmas, they should all go together to the king and demand the confirmation of the aforesaid liberties to them, and that they should in the meantime provide themselves with horses and arms, so that if the king should endeavour to depart from his oath, they might by taking his castles, compel him to satisfy their demands; and having arranged this, each man returned home . . .

AD 1215; which was the seventeenth year of the reign of king John; he held his court at Winchester at Christmas for one day, after which he hurried to London, and took up his abode at the New Temple; and at that place the above-mentioned nobles came to him in gay military array, and demanded the confirmation of the liberties and laws of king Edward, with other liberties granted to them and to the kingdom and church of England, as were contained in the charter, and above-mentioned laws of Henry the First; they also asserted that, at the time of his absolution at Winchester, he had promised to restore those laws and ancient liberties, and was bound by his own oath to observe them. The king, hearing the bold tone of the barons in making this demand, much feared an attack from them, as he saw that they were prepared for battle; he however made answer that their demands were a matter of importance and difficulty, and he therefore asked a truce till the end of Easter, that he might, after due deliberation, be able to satisfy them as well as the dignity of his crown. After much discussion on both sides, the king at-length, although unwillingly, procured the archbishop of Canterbury, the bishop of Ely, and William Marshal, as his sureties, that on the day pre-agreed on he would, in all reason, satisfy them all, on which the nobles returned to their homes. The king however, wishing to take precautions against the future, caused all the nobles throughout England to swear fealty to him alone against all men, and to renew their homage to him; and, the better to take care of himself, he, on the day of St. Mary's purification, assumed the cross of our Lord, being induced to this more by fear than devotion . . .

Of the Principal Persons who Compelled the King to Grant the Laws and Liberties

In Easter week of this same year, the above-mentioned nobles assembled at Stamford, with horses and arms; for they had now induced almost all the nobility of the whole kingdom to join them, and constituted a very large army; for in their army there were computed to be two thousand knights, besides horse soldiers, attendants, and foot soldiers, who were variously equipped . . . The king at this time was awaiting the arrival of his nobles at Oxford. On the Monday next after the octaves of Easter, the said barons assembled in the town of Brackley: and when the king learned this, he sent the archbishop of Canterbury, and William Marshal earl of Pembroke, with some other prudent men, to them to inquire what the laws and liberties were which they demanded. The barons then delivered to the messengers a paper, containing in great measure the laws and ancient customs of the kingdom, and declared that, unless the king immediately granted them and confirmed them under his own seal, they would, by taking possession of his fortresses, force him to give them sufficient satisfaction as to their before-named demands. The archbishop with his fellow messengers then carried the paper to the king, and read to him the heads of the paper one by one throughout. The king when he heard the purport of these heads, derisively said, with the greatest indignation, "Why, amongst these unjust demands, did not the barons ask for my kingdom also? Their demands are vain and visionary, and are unsupported by any plea of reason whatever." And at length he angrily declared with an oath, that he would never grant them such liberties as would render him their slave. The principal of these laws and liberties, which the nobles required to be confirmed to them, are partly described above in the charter of king Henry, and partly are extracted from the old laws of king Edward, as the following history will show in due time.

The Castle of Northampton Besieged by the Barons

As the archbishop and William Marshal could not by any
persuasions induce the king to agree to their demands they
returned by the king's order to the barons, and duly reported
all they had heard from the king to them; and when the nobles
heard what John said, they appointed Robert Fitz-Walter commander of their soldiers, giving him the title of "Marshal of the
army of God and the holy church," and then, one and all flying to
arms, they directed their forces towards Northampton. On their
arrival there they at once laid siege to the castle, but after having
stayed there for fifteen days, and having gained little or no
advantage, they determined to move their camp; for having come
without petrariæ and other engines of war, they, without accom-
plishing their purpose, proceeded in confusion to the castle of
Bedford . . .

How the City of London was Given up to the Barons

When the army of the barons arrived at Bedford, they were
received with all respect by William de Beauchamp. There also
came to them there messengers from the city of London, secretly
telling them, if they wished to get into that city, to come there
immediately. The barons, inspirited by the arrival of this agreeable
message, immediately moved their camp and arrived at Ware;
after this they marched the whole night, and arrived early in the
morning at the city of London, and, finding the gates open, they,
on the 24th of May, which was the Sunday next before our Lord's
ascension, entered the city without any tumult whilst the inhabitants were performing divine service; for the rich citizens were
favourable to the barons, and the poor ones were afraid to murmur
against them. The barons having thus got into the city, placed
their own guards in charge of each of the gates, and then arranged
all matters in the city at will. They then took security from the
citizens, and sent letters through England to those earls, barons,
and knights, who appeared to be still faithful to the king, though
they only pretended to be so, and advised them with threats, as
they regarded the safety of all their property and possessions, to
abandon a king who was perjured and who warred against his
barons, and together with them to stand firm and fight against the
king for their rights and for peace; and that, if they refused to do
this, they, the barons, would make war against them all, as against
open enemies, and would destroy their castles, burn their houses

and other buildings, and destroy their warrens, parks, and orch-ards. . . . The greatest part of these, on receiving the message of the barons, set out to London and joined them, abandoning the king entirely . . .

The Conference Between the King and the Barons

King John, when he saw that he was deserted by almost all, so that out of his regal superabundance of followers he scarcely retained seven knights, was much alarmed lest the barons would attack his castles and reduce them without difficulty, as they would find no obstacle to their so doing; and he deceitfully pretended to make peace for a time with the aforesaid barons, and sent William Marshal earl of Pembroke, with other trustworthy messengers, to them, and told them that, for the sake of peace, and for the exaltation and honour of the kingdom, he would willingly grant them the laws and liberties they required; he also sent word to the barons by these same messengers, to appoint a fitting day and place to meet and carry all these matters into effect. The king's messengers then came in all haste to London, and without deceit reported to the barons all that had been deceitfully imposed on them; they in their great joy appointed the fifteenth of June for the king to meet them, at a field lying between Staines and Windsor. Accordingly, at the time and place pre-agreed on, the king and nobles came to the appointed conference, and when each party had stationed themselves apart from the other, they began a long discussion about terms of peace and the aforesaid liberties. . . . At length, after various points on both sides had been discussed, king John, seeing that he was inferior in strength to the barons, without raising any difficulty, granted the underwritten laws and liberties, and confirmed them by his charter . . .

By the most famous clauses of the Magna Carta, everyone was granted justice and all free men secured from illegal interference with their person and property. The Carta, however, failed to prevent civil war. When John intentionally breached its terms, the barons offered the English crown to Louis of France in 1215. Not until 1217 was the "Barons' War" defeated, when the monarchy – now led by the deceased John's son Henry III – won the battle of Lincoln. There was a second round in 1264, with the rebellion led by Simon de Montfort. Although crushed by Edward I in 1267, the uprising secured more constraints on the royal prerogative.

THE WEATHER, 1236

Matthew Paris

. . . About the same time, for two months and more, namely, in January, February, and part of March, such deluges of rain fell as had never been seen before in the memory of any one. About the feast of St Scholastica (10 February), when the moon was new, the sea became so swollen by the river torrents which fell into it, that all the rivers, especially those which fell into the sea, rendered the fords impassable, overflowing their banks, hiding the bridges from sight, carrying away mills and dams, and overwhelming the cultivated lands, crops, meadows, and marshes. Amongst other unusual occurrences, the river Thames overflowed its usual bounds, and entered the grand palace at Westminster, where it spread and covered the whole area, so that small boats could float there, and people went to their apartments on horseback. The water also forcing its way into the cellars could with difficulty be drained off. The signs of this storm which preceded it, then gave proofs of their threats; for on the day of St Damasus (i.e. 11 December 1235), thunder was heard, and on the Friday next after the conception of St Mary (i.e. Friday, 14 December 1235), a spurious sun was seen by the side of the true sun. . . . In the summer of this year, after a winter beyond measure rainy, as has been mentioned, a constant drought, attended by an almost unendurable heat, succeeded, which lasted for four months and more. The marshes and lakes were dried up to their very bottoms; watermills stood uselessly still – the water being dried up; and the earth gaped with numerous fissures; the corn too in a great many places scarcely grew to the height of two feet. . . . Near about the same time too, namely on the Monday following that feast (Michaelmas), deluges of rain fell in the northern parts of England, to such a degree that the rivers and lakes, overflowing their usual bounds, caused great damage by destroying bridges, mills, and other property near the banks. . . . On the day after the feast of St Martin (11 November), and within the octaves of that feast, great inundations of the sea suddenly broke forth by night, and a fierce storm of wind arose, which caused inundations of the rivers, as well as of the sea, and in places, especially on the coast, drove the ships from their ports, tearing them from their anchors, drowned great numbers of people, destroyed flocks of sheep, and herds of cattle, tore up trees by the roots, overthrew houses, and ravaged the coast. The sea rose for two days and the intermediate night, a circumstance before unheard of, and did not ebb and flow in its usual way, being impeded (as was said) by the violence of the opposing winds. The dead bodies of those drowned were seen lying unburied in caves formed by the sea, near the coast, and at Wisbeach and the neighbouring villages, and along the sea-coast. An endless number of human beings perished.

CASTRATION OF A KNIGHT, 1248
Matthew Paris

I must not omit to mention, even if it seems ridiculous, the disgrace and irreparable harm which happened in this same most unlucky month to the knights. For a certain Norfolk knight of noble birth and accomplished prowess, named Godfrey de Millers, wretchedly led astray, one night secretly entered the house of a knight called John Brito to sleep with his daughter. But he was prevented by some people placed in ambush with the connivance of the whore, who was afraid of being found out. He was seized, savagely thrown to the ground and badly wounded. Then he was suspended from a beam by his feet with his legs stretched apart, so that he was completely at the mercy of his enemies, who disgracefully mutilated him by cutting off his genital organs, though he would have preferred to be beheaded. Thus wounded and castrated, he was thrown out half dead. The noise of complaint reached the king, the authors of this cruelty were arrested, and John Brito was convicted and sentenced to irrecoverable disinheritance and irrevocable exile. The adulteress managed to avoid death by going into hiding so that she could not be found. All who were present at this flagrant deed were dispersed and banished, exiles and fugitives, so that this inhuman and in every way merciless crime involved many nobles in a miserable calamity.

VIOLENT DEATHS, ENGLAND, 1267–87
Calendar of Inquisitions

Death by Misadventure, 1267
On Wednesday before Ascension day 51 Henry III William de Stangate came down a road called Burleyesdam (in Sussex) with a

cross-bow on his left shoulder and a poisoned arrow, and he met Desiderata, late the wife of Robert le Champeneys, who was his child's godmother, and a particular friend. And she asked him in jest, whether he were one of the men who were going about the country with cross-bows and other weapons, to apprehend robbers and evildoers by the king's order; adding that she could overcome and take two or three like him. And putting out her arm she caught him by the neck and crooking her leg behind his without his noticing it, she upset him and fell on him. And in falling she struck herself in the side with the arrow which he had under his belt, piercing to the heart, and died on the spot. *Verdict.* Death by misadventure.

A Wedding Brawl, 1268

A certain stranger being new-married was taking his wife and others who were with her to one end of the town of Byrun, when William Selisaule asked for a ball, which it is the custom to give: and they having no ball gave him a pair of gloves for a pledge; afterwards other men of Byrun asked for a ball, and they said they would not give one, because they had already given a pledge for one, and the men of Byrun would not believe them, but still asked for the said ball; and so there arose a dispute, and the wedding party, being slightly drunk, assaulted the men of Byrun with axes and bows and arrows, and wounded very many; and the said William hearing the noise, and thinking it was for the ball for which he had a pledge, ran with a stick to appease the dispute; and when he had come near, one William son of Ralph de Rotil(?) drew an arrow at him and hit him in the breast, so that he thought he had got his death; as the said William son of Ralph, not yet content, was meaning to shoot at him again, he saw that he could only escape the arrow by hitting him back, so as to hinder his drawing; so he ran up to the said William son of Ralph to hit him on the arm, but by mischance, hit the said Adam (de Auwerne), who unwittingly came between them, so he died." Thus the said William Selisaule killed the said Adam by mischance, and not of malice prepense.

A Stabbing, 1287

John de Quercubus of Scottes Acton killed Hugh de Weston, chaplain, in self defence. On Christmas day 16 Edward I after sunset there were some men singing outside a tavern kept by

Richard son of William de Skottesacton in that town. And Hugh came by the door immensely drunk, and quarreled with the singers. Now John was standing by, singing, and Hugh hated him a little because he sang well, and desired the love of certain woman who were standing by in a field and whom Hugh much affected. So Hugh took a naked sword in his hand and ran at John, striking him once, twice, thrice, on the head, and nearly cutting off two fingers of his left hand. And John went on his knees, and raised his hands asking God's peace and the king's, and then ran into a corner near the street under a stone wall. And Hugh ran after him and tried to kill him, so he drew his knife and wounded Hugh in the chest, killing him instantly.

MISADVENTURES IN CHILDHOOD, LONDON, 1301–1337

Calendar of the Coroner's Rolls

A Game on the Way to School, 1301
On Tuesday (19 July), Richard, son of John le Mazon, who was eight years old, was walking immediately after dinner across London Bridge to school. For fun, he tried to hang by his hands from a beam on the side of the bridge, but his hands giving way, he fell into the water and was drowned. Being asked who were present, the jurors say a great multitude of passers-by, whose names they know not, but they suspect no one of the death except mischance.

Playing on the Timber Pile, 1322
On the Sunday before the Feast of St Dunstan, Robert, son of John de St Botulph, a boy seven years old, Richard, son of John de Chesthunt, and two other boys whose names are unknown were playing on certain pieces of timber in the lane called "Kyroune-lane" in the ward of Vintry, and one piece fell on Robert and broke his right leg. In course of time Johanna his mother arrived and rolled the timber off him and carried him to the shop, where he lingered until the Friday before the Feast of St Margaret, when he died at the hour of prime, of the broken leg and of no other felony; nor do the jurors suspect anyone of the death, but only the accident and the fracture.

A Lost Ball, 1337

On Tuesday in Pentecost week John, son of William atte Noke, chandler, got out of a window in the rent of John de Wynton, plumber, to recover a ball lost in a gutter at play. He slipped and fell, and so injured himself that he died on the Saturday following, of the fall.

THE EXECUTION OF WILLIAM WALLACE, 23 AUGUST 1305

"Matthew of Westminster"

Sir William Wallace was the leader of the 1297 rebellion against English sovereighty over Scotland, secured by Edward I's defeat of the Scots at Dunbar.

Wilielmus Waleis, a man void of pity, a robber given to sacrilege, arson and homicide, more hardened in cruelty than Herod, more raging in madness than Nero . . . was condemned to a most cruel but justly deserved death. He was drawn through the streets of London at the tails of horses, until he reached a gallows of unusual height, especially prepared for him; there he was suspended by a halter; but taken down while yet alive, he was mutilated, his bowels torn out and burned in a fire, his head then cut off, his body divided into four, and his quarters transmitted to four principal parts of Scotland. Behold the end of the merciless man, who himself perishes without mercy.

THE BATTLE OF BANNOCKBURN, 24 JUNE 1314

Friar Barton

The decisive battle in the Anglo-Scottish wars; by virtue of victory, Scotland was never again conquered.

On the morrow – an evil, miserable and calamitous day for the English – when both sides had made themselves ready for battle, the English archers were thrown forward before the line, and the Scottish archers engaged them, a few being killed and wounded on either side; but the King of England's archers quickly put the others to flight. Now when the two armies had approached very near each other, all the Scots fell on their knees to repeat *Pater-Noster*, commending themselves to God and seeking help from heaven; after which they advanced boldly against the English. They had so arranged their army that two columns went abreast in advance of the third, so that neither should be in advance of the other; and the third followed, in which was Robert (the Bruce). Of a truth, when both armies engaged each other, and the great horses of the English charged the pikes of the Scots, as it were into a dense forest, there arose a great and terrible crash of spears broken and of destriers wounded to the death; and so they remained without movement for a while. Now the English in the rear could not reach the Scots because the leading division was in the way, nor could they do anything to help themselves, wherefore there was nothing for it but to take to flight. This account I heard from a trust-worthy person who was present as eyewitness.

In the leading division were killed the Earl of Gloucester, Sir John Comyn, Sir Pagan de Typtoft, Sir Edmund de Mauley and many other nobles, besides foot soldiers who fell in great numbers. Another calamity which befell the English was that, whereas they had shortly before crossed a great ditch called Bannockburn, into which the tide flows, and now wanted to recross it in confusion, many nobles and others fell into it with their horses in the crush, while others escaped with much difficulty, and many were never able to extricate themselves from the ditch; thus Bannockburn was spoken about for many years in English throats.

A BAKER'S TRICKS, 1327

Anon

A congregation of . . . aldermen, and Roger Chauntecler, one of the sheriffs of London, holden at the Guildhall, on Thursday in the week of Pentecost, that is, on the 4th day of June AD 1327 . . .

John Brid, baker, was attached to make answer as to certain falsehood, malice, and deceit, by him committed, to the nuisance of the common people; as to which, the mayor, aldermen, and sheriffs of the City were given to understand that the same John, for falsely and maliciously obtaining his own private advantage, did skilfully and artfully cause a certain hole to be made upon a table of his, called a "*moldingborde*," pertaining to his bakehouse, after the manner of a mouse-trap, in which mice are caught; there being a certain wicket warily provided for closing and opening such hole.

And when his neighbours and others, who were wont to bake their bread at his oven, came with their dough or material for making bread, the said John used to put such dough or other material upon the said table, called a *"moldingborde,"* as aforesaid, and over the hole before-mentioned for the purpose of making loaves therefrom, for baking; and such dough or material being so placed upon the table aforesaid, the same John had one of his household, ready provided for the same, sitting in secret beneath such table; which servant of his, so seated beneath the hole, and carefully opening it, piecemeal and bit by bit craftily withdrew some of the dough aforesaid, frequently collecting great quantities from such dough, falsely, wickedly, and maliciously; to the great loss of all his neighbours and persons living near, and of others, who had come to him with such dough to bake, and to the scandal and disgrace of the whole City, and, in especial, of the mayor and bailiffs for the safe-keeping of the assizes of the City assigned. Which hole, so found in his table aforesaid, was made of aforethought; and in like manner, a great quantity of such dough that had been drawn through the said hole, was found beneath the hole, and was . . . brought here into Court.

And the same John, here present in court, being asked how he will acquit himself of the fraud, malice, and deceit aforesaid, personally in court says that of such fraud, malice, and deceit, he is in no way guilty; and puts himself upon the country thereon, etc. Therefore, let inquisition as to the truth of the matter be made by the country, etc . . .

And after counsel and treaty had been held among the mayor and aldermen, as to passing judgment upon the falsehood, malice, and deceit aforesaid; seeing that, although there is no one who prosecutes them, or any one of them, the said deed is, as it were a certain species of theft, and that it is neither consonant with right nor pleasing to God that such falsehood, deceit, and malice shall go unpunished; the more especially as all those who have come to the said bakers, to bake their bread, have been falsely, wickedly, and maliciously deceived, they themselves being wholly ignorant thereof, and have suffered no little loss thereby; it was agreed and ordained, that all those of the bakers aforesaid, beneath whose tables with holes dough had been found, should be put upon the pillory, with a certain quantity of such dough hung from their necks; and that those bakers in whose houses dough was not found beneath the tables aforesaid, should be put upon the pillory, but without dough hung from their necks; and that they should so remain upon the pillory until vespers at St. Paul's in London should be ended.

THE BATTLE OF CRECY, FRANCE, 26 SEPTEMBER 1346

Sir John Froissart

Fought in pursuit of King Edward II's claim to the throne of France.

That night the King of France entertained at supper, in Abbeville, all the princes and chief lords of his army. There was much conversation relative to the war; and after supper the King entreated them always to remain in friendship with each other; "to be friends without jealousy, and courteous without pride". All the French forces had not yet arrived, for the King was still expecting the Earl of Savoy, who ought to have been there with a thousand lances, as he had well paid for them at Troyes in Champaign, three months in advance. That same evening the King of England also gave a supper to his earls and barons, and when it was over he withdrew into his oratory, where falling on his knees before the altar, he prayed to God that if he should combat his enemies on the morrow, he might come off with honour. About midnight he retired to rest, and rising early the next day, he and the Prince of Wales heard mass and communicated. The great part of his army did the same. After mass the King ordered his men to arm themselves and assemble on the ground which he had before fixed upon.

There was a large park near a wood, on the rear of the army, which King Edward enclosed, and in it placed all his baggage, wagons and horses; for his men-at-arms and archers were to fight on foot. He afterwards ordered, through his constable and his two marshals, that the army should be divided into three battalions. In the first, he placed the young Prince of Wales, and with him the Earls of Warwick and Oxford, Sir Godfrey de Harcourt, the Lord Reginald Cobham, Lord Thomas Holland, Lord Stafford, Lord Mauley, the Lord Delaware, Sir John Chandos, Lord Bartholomew Burghersh, Lord Robert Neville, Lord Thomas Clifford, the Lord Bouchier, the Lord Latimer, and many other knights and squires whom I cannot name. There might be, in this first division, about 800 men-at-arms, 2000 archers, and 1000 Welshmen; all of whom advanced in regular order to their ground, each lord under his banner and pennon, and in the centre of his men. In the second battalion were the Earl of Northampton, the Earl of Arundel, the Lords Ross, Willoughby, Basset, Saint Albans, Sir Lewis Tufton, Lord Multon, the Lord Lascels, and many others, amounting in the whole to about 800 men-at-arms, and 1200 archers. The third battalion was commanded by the King in person, and was composed of about 700 men-at-arms, and 2000 archers. The King was mounted on a small palfrey, having a white wand in his hand, and attended by his two marshals. In this manner he rode at a foot's pace through all the ranks, encouraging the army and entreating that they would guard his honour and defend his right; so sweetly and with such a cheerful countenance did he speak, that all who had been before dispirited, were directly comforted by hearing him. By the time he had thus visited all the battalions it was nearly ten o'clock: he then retired to his own division, having ordered the men to regale themselves, after which all returned to their own battalions, according to the marshal's orders, and seated themselves on the ground, placing their helmets and bows before them, in order that they might be the fresher when their enemies should arrive.

That same Saturday the King of France also rose betimes, heard mass in the monastery of St Peter's in Abbeville, where he lodged; and having ordered his army to do the same, left that town after sunrise. When he had marched about two leagues from Abbeville and was approaching the enemy, he was advised to form his army in order of battle, and to let those on foot march forward that they might not be trampled on by the horses. This being done, he sent off four knights, the Lord Moyne, of Bastleberg, the Lord of Noyers, the Lord of Beaujeu, and the Lord of Aubigny, who rode so near to the English, that they could clearly distinguish their position. The English plainly perceived that these knights came to reconnoitre; however, they took no notice of it, but suffered them to return unmolested.

When the King of France saw them coming back, he halted his army, and the knights pushing through the crowds came near to the King, who said to them, "My lords, what news?" Neither chose to speak first – at last the King addressed himself personally to the Lord Moyne, who said, "Sir, I will speak since it pleases you to order me, but under correction of my companions. We have advanced far enough to reconnoitre your · enemies. Know, then, that they are drawn up in three battalions, and are waiting for you. I would advise for my part (submitting, however, to your better counsel) that you halt your army here and quarter them for the night; for before the rear shall come up, and the army be properly drawn up, it will be very late, and your men will be tired and in disorder, whilst they will find your enemies fresh and properly arrayed. On the morrow you may draw up your army more at your ease, and may at leisure reconnoitre on what part it will be most advantageous to begin the attack, for be assured they will wait for you." The King commanded that it should so be done; and the two marshals rode, one to the front and the other to the rear, crying out, "Halt banners, in the name of God and St Denis." Those that were in front, halted; but those that were behind said they would not halt until they were as forward as the front. When the front perceived the rear pressing on, they pushed forward; and as neither the King nor the marshals could stop them, they marched on without any order until they came in sight of their enemies. As soon as the foremost rank saw the English they fell back at once in great disorder, which alarmed those in the rear, who thought they had been fighting. All the roads between Abbeville and Crécy were covered with common people, who, when they were come within three leagues of their enemies, drew their swords, bawling out, "Kill, kill"; and with them were many lords eager to make a show of their courage.

There is no man, unless he had been present, that can imagine or describe truly the confusion of that day, especially the bad management and disorder of the French, whose troops were out of number. What I know, and shall relate in this book, I have learned chiefly from the English, and from those attached to Sir John of Hainault, who was always near the person of the King of France. The English, who, as I have said, were drawn up in three divisions, and seated on the ground, on seeing their enemies advance, rose up undauntedly and fell into their ranks. The Prince's battalion, whose archers were formed in the manner of a portcullis, and the men-at-arms in the rear, was the first to do so. The Earls of Northampton and Arundel, who commanded the second division, posted themselves in good order on the Prince's wing to assist him if necessary.

You must know that the French troops did not advance in any regular order, and that as soon as their King came in sight of the English his blood began to boil, and he cried out to his marshals, "Order the Genoese forward and begin the battle in the name of God and St Denis." There were about 15,000 Genoese crossbow men; but they were quite fatigued, having marched on foot that day six leagues, completely armed and carrying their crossbows, and accordingly they told the Constable they were not in a condition to do any great thing in battle. The Earl of Alençon hearing this, said, "This is what one gets by employing such scoundrels, who fall off when there is any need for them." During this time a heavy rain fell, accompanied by thunder and a very terrible eclipse of the sun; and, before this rain, a great flight of crows hovered in the air over all the battalions, making a loud noise; shortly afterwards it cleared up, and the sun shone very bright; but the French had it in their faces, and the English on their backs. When the Genoese were somewhat in order they approached the English and set up a loud shout, in order to frighten them; but the English remained quite quiet and did not seem to attend to it. They then set up a second shout, and advanced a little forward; the English never moved. Still they hooted a third time, advancing with their crossbows presented, and began to shoot. The English archers then advanced one step forward, and shot their arrows with such force and quickness, that it seemed as if it snowed. When the Genoese felt these arrows, which pierced through their armour, some of them cut the strings of their crossbows, others flung them to the ground, and all turned about and retreated quite discomfited.

The French had a large body of men-at-arms on horseback to support the Genoese, and the King, seeing them thus fall back, cried out, "Kill me those scoundrels, for they stop up our road without any reason." The English continued shooting, and some of their arrows falling among the horsemen, drove them upon the Genoese, so that they were in such confusion, they could never rally again.

In the English army there were some Cornish and Welsh men on foot, who had armed themselves with large knives, these advancing through the ranks of the men-at-arms and archers, who made way for them, came upon the French when they were in this danger, and falling upon earls, barons, knights, and squires, slew many, at which the King of England was exasperated. The valiant King of

Bohemia was slain there; he was called Charles of Luxembourg, for he was the son of the gallant king and emperor, Henry of Luxembourg, and, having heard the order for the battle, he inquired where his son the Lord Charles was; his attendants answered that they did not know, but believed he was fighting. Upon this, he said to them, "Gentlemen, you are all my people, my friends, and brethren at arms this day; therefore, as I am blind, I request of you to lead me so far into the engagement that I may strike one stroke with my sword." The knights consented, and in order that they might not lose him in the crowd, fastened all the reins of their horses together, placing the King at their head that he might gratify his wish, and in this manner advanced towards the enemy. The Lord Charles of Bohemia, who already signed his name as King of Germany, and bore the arms, had come in good order to the engagement; but when he perceived that it was likely to turn out against the French he departed. The King, his father, rode in among the enemy, and he and his companions fought most valiantly; however, they advanced so far that they were all slain, and on the morrow they were found on the ground with all their horses tied together.

The Earl of Alençon advanced in regular order upon the English, to fight with them, as did the Earl of Flanders in another part. These two lords with their detachments, coasting, as it were, the archers, came to the Prince's battalion, where they fought valiantly for a length of time. The King of France was eager to march to the place where he saw their banners displayed, but there was a hedge of archers before him: he had that day made a present of a handsome black horse to Sir John of Hainault, who had mounted on it a knight of his, called Sir John de Fusselles, who bore his banner; the horse ran off with the knight and forced his way through the English army, and when about to return, stumbled and fell into a ditch and severely wounded him; he did not, however, experience any other inconvenience than from his horse, for the English did not quit their ranks that day to make prisoners: his page alighted and raised him up, but the French knight did not return the way he came, as he would have found it difficult from the crowd. This battle, which was fought on Saturday, between La Broyes and Crécy, was murderous and cruel; and many gallant deeds of arms were performed that were never known: towards evening, many knights and squires of the French had lost their masters, and wandering up and down the plain, attacked the English in small parties; but they were soon destroyed, for the English had determined that day to give no quarter, nor hear of ransom from anyone.

Early in the day some French, Germans, and Savoyards had broken through the archers of the Prince's battalion, and had engaged with the men-at-arms; upon this the second battalion came to his aid, and it was time they did so, for otherwise he would have been hard pressed. The first division, seeing the danger they were in, sent a knight off in great haste to the King of England, who was posted upon an eminence near a windmill. On the knight's arrival he said, "Sir, the Earl of Warwick, the Lord Stafford, the Lord Reginald Cobham, and the others who are about your son, are vigorously attacked by the French, and they entreat that you will come to their assistance with your battalion, for if numbers should increase against him, they fear he will have too much to do." The King replied, "Is my son dead, unhorsed, or so badly wounded that he cannot support himself?" "Nothing of the sort, thank God," rejoined the knight, "but he is in so hot an engagement that he has great need of your help." The King answered, "Now, Sir Thomas, return to those that sent you, and tell them from me not to send again for me this day, nor expect that I shall come, let what will happen, as long as my son has life; and say that I command them to let the boy win his spurs, for I am determined, if it please God, that all the glory of this day shall be given to him, and to those into whose care I have entrusted him." The knights returned to his lords and related the King's answer, which mightily encouraged them, and made them repent they had ever sent such a message.

It is a certain fact, that Sir Godfrey de Harcourt, who was in the prince's battalion, having been told by some of the English that they had seen the banner of his brother engaged in the battle against him, was exceedingly anxious to save him; but he was too late, for he was left dead on the field, and so was the Earl of Aumarle, his nephew. On the other hand, the Earls of Alençon and Flanders were fighting lustily under their banners with their own people; but they could not resist the force of the English, and were there slain, as well as many other knights and squires, who were attending on, or accompanying them.

The Earl of Blois, nephew to the King of France, and the Duke of Lorraine, his brother-in-law, with their troops, made a gallant defence; but they were surrounded by a troop of English and

Welsh, and slain in spite of their prowess. The Earl of St Pol, and the Earl of Auxerre, were also killed, as well as many others. Late after vespers, the King of France had not more about him than sixty men, every one included. Sir John of Hainault, who was of the number, had once remounted the King, for his horse had been killed under him by an arrow: and seeing the state he was in, he said, "Sir, retreat whilst you have an opportunity, and do not expose yourself so simply; if you have lost this battle, another time you will be the conqueror." After he had said this he took the bridle of the King's horse and led him off by force, for he had before entreated him to retire. The king rode on until he came to the castle of La Broyes, where he found the gates shut, for it was very dark: he ordered the Governor of it to be summoned, who, after some delay, came upon the battlements, and asked who it was that called at such an hour. The King answered, "Open, open, Governor, it is the fortune of France." The Governor hearing the King's voice immediately descended, opened the gate, and let down the bridge; the King and his company entered the castle, but he had with him only five barons: Sir John of Hainault, the Lord Charles of Montmorency, the Lord of Beaujeu, the Lord of Aubigny, and the Lord of Montfort. It was not his intention, however, to bury himself in such a place as this, but having taken some refreshments, he set out again with his attendants about midnight, and rode on under the direction of guides, who were well acquainted with the country, until about daybreak he came to Amiens, where he halted. This Saturday the English never quitted their ranks in pursuit of anyone, but remained on the field guarding their position and defending themselves against all who attacked them. The battle ended at the hour of vespers, when the King of England embraced his son and said to him, "Sweet son, God give you perseverance: you are my son; for most loyally have you acquitted yourself; you are worthy to be a sovereign." The Prince bowed very low, giving all honour to the King, his father. The English during the night made frequent thanksgivings to the Lord for the happy issue of the day; and with them there was no rioting, for the King had expressly forbidden all riot or noise.

On the following day, which was Sunday, there were a few encounters with the French troops; however, they could not withstand the English, and soon either retreated or were put to the sword. When Edward was assured that there was no appearance of the French collecting another army, he sent to have the number and rank of the dead examined. This business was entrusted to Lord Reginald Cobham and Lord Stafford, assisted by three heralds to examine the arms, and two secretaries to write down the names. They passed the whole day upon the field of battle, and made a very circumstantial account of all they saw: according to their report it appeared that 80 banners, the bodies of 11 princes, 1200 knights, and about 30,000 common men were found dead on the field.

THE BLACK DEATH, 1348–1350

Henry Knighton

A form of bubonic plague that may have carried away two million of Britain's six million population.

At this same time (1348) the pestilence became prevalent in England, beginning in the autumn in certain places. It spread throughout the land, ending in the same season of the following year. At the same time many cities in Corinth and Achaia were overturned, and the earth swallowed them. Castles and fortresses were broken, laid low, and swallowed up. Mountains in Cyprus were levelled into one, so that the flow of the rivers was impeded, and many cities were submerged and villages destroyed. Similarly, when a certain friar was preaching at Naples, the whole city was destroyed by an earthquake. Suddenly, the earth was opened up, as if a stone had been thrown into water, and everyone died along with the preaching friar, except for one friar who, fleeing, escaped into a garden outside the city. All of these things were done by an earthquake . . .

Then that most grievous pestilence penetrated the coastal regions (of England) by way of Southampton, and came to Bristol, and people died as if the whole strength of the city were seized by sudden death. For there were few who lay in their beds more than three days or two and a half days; then that savage death snatched them about the second day. In Leicester, in the little parish of St. Leonard, more than three hundred and eighty died; in the parish of the Holy Cross, more than four hundred, and in the parish of St. Margaret in Leicester, more than seven hundred. And so in each parish, they died in great numbers. Then the bishop of Lincoln sent through the whole diocese, and gave the general power to each and every priest, both regular and secular, to hear confessions and to absolve, by the full and entire power of the bishop, except only in the case of debt. And they might absolve in that case if satisfaction could be made by the person while he lived, or from his property after his death. Likewise, the pope granted full remission of all sins, to be absolved completely, to anyone who was in danger of death, and he granted this power to last until the following Easter. And everyone was allowed to choose his confessor as he pleased.

During this same year, there was a great mortality of sheep everywhere in the kingdom; in one place and in one pasture, more than five thousand sheep died and became so putrefied that neither beast nor bird wanted to touch them. And the price of everything was cheap, because of the fear of death; there were very few who took any care for their wealth, or for anything else. For a man could buy a horse for half a mark, which before was worth forty shillings, a large fat ox for four shillings, a cow for twelve pence, a heifer for sixpence, a large fat sheep for four pence, a sheep for threepence, a lamb for two pence, a fat pig for five pence, a stone of wool for nine pence. And the sheep and cattle wandered about through the fields and among the crops, and there was no one to go after them or to collect them. They perished in countless numbers everywhere, in secluded ditches and hedges, for lack of watching, since there was such a lack of serfs and servants, that no one knew what he should do. For there is no memory of a mortality so severe and so savage from the time of Vortigern, king of the Britons, in whose time, as Bede says, the living did not suffice to bury the dead. In the following autumn, one could not hire a reaper at a lower wage than eight pence with food, or a mower at less than twelve pence with food. Because of this, much grain rotted in the fields for lack of harvesting, but in the year of the plague, as was said above, among other things there was so great an abundance of all kinds of grain that no one seemed to have concerned himself about it.

The Scots, hearing of the cruel pestilence in England, suspected that this had come upon the English by the avenging hand of God, and when they wished to swear an oath, they swore this one, as the vulgar rumour reached the ears of the English, "be the foul deth of Engelond." And so the Scots, believing that the horrible vengeance of God had fallen on the English, came together in the forest of Selkirk to plan an invasion of the whole kingdom of

England. But savage mortality supervened, and the sudden and frightful cruelty of death struck the Scots. In a short time, about five thousand died; the rest, indeed, both sick and well, prepared to return home, but the English, pursuing them, caught up with them, and slew a great many of them.

Master Thomas Bradwardine was consecrated archbishop of Canterbury by the pope, and when he returned to England, came to London. In less than two days he was dead. He was famous above all other clerks in Christendom, in theology especially, but also in other liberal studies. At this same time there was so great a lack of priests everywhere that many widowed churches had no divine services, no masses, matins, vespers, sacraments, and sacramentals. One could hardly hire a chaplain to minister to any church for less than ten pounds or ten marks, and whereas, before the pestilence, when there were plenty of priests, one could hire a chaplain for five or four marks or for two marks, with board, there was scarcely anyone a this time who wanted to accept a position for twenty pounds or twenty marks. But within a short time a very great multitude whose wives had died of the plague rushed into holy orders. Of these many were illiterate and, it seemed, simply laymen who knew nothing except how to read to some extent. The hides of cattle went up from a low price to twelve pence, and for shoes the price went to ten, twelve, fourteen pence; for a pair of leggings, to three and four shillings.

Meanwhile, the king ordered that in every county of the kingdom, reapers and other labourers should not receive more than they were accustomed to receive, under the penalty provided in the statute, and he renewed the statute from this time. The labourers, however, were so arrogant and hostile that they did not heed the king's command, but if anyone wished to hire them, he had to pay them what they wanted, and either lose his fruits and crops or satisfy the arrogant and greedy desire of the labourers as they wished. When it was made known to the king that they had not obeyed his mandate, and had paid higher wages to the labourers, he imposed heavy fines on the abbots, the priors, the great lords and the lesser ones, and on others both greater and lesser in the kingdom. From certain ones he took a hundred shillings, from some, forty shillings, from others, twenty shillings, and from each according to what he could pay. And he took from each ploughland in the whole kingdom twenty shillings, and not one-fifteenth less than this. Then the king had many labourers arrested, and put them in prison. Many such hid themselves and ran away to the forests and woods for a while, and those who were captured were heavily fined. And the greater number swore that they would not take daily wages above those set by ancient custom, and so they were freed from prison. It was done in like manner concerning other artisans in towns and villages . . .

After the aforesaid pestilence, many buildings, both large and small, in all cities, towns, and villages had collapsed, and had completely fallen to the ground in the absence of inhabitants. Likewise, many small villages and hamlets were completely deserted; there was not one house left in them, but all those who had lived in them were dead. It is likely that many such hamlets will never again be inhabited. In the following summer (1350), there was so great a lack of servants to do anything that, as one believed, there had hardly been so great a dearth in past times. For all the beasts and cattle that a man possessed wandered about without a shepherd, and everything a man had was without a caretaker. And so all necessities became so dear that anything that in the past had been worth a penny was now worth four or five pence. Moreover, both the magnates of the kingdom and the other lesser lords who had tenants, remitted something from the rents, lest the tenants should leave, because of the lack of servants and the death of things. Some remitted half the rent, some more and others less, some remitted it for two years, some for three, and others for one year, according as they were able to come to an agreement with their tenants. Similarly, those who received day-work from their tenants throughout the year, as is usual from serfs, had to release them and to remit such services. They either had to excuse them entirely or had to fix them in a laxer manner at a small rent, lest very great and irreparable damage be done to the buildings, and the land everywhere remain completely uncultivated. And all foodstuffs and all necessities became exceedingly dear . . .

FLAGELLANTS, LONDON, MICHAELMAS 1349

Robert of Avesbury

Usually members of the Dominican and Franciscan orders, flagellants underwent public voluntary whipping in atonement for society's sins. Their numbers increased dramatically in the wake of the Black Death (which, in medieval eyes, was seeming punishment by God.)

About Michaelmas 1349 over six hundred men came to London from Flanders, mostly of Zeeland and Holland origin. Sometimes at St Paul's and sometimes at other points in the city they made two daily public appearances wearing cloths from the thighs to the ankles, but otherwise stripped bare. Each wore a cap marked with a red cross in front and behind. Each had in his right hand a scourge with three tails. Each tail had a knot and through the middle of it there were sometimes sharp nails fixed. They marched naked in a file one behind the other and whipped themselves with these scourges on their naked and bleeding bodies. Four of them would cant in their native tongue and, another four would chant in response like a litany. Thrice they would all cast themselves on the ground in this sort of procession, stretching out their hands like the arms of a cross. The singing would go on and, the one who was in the rear of those thus prostrate acting first, each of them in turn would step over the others and give one stroke with his scourge to the man lying under him. This went on from the first to the last until each of them had observed the ritual to the full tale of those on the ground. Then each put on his customary garments and always wearing their caps and carrying their whips in their hands they retired to their lodgings. It is said that every night they performed the same penance.

THE SURGEON'S CODE OF ETHICS, c. 1360

John of Arderne

First, it behoves a surgeon who wishes to succeed in this craft always to put God first in all his doings, and always meekly to call with heart and mouth for his help, and sometimes give of his earnings to the poor, so that they by their prayers may gain him grace of the Holy Ghost. And he must not be found rash or boastful in his sayings or in his deeds; and he must abstain from much speech, especially among great men; and he must answer cautiously to all questions, so that he may not be trapped by his own words. For if his works are known to disagree often with his words and his promises, he will be held more unworthy, and he will tarnish his own good fame. . . . A surgeon should not laugh or joke too much; and as far as he can without harm, he should avoid the company of knaves and dishonest persons. He should be always occupied in things that belong to his craft, whether reading, studying, writing, or praying; the study of books is of great advantage to the surgeon, both by keeping him occupied and by making him wiser. Above all, it helps him much to be found always sober; for drunkenness destroys all wisdom and brings it to nought. In strange places he should be content with the meats and drinks which he finds there, using moderation in all things. . . . He must scorn no man. . . . If anyone talks to him about another surgeon, he must neither set him at nought nor praise nor commend him too much, but he may answer courteously thus: "I have no real knowledge of him, but I have neither learnt nor heard anything of him but what is good and honest." . . . A surgeon should not look too boldly at the lady or the daughters or other fair women in great men's houses, nor offer to kiss them, nor to touch them secretly or openly . . . lest he arouses the indignation of the lord or one of his household. As far as possible, he should not annoy servants, but rather to try to gain their love and their good will. He must always abstain from harlotry in both word and deed, for if he practises harlotry in secret places, sometime he will be found out and publicly discredited for his evil practices. . . . If sick men or any of their friends come to the surgeon to ask help or advice, let him be neither too brusque nor too familiar, but adjust his manner according to the character of the person; to some respectful, to some friendly. . . . Also it is a help for him to have excuses ready for not being able to undertake a case so that he does not hurt or anger some great man or friend, and does not interrupt some necessary work. Otherwise he could pretend to be hurt or ill or give some other likely excuse if he does not want to undertake a case. If he does undertake a case, he should make a clear agreement about payment and take the money in advance. But the surgeon should be sure not to make any definite pronouncement in any illness, unless he has first seen the sickness and the signs of it. When he has made an examination, even though he may think that the patient may be cured, he should warn the patient in his prognosis of the perils to come if treatment should be deferred. And if he sees that the patient is eager for the cure, then the surgeon must boldly adjust his fee to the man's status in life. But the surgeon should always beware of asking too little, for this is bad both for the marker and the patient. Therefore for a case of fistula in ano, when it is curable, the surgeon may reasonably ask of a great man 100 marks or £40 with robes and fees to the value of 100 shillings each year for the rest of his life. From lesser men he may ask £40 or 40 marks without fees; but he must never take less than forty shillings. Never in my life have I taken less than 100 shillings for the cure of this disease, but of course every man must do what he thinks is right and most expedient. And if the patient or his friends and servants ask how long the cure will take, the surgeon had better always say twice as long as he really thinks; thus if a surgeon hopes to heal the patient in twenty weeks, which is the common period, let him add another twenty. For it is better to name a longer term for recovery than that the cure should drag on, a thing which might cause the patient to despair at the very time when confidence in the doctor is the greatest aid to recovery. For if the patient should later wonder or ask why the surgeon estimates so long for recovery when he was able to cure the patient in half the time, the surgeon should answer that it was because the patient had a strong heart and bore pain well and that he was of good complexion (that is, having such a combination of the four honours as would speed recovery) and that his flesh healed quickly; and he must think of other causes that would please the patient, for by such words are patients made proud and glad. And a surgeon should always be soberly dressed, not likening himself in clothing or bearing to minstrels, but rather after the manner of a clerk; for any discreet man clad in clerk's dress may sit at a gentleman's table. A surgeon must also have clean hands and well shaped nails, free from all blackness and dirt.

THE PEASANT'S LIFE, c. 1362

William Langland

From Langland's long poem *The Vision of Piers the Plowman*, the "first authentic cry of the poor" in British history.

> "Can you serve," he said, "or sing in churches,
> Or cock hay in my harvest, or handle a hay-fork,
> Mow or mound it or makes sheaves or bindings,
> Reap, or be an head reaper, and rise early,
> Or have an horn and be an hayward, and be out till morning,
> And keep my corn in my croft from pickers and stealers?
> Or make shoes, or sew cloth, or tend sheep or cattle,
> Or make hedges, or harrow, or drive geese, or be swineherd?

Or can you work at any craft which the commune calls for,
To be means of livelihood to the bed-ridden?"

"I have no penny," said Piers, "to buy pullets,
Nor geese nor pigs, but two green cheeses,
A few curds of cream, a cake of oatmeal,
Two loaves of beans and bran, baked for my children;
And, by my soul, I swear I have no salt bacon,
Nor cook to make collops, I take Christ to witness!
But I have parsley and pot herbs and a plenty of cabbages,
And a cow and a calf, and a cart mare
To draw my dung afield till the drought is over.
This is the little we must live on till the Lammas season.
And then I hope to have my harvest in the garner.
And then I may spread your supper to my soul's content."

So all the poor people fetched peascods,
And brought him beans and baked apples by the lapful,
Ripe cherries, chervils and many small onions,
And offered Piers the present to please Hunger.

The needy are our neighbours, if we note rightly;
As prisoners in cells, or poor folk in hovels,
Charged with children and overcharged by landlords.
What they may spare in spinning they spend on rental,
On milk, or on meal to make porridge
To still the sobbing of the children at meal time.
Also they themselves suffer much hunger.
They have woe in winter time, and wake at midnight
To rise and to rock the cradle at the bedside,
To card and to comb, to darn clouts and to wash them,
To rub and to reel and to put rushes on the paving.
The woe of these women who dwell in hovels
Is too sad to speak of or to say in rhyme.
And many other men have much to suffer
From hunger and from thirst; they turn the fair side outward,
For they are abashed to beg, lest it should be acknowledged
At their neighbours what they need at noon and even.

I know all this well; for the world has taught me
What befalls another who has many children,

With no claim but his craft to clothe and feed them,
When the mouths are many and the money scarce.
They have bread and penny ale in place of a pittance,
And cold flesh and cold fish for venison from the butcher.
On Fridays and fast days a farthing worth of mussels
Would be a feast for such folk, with a few cockles.
It were an alms to help all with such burdens,
And to comfort such cottagers and crooked men and blind folk.

FRAUDULENT BEGGARS, LONDON, 1380
City of London Letter-Book

On the 24th day of October, in the 4th year of Richard II, John
Warde, of the County of York, and Richard Lynham, of The
County of Somerset, two impostors, were brought to the Hall of the
Guildhall of London, before John Hadlee, Mayor, the Aldermen,
and the Sheriffs, and questioned for that, whereas they were stout
enough to work for their food and raiment, and had their tongues
to talk with, they, the same John Warde and Richard Lynham, did
there pretend that they were mutes, and had been deprived of their
tongues; and went about in divers places of the city aforesaid,
carrying in their hands two ell measures, an iron hook and pincers,
and a piece of leather, in shape like part of a tongue, edged with
silver, and with writing around it, to this effect – THIS IS THE TONGUE
OF JOHN WARDE – with which instruments, and by means of divers
signs, they gave many persons to understand that they were
traders, in token whereof they carried the said ell measures;
and that they had been plundered by robbers of their goods;
and that their tongues had also been drawn out with the said hook,
and then cut off with the pincers; they making a horrible noise, like
unto a roaring, and opening their mouths; where it seemed to all
who examined the same, that their tongues had been cut off: to the
defrauding of other poor and infirm persons, and in manifest deceit
of the whole of the people.

Wherefore, they were asked how they would acquit themselves
thereof; upon which, they acknowledged that they had done all
the things above imputed to them. And as it appeared to the
Court that of their evil intent and falsity they had done the
things aforesaid, and in deceit of all the people; and to the end

that other persons might beware of such and the like evil intent, falsity, and deceit, it was awarded that they should be put upon the pillory on three different days, each time for one hour in the day; namely, on the Wednesday, Friday, and Saturday, before the Feast of St Simon and St Jude; the said instruments being hung about their necks each day . . . which punishment being completed, they were instructed to have them taken back to the Gaol of Newgate, there to remain until orders should be given for their release.

THE PEASANTS' REVOLT, MAY–JUNE 1381

Sir John Froissart

Caused largely by the Poll Tax of 1379 and the Statute of Labourers of 1381. The latter fixed maximum wages in the wake of the Black Death.

In order that this disastrous rebellion may serve as an example to mankind, I will speak of all that was done from the information I had at the time. It is customary in England, as well as in several other countries, for the nobility to have great privileges over the commonality; that is to say, the lower orders are bound by law to plough the lands of the gentry, to harvest their grain, to carry it home to the barn, to thrash and winnow it; they are also bound to harvest and carry home the hay. All these services the prelates and gentlemen exact of their inferiors; and in the counties of Kent, Essex, Sussex, and Bedford, these services are more oppressive than in other parts of the kingdom. In consequence of this the evil disposed in these districts began to murmur, saying, that in the beginning of the world there were no slaves, and that no one ought to be treated as such, unless he had committed treason against his lord, as Lucifer had done against God; but they had done no such thing, for they were neither angels nor spirits, but men formed after the same likeness as these lords who treated them as beasts. This they would bear no longer; they were determined to be free, and if they laboured or did any work, they would be paid for it. A crazy priest in the county of Kent, called John Ball, who for his absurd preaching had thrice been confined in prison by the Archbishop of Canterbury, was greatly instrumental in exciting these rebellious ideas. Every Sunday after mass, as the people were coming out of church, this John Ball was accustomed to assemble a crowd around him in the marketplace and preach to them. On such occasions he would say, "My good friends, matters cannot go on well in England until all things shall be in common; when there shall be neither vassals nor lords; when the lords shall be no more masters than ourselves. How ill they behave to us! for what reason do they thus hold us in bondage? Are we not all descended from the same parents, Adam and Eve? And what can they show, or what reason can they give, why they should be more masters than ourselves? They are clothed in velvet and rich stuffs, ornamented with ermine and other furs, while we are forced to wear poor clothing. They have wines, spices, and fine bread, while we have only rye and the refuse of the straw; and when we drink, it must be water. They have handsome seats and manors, while we must brave the wind and rain in our labours in the field; and it is by our labour they have wherewith to support their pomp. We are called slaves, and if we do not perform our service we are beaten, and we have no sovereign to whom we can complain or who would be willing to hear us. Let us go to the King and remonstrate with him; he is young, and from him we may obtain a favourable answer, and if not we must ourselves seek to amend our condition." With such language as this did John Ball harangue the people of his village every Sunday after mass. The Archbishop, on being informed of it, had him arrested and imprisoned for two or three months by way of punishment; but the moment he was out of prison, he returned to his former course. Many in the city of London envious of the rich and noble, having heard of John Ball's preaching, said among themselves that the country was badly governed, and that the nobility had seized upon all the gold and silver. These wicked Londoners, therefore, began to assemble in parties, and to show signs of rebellion; they also invited all those who held like opinions in the adjoining counties to come to London; telling them that they would find the town open to them and the commonalty of the same way of thinking as themselves, and that they would so press the King, that there should no longer be a slave in England.

By this means the men of Kent, Essex, Sussex, Bedford, and the adjoining counties, in number about 60,000, were brought to London, under command of Wat Tyler, Jack Straw, and John Ball. This Wat Tyler, who was chief of the three, had been a tiler of houses – a bad man and a great enemy to the nobility. When these wicked people first began their disturbances, all London, with the exception of those who favoured them, was much alarmed. The Mayor and rich citizens assembled in council and debated whether they should shut the gate and refuse to admit them; however, upon mature reflection they determined not to do so, as they might run the risk of having the suburbs burned. The gates of the city were therefore thrown open, and the rabble entered and lodged as they pleased. True it is that full two-thirds of these people knew neither what they wanted, nor for what purpose they had come together; they followed one another like sheep. In this manner did many of these poor fellows walk to London from distances of one hundred, or sixty leagues, but the greater part came from the counties I have mentioned, and all on their arrival demanded to see the King. The country gentlemen, the knights and squires, began to be much alarmed when they saw the people thus assembling, and indeed they had sufficient reason to be so, for far less causes have excited fear. As the Kentish rebels were on their road towards London, the Princess of Wales, the king's mother, was returning from a pilgrimage to Canterbury; and when they saw her the scoundrels attacked her car and caused the good lady much alarm; but God preserved her from violence, and she came the whole journey from Canterbury to London without venturing to make any stoppage. On her arrival in London, King Richard was at the Tower; thither then the Princess went immediately, and found the King, attended by the Earl of Salisbury, the Archbishop of Canterbury, Sir Robert de Namur, and several others, who had kept near his person from suspicion of the rebels. King Richard well knew that this rebellion was in agitation long before it broke out, and it was a matter of astonishment to every one that he attempted to apply no remedy.

In order that gentlemen and others may take example and learn to correct such wicked rebels, I will most amply detail how the whole business was conducted. On the Monday preceding the feast of the Holy Sacrament in the year 1381, these people sallied forth from their homes to come to London, intending, as they said, to remonstrate with the King, and to demand their freedom. At Canterbury, they met John Ball, Wat Tyler, and Jack Straw. On entering this city they were well feasted by the inhabitants, who were all of the same way of thinking as themselves; and having held a council there, resolved to proceed on their march to London. They also sent emissaries across the Thames into Essex, Suffolk, and Bedford, to press the people of these parts to do the same, in order that the city might be quite surrounded. It was the intention of the leaders of this rabble, that all the different parties should be collected on the feast of the Holy Sacrament on the day following. At Canterbury the rebels entered the church of St Thomas, where they did much damage; they also pillaged the apartments of the Archbishop, saying as they were carrying off the different articles, "The Chancellor of England has had this piece of furniture very cheap; he must now give us an account of his revenues, and of the large sums which he has levied since the coronation of the King." After this they plundered the abbey of St Vincent, and then leaving Canterbury took the road towards Rochester. As they passed they collected people from the villages right and left, and on they went like a tempest, destroying all the houses belonging to attorneys, king's proctors, and the Archbishop, which came in their way. At Rochester they met with the same welcome as at Canterbury, for all the people were anxious to join them. Here they went at once to the castle, and seizing a knight by name Sir John de Newtoun, who was constable of the castle and captain of the town, told him that he must accompany them as their commander-in-chief and do whatever they wished. The knight endeavoured to excuse himself; but they met his excuses by saying, "Sir John, if you refuse you are a dead man." Upon which, finding that the outrageous mob were ready to kill him, he was constrained to comply with their request.

In other counties of England the rebels acted in a similar manner, and several great lords and knights, such as the Lord Manley, Sir Stephen Hales, and Sir Thomas Cossington, were compelled to march with them . . . When the rebels had done all they wanted at Rochester, they left that city and came to Dartford, continuing to destroy all the houses of lawyers and proctors on the right and left of the road; from Dartford they came to Blackheath, where they took up their quarters, saying, that they were armed for the King and commons of England. When the principal citizens of London found that the rebels were quartered so near them, they caused the gates of London Bridge to be closed, and placed guards there, by order of Sir William Walworth, Mayor of London; notwithstanding there were in the city more than 30,000 who favoured the Insurgents. Information that the gates of London Bridge had been closed against them soon reached Blackheath, whereupon the rebels sent a knight to speak with the King and to tell him that what they were doing was for his service; for the kingdom had now for many years been wretchedly governed, to the great dishonour of the realm and to the oppression of the lower orders of the people, by his uncles, by the clergy, and more especially by the Archbishop of Canterbury, his chancellor, from whom they were determined to have an account of his ministry. The knight who was appointed to this service would willingly have excused himself, but he did not dare to do it; so advancing to the Thames opposite the Tower, he took a boat and crossed over. The King and those who were with him in the Tower were in the greatest possible suspense and most anxious to receive some intelligence when the knight's arrival was announced, who was immediately conducted into the royal presence. With the King at this time were the Princess his mother, his two natural brothers, the Earl of Kent and Sir John Holland, the Earls of Salisbury, Warwick, and Suffolk, the Archbishop of Canterbury, the great Prior of the Templars, Sir Robert de Namur, the Mayor of London, and several of the principal citizens. Immediately upon entering the apartment the knight cast himself on his knees before the king, saying, "My much redoubted lord, do not be displeased with me for the message which I am about to deliver to you; for, my dear lord, I have been compelled to come hither." "By no means, sir knight," said the King. "Tell us what you are charged with, we hold you excused." "My most redoubted lord, the commons of this realm have sent me to entreat you to come to Blackheath and speak with them. They wish to have no one but yourself: and you need not fear for your person, as they will not do you the least harm; they always have respected you as their king, and will continue to do so; but they desire to tell you many things which they say it is necessary you should hear: with these, however, they have not empowered me to make you acquainted. Have the goodness, dear lord, to give me such an answer as may satisfy them, and that they may be convinced that I have really been in your presence; for they have my children as hostages for my return, and if I go not back they will assuredly put them to death." To this the King merely replied, "You shall have my answer speedily"; and when the knight had withdrawn, he desired his council to consider what was to be done; after some consultation, the King was advised to send word to the insurgents, that if on Thursday they would come down to the river Thames, he would without fail speak with them. The knight on receiving this answer was well satisfied, and taking leave of the King and his barons, returned to

Blackheath, where upwards of 60,000 men were assembled. He told them from the King, that if they would send their leaders the next morning to the Thames, the King would come and hear what they had to say. The answer was deemed satisfactory; and the rebels passed the night as well as they could, but you must know that one-fourth of them were without provisions.

On Corpus Christi day King Richard heard mass in the Tower of London, after which he entered his barge, attended by the Earls of Salisbury, Warwick, and Suffolk, and some other knights, and rowed down the Thames towards Rotherhithe, a royal manor, where upwards of 10,000 of the insurgents had assembled. As soon as the mob perceived the royal barge approaching, they began shouting and crying as if all the spirits of the nether world had been in the company. With them, also, was the knight whom they had sent to the Tower to the King; for if the King had not come, they determined to have him cut to pieces, as they had threatened him.

When the King and his lords saw this crowd of people, and the wildness of their manner, the boldest of the party felt alarm, and the King was advised not to land, but to have his barge rowed up and down the river. "What do you wish for?" he demanded of the multitude; "I am come hither to hear what you have to say." Those near him cried out, "We wish you to land, and then we will tell you what our wants are." Upon this the Earl of Salisbury cried out, "Gentlemen, you are not properly dressed, nor are you in a fit condition for a King to talk with." Nothing more was said on either side, for the King was prevailed upon at once to return to the Tower. The people seeing this were in a great passion, and returned to Blackheath to inform their companions how the King had served them; upon hearing which, they all cried out, "Let us instantly march to London." Accordingly they set out at once, and on the road thither destroyed all the houses of lawyers and courtiers, and all the monasteries they met with. In the suburbs of London, which are very handsome and extensive, they pulled down many fine houses: they demolished also the King's prison, called the Marshalsea, and set at liberty all who were confined in it; moreover, they threatened the Londoners at the entrance of the bridge for having shut the gates of it, declaring that they would take the city by storm, and afterwards burn and destroy it.

With regard to the common people of London, numbers entertained these rebellious opinions, and on assembling at the bridge asked of the guards, "Why will you refuse admittance to these honest men? They are our friends, and what they are doing is for our good." So urgent were they, that it was found necessary to open the gates, when crowds rushed in and took possession of those shops which seemed best stocked with provisions; indeed, wherever they went, meat and drink were placed before them, and nothing was refused in the hope of appeasing them. Their leaders, John Ball, Jack Straw, and Wat Tyler, then marched through London, attended by more than 20,000 men, to the palace of the Savoy, which is a handsome building belonging to the Duke of Lancaster, situated on the banks of the Thames on the road to Westminster: here they immediately killed the porters, pushed into the house, and set it on fire. Not content with this outrage, they went to the house of the Knight-hospitalers of Rhodes, dedicated to St John of Mount Carmel, which they burned, together with their church and hospital.

After this they paraded the streets, and killed every Fleming they could find, whether in house, church, or hospital; they broke open several houses of the Lombards, taking whatever money they could lay their hands upon. They murdered a rich citizen, by name Richard Lyon, to whom Wat Tyler had formerly been servant in France, but having once beaten him, the varlet had never forgotten it; and when he had carried his men to his house, he ordered his head to be cut off, placed upon a pike, and carried through the streets of London. Thus did these wicked people act, and on this Thursday they did much damage to the city of London. Towards evening they fixed their quarters in a square, called St Catherine's, before the Tower, declaring that they would not depart until they had obtained from the King everything they wanted – until the Chancellor of England had accounted to them, and shown how the great sums which were raised had been expended. Considering the mischief which the mob had already done, you may easily imagine how miserable, at this time, was the situation of the King and those who were with him. In the evening, he and his barons, together with Sir William Walworth, and some of the principal citizens, held a council in the Tower, when it was proposed to arm themselves and fall by night upon these wretches while they were drunk and asleep, for they might have been killed like so many fleas, as not one of them in twenty had arms: and the citizens were very capable of doing this, for they had secretly received into their house their friends and servants properly prepared for action. Sir Robert Knolles remained in his house guarding it, with more than six score companions completely armed, who could have sallied forth at a minute's notice. Sir Perducas d'Albret was also in London at this period, and would of course have been of great service, so that altogether they could have mustered upwards of 8000 men well armed. However, nothing was done; they were really too much afraid of the commonality; and the King's advisers, the Earl of Salisbury and others, said to him, "Sir, if you can appease them by fair words, it will be so much the better; for, should we begin what we cannot go through, it will be all over with us and our heirs, and England will be a desert." This council was followed, and the Mayor ordered to make no stir; who obeyed, as in reason he ought. On Friday morning the rebels, who lodged in the square of St Catherine's, before the Tower, began to make themselves ready. They shouted much and said, that if the King would not come out to them, they would attack the Tower, storm it, and slay all who were within. The King, alarmed at these menaces, resolved to speak with the rabble; he therefore sent orders for them to retire to a handsome meadow at Mile End, where, in the summertime, people go to amuse themselves, at the same time signifying that he would meet them there and grant their demands. Proclamation to this effect was made in the King's name, and thither, accordingly, the commonalty of the different villages began to march; many, however, did not care to go, but stayed behind in London, being more desirous of the riches of the nobles and the plunder of the city. Indeed, covetousness and the desire of plunder was the principal cause of these disturbances, as the rebels showed very plainly. When the gates of the Tower were thrown open, and the King, attended by his two brothers and other nobles, had passed through, Wat Tyler, Jack Straw, and John Ball, with upwards of 400 others, rushed in by force, and running from chamber to chamber, found the Archbishop of Canterbury, by name Simon, a valiant and wise man, whom the rascals seized and beheaded. The Prior of St John's suffered the same fate, and likewise a Franciscan friar, a doctor of physic, who was attached to the Duke of Lancaster, also a sergeant-at-arms whose name was John Laige.

The heads of these four persons the rebels fixed on long spikes and had them carried before them through the streets of London;

and when they had made sufficient mockery of them, they caused them to be placed on London Bridge, as if they had been traitors to their king and country. The scoundrels then entered the apartment of the Princess and cut her bed to pieces, which so terrified her that she fainted, and in this condition was carried by her servants and ladies to the riverside, when she was put into a covered boat and conveyed to a house called the Wardrobe, where she continued for a day and night in a very precarious state. While the King was on his way to Mile End, his two brothers, the Earl of Kent and Sir John Holland, stole away from his company, not daring to show themselves to the populace. The King himself, however, showed great courage, and on his arrival at the appointed spot instantly advanced into the midst of the assembled multitude, saying in a most pleasing manner, "My good people, I am your king and your lord, what is it you want? What do you wish to say to me?" Those who heard him made answer, "We wish you to make us free for ever. We wish to be no longer called slaves, nor held in bondage." The King replied, "I grant your wish; now therefore return to your homes, and let two or three from each village be left behind, to whom I will order letters to be given with my seal, fully granting every demand you have made: and in order that you may be the more satisfied, I will direct that my banners be sent to every stewardship, castlewick, and corporation."

These words greatly appeased the more moderate of the multitude, who said, "It is well: we wish for nothing more." The King, however, added yet further, "You, my good people of Kent, shall have one of my banners; and you also of Essex, Sussex, Bedford, Suffolk, Cambridge, Stafford, and Lincoln, shall each have one; I pardon you all for what you have hitherto done, but you must follow my banners and now return home on the terms I have mentioned," which they unanimously consented to do. Thus did this great assembly break up. The king instantly employed upwards of thirty secretaries, who drew up the letters as fast as they could, and when they were sealed and delivered to them, the people departed to their own counties. The principal mischief, however, remained behind: I mean Wat Tyler, Jack Straw, and John Ball, who declared, that though the people were satisfied, they were by no means so, and with them were about 30,000, also of the same mind. These all continued in the city without any wish to receive the letters or the King's seal, but did all they could to throw the town into such confusion, that the lords and rich citizens might be murdered and their houses pillaged and destroyed. The Londoners suspected this, and kept themselves at home, well armed and prepared to defend their property.

After he had appeased the people at Mile End Green, King Richard went to the Wardrobe, in order that he might console the Princess, who was in the greatest possible alarm. But I must not omit to relate an adventure which happened to these clowns before Norwich and to their leader, William Lister, who was from the county of Stafford. At the same time that a party of these wicked people in London burned the palace of the Savoy, the church and house of St John's, and the hospital of the Templars, there were collected numerous bodies of men from Lincolnshire, Norfolk, and Suffolk, who, according to the orders they had received, were marching towards London. On their road they stopped near Norwich, and forced everyone whom they met to join them.

The reason of their stopping near Norwich was, that the governor of the town was a knight, by name Sir Robert Salle, who was not by birth a gentleman; but who, because of his ability and courage, had been created a knight by King Edward: he was, moreover, one of the handsomest and strongest men in England. Lister and his companions took it into their heads that they would make this man their commander. They, therefore, sent orders to him to come out into the fields to speak with them, declaring, in case he refused, that they would attack and burn the city. The knight, considering it was much better for him to go to them than that they should commit such outrages, mounted his horse and went out of the town alone to hear what they had to say. On his approach they showed every mark of respect, and courteously entreated him to dismount and talk with them. He did dismount, and in so doing committed a great folly, for immediately the mob surrounded him, and at first conversed in a friendly way, saying, "Robert, you are a knight and a man of great weight in this country, renowned for your valour; yet, notwithstanding all this, we know who you are; you are not a gentleman, but the son of a poor mason, such as ourselves. Come with us therefore, as our commander, and we will make you so great a man that one-quarter of England shall be under your control."

The knight, on hearing them speak thus, was exceedingly enraged, and, eyeing them with angry looks, said, "Begone, scoundrels and false traitors, would you have me desert my natural lord for such a company of knaves as you are? Would you have me dishonour myself? I would rather have you all hanged, for that must be your end." On saying this, he attempted to mount his horse; but his foot slipping from the stirrup, the animal took fright, and the mob upon this cried out, "Put him to death." Upon hearing which, Sir Robert let go his horse, and drawing a handsome Bordeaux sword, began to skirmish, and soon cleared the crowd from about him in an admirable manner. Many attempted to close with him; but each stroke he gave cut off heads, arms feet, or legs so that the boldest became afraid to approach him. The wretches were 40,000 in number, and he killed twelve of them and wounded many before they overpowered him, which at last they did with their missiles; and as soon as he was down, they cut off his arms and legs and rent his body piecemeal. Such was the pitiable end of Sir Robert Salle.

On Saturday morning the King left the Wardrobe and went to Westminster, when he and his lords heard mass in the abbey. In this church there is a statue of Our Lady, in which the kings of England have much faith. To this on the present occasion King Richard and his nobles paid their devotions and made their offerings; they then rode in company along the causeway to London; but when they had proceeded a short distance, King Richard, with a few attendants, turned up a road on the left to go away from the city.

This day all the rabble again assembled under Wat Tyler, Jack Straw, and John Ball, at a place called Smithfield, where every Friday the horsemarket is kept. There were present about 20,000, and many more were in the city, breakfasting, and drinking Rhenish wine and Malmsey Madeira in the taverns and in the houses of the Lombards, without paying for anything; and happy was he who could give them good cheer to satisfy them. Those who collected in Smithfield had with them the King's banner, which had been given to them the preceding evening; and the wretches, notwithstanding this, wanted to pillage the city, their leaders saying, that hitherto they had done nothing. "The pardon which the King has granted will be of no use to us; but if we be of the same mind, we shall pillage this rich and powerful town of London before those from Essex, Suffolk, Cambridge, Bedford, Warwick, Reading, Lancashire, Arundel, Guildford, Coventry, Lynne, Lincoln, York and Durham shall arrive; for they are on their road, and we know for certain that Vaquier and Lister will conduct them hither. Let us, then, be beforehand in plundering the wealth of the city; for if we wait for their arrival, they will wrest it from us." To this opinion all had agreed, when the King, attended by sixty horses, appeared in sight; he was at the time not thinking of the rabble, but had intended to continue his ride, without coming into London; however, when he arrived before the Abbey of St Bartholomew, which is in Smithfield, and saw the crowd of people, he stopped, saying that he would ascertain what they wanted, and endeavour to appease them. Wat Tyler, seeing the King and his party, said to his men, "Here is the King, I will go and speak with him; do you not stir until I give you a signal." He then made a motion with his hand, and added, "When you shall see me make this signal, then step forward, and kill everyone except the King; but hurt him not, for he is young, and we can do what we please with him; carrying him with us through England, we shall be lords of the whole country, without any opposition." On saying which he spurred his horse and galloped up to the King, whom he approached so near that his horse's head touched the crupper of the King's horse.

His first words were these: "King, dost thou see all these men here?" "Yes," replied the King; "Why dost thou ask?" "Because they are all under my command, and have sworn by their faith and loyalty to do whatsoever I shall order." "Very well," said the King; "I have no objection to it." Tyler, who was only desirous of a riot, made answer: "And thou thinkest, King, that these people, and as many more in the city, also under my command, ought to depart without having thy letters? No, indeed, we will carry them with us." "Why," replied the King, "it has been so ordered, and the letters will be delivered out one after another; but, friend, return to thy companions, and tell them to depart from London; be peaceable and careful of yourselves; for it is our determination that you shall all have the letters by towns and villages according to our agreement." As the King finished speaking, Wat Tyler, casting his eyes round, spied a squire attached to the King's person bearing a sword. This squire Tyler mortally hated, and on seeing him cried out, "What has thou there? Give me thy dagger." "I will not," said the squire; "why should I give it thee?" The King upon this said, "Give it to him; give it to him"; which the squire did, though much against his will. When Tyler took the dagger, he began to play with it in his hand, and again addressing the squire, said, "Give me that sword." "I will not," replied the squire, "for it is the King's sword, and thou being but a mechanic art not worthy to bear it; and if only thou and I were together, thou wouldst not have dared to say what thou hast, for a heap of gold as large as this church." "By my troth," answered Tyler, "I will not eat this day before I have thy head." At these words the Mayor of London, with about twelve men, rode forward, armed under their robes, and seeing Tyler's manner of behaving, said "Scoundrel, how dare you to behave thus in the King's presence?" The King, also enraged at the fellow's impudence, said to the Mayor, "Lay hands on him." Whilst King Richard was giving this order, Tyler still kept up the conversation, saying to the Mayor, "What have you to do with it; does what I have said concern you?" "It does," replied the Mayor, who found himself supported by the King, and then added, "I will not live a day unless you pay for your insolence." Upon saying which he drew a kind of scimitar, and struck Tyler such a blow on the head as felled him to his horse's feet. As soon as the rebel was down, he was surrounded on all sides, in order that his own men might not see him; and one of the King's squires, by name John Standwich, immediately leaped from his horse, and drawing his sword, thrust it into his belly, so that he died.

When the rebels found that their leader was dead, they drew up in a sort of battle array, each man having his bow bent before him. The King at this time certainly hazarded much, though it turned out most fortunately for him; for as soon as Tyler was on the ground, he left his attendants, giving orders that no one should follow him, and riding up to the rebels, who were advancing to revenge their leader's death, said, "Gentlemen, what are you about? You shall have me for your captain: I am your King, remain peaceable." The greater part, on hearing these words, were quite ashamed, and those among them who were inclined for peace began to slip away; the riotous ones, however, kept their ground. The King returned to his lords, and consulted with them what next should be done. Their advice was to make for the fields; but the Mayor said that to retreat would be of no avail. "It is quite proper to act as we have done; and I reckon we shall very soon receive assistance from our good friends in London."

While things were in this state, several persons ran to London, crying out, "They are killing the King and our Mayor"; upon which alarm, all those of the King's party sallied out towards Smithfield, in number about seven or eight thousand. Among the first came Sir Robert Knolles and Sir Perducas d'Albret, well attended; then several aldermen, with upwards of 600 men-at-arms, and a powerful man of the city, by name Nicholas Bramber, the king's draper, bringing with him a large force on foot. These all drew up opposite to the rebels, who had with them the King's banner, and showed as if they intended to maintain their ground by offering combat.

The King created at this time three knights: Sir William Walworth, Sir John Standwich, and Sir Nicholas Bramber. As soon as Sir Robert Knolles arrived at Smithfield, his advice was immediately to fall upon the insurgents, and slay them; but King Richard would not consent to this. "You shall first go to them," he said, "and demand my banner; we shall then see how they will behave; for I am determined to have this by fair means or foul." The new knights were accordingly sent forward, and on approaching the rebels made signs to them not to shoot, as they wished to speak with them; and when within hearing said, "Now attend; the King orders you to send back his banners; and if you do so, we trust he will have mercy upon you." The banners, upon this, were given up directly, and brought to the King. It was then ordered, under pain of death, that all those who had obtained the King's letters should deliver them up. Some did so, but not all; and the King on receiving them had them torn in pieces in their presence. You must know that from the time the King's banners were surrendered, these fellows kept no order; but the greater part, throwing their bows upon the ground, took to their heels and returned to London. Sir Robert Knolles was very angry that the rebels were not attacked at once and all slain; however, the King would not consent to it, saying, that he would have ample revenge without doing so.

When the rabble had dispersed, the King and his lords, to their great joy, returned in good array to London, whence the King immediately took the road to the Wardrobe, to visit the Princess his mother, who had remained there two days and two nights under the greatest apprehension. On seeing her son, the good lady was much rejoiced, and said, "Ah, ah, fair son, what pain and anguish have I not suffered for you this day!" "Madam," replied the King, "I am well assured of that; but now rejoice, and thank God, for it behoves us to praise him, as I have this day regained my inheritance – the kingdom of England, which I had lost."

This whole day the King passed with his mother, and a proclamation was made through all the streets, that every person who was not an inhabitant of London, and who had not resided there for a whole year, should instantly depart; for if any of a contrary description were found in the city on Sunday morning at sunrise, they would be arrested as traitors to the King, and have their heads cut off. This proclamation no one dared to infringe, but all instantly departed to their homes quite discomfited.

John Ball and Jack Straw were found hidden in an old ruin, where they had secreted themselves, thinking to steal away when things were quiet; but this they were prevented doing, for their own men betrayed them. With this capture the King and his barons were much pleased, and had their heads cut off, as was that of Tyler's, and fixed on London Bridge, in the room of those whom these wretches themselves had placed there.

News of this total defeat of the rebels in London was sent throughout the neighbouring counties, in order that all those who were on their way to London might hear of it; and as soon as they did so, they instantly returned to their homes, without daring to advance farther.

EXCOMMUNICATION OF BOYS FOR PLAYING BALL IN ST PAUL'S CATHEDRAL, 1385

The Bishop of London

. . . Certain (boys), also, good for nothing in their insolence and idleness, instigated by evil minds and busying themselves rather in doing harm than good, throw and shoot stones, arrows, and different kinds of missiles at the rooks, pigeons, and other birds nesting in the walls and porches of the church and perching (there). Also they play ball inside and outside the church and engage in other destructive games there, breaking and greatly damaging the glass windows and the stone images of the church, which, having been made with the greatest skill, are a pleasure to the eyes of all be holders, adorning the fabric and adding to its refinement. This they do not without great offense to God and our church and to the prejudice and injury of us as well as to the grave peril of their souls.

THE DUTIES OF A VILLEIN, c. 1386

Customal of the Manor of Islip

Villeins, unfree peasants who cultivated land in village fields in return for labour services on the manorial farm, were the main class of medieval society. The villein whose duties are listed below was a tenant of West-minster Abbey at Islip, Oxfordshire.

William Cowpere holds in villeinage one messuage (a dwelling) and half-virgate of land (half the size of an average holding) lately held by Thomas Godhyne. This used to render 3s. a year or 2½ works a week throughout the year, value of work ½d.; afterwards, when Nicholas was Abbot of Westminster (1362–86), it was conceded to the said William and to all holding by like tenure that each of them should pay 6s. a year for the commutation of the said works and, in addition, he shall do one day's ploughing with half a plough at the winter sowing without food, value of work 2d., and one day's ploughing with half a plough at the Lenten sowing with food provided by the lord, value of work 1d., and give one hen worth ½d. at Christmas each year and 12 eggs worth ½d. at Easter. He used to pay ½d. a year at Whitsun for fencing for which he had a load of underwood, but this custom was to the lord's detriment, and so has ceased. He shall weed for 3 days, value of work ½d., mow for 3 days, value of work 4d., and carry hay for 3 days, value of work 1d. In autumn he shall do 3 boons (unpaid tasks) without food, value of work 2½d. and one boon with food at one meal provided by the lord, value of work 1½d. and one boon called the love boon for half a day without food or for the whole day with food at one meal provided by the lord, value of work 1½d. and he shall carry hay for one day and corn for one day, value of work 4d. He used to collect nuts for one day, value of work 1d., but, for the remission of this work, he and his peers shall mow all the second crop of hay in Le Mellehamme. He shall cut and carry wood for Christmas, value of work 1d. He used to do one day's carrying work each week with one horse and a sack, value of work 1½d., but this is remitted on account of the increase of the above-mentioned rent of 6s. He shall pay tallage (tax) and merchet (fine on child's marriage) with his peers and pay pannage, that is to say, for a pig a year or more old, 1d., for a pig of half a year, ½d., and for a pig three months old, ¼d.; and each customary tenant shall have free pannage for one full grown pig. If he threshes for one day he should have one truss of straw. If he mows for a whole day he should have one truss of grass. If he goes to the wood for a bundle of wood he should have a stick to carry it on. If he is reeve, or if he does the aforesaid works, he shall be quit of the aforesaid rent. He may collect dead wood if he wishes for his own use; the aforesaid hen and eggs are given in return for this. All the customary tenants below along with this customary shall have 3s. 4½d., and 1 quarter and 2 bushels of wheat for a custom called Mathshup (at Buckland, Gloucestershire, *Madschep* was a sheep given to the mowers). In addition, the said customary tenants shall have 6d. a year for mowing a certain piece of meadow in addition to their customary obligation. He shall not give his daughters in marriage, or sell a horse or ox of his own breeding without the lord's permission. He shall give heriot, do three-weekly suit to the lord's court and render yearly etc. 6s . . .

William Coupere holds 1 messuage and 9 acres of land formerly held by William Coupere his father. He shall plough, weed, mow and carry hay, reap, give tallage and merchet according to the entry under his name above. He shall stack hay for 1 day, value of work 2d., and corn for 1 day, value of work 2½d., give 1 cock and 4 hens at Martinmas and 9 eggs at Easter and render yearly 3s.

He also holds a certain parcel of demesne land (the lord's home farm) lying at Buryslade, rendering yearly etc. 16d.

A COMPLAINT AGAINST PETS IN THE NUNNERY, ENGLAND, 1387

William of Wykeham, Bishop of Winchester

A Letter Written to the Abbess of Romsey.

Item, because we have convinced ourselves by clear proofs that some of the nuns of your house bring with them to church birds, rabbits, hounds and such like frivolous things, whereunto they give more heed than to the offices of the church, with frequent hindrance to their own psalmody and that of their fellow nuns and to the grievous peril of their souls; therefore we strictly forbid you, all and several, in virtue of the obedience due unto us, that you presume henceforward to bring to church no birds, hounds, rabbits or other frivolous things that promote indiscipline; and any nun who does to the contrary, after three warnings shall fast on bread and water on one Saturday for each offence, notwithstanding one discipline to be received publicly in chapter on the same day . . . Item, whereas through the hunting-dogs and other hounds abiding within your monastic precincts, the alms that should be given to the poor are devoured and the church and cloister and other places

set apart for divine and secular services are foully defiled, contrary
to all honesty, and whereas, through their inordinate noise, divine
service is frequently troubled, therefore we strictly command and
enjoin you, Lady Abbess, in virtue of obedience, that you remove
these dogs altogether and that you suffer them never henceforth,
nor any other such hounds, to abide within the precincts of your
nunnery.

THE CAPTURE AND IMPRISONMENT OF
RICHARD II, 1399

Adam of Usk

Initially a moderate constitutional monarch, Richard II developed
Frenchified habits and a taste for despotism after his marriage to Isabella
of France in 1396. With the connivance of much of the baronial party,
Richard's cousin Henry Bolingbroke, Duke of Lancaster, invaded England in July 1399.

On the eve of the Assumption of the Blessed Virgin (14 August),
my lord of Canterbury and the Earl of Northumberland went
away to the king at the castle of Conway, to treat with him on the
duke's behalf; and the king, on condition of saving his dignity,
promised to surrender to the duke at the castle of Flint. And so,
delivering up to them his two crowns, valued at one hundred
thousand marks, with other countless treasure, he straightaway set
forth to Flint. There the duke coming to him with twenty thousand
chosen men – the rest of his host being left behind to guard his
quarters and the country and castle and city of Chester – sought
the king within the castle, for he would not come forth [girding it
round with his armed men on the one side and with his archers on
the other; whereby was fulfilled the prophecy: "The white king
shall array his host in form of a shield"]. And he led him away
prisoner to Chester castle, where he delivered him into safe
keeping. Thus, too, he placed in custody certain lords, taken along
with the king, to be kept till the parliament which was to begin on
the morrow of Michaelmas-day.

. While the duke was then at Chester, three of the twenty-four
aldermen of the city of London, on behalf of the same city,
together with fifty other citizens, came to the duke, and recommended their city to him, under their common seal, renouncing
their fealty to King Richard. And so the duke, having gloriously,

within fifty days, conquered both king and kingdom, marched to London; and there he placed the captive king in the Tower, under fitting guard.

On St Matthew's day (21 September) just two years after the beheading of the Earl of Arundel, I, the writer of this history, was in the Tower, wherein King Richard was a prisoner, and I was present when he dined, and I marked his mood and bearing, having been taken thither for that very purpose by Sir William Beauchamp. And there and then the king discoursed sorrowfully in these words: "My God!, a wonderful land is this, and a fickle; which hath exiled, slain, destroyed or ruined so many kings, rulers, and great men, and is ever tainted and toileth with strife and variance and envy"; and then he recounted the histories and names of sufferers from the earliest habitation of the kingdom. Perceiving then the trouble of his mind, and how that none of his own men, nor such as were wont to serve him, but strangers who were but spies upon him, were appointed to his service, and musing on his ancient and wonted glory and on the fickle fortune of the world, I departed thence much moved at heart.

THE ENGLISH LONGBOW WINS THE BATTLE OF AGINCOURT, FRANCE, 25 OCTOBER 1415

Jehan de Wavrin

A battle in the Hundred Years War between England and France in which, as at Crécy, the superior technology of the English defeated the greater numbers of the French. Around 10,000 men under Henry V faced the 50,000 French troops of Constable Charles I d'Albret.

Of the mortal battle of Agincourt, in which the King of England discomfited the French.

It is true that the French had arranged their battalions between two small thickets, one lying close to Agincourt, and the other to Tramecourt. The place was narrow, and very advantageous for the English, and, on the contrary, very ruinous for the French, for the said French had been all night on horseback, and it rained, and the pages, grooms, and others, in leading about the horses, had broken up the ground, which was so soft that the horses could with difficulty step out of the soil. And also the said French were so loaded with armour that they could not support themselves or move forward. In the first place they were armed with long coats of steel, reaching to the knees or lower, and very heavy, over the leg harness, and besides plate armour also most of them had hooded helmets; wherefore this weight of armour, with the softness of the wet ground, as has been said, kept them as if immovable, so that they could raise their clubs only with great difficulty, and with all these mischiefs there was this, that most of them were troubled with hunger and want of sleep. There was a marvellous number of banners, and it was ordered that some of them should be furled. Also it was settled among the said French that everyone should shorten his lance, in order that they might be stiffer when it came to fighting at close quarters. They had archers and cross-bowmen enough, but they would not let them shoot, for the plain was so narrow that there was no room except for the men-at-arms.

Now let us return to the English. After the parley between the two armies was finished, as we have said, and the delegates had returned, each to their own people, the King of England, who had appointed a knight called Sir Thomas Erpingham to place his archers in front in two wings, trusted entirely to him, and Sir Thomas, to do his part, exhorted every one to do well in the name of the king, begging them to fight vigorously against the French in order to secure and save their own lives. And thus the knight, who rode with two others only in front of the battalion, seeing that the hour was come, for all things were well arranged, threw up a baton which he held in his hand, saying "Nestrocq" (? "Now Strike!"), which was the signal for attack; then dismounted and joined the king, who was also on foot in the midst of his men, with his banner before him. Then the English, seeing this signal, began suddenly to march, uttering a very loud cry, which greatly surprised the French. And when the English saw that the French did not approach them, they marched dashingly towards them in very fine order, and again raised a loud cry as they stopped to take breath.

Then the English archers, who, as I have said, were in the wings, saw that they were near enough, and began to send their arrows on the French with great vigour. The said archers were for the most part in their doublets, without armour, their stockings rolled up to their knees, and having hatchets and battle-axes or great swords hanging at their girdles; some were bare-footed and bare-headed, others had caps of boiled leather, and others of osier, covered with harpoy or leather.

Then the French, seeing the English come towards them in this fashion, placed themselves in order, every one under his banner, their helmets on their heads. The constable, the marshal, the admirals, and the other princes earnestly exhorted their men to fight the English well and bravely; and when it came to the approach the trumpets and clarions resounded everywhere; but the French began to hold down their heads, especially those who had no bucklers, for the impetuosity of the English arrows, which fell so heavily that no one durst uncover or look up. Thus they went forward a little, then made a little retreat, but before they could come to close quarters, many of the French were disabled and wounded by the arrows; and when they came quite up to the English, they were, as has been said, so closely pressed one against another that none of them could lift their arms to strike against their enemies . . .

RECIPES, 1420–1450

Anon

Strawberries
Take strawberries, and wash them, in season, in good red wine; then strain through a cloth, and put them in a pot with good almond milk; cover it with wheat flour or rice flour, and make it thick, and let it boil, and add currants, saffron, pepper, plenty of sugar, powdered ginger, cinnamon, galingale; make it acid with vinegar, and add a little white grease; colour it with alkanet, and mix it together, sprinkle it with the grains of pomegranate, and then serve it up.

Pork Pie
Take fresh pork, cut it and grind it on a mortar, and put it into a fair vessel. Take the white and the yokes of eggs, and strain into a vessel through a strainer, and mix with the pork. Then take pines [seeds of fir or pepper pines], currants, and fry them in fresh grease, and add powdered pepper, ginger, cinnamon, sugar, saffron, and salt; and put in the vessel with the grinded pork. And then make a pie crust and cover pie with same pastry. Set in oven and bake.

Roasted Peacock

Take a peacock, break its neck, and cut its throat, and flay it, skin and feathers together, with the head still attached to the skin of the neck, and keep the skin and the feathers whole together. Draw the bird like a hen, and keep the bone to the neck whole, and roast it. And set the bone of the neck above the spit, as the bird was wont to sit when it was alive, and bend the legs to the body, as it was wont to sit when it was alive. And when it is roasted enough, take it off and let it cool, and then wind the skin with the feathers and the tail about the body, and serve as if the bird were still alive; or else pluck it clean and roast it and serve it as you do a hen.

Fritters

Take the yolks of eggs, put them through a strainer, add fair flour, yeast, and ale; stir it together until it is thick. Take pared apples, cut them thick like sacramental wafers, lay them in butter; then put them into a frying pan, and fry them in fair grease or butter until they are golden brown. Then put them in dishes and strew sugar on them enough, and serve.

Fruit Tart

Take figs, and boil them in wine, and grind them small, and put them in a vessel. And take powdered pepper, cinnamon, cloves, mace, powdered ginger, pines, raisins or currants, saffron, and salt, and add. And then make a fair low pie crust, and put the mixture in it, and put pines on top. And cut dates and fresh salmon in fair pieces or else fresh eels, and parboil them a little in wine, and place on top of the mixture in the pie. And cover the pie fair with the same pastry, and gild the crust outside with saffron and almond milk. Set it in the oven and let it bake.

THE CORONATION FEAST OF HENRY VI, 1429

Anon

This was the first course at his coronation; that is to say, first:

Frumenty, with venison. Meat royal, planted with lozenges of gold. Boars heads in castles of . . . armed with gold. Beef. Mutton. Cygnet. Stewed capon. Heron. Great pike. A red leach with lions carved therein in white. Custard royal with a leopard of gold sitting therein. Fritter like a sun, with a fleur-de-lis therein. A subtlety, St Edward and St Louis, clad in coat armour bringing in between the king in his coat armour with this writing as follows:

> Lo, here are two kings right profitable and good,
> Holy St Edward and St Louis
> And see the branch borne of their blessèd blood,
> Live among Christians most sovereign of price
> Inheritor of the fleur-de-lis;
> God grant he may through help of Christ Jesu
> This sixth Henry to reign and be as wise,
> And them resemble in knighthood and virtue.

Here follows the second course, that is to say:

Meat blanched, barred with gold. Jelly divided by the writing and musical notation. Te Deum Laudamus. Pig gilded. Crane Bittern. Rabbits; Chickens gilded. Partridge. Peacock adorned. Great bream. White leach, with an antelope of red carved therein a crown about his neck with a chain of gold. Flampayne powdered with leopards and fleurs de lis of gold. Fritters, a leopard's head with two ostrich feathers. A subtlety, the emperor and the king who is dead, armed, and their mantles of the Garter; and the king that now is, kneeling before them with this reason:

> Against miscreants the emperor Sigismund
> Has shown his might, which is imperial:
> Since Henry the Fifth so noble a knight was found
> For Christ's dear cause in acts full martial
> Cherished the church so that Lollards had a fall
> To give example to kings that followèd
> And to this branch here in especi-all
> While he does reign to love the Lord and dread.

The third course follows, that is to say:

Bland surrey powdered with gilt quatrefoils. Roasted venison. Aigrettes. Curlew. Cocks. Plover. Quails. Snipes. Great birds. Larks. Carp-Crab. Leach of three colours. A cold baked meat like a shield quarterly, red and white, set with lozenges and gilt, and flowers of borage. Fritter crisps. A subtlety of Our Lady sitting and her child in her lap, and she holding in her hand a crown and St George kneeling on one side and St Denis on the other, presenting the king, kneeling to Our Lady, with this reason following:

> O blessed Lady, Christ's own mother dear,
> And thou St George, that called art her knight,
> Holy St Denis, O martyr most entire,
> The sixth Henry here present in your sight,
> Shed, of your grace, on him your heavenly light,
> His tender youth with virtue does advance,
> Born by descent and by title of right,
> Justly to reign in England and in France.

THE HUNDRED YEARS WAR: "HEAR THE WORDS OF THE MAID", 22 MARCH 1429

Joan of Arc

A letter from Joan of Arc, the seventeen year old peasant commander of the French army, to Henry VI of England at the siege of Orleans.

JESUS, MARY

King of England, render account to the King of Heaven of your royal blood. Return the keys of all the good cities which you have seized, to the Maid. She is sent by God to reclaim the royal blood, and is fully prepared to make peace, if you will give her satisfaction; that is, you must render justice, and pay back all that you have taken.

King of England, if you do not do these things, I am the commander of the military; and in whatever place I shall find your men in France, I will make them flee the country, whether they wish to or not; and if they will not obey, the Maid will have them all killed. She comes sent by the King of Heaven, body for body, to take you out of France, and the Maid promises and certifies to you that if you do not leave France she and her troops will raise a mighty outcry as has not been heard in France in a thousand years. And believe that the King of Heaven has sent her so much power that you will not be able to harm her or her brave army.

To you, archers, noble companions in arms, and all people who are before Orleans, I say to you in God's name, go home to your own country; if you do not do so, beware of the Maid, and of the damages you will suffer. Do not attempt to remain, for you have no rights in France from God, the King of Heaven, and the Son of the Virgin Mary. It is Charles, the rightful heir, to whom God has given France, who will shortly enter Paris in a grand company. If you do not believe the news written of God and the Maid, then in whatever place we may find you, we will soon see who has the better right, God or you.

William de la Pole, Count of Suffolk, Sir John Talbot, and Thomas, Lord Scales, lieutenants of the Duke of Bedford, who calls himself regent of the King of France for the King of England, make a response, if you wish to make peace over the city of Orleans! If you do not do so, you will always recall the damages which will attend you.

Duke of Bedford, who call yourself regent of France for the King of England, the Maid asks you not to make her destroy you. If you do not render her satisfaction, she and the French will perform the greatest feat ever done in the name of Christianity.

Done on the Tuesday of Holy Week (March 22, 1429). HEAR THE WORDS OF GOD AND THE MAID.

By 8 May Joan of Arc had lifted the siege of the city. A year later she was captured and tried by the English for heresy. She was burned at the stake on 30 May 1331.

HOW TO PREPARE THE MASTER'S BATH, c. 1460

John Russell

If your lord wishes to bathe and wash his body clean, hang sheets round the roof, every one full of flowers and sweet green herbs, and have five or six sponges to sit or lean upon, and see that you have one big sponge to sit upon, and a sheet over so that he may bathe there for a while, and have a sponge also for under his feet, if there be any to spare, and always be careful that the door is shut. Have a basin full of hot fresh herbs and wash his body with a soft sponge, rinse him with fair rose-water, and throw it over him; then let him go to bed; but see that the bed be sweet and nice; and first put on his socks and slippers that he may go near the fire and stand on his foot-sheet, wipe him dry with a clean cloth, and take him to bed to cure his troubles.

THE WARS OF THE ROSES: MARGARET D'ANJOU FLEES THE YORKISTS, 1463

George Chastellain

Margaret D'Anjou, Queen Consort of Henry VI, was a principal figure on the Lancastrian side in the long dynastic struggle with the Yorkists for the throne of England. After Edward VI's victory at Towton, she escaped with her son to the protection of the Duke of Burgundy.

The Queen related some of her adventures . . . saying that it happened, for the space of five days, that her husband the King, her son, and she had for their three selves only one herring, and not one day's supply of bread; and that on a holy day she found herself at mass without a brass farthing to offer; wherefore, in her beggary and need, she prayed a Scottish archer to lend her something, who, half loth and regretfully, drew a Scots groat from his purse and lent it to her. She also related how, at her last unfortunate discomfiture, she was robbed and despoiled of all she had, of her royal jewels and dresses, of her plate and treasures, with which she thought to escape into Scotland; and when all this had been taken from her, she herself was seized upon, villainously reviled, run upon with a drawn sword, caught hold of her head-gear to have her neck severed, menaced with divers torments and cruelties, while she, on her knees and with clasped hands, wailing and weeping, prayed that, for the sake of divine and human pity, they would have mercy upon her. Withal she perseveringly called upon God's mercy; and Heaven heard her appeal; for speedily there arose such a discord and dissension among her captors about the booty, that, furiously slaughtering each other like madmen, they concerned themselves no more about the dolorous and discomfited Queen their princess . . . When the poor Queen saw this, she piteously addressed an esquire who was by, and prayed him that, for the sake of Our Saviour's passion, he would help her to escape. Then the esquire looked at her, and God caused him to conceive a pity for her, so that he said, "Madam, mount behind me, and my lord the Prince before, and I will save you or die, although death seems to me more likely than not." So the Queen and her son mounted . . .

The esquire, at the Queen's desire, makes for a neighbouring forest.

Now there was in this forest a place haunted by brigands, who were reported throughout the country to be pitiless cutthroats. It befell that there came up a brigand, hideous and horrible of aspect, and, roused by the sight of prey, he approached the Queen with intent to lay hands upon her. Then when the noble Queen thought that nothing but death was before her, either from the enemies from whom she had escaped, or from the brigands of whom she now saw a specimen, she called the robber up to her, and thus addressed him;

Margaret declares herself to be the Queen, and adjures the robber to save the son of his King.

In such words, or to such effect, the poor Queen reasoned with the brigand, who, seeing her tears and her distress, and also because she was Queen of the land, conceived a great pity for her; and, the Holy Spirit softening his heart, he fell at her feet, saying that he would die by a thousand deaths and as many torments rather than abandon the noble youth until he had brought him to the haven of safety. And praying mercy of the Queen for his misdeeds, as if she were reigning in London, he vowed to God and to her never to revert to his present courses, and to amend his life in expectation of mercy. So he took the youth in haste, for the Queen was ever in fear of being overtaken; wherefore she sought only to separate from the child, and to put him into God's guiding hand. Thus, kissing her son, weeping and lamenting, she left him in the hands of the brigand, who nobly did his duty by him afterwards. And the Queen, riding behind the esquire, made straight for a foreign march, where she expected to find her husband the King. Which having reached by long weary travelling, she related to him these adventures . . . The Duchess felt great pity for her, and said that certainly, short of having passed through the anguish of death, never had so high a princess a harder fortune, and that therefore, if God did not raise her up again, she ought to be put in the book of noble unhappy women, as having surpassed them all.

A GERMAN AT THE COURT OF EDWARD IV, 1466

Gabriel Tetzel

From this town (Canterbury) we rode through the kingdom of England to the capital, called London, where the king of England holds court . . . In this city we found the king, and when he was aware of my lord's arrival he ordered an excellent inn to be prepared for him, and sent his herald far along the road with some of his council to meet him and they all rode in with my lord. The king soon allowed my lord to appear before him. Then we saw the tremendously great reverence which his servants showed towards him, and how mighty earls had to kneel before him. But he gave my lord and his noble companions his hand, and my lord then told him about his journey, and the reasons for his itinerary. The king took a great delight in this recital and showed himself very friendly to my lord. The king is a very handsome upright man and has the most splendid court that one can find in all Christendom. After this, nine days later, he entertained my lord Leo and all his noble companions and gave him a very splendid meal, of over fifty courses, according to their custom.

On another day the king summoned us to his court, on the morning when the queen left her childbed to go to church with a splendid procession, accompanied by many priests carrying relics and many school-boys singing and carrying lights. Then followed a great band of matrons and maidens from the country and from London too, who had been invited to attend. Then came a great number of trumpeters, pipers, and drummers. Then followed the king's choristers, about 42 of them, who sang excellently. Then marched 24 heralds and pursuivants, followed by about 60 earls and knights. After them came the queen, escorted by two dukes, with a canopy carried over her. Behind her walked her mother, with about 60 maidens and ladies. So she heard a sung office and then she left the church with the same procession as before and returned to her palace. Then all who had taken part in the procession stayed to the banquet. They seated themselves, men and women, clerical and lay, each according to his rank, and they filled four large halls.

So my lord and his companions and the noblest lords were specially served in the hall and at the tables where the king and his court are accustomed to dine. And one of the king's mightiest earls sat at the head of the king's table, in the king's chair in the king's stead. My lord was also seated at the same table only two paces away from him, and no one else sat at that table. All the honours that would have been paid to the king as in carving and tasting and the serving of courses, were paid to the earl in the king's stead, in like measure as though the king himself were seated there; and they entertained my lord so splendidly that you would not believe how lavish was the feast.

While we were eating, the king's gifts were distributed to all the trumpeters, pipers, jesters, and heralds, the heralds alone receiving 400 nobles. Every man to whom a reward had been given went about the tables, and called out aloud the sum which the king had given to him.

When my lord and the earl had finished their meal, the earl led my lord and his companions into a particularly splendid and decorated hall, where the queen was now to have her meal. My lord and his companions were seated in a corner, so that they might witness the great splendour of the arrangements. The queen sat alone at table in a costly golden chair. The queen's mother and the king's sister had to stand below. And if the queen talked with her mother or the king's sister, they had to kneel before the queen until she drank water. Not until the first dish was set before her were they allowed to sit down. The ladies and maidens and all who served dishes to the queen, even if they were powerful earls, had nevertheless to kneel, as long as she was eating. The feast lasted for three hours, and many costly dishes were served to the queen, and her mother, and the king's sister and others; of these dishes it would take too long to write. And all were silent; not a word was spoken. My lord with his companions stood all the time in the alcove and looked on.

After the banquet the dancing began. The queen remained seated in her chair. Her mother knelt before her, standing up only at intervals. The king's sister danced with two dukes in stately dances, and made impressive courtesies to the queen such as I have never seen elsewhere; nor have I witnessed such outstandingly beautiful maidens. Among these young ladies were eight duchesses and about thirty countesses, and the others were all daughters of men of high lineage. After the dancing the king's choristers entered and sang.

When the king heard mass in his chapel, they admitted my lord with his companions, and I think there can be no better singers in all the world. Then the king allowed us to see his relics and many shrines which are to be found in London. Among them especially we saw a stone which had come from the Mount of Olives, bearing the footprint of Jesus Christ, and Our Lady's girdle and ring and many other relics.

Soon afterwards my lord and his companions were invited by two earls to their house. They gave us indescribably splendid dishes to the number of about sixty according to their customs. We saw there exceptionally precious tapestries. After this my lord invited many earls and lords to his house, and provided a banquet in the Bohemian fashion. They thought this very strange. My lord was anxious to have the opportunity along with his companions, of taking part in tournaments; but the king would not allow it. So my Lord Leo, Frodner, and Gabriel Tetzel presented all their gear and tournament horses to the king, and left all their racing gear in England. After this, my lord took leave of the king, and the king paid all his expenses at his inn, after a stay of about 40 days there.

A VALENTINE, FEBRUARY 1477
Margery Brews

Sent to John Paston III of Norfolk. The couple later married.

Right reverend and worshipful and my right well beloved Valentine. I recommend me unto you full heartily, desiring to hear of your welfare, which I beseech Almighty God long for to preserve unto His pleasure and your heart's desire. And if it please you to hear of my welfare, I am not in good hele of body nor of heart, nor shall be till I hear from you:

> For there wots no creature what pain that I endure
> And for to be dead I dare it not discure (discover).

And my lady my mother hath laboured the matter to my father full diligently, but she can no more get than ye know of; for the which God knoweth I am full sorry. But if that ye love me, as I trust verily that ye do, ye will not leave me therefore. For if that ye had not half the livelihood that ye have, for to do the greatest labour that any woman alive might I would not forsake you:

> And if ye command me to keep me true wherever I go
> I wiss I will do all my might you to love and never no mo
> And if my friends say that I do amiss
> They shall not me let [prevent] so for to do.
> Mine heart me bids ever more to love you
> Truly over all earthly thing
> And if they be never so wroth
> I trust it shall, be better in time coming.

No more to you at this time, but the Holy Trinity have you in keeping. And I beseeh you that this bill be not seen of none earthly creature save only yourself.

And this letter was indited at Topcroft, with full heavy heart

By your own

MARGERY BREWS

RICHARD III MURDERS THE PRINCES IN THE TOWER, 1483

Polydore Vergil

Made Protector of the twelve year old Edward V, Uncle Richard unsurped power to become king in June 1483, quite possibly murdering his nephews in the process. Polydore Vergil was an Italian scholar encouraged by Richard's nemesis, Henry VII, to write a history of England, *Anglicae historia libri XXVI*.

Richard determined by death to despatch his nephews because so long as they lived he could never be out of hazard; wherefore he sent warrant to Robert Brackenbury, lieutenant of the Tower of London, to procure their death with all diligence by some convenient means . . . But after he had received the king's horrible commission, he was astonished with the cruelty of the fact, and fearing lest if he should obey the same it might at one time or other turn to his own harm, and did therefore defer the doing thereof in the hope that the king would spare his own blood, or their tender age, or alter that heavy determination . . . When Richard understood the lieutenant to make delay of that which he had commanded, he anon committed the charge of hastening that slaughter unto . . . James Tyrell who, being forced to do the king's commandment, rode sorrowfully to London, and, to the worst example that has almost ever been heard of, murdered those babes of the royal issue.

This end had Prince Edward and Richard his brother; but with what kind of death these children were executed is not certainly known. But King Richard, delivered by this fact from his care and fear, kept the slaughter not long secret, who, within a few days after, permitted the rumour of their death to go abroad, to the intent, as we may well believe, that after the people understood no male issue of King Edward to be now left alive, they might with better mind and goodwill bear and sustain his government. But when the fame of this notable foul fact was dispersed through the realm, so great grief struck generally to the hearts of all men, that the same, subduing all fear, they wept everywhere . . . What man is there in this world who, if he has regard to such noble children thus shamefully murdered, will not tremble and quake . . .

THE BATTLE OF BOSWORTH, 22 AUGUST 1485
Polydore Vergil

The battle that ended the Wars of the Roses. It was won by the Lancastrian claimant to the throne, Henry Tudor, after Richard III ("deformed of body, the one shoulder being higher than the other, a short and sour countenance", according to Vergil) was treasonably deserted in mid battle by the Stanley family. Following his victory, Henry was crowned King Henry VII – the first Tudor monarch – and three months later astutely married Elizabeth of York, thus uniting the houses of Lancaster and York.

At the battle of Bosworth the number of all Henry Tudor's soldiers, altogether, was scarcely 5000, beside the Stanleyans, of whom about 3000 were at the battle, under the conduct of William . . . The king's forces were twice as many and more.

. . . Henry bore the brunt of the fighting longer than even his own soldiers would have thought, who were now almost out of hope of victory, when, behold, William Stanley with 3000 men came to the rescue; then truly in a very moment the residue all fled, and King Richard alone was killed fighting manfully in the thickest press of his enemies. In the meantime also the Earl of Oxford, after a little skirmishing, put to flight those that fought in the forward, whereof a great company were killed in the chase. But many more forebore to fight, who came to the field with King Richard for awe, and for no goodwill and departed without any danger, as men who desired not the safety but destruction of that prince whom they hated.

There were killed about 1000 men, and amongst them (were) John Duke of Norfolk, Walter Lord Ferrers, Robert Brackenbury, Richard Ratcliffe and many more. Two days after at Leicester, William Catesby, lawyer, with a few that were his fellows, were executed. And of those who took to their feet Francis Lord Lovell, Humphrey Stafford, with Thomas his brother and much more company, fled into sanctuary . . . As for the number of captives, it was very great; for when King Richard was killed, all men forthwith threw away weapon and freely submitted themselves to Henry's obedience, whereof the most part would have done the same at the beginning (but) for King Richard's scouts . . . Amongst them the chief were Henry Earl of Northumberland and Thomas Earl of Surrey . . . Henry lost in that battle scarcely a hundred soldiers . . .

The report is that King Richard might have sought to save himself by flight; for they who were about him, seeing the soldiers even from the first stroke to lift up their weapons feebly and faintly, and some of them to depart the field privily, suspected treason, and exhorted him to fly, and when the matter began manifestly to falter, they brought him swift horses; but he, who was not ignorant that the people hated him, is said to have answered that that very day he would make an end either of war or life . . .

Henry, after the victory obtained, gave forthwith thanks unto Almighty God for the same . . . The soldiers cried, "God save King Henry, God save King Henry!", and with heart and hand uttered all the show of joy that might be; which, when Thomas Stanley did see, he set at once King Richard's crown, which was found among the spoil in the field, upon his head . . .

The body of King Richard, naked of all clothing, and laid upon a horse's back, with the arms and legs hanging down on both sides, was brought to the abbey of Franciscan monks at Leicester, a miserable spectacle in good truth, but not unworthy for the man's life, and there was buried two days after without any pomp or solemn funeral.

Part Three

The Tudors & The Stuarts, Britain 1486–1688

"I know I have but the body of a weak and feeble woman; but I have the heart of a king, and a king of England too."
Elizabeth I, on the eve of the Armada

"The poorest he that is in England has a life to live as the greatest he, and therefore . . . every man that is to live under a government ought first by his own consent to put himself under that government"
Colonel Thomas Rainborough, Leveller

INTRODUCTION

The Britain of 1485, the year in which Henry Tudor by dint of arms secured the English throne, was a divided feudal island off the coast of Europe of no particular importance. When Henry Tudor's heirs the Stuarts were eased from power in the Glorious Revolution of 1688, Britain was a united kingdom poised for world domination.

This transformation in fortunes was due in no small measure to Henry VII himself, partly because the sheer longevity of his reign – he died in 1509 – brought stability at a time when the Continent was wracked by wars. This stability, helped by the aristocracy's near self-immolation in the Wars of the Roses, allowed the mercantilist basis of society to burgeon. So it was that Henry's son, Henry VIII, inherited a personal fortune of £1.5 million and a commercially prosperous realm. The son squandered the personal inheritance on a round of glory-seeking wars, but his love-life and dynastic ambition changed the course of British history forever. If accidentally.

In 1528 Henry having fallen out of love with his first wife (not least because of her inability to produce a male heir) and into love with Anne Boleyn, determined on divorce. The Pope refused to grant one. To settle the "Great Matter", Henry broke with Rome and set up a new Church with himself at the head. Moreover, he suppressed the monasteries and sold them off cheap to the local squirearchy. Newly enriched, the squirearchy had a direct stake in the new order. Although Henry himself remained until his death a Catholic-without-the-Pope, the logic of his reformation was towards the new theology of Protestantism – which is where it ended up with his son, Edward VI. When Edward died at the premature age of 16 in 1553, the English throne passed to his sister Mary. Although the "Marian Reaction" tried to return Britain to the Catholic fold by the public burning of Protestants, it failed. Mary herself expired after five years on the throne; her brutality – recorded so lucidly in *Foxe's Book of the Martyrs* – turned Englishmen away; and there were simply too many people with a vested interest in Protestantism. Not just the squirearchy, but the mercantilists and manufacturers, who found in the new faith a justification of their ways and beliefs. Protestantism preached thriftiness, industriousness, this wordliness.

A mistress of realpolitik, Elizabeth I understood that the English future was Protestant; and anyway, her taste ran in that direction. Abroad, she supported Protestant powers, at home she practised a moderate Protestantism, almost indistinguishable from modern Anglicanism, which stabilized the realm for the duration of her long reign (1558–1603). Like her grandfather, she proved adept at checking the nobility; the House of Commons gained in importance, as did the gentry who flocked to fill it. The self-confidence of Elizabeth's England knew few bounds; English seamen like Drake and Raleigh roamed the world's oceans (pilfering and pirating as they did so), while Shakespeare, Marlowe and Jonson created some of the world's greatest theatre. Elizabeth's England was God's chosen land for his chosen people (who were rapidly growing in numbers: between 1561 and 1601, the population of England climbed from 2.98 million to 4.10 million). This sense of national blessedness and destiny was caught perfectly by Shakespeare in *Richard II*: "This precious stone set in the silver sea . . . This blessed plot, this earth, this realm, this England . . . This land of such dear souls, this dear, dear land".

And then, in 1603, came the Stuarts. James I, the Virgin Queen's appointed successor, was a Scottish homosexual, forever playing with his genitals and landing slobbering kisses on the lips of court favourites like Buckingham ("Christ had his John and I have my George"). He ruled uneasily and unwell, and virtually cut dead English expansionism overseas. His son, Charles I, was a greater disaster, for he had an even more marked tendency to impersonate the regal autocrats of the continent. This, of course, ran headlong into the long march of English Parliamentarianism.

Constitutionalism was but one cause of the English Civil War.

There were others. Charles's I crypto-Catholicism alienated most of his subjects, notably the Presbyterian Scots with whom he blunderingly went to war in 1637. Meanwhile, men of commerce, outside a charmed ring of London financiers who subsidized the monarchy in return for baubles and privileges, chafed at government policies, monopolies and over-regulation. When Charles I raised his standard at Nottingham on 22 August 1642 (effectively declaring war against his own nation) he was overwhelmed by the forces against him, especially since these were spearheaded by Parliament's New Model Army. By 1646, it was all over and the King surrendered. Although a peacably-inclined Parliament tried to treat with him, he continued to scheme and started another Civil War by hiring the Scots in return for the promise of Presbyterianism north of the border. Unfortunately for Charles I, the Scots were no match for Oliver Cromwell who defeated them at Preston in August 1648. This time Parliament was less lenient and Charles's head, with its flowing locks, was lopped off.

Revolutionary England was a ferment of radical democratic ideas, but lapsed into a military dicatorship under Lord Protector Oliver Cromwell as the only system and only man who could save the nation from anarchy. The Interregnum is invariably portrayed as a joyless terror, whereas in reality it was the making of modern Britain. Cromwell achieved something that eluded even Elizabeth, the uniting of the isles (by conquering Scotland and Ireland), before turning Britain outwards into the world once more. Decisively, the Navigation Act of 1651 massively expanded British commerce and the mercantile marine, the latter protected by big warships with big cannon. Oliver Cromwell, in short, made Britain and made it safe for capitalism.

When Cromwell was eventually defeated by bronchitis, the degree to which the success of the whole enterprise depended upon his persona was starkly obvious. His son Richard carried on for a while as Lord Protector, before (wisely) relinquishing the task as beyond him. A vacuum yawned, and the Army invited the restoration of the Stuarts. The clock was not turned back to the "good old days" of James I, however. The royal prerogative was gone for ever, Parliament more powerful than ever, *laissez faire* capitalism here to stay. The latter Stuarts, Charles II and James II, were as inclined to foreign ideas in religion and politics as the earlier Stuarts.

Thus in 1688 they too were dispensed with.

THE PRETENCE OF PERKIN WARBECK, 1498

Raimondo de Soncino

The son of the Controller of Tournai, Warbeck was persuaded to impersonate Richard, duke of York, one of the princes murdered in the Tower in 1483. Acknowledged by a scheming James IV of Scotland (among others), Warbeck invaded Cornwall in 1498 to claim 'his' throne from Henry VII.

On the 19th inst., by Vadino Gambarana of Saona, I advised your Excellency of the coming of Perkin to this realm and what was the general opinion about it; and on the 25th by way of the Genoese at Bruges, I sent word that Perkin had fled. Now with the arrival of the Venetian packet I will send a detailed account of what has taken place according to the relation of Messer Fra Zoan Antonio de Carbonariis of Milan, who was actually present in the city of Exeter.

On the 6th of this month Perkin landed in Cornwall at a port called Mount St. Michael with three small ships and about three hundred persons of various nationalities, who had followed him for some time before. As he had so few with him, it is thought that the Cornishmen must have invited him. In fact eight thousand peasants were forthwith in arms with him, although ill disciplined and without any gentlemen, who form the governing class of England.

They proclaimed Perkin as King Richard, and they paid for the victuals with which the commune provided them, as they had done when the Cornishmen were routed at London. They marched towards his Majesty, who did not hear of this movement until the 10th . . .

Without waiting the royal command, the Earl of Devon, a lord of the County, opposed these people with about 1,500 men, but owing to the multitude of the enemy he withdrew to the city of Exeter. Perkin arrived at that place at the 22nd hour of the 17th of the month, and being refused admission, he began the attack on two of the gates. He burned one, but the Earl drove him off with stones, so that at the second hour on the following day Perkin asked for a truce for six hours. This was granted on the understanding that no one of Exeter should be allowed to follow him. The moment the truce was made, Perkin departed and went to a village called Minet, ten miles from Exeter, where he passed the night. On the 19th he came to another good village called

Taunton, twenty-four miles from Exeter, and stayed there until the 21st. Among other things he published certain apostolic bulls affirming that he was the son of King Edward and that he meant to coin money and give money to all.

In the meantime his Majesty had sent the Lord Chamberlain against him with a good number of men, and announced that he would pardon all who laid down their arms. Accordingly the numbers with Perkin constantly lessened. He began to declare that he had a close understanding with some lords of the realm. As the bridges on the straight road were cut, he proposed to turn somewhat to the right and take another way. Subsequently at the fourth hour of the night, he silently departed from the camp with some ten thousand persons and at dawn the next morning the unfortunate Cornishmen discovered their plight and took to flight, to such an extent that by the third hour of the day not one was left in Taunton. . . . When Perkin fled from Taunton, in the company of John Aeron (Heron) sometime a merchant of London, and two other English gentlemen, he came to an abbey called Diodle (Beaulieu). . . . The abbot of this happened to know the said John and the two gentlemen, and sent word to his Majesty about them, feeling sure that the youth must be with them, as indeed he was. Some of the Royal Council sent thither, and came to the following arrangement with John and his fellows, to wit, that John should go to his Majesty and either bring back a pardon for himself and his companions, or should be put back into sanctuary, while in the meantime the two companions should stay behind and guard the youth, so that he should not escape. . . .

John, who swore to the King that he had never known Perkin except as Richard II [sic] son of King Edward, returned with the offer of a pardon to the young man if he would go to the King's presence. The youth agreed to go. . . . He tells me that the young man is not handsome, indeed his left eye rather lacks lustre, but he is intelligent and well spoken.

The young man was brought into the royal presence, where many nobles of the realm were assembled, some of whom had been companions of Richard, Duke of York. He kneeled down and asked for mercy. The King bade him rise and then spoke as follows: We have heard that you call yourself Richard, Son of King Edward. In this place are some who were companions of that lord, look and see if you recognise them. The young man answered that he knew none of them, he was not Richard, he had never come to England except that once, and he had been induced by the English and Irish to commit this fraud and to learn English. For quite two years he had longed to escape from these troubles, but Fortune had not allowed him.

Richmond was not present at this interview, at which there were none besides princes, but I believe it all, because he is a wise man, and because he shewed me a sheet, written in French, signed in a different hand, thus "Pet Pero Osbeck", which he says is Perkin's hand. . . .

I asked Richmond if Perkin would escape with his life. He told me that he would, but it was necessary to guard him well, in order that the men of Cornwall may not murder him, as they are incensed since they have learned from the King that they have been worshipping a low born foreigner as their sovereign. . . .

Warbeck was executed in 1499 following two attempted escapes from the Tower.

A PORTRAIT OF HENRY VIII, 1519

Sebastian Giustinian

A portrait of the monarch at the zenith of his reign, a year after the Treaty of London, the glories of the wars against France and Scotland behind him. Giustinian was the Venetian ambassador to England 1515–19.

His majesty is twenty-nine years old and extremely handsome. Nature could not have done more for him. He is much handsome than any other sovereign in Christendom; a great deal handsomer than the King of France; very fair, and his whole frame admirably proportioned. On hearing that Francis I wore a beard, he allowed his own to grow, and as it is reddish, he has now a beard that looks like gold. He is very accomplished, a good musician, composes well, is a most capital horseman, a fine jouster, speaks good French, Latin, and Spanish, is very religious, hears three masses daily when he hunts, and sometimes five on other days. He hears the office every day in the queen's chamber, that is to say vesper and compline. He is very fond of hunting, and never takes his diversion without tiring eight or ten horses, which he causes to be stationed beforehand along the line of country he means to take, and when one is tired he mounts another, and before he gets home they are all exhausted. He is extremely fond of tennis, at which game it is the prettiest thing in the world to see him play, his fair skin glowing through a shirt of the finest texture. He gambles with the French hostages, to the amount occasionally, it is said, of from 6000 to 8000 ducats in a day. He is affiable and gracious, harms no one, does not covet his neighbour's goods, and is satisfied with his own dominions, having often said to me, "Sir Ambassador, we want all potentates to content themselves with their own territories; we are satisfied with this island of ours." He seems extremely desirous of peace.

He is very rich. His father left him ten millions of ready money in gold, of which he was supposed to have spent one-half in the war against France, when he had three armies on foot; one crossed the Channel with him, another was in the field against Scotland, and the third remained with the queen in reserve.

His revenues amount to about 350,000 ducats annually, and are derived from estates, forests, and meres, the customs, hereditary and confiscated property, the duchies of Lancaster, York, Cornwall and Suffolk, the county palatine of Chester, and others, the principality of Wales, the export duties, the wool staple, the great seal, the annates yielded by Church benefices, the Court of Wards, and from New Year's gifts; for on the first day of the year it is customary for his majesty to make presents to everybody, but the value of those he receives in return greatly exceeds his own outlay. His majesty's expenses may be estimated at 100,000 ducats, those in ordinary having been reduced from 100,000 to 56,000 to which must be added 16,000 for salaries, 5000 for the stable, 5000 for the halberdiers, who have been reduced from 500 to 150, and 16,000 for the wardrobe, for he is the best dressed sovereign in the world. His robes are very rich and superb, and he puts on new clothes every holyday.

The queen is the sister of the mother of the king of Spain, now styled King of the Romans. She is thirty-five years old and not handsome, though she has a very beautiful complexion. She is religious and as virtuous as words can express.

THE MAGNIFICENCE OF CARDINAL WOLSEY, c. 1525

George Cavendish

A butcher's son, Thomas Wolsey rose to be Henry VIII's chief minister, following his planning of the French campaign of 1512–13. He was appointed Archbishop of York in 1514, cardinal and lord chancellor in the following year. He lived thereafter in a sumptuousness which rivalled the King's. Wolsey fell from favour following his resort to the forced loan inflicted on men of property in 1524 and his failure to secure Papal approval for Henry's divorce from Catherine of Aragon. George Cavendish was usher to Wolsey.

Truth it is, Cardinal Wolsey, sometime Archbishop of York, was an honest poor man's son, born at Ipswich, within the county of Suffolk; and being but a child, was very apt to learning; by means whereof his parents, or his good friends and masters, conveyed him to the University of Oxford, where he prospered so in learning, that, as he told me in his own person, he was called the boy-bachelor, forasmuch as he was made a Bachelor of Arts at fifteen years of age, which was a rare thing and seldom seen . . .

Now will I declare unto you his order in going to Westminster Hall, daily in the term of season. First, before his coming out of his privy chamber, he heard most commonly every day two masses in his privy closet; and there then said his daily service, with his chaplain; and as I heard his chaplain say, being a man of credence and of excellent learning, that the cardinal, what business or weighty matters soever he had in the day, he never went to his bed with any part of his divine service unsaid, yea not so much as one collect; wherein I doubt not but he deceiveth the opinion of divers persons. After mass he would return in his privy chamber again, and being advertised of the furniture of his chambers without, with noblemen, gentlemen, and other persons, would issue out into them, apparelled all in red, in the habit of a cardinal; which was either of fine scarlet, or else of crimson satin, taffety, damask, or caffa, the best that he could get for money: and upon his head a round pillion, with a noble of black velvet set to the same in the inner side; he had also a tippet of fine sables about his neck; holding in his hand a very fair orange, whereof the meat or substance within was taken out, and filled up again with the part of a sponge, wherein was vinegar, and other confections against the pestilent airs; the which he most commonly smelt unto, passing amongst the press, or else when he was pestered with many suitors. There was also borne before him first, the great seal of England, and then his cardinal's hat, by a nobleman or some worthy gentleman, right solemnly, bareheaded. And as soon as he was entered into his chamber of presence, where there was attending his coming to await upon him to Westminster Hall, as well noblemen and other worthy gentlemen, as noblemen and gentlemen of his own family; thus passing forth with two great crosses of silver borne before him; with also two great pillars of silver, and his pursuivant at arms with a great mace of silver gilt. Then his gentlemen ushers cried, and said: "On, my lords and masters, on before; make way for my Lord's Grace". Thus passed he down from his chamber through the hall; and when he came to the hall door, there was attendant for him his mule, trapped all together in crimson velvet, and gilt stirrups. When he was mounted, with his cross bearers, and pillar bearers, also upon great horses trapped with fine scarlet. Then marched he forward, with his train and furniture in manner as I have declared, having about him four footmen, with gilt pollaxes in their hands; and thus he went until he came to Westminster Hall door. And there alighted, and went after this manner, up through the hall into the chancery; howbeit he would most commonly stay awhile at a bar, made for him, a little beneath the chancery on the right hand, and there commune sometime with the judges, and sometime with other persons. And that done he would repair into the chancery, sitting there till eleven of the clock, hearing suitors, and determining of divers matters. And from thence, he would divers times go into the star chamber, as occasion did serve; where he spared neither high nor low, but judged every estate according to their merits and deserts . . .

Thus in great honour, triumph, and glory, he reigned a long season, ruling all things within this realm, appertaining unto the king, by his wisdom, and also all other weighty matters of foreign regions, with which the king of this realm had any occasion to intermeddle. All ambassadors of foreign potentates were always dispatched by his discretion, to whom they had always access for their dispatch. His house was also always resorted and furnished with noblemen, gentlemen, and other persons, with going and coming in and out, feasting and banqueting all ambassadors diverse times, and other strangers right nobly . . .

"MINE OWN SWEETHEART": HENRY VIII WRITES TO ANNE BOLEYN, c. 1526

Henry VIII

Tiring of his first wife, Catherine of Aragon (and her inability to produce a son and heir), Henry VIII turned to the charms of Anne Boleyn, niece of the Duke of Norfolk, whom he determined to marry. When the Pope

refused Henry's divorce from Catherine, Henry set in the train the break
with Rome that reformed the monasteries and founded the Protestant
Church of England

Mine own sweetheart, this shall be to advertise you of the great
melancholy that I find here since your departing; for, I ensure you,
methinketh the time longer since your departing now last than I
was wont to do a whole fortnight. I think your kindness and my
fervency of love causeth it; for, otherwise I would not have thought
it possible that for so little a while it should have grieved me. But
now I am coming towards you, methinketh my pains by half
removed; and also I am right well comforted insomuch that my
book maketh substantially for my matter; in looking where of I
have spent above four hours this day, which causeth me now to
write the shorter letter to you at this time, because of some pain in
my head. Wishing myself (especially an evening) in my sweetheart's arms whose pretty duckies* I trust shortly to kiss. Written
by the hand of him that was, is, and shall be yours by his own will,

H. R.

THE CORONATION OF ANNE BOLEYN, 1 JUNE 1533

Archbishop Cranmer

Henry VIII secretly married Anne Boleyn on 25 January 1533. Four
months later, after Archbishop Cranmer had declared his previous
marriage, to Catherine of Aragon, null and void Henry had Anne
crowned Queen.

. . . The Thursday next before the Feast of Pentecost, the King
and the Queen being at Greenwich, all the Crafts of London
thereunto well appointed, in several barges decked after the most
gorgeous and sumptuous manner, with divers pageants thereunto
belonging, repaired and waited all together upon the Mayor of
London; and so, well furnished, came all unto Greenwich, where
they tarried and waited for the Queen's coming to her barge;
which so done, they brought her unto the Tower, trumpets,
shawms, and other divers instruments playing and making great
melody, which, as is reported, was as comely done as never was like
in any time nigh to our remembrance. And so her Grace came to

* Breasts

the Tower on Thursday at night, about five of the clock, where also was such a peal of guns as hath not been heard the like a great while before. And the same night, and Friday all day, the King and Queen tarried there; and on Friday at night the King's Grace made eighteen knights of the Bath, whose creation was not only so strange to hear of, as also their garments stranger to behold or look upon; which said knights, the next day, which was Saturday, rode before the Queen's Grace throughout the City of London towards Westminster Palace, over and besides the most part of the nobles of the realm, which like accompanied her Grace throughout the said city; she sitting in her hair (i.e. her hair flowing down), upon a horse litter, richly apparelled, and four knights of the Five Ports bearing a canopy over her head. And after her came four rich chariots, one of them empty, and three other furnished with divers ancient old ladies; and after them came a great train of other ladies and gentlewomen; which said progress, from the beginning to the ending, extended half a mile in length by estimation or thereabout. To whom also, as she came along the City, were shewn many costly pageants, with divers other encomiums spoken of children to her; wine also running at certain conduits plenteously. And so proceeding throughout the streets, passed further unto Westminster Hall, where was a certain banquet prepared for her, which done, she was conveyed out of the back side of the Palace into a barge, and so unto York Place, where the King's Grace was before her coming, for this you must ever presuppose that his Grace came always before her secretly in a barge as well from Greenwich to the Tower as from the Tower to York Place.

Now then on the Sunday was the Coronation, which also was of such a manner.

In the morning there assembled with me at Westminster Church the Bishop of York, the Bishop of London, the Bishop of Winchester, the Bishop of Lincoln, the Bishop of Bath, and the Bishop of St. Asaph, the Abbot of Westminster with ten or eleven more Abbots, which all revestred ourselves in our pontificalibus, and, so furnished, with our Crosses and Croziers, proceeded out of the Abbey in a procession into Westminster Hall, where we received the Queen apparelled in a robe of purple velvet, and all the ladies and gentlewomen in robes and gowns of scarlet according to the manner used beforetime in such business; and so her Grace sustained of each side with two bishops, the Bishop of London and the Bishop of Winchester, came forth in procession unto the Church of Westminster, she in her hair, my Lord of Suffolk bearing before her the Crown, and two other Lords bearing also before her a sceptre and a white rod, and so entered up into the High Altar, where divers ceremonies used about her, I did set the Crown on her head, and then was sung *Te Deum* & c. And after that was sung a solemn Mass, all which while her Grace sat crowned upon a scaffold which was made between the High Altar and Choir in Westminster Church; which Mass and ceremonies done and finished, all the assembly of noblemen brought her into Westminster Hall again, where was kept a great solemn feast all that day; the good order thereof were too long to write at this time to you.

But now, Sir, you may not imagine that this Coronation was before her marriage, for she was married much about St. Paul's Day last, as the condition thereof doth well appear by reason she is now somewhat big with child.

Within three months of the coronation, Henry's passion for Boleyn had cooled, and was not revived by the birth of a daughter (later to rule as Elizabeth I). In 1536 Boleyn was beheaded for adultery with her own brother, plus four commoners. Eleven days after the execution, Henry married Jane Seymour. The other three of Henry's six wives were: Anne of Cleves, Catherine Howard, and Catherine Parr.

INCONTINENT WITH PISS, ENGLAND, c. 1535

Lord Edmund Howard

The medicine mentioned in Howard's letter to Lady Lisle was probably derived from dandelion, a common medieval diuretic (hence its colloquial name, "pissabed"). Howard was the father of the future queen, Catherine Howard.

Madame,

So it is I have this night after midnight taken your medicine, for the which I heartily thank you, for it hath done me much good, and hath caused the stone to break; so that now I void much gravel. But for all that, your said medicine hath done me little honesty, for it made me piss my bed this night, for the which my wife hath sore beaten me, and saying it is children's parts to bepiss their bed. Ye have made me such a pisser that I dare not this day go abroad, wherefore I beseech you to make mine excuse to my Lord and Master Treasurer, for that I shall not be with you this day at dinner. Madame, it is showed me that a wing or a leg of a stork, if I eat thereof, will make me that I shall never piss more in bed, and though my body be simple yet my tongue shall be ever good, and especially when it speaketh of women; and sithence such a medicine will do such a great cure God send me a piece thereof.

all yours,
Edmund Howard

THE REFORMATION IN ENGLAND: A VISITATION TO THE MONASTERIES OF BUCKINGHAMSHIRE, KENT AND SUFFOLK, 1535–8

John London, John Ap Rice, Richard Layton, Geoffrey Chamber, Roger Townsend

The authors were agents of Thomas Cromwell, Henry VIII's Lord Privy Seal, sent to report on the state of the monasteries prior to dissolution.

In my most humble manner I have me commended unto your good lordship, ascertaining the same that I have pulled down the image of Our Lady at Caversham, whereunto was great pilgrimage. The image is plated over with silver, and I have put it in a chest fast locked and nailed up, and by the next barge that cometh from Reading to London it shall be brought to your lordship. I have also pulled down the place she stood in, with all other ceremonies, as lights, shrouds, crosses, and images of wax hanging about the chapel, and have defaced the same thoroughly in eschewing of any further resort thither. This chapel did belong to Notley Abbey, and there always was a canon of that monastery which was called the Warden of Caversham, and he sung in this chapel and had the offerings for his living. He was accustomed to show many pretty relics, among the which were (as he made report) the holy dagger that killed King Henry, and the holy knife that killed St Edward. All these with many other, with the coats of this image, her cap and hair, my servants shall bring unto your lordship this week, with the surrender of the friars under their convent seal, and their seal also. I have sent the canon home again to Notley, and have made fast the doors of the chapel, which is thoroughly well covered with lead, and if it be your lordship's pleasure I shall see it made sure to the King's grace's use. And if it be not so ordered, the chapel standeth so wildly that the lead will be stolen by night, as I was served at the Friars. For as soon as I had taken the Friars' surrender, the multitude of the poverty of the town resorted thither, and all things that might be had they stole away, insomuch that they had conveyed the very clappers of the bells. And saving that Mr Fachell, which made me great cheer at his house, and the Mayor did assist me, they would have made no little spoil . . .

Please it your good lordship to be advertised that . . . the Abbot of Langdon passeth all other that ever I knew in profound bawdry; the drunkennest knave living. All his canons be even as he is, not one spark of virtue amongst them; arrant bawdy knaves every man. The Abbot caused his chaplain to take an whore, and instigate him to it, brought her up into his own chapter, took one of his feather-beds off his own bed, and made his chaplain's bed in the inner chamber, within him, and there caused him to go to bed with his whore that the Abbot had provided for him. To rehearse you the whole story, it were long and too abominable to hear. The house is in utter decay and will shortly fall down. You must needs depose him and suddenly sequestrate the fruits, and take an inventory of the goods. You can do no less of justice . . .

My singular good lord, my duty remembered unto your lordship, this shall be to advertise the same that upon the defacing of the late monastery of Boxley, and plucking down the images of the same, I found in the image of the Rood called the Rood of Grace, the which heretofore hath been had in great veneration of the people, certain engines and old wire, with old rotten sticks in the back of the same, that did cause the eyes of the same to move and stare in the head thereof, like unto a living thing; and also the nether lip in like wise to move as though it should speak, which, so famed, was not a little strange to me and other that was present at the plucking down of the same, whereupon the abbot, hearing this bruit, did thither resort, whom to my little wit and cunning, with other of the old monks, I did examine of their knowledge of the premises; who do declare themselves to be ignorant of the same

Please it your goodness to understand that on Friday 22 October I rode back with speed to take an inventory of Folkestone (priory), and from thence went to Langdon. Whereas immediately descending from my horse, I sent Bartelot your servant, with all my servants to circumcept the abbey, and surely to keep all back doors and startyng hoilles*, etc. I myself went alone to the abbot's lodging joining upon the fields and wood, even like a cony clapper† full of private ways; a good space knocking at the abbot's door, neither sound nor sign of life appearing, saving the abbot's little dog, that within his door fast locked, bayed and barked. I found a short pole-axe standing behind the door, and with it I dashed the abbot's door in pieces, and set one of my men to keep that door, and about the house I go with the pole-axe in my hand, for the abbot is a dangerous desperate knave and a hardy. But for a conclusion, his whore alias his gentlewoman bestirred her stumps towards her startyng hoilles, and there Bartelot watching the pursuit took the tender damsel, and after I had examined her, to Dover there to the mayor to set her in some cage or prison for 8 days, and I brought holy father abbot to Canterbury, and there in Christ Church (priory) I will leave him in prison. In this sudden doing extempore, to circumcept the house and to search, your servant John Antony and his men marvelled what fellow I was, and so did the rest of the abbey, for I was unknown there of all men. At last I found her apparel in the abbot's coffer. To tell you all this comedy, but for the abbot a tragedy, it were too long.

Please it your mastership, forasmuch as I suppose ye shall have suit made unto you touching Bury ere we return, I thought convenient to advertise you of our proceedings there, and also of the comperta of the same. As for the abbot, we found nothing suspect as touching his living, but it was detected that he lay much forth in his granges, that he delighted much in playing at dice and cards, and therein spent much money, and in building for his pleasure. He did not preach openly. Also that he converted divers farms into copyholds, whereof poor men doth complain. Also he seemeth to be addict to the maintaining of such superstitious ceremonies as hath been used heretofore.

As touching the convent, we could get little or no reports among them, although we did use much diligence in our examination, and thereby, with some other arguments gathered of their examinations, I firmly believe and suppose that they had conferred and compacted before our coming that they should disclose nothing. And yet it is confessed and proved, that there was here such frequence of women coming and resorting to this monastery as to

* Private posterns.
† A rabbit's burrow.

no place more. Amongst the relics we found much vanity and superstition, as the coals that Saint Lawrence was toasted withal, the parings of S. Edmund's nails, S. Thomas of Canterbury's penknife and his boots, and divers skills for the headache; pieces of the holy cross able to make a holy cross of . . .

THE MARRIAGE OF QUEEN MARY AND PHILIP II OF SPAIN, 25 JULY 1554

John Elder

On the death of Henry VIII in 1537, the throne was assumed by Edward VI, his son by Jane Seymour. Never robust, Edward VI reigned for six years, dying at the age of sixteen. The crown was then held for nine days by Lady Jane Grey in a coup d'état engineered by her father-in-law, the Earl of Northumberland, before Henry's daughter Mary Tudor became queen.

Then Wednesday, being St James's Day and the 25th of July, His Highness at 10 of the clock and his nobles before him went to the Cathedral Church (of Winchester) and remained there . . . until the Queen's Highness came, whose Majesty with all her Council and nobility before her came thither at half hour to eleven. And entering at the west door of the said Cathedral Church . . . Her Majesty ascended the foresaid steps and came toward the choir door, where a little without the same door was made a round mount of boards ascending also five steps above the scaffold. On which mount immediately after Her Majesty and the King were shriven (i.e. confessed) they were married by my lord the Bishop of Winchester, Lord Chancellor of England, Her Majesty standing on the right side of the said mount and the King on the left side.

And this marriage being ended and solemnized, which . . . was declared and done by the said Lord Chancellor both in Latin and in English, his Lordship also declared there that the Emperor's Majesty signed under his Imperial Seal the Kingdoms of Naples and Jerusalem to his son Philip, Prince of Spain, whereby it might well appear to all men that the Queen's Highness was then married not only to a Prince but also to a King.

The Queen's marriage ring was a plain hoop of gold without any stone in it, for that was her pleasure, because maidens were so married in old times.

This being done . . . the Earl of Derby before the Queen's

Majesty and the Earl of Pembroke before the King's Highness did
bear each of them a sword of honour. And so both their majesties
entered the Choir hand in hand under a canopy borne by four
knight towards the high altar, where – after they had kneeled a
while with each of them a taper – they arose, and the Queen went
to a seat [on] the right hand of the altar and the King to another
seat to the left hand and where they continued thus . . . their
meditations and prayers until the gospel was said and then they
came out and knelt all the high mass time, openly before the high
altar . . . Where during the mass time the Queen's Chapel,
matched with the Choir and the organs, used such sweet proportion of music and harmony as the like (I suppose) was never before
invented or heard.

The High Mass being done . . . by my lord Bishop of Winchester
and the Bishops of Durham, Ely, London, Lincoln and Chichester,
the King of Heralds openly in preface of both their majesties and
the whole audience so solemnly proclaimed this their new style and
title in Latin, French and English.

. . . And thus shortly to conclude, there was for certain days
after this most noble marriage such triumphing, banqueting,
singing, masquing, and dancing as was never in England heretofore. Wherefore, to see the King's majesty and the Queen sitting
under the cloth of state, in the hall where they dined, and also in
the Chamber of presence at dancing time, where both their
majesties danced, and also to behold the dukes and noble men
of Spain dance with the fair ladies and most beautiful nymphs in
England, it should seem to him to be another world.

THE MARTYRDOM OF DOCTOR TAYLOR, 1555

John Foxe

An ardent Roman Catholic, Mary I sought the reversal of the Protestant
Reformation of her father and brother. In 1555 the persecution of
Protestants began. Taylor was sentenced to death for trying to prevent
Mass being celebrated in his parish church at Hadleigh, Suffolk.

When Taylor in the company of the Sheriff and the latter's escort
were come to Hadleigh bridge, at the footbridge waited a poor
man with five small children; who held up their hands, and he
cried, "O dear father and good shepherd, Dr Taylor, God help and
succour thee as thou hast many a time succoured me and my poor

children!" The streets of Hadleigh were beset on both sides . . . with the men and women of the town and country who waited to see and bless him. Coming against the alms-houses, which he well knew, he cast to the poor people money, some of which remained out of what had been given him in the time of his imprisonment . . .

His head had been notched and clipped as a man would clip a fool's, which cost the good Bishop Bonner had bestowed upon him. But when people saw his reverend and ancient face, with a long white beard, they burst out with weeping tears, and cried, saying "God save thee, good Dr Taylor! . . ."

Dr Taylor, perceiving that he should not be suffered to speak, sat down. On seeing one named Soyce, he called to him and said, "Soyce, I pray thee come and pull off my boots, and take them for thy labour; thou hast long looked for them, now take them." Then he rode up, and put off his clothes unto his shirt, and gave them away. Which done, he said with a loud voice, "Good people, I have taught you nothing but God's holy word, and those lessons that I have taken out of God's blessed book, the Holy Bible, and I am come hither this day to seal it with my blood."

With that word Holmes, yeoman of the guard, who used Dr Taylor very cruelly all the way, gave him a heavy stroke upon the head, and said, "Is that the keeping of thy promise of silence, thou heretic?" Then the doctor knelt down and prayed, and a poor woman that was among the people stepped in and prayed with him. When he had prayed, he went to the stake and kissed it, and set himself into a pitch-barrell which they had put for him to stand in, and stood with his back upright against the stake, with his hands folded together, and his eyes toward heaven, and continually prayed.

Then they bound him with the chains, and having set up the faggots, one Warwick cruelly cast a faggot at him, which struck him on his head and cut his face, so that the blood ran down. Then said Dr Taylor, "O friend, I have harm enough, what needed that?" . . . At last they kindled the fire, and Dr Taylor, holding up both his hands called upon God and said, "Merciful Father of Heaven! . . . receive my soul into Thy hands!" So he stood still without either crying or moving with his hands folded together till Soyce with a halbert struck him on the head . . . and the corpse fell down into the fire.

THE BURNING OF ARCHBISHOP CRANMER, 21 MARCH 1556

A Bystander

The first Protestant Archbishop of Canterbury, Thomas Cranmer was convicted of heresy under Mary I. He recanted no less than seven times, before publically and dramatically affirming his Protestatism on the day of his execution.

But that I know for our great friendships, and long continued love, you look even of duty that I should signify to you of the truth of such things as here chanceth among us; I would not at this time have written to you the unfortunate end, and doubtful tragedy, of Thomas Cranmer late bishop of Canterbury: because I little pleasure take in beholding of such heavy sights. And, when they are once overpassed, I like not to rehearse them again; being but a renewing of my woe, and doubling my grief. For although his former life, and wretched end, deserves a greater misery, (if any greater might have chanced than chanced unto him), yet, setting aside his offences to God and his country, and beholding the man without his faults, I think there was none that pitied not his case, and bewailed not his fortune, and feared not his own chance, to see so noble a prelate, so grave a counsellor, of so long continued honour, after so many dignities, in his old years to be deprived of his estate, adjudged to die, and in so painful a death to end his life. I have no delight to increase it. Alas, it is too much of itself, that ever so heavy a case should betide to man, and man to deserve it.

But to come to the matter: on Saturday last, being 21 of March, was his day appointed to die. And because the morning was much rainy, the sermon appointed by Mr Dr Cole to be made at the stake, was made in St Mary's church: whither Dr Cranmer was brought by the mayor and aldermen, and my lord Williams: with whom came divers gentlemen of the shire, sir T. A. Bridges, sir John Browne, and others. Where was prepared, over against the pulpit, an high place for him, that all the people might see him. And, when he had ascended it, he kneeled him down and prayed, weeping tenderly: which moved a great number to tears, that had conceived an assured hope of his conversion and repentance . . .

When praying was done, he stood up, and, having leave to speak, said, "Good people, I had intended indeed to desire you to pray for me; which because Mr Doctor hath desired, and you have done already, I thank you most heartily for it. And now will I pray for myself, as I could best devise for mine own comfort, and say the prayer, word for word, as I have here written it." And he read it standing: and after kneeled down, and said the Lord's Prayer; and all the people on their knees devoutly praying with him . . .

And then rising, he said, "Every man desireth, good people, at the time of their deaths, to give some good exhortation, that other may remember after their deaths, and be the better thereby. So I beseech God grant me grace, that I may speak something, at this my departing, whereby God may be glorified, and you edified . . .

"And now I come to the great thing that troubleth my conscience more than any other thing that ever I said or did in my life: and that is, the setting abroad of writings contrary to the truth. Which here now I renounce and refuse, as things written with my hand, contrary to the truth which I thought in my heart, and written for fear of death, and to save my life, if it might be: and that is, all such bills, which I have written or signed with mine own hand since my degradation: wherein I have written many things untrue. And forasmuch as my hand offended in writing contrary to my heart, therefore my hand shall first be punished: for if I may come to the fire, it shall be first burned. And as for the pope, I refuse him, as Christ's enemy and antichrist, with all his false doctrine."

And here, being admonished of his recantation and dissembling, he said, "Alas, my lord, I have been a man that all my life loved plainness, and never dissembled till now against the truth; which I am most sorry for it." He added hereunto, that, for the sacrament, he believed as he had taught in his book against the bishop of Winchester. And here he was suffered to speak no more . . .

Then was he carried away; and a great number, that did run to see him go so wickedly to his death, ran after him, exhorting him, while time was, to remember himself. And one Friar John, a godly and well learned man, all the way travelled with him to reduce him. But it would not be. What they said in particular I cannot tell, but the effect appeared in the end: for at the stake he professed, that he died in all such opinions as he had taught, and oft repented him of his recantation.

Coming to the stake with a cheerful countenance and willing mind, he put off his garments with haste, and stood upright in his shirt: and a bachelor of divinity, named Elye, of Brazen-nose college, laboured to convert him to his former recantation, with the two Spanish friars. And when the friars saw his constancy, they said in Latin one to another "Let us go from him: we ought not to be nigh him: for the devil is with him." But the bachelor in divinity was more earnest with him: unto whom he answered, that, as concerning his recantation, he repented it right sore, because he knew it was against the truth; with other words more. Whereby the Lord Williams cried, "Make short, make short." Then the bishop took certain of his friends by the hand. But the bachelor of divinity refused to take him by the hand, and blamed all others that so did, and said, he was sorry that ever he came in his company. And yet again he required him to agree to his former recantation. And the bishop answered, (shewing his hand), "This was the hand that wrote it, and therefore shall it suffer first punishment."

Fire being now put to him, he stretched out his right hand, and thrust it into the flame, and held it there a good space, before the fire came to any other part of his body; where his hand was seen of every man sensibly burning, crying with a loud voice, "This hand hath offended." As soon as the fire got up, he was very soon dead, never stirring or crying all the while.

His patience in the torment, his courage in dying, if it had been taken either for the glory of God, the wealth of his country, or the testimony of truth, as it was for a pernicious error, and subversion of true religion, I could worthily have commended the example, and matched it with the fame of any father of ancient time: but, seeing that not the death, but cause and quarrel thereof, commendeth the sufferer, I cannot but much dispraise his obstinate stubbornness and sturdiness in dying, and specially in so evil a cause. Surely his death much grieved every man; but not after one sort. Some pitied to see his body so tormented with the fire raging upon the silly carcass, that counted not of the folly. Other that passed not much of the body, lamented to see him spill his soul, wretchedly, without redemption, to be plagued for ever. His friends sorrowed for love; his enemies for pity: strangers for a common kind of humanity, whereby we are bound one to another. Thus I have enforced myself, for your sake, to discourse this heavy narration, contrary to my mind: and, being more than half weary, I make a short end, wishing you a quieter life, with less honour; and easier death, with more praise.

Almost another 300 Protestants followed Taylor and Cranmer to the stake in the reign of "Bloody Queen Mary".

THE FALL OF CALAIS, 5 JANUARY 1558

John Highfield

Courtesy of Mary's marriage to Philip II, England was dragged into Spain's war with France. This proceeded disastrously, and the French captured Calais, the last English possession on French soil.

On Wednesday (5th January), the enemy continued their battery on the town, without great hurt done, because they could not beat the foot of the wall, for that the *contremure* was of a good height, and we reinforced the breach, in the night, with timber wool, and other matter sufficiently; and we looked that the enemy would have attempted the assault the same evening; whereupon I caused two flankers to be made ready, and also placed two bombards, by the help of the soldiers, appointing weapons and fireworks to be in readiness at the said breach. At which time, my Lord commanded the soldiers of the garrison to keep their ordinary wards, and Master Grimston to the breach with the residue of the best soldiers. And then my Lord exhorted all men to fight, with other good words as in such cases appertaineth. And my Lord told me, divers times, that "although there came no succour; yet he would never yield, nor stand to answer the loss of such a town."

On Thursday, began one other battery to the Castle; which being a high and weak wall without ramparts, was made saultable the same day. Whereupon, the Captain of the Castle desired some more help to defend this breach, or else to know what my Lord thought best in that behalf. Then, after long debating, my Lord determined to have the towers overthrown, which one Saulle took upon him to do; notwithstanding, I said openly that "if the Castle were abandoned, it should be the loss of the Town."

The same night, my Lord appointed me to be at the breach of the town with him: and, about eight of the clock, the enemy waded over the haven, at the low water, with certain harquebussiers, to view the breaches; and coming to the Castle, found no resistance, and so entered. Then the said Saulle failed to give fire unto the train of powder.

Then my Lord, understanding that the enemy were entered into the Castle, commanded me to give order for battering of the Castle: whereupon incontinent there were bent three cannons and one saker before the gate, to beat the bridge; which, being in the night, did not greatly annoy.

The same time, Master Marshall with divers soldiers, came towards the Castle, lest the enemy should enter the town also. And after we had skirmished upon the bridge, seeing no remedy to recover the Castle, we did burn and break the said bridge: and there was a trench immediately cast before the Castle, which was only help at that time.

Within one hour after, upon a necessity of things (my Lord) determined to send a trumpet with a herald, declaring that "If the Frenchmen would send one gentleman, then he would send one other in gage". Whereupon my Lord sent for me, and commanded that I should go forth of the town for the same purpose; wherein I desired his Lordship that he would send some other, and rather throw me over the walls. Then he spake likewise to one Windebanke, and to Massingberd, as I remember, which were both to go unto such service.

Then my Lord sent for me again, in Peyton's house; and being eftsoons commanded by the Council there, I went forth with a trumpet, and received in a French gentleman: who, as I heard, was brought to my Lord Deputy's house, and treated upon some articles; which were brought, within one hour, by one Hall, merchant of the staple.

Then Monsieur D'Andelot entered the town with certain French gentlemen; and the said Hall and I were brought to Monsieur De Guise, who lay in the sand hills by Rysbank, and there the said Hall delivered a bill: we were sent to Monsieur D'Estrees' tent.

The Friday after (7th January), Monsieur D'Estrees told me that my Lord Deputy had agreed to render the town with loss of all the goods, and fifty prisoners to remain . . .

ELIZABETH I REJECTS A SUITOR, 25 FEBRUARY 1561

Elizabeth I

Elizabeth I, daughter of Henry VIII and Anne Boleyn, acceeded to the English throne in 1558 on Mary Tudor's death. There were many suitors for Elizabeth's hand; she dallied with some, but eventually declared her marriage to her country, in whose honour she wore a token ring. The rejection letter below was addressed to Erik of Sweden, one of the first to try his luck.

Most Serene Prince Our Very Dear Cousin,

A letter truly yours both in the writing and sentiment was given, us on 30 December by your very dear brother, the Duke of Finland. And while we perceive therefrom that the zeal and love of your mind towards us is not diminished, yet in part we are grieved that we cannot gratify your Serene Highness with the same kind of affection. And that indeed does not happen because we doubt in any way of your love and honour, but, as often we have testified both in words and writing, that we have never yet conceived a feeling of that kind of affection towards anyone. We therefore beg your Serene Highness again and again that you be pleased to set a limit to your love, that it advance not beyond the laws of friendship for the present nor disregard them in the future. And we in our turn shall take care that whatever can be required for the holy preservation of friendship between Princes we will always perform towards your Serene Highness. It seems strange for your Serene Highness to write that you understand from your brother and your ambassadors that we have entirely determined not to marry an absent husband; and that we will give you no certain reply until we shall have seen your person.

We certainly think that if God ever direct our heart to consideration of marriage we shall never accept or choose any absent husband how powerful and wealthy a Prince soever. But that we are not to give you an answer until we have seen your person is so far from the thing itself that we never even considered such a thing. But I have always given both to your brother, who is certainly a most excellent prince and deservedly very dear to us, and also to your ambassador likewise the same answer with scarcely any variation of the words, that we do not conceive in our heart to take a husband, but highly commend this single life, and hope that your Serene Highness will no longer spend time in waiting for us.

God keep your Serene Highness for many years in good health and safety. From our Palace at Westminster, 25 February

Your Serene Highness' sister and cousin,

Elizabeth

THE MURDER OF RIZZIO, EDINBURGH, 9 MARCH 1566

Lord Ruthven

David Rizzio was an Italian chorister who rose to become the favourite and private secretary of Mary, Queen of Scots. His influence discontented the nobility, who conspired to be rid of him. The conspirators included Mary's husband, Lord Darnley.

The said Earl Morton, Lords Ruthven and Lindsay, with their accomplices, entering the Palace . . . and through the chamber to the cabinet, where they found her Majesty at supper, at a little table, the Lady Argyll at the one end, and David at the other end, his cap on his head, the King speaking with her Majesty, with his hand about her waist.

The said Lord Ruthven at his entering in, said unto the Queen's Majesty, "let it please your Majesty that yonder man David come forth of your privy chamber, where he hath been overlong". The Queen answered, "what offence hath he done?" Ruthven answered, that he made a greater and more heinous offence to her Majesty's honour, the King her husband, the Nobility and the Commonwealth. "If it please your Majesty, he hath offended your honour, which I dare not be so bold to speak of. As to the King your husband's honour, he hath hindered him of the Crown-Matrimonial, which your Grace promised him, besides many other things which are not necessary to be expressed; and hath caused your Majesty to banish a great part of the Nobility, and to forfeit them, that he might be made a Lord . . .

Then the said Lord Ruthven said to the King, "Sir, take the Queen your wife and sovereign to you", who stood all amazed, and wist not what to do. Then her Majesty rose upon her feet, and stood before David, he holding her Majesty by the plates of her gown, leaning back over the window, his dagger drawn in his hand, and Arthur Erskine, and the Abbot of Holyroodhouse, and the Lord Keith, master of the household, with the French pothecary; and one of the chamber began to lay hands on the Lord Ruthven, none of the King's party being there present. Then the said Lord Ruthven pulled out his dagger, and defended himself until more came in, and said to them, "Lay no hands on me, for I will not be handled." At the coming in of others into the cabinet, the said Lord Ruthven put up his dagger; and with the rushing in of men, the board fell into the wall, meat and candles being thereon, and the Lady of Argyll took one of the candles in her hand. At the same instant the Lord Ruthven took the Queen in his arms and put her into the King's arms, beseeching her Majesty not to be afraid, for there was no man there that would do her body any more harm than they would do their own hearts; and assured her Majesty that all that was done was the King's own deed. And the remnant of the gentlemen being in the cabinet took David out of the window, and after they had him out of the Queen's chamber, the said Lord Ruthven followed, and bade take him away down to the King's chamber the privy way; and the said Lord returned to the cabinet, thinking that the said David had been taken down to the King's chamber; the press of the people hurled him forth to the outer-chamber, where there was a great number standing who were vehemently moved against him, so that they could not abide any longer, but slew him at the "Queen's foredoor in the other chamber . . . and David was thrown down the stairs from the Palace where he was slain, and brought to the Porter's lodge, who taking off his clothes said, this was his destiny; for upon this chest was his first bed when he came to this place, and now he lieth a very niggard and misknown knave. The King's dagger was found sticking in his side. The Queen enquired at the King where his dagger was? who answered that he wist not well. "Well," said the Queen, "it will be known hereafter."

A PRISONER OF THE INQUISITION, MEXICO CITY, 1574–5

Miles Phillips

The author, along with 140 other English sailors, had been abandoned on the coast of Spanish Mexico by Sir John Hawkins' disastrous third slave-trading expedition (1567).

Now after that six years were fully expired since our first coming into the Indies, in which time, we had been imprisoned and served in the said country, as is before truly declared: in the year of our Lord 1574, the Inquisition began to be established in the Indies; very much against the minds of many of the Spaniards themselves. For never until this time, since their first conquering and planting in the Indies, were they subject to that bloody and cruel Inquisition.

The Chief Inquisitor was named Don Pedro Moya de Contreres, and Juan de Bouilla, his companion; and Juan Sanchis, the Fiscal; and Pedro de la Rios, the Secretary.

They being come and settled, and placed in a very fair house near unto the White Friars (considering with themselves that they must make an entrance and beginning of that their most detestable Inquisition here in Mexico, to the terror of the whole country) thought it best to call us that were Englishmen first in question. We were sent for, and sought out in all places of the country, and Proclamation made, upon pain of losing of goods and excommunication, that no man should hide or keep secret any Englishman or any part of his goods.

By means whereof, we were all soon apprehended in all places, and all our goods seized and taken for the Inquisitors' use. And so, from all parts of the country, we were conveyed and sent as prisoners to the city of Mexico; and there committed to prison, in sundry dark dungeons, where we could not see but by candle light; and were never past two together in one place: so that we saw not one another, neither could one of us tell what was become of another.

Thus we remained close imprisoned for the space of a year and a half, and others for some less time: for they came to prison ever as they were apprehended.

During which time of our imprisonment, at the first beginning, we were often called before the Inquisitors alone; and there severely examined of our faith; and commanded to say the *Pater noster*, the *Ave Maria*, and the *Creed* in Latin: which, God knoweth! a great number of us could not say otherwise than in the English tongue. And having the said Robert Sweeting, who was our friend at Tescuco always present with them for an interpreter, he made report for us, that in our own country speech, we could say them perfectly, although not word for word as they were in the Latin.

Then did they proceed to demand of us, upon our oaths, "What we did believe of the Sacrament?" and "Whether there did remain any bread or wine, after the words of consecration, Yea or No?" and "Whether we did not believe that the Host of bread which the priest did hold up over his head, and the wine that was in the chalice, was the very true and perfect body and blood of our Saviour Christ, Yea or No?"

To which, if we answered not "Yea!" then there was no way but death.

Then they would demand of us, "What did we remember of ourselves, what opinions we had held or been taught to hold contrary to the same, whiles we were in England?"

So we, for the safety of our lives, were constrained to say that, "We never did believe, nor had been taught otherwise than as before we had said."

Then would they charge us that "We did not tell them the truth. That they knew to the contrary, and therefore we should call ourselves to remembrance, and make them a better answer at the next time, or else we should be racked, and made to confess the truth whether we would or not!"

And so coming again before them, the next time, we were still demanded of "our belief whiles we were in England, and how we had been taught"; and also what we thought, or did know of such of our own company as they did name unto us. So that we could never be free from such demands.

And, at other times, they would promise us that if we would tell them truth, then should we have favour and be set at liberty; although we very well knew their fair speeches were but means to intrap us, to the hazard and loss of our lives.

Howbeit, God so mercifully wrought for us, by a secret means that we had, that we kept us still to our first answer; and would still say that "we had told the truth unto them; and knew no more by ourselves, nor any other of our fellows than as we had declared; and that for our sins and offences in England, against God, and Our Lady, and any of His blessed Saints; we were right heartily sorry for the same, and did cry God, mercy!" And besought the Inquisitors, "For God's sake, considering that we came unto those countries by force of weather, and against our wills; and that we had never, in all our lives, either spoken or done anything contrary to their laws; that therefore they would have mercy upon us!" Yet all this would not serve.

About the space of three months before (i.e., in January 1575) they proceeded to their severe judgement, we were all racked; and some enforced to utter against themselves, which afterwards cost them their lives.

And having thus got, from our own mouths, sufficient for them to proceed in judgment against us; they caused a large scaffold to be made in the midst of the Market Place in Mexico, right over against the Head Church: and fourteen or fifteen days before the day of their judgment, with the sound of trumpet and the noise of their *attabalies* (which are a kind of drums) they did assemble the people in all parts of the city; before whom it was then solemnly proclaimed that "whosoever would, upon such a day, repair to the Market Place, they should hear the sentence of the Holy Inquisition against the English heretics, Lutherans; and also see the same put in execution".

Which being done, and the time approaching of this cruel judgment; the night before, they came to the prison where we were, with certain Officers of that Holy Hellish House, bringing with them certain fools' coats, which they had prepared for us, being called in their language, *San Banitos*, which coats were made of yellow cotton, and red crosses upon them both before and behind.

They were so busied in putting on their coats about us, and in bringing us out into a large yard, and placing and pointing us in what order we should go to the scaffold or place of judgment upon the morrow, that they did not once suffer us to sleep all that night long.

The next morning being come, there was given to every one of us, for our breakfast, a cup of wine and a slice of bread fried in honey; and so about eight of the clock in the morning, we set forth of the prison: every man alone, in his yellow coat, and a rope about his neck, and a great green wax candle in his hand unlighted; having a Spaniard appointed, to go upon either side of every one of us.

So marching in this order and manner towards the Scaffold in the Market Place, which was a bow shot distant or thereabouts, we found a great assembly of people all the way, and such a throng that certain of the Inquisitors' Office, on horseback, were constrained to make way.

So coming to the Scaffold, we went up by a pair of stairs, and found seats ready made, and prepared for us to sit down on, every man in the order as he should be called to receive his judgment.

We being thus set down as we were appointed: presently the Inquisitors came up another pair of stairs, and the Viceroy and all the Chief Justices with them.

When they were set down under the Cloth of Estate, and placed according to their degrees and calling; then came up also a great number of Friars, White, Black, and Grey. They, being about the number of 300 persons, were set in the places appointed for them there.

There was there a solemn *Oyez!* made; and silence commanded. And then presently began their severe and cruel judgment.

The first man that was called, was one Roger, the Chief Armourer of the *Jesus*: and he had judgment to have 300 stripes on horseback; and, after, was condemned to the galleys, as a slave, for ten years.

After him, were called John Gray, John Browne, John Rider, John Moon, James Collier, and one Thomas Browne. These were adjudged to have 200 stripes on horseback; and, after, to be committed to the galleys for the space of eight years.

Then was called John Keies, and was adjudged to have 100 stripes on horseback; and condemned to serve in the galleys for the space of six years.

Then were severally called, to the number of fifty-three; one after another: and every man had his several judgment. Some to have 200 stripes on horseback, and some 100; and condemned for slaves in the galleys, some for six years, some for eight, and some for ten.

And then was I, Miles Phillips, called; and was adjudged to serve in a Monastery for five years without any stripes; and to wear a fool's coat, or *San Benito*, during all that time.

Then were called John Story, Richard Williams, David Alexander, Robert Cooke, Paul Horsewell, and Thomas Hull. These six were condemned to serve in Monasteries without stripes; some for three years, and some for four, and to wear the *San Banito* during all the said time.

Which being done, and it now drawing towards night, George Rivelie, Peter Momfrie, and Cornelius the Irishman were called: and had their judgment to be burnt to ashes. And so were presently sent away to the place of execution in the Market Place, but a little from the Scaffold: where they were quickly burned and consumed.

And as for us that had received our judgment, being 68 in number; we were carried back that night to prison again.

And the next day, in the morning, being Good Friday, the year of our Lord 1575, we were all brought into a court of the Inquisitors' Palace; where we found a horse in a readiness for every one of our men which were condemned to have stripes, and to be committed to the galleys, which were in number 61.

So they being enforced to mount up on horseback, naked from the middle upwards, were carried to be shewed as a spectacle for all the people to behold throughout the chief and principal streets of the city; and had the number of stripes appointed to every one of them, most cruelly laid upon their naked bodies with long whips, by sundry men appointed to be the executioners thereof. And before our men there went a couple of Criers, which cried as they went, "Behold these English dogs! Lutherans! enemies to God!" And all the way as they went, there were some of the Inquisitors themselves, and of the Familiars of that rakehell Order, that cried to the executioners, "Strike! Lay on those English heretics! Lutherans! God's enemies!"

So this horrible spectacle being shewed round about the city; and they returned to the Inquisitor's House, with their backs all gore blood, and swollen with great bumps: they were then taken from their horses; and carried again to prison, where they remained until they were sent into Spain to the galleys, there to receive the rest of their martyrdom.

I, and the six others with me, which had judgment, and were condemned amongst the rest, to serve an apprenticeship in the Monasteries, were taken presently, and sent to certain Religious Houses appointed for the purpose.

THE DISCOVERY OF VIRGINIA, 1576

Captain John Smith

The second of July they fell with the coast of Florida in shoal water, where they felt a most delicate sweet smell, though they saw no land, which ere long they espied, thinking it the continent: an hundred and twenty miles they sailed not finding any harbour. The first that appeared with much difficulty they entered, and anchored; and after thanks to God they went to view the next land adjoining, to take possession of it for the Queen's most excellent Majesty: which done, they found their first landing place very sandy and low, but so full of grapes that the very surge of the sea sometimes overflowed them: of which they found such plenty in all places, both on the sand, the green soil and hills, as in the plains as well on every little shrub, as also climbing, towards the tops of high cedars, that they did think in the world were not the like abundance.

We passed by the sea-side towards the tops of the next hills being not high: from whence we might see the sea on both sides, and found it an isle of twenty miles in length and six in breadth, the valleys replenished with goodly tall cedars. Discharging our muskets, such a flock of cranes, the most white, arose by us, with such a cry as if an army of men had shouted all together. This isle hath many goodly woods and deer, conies, and fowl in incredible abundance, and using the author's own phrase, the woods are not such as you find in Bohemia, Muscovy, or Hercynia, barren and fruitless, but the highest and reddest cedars of the world, bettering those of the Azores, Indies, or Libanus; pines, cypress, sassafras, the lentisk that beareth mastic, and many other of excellent smell and quality. Till the third day we saw not any of the people, then in a little boat three of them appeared. One of them went on shore, to whom we rowed, and he attended us without any sign of fear; after he had spoke much though we understood not a word, of his own accord he came boldly aboard us. We gave him a shirt, a hat, wine and meat, which he liked well; and after he had well viewed the barks and us, he went away in his own boat; and within a quarter of a mile of us in half an hour, had laden his boat with fish, with which he came again to the point of land, and there divided it in two parts, pointing one part to the ship, the other to the pinnace, and so departed.

The next day came divers boats, and in one of them the king's brother, with forty or fifty men, proper people, and in their behaviour very civil; his name was Granganameo, the king is called Wingina, the country Wingandacoa. Leaving his boats a little from our ships, he came with his train to the point, where spreading a mat he sat down. Though we came to him well armed, he made signs to us to sit down without any show of fear, stroking his head and breast, and also ours, to express his love. After he had made a long speech unto us, we presented him with divers toys, which he kindly accepted. He was greatly regarded by his people, for none of them did sit nor speak a word, but four, on whom we bestowed presents also, but he took all from them, making signs all things did belong to him.

The king himself, in a conflict with a king, his next neighbour and mortal enemy, was shot in two places through the body and the thigh, yet recovered: whereby he lay at his chief town six days' journey from thence.

A day or two after showing them what we had, Granganameo taking most liking to a pewter dish, made a hole in it, hung it about his neck for a breastplate: for which he gave us twenty deer skins, worth twenty crowns: and for a copper kettle, fifty skins, worth fifty crowns. Much other truck we had, and after two days he came aboard, and did eat and drink with us very merrily. Not long after he brought his wife and children; they were of mean stature, but well favoured and very bashful. She had a long coat of leather, and about her forehead a band of white coral, and so had her husband; in her ears were bracelets of pearl, hanging down to her middle, of the bigness of great peas. The rest of the women had pendants of copper, and the noblemen five or six in an ear; his apparel as his wives', only the women wear their hair long on both sides, and the men but on one; they are of colour yellow, but their hair is black, yet we saw children that had very fair chestnut coloured hair.

After that these women had been here with us, there came down from all parts great store of people, with leather, coral, and divers kind of dyes, but when Granganameo was present, none durst trade but himself and them that wore red copper on their heads, as he did. Whenever he came, he would signify by so many fires he came with so many boats, that we might know his strength. Their boats are but one great tree, which is but burnt in the form of a trough with gins and fire, till it be as they would have it. For an armour he would have engaged us a bag of pearl, but we refused, as not regarding it, that we might the better learn where it grew. He was very just of his promise, for oft we trusted him, and he would come within his day to keep his word. He sent us commonly every day a brace of bucks, conies, hares and fish, sometimes melons, walnuts, cucumbers, peas and divers roots. This author saith, their corn growth three times in five months; in May they sow, in July reap; in June they sow, in August reap; in July sow, in August reap. We put some of our peas in the ground, which in ten days were fourteen inches high.

The soil is most plentiful, sweet, wholesome, and fruitful of all other; there are about fourteen several sorts of sweet smelling timber trees; the most parts of the underwood, bays and such like, such oaks as we, but far greater and better . . .

This discovery was so welcome into England that it pleased her Majesty to call this country of Wingandacoa, Virginia.

THE FORGOTTEN FART, 1580

John Aubrey

This Earl of Exford, making on his low obeisance to Queen Elizabeth, happened to let a Fart, at which he was so abashed

and ashamed that he went to travel, 7 years. On his return the
Queen welcomed him home, and said, My Lord, I had forgot the
Fart.

"A BLOODY AND MURDERING PRACTICE"; FOOTBALL, c. 1581

Philip Stubbes

For as concerning football playing, I protest unto you it may
rather be called a friendly kind of fight, than a play or recreation; a
bloody and murdering practice, than a fellowly sport or pastime.
For doth not every one lie in wait for his adversary, seeking to
overthrow him and to pick him on his nose, though it be upon hard
stones, in ditch or dale, in valley or hill, or what place soever it be
he careth not, so he have him down. And he that can serve the
most of this fashion, he is counted the only fellow, and who but he?
So that by this means, sometimes their necks are broken, sometimes their backs, sometimes their legs, sometime their arms,
sometime their noses gush out with blood, sometime their eyes
start out, and sometimes hurt in one place, sometimes in another.
But whosoever scapeth away the best goeth not scot-free, but is
either sore wounded, and bruised, so as he dieth of it, or else
scapeth very hardly. And no marvel, for they have sleights to meet
one betwixt two, to dash him against the heart with their elbows,
to hit him under the short ribs with their gripped fists, and with
their knees to catch him upon the hip, and to pick him on his neck,
with an hundred such murdering devices. And hereof groweth
envy, malice, rancour, choler, hatred, displeasure, enmity and
what not else: and sometimes fighting, brawling, contention,
quarrel picking, murder, homicide and great effusion of blood,
as experience daily teacheth.

THE ARREST OF THE CATHOLIC PRIEST EDMUND CAMPION, 17 JULY 1581

A Government Agent

Campion was a Jesuit missionary to England. He was later beatified.

It happened that after the receipt of our Commission, we consulted
between ourselves, What way were best to take first? For we were

utterly ignorant where, or in what place, certainly to find out the said Campion, or his compeers. And our consultation was shortly determined: for the greatest part of our travail and dealings in this service did lie chiefly upon mine own determination, by reason of mine acquaintance and knowledge of divers of the like sect.

It then presently came to my remembrance of certain acquaintance which I once had with one Thomas Cooper a cook, who, in November (1578) was two years, served Master Thomas Roper of (Orpington in) Kent; where, at that time, I in like manner served: and both of us, about the same month, departed the said Master Roper his service; I into Essex, and the said Cooper to Lyford in Berkshire, to one Master Yate. From whence, within one half year after, I was advertised in Essex, that the said Cook was placed in service; and that the said Master Yate was a very earnest Papist, and one that gave great entertainment to any of that sect.

Which tale, being told me in Essex two years before we entered (on) this journey, by God's great goodness, came to my memory but even the day before we set forth. Hereof I informed the said David Jenkins, being my fellow in Commission, and told him it would be our best way to go thither first: for that it was not meant that we should go to any place but where indeed I either had acquaintance; or by some means possible in our journey, could get acquaintance. And told him we would dispose of our journey in such sort as we might come to the said Master Yate's upon the Sunday about eight of the clock in the morning: "where," said I, "if we find the said Cook, and that there be any Mass to be said there that day, or any massing Priest in the house; the Cook, for old acquaintance and for that he supposeth me to be a Papist, will bring me to the sight thereof."

And upon this determination, we set from London the 14th day of July last; and came to the said Master Yate's house, the 16th of the same month, being Sunday, about the hour aforesaid.

Where, without the gates of the same house, we espied one of the servants of the house, who most likely seemed, by reason of his lying aloof, to be as it were a Scout Watcher, that they within might accomplish their secret matters more safely.

I called the said servant, and inquired of him for the said Thomas Cooper the Cook.

Who answered, That he could not well tell, whether he were within or not.

I prayed him that he would friend me so much as to see; and told him my name.

The said servant did so, it seemed; for the Cook came forth presently unto us where we sat still upon horseback. And after a few such speeches, as betwixt friend and friend when they have been long asunder, were passed; still sitting upon our horses, I told him that I had longed to see him; and that I was then travelling into Derbyshire to see my friends, and came so far out of my way to see him. And said I, "Now I have seen you, my mind is well satisfied; and so fare you well!"

"No," saith he, "that shall you not do before dinner."

I made the matter very earnest to be gone; and he, more earnest and importune to stay me. But in truth I was as willing to stay as he to have me.

And so, perforce, there was no remedy but stay we must. And having lighted from horseback; and being by him brought into the house, and so into the buttery, and there caused to drink: presently after, the said Cook came and whispered with me, and asked, Whether my friend (meaning the said Jenkins) were within the Church or not? Therein meaning, Whether he were a Papist or no?

To which I answered, "He was not; but yet," said I, "he is a very honest man, and one that wisheth well that way."

Then said the Cook to me, "Will you go up?" By which speech, I knew he would bring me to a Mass.

And I answered him and said, "Yea, for God's sake, that let me do: for seeing I must needs tarry, let me take something with me that is good."

And so we left Jenkins in the buttery; and I was brought by the Cook through the hall, the dining parlour, and two or three other odd rooms, and then into a fair large chamber: where there was, at the same instant, one Priest, called Satwell, saying Mass; two other Priests kneeling by, whereof one was Campion, and the other called Peters *alias* Collington; three Nuns, and 37 other people.

When Satwell had finished his Mass; then Campion he invested himself to say Mass, and so he did: and at the end thereof, made holy bread and delivered it to the people there, to every one some, together with holy water; whereof he gave me part also.

And then was there a chair set in the chamber something beneath the altar, wherein the said Campion did sit down; and there made a sermon very nigh an hour long: the effect of his text

being, as I remember, "That Christ wept over Jerusalem, &cc."
And so applied the same to this our country of England for that the
Pope his authority and doctrine did not so flourish here as the same
Campion desired.

At the end of which sermon, I gat down unto the said Jenkins so
soon as I could. For during the time that the Masses and the
sermon were made, Jenkins remained still beneath in the buttery
or hall; not knowing of any such matter until I gave him some
intelligence what I had seen.

And so we departed, with as convenient expedition as we might,
and came to one Master Fettiplace, a Justice of the Peace in the
said country: whom we made privy of our doings therein; and
required him that, according to the tenour of our Commission, he
would take sufficient Power, and with us thither.

Whereupon the said Justice of Peace, within one quarter of an
hour, put himself in a readiness, with forty or fifty men very well
weaponed: who went, in great haste, together with the said Master
Fettiplace and us, to the said Master Yate his house.

Where, at our coming upon the sudden, being about one of the
clock in the afternoon of the same day, before we knocked at the
gates which were then (as before they were continually accustomed
to be) fast shut (the house being moated round about; within
which moat was great store of fruit trees and other trees, with thick
hedgerows: so that the danger for fear of losing of the said Campion
and his associates was the more doubted); we beset the house with
our men round about the moat in the best sort we could devise: and
then knocked at the gates, and were presently heard and espied;
but kept out by the space of half an hour.

In which time, as it seemeth, they had hidden Campion and the
other two Priests in a very secret place within the said house; and
had made reasonable purveyance for him as hereafter is mentioned: and then they let us into the house.

Where came presently to our sight, Mrs Yate, the good wife of
the house; five Gentlemen, one Gentlewoman, and three Nuns: the
Nuns being then disguised in Gentlewomen's apparel, not like unto
that they heard Mass in. All which I well remembered to have
seen, the same morning, at the Masses and Sermon aforesaid: yet
every one of them a great while denied it. And especially the said
Mistress Yate; who could not be content only to make a plain
denial of the said Masses and the Priests: but, with great and
horrible oaths, forsware the same, betaking herself to the Devil if

any such there were; in such sort as, if I had not seen them with mine own eyes, I should have believed her.

But knowing certainly that these were but bare excuses, and that we should find the said Campion and his compeers if we made narrow search; I eftsoons put Master Fettiplace in remembrance of our Commission: and so he, myself, and the said Jenkins Her Majesty's Messenger, went to searching the house; where we found many secret corners.

Continuing the search, although with no small toil, in the orchards, hedges, and ditches, within the moat and divers other places; at the last found out Master Edward Yate, brother to the good man of the house, and two countrymen called Weblin and Mansfield, fast locked together in a pigeon house: but we could not find, at that time, Campion and the other two Priests whom we specially sought for.

It drew then something towards evening, and doubting lest we were not strong enough; we sent our Commission to one Master Foster, High Sheriff of Berkshire; and to one Master Wiseman, a Justice of Peace within the same Country; for some further aid at their hands.

The said Master Wiseman came with very good speed unto us the same evening, with ten or twelve of his own men, very able men and well appointed: but the said Master Foster could not be found, as the messenger that went for him returned us answer.

And so the said house was beset the same night with at the least three score men well weaponed; who watched the same very diligently.

And the next day, being Monday, in the morning very early, came one Master Christopher Lydcot, a Justice of Peace of the same shire, with a great sort of his own men, all very well appointed: who, together with his men, shewed such earnest loyal and forward service in those affairs as was no small comfort and encouragement to all those which were present, and did bear true hearts and good wills to Her Majesty.

The same morning, began a fresh search for the said Priests; which continued with very great labour until about ten of the clock in the forenoon of the same day: but the said Priests could not be found, and every man almost persuaded that they were not there. Yet still searching, although in effect clean void of any hope for finding of them, the said David Jenkins, by God's great goodness, espied a certain secret place, which he quickly found to be hollow;

and with a pin of iron which he had in his hand much like unto a harrow tine, he forthwith did break a hole into the said place: where then presently he perceived the said Priests lying all close together upon a bed, of purpose there laid for them; where they had bread, meat, and drink sufficient to have relieved them three or four days together.

The said Jenkins then called very loudly, and said, "I have found the traitors!"; and presently company enough was with him: who there saw the said Priests, when there was no remedy for them but *nolens volens*, courteously yielded themselves.

Shortly after came one Master Reade, another Justice of the Peace of the said shire, to be assistant in these affairs.

Of all which matters, news was immediately carried in great haste to the Lords of the Privy Council: who gave further Commission that the said Priests and certain others their associates should be brought to the Court under the conduction of myself and the said Jenkins; with commandment to the Sheriff to deliver us sufficient aid forth of his shire, for the safe bringing up of the said people.

After the rumour and noise for the finding out of the said Campion, Satwell, and Peters *alias* Collington, was in the said house something assuaged; and that the sight of them was to the people there no great novelty: then was the said High Sheriff sent for once again; who all that while had not been seen in this service. But then came, and received into his charge the said Priests and certain others from that day until Thursday following.

The fourth Priest which was by us brought up to the Tower, whose name is William Filbie, was not taken with the said Campion and the rest in the said house: but was apprehended and taken in our watch by chance, in coming to the said house to speak with the said Peters, as he said; and thereupon delivered likewise in charge to the Sheriff, with the rest.

Upon Thursday, the 20th day of July last, we set forwards from the said Master Yate his house towards the Court, with our said charge; being assisted by the said Master Lydcot and Master Wiseman, and a great sort of their men; who never left us until we came to the Tower of London. There were besides, that guarded us thither, 50 or 60, Horsemen; very able men and well appointed: which we received by the said Sheriff his appointment.

We went that day to Henley upon Thames, where we lodged that night.

And about midnight we were put into great fear by reason of a very great cry and noise that the said Filbie made in his sleep; which wakened the most that were that night in the house, and that in such sort that every man almost thought that some of the prisoners had been broken from us and escaped; although there was in and about the same house a very strong watch appointed and charged for the same. The aforesaid Master Lydcot was the first that came unto them: and when the matter was examined, it was found no more but that the said Filbie was in a dream; and, as he said, he verily thought one to be a ripping down his body and taking out his bowels.

THE VIRTUES OF TOBACCO, VIRGINIA, AMERICA, 1585

Thomas Heriot

The writer was a member of Sir Richard Grenville's unsuccessful attempt to establish an English colony at Roanoke.

There is an herbe which is sowed apart by itselfe, and is called by the inhabitants Uppowoc; in the West Indies it hath divers names, according to the severall places and countreys where it groweth and is used; the Spanyards generally call it Tabacco. The leaves thereof being dried and brought into pouder, they use to take the fume or smoke thereof, by sucking it thorow pipes made of clay, into their stomacke and head; from whence it purgeth superfluous fleame and other grosse humours, and openeth all the pores and passages of the body; by which meanes the use thereof not onely preserveth the body from obstructions, but also (if any be, so that they have not bene of too long continuance) in short time breaketh them; whereby their bodies are notably preserved in health, and know not many grievous diseases, wherewithall we in England are often times afflicted.

This Uppowoc is of so precious estimation amongst them, that they thinke their gods are marvellously delighted therewith: whereupon sometime they make hallowed fires, and cast some of the pouder therin for a sacrifice: being in a storme upon the waters, to pacific their gods, they cast some up into the aire and into the water: so a weare for fish being newly set up, they cast some therein and into the aire: after an escape from danger, they cast some into the aire likewise: but all done with strange gestures, stamping, sometime dancing, clapping of hands, holding up of hands, and staring up into the heavens, uttering therewithall, and chattering strange words and noises.

FRIAR WILLIAM WESTON DASHES FOR THE PRIEST-HOLE, 1585

Friar William Weston

Catholic priests were subject to execution in Elizabeth's England. To avoid this fate they were often obliged to hide in secret places in houses of supporters.

A house where I used secretly to be given hospitality was visited once by certain Catholics, who gave a satisfactory account of themselves, both to me and to the head of the family, and said that they wished to hear Mass. After the end of Mass, when the people had left, I stayed on as usual and went upstairs to the room where I kept my books and resumed my work. Not quite two hours later the house was surrounded by a large mob of men. Whether they came on information or on chance, I do not know. But the servant rushed up to my room – I was still there – and warned me of the danger. She made me come downstairs at once and showed me a hiding-place underground: Catholic houses have several places like this, otherwise there would be no security. I got down into it, taking my breviary with me – it was all I had near me at the time, and to loiter would have been dangerous. Meantime the heretics had already made their way into the house and were examining the remoter parts. From my cave-like hide I could follow their movements by the noise and uproar they raised. Step by step they drew closer, and when they entered my room the sight of my books was an added incentive to their search. In that room also there was a secret passage-way for which they demanded the key, and as they opened the door giving on to it they were standing immediately above my head. I could hear practically every word they said. "Here! Look!" they called out. "A chalice! And a missal!" The things were, in fact, there. There had been no time to hide them, and, in any case, it would have been impossible. Then they demanded a hammer and other tools, to break through the wall and panelling. They were certain now that I could not be far away.

Meanwhile I was praying fervently to God that He would avert the danger. At the same time I reflected that it would be better to surrender myself into the enemy's hands than be dragged out ignominiously. I believed that some Judas had given information and betrayed me, but, to cover up the traitor, they wanted my discovery to appear accidental, and not the result of treachery.

While I was reflecting in this way, one of the men, either by mistake or on purpose or at the prompting of a good angel, shouted out: "Why waste time getting hammers and hatchets? There's not enough space here for a man. Look at the corners. You can see where everything leads to. There can't be a hiding-place here."

They took the fellow's word for it, and the party abandoned their plan of search and destruction.

THE EXECUTION OF MARY, QUEEN OF SCOTS, FOTHERINGAY, ENGLAND, 8 FEBRUARY 1586

R. K. Wynkfielde

After fleeing the 1567 revolt of the confederated lords, Mary Stuart threw herself on the mercy of her English cousin Elizabeth I. But Mary's presence was a constant source of unease to the English government, since the country's catholic minority looked to her as a potential restorer of the old faith. On the evidence of letters seemingly approving Elizabeth's murder, Mary was sentenced to death.

Then, silence being made, the Queenes Majesties Commission for the execution of the Queen of Scots was openly redd by Mr. Beale clarke of the Counsell; and thes wordes pronounced by the Assembly, "God save the Queene." During the reading of which Commission the Q. of Sc. was silent, listening unto it with as small regarde as if it had not concerned her at all; and with as cheerful a countenaunce as if it had been a Pardon from her Majestie for her life; using as much straungenes in worde and deede as if she had never knowne any of the Assembly, or had been ignorant of the English language.

Then on Doctor Fletcher, dean of Peterborowe, standing directly before her, without the rayle, bending his body with great reverence, began to utter this exhortacion following: "Madame the Q. most excellent Matie &c." and iterating theis wordes three or fowre tymes, she told him, "Mr. Dean, I am settled in the auncient Catholique Romayne, religion, and mynd to spend my bloode in defence of it." Then Mr. Dean said, "Madame, chaung your opinion and repent you of your former wickedness, and settle

your faith onely in Jesus Christ, by him to be saved." Then she
aunswered agayne and againe, "Mr. Deane, trouble not yourselfe
any more, for I am settled and resolved in this my religion, and am
purposed therein to die." Then the Earle of Shrewsbury and the
Earl of Kente, perceavinge her so obstinate, tolde her that sithence
she wold not heere the exhortacion begonn by Mr. Dean, "We will
pray for your Grace, that it stande with Gods will you may have
your harte lightened, even at the last howre, with the true knowledge of God, and so die therein." Then she aunswered "If you will
pray for me, my Lordes, I will thanke you; but to joyne in prayer
with you I will not, for that you and I are not of one religion."

Then the Lordes called for Mr. Dean, who kneeling on the
scaffold staires, began this Prayer, "O most gracious God and
merciful Father," &c. all the Assembly, saving the Queen of Scots
and her servauntes, saying after him. During the saying of which
prayer, the Queen of Scots, sitting upon a stoole, having about her
necke an *Agnus Die*, in her hand a crucifix, at her girdle a pair of
beades with a golden crosse at the end of them, a Latin booke in
her hand, began with teares and with loud and fast voice to pray in
Latin; and in the middest of her prayers she slided off from her
stoole, and kneeling, said divers Latin prayers; and after the end of
Mr. Deans prayer, she kneelinge, prayed in Englishe to this effecte:
"for Christ his afflicted Church, and for an end of their troubles;
for her sonne; and for the Queen's Majestie, that she might prosper
and serve God aright." She confessed that she hoped to be saved
"by and in the bloode of Christ, at the foote of whose Crucifix she
wold shedd her bloode". . . .

Her prayer being ended, the Executioners, kneeling, desired her
Grace to forgive them her death: who aunswered, "I forgive you
with all my harte, for now, I hope, you shall make an end of all my
troubles." Then they, with her two women, helping of her up,
began to disrobe her of her apparell; then, She, laying her crucifix
upon the stoole, one of the executioners tooke from her necke the
Agnus Dei, which she, laying handes of it, gave it to one of her
women, and told the executioner that he should be aunswered
mony for it . . .

All this tyme they were pulling off her apparell, she never
chaunged her countenance, but with smiling cheere she uttered
thes wordes, "that she never had such groomes to make her
unready, and that she never put off her clothes before such a
company."

Then She, being stripped of all her apparell saving her peticote and kirtle, her two women beholding her made great lamentacion, and crying and crossing themselves prayed in Latin; She, turning herselfe to them, imbrasinge them, said thes wordes in French, "*Ne crie vous, j'ay prome pour vous,*" and so crossing and kissing them, bad them pray for her and rejoyce and not weepe, for that now they should see an ende of all their Mistris troubles.

Then She, with a smiling countenaunce, turning to her men servauntes, as Melvin and the rest, standing upon a bench nigh the Scaffold, who sometyme weeping sometyme crying out alowde, and continually crossing themselves, prayed in Latin, crossing them with her hand bad them farewell; and wishing them to pray for her even until the last howre.

This donn, one of the women having a Corpus Christicloth lapped up three-corner-wayes, kissing it, put it over the Q. of Sc. face, and pinned it fast to the caule of her head. Then the two women departed from her, and she kneeling downe upon the cusshion most resolutely, and without any token or feare of death, she spake alowde this Psalme in Latin, "*In te Dominc confido, non confundar in eternam,*" &c. . . . Then lying upon the blocke most quietly and stretching out her armes cryed, "*In manus tuas, Domine,*" etc. three or fowre times . . .

THE ARMADA: THE ENGLISH ENGAGE, 21 JULY 1588

Lord Howard of Effingham

Intent on dethroning the "heretical" Elizabeth I and curbing English seapower in the New World, Philip II of Spain dispatched an invasion fleet to the isles. Some 130 Spanish ships, carrying 24,000 soldiers and sailors, reached the English Channel. Howard was Lord High Admiral; he writes to Sir Francis Walsyngham, principal Secretary of State.

Sir: – I will not trouble you with any long letter; we are at this present otherwise occupied than with writing. Upon Friday, at Plymouth, I received intelligence that there were a great number of ships described off of the Lizard; whereupon, although the wind was very scant, we first warped out of harbour that night, and upon Saturday turned out very hardly, the wind being at South-West; and about three of the clock in the afternoon, described the Spanish fleet, and did what we could to work for the wind, which (by this) morning we had recovered, descrying their f(leet to) consist of 120 sail, whereof, there are 4 g(allesses) and many ships of great burden.

At nine of the (clock) we gave them fight, which continued until one. (In this fight) we made some of them to bear room to stop their leaks; notwithstanding we durst not adventure to put in among them, their fleet being so strong. But there shall be nothing either neglected or unhazarded, that may work their overthrow.

Sir, the captains in her Majesty's ships have behaved themselves most bravely and like men hitherto, and I doubt not will continue, to their great commendation. And so, recommending our good success to your godly prayers, I bid you heartily farewell. From aboard the Ark, thwart of Plymouth, the 21st of July, 1588.

Your very loving friend,
C. HOWARD.

Sir, the southerly wind that brought us back from the coast of Spain brought them out. God blessed us with turning us back. Sir, for the love of God and our country, let us have with some speed some great shot sent us of all bigness; for this service will continue long; and some powder with it.

THE ARMADA: A SPANISH GALLEASS IS ATTACKED OFF CALAIS, 29 JULY 1588

Richard Tomson

After a six-day running fight up the Channel, the Spanish fleet anchored near Calais. On 28 July the English sent in eight fire ships among the Spaniards, which forced them to sea. The battle of Gravelines which followed the next day saw the Armada defeated.

At the break of day upon Monday morning, my Lord and all the fleet setting sail after our enemies, we espied riding within shot of the town of Calais the greatest of the King's galleasses, the rest of the Spanish fleet being two leagues to leeward of her.

My Lord Admiral began to go toward the galleass with his ship, the *Ark*, but finding the water to be shallow, other ships of less draught bare in with her and shot at her; whereupon she let slip and run the galleass aground hard before the town.

In our ship, which was the *Margaret and John of London*, we approached so near that we came on ground also; but afterwards came safely off again with the flood, being damaged by nothing but by the town of Calais, who, off the bulwarks, shot very much at us, and shot our ship twice through. And the like powder and shot did Monsieur Gourdan* bestow upon sundry of our countrymen, and make us relinquish the galleass which otherwise we had brought away, being master of her above two hours, and gotten by hard assault, to the great credit of our country, if Monsieur Gourdan herein had not showed his affection to the Spaniards to be greater than our nation, or seemed by force to wrest from us that which we had gotten with bloody heads.

My Lord Admiral, seeing he could not approach the galleass with his ship, sent off his long boat unto her with 50 or 60 men, amongst whom were many gentlemen as valiant in courage as gentle in birth, as they well showed. The like did our ship send off her pinnace, with certain musketeers, amongst whom myself went. These two boards came hard under the galleass sides, being aground; where we continued a pretty skirmish with our small shot against theirs, they being ensconced within their ship and very high over us, we in our open pinnaces and far under them, having nothing to shroud and cover us; they being 300 soldiers, besides 450 slaves, and we not, at the instant, 100 persons. Within one half hour it pleased God, by killing the captain with a musket shot, to give us victory above all hope or expectation; for the soldiers leaped overboard by heaps on the other side, and fled with the shore, swimming and wading. Some escaped with being wet; some, and that very many, were drowned. The captain of her was called Don Hugo de Moncada, son to the viceroy of Valencia. He being slain, and the most part of their soldiers fled, some few soldiers remaining in her, seeing our English boats under her sides and more of ours coming rowing towards her, some with 10 and some with 8 men in them, for all the smallest shipping were the nearest the shore, put up two handkerchiefs upon two rapiers, signifying that they desired a truce. Hereupon we entered, with much difficulty, by reason of her height over us, and possessed us of her by the space of an hour and a half as I judge; each man seeking

* The Governor of Calais.

his benefit of pillage until the flood came, that we might haul her
off the ground and bring her away . . .

THE ARMADA: THE SAN PEDRO FLOUNDERS IN
A STORM, DECEMBER 1588

Captain Francisco De Cuellar

In consequence of the battle of Gravelines, the Armada was driven into the
North Sea, where the English were forced to abandon the chase due to a
lack of gunpowder. The surviving Spanish ships rounded Scotland and
sailed down past the coast of Donegal, encountering merciless weather
almost all the way. The San Pedro sank off Ireland; De Cuellar, after
swimming ashore was returned to Spain by the Irish Catholic underground.
Of the 130 Spanish ships that started on the invasion, only 86 reached home.

I placed myself on the top of the poop of my ship, after having
commended myself to God and Our Lady, and from thence I
gazed at the terrible spectacle. Many were drowning in the ships,
others, casting themselves into the water, sank to the bottom
without returning to the surface; others on rafts and barrels,
and gentlemen on pieces of timber; others cried out aloud in
the ships calling upon God; captains threw their jewelled chains
and crown-pieces into the sea; the waves swept others away,
washing them out of the ships. While I was watching this sorrowful
scene, I did not know what to do, nor what means to adopt as I did
not know how to swim and the waves and storm were very great;
and, on the other hand, the land and the shore were full of enemies,
who went about jumping and dancing with delight at our misfortunes; and when any one of our people reached the beach two
hundred savages and other enemies fell upon him and stripped him
of what he had on until he was left in his naked skin. Such they
maltreated and wounded without pity, all of which was plainly
visible from the battered ships.

I went to the Auditor–God pardon him! – he was very sorrowful
and depressed, and I said to him that he should make some
provision for saving his life before the ship went to pieces, as
she could not last for half a quarter of an hour longer; nor did she
last it. Most of her complement of men and all the captains and
officers were already drowned and dead when I determined to seek
means of safety for my life, and placed myself upon a piece of the
ship that had broken off, and the Auditor followed me, loaded with

crown-pieces which he carried stitched up in his waistcoat and trousers.

HOUSEKEEPING LIST FOR CHRISTMAS WEEK, 1594

Lady Mildmay

Wheaten bread 16 dozen (40 oz) loaves
Brown bread 28 dozen loaves
Beer 8 hogsheads (each 52½ gallons)
Beef 50 stone
Mutton 6 carcases, 1 joint
Pork 27 joints 8 pigs
Blackbirds 6 dozen
Larks 8 dozen
Rabbits 50; also geese, hens and wild game
Flour 9 pottles (each half a gallon)
Candles 36 lbs
Butter (fresh) 15 lbs
Butter (salt) 35 lbs

The domestic labour of three maids and seven men:

Of the three maids one is to serve for cook, one for tending of poultry, making butter and cheese and necessaries, the third for a chambermaid or otherwise at your pleasure; of the seven men servants, one to bake and brew, one to tend your ground and make your provisions of beef and mutton and to serve as caterer. Two to attend on yourself, one of them to serve in the buttery, and in his absence one of the maids or the brewer. One to keep the horse. A warrener to serve as a caterer when your other servant shall be abroad for making other provisions, lastly a footboy.

SIR WALTER RALEIGH SACKS CADIZ, 1596

Sir Walter Raleigh

The sack of the Spanish port of Cadiz secured considerable booty; it also prevented Philip II from sending another Armada against England.

Having, as aforesaid, taken the leading, I was first saluted by the fort called *Philip*, afterwards by the ordnance on the curtain, and lastly by all the galleys, in good order. To show scorn to all which, I only answered first the fort, and thereafter the galleys, to each piece a burr with a trumpet: disdaining to shoot one piece at any one or all of those esteemed dreadful monsters. The ships that followed beat upon the galleys so thick that they soon be took them to their oars, and got up to join with the galleons in the strait, as aforesaid; and then, as they were driven to come near me, and enforced to range their sides towards me, I bestowed a benediction amongst them.

But the *St Philip*, the great and famous Admiral of Spain, was the mark I shot at; esteeming those galleys but as wasps in respect of the powerfulness of the other; and being resolved to be avenged for the *Revenge*, or to second her with mine own life, I came to anchor by the galleons; of which the *Philip* and *Andrew* were two that boarded the *Revenge*. I was formerly commanded not to board, but was promised fly-boats, in which, after I had battered a while, I resolved to join unto them.

My Lord Thomas came to anchor by me, on the one hand, with the *Lyon*; the *Mary Rose*, on the other, with the *Dreadnaughi*; the Marshall (Sir Francis Vere) towards the side of Puntall; and towards ten of the clock, my Lord General Essex, being impatient to abide far off, hearing so great athunder of ordnance, thrust up through the fleet, and headed all those on the left hand, coming to anchor next unto me on that side; and afterward came in the *Swiftsure*, as near as she could. Always I must, without glory, say for myself, that I held single in the head of all.

Now, after we had beat, as two butts, one upon another almost three hours (assuring your Honour that the volleys of cannon and culverin came as thick as if it had been a skirmish of musketeers), and finding myself in danger to be sunk in the place, I went to my Lord General in my skiff, to desire him that he would enforce the promised fly-boats to come up, that I might board; for as I rid, I could not endure so great battery any long time. My Lord General was then coming up himself; to whom I declared that if the fly-boats came not, I would board with the Queen's ship, for it was the same loss to burn, or sink, for I must endure the one. The Earl finding that it was not in his power to command fear, told me that, whatsoever I did, he would second me in person, upon his honour. My Lord Admiral, having also a disposition to come up at first, but the river was so choked as he could not pass with the *Ark*, came up in person into the *Nonpareill*, with my Lord Thomas.

While I was thus speaking with the Earl, the Marshall who thought it some touch to his great esteemed valour to ride behind me so many hours, got up ahead my ship; which my Lord Thomas perceiving headed him again; – myself being but a quarter of an hour absent. At my return, finding myself from being the first to being but the third, I presently let slip anchor, and thrust in between my Lord Thomas and the Marshall, and went up further ahead than all them before, and thrust my self athwart the channel; so as I was sure none should outstart me again, for that day. My Lord General Essex, thinking his ship's side stronger than the rest thrust the *Dreadnaught* aside, and came next the *Warspight* on the left hand; ahead all that rank, but my Lord Thomas. The Marshall, while we had no leisure to look behind us, secretly fastened a rope on my ship's side towards him, to draw himself up equally with me; but some of my company advertising me thereof, I caused it to be cut off, and so he fell back into his place, whom I guarded, all but his very prow, from the sight of the enemy.

Now, if it please you to remember, that having no hope of my fly-boats to board, and that the Earl and my Lord Thomas both promised to second me, I laid out a warp by the side of the *Philip* to shake hands with her (for with the wind we could not get aboard): which when she and the rest perceived, finding also that the *Repulse* (seeing mine) began to do the like, and the Rear-Admiral my Lord Thomas, they all let slip, and ran aground, tumbling into the sea heaps of soldiers, so thick as if coals had been poured out of a sack in many ports at once; some drowned and some sticking in the mud. The *Philip* and the *St Thomas* burnt themselves: the *St Matthew* and the *St Andrew* were recovered with our boats ere they could get out to fire them. The spectacle was very lamentable on their side, for many drowned themselves; many, half burnt, leapt into the water; very many hanging by the ropes' ends by the ships' side, under the water even to the lips; many swimming with grievous wounds, strucken under water, and put out of their pain: and withal so huge a fire, and such tearing of the ordnance in the great *Philip*, and the rest, when the fire came to them, as, if any man had a desire to see Hell itself, it was there most lively figured. Ourselves spared the lives of all, after the victory; but the Flemings, who did little or nothing in the fight, used merciless slaughter, till they were by myself, and afterwards by my Lord Admiral, beaten off . . . this being happily finished, we prepared to land the army . . .

The town . . . was very rich in merchandize, in plate, and money; many rich prisoners given to the land commanders; so as that sort are very rich. Some had prisoners for sixteen thousand ducats; some for twenty thousand; some for ten thousand; and besides, great houses of merchandize. What the Generals have gotten, I know least; they protest it is little. For my part, I have gotten a lame leg, and a deformed.

THE TORTURING OF A JESUIT PRIEST, THE TOWER OF LONDON, ENGLAND, APRIL 1597

Father John Gerard

On the third day the warder came to my room straight from his dinner. Looking sorry for himself, he said the Lords Commissioners had arrived with the Queen's Attorney-General and that I had to go down to them at once.

"I am ready," I said, "but just let me say an *Our Father* and *Hail Mary* downstairs."

He let me go, and then we went off together to the Lieutenant's lodgings inside the walls of the Tower. Five men were there waiting for me, none of whom, except Wade, had examined me before. He was there to direct the charges against me . . .

"You say," said the Attorney-General, "you have no wish to obstruct the Government. Tell us, then, where Father Garnet is. He is an enemy of the state, and you are bound to report on all such men."

"He isn't an enemy of the state," I said . . . "But I don't know where he lives, and if I did, I would not tell you."

"Then we'll see to it that you tell us before we leave this place."

"Please God you won't," I answered.

Then they produced a warrant for putting me to torture. They had it ready by them and handed it to me to read. (In this prison a special warrant is required for torture.)

I saw the warrant was properly made out and signed, and then I answered: "With God's help I shall never do anything which is unjust or act against my conscience or the Catholic faith. You have me in your power. You can do with me what God allows you to do – more you cannot do."

Then they began to implore me not to force them to take steps they were loath to take. They said they would have to put me to torture every day, as long as my life lasted, until I gave them the information they wanted.

"I trust in God's goodness," I answered, "that He will prevent me from ever committing a sin such as this – the sin of accusing innocent people. We are all in God's hands and therefore I have no fear of anything you can do to me."

This was the sense of my answers, as far as I can recall them now.

We went to the torture-room in a kind of solemn procession the attendants walking ahead with lighted candles.

The chamber was underground and dark, particularly near the entrance. It was a vast place and every device and instrument of human torture was there. They pointed out some of them to me and said I would try them all. Then they asked me again whether I would confess.

"I cannot," I said.

I fell on my knees for a moment's prayer. Then they took me to a big upright pillar, one of the wooden posts which held the roof of this huge underground chamber. Driven into the top of it were iron staples for supporting heavy weights. Then they put my wrists into iron gauntlets and ordered me to climb two or three wicker steps. My arms were then lifted up and an iron bar was passed through the rings of one gauntlet, then through the staple and rings of the second gauntlet. This done, they fastened the bar with a pin to prevent it slipping, and then, removing the wicker steps one by one from under my feet, they left me hanging by my hands and arms fastened above my head. The tips of my toes, however, still touched the ground, and they had to dig away the earth from under them. They had hung me up from the highest staple in the pillar and could not raise me any higher, without driving in another staple.

Hanging like this I began to pray. The gentlemen standing around asked me whether I was willing to confess now.

"I cannot and I will not," I answered.

But I could hardly utter the words, such a gripping pain came over me. It was worst in my chest and belly, my hands and arms. All the blood in my body seemed to rush up into my arms and hands and I thought that blood was oozing from the ends of my fingers and the pores of my skin. But it was only a sensation caused by my flesh swelling above the irons holding them. The pain was so intense that I thought I could not possibly endure it, and added to it, I had an interior temptation. Yet I did not feel any inclination or wish to give them the information they wanted. The Lord saw my weakness with the eyes of His mercy, and did not permit me to be tempted beyond my strength. With the temptation He sent me relief. Seeing my agony and the struggle going on in my mind, He gave me this most merciful thought: the utmost and worst they can do is to kill you, and you have often wanted to give your life for your Lord God. The Lord God sees all you are enduring – He can do all things. You are in God's keeping. With these thoughts, God in His infinite goodness and mercy gave me the grace of resigna- tion, and with a desire to die and a hope (I admit) that I would, I offered Him myself to do with me as He wished. From that moment the conflict in my soul ceased, and even the physical pain seemed much more bearable than before, though it must, in fact, I am sure, have been greater with the growing strain and weariness of my body . . .

Sometime after one o'clock, I think, I fell into a faint. How long I was unconscious I don't know, but I think it was long, for the men held my body up or put the wicker steps under my feet until I came to. Then they heard me pray and immediately let me down again. And they did this every time I fainted – eight or nine times that day – before it struck five . . .

A little later they took me down. My legs and feet were not damaged, but it was a great effort to stand upright . . .

A PETITION FOR THE SUPPRESSION OF UNGODLY STAGE-PLAYS, 28 JULY 1597

The Lord Mayor and Aldermen of London

The Elizabethan era saw the flowering of English theatre, in the works of Shakespeare, Jonson and Marlowe. Their largely secular entertainments, however, and the "ungodly" audiences they attracted, were not to the taste of Puritans or city authorities.

To the Privy Council:
Our humble duties remembered to your good Lords and the rest. We have signified to your Honours many times heretofore the great inconvenience which we find to grow by the common exercise of stage-plays. We presumed to do so, as well in respect of the duty we bear towards her Highness for the good government

of this her city, as for conscience sake, being persuaded (under correction of your Honours' judgment) that neither in polity nor in religion they are to be suffered in a Christian commonwealth, specially being of that frame and matter as usually they are, containing nothing but profane fables, lascivious matters, cozening devices, and scurrilous behaviours, which are so set forth as that they move wholly to imitation and not to the avoiding of those faults and vices which they represent. Among other inconveniences it is not the least that they give opportunity to the refuse sort of evil-disposed and ungodly people that are within and about this city to assemble themselves and to make their matches for all their lewd and ungodly practices; being as heretofore we have found by the examination of divers apprentices and other servants who have confessed unto us that the said stage-plays were the very places of their rendezvous, appointed by them to meet with such other as were to join with them in their designs and mutinous attempts, being also the ordinary places for masterless men to come together and to recreate themselves. For avoiding whereof we are now again most humble and earnest suitors to your honours to direct your letters as well to ourselves as to the justices of peace of Surrey and Middlesex for the present stay and final suppressing of the said stage-plays, as well at the Theater, Curtain and Bankside as in all other places in and about the city; whereby we doubt not but the opportunity and the very cause of many disorders being taken away, we shall be more able to keep the worse sort of such evil and disordered people in better order than heretofore we have been. And so most humbly we take our leaves. From London the 28th of July 1597.

1. They are a special cause of corrupting their youth, containing nothing but unchaste matters, lascivious devices, shifts of cozenage, and other lewd and ungodly practices, being so as that they impress the very quality and corruption of manners which they represent, contrary to the rules and art prescribed for the making of comedies even among the heathen, who used them seldom and at certain set times, and not all the year long as our manner is. Whereby such as frequent them, being of the base and refuse sort of people or such young gentlemen as have small regard of credit or conscience, draw the same into imitation and not to the avoiding the like vices which they represent.

2. They are the ordinary places for vagrant persons, masterless men, thieves, horse-stealers, whoremongers, cozeners, coney-catchers, contrivers of treason and other idle and dangerous persons to meet together and to make their matches to the great displeasure of Almighty God and the hurt and annoyance of her Majesty's people; which cannot be prevented nor discovered by the governors of the city for that they are out of the city's jurisdiction.

3. They maintain idleness in such persons as have no vocation, and draw apprentices and other servants from their ordinary works and all sorts of people from the resort unto sermons and other Christian exercises to the great hindrance of trades and profanation of religion established by her Highness within this realm.

4. In the time of sickness it is found by experience that many, having sores and yet not heart-sick, take occasion hereby to walk abroad and to recreate themselves by hearing a play. Whereby others are infected, and themselves also many things miscarry.

AN AUDIENCE WITH QUEEN ELIZABETH I, LONDON, 8 DECEMBER 1597

André Hurault

Hurault was an Ambassador Extraordinary from Henry IV of France to the court of Queen Elizabeth. In 1597 Elizabeth was sixty years old, and in the fortieth year of her reign.

She kept the front of her dress open, and one could see the whole of her bosom, and passing low, and often she would open the front of this robe with her hands as if she was too hot. The collar of the robe was very high, and the lining of the inner part all adorned with rubies and pearls, very many, but quite small. She had also a chain of rubies and pearls about her neck. On her head she wore a garland of the same material and beneath it a great-reddish coloured wig, with a great number of spangles of gold and silver, and hanging down over her forehead some pearls, but of no great worth. On either side of her ears hung two great curls of hair, almost down to her shoulders and within the collar of her robe, spangled as the top of her head. Her bosom is somewhat wrinkled, as well as one can see for the collar that she wears round her neck, but lower down her flesh is exceeding white and delicate, so far as one could see.

As for her face, it is and appears to be very aged. It is long and thin, and her teeth are very yellow and unequal, compared with what they were formerly, so they say, and on the left side less than on the right. Many of them are missing, so that one cannot understand her easily when she speaks quickly. Her figure is fair and tall and graceful in whatever she does; so far as may be she keeps her dignity, yet humbly and graciously withal.

All the time she spoke she would often rise from her chair and appear to be very impatient with what I was saying. She would complain that the fire was hurting her eyes, though there was a great screen before it and she six or seven feet away; yet did she give orders to have it extinguished, making them bring water to pour on it. She told me she was well pleased to stand up, and that she used to speak thus with ambassadors who came to seek her, and used sometimes to tire them, of which they would on occasion complain. I begged her not to overtire herself in any way, and I rose when she did; and then she sat down again, and so did I.

THE DEATH OF QUEEN ELIZABETH I, RICHMOND PALACE, SURREY, 24 MARCH 1603

Sir Robert Carey

When I came to court, I found the Queen ill disposed, and she kept her inner lodging; yet she, hearing of my arrival, sent for me. I found her in one of her withdrawing chambers sitting low upon her cushions. She called me to her; I kissed her hand, and told her, it was my chiefest happiness to see her in safety and in health, which I wished might long continue. She took me by the hand, and wrung it hard; and said "No, Robin, I am not well!" and then discoursed with me of her indisposition, and that her heart had been sad and heavy for ten or twelve days; and, in her discourse, she fetched not so few as forty or fifty great sighs. I was grieved, at the first, to see her in this plight: for, in all my lifetime before, I never knew her fetch a sigh, but when the Queen of Scots was beheaded; then, upon my knowledge, she shed many tears and sighs, manifesting her innocence that she never gave consent to the death of that Queen. I used the best words I could to persuade her

from this melancholy humour; but I found by her it was too deep
rooted in her heart, and hardly to be removed. This was upon a
Saturday night: and she gave command that the great closet
should be prepared for her to go to chapel the next morning.

The next day, all things being in a readiness, we long expected
her coming. After eleven o'clock, one of the grooms came out, and
bade make ready for the private closet; she would not go to the
great. There we stayed long for her coming: but at last she had
cushions laid for her in the privy chamber, hard by the closet door;
and there she heard service. From that day forwards she grew
worse and worse. She remained upon her cushions four days and
nights, at the least. All about her could not persuade her, either to
take any sustenance or go to bed. I, hearing that neither the
physicians, nor none about her, could persuade her to take any
course for her safety, feared her death would soon after ensue. I
could not but think in what a wretched estate I should be left, most
of my livelihood depending on her life. And hereupon I bethought
myself with what grace and favour I was ever received by the King
of Scots, whensoever I was sent to him. I did assure myself it was
neither unjust nor unhonest for me to do for myself, if God at that
time should call her to his mercy. Hereupon I wrote to the King of
Scots, knowing him to be the right heir to the crown of England,
and certified him in what state her Majesty was. I desired him not
to stir from Edinburgh: if of that sickness she should die, I would be
the first man that should bring him news of it.

The Queen grew worse and worse, because she would be so:
none about her being able to persuade her to go to bed. My Lord
Admiral was sent for, who, by reason of my sister's death that was
his wife, had absented himself some fortnight from court. What by
fair means, what by force, he gat her to bed. There was no hope of
her recovery, because she refused all remedies. On Wednesday, the
23rd of March, she grew speechless. That afternoon, by signs, she
called for her Council: and by putting her hand to her head, when
the King of Scots was named to succeed her, they all knew he was
the man she desired should reign after her. About six at night, she
made signs for the Archbishop, and her chaplains to come to her;
at which time, I went in with them, and sat upon my knees full of
tears to see that heavy sight. Her Majesty lay upon her back, with
one hand in the bed and the other without. The bishop kneeled
down by her, and examined her first of her faith; and she so
punctually answered all his several questions by lifting up her eyes

and holding up her hand, as it was a comfort to all beholders. Then the good man told her plainly, what she was and what she was to come to, and though she had been long a great Queen here upon earth, yet shortly she was to yield an accompt of her stewardship to the King of Kings. After this he began to pray, and all that were by did answer him. After he had continued long in prayer, till the old man's knees were weary, he blessed her, and meant to rise and leave her. The Queen made a sign with her hand. My sister Scroop, knowing her meaning, told the bishop, the Queen desired he would pray still. He did so for a long half-hour after, and then thought to leave her. The second time she made sign to have him continue in prayer. He did so for half an hour more, with earnest cries to God for her soul's health, which he uttered with that fervency of spirit as the Queen, to all our sight, much rejoiced thereat, and gave testimony to us all of her Christian and comfortable end. By this time, it grew late, and every one departed, all but her women that attended her. This that I heard with my ears and did see with my eyes, I thought it my duty to set down, and to affirm it for a truth upon the faith of a Christian; because I know there have been many false lies reported of the end and death of that good lady.

I went to my lodging, and left word with one in the cofferer's chamber to call me, if that night it was thought she would die; and gave the porter an angel to let me in at any time, when I called. Between one and two of the clock on Thursday morning, he that I left in the cofferer's chamber, brought me word the Queen was dead. I rose and made all haste to the gate, to get in. There I was answered, I could not enter: the Lords of the Council having been with him and commanded him that none should go in or out, but by warrant from them. At the very instant, one of the Council, the Comptroller, asked whether I was at the gate. I said "Yes." He said, if I pleased, he would let me in. I desired to know how the Queen was. He answered, "Pretty well." I bade him good night. He replied and said, "Sir, if you will come in, I will give you my word and credit you shall go out again at your own pleasure." Upon his word, I entered the gate, and came up to the cofferer's chamber: where I found all the ladies weeping bitterly. He led me from thence to the privy chamber, where all the Council was assembled. There I was caught hold of; and assured I should not go for Scotland till their pleasures were further known. I told them I came of purpose to that end. From thence, they all went to the secretary's chamber; and, as they went, they gave a special command to the porters, that none should go out at the gates but such servants as they should send to prepare their coaches and horses for London.

There was I left, in the midst of the court, to think my own thoughts till they had done counsel. I went to my brother's chamber, who was in bed, having been overwatched many nights before. I got him up with all speed; and when the Council's men were going out of the gate, my brother thrust to the gate. The porter, knowing him to be a great officer, let him out. I pressed after him, and was stayed by the porter. My brother said angrily to the porter, "Let him out, I will answer for him!" Whereupon I was suffered to pass; which I was not a little glad of. I got to horse, and rode to the Knight Marshal's lodging by Charing Cross; and there stayed till the Lords came to Whitehall Garden. I stayed there till it was nine o'clock in the morning; and hearing that all the Lords were in the old orchard at Whitehall, I sent the Marshal to tell them that I had stayed all that while to know their pleasures; and that I would attend them, if they would command me any service. They were very glad when they heard I was not gone: and desired the marshal to send for me; and I should, with all speed, be dispatched for Scotland. The Marshal believed them; and sent Sir Arthur Savage for me. I made haste to them. One of the Council, my Lord of Banbury that now is, whispered the Marshal in the ear, and told him, if I came they would stay me and send some other in my stead. The Marshal got from them and met me coming to them, between the two gates. He bade me be gone, for he had learned, for certain, that if I came to them, they would betray me.

I returned, and took horse between nine and ten o'clock; and that night rode to Doncaster. The Friday night I came to my own house at Witherington, and presently took order with my deputies to see the Borders kept in quiet; which they had much to do: and gave order, the next morning, the King of Scotland should be proclaimed King of England, and at Morpeth and Alnwick. Very early, on Saturday, I took horse for Edinburgh, and came to Norham about twelve at noon, so that I might well have been with the King at supper time. But I got a great fall by the way; and my horse, with one of his heels, gave me a great blow on the head, that made me shed much blood. It made me so weak, that I was forced to ride a soft pace after: so that the King was newly gone to bed by the time I knocked at the gate. I was quickly let in; and carried up to the King's Chamber. I kneeled by him, and saluted him by his title of "England, Scotland, France and Ireland." He gave me his hand to kiss, and bade me welcome. After he had long discoursed of the manner of the Queen's sickness, and of her death, he asked what letters I had from the Council. I told him, none: and acquainted him how narrowly I escaped from them. And yet I brought him a blue ring from a fair lady, that I hoped would give him assurance of the truth that I had reported. He took it, and looked upon it, and said, "It is enough. I know by this you are a true messenger." Then he committed me to the charge of my Lord Hume, and gave straight command that I should want nothing. He sent for his chirurgeons to attend me; and when I kissed his hand, at my departure, he said to me these gracious words: "I know you have lost a near kinswoman and a loving mistress: but take here my hand, I will be as good a master to you, and will requite you this service with honour and reward." So I left him that night, and went with my Lord Hume to my lodging, where I had all things fitting for so weary a man as I was. After my head was dressed, I took leave of my Lord and many others that attended me, and went to my rest.

The next morning, by ten o'clock, my Lord Hume was sent to me from the King, to know how I had rested: and withal said, that his Majesty commanded him to know of me, what it was that I desired most that he should do for me; bade me ask, and it should be granted. I desired my Lord to say to his Majesty from me, that I had no reason to importune him for any suit; for that I had not, as yet, done him any service: but my humble request to his Majesty was to admit me a gentleman of his bedchamber; and hereafter, I knew, if his Majesty saw me worthy, I should not want to taste his bounty. My Lord returned this answer, that he sent me word back, "With all his heart, I should have my request." And the next time I came to court, which was some four days after at night, I was called into his bedchamber: and there, by my Lord of Richmond, in his presence, I was sworn one of the gentlemen of his bed-chamber; and presently I helped to take off his clothes, and stayed till he was in bed. After this, there came, daily, gentlemen and noblemen from our court; and the King set down a fixed day for his departure towards London.

THE GUNPOWDER PLOT, ENGLAND, 5 NOVEMBER 1605

Guy Fawkes

The Gunpowder Plot was a conspiracy to advance the Catholic cause in England by blowing up the King and the Houses of Parliament. The foiling of the plot is still celebrated in England, with an annual burning of an effigy of the conspirator Guy Fawkes.

I confesse, that a practise in generall was first broken unto me, against his Maiestie for reliefe of the Catholic cause, and not invented or propounded by my selfe. And this was first propounded unto me about Easter Last was twelve moneth beyond the seas, in the Lowe Countreys of the *Archdukes* obeissance, by *Thomas Winter*, who came thereupon with mee into England, and there we imparted our purpose to three other Gentlemen more, namely, *Robert Catesby*, *Thomas Percy* and *Iohn Wright*, who all five consulting together of the means how to execute the same, and taking a vow among our selves for secrecie, *Catesby* propounded to have it performed by Gunpowder, and by making a Myne under the upper House of Parliament: which place wee made a choice of the rather because Religion having been unjustly suppressed there, it was fittest that Justice and punishment should be executed there.

This being resolved amongst us, *Thomas Percy* hired an House at Westminster for that purpose, neere adioyning to the Parliament House, and there we begun to make our Myne about the II of December 1604.

The five that first entred into the worke were *Thomas Percy*, *Thomas Catesby*, *Thomas Winter*, *Iohn Wright* and myselfe: and soone after wee tooke another unto us, *Christopher Wright* having Sworne him also, and taken the Sacrament for secrecie.

When we came to the very foundation of the Wall of the House, which was about three yards thicke, and found it a matter of great difficultie, wee tooke unto us another Gentleman *Robert Winter*, in like maner with oath and sacrament as afore said.

It was about Christmas when we brought our myne unto the Wall, and about Candlemas we had wrought the wall halfe through: and whilst they were in working, I stood as Sentinell to descrie any man that came neere, whereof I gave them warning, and so they ceased until I gave notice againe to proceede.

All we seven lay in the House, and had Shot and Powder, being resolved to die in that place before we should yield or be taken. As they were working upon the wall they heard a rushing in the Cellar of remooving of Coales, whereupon we feared we had been discovered: and they sent me to go to the Cellar, who finding that the Coales were a-selling and that the Cellar was to bee let, viewing the commoditie thereof for our purpose, *Percy* went and hired the same for yeerely rent.

We had before this provided and brought into the House twentie Barrels of Powder, which we removed into the Cellar, and covered the same with Billets and Faggots, which were provided for that purpose.

About Easter, the Parliament being prorogued till October next, we dispersed ourselves and I retired into the Low countreys by advice and direction of the rest, as well to aquaint *Owen* with the particulars of the Plot, as also lest by my longer stay I might have growen suspicious, and so have come in question.

In the meantime *Percy* having the key of the Cellar, laide in more Powder and wood into it. I returned about the beginning of September next, and then receiving the key againe of Percy, we brought in more Powder and Billets to cover the same againe, and so I went for a time into the Countrey till the 30 of October.

It was a further resolve amongst us that the same day that this act should have been performed, some other of our Confederates should have surprised the person of Lady Elizabeth the King's eldest daughter, who was kept in Warwickshire at Lo. *Harrington's* house, and presently have her proclaimed as Queen, having a project of a Proclamation ready for that purpose, wherein we made no mention of altering of Religion, nor would have avowed the deede to be ours, until we should have had power enough to make our partie good and then we would have avowed both.

Concerning Duke Charles, the King's second sonne, wee had sundry consultations how to seise on his Person. But because we found no means how to to compasse it (the Duke being kept neere London, where we had not Forces y-nough) we resolved to serve our turn with the Lady Elizabeth.

THE NAMES OF OTHER PRINCIPALL
persons, that were made privy
afterwards to this horrible
conspiracie

A SKETCH OF KING JAMES, 1603–25

Sir Anthony Weldon

A Clerk of the Green Cloth, Weldon was removed from his post when a satire of his on the Scots was found wrapped in departmental records. He sided with Parliament during the Civil War.

He was of a middle stature, more corpulent through his clothes than in his body, yet fat enough, his clothes ever being made large and easy, the doublets quilted for stiletto proof, his breeches in great pleats and full stuffed. He was naturally of a timorous disposition, which was the reason of his quilted doublets: his eyes large, ever rolling after any stranger that came into his presence, insomuch as many for shame have left the room, as being out of countenance; his beard was very thin: his tongue too large for his mouth which ever made him speak full in the mouth, and made him drink very uncomely, as if eating his drink, which came out into the cup of each side of his mouth; his skin was as soft as taffeta sarsnet, which felt so, because he never washed his hands, only rubbed his fingers ends slightly with the wet end of a napkin. His legs were very weak, having had (as was thought) some foul play in his youth, or rather before he was born, that he was not able to stand at seven years of age, that weakness made him ever leaning on other men's shoulders: his walk was ever circular, his fingers ever in that walk fiddling about his cod-piece.

He was very temperate in his exercises and in his diet, and not intemperate in his drinking; however, in his old age, at Buckingham's jovial suppers. when he had any turn to do with him, made him sometimes overtaken, which he would the very next day remember and repent with tears; it is true he drank very often, which was rather out of a custom than any delight, and his drinks were of the kind for strength, as Frontinack, Canary, High Country Wine, Tent Wine and Scottish Ale, that, had he not had a very strong brain, might have daily been overtaken, although he seldom drank at any one time above four spoonfuls, many times not above one or two.

He was very constant in all things (his favourites excepted), in which he loved change, yet never cast down any (he once raised) from the height of greatness, though from their wonted nearness and privacy, unless by their own default . . . In his diet, apparel and journeys, he was very constant . . . that the best observing courtier of our time was wont to say, were he asleep seven years, and then awakened, he would tell where the King every day had been, and every dish he had had at table.

He was not very uxorious, though he had a very brave queen that never crossed his designs, nor intermeddled with State affairs, but ever complied with him . . . in the change of favourites; for he was ever best when furthest from his queen, and that was thought to be the first grounds of his often removes, which afterwards proved habitual . . .; he naturally loved not the sight of a soldier, nor of any valiant man . . .

He was very witty, and had as many ready witty jests as any man living, at which he would not smile himself, but deliver them in a grave and serious manner. He was very liberal of what he had not in his own grip, and would rather part with 100 *li.* he never had in his keeping than one twenty shilling piece within his own custody; he spent much, and had much use of his subjects' purses, which bred some clashings with them in parliament, yet would *always* come off, and end with a sweet and plausible close.

TREATMENT FOR THE PLAGUE, 1615

Gervase Markham

The plague was an almost annual visitor to London during the Tudor and Stuart era. Thirty deaths a week during summer was routine. The Great Plague of 1665 was only exceptional for its severity.

To preserve your body from the infection of the plague, you shall take a quart of old ale, and after it hath risen upon the fire and hath been scummed, you shall put thereinto of aristolochia longa, of angelica and of celandine of each half an handful, and boil them well therein; then strain the drink through a clean cloth, and dissolve therein a drachm of the best mithridate, as much ivory finely powdered and searced, and six spoonful of dragon-water, then put it in a close glass; and every morning fasting take five spoonful thereof, and after bite and chew in your mouth the dried root of angelica, or smell, as on a nosegay, to the tasselled end of a ship rope, and they will surely preserve you from infection.

But if you be infected with the plague, and feel the assured signs thereof, as pain in the head, drought, burning, weakness of stomach and such like: then you shall take a drachm of the best mithridate, and dissolve it in three or four spoonful of dragon-water, and immediately drink it off, and then with hot cloths or bricks, made extreme hot and laid to the soles of your feet, after you have been wrapt in woollen cloths, compel the sick party to sweat, which if he do, keep him moderately therein till the sore begin to rise; then to the same apply a live pigeon cut in two parts, or else a plaster made of the yolk of an egg, honey, herb of grace chopped exceeding small, and wheat flour, which in very short space will not only ripen, but also break the same without any other incision; then after it hath run a day or two, you shall apply a plaster of melilot into it until it be whole.

THE LAND AND PEOPLE OF ENGLAND, 1617

Fynes Moryson

The air of England is temperate, but thick, cloudy and misty, and Caesar witnesseth that the cold is not so piercing in England as in France. For the sun draweth up the vapours of the sea which compasseth the island, and distills them upon the earth in frequent showers of rain, so that frosts are somewhat rare; and howsoever snow may often fall in the winter time, yet in the southern parts (especially) it seldom lies long on the ground. Also the cool blasts of sea winds mitigate the heat of summer.

By reason of this temper, laurel and rosemary flourish all winter, especially in the southern parts, and in summer time. England yields apricots plentifully, musk melons in good quantity, and figs in some places, all which ripen well, and happily imitate the taste and goodness of the same fruits in Italy. And by the same reason all beasts bring forth their young in the open fields, even in the time of winter. And England hath such abundance of apples, pears, cherries and plums, such variety of them and so good in all respects, as no country yields more or better, for which the Italians would gladly exchange their citrons and oranges. But upon the sea coast the winds many times blast the fruits in the very flower.

The English are so naturally inclined to pleasure, as there is no country wherein the gentlemen and lords have so many and large parks only reserved for the pleasure of hunting, or where all sorts of men allot so much ground about their houses for pleasure of gardens and orchards. The very grapes, especially towards the south and west, are of a pleasant taste, and I have said, that in some counties, as in Gloucestershire, they made wine of old, which

no doubt many parts would yield at this day, but that the
inhabitants forbear to plant vines, as well because they are served
plentifully and at a good rate with French wines, as for that the
hills most fit to bear grapes yield more commodity by feeding of
sheep and cattle. Caesar writes in his Commentaries, that Britanny
yields white lead within land, and iron upon the sea coasts. No
doubt England hath inexhaustible veins of both, and also of tin,
and yields great quantity of brass, and of alum and iron, and
abounds with quarries of freestone, and fountains of most pure salt;
and I formerly said that it yields some quantity of silver, and that
the tin and lead is mingled with silver, but so, as it doth not largely
quit the cost of the labour in separating or trying it. Two cities
yield medicinal baths, namely Buxton and Bath, and the waters of
Bath especially have great virtue in many diseases. England
abounds with sea-coals upon the sea coast, and with pit coals
within land. But the woods at this day are rather frequent and
pleasant than vast, being exhausted for fire, and with iron-mills, so
as the quantity of wood and charcoal for fire is much diminished,
in respect of the old abundance; and in some places, as in the Fens,
they burn turf, and the very dung of cows. Yet in the meantime
England exports great quantity of sea-coal to foreign parts. In like
sort England hath infinite quantity, as of metals, so of wool, and of
woollen clothes to be exported. The English beer is famous in
Netherlands and longer Germany, which is made of barley and
hops; for England yields plenty of hops, howsoever they also use
Flemish hops. The cities of lower Germany upon the sea forbid the
public selling of English beer, to satisfy their own brewers, yet
privately swallow it like nectar. But in Netherland great and
incredible quantity thereof is spent. England abounds with corn,
which they may transport, when a quarter in some places containing six, in others eight bushells) is sold for twenty shillings, or
under; and this corn not only serves England, but also served the
English army in the civil wars of Ireland, at which time they also
exported great quantity thereof into foreign parts and by God's
mercy England scarce once in ten years needs supply of foreign
corn, which want commonly proceeds of the coveteousness of
private men, exporting or hiding it. Yet I must confess, that daily
this plenty of coin decreaseth, by reason that private men, finding
greater commodity in feeding of sheep and cattle than in the
plough requiring the hands of many servants, can by no law be
restrained from turning corn-fields into enclosed pastures, espe-

cially since great men are the first to break these laws. England abounds with all kinds of fowl as well of the sea as of the land, and hath more tame swans swimming in the rivers, than I did see in any other part. It hath multitudes of hurtful birds, as crows, ravens and kites, and they labour not to destroy the crows consuming great quantity of corn, because they feed on worms and other things hurting the corn. And in great cities it is forbidden to kill kites and ravens, because they devour the filth of the streets. England hath very great plenty of sea and river fish, especially above all other parts abundance of oysters, mackerel and herrings, and the English are very industrious in fishing, though nothing comparable to the Flemings therein.

BESS BROUGHTON SETS UP FOR HERSELF, c. 1625

John Aubrey

Bess Broughton (Mistress Elizabeth Broughton) was daughter of (Edward) Broughton of (Kington) in Herefordshire an ancient Family. Her father lived at the Mannour-house at Canon-Peon. Whether she was borne there, or no I know not: but there she lost her Mayden-head to a poor young fellow, then I beleeve handsome, but in 1660 a pittifull poor old weaver (he had a fine curled haire, but gray) clarke of the parish. Her father at length discovered her inclinations, and locked her up in the Turret of the house; but she (like a . . .) getts downe by a rope, and away she gott to London, and did sett-up for her selfe.

She was a most exquisite beautie, as finely shaped as nature could frame, and had a delicate Witt. She was soon taken notice of at London; and her price was very deare. A second Thais. Richard Earle of Dorset kept her (whether before or after Venetia [Stanley] I know not, but I guesse before). At last she grew common and infamous and gott the Pox, of which she died. I remember thus much of an old Song of those dayes which I have seen in a Collection. 'Twas by way of Litanie. viz.

From the Watch at Twelve a Clock
And from Bess Broughton's buttond smock.
Libera nos Domine.

In Ben Johnson's 'Execrations against Vulcan', he concludes thus.

> Pox take thee Vulcan, may Pandora's pox
> And all the Ills that flew out of her Box
> Light on thee, and if these plagues will not doe.
> Thy Wive's Pox take thee, and Bess Broughton's too.

THE MURDER OF THE DUKE OF BUCKINGHAM, 23 AUGUST 1628

Sir Dudley Carleton

George Villiers (aka "Steenie"), Duke of Buckingham, was the royal favourite of both James I and Charles I. Loathed by Parliament for his arrogance, for his wealth, for his abortive expedition against Cadiz in 1625, he was only saved from impeachment by a dissolution and a prorogue. He was assassinated by John Felton, a subaltern who had been refused promotion by him.

This day betwixt nine and ten of the clocke in the morning, the Duke of Buckingham, then coming out of a Parlor, into a Hall, to go to his coach and soe to the King (who was four miles off), having about him diverse Lords, Colonells, and Captains, & many of his own Servants, was by one Felton (once a Lieutenant of this our Army) slain at one blow, with a dagger knife. In his staggering he turn'd about, uttering onely this word, "Villaine!" & never spake a word more, but presently plucking out the knife from himself, before he fell to the ground, he made towards the Traytor, two or three paces, and then fell against a Table although he were upheld by diverse that were neare him, that (through the villain's close carriage in the act) could not perceive him hurt at all, but guessed him to be suddenly oversway'd with some apoplexie, till they saw the blood come gushing from his mouth and the wound, soe fast, that life, and breath, at once left his begored body.

You may easily guess what outcries were then made, by us that were Commanders and Officers there present, when once we saw him thus dead in a moment, and slaine by an unknowne hand; for it seems that the Duke himself onely knew who it was that had murdered him, and by meanes of the confused presse at the instant about his person, wee neither did not could. The Souldiers feare his losse will be their utter ruine, wherefore att that instant the house and court about it were full, every man present with the Dukes body, endeavouring a care of itt. In the meane time Felton pass'd the throng, which was confusedly great, not so much as mark'd or followed, in soe much that not knowing where, nor who he was that had done that fact, some came to keepe guard at the gates, and others went to the Ramports of the Towne; in all which time the villaine was standing in the kitchin of the same house, and after inquiry made by a multitude of captaines and gentlemen then pressing into the house and court, and crying out a maine "Where is the villain? Where is the butcher?" he most audaciously and resolutely drawing forth his sword, came out and went amongst them, saying boldly, "I am the Man, here I am"; upon which diverse drew upon him, with the intent to have dispatch him; but Sir Thomas Morton, myself, and some others, us'd such means (though with much trouble and difficulty) that we drew him out of their hands, and by order of my Lord High Chamberlaine, wee had the charge of keeping him from any comming to him untill a guard of muskateers were brought, to convey him to the Governor's House, where wee were discharg'd.

My Lord High Chamberlaine and Mr Secretary Cooke that were then at the Governor's House, did there take his examination of which as yet there is nothing knowne, onely whilst he was in our custody I asked him several questions, to which he answer'd; viz. He sayd, he was a Protestant in Religion; he also express'd himself that he was partly discontented for want of eighty pounds pay which was due unto him; and for that he being Lieutenant of a company of foot, the company was given over his head unto another, and yett, he sayd, that that did not move him to this resolution, but that he reading the Remonstrance of the house of Parliament it came into his mind, that in committing the Act of killing the Duke, hee should do his Country great good service. And he sayd that to-morrow he was to be prayd for in London. I then asked him att what Church, and to what purpose; he told me at a Church by Fleet-Street-Conduit, and, as for a man much discontented in mind. Now wee seeing things to fall from him in this manner, suffer'd him not to be further question'd, thinking it much fitter for the Lords to examine him, and to finde it out, and knowe from him whether he was encouraged and sett on by any to perform this wicked deed.

But to returne to the screeches made att the fatall blow given, the Duchesse of Buckingham and the Countesse of Anglesey came forth into a Gallery which look'd into a Hall where they might behold the blood of their dearest Lord gushing from him; ah, poor Ladies, such was their screechings, teares, and distractions, that I never in my Life heard the like before, and hope never to heare the like againe. His Majesties griefe for the losse of him, was express'd to be more than great, by the many teares hee shed for him, with which I will conclude this sad and untimely News.

Felton had sowed a writing in the crowne of his hatt, half within lyning, to shew the cause why he putt this cruell act in excution; thinking hee should have beene slaine in the place: and it was thus: "If I bee slaine, let no man condemne me, but rather condemne himself; it is for our sinns that our harts are hardned, and become sencelesse, or else hee had not gone soe long unpunished. John Felton." "He is unworthy of the name of a Gentleman, or Soldier, in my opinion, that is afraid to sacrifice his life for the honor of God, his King and Country. John Felton."

A PORTRAIT OF OLIVER CROMWELL, LONDON, NOVEMBER 1640

Sir Philip Warwick

Born in 1599, the son of a country squire, Cromwell rose to become commander of the New Model Army in the English Civil War. After the eventual defeat of the Royalist side, Cromwell was declared the Lord Protector of England.

I have no mind to give an ill character of Cromwell, for in his conversation towards me he was ever friendly, though at the latter end of the day, finding me ever incorrigible and having some inducements to suspect me a tamperer, he was sufficiently rigid. The first time that ever I took notice of him was in the very beginning of the Parliament held in November 1640, when I vainly thought myself a courtly young gentleman (for we courtiers valued ourselves much upon our good clothes). I came one morning into the House well clad, and perceived a gentleman speaking (whom I knew not) very ordinarily apparelled, for it was a plain-cloth suit, which seemed to have been made by an ill country tailor: his linen was plain and not very clean, and I remember a speck or two of blood upon his little band, which was not much larger than his collar. His hat was without a hatband. His stature was of good size, his sword stuck close to his side, his countenance swollen and reddish, his voice sharp and untunable, and his eloquence full of fervour, for the subject matter would not bear much of reason, it being in behalf of a servant of Mr Prynne's, who had dispersed libels against the Queen for her dancing and such like innocent and courtly sports: and he aggravated the imprisonment of this man by the Council-Table unto that height that one would have believed the very government itself had been in great danger by it.

THE ATTEMPTED ARREST OF THE FIVE MEMBERS, 4 JANUARY 1642

John Rushworth

The reign of Charles I, begun in 1625, was dominated by constitutional and religious struggle with Parliament, which viewed askance the King's use of the royal prerogative and his resistance to the Puritanisation of the Anglican Church. The breach between monarch and Parliament became absolute in early 1642 when Charles tried to arrest five members of the Commons – MPs Pym, Hampden, Hesilrige, Holles and Strode – for treason.

. . . The said five accused Members this day *after dinner* came into the House, and did appear according to the special Order and Injunction of the House laid upon them yesterday, to give their attendance upon the House, *de die in diem* and their appearance was entred in the Journal.

They were no sooner sate in their places, but the House was informed by one Captain *Langrish*, lately an Officer in Arms in *France*, that he came from among the Officers, and souldiers at *White Hall*, and understanding by them, that his Majesty was coming with a Guard of Military Men, Commanders and Souldiers, to the House of Commons, he passed by them with some difficulty to get to the House before them, and sent in word how near the said Officers and Souldiers were come; Whereupon a certain Member of the House having also private Intimation from the Countess of *Carlile*, Sister to the Earl of *Northumberland*, that endeavours would be used this day to apprehend the five Members, the House required the five Members to depart the House forthwith, to the end to avoid Combustion in the House, if the said Souldiers should use Violence to pull any of them out. To which Command of the House, four of the said Members yielded ready

Obedience, but Mr. *Stroud* was obstinate, till Sir *Walter Earle* (his ancient acquaintance) pulled him out by force, the King being at that time entring into the *New Pallace-yard*, in *Westminster:* And as his Majesty came through *Westminster Hall*, the Commanders, Reformadoes, &c. that attended him, made a Lane on both sides the Hall (through which his Majesty passed and came up the Stairs to the House of Commons) and stood before the Guard of Pentioners, and Halberteers, (who also attended the King Person,) and the door of the House of Commons being thrown open, his Majesty entred the House, and as he passed up towards *the Chair* he cast his eye on the Right-hand near the Bar of the House, where Mr. *Pym* used to sit, but his Majesty not seeing him there (knowing him well) went up to the Chair, and said, "By your leave, (Mr. Speaker) I must borrow your Chair a little," whereupon the Speaker came out of the Chair, and his Majesty stept up into it, after he had stood in the Chair a while, casting his Eye upon the Members as they stood up *uncovered*, but could not discern any of the five Members to be there, nor indeed were they easie to be discerned (had they been there) among so many bare Faces all standing up together.

Then his Majesty made this Speech,

"Gentlemen,

I Am sorry for this occasion of coming unto you: Yesterday I sent a Serjeant at Arms upon a very Important occasion to apprehend some that by my command were accused of High Treason, whereunto I did expect Obedience and not a Message. And I must declare unto you here, that albeit, no King that ever was in *England*, shall be more careful of your Priviledges, to maintain them to the uttermost of his power then I shall be; yet you must know that in Cases of Treason, no person hath a priviledge. And therefore I am come to know if any of these persons that were accused are here: For I must tell you Gentlemen, that so long as these persons that I have accused (for no slight Crime but for Treason) are here, I cannot expect that this House will be in the Right way that I do heartily wish it: Therefore I am come to tell you that I must have them wheresoever I find them. Well since I see all the Birds are Flown, I do expect from you, that you shall send them unto me, as soon as they return hither. But I assure you, in the word of a King, I never did intend any Force, but shall proceed against them in a legal and fair way, for I never meant any other.

And now since I see I cannot do what I came for, I think this no unfit occasion to repeat what I have said formerly, That whatsoever I have done in favour, and to the good of my Subjects, I do mean to maintain it.

I will trouble you no more, but tell you I do expect as soon as they come to the House, you will send them to me; otherwise I must take my own Course to find them."

When the King was looking about the House, the Speaker standing below by the Chair, his Majesty ask'd him, whether any of these persons were in the House? Whether he saw any of them? and where they were? To which the Speaker falling on his Knee, thus Answered.

"*May it please your Majesty*, I Have neither Eyes to see, nor Tongue to speak in this place, but as the House is pleased to direct me, whose Servant I am here, and humbly beg your Majesties Pardon, that I cannot give any other Answer than this, to what your Majesty is pleased to demand of me."

The King having Concluded his Speech, went out of the House again which was in great disorder, and many Members cried out, aloud so as he might hear them, "Priviledge! Priviledge!" and forthwith Adjourned till the next Day at One of the Clock . . .

For the next seven months the King and Parliament built up their military strength. On 22 August 1642 Charles I raised the royal standard at Nottingham. The English Civil War had begun.

THE ENGLISH CIVIL WAR: NEHEMIAH WHARTON SKIRMISHES, PILLAGES AND STARVES IN WARWICKSHIRE, AUGUST 1642

Nehemiah Wharton

Wharton was a young subaltern in the Parliamentary Army commanded by the Earl of Essex.

August 17, our companies, after they had taken six delinquents and sent them to London, returned to Alesbury this day; we retained two feild pieces and two troopes of horse, with other necessaries for warre. Wensday morning, a Warwickshire minister, which the Calualleres* had pillaged to the skin, gave us a sermon. After noone our regiment marched into the field and skirmished.

* Cavaliers.

Thursday morning another sermon was given us. After noone our regiment marched into the feild, but by reason of foule weather were immediately definished. This night our regiment was commanded to march the next morninge by four of the clock under our Leiftenant Colonell, but our sargeants refused to surrender their halberts, and the souldiers their armes, and not to march. Friday, very early in the morninge, our Lieftenant Colonell was cashiered, for which I give you hearty thanks, and Sergeant-Major Quarles imployed in his roome, whereat both commaunders, officers, and souldiers exceedingly rejoysed. This morninge wee cherfully marched towards Buckingham in the rear of Colonell Chomley's regiment, by reason whereof we could get no quarter there, but were constrained to quarter ourselves about the countrey, whereupon I and three gentlemen of my company visited that thrice noble gentleman Sr Richard Inglisby, where his owne table was our quarter, and Sergeant-Major Burrif, and his sonne Captaine Inglisby, and several other noble gentlemen were our comrades.

Saturday, early in the morning, I departed hence and gathered a compliete file of my owne men about the countrey, and marched to Sir Alexander Denton's parke, who is a malignant fellow, and killed a fat buck, fastened his head upon my halbert, and commanded two of my pickes to bring the body after me to Buckingham, with a guard of musquetteers comminge theither. With part of it I feasted my captaine, Captaine Parker, Captaine Beacon, and Colonell Hamden's sonne, and with the rest severall leiftenants, enseignes, and serjeants, and had much thankes for my paines. This day Sergeant Major our Generall came unto us, and declared the commaund given him over our regiments. Sunday morninge wee marched from Buckingham into Northamptonshire, a longe and tedious jorney, wantinge both bread and water, and about ten at night came unto Byfeild in dispight of our enemies, at which towne we could get no quarter, neither meate, drinke, nor lodginge, and had we not bin suplyed with ten cart loade of provision and beare from Banbury, many of us had perished. This night our company was commanded to guard the towne all night, whiche after a longe and tedious marche, was very grevious unto me. Monday morninge wee marched into Warwick-shere with about three thousand foote and four hundred horse, until we came to Southam. In the way we tooke two Calvalleres spies. This is a very malignant towne, both minister and people. We pillaged the minister, and tooke from him a drum and severall armes. This night our soildiers, wearied out, quartered themselves about the towne for foode and lodginge, but before we could eat or drinke an alarum cryed "arme, arme, for the enemy is commenge," and in halfe an hower all our soildiers, though dispersed, were cannybals in armes, ready to encounter enemy, cryinge out for a dish of Calvellaers to supper. Our horse were quartered about the countrey, but the enemy came not, whereupon our soildiers cryed out to have a breakefast of Cauallers. We barecaded the towne, and at every passage placed our ordinance and watched it all night, our soildiers contented to lye upon hard stones. In the morning early our enemise, consisting of about eight hundred horse and three hundred foote, with ordinance, led by the Earl of Northampton, the Lord of Carnarvan, and the Lord Compton and Captn Legge, and other, intended to set upon us before we could gather our companies together, but beinge ready all night, early in the morninge wee went to meet them with a few troopes of horse and sixe feild pieces, and beinge on fier to be at them wee marched thorow the coarn and got the hill of them, wherupon they played upon us with their ordinances, but they came short. Our gunner tooke theire owne bullet, sent it to them againe, and killed a horse and a man. After we gave them eight shot more, whereupon all their foote companies fled and offered their armes in the townes adjacent for twelve pence a peece.

Ther troopse, whelinge about, toke up their dead bodies and fled; but the horse they left behind, some of them having ther guts beaten out on both sides. One drummer, being dead at the bottom of the hill, our knapsack boyes rifled to the shirt, which was very louzy. Another drummer wee found two miles of, with his arme shot of, and lay a dieinge. Severall dead corps wee found in corne feilds, and amongst them a trumpeter, whose trumpet our horsemen sounded into Coventry. Wee tooke severall prisoners, and amongst them Capt. Legge and Captaine Clarke. From thence wee marched valiantly after them toward Coventry, and at Dunsmore Heath they threatned to give us battaile, but we got the hill of them, ordered our men, and cryed for a messe of Calualleres to supper, as we had to breakefast; but they all fled, and we immediately marched into Coventry, where the countrey met us in armes and welcomed us, and gave us good quarter both for horse and foote. In this battell I met with your horseman Davy, and he and I present you and my Mistris with our most humble service, desiringe you to pray for us, and doubt not that both of (us) will valiantly fight the Lord's battaile. Thus, with my service to Mrs. Elizabeth, Anne, John, and Samuell, and my love to all my fellow servants, I rest,

> Yours, in all good services,
> NEHEMIAH WHARTON.

THE ENGLISH CIVIL WAR: EDGEHILL, 23 OCTOBER 1642

C. H.

A Royalist view of the first battle of the Civil War.

On Sunday last I saw the Battle which was the bloudiest I believe the oldest soldiers in the field ever saw. We have routed utterly their horse and slain & chased away so considerable a party of their foot, that the Enemy is very weak. Though we have lost some, yet few of eminency, save some prisoners. The Earl of Lindsey, Willoughby, and Colonel Lunston, the Lord St. John, with the Lord Fielding are slain, with many others. My Lord of Essex escaped us by being in an alehouse. We have his coach and much money in it. There needs no more to assure any understanding man we had the day, than to tell them (which is true) we had all their ordnances in the field and fetcht them out next morning in their sight. They are so weak they have entrenched themselves, and we are now going on our intended march to Oxford, having only gone backward on Sunday to bestow this breathing on them. We have taken about five colours and cornetts, and lost about five or six colours, but never a cornett. The King hath five hundred of their horse alive, and of eighteen hundred not one horse is left them. At the beginning of the fight, two double troops came over to the King's party commanded by Sir Faithfeill Fortescue and Mr. Gervase Pain, & fought on that side. It is commonly reported the Earl of Essex his soldiers ran away dayly. Three hundred prisoners are taken, among which is Sergeant Major Barrey, a recusant of the Irish. My Lord Albany is slain on the King's side, and Dr. Lake. The King gave fire to the first piece, the Lord General having first demanded the word, which was *"Go in the name of God and I'll lay my bones with yours."* Marquis Hartford is now on the march with ten thousand men armed out of Wales, and intends to meet the King at Oxford. Sir R. Hopton and Mr. Rogers bring as many from the West Country.

C.H.

THE ENGLISH CIVIL WAR: THE DEATH OF A NEPHEW AT MARSTON MOOR, YORKSHIRE, 1 JULY 1644

Oliver Cromwell

It was Cromwell's surprise cavalry charge late in the day that won Marston Moor for the roundheads. With the Royalist Northern Army routed, the tide of the Civil War turned ineluctably in Parliament's favour. Cromwell's letter below is addressed to his brother-in-law, Colonel Valentine Walton.

It's our duty to sympathize in all mercies; and to praise the Lord together in chastisements or trials, that so we may sorrow together.

Truly England and the Church of God hath had a great favour from the Lord, in this great Victory given unto us, such as the like never was since this War began. It had all the evidences of an absolute Victory obtained by the Lord's blessing upon the Godly Party principally. We never charged but we routed the enemy. The Left Wing, which I commanded, being our own horse, saving a few Scots in our rear, beat all the Prince's horse. God made them as stubble to our swords. We charged their regiments of foot with our horse, and routed all we charged. The particulars I cannot relate now; but I believe, of Twenty-thousand the Prince hath not Four-thousand left. Give glory, all the glory, to God. . . .

Sir, God hath taken away your eldest Son by a cannon-shot. It brake his leg. We were necessitated to have it cut off, whereof he died.

Sir, you know my own trials this way: but the Lord supported me with this, That the Lord took him into the happiness we all pant for and live for. There is your precious child full of glory, never to know sin or sorrow any more. He was a gallant young man, exceedingly gracious. God give you His comfort. Before his death he was so full of comfort that to Frank Russel and myself he could not express it, "It was so great above his pain." This he said to us. Indeed it was admirable. A little after, he said, One thing lay upon his spirit. I asked him, What that was? He told me it was, That God had not suffered him to be any more the executioner of His enemies. At his fall, his horse being killed with the bullet, and as I am informed three horses more, I am told he bid them, Open to the right and left, that he might see the rogues run. Truly he was exceedingly beloved in the Army, of all that knew him. But few

knew him; for he was a precious young man, fit for God. You have
cause to bless the Lord. He is a glorious Saint in Heaven; wherein
you ought exceedingly to rejoice. Let this drink up your sorrow;
seeing these are not feigned words to comfort you, but the thing is
so real and undoubted a truth. You may do all things by the
strength of Christ. Seek that, and you shall easily bear your trial.
Let this public mercy to the Church of God make you to forget
your private sorrow. The Lord be your strength: so prays

    Your truly faithful and loving brother

My love to your Daughter, and my Cousin Perceval, Sister
Desborow and all friends with you.

THE ENGLISH CIVIL WAR: THE EXECUTION OF CHARLES I, LONDON, 30 JANUARY 1649

Robert Crotchett

On his defeat in the Civil War in 1646, Charles I surrendered to
Parliamentary forces, before spending the next two years politicking
and scheming. An agreement with the Scots (who had opposed him in
the Civil War) whereby they would support his restoration in return for
the establishment of Presbyterianism in Britain, led to another round of
Civil War in 1648, which was efficiently crushed by Cromwell's New
Model Army. Charles was once again captured. The Army demanded the
head of the "tyrant, traitor and murderer, Charles Stuart".

The scaffold erected before Whitehall, the King about 2 of the
clocke came out of the banqueting house at a passage made
through a window upon the scaffold, where the block and axe
lay, at which he smilingly looking found fault with the block for
being made too lowe. The scaffold was covered with black cloth.
His Majestie turned about and spake something to the Bishop of
London who replied to him and administered the Lord's supper. I
think none heard what was said, but only those few on the scaffold
with him, being about 14. Haveing spoke a quarter of an hour he
putt off his hat and one of the executioners putt on his head a white
capp and gathered upp his hair under it. Then he putt off his
doublet and lay flatt downe on his belly with his neck on the block
with his arms spread out giving the signe by spreading his hands
wider. The executioner, haveing on his knees asked him pardon,

cutt off his head at one blow and his mate took it upp and held it up
to the spectators which was very many. The executioners were
disguised being masqued with great beards and I believe not
known to many. The King seemed to dye resolutely. I heard he
left a speech in writing to be published. It may be it will come forth
the morrow. I shall send it as soon as I can gett it.

All the army was uppon guard at their severall posts at Whitehall, Charing Cross, Westminster, St James parke and fields,
Covent Garden etc.

Two Ambassadors at the importunity of the Prince are come
from ye States of Holland to intercede but too late. They delivered
the message yesterday in French and Dutch to the House, which
the House not skilled at required the message in plain English,
which is thought but a dilatory complaint on both sides. The Lord
Loughborough is escaped from Windsor. There was much scrab-
bling for the King's blood.

THE ENGLISH CIVIL WAR: THE STORMING OF DROGHEDA, IRELAND, 10–11 SEPTEMBER 1649

Oliver Cromwell

In May 1649 England became a republic. To protect the new "Commonwealth", Parliament ruthlessly subjugated Royalist-inclined Ireland.

It hath pleased God to bless our endeavours at Tredah (Drogheda). After battery, we stormed it. The enemy were about 3000
strong in the Town. They made a stout resistance; and near 1000 of
our men being entered, the Enemy forced them out again. But God
giving a new courage to our men, they attempted again, and
entered; beating the enemy from their defences.

The Enemy had made three retrenchments, both to the right
and left of where we entered; all which they were forced to quit.
Being thus entered, we refused them quarter; having, the day
before, summoned the Town. I believe we put to the sword the
whole number of the defendants. I do not think Thirty of the whole
number escaped with their lives. Those that did, are in safe custody
for the Barbadoes. Since that time, the Enemy quitted to us Trim
and Dundalk. In Trim they were in such haste that they left their
guns behind them.

This hath been a marvellous great mercy. The Enemy, being not
without some considerable loss; Colonel Castle being there shot in

the head, whereof he presently died; and divers officers and soldiers doing their duty killed and wounded. There was a Tenalia to flanker the south Wall of the Town, between Duleek Gate and the corner Tower before mentioned; – which our men entered, wherein they found some forty or fifty of the Enemy, which they put to the sword. And this "Tenalia" they held: but it being without the Wall, and the sally-port through the Wall into that Tenalia being choked up with some of the Enemy which were killed in it, it proved of no use for an entrance into the Town that way.

Although our men that stormed the breaches were forced to recoil, as is before expressed; yet, being encouraged to recover their loss, they made a second attempt; wherein God was pleased so to animate them that they got ground of the enemy, and by the goodness of God, forced him to quit his entrenchments. And after a very hot dispute, the Enemy having both horse and foot, and we only foot, within the Wall – they gave ground, and our men became masters both of their retrenchments and of the Church; which, indeed, although they made our entrance the more difficult, yet they proved of excellent use to us; so that the Enemy could not now annoy us with their horse, but thereby we had the advantage to make good the ground, that so we might let in our own horse; which accordingly was done, though with much difficulty.

Divers of the Enemy retreated into the Mill-Mount: a place very strong and difficult of access; being exceedingly high, having a good graft, and strong palisadoed. The Governor, Sir Arthur Ashton, and divers considerable Officers being there, our men getting up to them, were ordered by me to put them all to the sword. And indeed, being in the heat of action, I forbade them to spare any that were in arms in the Town: and, I think, that night they put to the sword about 2000 men; – divers of the officers and soldiers being fled over the Bridge into the other part of the Town, where about 100 of them possessed St Peter's Church-steeple, some the west Gate, and others a strong Round Tower next the Gate called St Sunday's. These being summoned to yield to mercy, refused. Whereupon I ordered the steeple of St Peter's Church to be fired, when one of them was heard to say in the midst of the flames: "God damn me, God confound me; I burn, I burn."

The next day, the other two Towers were summoned; in one of which was about six or seven score; but they refused to yield themselves: and we knowing that hunger must compel them, set only good guards to secure them from running away until their stomachs were come down. From one of the said Towers, notwith-standing their condition, they killed and wounded some of our men. When they submitted, their officers were knocked on the head; and every tenth man of the soldiers killed; and the rest shipped for the Barbadoes. The soldiers in the other Tower were all spared, as to their lives only; and shipped likewise for the Barba-does.

I am persuaded that this is a righteous judgement of God upon these barbarous wretches, who have imbrued their hands in so much innocent blood; and that it will tend to prevent the effusion of blood for the future. Which are the satisfactory grounds to such actions, which otherwise cannot but work remorse and regret. The officers and soldiers of this Garrison were the flower of their army. And their great expectation was, that our attempting this place would put fair to ruin us . . . And now give me leave to say how it comes to pass that this work is wrought. It was set upon some of our hearts, That a great thing should be done, not by power or might, but by the Spirit of God. And is it not so, clearly? That which caused your men to storm so courageously, it was the Spirit of God, who gave your men courage, and took it away again; and gave the Enemy courage, and took it away again; and gave your men courage again, and therewith this happy success. And therefore it is good that God alone have all the glory . . .

Your most obedient servant,

OLIVER CROMWELL.

UNCONSUMMATED CHILD MARRIAGE, ENGLAND, 1651

Court Records

John Bridge v Elizabeth Bridge

. . . the said John wold Eate no meate at supper . . . and whan hit was bed tyme, the said John did wepe to go home with his father, he beynge at that tyme at her brothers house. Yet nevertheles, bie his fathers intreating, and bie the perswasion of the priest, the said John did comme to bed to this Respondent far in the night; and there lay still, till in the morning, in suche sort as this deponent might take unkindnes with hym; for he lay with his backe toward her all night; and neither then, nor anie tyme els, had carnall dole with her, nor never after came in her companie, more than he had never knowne her.

. . . the said John was, at the tyme of the said marriage, above the age of xii yeres, and vnder xiii.

HIGHWAY ROBBERY, KENT, ENGLAND, 11 JUNE 1652

John Evelyn

The weather being hot, and having sent my man on before, I rode negligently under favour of the shade, till within three miles of Bromley, at a place called Procession Oak, two cut-throats started out, and striking with long staves at the horse and taking hold of the reins threw me down, took my sword, and haled me into a deep thicket some quarter of a mile from the highway, where they did might securely rob me, as they soon did. What they got of money was not considerable, but they took two rings, the one an emerald with diamonds, the other an onyx, and a pair of buckles set with rubies and diamonds, which were of value, and after all bound my hands behind me, and my feet, having before pulled off my boots; they then set me up against an oak, with the most bloody threats to cut my throat if I offered to cry out or make any noise, for they should be within hearing, I not being the person they looked for. I told them, if they had not basely surprised me they should not have had so easy a prize, and that it would teach me never to ride near a hedge, since had I been midway they durst not have adventured on me; at which they cocked their pistols, and told me they had long guns too, and were 14 companions. I begged for my onyx, and told them it being engraven with my arms would betray them, but nothing prevailed. My horse's bridle they slipt, and searched the saddle, which they pulled off, but let the horse graze, and then turning again bridled him and tied him to a tree, yet so as he might graze, and thus left me bound. My horse was perhaps not taken because he was marked and cropped on both ears, and well known on that road. Left in this manner grievously was I tormented with flies, ants, and the sun, nor was my anxiety little how I should get loose in that solitary place, where I could neither hear or see any creature but my poor horse, and a few sheep straggling in the copse.

Afternear two hours attempting I got my hands to turn palm to palm, having been tied back to back, and then it was long before I could slip the cord over my wrists to my thumb, which at last I did, and then soon unbound my feet, and saddling my horse and roaming awhile about I at last perceived dust to rise, and soon after heard the rattling of a cart, towards which I made, and by the help of two countrymen I got back into the highway. I rode to Col. Blount's, a great judiciary of the times, who sent out hue and cry immediately. The next morning, sore as my wrists and arms were, I went to London and got 500 tickets printed and dispersed by an officer of Goldsmiths Hall, and within two days had tidings of all I had lost except my sword which had a silver hilt and some trifles. The rouges had pawned one of my rings for a trifle to a goldsmith's servant before the tickets had come to the shop, by which means they escaped; the other ring was bought by a victualler, who brought it to a goldsmith, but he having seen the ticket seized the man. I afterwards discharged him on protestation of innocence. Thus did God deliver me from these vilains, and not only so, but restored what they took, as twice before he had graciously done, both at sea and land; I mean when I was robbed by pirates, and was in danger of a considerable loss at Amsterdam; for which, and many, many signal preservations, I am extremely obliged to give thanks to God my Saviour.

WHALE HARPOONED IN THE THAMES, 3 JUNE 1658

John Evelyn

A large whale was taken betwixt my land butting on the Thames and Greenwich, which drew an infinite concourse to see it, by water, coach and on foot, from London and all parts. It appeared first below Greenwich at low water, for at high water it would have destroyed all the boats, but lying now in shallow water encompassed with boats after a long conflict it was killed with a harping iron (*harpoon*), struck in the head, out of which spouted blood and water by two tunnels, and after an horrid groan it ran quite on shore and died. Its length was fifty-eight foot, height sixteen; black-skinned like coach leather, very small eyes, great tail, only two small fins, a picked (*tapering*) snout, and a mouth so wide that divers men might have stood upright in it; no teeth, but sucked the slime only as through a grate of that bone which we call whalebone; the throat yet so narrow as would not have admitted the least of fishes. The extremes of the cetaceous bones hang downwards from the upper jaw, and was hairy towards the ends and bottom within side: all of it prodigious, but in nothing more wonderful than that an animal of so great a bulk should be nourished only by slime through those grates.

THE PRODIGIOUS BOYHOOD OF SIR ISAAC NEWTON, c. 1660

Dr Stukeley

Every one that knew Sir Isaac, or have heard of him, recount the pregnancy of his parts when a boy, his strange inventions, and extraordinary inclination for mechanics. That instead of playing among the other boys, when from school, he always busied himself in making knick-knacks and models of wood in many kinds. For which purpose he had got little saws, hatchets, hammers, and all sorts of tools, which he would use with great dexterity. In particular they speak of his making a wooden clock. About this time, a new windmill was set up near Grantham, in the way to Gunnerby, which is now demolished, this country chiefly using water mills. Our lad's imitating spirit was soon excited and by frequently prying into the fabric of it, as they were making it, he became master enough to make a very perfect model thereof, and it was said to be as clean and curious a piece of workmanship, as the original. This sometimes he would set upon the house-top, where he lodged, and clothing it with sail-cloth, the wind would readily turn it; but what was most extraordinary in its composition was, that he put a mouse into it, which he called the miller, and that the mouse made the mill turn round when he pleased; and he would joke too upon the miller eating the corn that was put in. Some say that he tied a string to the mouse's tail, which was put into a wheel, like that of turn-spit dogs, so that pulling the string, made the mouse go forward by way of resistance, and this turned the mill. Others suppose there was some corn placed above the wheel, this the mouse endeavouring to get to, made it turn.

THE RESTORATION: CHARLES II RETURNS TO ENGLAND, MAY 1660

Anon

On Oliver Cromwell's death in 1658 his son Richard assumed the title of Lord Protector, but was dismissed by the "Rump Parliament" for showing little aptitude and less enthusiasm. After a year of instability, the Army negotiated the restoration of the monarchy, in the shape of Charles I's son, then in exile in Holland.

Being come aboard one of the fairest of those ships, which attended at Sluys, for wafting him over from the Hague in Holland; and, therein having taken leave of his sister, the princess royal, he set sail for England on Wednesday evening, May 23, 1660. And having, during his abode at sea, given new names to that whole navy (consisting of twenty-six goodly vessels) he arrived at Dover on the Friday following (viz. May the 25th) about two of the clock in the afternoon. Ready on the shore to receive him, stood the Lord General Monk, as also the Earl of Winchelsea, constable of Dover castle, with divers persons of quality on the one hand, and the mayor of Dover, accompanied by his brethren of that corporation on the other, with a rich canopy.

As soon as he had set foot on the shore, the lord general, presenting himself before him on his knee, and kissing his royal hand, was embraced by his majesty, and received divers gracious expressions of the great sense he had of his loyalty, and in being so instrumental in this his restoration. . . .

From thence taking coach immediately, with his royal brothers, the Dukes of York and Gloucester, he passed to Barham-down . . . where multitudes of the country people stood, making loud shouts, he rode to the head of each troop (they being placed on his left hand, three deep) who, bowing to him, kissed the hilts of their swords, and then flourished them above their heads, with no less acclamations; the trumpets, in the mean time, also echoing the like to them.

In the suburb at Canterbury stood the mayor and aldermen of that ancient city, who received him with loud musick, and presented him with a cup of gold, of two-hundred and fifty pounds value. Whence after a speech made to him by the recorder, he passed to the Lord Camden's house, the mayor carrying the sword before him. . . .

From Canterbury he came, on Monday, to Rochester, where the people had hung up, over the midst of the streets, as he rode, many beautiful garlands, curiously made up with costly scarfs and ribbands, decked with spoons and bodkins of silver, and small plate of several sorts; and some with gold chains, in like sort as at Canterbury; each striving to outdoe others in all expressions of joy.

On Tuesday, May the 29th (which happily fell out to be the anniversary of his majesty's birth-day) he set forth of Rochester in his coach; but afterwards took horse on the farther side of Black-heath, on which spacious plain he found divers great and eminent troops of horse, a most splendid and glorious equipage; and a kind of rural triumph, expressed by the country swains, in a Morrice-dance, with the old musick of taber and pipe, which was performed with all agility and chearfulness imaginable. . . .

In this order proceeding towards London, there were placed in Deptford, on his right hand (as he passed through the town) above an hundred proper maids, clad all alike, in white garments, with scarfs about them; who, having prepared many flaskets covered with fine linnen, and adorned with rich scarfs and ribbands, which flaskets were full of flowers and sweet herbs, strowed the way before him as he rode.

From thence passing on, he came to St. George's Fields in Southwark, where the lord mayor and aldermen of London, in their scarlet, with the recorder, and other city council, waited for him in a large tent, hung with tapestry; in which they had placed a chair of state, with a rich canopy over it. When he came thither, the lord mayor presented him with the city sword, and the recorder made a speech to him; which being done, he alighted, and went into the tent, where a noble banquet was prepared for him. . . .

In . . . magnificent fashion his majesty entered the borough of Southwark, about half an hour past three of the clock in the afternoon; and, within an hour after, the city of London at the Bridge; where he found the windows and streets exceedingly thronged with people to behold him; and the walls adorned with hangings and carpets of tapestry and other costly stuff; and in many places sets of loud musick; all the conduits, as he passed, running claret wine; and the several companies in their liveries, with the ensigns belonging to them; as also the trained bands of the city standing along the streets as he passed, welcoming him with joyful acclamations.

And within the rails where Charing-cross formerly was, a stand of six-hundred pikes, consisting of knights and gentlemen, as had been officers of the armies of his majesty of blessed memory; the truly noble and valiant Sir John Stowell, Knight of the honourable Order of the Bath, a person famous for his eminent actions and sufferings, being in the head of them.

From which place, the citizens, in velvet coats and gold chains, being drawn up on each hand, and divers companies of foot soldiers; his majesty passed betwixt them, and entered White-hall at seven of the clock, the people making loud shouts, and the horse and foot several vollies of shot, at this his happy arrival. Where the house of lords and commons of parliament received him, and kissed his royal hand. At the same time likewise the Reverend Bishops of Ely, Salisbury, Rochester, and Chichester, in their episcopal habits, with divers of the long oppressed orthodox clergy, met in that royal chapel of king Henry the Seventh, at Westminster; there also sung *Te Deum, & c.* in praise and thanks to Almighty God, for this his unspeakable mercy, in the deliverance of his majesty from many dangers, and so happily restoring him to rule these kingdoms, according to his just and undoubted right.

LOST: THE KING'S DOG, JUNE–JULY 1660

John Ellis and Charles II

Charles II was a noted dog lover. The second of these advertisements for a lost dog, though placed anonymously in *Mercurius Publicus*, was certainly written by the witty monarch himself.

A Smooth Black DOG, less than a Greyhound, with white under his breast, belonging to the King's Majesty, was taken from Whitehal, the eighteenth day of this instant June, or thereabout. If any one can give notice to John Ellis, one of his Majesties Servants, or to his Majesties Back-Stayrs, shal be well rewarded for their labour.

Mercurius Publicus, June 21–28, 1660.

We must call upon you again for a Black Dog between a Greyhound and a Spaniel, no white about him onely a streak on his Brest and his Tayl a little bobbed. It is His Majesties own

Dog, and doubtles was stoln, for the Dog was not born nor bred in England, and would never forsake his Master. Whosoever findes him may acquaint any at Whitehal, for the Dog was better known at Court than those who stole him. Will they never leave robbing His Majesty? Must he not keep a Dog? This Dog's place (though better than some imagine) is the only place which nobody offers to beg.

Mercurius Publicus, June 28–July 5, 1660.

JOURNAL OF THE PLAGUE YEAR, 1665
John Evelyn

At the time of the Great Plague the diarist Evelyn was an Admiralty official.

Diary 1665, July 7. To London, to Sir William Coventrie; and so to Sion, where his Majesty sat at Council during the contagion; when business was over, I viewed that seat belonging to the Earl of Northumberland, built out of an old Nunnery, of stone, and fair enough, but more celebrated for the garden than it deserves; yet there is excellent wall-fruit, and a pretty fountain; nothing else extraordinary.

9. I went to Hampton Court, where now the whole Court was, to solicit for money; to carry intercepted letters; confer again with Sir Wm. Coventrie, the Duke's secretary; and so home, having dined with Mr. Secretary Morice.

16. There died of the plague in London this week 1100, and in the week following above 2000. Two houses were shut up in our parish.

Aug. 2. A solemn fast through England to deprecate God's displeasure against the land by pestilence and war; our Dr. preaching on 26 Levit: 41, 42. that the means to obtain remission of punishment was not to repine at it, but humbly submit to it.

3. Came his Grace the Duke of Albemarle, L. General of all his Majesty's Forces, to visit me, and carried me to dine with him.

4. I went to Wotton to carry my son and his tutor Mr. Bohun, Fellow of New Coll. (recommended to me by Dr. Wilkins and the Pres. of New Coll. Oxford), for fear of the pestilence, still increasing in London and its environs. On my return I called at Durdans, where I found Dr. Wilkins, Sir Wm. Petty, and Mr. Hooke, contriving chariots, new rigging for ships, a wheel for one to run races in, and other mechanical inventions; perhaps three such persons together were not to be found elsewhere in Europe, for parts and ingenuity.

8. I waited on the D. of Albemarle, who was resolved to stay at the Cock-pit in St. James's Park. Died this week in London 4000.

15. There perished this week 5000.

28. The contagion still increasing and growing now all about us, I sent my wife and whole family (two or three necessary servants excepted) to my brother's at Wotton, being resolved to stay at my house myself and to look after my charge, trusting in the providence and goodness of God.

Sept. 5. To Chatham to inspect my charge, with £900 in my coach.

7. Came home, there perishing near 10,000 poor creatures weekly; however I went all along the City and suburbs from Kent Street to St. James's, a dismal passage, and dangerous to see so many coffins exposed in the streets, now thin of people; the shops shut up, and all in mournful silence, as not knowing whose turn might be next. I went to the Duke of Albemarle for a pest-ship, to wait on our infected men, who were not a few.

14. I went to Wotton; and on 16 Sept. to visit old Secretary Nicholas, being now at his new purchase of West Horsley, once mortgaged to me by Lord Visct. Montagu: a pretty dry seat on the Down, Returned to Wotton.

17. Received a letter from Lord Sandwich of a defeat given to the Dutch, I was forced to travel all Sunday. I was exceedingly perplexed to find that near 3000 prisoners were sent to me to dispose of, being more than I had places fit to receive and guard.

25. My Lord Admiral being come from the Fleet to Greenwich, I went thence with him to the Cock-pit to consult with the Duke of Albemarle. I was peremptory that unless we had £10,000 immediately, the prisoners would starve, and 'twas proposed it should be raised out of the E. India prizes now taken by Lord Sandwich. They being but two of the Commission, and so not empowered to determine, sent an express to his Majesty and Council to know what they should do. In the meantime I had 5 vessels with competent guards to keep the prisoners in for the present, to be placed as I should think best. After dinner (which was at the Generals) I went over to visit his Grace the A. Bishop of Canterbury at Lambeth.

28. To the General again, to acquaint him of the deplorable state of our men for want of provisions; returned with orders.

29. To Erith to quicken the sale of the prizes lying there, with order to the Commissioner who lay on board till they should be disposed of, £5000 being proportioned for my quarter. Then I delivered the Dutch Vice-Admiral, who was my prisoner, to Mr. Lowman, of the Marshalsea, he giving me bond in £500 to produce him at my call. I exceedingly pitied this brave unhappy person, who had lost with these prizes £40,000 after 20 years negotiation (trading) in the East Indies. I dined in one of these vessels, of 1200 tons, full of riches.

October 1. This afternoon, whilst at evening prayers, tidings were brought me of the birth of a daughter at Wotton, after six sons, in the same chamber I had first took breath in, and at the first day of that month, as I was on the last, 45 years before.

4. The monthly fast.

11. To London, and went through the whole City, having occasion to alight out of the coach in several places about business of money, when I was environed with multitudes of poor pestiferous creatures begging alms; the shops universally shut up, a dreadful prospect! I dined with my Lord General; was to receive £10,000 and had guards to convey both myself and it, and so returned home, through God's infinite mercy.

17. I went to Gravesend, next day to Chatham, thence to Maidstone, in order to the march of 500 prisoners to Leeds Castle, which I had hired of Lord Culpeper. I was earnestly desired by the learned Sir Roger Twisden and Deputy Lieutenants to spare Maidstone from quartering any of my sick flock. Here Sir Edw. Brett sent me some horse to bring up the rear. This country from Rochester to Maidstone by the Medway and the Downs is very agreeable for the prospect.

21. I came from Gravesend, where Sir Jo. Griffith, the Governor of the Fort, entertained me very handsomely.

31. I was this day 45 years of age, wonderfully preserved, for which I blessed God for his infinite goodness towards me.

November 23. Went home, the contagion having now decreased considerably.

THE GREAT FIRE OF LONDON, 2 SEPTEMBER 1666

Samuel Pepys

After the Great Plague of 1665, fire visited the English capital. The son of a tailor, Samuel Pepys was an official with the Admiralty. He was also an assiduous diarist, recording entries daily from 1660 until 1669, when his eyesight failed him. Written in shorthand code, the diary was not deciphered until 1825.

Diary: 1666, September 2 (Lord's day). Some of our maids sitting up late last night to get things ready against our feast to-day, Jane called us up about three in the morning, to tell us of a great fire they saw in the City. So I rose, and slipped on my night-gown, and went to her window; and thought it to be on the backside of Mark Lane at the farthest; but being unused to such fires as followed, I thought it far enough off; and so went to bed again, and to sleep. About seven rose again to dress myself, and there looked out at the window, and saw the fire not so much as it was, and farther off. So to my closet to set things to rights, after yesterday's cleaning. By and by Jane comes and tells me that she hears that above 300 houses have been burned down to-night by the fire we saw, and that it is now burning down all Fish Street, by London Bridge. So I made myself ready presently, and walked to the Tower; and there got up upon one of the high places, Sir J. Robinson's little son going up with me; and there I did see the houses at that end of the bridge all on fire, and an infinite great fire on this and the other side the end of the bridge; which, among other people, did trouble me for poor little Michell and our Sarah on the bridge. So down, with my heart full of trouble, to the Lieutenant of the Tower, who tells me that it began this morning in the King's baker's house in Pudding Lane, and that it hath burned down St Magnus's Church and most part of Fish Street already. So I down to the waterside, and there got a boat, and through bridge, and there saw a lamentable fire. Poor Michell's house, as far as the Old Swan, already burned that way, and the fire running farther, that in a very little time it got as far as the Steelyard, while I was there. Everybody endeavouring to remove their goods, and flinging into the river, or bringing them into lighters that lay off; poor people staying in their houses as long as till the very fire touched them, and then running into boats, or clambering from one pair of stairs, by the waterside, to another. And, among other things, the poor pigeons, I perceive, were loath to leave their houses, but hovered about the windows and balconies, till they burned their wings, and fell down. Having stayed, and in an hour's time seen the fire rage every way; and nobody, to my sight, endeavouring to quench it, but to remove their goods, and leave all to the fire; and having seen it get as far as the Steelyard, and the wind mighty high and driving it into the City; and everything, after so long a drought, proving combustible, even the very stones of churches, and, among other things, the poor steeple by which pretty Mrs— lives, and whereof my old schoolfellow Elborough is parson, taken fire in the very top, and there burned till it fell down; I to Whitehall, with a gentleman with me, who desired to go off from the Tower, to see the fire, in my boat; and there up to the King's closet in the Chapel, where people came about me, and I did give them an account dismayed them all, and word was carried in to the King. So I was called for, and did tell the King and Duke of York what I saw; and that unless his Majesty did command houses to be pulled down nothing could stop the fire. They seemed much troubled, and the King commanded me to go to my Lord Mayor from him, and command him to spare no houses, but to pull down before the fire every way. The Duke of York bid me tell him that if he would have any more soldiers he shall; and so did my Lord Arlington afterwards, as a great secret. Here meeting with Captain Cocke, I in his coach, which he lent me, and Creed with me to Paul's; and there walked along Watling Street as well as I could, every creature coming away loaden with goods to save, and here and there sick people carried away in beds. Extraordinary good goods carried in carts and on backs. At last met my Lord Mayor in Canning Street, like a man spent, with a handkercher about his neck. To the King's message he cried, like a fainting woman, "Lord! what can I do? I am spent: people will not obey me. I have been pulling down houses; but the fire overtakes us faster than we can do it." That he needed no more soldiers; and that, for himself, he must go and refresh himself, having been up all night. So he left me, and I him, and walked home, seeing people all almost distracted, and no manner of means used to quench the fire. The houses, too, so very thick thereabouts, and full of matter for burning, as pitch and tar, in Thames Street; and warehouses of oil, and wines, and brandy, and other things. Here I saw Mr Isaac Houblon, the handsome man, prettily dressed and dirty, at his door at Dowgate, receiving some of his brother's things, whose houses were on fire; and, as he says, have been removed twice already; and he doubts, as it soon proved, that they must be in a little time removed from his house also, which was a sad consideration. And to see the churches all filling with goods by people who themselves should have been quietly there at this time. By this time it was about twelve o'clock; and so home, and there find my guests, who were Mr Wood and his wife Barbary Sheldon, and also Mr Moone; she mighty fine, and her husband, for aught I see, a likely man. But Mr Moone's design and mine, which was to look over my closet, and please him with the sight thereof, which he hath long desired, was wholly disappointed; for we were in great trouble and disturbance at this fire, not knowing what to think of it. However, we had an extraordinary good dinner, and as merry as at this time we could be. While at dinner, Mrs Batelier came to enquire after Mr Woolfe and Stanes, who, it seems, are related to them, whose houses in Fish Street are all burned, and they in a sad condition. She would not stay in the fright. Soon as dined, I and Moone away, and walked through the City, the streets full of nothing but people and horses and carts loaden with goods, ready to run over one another, and removing goods from one burned house to another. They now removing out of Canning Street, which received goods in the morning, into Lombard Street, and farther; and, among others, I now saw my little goldsmith, Stokes receiving some friend's goods, whose house itself was burned the day after. We parted at Paul's; he home, and I to Paul's Wharf, where I had appointed a boat to attend me, and took in Mr Carcasse and his brother, whom I met in the street, and carried them below and above bridge to and again to see the fire, which was now got farther, both below and above, and no likelihood of stopping it. Met with the King and Duke of York in their barge, and with them to Queenhithe, and there called Sir Richard Browne to them. Their order was only to pull down houses apace, and so below bridge at the waterside; but little was or could be done, the fire coming upon them so fast. Good hopes there was of stopping it at the Three Cranes above and at Buttulph's Wharf below bridge, if care be used; but the wind carries it into the City, so as we know not by the waterside what it do there. River full of lighters and boats taking in goods, and good goods swimming in the water; and only I observed that hardly one lighter or boat in three that had the goods of a house in, but there was a pair of virginals in it. Having seen as much as I could now, I away to Whitehall by appointment, and there walked to St James's Park; and there met my wife, and Creed, and Wood and his wife, and walked to my boat; and there upon the water again, and to the fire up and down, it still increasing, and the wind great. So near the fire as we could for smoke; and all over the Thames, with one's face in the wind, you were almost burned with a shower of firedrops. This is very true; so as houses were burned by these drops and flakes of fire, three or four, nay, five or six houses, one from another. When we could endure no more upon the water, we to a little alehouse on the Bankside, over against the Three Cranes, and there stayed till it was dark almost, and saw the fire grow; and, as it grew darker, appeared more and more, and in corners and upon steeples, and between churches and houses, as far as we could see up the hill of the City, in a most horrid, malicious, bloody flame, not like the fine flame of an ordinary fire. Barbary and her husband away before us. We stayed till, it being darkish, we saw the fire as only one entire arch of fire from this to the other side the bridge, and in a bow up the hill for an arch of above a mile long: it made me weep to see it. The churches, houses, and all on fire, and flaming at once; and a horrid noise the flames made, and the cracking of houses at their ruin.

ISAAC NEWTON EXPERIMENTS ON LIGHT, CAMBRIDGE, 1666

Sir Isaac Newton

Principally remembered for his discoveries in mathematics and gravity, Newton was also a pioneering researcher in 'Opticks'. His experiments refracting sunlight through a prism eventually led to the construction of reflecting telescopes.

I procured me a Triangular glass-Prisme, to try therewith the celebrated *Phaenomena of Colours*. And in order thereto having darkened my chamber, and made a small hole in my window-shuts, to let in a convenient quantity of the Suns light, I placed my Prisme at his entrance, that it might be thereby refracted to the opposite wall. It was at first a very pleasing divertisement, to view the vivid and intense colours produced thereby; but after a while applying myself to consider them more circumspectly, I became surprised to see them in an *oblong* form; which, according to the received laws of Refraction, I expected should have been *circular*.

And I saw that the light, tending to [one] end of the Image, did suffer a Refraction considerably greater than the light tending to the other. And so the true cause of the length of that Image was detected to be no other, then that *Light* consists of *Rays differently refrangible*, which, without any respect to a difference in their incidence, were, according to their degrees of refrangibility, transmitted towards divers parts of the wall.

Then I placed another Prisme . . . so that the light . . . might pass through that also, and be again refracted before it arrived at the wall. This done, I took the first Prisme in my hand and turned it to and fro slowly about its *Axis*, so much as to make the several parts of the Image . . . successively pass through . . . that I might observe to what places on the wall the second Prisme would refract them.

When any one sort of Rays hath been well parted from those of other kinds, it hath afterwards obstinately retained its colour, notwithstanding my utmost endeavours to change it.

I have refracted it with Prismes, and reflected with it Bodies which in Day-light were of other colours; I have intercepted it with the coloured film of Air interceding two compressed plates of glass; transmitted it through coloured Mediums, and through mediums irradiated with other sorts of Rays, and diversely terminated it; and yet could never produce any new colour out of it.

But the most surprising, and wonderful composition was that of *Whiteness*. There is no one sort of Rays which alone can exhibit this. 'Tis ever compounded, and to its composition are requisite all the aforesaid primary Colours, mixed in a due proportion. I have often with Admiration beheld, that all the Colours of the Prisme being made to converge, and thereby to be again mixed, reproduced light, intirely and perfectly white.

Hence therefore it comes to pass, that *Whiteness* is the usual colour of *Light*; for, Light is a confused aggregate of Rays indued with all sorts of Colours, as they are promiscuously darted from the various parts of luminous bodies.

A NAVAL CUCKOLD SPARED, 28 SEPTEMBER 1675

Henry Teonge

Teonge was a Warwickshire clergyman who, in his fifties, decided to go to sea as a chaplain aboard a man-of-war.

This morning one of our men, viz. Skinner, a known cuckold, for going on shore without leave had his legs tied together, his hands tied to a great rope, and stood on the side of the ship to be hoisted up to the yard arm, and from thence to drop down into the water 3 times: but he looking so very pitifully, and also by the gentlemen's entreaties to the Captain for him, who alleged that he had injuries enough already, as having a wife, a whore and a scold, to injure him at home, *ergo* had the more need to be pitied abroad, was spared.

THE GREAT FROST, LONDON, 1684

John Evelyn

Diary [Sunday] Jan. Ist, 1684. The weather continuing intolerably severe, streetes of booths were set upon the Thames; the air was so very cold and thick, as of many years there had not ben the like. The small pox was very mortal . . .

9th. I went cross the Thames on the ice, now become so thick as to beare not onely streetes of boothes, in which they roasted meate, and had divers shops of wares, quite across as in a towne, but coaches, carts and horses, passed over. So I went from Westminster Stayres to Lambeth, and din'd with the Archbishop . . .

16th. The Thames was fill'd with people and tents, selling all sorts of wares as in the Citty.

24th. The frost continuing more and more severe, the Thames before London was still planted with boothes in formal streetes, all sortes of trades and shops furnish'd and full of commodities, even to a printing presse, where the people and ladyes tooke a fancy to have their names printed, and the day and yeare set down when printed on the Thames: this humour tooke so universally, that 'twas estimated the printer gain'd £5 a day, for printing a line onely, at sixpence a name, besides what he got by ballads, &c. Coaches plied from Westminster to the Temple, and from several other staires to and fro, as in the streetes, sleds, sliding with skeetes, a bull-baiting, horse and coach races, puppet plays and interludes, cookes, tipling, and other lewd places, so that it seem'd to be a bacchanalian triumph or carnival on the water, whilst it was a severe judgement on the land, the trees not onely splitting as if lightning-struck, but men and cattle perishing in divers places, and the very seas so lock'd up with ice, that no vessels could stir out or

come in. The fowles, fish, and birds, and all our exotiq plants and
greenes universally perishing. Many parkes of deer were destroied,
and all sorts of fuell so deare that there were great contributions to
preserve the poore alive. Nor was this severe weather much less
intense in most parts of Europe, even as far as Spaine and the most
southern tracts. London, by reason of the excessive coldnesse of the
aire hindering the ascent of the smoke, was so filled with the
fuliginous steame of the sea-coale, that hardly could one see crosse
the streets, and this filling the lungs with its grosse particles,
exceedingly obstructed the breast, so as one could hardly breath.
Here was no water to be had from the pipes and engines, nor could
the brewers and divers other tradesmen worke, and every moment
was full of disastrous accidents.

Feb. 4th. I went to Says Court to see how the frost had dealt with
my garden, where I found many of the greenes and rare plantes
utterly destroied. The oranges and mirtalls very sick, and rosemary
and laurells dead to all appearance, but ye cypress likely to indure
it.

5th. It began to thaw, but froze againe. My coach crossed from
Lambeth to the Horseferry at Millbank, Westminster. The booths
were almost all taken downe, but there was first a map or landskip
cut in copper representing all the manner of the camp, and the
several actions, sports, and pastimes thereon, in memory of so
signal a frost . . .

8th. The weather was set in to an absolute thaw and raine, but
ye Thames still frozen.

THE GLORIOUS REVOLUTION: WILLIAM OF ORANGE INVADES ENGLAND, OCTOBER–NOVEMBER 1688

Anon

Anxiety over the unconstitutional rule and pro-Catholic policies of James
II led disaffected parliamentarians to invite William of Orange (James II's
Dutch Protestant son-in-law) to invade England.

. . . First you are to take notice that his Highness set sail from
Holland with fifty-one men of war, eighteen fire ships, and about
three hundred and thirty tenders, being ships hired of merchants,
for the carriage of horse and foot, arms, ammunition, &c. The fleet
stood out to sea to the northward, which met with horrid storms for

two days and two nights together; in which bad weather there were lost above five hundred horse, and a vessel parted from the fleet, wherein were four hundred foot, supposed to be lost, but now known to be arrived at the Texel, though grievously shattered and torn by the storm; two of the Prince's principal men of war were forced to new-rig at Helvetsluce.

The Prince, immediately on his return back, informed the States of the condition of the fleet (which was not so damnified as was presented by the vulgar and ignorant) who, thereupon, to lull a great man* asleep, the States, or some one employed by them, ordered that the Haarlem and Amsterdam Courantier should make a dismal story of it, by representing to the world, that the Prince returned with his fleet miserably shattered and torn, having lost nine men of war, and divers others of less concern; a thousand horse ruined; a calenture among the seamen; the loss of Dr. Burnet, and the chief ministers under the Prince; the ill opinion the States had of the expedition; in short, that one hundred thousand pounds would not repair the damage sustained; and, almost next to an impossibility, that the Prince should be in a condition to pursue his design, till the spring . . .

In eight days' time they were all refitted. The signal being given by the discharge of a gun, all the fleet immediately weighed anchor, and stood out at sea, steering their course northwards, all that night; next day upon tide of ebb, they made a stretch, and made a watch above a league, and then stood westward, and lay all night in the same posture, not making two leagues a watch.

In the middle of the night, an advice-boat brought us an account, that the English fleet, consisting of thirty-three sail, lay to the westward of ours. Upon which the Prince fired a gun, which caused a great consternation in the whole fleet; we, having a brisk easterly wind, concluded ourselves to be all ruined; but the small advice-boats, cruising for a more certain account of the English, brought us back word, that, instead of the English fleet, which the former advice had alarmed us with, it was Admiral Herbert with part of our fleet, which had been separated some hours from the body of our fleet. Upon whose arrival great rejoicing was among us all, and a signal of joy was given for it by the Prince.

In the morning, about eight, the Prince gave a signal, that the

* i.e. James II.

Admiral should come a-board him. Immediately after the whole fleet was got into the North Foreland, upon which the Prince gave the usual sign (according to the printed book), and ordered that the fleet should all come up in a body, some fifteen or sixteen deep, his Highness leading the van in the ship the Brill (in English, Spectacles): his flag was English colours, the motto impaled thereon, was, 'The Protestant Religion, and the Liberties of England', and underneath, instead of *Dieu & mon droit*, was, 'And I will maintain it'.

The council of war, from on board the Prince, sent three small frigates into the mouth of the Thames . . . who, on their return, brought us word, that the English fleet lay in the Buoy of the Nore, consisting of thirty-four sail, and three more which lay in the Downs. The wind continuing at E.N.E.

The Prince immediately thereupon gave another signal of stretching the whole fleet in a line, from Dover to Calais, twenty-five deep. This sight would have ravished the most curious eyes of Europe: when our fleet was in its greatest splendour, the trumpets and drums playing various tunes to rejoice our hearts; this continued for above three hours.

Immediately after, the Prince gave us a sign to close, and sailed that night as far as Beach, and commanded us to follow the signal by lights he had hung out to us, viz. all the small sail should come up to him by morning.

By the morning we espied the Isle of Wight, and then the Prince ordered the fleet to be drawn into the same posture, as before related . . . about five in the morning we made the Start, the wind chopping about to the westward; upon which we stood fair by Dartmouth, and so made for Torbay, where the Prince again ordered the whole fleet into the same posture as at Dover and Calais.

Upon his arrival at Torbay, the people on land, in great numbers, welcomed his Highness with loud acclamations of joy.

Immediately after the Prince gave two signals, that the Admirals should come aboard him, which they did: and then ordered, that the whole fleet should come to anchor, and immediately land; and further ordered that the Admirals should stand out at sea, as a guard, as well as the smaller men of war, to attend and guard their landing; and also ordered six men of war to run in, to guard Torbay.

The Prince then put out a red flag at the mizzen-yard-arm, and provided to land in sixty boats, laid ready for that purpose. Upon which the Prince signified that General Mackay with his six regiments of English and Scotch should first land; also, that the little Porpus, with eighteen guns, should run aground, to secure their landing; but there was no opposition; for the people bid us heartily welcome to English, and gave us all manner of provisions for our refreshment.

The fifth of November (a day never to be blotted out of the Englishman's heart) the Prince caused to be landed about two thousand. On the sixth we landed as many horse and foot as we could possibly, and so it continued the seventh: the country bringing in all manner of provision, both for man and horse, and were paid their price honestly for it.

The Prince the same day commanded Captain M— to search the Lady Cary's house, at Tor-Abbey, for arms and horses, and so all other houses which were Roman Catholicks. The Lady, entertaining them civilly, said her husband was gone to Plymouth. They brought from thence some horses and a few arms, but gave no further disturbance to the Lady or her house. Nor shall it be forgotten what was faithfully acted at this Lady's house, immediately on our arrival at Torbay: There were a priest and some others with him on a watch-tower, to discover what our fleet was, whether French or Dutch. At last they discovered the white flags on some of our men of war; the ignorant priest concluded absolutely we were the French fleet, which, with great impatience, they had so long expected; and having laid up great provisions for their entertainment; the priest ordered all to the chapel to sing *Te Deum*, for the arrival of their supposed forces; but being soon undeceived on our landing, we found the benefit of their provisions; and instead of *Vostre Serviteur Monsieur*, they were entertained with *Yeen Mynbeer*, Can you Dutch spraken? Upon which they all ran away from the house, but the Lady and a few old servants . . .

November the eighth, the Prince came from Chudleigh towards Exeter, with the greatest part of his army attending him; and about one of the clock entered at the west-gate of the city, welcomed with loud acclamations by the people.

THE GLORIOUS REVOLUTION: JAMES II FALLS, NOVEMBER–DECEMBER 1688

John Evelyn

Diary Nov 14. The Prince increases every day in force. Several Lords go in to him. Lord Cornburry carries some regiments, marches to Honiton, the Prince's headquarters. The City of London in disorder; the rabble pulled down the Nunnery newly bought by the Papists of Lord Berkeley at St. John's. The Queen prepares to go to Portsmouth for safety, to attend the issue of this national commotion, which has a dreadful aspect.

18. It was now very hard frost. The King goes to Salisbury to rendezvous the army, and returns to London. Lord Delamere appears for the Prince in Cheshire. The Nobility meet in Yorkshire. The Archbishop of Canterbury and some Bishops, and such Peers as were in London, address his Majesty to call a Parliament. The King invites all foreign nations to come over. The French take all the Palatinate, and alarm the Germans more than ever.

29. I went to the Royal Society. We adjourned the election of a President to 23 April by reason of the public commotions, yet dined together as of custom this day.

Dec. 2. Dr. Tenison preached at St. Martin's on 36 Psalm 5, 6, 7, concerning Providence. I received the blessed Sacrament. Afterwards visited my Lord Godolphin, then going with the Marquess of Halifax and Earl of Nottingham as Commissioners to the Prince of Orange; he told me they had little power. Plymouth declared for the Prince. Bath, York, Hull, Bristol, and all the eminent nobility and persons of quality through England, declare for the Protestant religion and laws, and go to meet the Prince, who every day sets forth new declarations against the Papists. The great favourites at Court, Priests and Jesuits, fly or abscond. Everything, till now concealed, flies abroad in public print, and is cried about the streets. Expectation of the Prince coming to Oxford. The Prince of Wales and great treasure sent privily to Portsmouth, the Earl of Dover being Governor. Address from the Fleet not grateful to his Majesty. The Papists in offices lay down their commissions, and fly. Universal consternation amongst them; it looks like a Revolution.

7. My son went towards Oxford. I returned home.

9. Lord Sunderland meditates flight. The rabble demolished all Popish Chapels, and several Papist Lords and gentlemen's houses, especially that of the Spanish Ambassador, which they pillaged, and burnt his Library.

13. The King flies to sea, puts in at Faversham for ballast; is rudely treated by the people; comes back to Whitehall.

The Pr. of Orange is advanced to Windsor, is invited by the King to St. James's, the messenger sent was the Earl of Faversham,

the General of the Forces, who going without trumpet or passport
is detained prisoner by the Prince, who accepts the invitation, but
requires his Majesty to retire to some distant place, that his own
guards may be quartered about the Palace and City. This is taken
heinously, and the King goes privately to Rochester; is persuaded
to come back; comes on the Sunday; goes to mass, and dines in
public, a Jesuit saying grace. (I was present.)

17. That night was a Council; his Majesty refuses to assent to all
the proposals; goes away again to Rochester.

18. I saw the King take barge to Gravesend at 12 o'clock – a sad
sight! The Prince comes to St. James's, and fills Whitehall with
Dutch guards. A council of Peers meet about an expedient to call a
Parliament; adjourn to the House of Lords. The Chancellor, Earl
of Peterborough, and divers others taken. The Earl of Sunderland
flies; Sir Edward Hales, Walker and others, taken and secured.

All the world go to see the Prince at St. James's, where there is a
great Court. There I saw him, and several of my acquaintance who
came over with him. He is very stately, serious and reserved. The
English soldiers sent out of town to disband them; not well pleased.

24. The King passes into France, whither the Queen and Child
were gone a few days before.

26. The Peers and such Commoners as were Members of the
Parliament at Oxford, being the last of Charles II meeting, desire
the Pr. of Orange to take on him the disposal of the public revenue
till a Convention of Lords and Commons should meet in full body,
appointed by his circular letters to the Shires and Boroughs, *22 Jan*.
– I had now quartered upon me a Lieutenant Col. and 8 horses.

30. This day Prayers for the Prince of Wales were first left off in
our Church.

Part Four

The Age of Empire
1689–1899

"Fix bayonets and die like British soldiers do"
> Last order given to British troops
> at Isandhlwana, Zululand, 1879

INTRODUCTION

The Revolution of 1688 was Glorious, of course, because it was bloodless. The stability of Britain was hardly affected, while William's financial dependence on Parliament – made even greater when he dragged Britain into the European War against France and Spain – ensured his promises to curtail the royal prerogative were kept. His successors, despite their absolutist inclinations, fared little better. Indeed, the next century saw the flourishing of Parliament, the growth of parliamentary politics and, in the career of Robert Walpole between 1721 and 1742, the establishment of the office of Prime Minister.

Not everyone was delighted by the rise and rise of Parliament. Or the consolidation of Anglicanism. The loyalty of the Tories was strained and even snapped by the passing of the throne to the Lutheran Hanoverians in 1714. Many Tories turned secret "Jacobite" (that is, supporters of James II); however the rebellions of 1715 and 1745 to restore the Stuarts to the throne came to nought. The Hanoverians might have been German and unpopular, but the mass of the British had little wish to upset the national apple-cart.

And the apple-cart was doing very nicely. By a combination of naval mastery, credit expansion (the Bank of England was founded in 1694), mercantilist expertise, Britain had developed a network of trading posts and colonies across the world. Further use of military power wrested Canada – by the battle of Quebec, 1759 – and much of India from France. Trade, colonies and the navy formed a tryptych of mutual love and massage.

All this was enough to establish Britain as the pre-eminent nation in the world by the mid eighteenth century. But there was more to come. Already Britain was on the eve of the Industrial Revolution and, with it, super-power status.

Why Britain entered the Industrial Revolution first among the nations of the world has been explained by everything from Providence to native wit to the reinvestment of the hyper-profits of slave-and-sugar trading. Certainly the lack of internal customs barriers, especially after the 1707 Act of Union played a part, so did the natural abundance of coal and iron, as did a growing population which stimulated consumer spending. (The population of Britain rose from 9 million in 1700 to 16 million in 1800, more because of better sanitation and diet than through a rise in the birth rate, the with improved diet underpinned by agricultural improvements and increased cultivation of the potato.) Whatever, enormous capital investment by the City of London moneymen in the machine inventions of James Watt (the steam engine, 1765), Edmund Cartwright (the power loom, 1785) et al, begat the factory system, the spread of communications (roads, canals, rail) and the domination of town over country, as rural people flocked to the new urban centres.

For almost a century and a half, Britain retained its lead in the Industrial Revolution. At its peak, around 1860, Britain produced 53 per cent of the world's coal and traded 40 per cent of the world's goods. This on just 2 per cent of the globe's population.

Deep pockets also paid for the winning of wars. Aside from the military genius of Nelson and Wellington, Britain emerged triumphant in the close-run Napoleonic conflict because it was better able to finance the job. Bonaparte defeated, British forces successively seized and held more and more of the globe, until in the reign of Victoria (1837–1901) one quarter of the map was pink – the largest empire the world had ever known.

Imperial triumph brought an overweening self-confidence to Victorian society. Architects threw up enormous, imposing monuments to Britannia's glory. Robert Peel dropped protectionism for free trade in the pure knowledge that Great Britain Ltd could out-trade any other country, and the Great Exhibition of 1851 advertised Britain as the "Workshop of the World".

The delights of the Great Exhibition at Crystal Place, however, were probably lost on the new industrial working class, crowded into the slums of Britain as wage-slaves for manufacturers. Their piteous condition aroused the sympathy of social reformers like Henry Mayhew and Charles Dickens; their improvement came largely through trade unions and political struggle – the "Tolpuddle Martyrs", the Chartists, and the National Agricultural Labourers Union of Joseph Arch. The struggles of Everyman would continue beyond the Age of Empire and the death of Victoria in 1901. Indeed, the fruits of this struggle – universal extension of the franchise, a welfare state – belonged to another era, the twentieth century.

THE BATTLE OF THE BOYNE, 1 JULY 1690

Reverend Rowland Davies

In 1690, the exiled James II landed in Ireland with the intention of launching a "Jacobite" invasion of the mainland; he was countered by the new monarch, William of Orange, at the river Boyne, north of Dublin. Rowland Davies was chaplain to an Orange cavalry regiment.

June 30th – At two in the morning we decamped again, and marched towards Drogheda, where we found King James encamped on the other (side) of the Boyne; we drew up all our horse in a line opposite him within cannon-shot, and as his Majesty passed our line they fired six shot at him, one whereof fell and struck off the top of the Duke of Wurtemberg's pistol, and the whiskers off his horse, and another tore the King's coat on the shoulder. We stood open during at least twenty shot, until, a man and two horses being killed among the Dutch Guards, we all retired into a trench behind us, where we lay safe while much mischief was done to other regiments, and in the evening drew off and encamped behind the hill.

July 1st – About six in the morning the Earl of Portland marched up the river almost to the bridge of Slane, with the right wing, consisting of twenty-four squadrons of horse and dragoons and six regiments of foot, and at two fords we passed the river where there were six squadrons of the enemy to guard the pass; but, at the first firing of our dragoons and three pieces of cannon that marched with us, they all ran away killing nothing but one of our dragoon's horses. As soon as we passed the river, we saw the enemy marching towards us, and that they drew up on the side of a hill in two lines; the river on their right, and all their horse on the left wing: their foot appeared very numerous, but in horse we far exceeded. Whereupon the Earl of Portland drew us up also in two lines, intermixing the horse and foot by squadron and battalion, and sent away for more foot to enforce us; and thus the armies stood for a considerable time, an impassable bog being between them. At length six regiments of foot more joined us, and we altered our line of battle, drawing all our horse into the right wing: and so outflanking the enemy we marched round the bog and engaged them, rather pursuing than fighting them, as far as Duleek. In the interim Count Solmes with the foot forced the pass under our camp and marched over the river with the Blue Dutch regiment of Guards; no sooner were they up the hill but the enemy's horse fell on them, ours with the King being about half a mile lower passing at another ford. At the first push the front rank only fired and then fell on their faces, loading their muskets again as they lay on the ground; at the next charge they fired a volley of three ranks; then, at the next, the first rank got up and fired again, which being received by a choice squadron of the enemy, consisting mostly of officers, they immediately fell in upon the Dutch as having spent all their front fire; but the two rear ranks drew up in two platoons and flanked the enemy across, and the rest, screwing their swords into their muskets, received the charge with all imaginable bravery and in a minute dismounted them all. The Derry Regiment also sustained them bravely, and as they drew off maintained the same ground with a great slaughter. His Majesty then came up and charged at the head of the Enniskilling horse, who deserted him at the first charge, and carried with them a Dutch regiment that sustained them; but the King's blue troop of Guards soon supplied their place, and with them he charged in person and routed the enemy, and coming over the hill near Duleek appeared on our flank, and, not being known at first, made all our forces halt and draw up again in order, which gave the enemy time to rally also, and draw up on the side of the hill, a bog and river being between us, and then they fired two pieces of cannon on us, but did no mischief; but, as soon as our foot and cannon came up, they marched on, and we after them, but, our foot being unable to march as they did, we could not come up to fight again, but, on the night coming on, were forced to let them go; but had we engaged half an hour sooner, or the day held an hour longer, we had certainly destroyed that army. However we killed the Lord Dungane, Lord Carlingford, Sir Neal O'Neal, and about three thousand others, and lost Duke Schomberg, Dr.

Walker, Colonel Caillimotte, and about three hundred more. We took Lieutenant-General Hamilton and several officers and soldiers prisoners, and, it being very dark, were forced to lie in the field all night with our horses in our hands.

July 2nd – In the morning as soon as it was light we returned to Duleek, where our foot was, and sent a detachment to bring up our baggage from the last camp. In the afternoon six troops of horse and three regiments of foot that came from Munster to join King James appeared on the flank and alarmed us, and, sending two spies to discover who we were, we took and hanged them, the rest marching back without any engagement.

THE MASSACRE OF GLENCOE, 13 FEBRUARY 1692

Anon

Some 38 MacDonalds of Glencoe in Scotland were killed by the Campbell clan for their suspected Stuart (Jacobite) sympathies and delay in taking an oath of allegiance to William of Orange.

Sir,

The Account you desir'd of that strange and surprizing Massacre of *Glenco* take as follows:—

Mac-jan Mac-donald, Laird of *Glenco*, a Branch of the *Mackdonalds*, one of the greatest Clans (or Tribes) in the North of *Scotland*, came with the most considerable Men of his Clan to Coll. *Hill*, Governour of *Fort William* at *Inverlochy*, some few days before the Expiring of the time for receiving the Indemnity appointed by Proclamation, which as I take it, was the First of *January* last, entreating he would administer unto him the *Oaths* which the foresaid Proclamation requir'd to be taken; that so submitting himself to the Government, he might have its Protection. The Colonel receiv'd him with all Expressions of Kindness; nevertheless shifted the administring the *Oaths* to him, alledging that by the Proclamation it did not belong to him, but to the Sheriffs, Bailyffs of Regalities, and Magistrates of Burghs, to administer them. *Mac-jan* Complaining that by this *Disappointment* he might be wrong'd, the Time being now near the Expiring, and the Weather so extreme, and the ways so very bad, that it was not possible for him so soon to reach any Sheriff,

&c. got from Coll. *Hill*, under his Hand, his Protection; and withal he was assur'd, that no Orders from the Government against him should be put in Execution, until he were first advertis'd, and had time allow'd him to apply himself to King or Council for his Safety. But the better to make all sure, (tho' this might have seem'd Security enough for that time) with all dispatch imaginable he posted to *Inverary*, the Chief Town of *Argyleshire*, there he found Sir *Collin Campbel* of *Arakinlis*, Sheriff of that Shire, and crav'd of him the Benefit of the Indemnity, according to the Proclamation, he being willing to perform all the Conditions requir'd. Sir *Collin* at first scrupled to admit him to the Oaths, the Time which the Proclamation did appoint being elapsed by one day, alledging it would be of no use to him then to take them: But *Mac-jan* represented that it was not his Fault, he having come in time enough to Colonel *Hill*, not doubting but he could have administred the Oaths to him, and that upon his refusal he had made such hast to *Inverary*, that he might have come in time enough, had not the extremity of the Weather hinder'd him; and even as it was, he was but one day after the Time appointed; and that would be very unbecoming the Government to take Advantage of a Man's coming late by one Day, especially when he had done his utmost to have come in time. Upon this, and his threatning to protest against the Sheriff for the Severity of this Usage, he administred to him and his Attendants the Oaths, *Mac-jan* depending upon the Indemnity granted to those who should take them; and having so done, he went home, and lived quietly and peaceably under the Government, till the day of his Death.

In *January* last, a Party of the Earl of *Argile's* Regiment came to that Country: the Design of their coming was then suspected to be to take course with those who should stand out, and not submit, and take the Oaths. The Garison of *Inverlochy* being throng'd, and *Glenco* being commodious for quartering, as being near that Garison, those Soldiers were sent thither to Quarter; . . . ere they entered *Glenco*, that Laird, or his Sons, came out to meet them, and asked them if they came as Friends or as Enemies? The Officers answer'd as Friends; and gave their Paroll of Honour, that they would do neither him nor his Concerns any harm; upon which he welcom'd them, promising them the best Entertainment the Place could afford. This he really perform'd, as all the Soldiers confess. He and they lived together in mutual Kindness and Friendship fifteen days or thereabouts; so far was he from fearing any Hurt from them. And the very last Day of his Life he spent in keeping Company with the Commander of that Party, Capt. *Campbell* of *Glenlyon*, playing at Cards with him till 6 or 7 at Night, and at their parting mutual Protestations of Kindness were renew'd. Some time that very day, but whether before or after their parting, I know not, Capt. *Campbell* had these Orders sent him from Major *Duncanson*, a Copy whereof I here send you.

> "Ballacholis, *Feb.* 12, 1692.

"Sir,

"You are hereby ordered to fall upon the Rebels the *Mac-Donalds* of *Glenco*, and put all to the Sword under 70. You are to have especial Care, that the Old Fox and his Sons do upon no account escape your Hands; You are to secure all the Avenues, that no Man escape: This you are to put in Execution at five a Clock in the Morning precisely, and by that time or very shortly after it, I'll strive to be at you with a stronger Party; If I do not come to you at five, you are not to tarry for me, but to fall on. *This is by the King's* SPECIAL COMMAND, for the Good and Safety of the Country, that these Miscreants may be cut off, Root and Branch. See that this be put in Execution without Feud or Favour, else you may expect to be Treated as not true to the King or Government, nor a Man fit to carry Commission in the King's Service. Expecting you will not fail in the fulfilling hereof, as you love your self. I subscribe these with my Hand,

> "ROBERT DUNCANSON.

"For Their Majesties Service, to Capt. *Robert Campbell* of *Glenlyon*."

. . . The Soldiers being disposed five or three in a House, according to the Number of the Family they were to Assassinate, had their Orders given them secretly. They had been all receiv'd as Friends by those poor people, who intended no Evil themselves, and little suspected that their Guests were design'd to be their Murtherers. At 5 a Clock in the Morning they began their bloody Work, Surpris'd and Butcher'd 38 Persons, who had kindly receiv'd them under their Roofs. *Mac-jan* himself was Murther'd, and is much bemoan'd; He was a stately well-favour'd Man, and of good Courage and Sense: As also the Laird *Archintrikin*, a Gentleman of more than ordinary Judgment and Understanding, who had submitted to the Government, and had Coll. *Hill's* Protection in his Pocket, which he had got three Months before. I cannot without Horror represent how that a Boy about Eight Years of Age was murthered; he seeing what was done to others in the House with him, in a terrible Fright run out of the House, and espying Capt. *Campbell*, grasp'd him about the Legs, crying for Mercy, and offering to be his Servant all his Life. I am informed Capt. *Campbell* inclined to spare him; but one *Drummond*, an Officer, barbarously run his Dagger through him; whereof he died immediately, The rehearsal of several Particulars and Circumstances of this Tragical Story, makes it appear most doleful; as that *Mac-jan* was killed as he was drawing on his Breeches, standing before his Bed, giving Orders to his Servants for the good Entertainment of those who murthered him; While he was speaking the Words, he was shot through the Head, and fell dead in his Ladies Arms, who through the Grief of this and other bad Usages she met with, died the next day. It is not to be omitted, that most of those poor People were killed when they were asleep, and none was allowed to pray to *God* for Mercy. Providence ordered it so, that that Night was most boisterous; so as a Party of 400 Men, who should have come to the other End of the *Glen*, and begun the like work there at the same Hour, (intending that the poor Inhabitants should be enclosed, and none of them escape) could not march at length, until it was 9 a Clock, and this afforded to many an Opportunity of escaping, and none were killed but those in whose Houses *Campbell* and *Glenlyon's* Men were Quartered, otherwise all the Male under 70 Years of Age, to the number of 200, had been cut off, for that was the Order; and it might have been easily executed, especially considering that the Inhabitants had no Arms at that time; for upon the first hearing that the Soldiers were coming to the *Glen*, they had conveyed them all out of the way: For though they relyed on the promises which were made them for their Safety; yet they thought it not improbable that they might be disarmed. I know not whether to impute it to difficulty of distinguishing the difference of a few Years, or to the fury of the Souldiers, who being once glutted with *Blood*, stand at nothing, that even some above Seventy Years of Age were destroyed. They set all the Houses on Fire, drove off all the Cattle to the Garison of *Inverlochy, viz*. 900 Cows, 200 Horses, and a great many Sheep and Goats, and there they were divided amongst the Officers. And how dismal may you imagine the Case of the poor Women and Children was then! It was lamentable, past expression; their Husbands and Fathers, and near Relations were forced to flee for their Lives; they themselves almost stript, and nothing left them, and their Houses being burnt, and not one House nearer than six Miles; and to get thither they were to pass over Mountains, and Wreaths of Snow, in a vehement Storm, wherin the greatest part of them perished through Hunger and Cold. . . .

There is enough of this mournful Subject.

TRIAL FOR WITCHCRAFT, ESSEX, 1699

John Bufton

Although England escaped the worst excesses of the great witch-hunt, which began in the Western world in the fifteenth century, there were isolated trials for witchcraft as late as the 1690s (as there were in America, notably at Salem) and early 1700s.

Diary: 1699, July 13. The widow Comon was put into the river to see if she would sink, because she was suspected to be a witch – and she did not sink, but swim. And she was tried again July 19, and then she swam again, and did not sink.

24. The widow Comon, was tried a third time by putting her into the river, and she swum and did not sink.

Dec. 27. The widow Comon, that was counted a witch, was buried.

BATH UNDER THE CODE OF BEAU NASH, c. 1710

Oliver Goldsmith

The dandy Richard "Beau" Nash established Bath as the leading English spa; he also introduced a code of upper-class manners and fashion which was hugely influential in the eighteenth century.

Upon a stranger's arrival at Bath he is welcomed by a peal of the Abbey Bells, and, in the next place, by the voice and music of the city waits. For these civilities, the ringers have generally a present made them of half-a-guinea, and the waits of half-a-crown, or more, in proportion to the person's fortune, generosity, or ostentation. These customs, though disagreeable, are however, liked or they would not continue. The greatest incommodity attending them is the disturbance the bells must give the sick. But the pleasure of knowing the name of every family that comes to town recompenses the inconvenience. Invalids are fond of news, and upon the first sound of the bells everybody sends out to inquire for whom they ring.

After the family is thus welcomed to Bath, it is the custom for the master of it to go to the public places, and subscribe two guineas at the assembly-houses towards the balls and music in pump-house, for which he is entitled to three tickets every ball night. His next subscription is a crown, half-a-guinea, or a guinea, according to his rank and quality, for the liberty of walking in the private walks belonging to Simpson's assembly-house; a crown or half-a-guinea is also given to the booksellers, for which the gentleman is to have what books he pleases to read at his lodgings, and at the coffee-house another subscription is taken for pen, ink, and paper, for such letters as the subscriber shall write at it during his stay. The ladies, too, may subscribe to the booksellers, and to a house by the pump-room, for the advantage of reading the news, and for enjoying each other's conversation.

Things being thus adjusted, the amusements of the day are generally begun by bathing, which is no unpleasing method of passing away an hour or so.

The baths are five in number. On the south-west side of the Abbey Church is the King's Bath, which is an oblong square; the walls are full of niches, and at every corner are steps to descend into it: this bath is said to contain 427 tons and 50 gallons of water; and on its rising out of the ground over the springs, it is sometimes too hot to be endured by those who bathe therein. Adjoining to the King's Bath, there is another, called the Queen's Bath; this is of a more temperate warmth, as borrowing its water from the other.

In the south-west part of the city are three other baths, viz: the Hot Baths, which is not much inferior in heat to the King's Bath, and contains 53 tons, 2 hogsheads, and 11 gallons of water; the Cross Bath, which contains 52 tons, 3 hogsheads, and 11 gallons; and the Leper's Bath, which is not so much frequented as the rest.

The King's Bath (according to the best observations) will fill in about nine hours and a half; the Hot Bath in about eleven hours and a half; and the Cross Bath in about the same time.

The hours for bathing are commonly between six and nine in the morning, and the baths are every morning supplied with fresh water; for when the people have done bathing, the sluices in each bath are pulled up, and the water is carried off by drains into the River Avon.

In the morning the lady is brought in a close chair, dressed in her bathing clothes, to the bath; and, being in the water, the woman who attends presents her with a little floating dish like a basin; into which the lady puts a handkerchief, a snuff-box, and a nosegay. She then traverses the bath; if a novice, with a guide; if otherwise, by herself; and having amused herself thus while she thinks proper, calls for her chair, and returns to her lodgings.

The amusement of bathing is immediately succeeded by a general assembly of people at the pump-room; some for pleasure, and some to drink the hot waters. Three glasses at three different times is the usual portion for every drinker; and the intervals between every glass are enlivened by the harmony of a small band of music, as well as by the conversation of the gay, the witty, or the forward.

From the pump-room the ladies, from time to time, withdraw to a female coffee-house, and from thence return to their lodgings to breakfast. The gentlemen withdraw to their coffee-houses, to read the papers, or converse on the news of the day, with a freedom and ease not to be found in the metropolis.

People of fashion make public breakfasts at the assembly-houses, to which they invite their acquaintances, and they sometimes order private concerts; or, when so disposed, attend lectures on the arts and sciences, which are frequently taught there in a pretty superficial manner, so as not to tease the understanding, while they afford the imagination some amusement. The private concerts are performed in the ball-rooms; the tickets a crown each.

Concert breakfasts at the assembly-houses sometimes make also a part of the morning's amusement here, the expenses of which are defrayed by a subscription among the men. Persons of rank and fortune who can perform are admitted into the orchestra, and find a pleasure in joining with the performers.

Thus we have the tedious morning fairly over. When noon approaches, and church (if any please to go there) is done, some of the company appear upon the parade, and other public walks, where they continue to chat and amuse each other, till they have formed parties for the play, cards, or dancing for the evening.

Another part of the company divert themselves with reading in the booksellers' shops, or are generally seen taking the air and exercise, some on horseback, some in coaches. Some walk in the meadows round the town, winding along the side of the River Avon and the neighbouring canal; while others are seen scaling some of those romantic precipices that overhang the city.

When the hour of dinner draws nigh, and the company are returned from their different recreations, the provisions are generally served with the utmost elegance and plenty. Their mutton, butter, fish, and fowl, are all allowed to be excellent, and their cookery still exceeds their meat.

After dinner is over, and evening prayers ended, the company meet a second time at the pump-house. From this they retire to the walks, and from thence go to drink tea at the assembly-houses, and the rest of the evenings are concluded either with balls, plays, or visits. A theatre was erected in the year 1705, by subscription, by people of the highest rank, who permitted their arms to be engraven on the inside of the house, as a public testimony of their liberality towards it. Every Tuesday and Friday evening is concluded with a public ball, the contributions to which are so numerous, that the price of each ticket is trifling. Thus Bath yields a continued rotation of diversions, and people of all ways of thinking, even from the libertine to the methodist, have it in their power to complete the day with employments suited to their inclinations.

SMALL AD: SLAVE BOY FOR SALE, 9–11 FEBRUARY 1709

The Tatler

A Black Indian Boy, 12 Years of age, fit to wait on a Gentleman, to be disposed of at Denis's Coffee-House in Finch Lane near the Royal Exchange.

BULL-BAITING, 1710

Zacharias von Uffenbach

Von Uffenbach was a German visitor to London.

June 23, 1710: Towards evening we drove to see the bull-baiting, which is held here nearly every Monday in two places. On the morning of the day the bull, or any other creature that is to be baited, is led round. It takes place in a large open space or courtyard, on two sides of which high benches have been made for the spectators. First a young ox or bull was led in and fastened by a long rope to an iron ring in the middle of the yard; then about thirty dogs, two or three at a time, were let loose on him, but he made short work of them, goring them and tossing them high in the air above the height of the first storey. Then amid shouts and yells the butchers to whom the dogs belonged sprang forward and caught their beasts right side up to break their fall. They had to keep fast hold of the dogs to hinder them from returning to the attack without barking. Several had such a grip of the bull's throat or ear that their mouths had to be forced open with poles. When the bull had stood it tolerably long, they brought out a small bear and tied him up in the same fashion. As soon as the dogs had at him, he stood up on his hind legs and gave some terrific buffets; but if one of them got at his skin, he rolled about in such a fashion that the dogs thought themselves lucky if they came out safe from beneath him. But the most diverting and worst of all was a common little ass, who was brought out saddled with an ape on his back. As soon as a couple of dogs had been let loose on him, he broke into a prodigious gallop – for he was free, not having been tied up like the other beasts – and he stamped and bit all round himself. The ape began to scream most terribly for fear of falling off. If the dogs came too near him, he seized them with his mouth and twirled them round, shaking them so much that they howled prodigiously. Finally another bull appeared, on whom several crackers had been hung: when these were lit and several dogs let loose on him on a sudden, there was a monstrous hurly-burly. And thus was concluded this truly English sport, which vastly delights this nation but to me seemed nothing very special.

PUBLIC EXECUTIONS AT TYBURN, c. 1725

C. de Saussure

Some time after my arrival in London I witnessed a spectacle which certainly was not as magnificent or as brilliant as the Lord Mayor's Show; it is true it was quite a different kind of entertainment. I saw thirteen criminals all hanged at the same time. It will interest you, no doubt, to know something about justice in England, how it is practised, how criminals are punished, in what manner they are executed, as here it is done in quite a different way to what it is in other countries.

The day before the execution those who desire it may receive the sacrament, provided the chaplain thinks that they have sincerely repented and are worthy of it. On the day of execution the condemned prisoners, wearing a sort of white linen shirt over their clothes and a cap on their heads, are tied two together and placed on carts with their backs to the horses' tails. These carts are guarded and surrounded by constables and other police officers on horseback, each armed with a sort of pike. In this way part of the town is crossed, and Tyburn, which is a good half-mile from the last suburb, is reached, and here stands the gibbet. One often sees criminals going to their death perfectly unconcerned, others so impenitent that they fill themselves full of liquor and mock at those who are repentant. When all the prisoners arrive at their destination they are made to mount on a very wide cart made expressly for the purpose, a cord is passed round their necks and the end fastened to the gibbet, which is not very high. The chaplain who accompanies the condemned men is also on the cart; he makes them pray and sing a few verses of the Psalms. The relatives are permitted to mount the cart and take fare-well. When the time is up – that is to say about a quarter of an hour – the chaplain and the relations get off the cart, which slips from under the condemned men's feet, and in this way they remain all hanging together. You often see friends and relations tugging at the hanging men's feet so that they should die quicker and not suffer. The bodies and clothes of the dead belong to the executioner; relatives must, if they wish for them, buy them from him, and unclaimed bodies are sold to surgeons to be dissected. You see most amusing scenes between the people who do not like the bodies to be cut up and the messengers the surgeons have sent for the bodies; blows are given and returned before they can be got away, and sometimes in the turmoil the bodies are quickly removed and buried. Again, the populace often come to blows as to who will carry the bought corpses to the parents who are waiting in coaches and cabs to receive them, for the carriers are well paid for their trouble. All these scenes are most diverting, the noise and confusion is unbelievable, and can be witnessed from a sort of amphitheatre erected for spectators near the gibbet.

THE LEEDS CLOTH-MARKET, c. 1725

Daniel Defoe

From *Aberforth* we turned West, and went to *Leeds*, which is a large, wealthy, and populous Town, standing on the North Side of the River *Aire*, with great Suburbs on the South Side, and both joined by a stately, strong, Stone Bridge, so large, and so wide, that formerly the Cloth-market was kept upon it; and therefore the Refreshment given the Clothiers by the Inn-keepers (being a Pot of Ale, a Noggin of Pottage, and a Trencher of boil'd or roast Beef, for Two-pence) is called the *Brigg-shot* to this Day.

The Increase of the Manufactures, and of the Trade, soon made the Market too great to be confined to the *Brigg*; so that it is now kept in the High-street, beginning from the Bridge, and running up North almost to the Market-house, where the ordinary Market for Provisions begins; which also is the greatest of its kind in all the North of *England*. You may judge of the Plenty of it, when 500 Load of Apples have been numbered by the Mayor's Officers in a Day.

But the Cloth-market is chiefly to be admired, as a Prodigy of its Kind, and perhaps not to be equalled in the World. The Market for Serges at *Exeter* is indeed a wonderful Thing, and the Money returned very great; but it is there only once a Week, whereas here it is every *Tuesday* and *Saturday*.

Early in the Morning, Tressels are placed in two Rows in the Street, sometimes two Rows on a Side, cross which Boards are laid, which make a kind of temporary Counter on either Side, from one End of the Street to the other.

The Clothiers come early in the Morning with their Cloth; and, as few bring more than one Piece, the Market-days being so frequent, they go into the Inns and Public-houses with it, and there set it down.

At about Six o'Clock in the Summer, and about Seven in the Winter, the Clothiers being all come by that Time, the Market Bell at the Old Chapel by the Bridge rings; upon which it would surprise a Stranger, to see in how few Minutes, without Hurry, Noise, or the least Disorder, the whole Market is filled, and all the Boards upon the Tressels covered with Cloth, as close to one another as the Pieces can lie longways, each Proprietor standing behind his own Piece, who form a Mercantile Regiment, as it were, drawn up in a double Line, in as great Order as a Military one.

As soon as the Bell has ceased ringing, the Factors and Buyers of all Sorts enter the Market, and walk up and down between the Rows, as their Occasions direct. Some of them have their foreign Letters of Orders, with Patterns sealed on them, in their Hands; the Colours of which they match, by holding them to the Cloths they think they agree to. When they have pitched upon their Cloth, they lean over to the Clothier, and, by a Whisper, in the fewest Words imaginable, the Price is stated; one asks, the other bids; and they agree or disagree in a Moment.

The Reason of this prudent Silence is owing to the Clothiers standing so near to one another; for it is not reasonable, that one Trader should know another's Traffick.

If a Merchant has bidden a Clothier a Price, and he will not take it, he may go after him to his House, and tell him he has considered of it, and is willing to let him have it; but they are not to make any new Agreement for it, so as to remove the Market from the Street to the Merchant's House.

The Buyers generally walk up and down twice on each Side of the Rows, and in little more than an Hour all the Business is done. In less than half an Hour you will perceive the Cloth begin to move off, the Clothier taking it up upon his Shoulder to carry it to the Merchant's House. At about half an Hour after Eight the Market Bell rings again, upon which the Buyers immediately disappear, the Cloth is all sold; or if any remains, it is carried back into the Inn. By Nine o'Clock the Boards and Tressels are removed, and the Street left at Liberty for the Market-people of other Professions, the Linendrapers, Shoemakers, Hard-waremen, and the like.

Thus you see 10 or 20,000*l*. worth of Cloth, and sometimes much more, bought and sold in little more than an Hour, the Laws of the Market being the most strictly observed that I ever saw in any Market in *England*.

If it be asked, How all these Goods at this Place, at *Wakefield*, and at *Halifax*, are vended and disposed of? I would observe,

First, That there is an Home-consumption; to supply which, several considerable Traders in *Leeds* go with Droves of Pack-horses, loaden with those Goods, to all the Fairs and Market-towns almost over the whole Island, not to sell by Retail, but to the Shops by Wholesale; giving large Credit. 'Tis ordinary for one of these Men to carry a thousand Pounds worth of Cloth with him at a time; and, having sold that, to send his Horses back for as much more; and this very often in a Summer; for they travel chiefly at that Season, because of the Badness of the Roads.

There are others, who have Commissions from *London* to buy, or who give Commissions to Factors and Warehouse-keepers in *London* to sell for them, who not only supply all the Shop-keepers and Wholesale Men in London, but sell also very great Quantities to the Merchants, as well for Exportation to the *English* Colonies in *America*, which take off great Quantities of the coarse Goods, especially *New England, New York, Virginia*, &c. as also to the *Russia Merchants*, who send exceeding great Quantities to *Petersburg, Riga, Dantzick, Narva, Sweden*, and *Pomerania*; tho' of late the Manufactures of this kind set up in *Prussia*, and other Northern Parts of *Germany*, interfere a little with them.

The third Sorts are such as receive Commissions from abroad, to buy Cloth for the Merchants chiefly in *Hamburg*, and in *Holland*, &c. These are not only many in Number, but some of them very considerable in their Dealings, and correspond with the farthest Provinces in *Germany*.

A DAY AT THE SEASIDE, BRIGHTON, 22 JULY 1736

William Clarke

We are now sunning ourselves upon the beach at Brighthelmston, and observing what a tempting figure this island must have made formerly in the eyes of those gentlemen who were pleased to civilize and subdue us. The place is really pleasant; I have seen nothing in its way that outdoes it: such a tract of sea, such regions of corn, and such an extent of fine carpet, that gives your eye the command of it all. But then the mischief is, that we have little conversation besides the *clamor nauticus*, which is here a sort of treble to the plashing of the waves against the cliffs. My morning business is, bathing in the sea, and then buying fish; the evening is, riding out for air, viewing the remains of old Saxon camps, and counting the ships in the road – and the boats that are trawling. Sometimes we give the imagination leave to expatiate a little – fancy that you are coming down, and that we intend next week to dine one day at Dieppe in Normandy; the price is already fixed, and the wine and lodging there tolerably good. But, though we build these castles in the air, I assure you we live here almost underground. I fancy the architects here usually take the altitude of the inhabitants, and lose not an inch between the head and the ceiling, and then dropping a step or two below the surface, the second story is finished – something under 12 feet. I suppose this was a necessary precaution against storms, that a man should not be blown out of his bed into New England, Barbary, or God knows where. But, as the lodgings are low, they are cheap: we have two parlours, two bedchambers, pantry, &c. for 5s. per week; and if you really will come down, you need not fear a bed of proper dimensions. And then the coast is safe, the cannons all covered with rust and grass, the ships moored – no enemy apprehended. Come and see,

> "*Nec tela timeres*
> *Gallica, nec Pictum tremeres, nec littore toto*
> *Prospiceres dubiis venturum Saxona ventis.*"

My wife does not forget her good wishes and compliments upon this occasion. How would you surprise all your friends in Fleet Street, to tell them that you were just come from France, with a vivacity that everybody would believe to be just imported from thence!

Later.

We are now about taking our leave of that very variable element the sea. After it had smiled upon us for a month, it is at present so black and angry, that there is no seeing or approaching it. It is all either fog or foam; and I truly pity everybody who cannot fly from it. We had this morning some hopes of entertaining your Society with our discoveries upon the beach. The sea had thrown up a piece of an old coin, grown green with salt water: but, instead of an Otho's head, it proved only a fragment of Charles I. Pray let me know which way your researches run at present in that Society. We have here a very curious old font, covered over with hieroglyphics, representing the two Sacraments, which rise in very bold but bad relievos on each side of it.

JOHN WESLEY PREACHES, 1742–69

John Wesley

Wesley was the founder of Methodism, an evangelical offshoot of the Anglican Church. Following his "conversion" in 1738, Wesley spent 51 years open-air preaching, in the process walking upwards of 250,000 miles.

Friday, March 19, 1742 – I rode once more to Pensford, at the earnest request of several serious people. The place where they desired me to preach was a little green spot near the town. But I had no sooner begun, than a great company of rabble, hired (as we afterwards found) for that purpose, came furiously upon us, bringing a bull which they had been baiting and now drove in among the people. But the beast was wiser than his drivers, and continually ran either on one side of us or the other, while we quietly sang praise to God and prayer for about an hour. The poor wretches finding themselves disappointed, at length seized upon the bull, now weak and tired after being so long torn and beaten both by dogs and men, and by main strength partly dragged and partly thrust him in among the people. When they had forced their way to the little table on which I stood, they strove several times to throw it down by thrusting the helpless beast against it, who of himself stirred no more than a log of wood. I once or twice put aside his head with my hand, that the blood might not drop upon my clothes, intending to go on as soon as the hurry should be a little over. But the table falling down, some of our friends caught me in their arms and carried me right away on their shoulders, while the rabble wreaked their vengeance on the table which they tore bit from bit. We went a little way off, where I finished my discourse without any noise or interruption.

Wednesday, June 9, 1742 – I rode over to a neighbouring town to wait upon a Justice of Peace, a man of candour and understanding, before whom their angry neighbours had carried a whole waggon-load of these new heretics. But when he asked what they had done there was a deep silence; for that was a point their conductors had forgot. At length one said, "Why, they pretended to be better than other people. And besides, they prayed from morning to night." Mr. S. asked, "But have they done nothing besides?" "Yes, Sir," said an old man, "An't please your worship, they have *converted* my wife. Till she went among them she had such a tongue! And now she is as quiet as a lamb." "Carry them back, carry them back", replied the Justice, "and let them convert all the scolds in the town".

Thursday, April 17, 1743. As I was preaching at Pelton, one of the colliers, not much accustomed to things of this kind, in the middle of the sermon began shouting amain for mere satisfaction and joy of heart. But their usual token of approbation (which somewhat surprised me at first) was clapping me on the back.

Wednesday, October 18, 1749. I rode, at the desire of John Bennet, to Rochdale, in Lancashire. As soon as ever we entered the town, we found the streets lined on both sides with multitudes of people, shouting, cursing, blaspheming and gnashing upon us with their teeth. Perceiving it would not be practicable to preach abroad, I went into a large room, open to the street and called aloud "Let the wicked forsake his way, and the unrighteous man his thoughts." . . . None opposed or interrupted; and there was a very remarkable change in the behaviour of the people as we afterwards went through the town.

We came to Bolton about five in the evening. We had no sooner entered the main street than we perceived the lions at Rochdale were lambs in comparison of those at Bolton. Such rage and bitterness I scarce ever saw before in any creatures that bore the form of men. They followed us in full cry to the house where we went and, as soon as we were gone in, took possession of all the avenues to it, and filled the street from one end to the other. . . . When the first stone came among us through the window, I expected a shower to follow, and the rather because they had now procured a bell to call their whole forces together; but they did not design to carry on the attack at a distance. Presently one ran up and told us the mob had bursted into the house; he added that they had got J[ohn] B[ennet] in the midst of them. They had; and he laid hold on the opportunity to tell them of "the terrors of the Lord".

Meantime D[avid] T[aylor] engaged another part of them with smoother and softer words. Believing the time was now come, I walked down into the thickest of them. They had now filled all the rooms below. I called for a chair. The winds were hushed and all was calm and still. My heart was filled with love, my eyes with tears, and my mouth with arguments. They were ashamed that they were melted down, they devoured every word.

1753, Aug. 28 (Tues.). I reached Cardiff. Finding I had all here to begin anew, I set out as at first, by preaching in the Castle Yard on

"Lord, are there few that be saved?" I afterwards met what was once a society, and in the morning spoke severally to a few who were still desirous to join together, and build up, not devour, one another.

I preached in the evening at Fonmon, and on *Thursday* the 30th spake to many at Cardiff who were resolved to set out once more in the Bible-Way and strengthen each other's hands in God.

31 (Fri.). We had a pleasant ride and a ready passage; so that we reached Bristol in the afternoon. I preached in the evening over the remains of Mary Henley, a good soldier of Jesus Christ, who died rejoicing in His love the same day I set out for Cardiff.

Sept. 3 (Mon.). I began visiting the little societies in Somerset-shire and Wiltshire. This evening I preached at Shepton Mallet, and found much life among the poor plain people. It was not so at Oakhill the next day, where many once alive have drawn back to perdition. But at Coleford, in the evening, I found many living souls, though joined with some who did not adorn the gospel.

5 (Wed.). I rode over to Kingswood, a little town near Wotton-under-Edge. Some weeks since W— S— was invited to preach at Wotton; which he did once, in great peace. But the next time he went the mob was so turbulent that he could not finish his sermon, upon which one desired him to come to Kingswood; which he did, and many people heard him gladly. Soon after I came in, a multitude of people was gathered from all parts. A large congregation was there at five in the morning, and a larger than ever in the evening. The next morning I accepted of Mr. Baylis's offer, and after reading prayers, preached at the church. All the people expressed huge good-will, but none appeared to be deeply affected.

At half an hour after twelve I preached in the street at Wickwar, about four miles from Kingswood, where there was a small society for some years, many of whom can rejoice in God. The rest of the audience gave a civil attention, and seemed little pleased or displeased at the matter.

10 (Mon.). I preached to condemned malefactors in Newgate, but I could make little impression upon them. I then took horse for Paulton, where I called on Stephen Plummer, one of our society, but now a zealous Quaker. He was much pleased with my calling, and came to hear me preach. Being straitened for time, I concluded sooner than usual; but as soon as I had done Stephen began. After I had listened half an hour, finding he was no nearer the end, I rose up to go away. His sister then begged him to leave off, on which he flew into a violent rage, and roared louder and louder, till an honest man took him in his arms and gently carried him away.

What a wise providence was it that this poor young man turned Quaker some years before he ran mad! So the honour of turning his brain now rests upon them, which otherwise must have fallen upon the Methodists.

March 1 (Sun.). We had a happy love feast at the chapel. Many of our brethren spoke plainly and artlessly what God had done for their souls. I think none were offended; but many were strengthened and comforted.

4 (Wed.). I was scarce come into the room where a few believers were met together when one began to tremble exceedingly, and soon after sunk to the floor. After a violent struggle she burst out into prayer, which was quickly changed into praise. She then declared, "The Lamb of God has taken away all my sins." She spoke many strong words to the same effect, rejoicing with joy unspeakable.

6 (Fri.). I met again with those who believe God has delivered them from the root of bitterness. Their number increases daily. I know not if fifteen or sixteen have not received the blessing this week.

9 (Mon.). I set out early and about noon preached at High Wycombe, where the dry bones begin to shake again. In the afternoon I rode on to Oxford, and spent an agreeable evening with Mr. H. His openness and frankness of behaviour were both pleasing and profitable. Such conversation I want; but I do not wonder it is offensive to men of nice ears.

10 (Tues.). We rode to Evesham, where I found the poor shattered society almost sunk to nothing. And no wonder, since they have been almost without help, till Mr. Mather came. In the evening I preached in the town hall. Both at this time and at five in the morning God applied His word, and many found a desire to "strengthen the things that remained." I designed to have rested on *Wednesday* but finding that notice had been given of my preaching at Stanley we got thither through roads almost impassable, about noon, and found more people than the house could contain; so I stood in the yard, and proclaimed free salvation to a loving, simple people. Several were in tears, and all of them so thankful that I could not repent of my labour.

The congregation at Evesham in the evening was thrice as large as the night before. Indeed many of them did not design to hear, or to let any one else hear; but they were over-ruled, and behaved with tolerable decency till the service was over. Then they roared amain; but I walked straight through them, and none offered the least rudeness.

Sunday, May 6, 1750 [Athlone]. . . . In the midst of the sermon, a man with a fine curveting horse drew off a large part of the audience. I paused a little, and then, raising my voice, said, "If there are any more of you who think it is of more concern to see a dancing horse than to hear the Gospel of Christ, pray go after them." They took the reproof; the greater part came back directly and gave double attention.

Tuesday, 19 September, 1769 – Between twelve and one I preached at Freshford, and on White's Hill, near Bradford, in the evening. I had designed to preach there again the next evening, but a gentleman in the town desired me to preach at his door. The beasts of the people were tolerably quiet till I had nearly finished my sermon. Then they lifted up their voice, especially one, called a gentleman, who had filled his pocket with rotten eggs. But a young man coming unawares, clapped his hands on each side and mashed them all at once. In an instant he was perfume all over, though it was not so sweet as balsam!

DRAWING THE BOUNDARIES: THE RULES OF CRICKET, 1744

Anon

The earliest surviving rules of cricket were drawn up by gentleman players at the Artillery Ground in Islington, London.

The Pitch

The pitching of ye first Wicket is to be determined by ye cast of a Piece of Money. When ye first Wicket is pitched & the Popping Crease cut, which must be exactly 3 Feet 10 inches from the Wicket, ye other Wicket is to be pitched directly opposite at 22 yards Distance & ye other Popping Crease cut 3 Feet 10 Inches before it. The Bowling Creases must be cut in a direct line from each Stump. Ye stumps must be 22 Inches long & ye Bail 6 Inches. Ye Ball must weigh between 5 & 6 Ounces. When ye Wickets are both pitched & all ye creases cut ye Party that wins the toss-up may order which side shall go in first at his Option.

Laws for the Bowlers
Ye Bowler must deliver ye Ball with 1 foot behind ye crease even with ye Wicket & when he has bowled 1 Ball or more shall bowl to ye Number 4 before he changes Wickets & he shall change but once in ye same Innings. He may order ye Player that is in at his Wicket to stand on which side of it he pleases at a reasonable Distance. If he delivers ye Ball with his hinder foot over ye Bowling crease ye Umpire shall call no Ball though she be struck or ye Player is bowled out, which he shall do without being asked and no Person shall have any Right to ask him.

Laws for Wicket Keepers
The Wicket-Keepers shall stand at a reasonable Distance behind ye Wicket & shall not move till ye Ball is out of ye Bowler's Hand & shall not by any noise incommode the Striker & if his Hands, Knees, foot or Head be over or before ye Wicket though ye Ball hit it, it shall not be out.

Bat, Foot, or Hand Over the Crease
When ye ball has been in Hand by one of ye Keepers or Stoppers and ye Player has been at home he may go where he pleases till ye next Ball is bowled. If either of ye Strikers is cross'd in his running Ground designedly, which design must be determined by ye Umpires: NB Ye Umpires may order that Notch to be scor'd. When the Ball is hit up either of ye Strikers may hinder ye catch in his running Ground or if she's hit directly across ye Wickets ye other Player may place his Body any where within ye Swing of the Batt so as to hinder ye Bowler from catching her, but he must neither strike at her nor touch her with his Hands. If a Striker nipps a Ball up just before him he may fall before his Wicket, or pop down his Batt before she comes to save it. The Bail hanging on one Stump, though the Ball hit ye Wicket it's not out.

Laws for the Strikers
If ye Wicket is bowled down it's out. If he strikes or treads down or falls himself upon his Wicket in Striking (but not in over-running) it's out. A Stroke or Nipp over or under his Batt or upon his hands (but not Arms) if ye Ball be held before she touches Ground, though she be

hug'd to ye Body it's out. If in striking both his Feet are over the Popping Crease & his Wicket put down except his Batt is down within it's out. If he runs out [of] his ground to hinder a Catch it's out. If a Ball is nipp'd up & he strikes her again wilfully before she comes to the Wicket it's out. If ye Players have cross'd each other that runs for ye Wicket that is put down is out, if they are not cross'd he that returns is out. If in running a Notch ye Wicket is struck down by a throw before his foot Hand or Batt is over ye Popping crease or a Stump hit by ye Ball though ye Bail was down it's out. But if ye bail is down before, he that catches ye Ball must strike a Stump out of ye Ground Ball in hand, then it's out. If ye Striker touches or takes up ye Ball before she is lain quite still unless asked by ye Bowler or Wicket-Keeper it's out.

Laws for the Umpires

To allow 2 Minutes for each Man to come in when one is out, & 10 Minutes between each Hand. To mark ye Ball that it may not be changed. They are sole judges of all Outs and In's, of all fair & unfair Play or frivolous Delays, of all Hurts whether real or pretended & discretionally to allow what Time they think proper before ye Game goes on again. In case of a real Hurt to a Striker they are to allow another to come in & ye Person hurt to come in again. But are not to allow a fresh Man to Play on either Side on any Acount. They are sole Judges of all Hindrances, crossing ye Players in running & standing unfair to strike & in Case of Hindrance may order a Notch to be scor'd. They are not to order any Man out unless appeal'd to by any 1 of ye Players. These laws are to ye Umpires jointly. Each Umpire is ye sole Judge of all Nips & Catches, Ins & Outs, good or bad Runs at his own Wicket & his determination shall be absolute & he shall not be chang'd for another Umpire without ye Consent of both Sides. When ye 4 Balls are bowl'd he is to call over. These Laws are separately. When both Umpires shall call Play 3 Times 'at ye Peril of giving ye Game from them that refuse to Play.

BONNIE PRINCE CHARLIE INVADES MANCHESTER, 26–29 NOVEMBER 1745

Elizabeth Byrom

In the last Stuart attempt to regain the thrones of Scotland and England, Charles Edward Stuart, the young pretender, landed in Scotland in July 1745 and led an army of sympathisers southwards.

1745, Nov. 26. They are at Preston this morning, came in there at ten o'clock, behaved very civilly; everybody is going out of town and sending all their effects away, there is hardly any family left but ours and our kin; they have sent their shops and shut up shop, and all the warehouses in town almost are empty, tonight the bellman is going about to forbid anybody sending provision out of town, for a great many have today; Dr. Mainwaring says the rebels have done nothing but what a rabble without a head might have done.

They pulled up Stockport bridge and Barton bridge, and we expect every minute they will begin at Salford bridge (they have begun at Cross Street), if they do, some folks say they will set the fire bells of ringing to raise a mob to stop them. Last Sunday Mr. Lewthwaite preached, and his text was, "He that has no sword, let him sell his garment and buy one"; about a fortnight since his text was, "Is thy servant a dog that he should do this thing?" I have been laughing at him tonight about it.

27. The postmaster is gone to London today, we suppose to secure the money from falling into the hands of the rebels; we expect a party of them here tomorrow. The Prince lay at Lawyer Starkey's at Preston last night; he has marched from Carlisle on foot at the head of his army; he was dressed in a Scotch plaid, a blue silk waistcoat with silver lace, and a Scotch bonnet with J. R. on it. My aunt Ann is gone to Dr. Dunster's and Mrs. Mainwaring; Mr. Hoole is dead. Tonight there's not above four women hardly left in the Square. Mr. H. Goddard is left in Mrs. Wilson's house; I just called there. Mr. W. Blackburn and Coz Wright drank tea here this afternoon.

Yesterday the militia was all discharged and sent home, but just in time before the Highlanders come, – well contrived.

28 (Thursday). About three o'clock today came into town two men in Highland dress, and a woman behind one of them with a drum on her knee, and for all the loyal work that our Presbyterians have made, they took possession of the town as one may say, for immediately after they were 'light they beat up for volunteers for Prince Charles: "All gentlemen that have a mind to serve His Royal Highness Prince Charles with a willing mind, etc., five guineas advance," and nobody offered to meddle with them. They were directly joined by Mr. J. Bradshaw, Tom Lydall, Mr. Tom Deacon, Mr. Fletcher, Tom Chaddock, and several others have listed, above eighty men by eight o'clock, when my papa came down to tell us there was a party of horse come in; he took care of me to the Cross, where I saw them all; it is a very fine moonlight night; Mr. Walley, Mr. Foden and Deputy billeted them. They are my Lord Pitsligo's Horse, and Hugh Sterling, that was 'prentice at Mr. Hibbert's, is with them, and the streets are exceeding quiet, there is not one person to be seen nor heard. One of the Highlanders that came today is a Yorkshireman, and is gone tonight to see his sister that lives at Sleat Hall; he took his drawn sword in his hand and went by himself. My papa and my uncle are gone to consult with Mr. Croxton, Mr. Feilden and others, how to keep themselves out of any scrape, and yet behave civilly. All the justices fled and lawyers too but Coz Clowes.

29 (Friday). They are beating up for the Prince; eleven o'clock we went up to the Cross to see the rest come in; there came small parties of them till about three o'clock, when the Prince and the main body of them came, I cannot guess how many. The Prince went straight up to Mr. Dickenson's, where he lodges, the Duke of Athol at Mr. Marsden's, the Duke of Perth at Gartside's. There came an officer up to us at Cross and gave us the manifests and declarations; the bells they rung, and P. Cotterel made a bonfire, and all the town was illuminated, every house except Mr. Dickenson's, my papa mamma and sister, and my uncle and I walked up and down to see it; about four o'clock the King was proclaimed, the mob shouted very cleverly, and then we went up to see my aunt Brearcliffe and stayed till eleven o'clock making St. Andrew's crosses for them; we sat up making till two o'clock. Miss Vigor lies here.

Stuart then marched on Derby, before retreating; his army was destroyed at Culloden in April 1746, but the young pretender himself escaped to France.

THE EFFECTS OF AN EARTHQUAKE, LONDON, APRIL 1750

Horace Walpole

You will not wonder so much at our earthquakes as at the effects they have had. All the women in town have taken them up upon the foot of *Judgments*; and the clergy, who have had no windfalls of a long season, have driven horse and foot into this opinion. There has been a shower of sermons and exhortations: Secker, the jesuitical Bishop of Oxford, began the mode. He heard the women were all going out of town to avoid the next shock; and so, for fear of losing his Easter offerings, he set himself to advise them to await God's good pleasure in fear and trembling. But what is more astonishing, Sherlock, who has much better sense, and much less of the Popish confessor, has been running a race with him for the old ladies, and has written a pastoral letter, of which ten thousand were sold in two days; and fifty thousand have been subscribed for, since the two first editions.

I told you the women talked of going out of town: several families are literally gone, and many more going to-day and to-morrow; for what adds to the absurdity, is, that the second shock having happened exactly a month after the former, it prevails that there will be a third on Thursday next, another month, which is to swallow up London. I am almost ready to burn my letter now I have begun it, lest you should think I am laughing at you: but it is so true, that Arthur of White's told me last night, that he should put off the last ridotto, which was to be on Thursday, because he hears nobody would come to it. I have advised several, who are going to keep their next earthquake in the country, to take the bark for it, as it is so periodic. Dick Leveson and Mr. Rigby, who had supped and stayed late at Bedford House the other night, knocked at several doors, and in a watchman's voice cried, "Past four o'clock, and a dreadful earthquake!" . . .

This frantic terror prevails so much, that within these three days seven hundred and thirty coaches have been counted passing Hyde Park corner, with whole parties removing into the country. Here is a good advertisement which I cut out of the papers to-day:–

"On Monday next will be published (price 6d.) A true and exact List of all the Nobility and Gentry who have left, or shall leave, this place through fear of another Earthquake."

Several women have made earthquake gowns; that is, warm gowns to sit out of doors all to-night. These are of the more courageous. One woman, still more heroic, is come to town on purpose: she says, all her friends are in London, and she will not survive them. But what will you think of Lady Catherine Pelham, Lady Frances Arundel, and Lord and Lady Galway, who go this evening to an inn ten miles out of town, where they are to play at brag till five in the morning, and then come back – I suppose, to look for the bones of their husbands and families under the rubbish. The prophet of all this (next to the Bishop of London) is a trooper of Lord Delawar's, who was yesterday sent to Bedlam. His *colonel* sent to the man's wife, and asked her if her husband had ever been disordered before. She cried, "Oh dear! my lord, he is not mad now; if your *lordship* would but get any *sensible* man to examine him, you would find he is quite in his right mind." . . .

THE BLACK HOLE OF CALCUTTA, 21 JUNE 1756

J. Z. Holwell

Having captured Calcutta's Fort William, the nawab of Bengal confined 146 British prisoners to the military goal there – the 300-square-foot "Black Hole".

We had been but few minutes confined before every one fell into a perspiration so profuse, you can form no idea of it. This brought on a raging thirst, which increased in proportion as the body was drained of its moisture.

Various expedients were thought of to give more room and air. To obtain the former, it was moved to put off their cloaths; this was approved as a happy motion, and in a few minutes I believe every man was stripped (myself, Mr Court, and the two young gentlemen by me excepted). For a little time they flattered themselves with having gained a mighty advantage; every hat was put in motion to produce a circulation of air, and Mr Baillie proposed that every man should sit down on his hams. This expedient was several times put in practice, and at each time many of the poor creatures, whose natural strength was less than that of others, or who had been more exhausted and could not immediately recover their legs, as others did when the word was given to rise, fell to rise no more; for they were instantly trod to death or suffocated. When the whole body sat down, they were so closely wedged together, that they were obliged to use many efforts before they could put themselves in motion to get up again.

Before nine o'clock every man's thirst grew intolerable, and respiration difficult. Efforts were made again to force the door, but in vain. Many insults were used to the guard to provoke them to fire in upon us. For my own part, I hitherto felt little pain or uneasiness, but what resulted from my anxiety for the sufferings of those within. By keeping my face between two of the bars, I obtained air enough to give my lungs easy play, though my perspiration was excessive, and thirst commencing. At this period, so strong a urinous volatile effluvia came from the prison, that I was not able to turn my head that way, for more than a few seconds at a time.

Now every body, excepting those situated in and near the windows, began to grow outrageous, and many delirious: *Water, water,* became the general cry. And the old Jemmautdaar before mentioned, taking pity on us, ordered the people to bring some skins of water. This was what I dreaded. I foresaw it would prove the ruin of the small chance left us, and essayed many times to speak to him privately to forbid its being brought; but the clamour was so loud, it became impossible. The water appeared. Words cannot paint to you the universal agitation and raving the sight of it threw us into. I flattered myself that some, by preserving an equal temper of mind, might out-live the night; but now the reflection, which gave me the greatest pain, was, that I saw no possibility of one escaping to tell the dismal tale.

Until the water came, I had myself not suffered much from thirst, which instantly grew excessive. We had no means of conveying it into the prison, but by hats forced through the bars; and thus myself and Messieurs Coles and Scott (notwithstanding the pains they suffered from their wounds) supplied them as fast as possible. But those who have experienced intense thirst, or are acquainted with the cause and nature of this appetite, will be sufficiently sensible it could receive no more than a momentary alleviation; the cause still subsisted. Though we brought full hats within the bars, there ensued such violent struggles, and frequent contests to get at it, that before it reached the lips of any one, there would be scarcely a small tea cup full left in them. These supplies, like sprinkling water on fire, only served to feed and raise the flame.

Oh! my dear Sir, how shall I give you a conception of what I felt at the cries and ravings of those in the remoter parts of the prison, who could not entertain a probable hope of obtaining a drop, yet could not divest themselves of expectation, however unavailing! and calling on me by the tender considerations of friendship and affection, and who knew they were really dear to me! Think, if possible, what my heart must have suffered at seeing and hearing their distress, without having it in my power to relieve them: for the confusion now became general and horrid. Several quitted the other window (the only chance they had for life) to force their way to the water, and the throng and press upon the window was beyond bearing; many forcing their passage from the further part of the room, pressed down those in their way, who had less strength, and trampled them to death.

From about nine to near eleven, I sustained this cruel scene and painful situation, still supplying them with water, though my legs were almost broke with the weight against them. By this time I myself was near pressed to death, and my two companions, with Mr William Parker (who had forced himself into the window) were really so . . .

For a great while they preserved a respect and regard to me, more than indeed I could well expect, our circumstances considered; but now all distinction was lost. My friend Baillie, Messrs Jenks, Revely, Law, Buchanan, Simpson, and several others, for whom I had a real esteem and affection, had for some time been dead at my feet: and were now trampled upon by every corporal or common soldier, who, by the help of more robust constitutions, had forced their way to the window, and held fast by the bars over me, till at last I became so pressed and wedged up, I was deprived of all motion.

Determined now to give every thing up, I called to them, and begged, as the last instance of their regard, they would remove the pressure upon me, and permit me to retire out of the window, to die in quiet. They gave way; and with much difficulty I forced a passage into the centre of the prison, where the throng was less by the many dead, (then I believe amounting to one-third) and the numbers who flocked to the windows; for by this time they had water also at the other window.

In the black hole there is a platform corresponding with that in the barrack: I travelled over the dead, and repaired to the further end of it, just opposite to the other window. Here my poor friend Mr Edward Eyre came staggering over the dead to me, and with his usual coolness and good-nature, asked me how I did? but fell and expired before I had time to make him a reply. I laid myself down on some of the dead behind me, on the platform; and, recommending myself to heaven, had the comfort of thinking my sufferings could have no long duration.

My thirst grew now insupportable, and the difficulty of breathing much increased; and I had not remained in this situation, I believe, ten minutes, when I was seized with a pain in my breast, and palpitation of heart, both to the most exquisite degree. These roused and obliged me to get up again; but still the pain, palpitation, thirst, and difficulty of breathing increased. I retained my senses notwithstanding; and had the grief to see death not so near me as I hoped; but could no longer bear the pains I suffered without attempting a relief, which I knew fresh air would and could only give me. I instantly determined to push for the window opposite to me; and by an effort of double the strength I had ever before possessed, gained the third rank at it, with one hand seized a bar, and by that means gained the second, though I think there were at least six or seven ranks between me and the window.

In a few moments the pain, palpitation, and difficulty of breathing ceased; but my thirst continued intolerable. I called aloud for *Water for God's sake*. I had been concluded dead; but as soon as they found me amongst them, they still had the respect and tenderness for me, to cry out, *Give him water, give him water!* nor would one of them at the window attempt to touch it until I had drank. But from the water I had no relief; my thirst was rather increased by it; so I determined to drink no more, but patiently wait the event; and kept my mouth moist from time to time by sucking the perspiration out of my shirt sleeves, and catching the drops as they fell, like heavy rain, from my head and face; you can hardly imagine how unhappy I was if any of them escaped my mouth.

I came into the prison without coat or waistcoat; the season was too hot to bear the former, and the latter tempted the avarice of one of the guards, who robbed me of it, when we were under the Veranda. Whilst I was at this second window, I was observed by one of my miserable companions on the right of me, in the expedient of allaying my thirst by sucking my shirt-sleeve. He took the hint, and robbed me from time to time of a considerable part of my store; though after I detected him, I had even the address to begin on that sleeve first, when I thought my reservoirs were sufficiently replenished; and our mouths and noses often met in the contest. This plunderer I found afterwards was a worthy young gentleman in the service, Mr Lushington, one of the few who escaped from death, and since paid me the compliment of assuring me, he believed he owed his life to the many comfortable draughts he had from my sleeves. Before I hit upon this happy expedient, I had in an ungovernable fit of thirst, attempted drinking my urine; but it was so intensely bitter, there was no enduring a second taste, whereas no Bristol water could be more soft or pleasant than what arose from perspiration . . .

Many to the right and left sunk with the violent pressure, and were soon suffocated; for now a steam arose from the living and the dead, which affected us in all its circumstances, as if we were forcibly held by our heads over a bowl of strong volatile spirit of hartshorn, until suffocated; nor could the effluvia of the one be distinguished from the other; and frequently, when I was forced by the load upon my head and shoulders, to hold my face down, I was obliged, near as I was to the window, instantly to raise it again, to escape suffocation . . .

When the day broke, and the gentlemen found that no intreaties could prevail to get the door opened, it occurred to one of them (I think to Mr Secretary Cooke) to make a search for me, in hopes I might have influence enough to gain a release from this scene of misery. Accordingly Messrs Lushington and Walcot undertook the search, and by my shirt discovered me under the dead upon the platform. They took me from thence, and imagining I had some signs of life, brought me towards the window I had first possession of.

But as life was equally dear to every man (and the stench arising from the dead bodies was grown so intolerable) no one would give up his station in or near the window: so they were obliged to carry me back again. But soon after Captain Mills, (now captain of the company's yacht) who was in possession of a seat in the window, had the humanity to offer to resign it. I was again brought by the same gentlemen and placed in the window.

At this juncture the suba (viceroy of Bengal), who had received an account of the havock death had made amongst us, sent one of his Jemmautdaars to enquire if the chief survived. They shewed me to him; told I had appearance of life remaining; and believed I might recover if the door was opened very soon. This answer being returned to the suba, an order came immediately for our release, it being then near six in the morning.

As the door opened inwards, and as the dead were piled up against it, and covered all the rest of the floor, it was impossible to open it by any efforts from without; it was therefore necessary that the dead should be removed by the few that were within, who were become so feeble, that the task, though it was the condition of life, was not performed without the utmost difficulty, and it was twenty minutes after the order came before the door could be opened.

About a quarter after six in the morning, the poor remains of 146 souls, being no more than three and twenty, came out of the black hole alive, but in a condition which made it very doubtful whether they would see the morning of the next day; among the living was Mrs Carey, but poor Leech was among the dead. The bodies were dragged out of the hole by the soldiers, and thrown promiscuously into the ditch of an unfinished ravelin, which was afterwards filled with earth.

THE DEATH OF GENERAL WOLFE, QUEBEC, 13 SEPTEMBER 1759

Captain John Knox

Wolfe's victory over the French at Quebec secured British control of Canada. He was mortally wounded in the attack.

Before day-break this morning we made a descent upon the north shore, about half a quarter of a mile to the eastward of Sillery; . . . we had, in this debarkation, thirty flat-bottomed boats, containing about sixteen hundred men. This was a great surprise on the enemy, who, from the natural strength of the place, did not suspect, and consequently were not prepared against, so bold an attempt. . . . As fast as we landed, the boats put off for reinforcements . . . the General, with Brigadiers Monckton and Murray, were a-shore with the first division. We lost no time here, but clambered up one of the steepest precipices that can be conceived, being almost a perpendicular, and of an incredible height. As soon as we gained the summit, all was quiet, and not a shot was heard, owing to the excellent conduct of the light infantry under Colonel Howe; it was by this time clear day-light. Here we formed again . . . we then faced to the right, and marched towards the town by files, till we came to the plains of Abraham; an even piece of ground which Mr. Wolfe had made choice of, while we stood forming upon the hill. Weather showery: about six o'clock the enemy first made their appearance upon the heights, between us and the town; whereupon we halted, and wheeled to the right, thereby forming the line of battle. . . . The enemy had now likewise formed the line of battle, and got some cannon to play on us, with round and canister shot; but what galled us most was a body of Indians and other marksmen they had concealed in the corn opposite to the front of our right wing . . . but Colonel Hale . . . advanced some platoons . . . which, after a few rounds, obliged these skulkers to retire. We were now ordered to lie down, and remained some time in this position. About eight o'clock we had two pieces of short brass six-pounders playing on the enemy, which threw them into some confusion. . . . About ten o'clock the enemy began to advance briskly in three columns, with loud shouts and recovered arms, two of them inclining to the left of our army, and the third towards our right, firing obliquely at the two extremities of our line, from the distance of one hundred and thirty, until they came within forty yards; which our troops withstood with the greatest intrepidity and firmness, still reserving their fire, and paying the strictest obedience to their Officers: this uncommon steadiness, together with the havoc which the grape-shot from our field-pieces made among them, threw them into some disorder, and was most critically maintained by a well-timed, regular and heavy discharge of our small arms, such as they could no longer oppose; hereupon they gave way, and fled with precipitation, so that, by the time the cloud of smoke was vanished, our men were again loaded, and profiting by the advantage we had over them, pursued them almost to the gates of the town, and the bridge over the little river, redoubling our fire with great eagerness, making many Officers and men prisoners. The weather cleared up, with a comfortably warm sunshine. . . . Our joy at this success is inexpressibly damped by the loss we sustained of one of the greatest heroes which this or any other age can boast of – General James Wolfe, who received his mortal wound as he was exerting himself at the head of the grenadiers of Louisbourg. . . . The officers who are prisoners say that Quebec will surrender in a few days: some deserters, who came out to us in the evening, agree in that opinion, and inform us, that the Sieur de Montcalm is dying, in great agony, of a wound he received today in their retreat . . .

After our late worthy general, of renowned memory, was carried off wounded, to the rear of the front line, he desired those who were about him to lay him down; being asked if he would have a Surgeon, he replied, "It is needless; it is all over with me". One of them then cried out, "They run, see how they run". "Who runs?" demanded our hero, with great earnestness, like a person roused from sleep. The Officer answered, "The enemy, Sir, Egad they give way everywhere". Thereupon the General rejoined, "Go one of you, my lads, to Colonel Burton; tell him to march Webb's regiment with all speed down to Charles's river, to cut off the retreat of the fugitives from the bridge". Then, turning on his side, he added, "Now, God be praised, I will die in peace:" and thus expired.

GEORGE II INTERRED, 13 NOVEMBER 1760

Horace Walpole

Do you know I had the curiosity to go to the burying t'other night; I had never seen a royal funeral. Nay, I walked as a rag of quality, which I found would be, and so it was, the easiest way of seeing it. It is absolutely a noble sight. The Prince's Chamber hung with purple and a quantity of silver lamps, the coffin under a canopy of purple velvet, and six vast chandeliers of silver on high stands had a very good effect: the ambassador from Tripoli and his son were carried to see that chamber. The procession through a line of footguards, every seventh man bearing a torch, the horse-guards lining the outside, their officers with drawn sabres and crape sashes, on horseback, the drums muffled, the fifes, bells tolling and minute guns, all this was very solemn. But the charm was the entrance of the Abbey, where we were received by the Dean and chapter in rich copes, the choir and almsmen all bearing torches; the whole Abbey so illuminated, that one saw it to greater advantage than by day; the tombs, long aisles, and fretted roof all appearing distinctly, and with the happiest chiaroscuro. There wanted nothing but incense, and little chapels here and there with priests saying mass for the repose of the defunct – yet one could not complain of its not being Catholic enough. I had been in dread of being coupled with some boy of ten years old – but the heralds were not very accurate, and I walked with George Grenville, taller and older enough to keep me in countenance. When we came to the chapel of Henry VII all solemnity and decorum ceased – no order was observed, people sat or stood where they could or would, the yeomen of the guard were crying out for help, oppressed by the immense weight of the coffin, the Bishop read sadly, and blundered in the prayers, the fine chapter, *Man that is born of a woman*, was chanted not read, and the anthem, besides being unmeasurably tedious, would have served as well for a nuptial. The real serious part was the figure of the Duke of Cumberland, heightened by a thousand melancholy circumstances. He had a dark brown adonis [wig] and a cloak of black cloth with a train of five yards.

Attending the funeral of a father, how little reason soever he had to love him, could not be pleasant. His leg extremely bad, yet forced to stand upon it near two hours, his face bloated and distorted with his late paralytic stroke, which has affected too one of his eyes, and placed over the mouth of the vault, into which in all probability he must himself so soon descend – think how unpleasant a situation! He bore it all with a firm and unaffected countenance. This grave scene was fully contrasted by the burlesque Duke of Newcastle – he fell into a fit of crying the moment he came into the chapel and flung himself back in a stall, the Archbishop hovering over him with a smelling bottle – but in two minutes his curiosity got the better of his hypocrisy and he ran about the chapel with his glass to spy who was or was not there, spying with one hand and mopping his eyes with t'other. Then returned the fear of catching cold, and the Duke of Cumberland, who was sinking with heat, felt himself weighed down, and turning round, found it was the Duke of Newcastle standing upon his train to avoid the chill of the marble. It was very theatric to look down into the vault, where the coffin lay, attended by mourners with lights. Clavering, the Groom of the Bedchamber, refused to sit up with the body, and was dismissed by the King's order.

A RAKE'S PROGRESS, 1763

James Boswell

Boswell was the biographer of Dr Samuel Johnson. He was also a libertine.

I came softly into the room, and in a sweet delirium slipped into bed and was immediately clasped in her snowy arms and pressed to her milk-white bosom. Good heavens, what a loose did we give to amorous dalliance! The friendly curtain of darkness concealed our blushes. In a moment I felt myself animated with the strongest powers of love, and, from my dearest creature's kindness, had a most luscious feast. Proud of my godlike vigour, I soon resumed the noble game. I was in full glow of health. Sobriety had preserved me from effeminacy and weakness, and my bounding blood beat quick and high alarms. A more voluptuous night I never enjoyed. Five times was I fairly lost in supreme rapture. Louisa was madly fond of me; she declared I was a prodigy, and asked me if this was not extraordinary for human nature. I said twice as much might be, but this was not, although in my own mind I was somewhat proud of my performance. She said it was what there was no just reason to be proud of. But I told her I could not help it. She said it was what we had in common with the beasts. I said no. For we had it highly improved by the pleasures of sentiment. I asked her what she thought enough. She gently chid me for asking such questions, but said two times. I mentioned the Sunday's assignation, when I was in such bad spirits, told her in what agony of mind I was, and asked her if she would not have despised me for my imbecility. She declared she would not, as it was what people had not in their own power.

She often insisted that we should compose ourselves to sleep before I would consent to it. At last I sunk to rest in her arms and she in mine. I found the negus, which had a fine flavour, very refreshing to me. Louisa had an exquisite mixture of delicacy and wantonness that made me enjoy her with more relish. Indeed I could not help roving in fancy to the embraces of some other ladies which my lively imagination strongly pictured. I don't know if that was altogether fair. However, Louisa had all the advantage. She said she was quite fatigued and could neither stir leg nor arm. She begged I would not despise her, and hoped my love would not be altogether transient. I have painted this night as well as I could. The description is faint; but I surely may be styled a Man of Pleasure.

A PERFECT STEAM ENGINE, SCOTLAND, c. 1765

John Robinson

At the breaking-up of the College (I think in 1765), I went to the country. About a fortnight after this, I came to town, and went to have a chat with Mr Watt, and to communicate to him some observations I had made on Desaguiliers' and Belidor's account of the steam-engine. I came into Mr Watt's parlour without ceremony, and found him sitting before the fire, having lying on his knee a little tin cistern, which he was looking at. I entered into conversation on what we had been speaking of at last meeting, – something about steam. All the while, Mr Watt kept looking at the fire, and laid down the cistern at the foot of his chair. At last he looked at me, and said briskly, "You need not *fash* yourself any more about that, man; I have now got an engine that shall not waste a particle of steam. It shall be all boiling hot; – aye, and hot water injected if I please." So saying, Mr Watt looked with complacency at the little thing at his feet, and, seeing that I observed him, he shoved it away under a table with his foot. I put a question to him about the nature of his contrivance. He answered me rather drily. I did not press him to a further explanation at that time, knowing that I had offended him a few days before by blabbing a pretty contrivance which he had hit on for turning the cocks of the engine. I had mentioned this in presence of an engine-builder who was going to erect one for a friend of mine; and this having come to Mr Watt's ears, he found fault with it.

I was very anxious, however, to learn what Mr Watt had contrived, but was obliged to go to the country in the evening. A gentleman who was going to the same house said he would give me a place in his carriage, and desired me to wait for him on the walk by the river-side. I went thither, and found Mr Alexander Brown; a very intimate acquaintance of Mr Watt's, walking with another gentleman, (Mr Craig, architect). Mr Brown immediately accosted me with, "Well, have you seen Jamie Watt?" – "Yes." – "He'll be in high spirits now with his engine, isn't he?" "Yes," said I, "very fine spirits." "Gad," says Mr Brown, "the condenser's the thing: keep it but cold enough, and you may have perfect vacuum, whatever be the heat of the cylinder." The instant he said this, the whole flashed on my mind at once. I did all I could to encourage the conversation, but was much embarrassed. I durst not appear ignorant of the apparatus, lest Mr Brown should find he had communicated more than he ought to have done. I could only learn that there was a vessel called a condenser which communicated with the cylinder, and that this condenser was immersed in cold water, and had a pump to clear it of the water which was formed in it. I also learned that the great difficulty was to make the piston tight; and that leather and felt had been tried, and were found quite unable to stand the heat. I saw that the whole would be perfectly dry, and that Mr Watt had used steam instead of air to press up his piston, which I thought, by Mr Brown's description was inverted. We parted, and I went home, a very silent companion to the gentleman who had given me a seat. Next day, impatient to see the effects of the separate condensation, I sent to Paisley and got some tin things made there, in completion of the notion I had formed. I tried it as an air-pump, by making my steam-vessel communicate with a tea-kettle, a condenser, and a glass receiver. In less than two minutes I rarefied the air in a pretty large receiver more than twenty times. I could go no farther in this process, because my pump for taking out the air from my condenser was too large, and not tight enough; but I saw that when applied to the mere process of taking out the air generated from the water, the vacuum might be made almost complete. I saw, too, (in consequence of a conversation the preceding day with Mr Watt about the eduction-pipe in Beighton's engine), that a long suckpipe; or syphon, would take off all the water. In short, I had no doubt that Mr Watt had really made a perfect steam-engine.

MOZART PLAYS LONDON, 1765

Daines Barrington

The Austrian musical prodigy stayed in London for fifteen months during his European tour of 1763–6. He was nine at the time of the performance below.

Having been informed that he was often visited with musical ideas, to which, even in the midst of the night, he would give utterance on his harpsichord; I told his father that I should be glad to hear some of his extemporary compositions.

The father shook his head at this, saying, that it depended entirely upon his being as it were musically inspired, but that I might ask him whether he was in humour for such a composition.

Happening to know that little Mozart was much taken notice of by Manzoli, the famous singer, who came over to England in 1764, I said to the boy, that I should be glad to hear an extemporary *Love Song*, such as his friend Manzoli might choose in an opera.

The boy on this (who continued to sit at his harpsichord) looked back with much archness, and immediately began five or six lines of a jargon recitative proper to introduce a love song.

He then played a symphony which might correspond with an air composed to the single word, *Affetto*.

It had a first and second part, which, together with the symphonies, was of the length that opera songs generally last: if this extemporary composition was not amazingly capital, yet it was really above mediocrity, and shewed most extraordinary readiness of invention.

Finding he was in humour, and as it were inspired, I then

desired him to compose a *Song of Rage*, such as might be proper for the opera stage.

The boy again looked back with much archness, and began five or six lines of a jargon recitative proper to precede a *Song of Anger*.

This lasted also about the same time with the *Song of Love*; and in the middle of it, he had worked himself up to such a pitch, that he beat his harpsichord like a person possessed, rising sometimes in his chair.

Witness as I was myself of most of these extraordinary facts, I must own that I could not help suspecting his father imposed with regard to the real age of the boy, through he had not only a most childish appearance, but likewise had all the actions of that stage of life.

For example, whilst he was playing to me, a favourite cat came in, upon which he immediately left his harpsichord, nor could we bring him back for a considerable time.

He would also sometimes run about the room with a stick between his legs by way of a horse. . . .

CAPTAIN COOK DISCOVERS BOTANY BAY, AUSTRALIA, APRIL–MAY 1770

Captain James Cook

Saturday 28 April. At daylight in the morning we discovered a bay which appeared to be tolerably well sheltered from all winds, into which I resolved to go with the ship, and with this view sent the master in the pinnace to sound the entrance while well kept turning up with the ship, having the wind right out. At noon the entrance bore NNW distance I mile.

Sunday 29 April. Saw as we came in, on both points of the bay, several of the natives and a few huts, men, women, and children on the south shore abreast of the ship, to which place I went in the boats in hopes of speaking with them, accompanied by Mr Banks, Dr Solander, and Tupia. As we approached the shore they all made off, except two men who seemd resolved to oppose our landing. As soon as I saw this I ordered the boats to lay upon their oars in order to speak to them, but this was to little purpose, for neither us nor Tupia could understand one word they said. We then threw them some nails, beads, etc., ashore, which they took up and seemed not ill-pleased, insomuch that I thought that they beckoned to us to come ashore; but in this we were mistaken, for as soon as we put the boat in they again came to oppose us, upon which I fired a musket between the two, which had no other effect than to make them retire back where bundles of their darts lay; and one of them took up a stone and threw at us, which caused my firing a second musket loaded with small shot, and although some of the shot struck the man yet it had no other effect than to make him lay hold of shield or target to defend himself. Immediately after this we landed, which we had no sooner done than they throwed two darts at us. This obliged me to fire a third shot, soon after which they both made off, but not in such haste but what we might have taken one, but Mr Banks, being of opinion that the darts were poisoned, made me cautious how I advanced into the woods. We found here a few small huts made of the bark of trees, in one of which were four or five small children, with whom we left some strings of beads, etc. A quantity of darts lay about the huts; these we took away with us. . . .

Friday 4 May. In the a.m., as the wind would not permit us to sail, I sent out some parties into the country to try to form some connections with the natives. One of the midshipmen met with a very old man and woman and two small children; they were close to the waterside, where several more were in their canoes gathering shellfish, and he being alone was afraid to make any stay with the two old people lest he should be discovered by those in the canoes. He gave them a bird he had shot, which they would not touch, neither did they speak one word but seemed to be much frightened; they were quite naked, even the woman had nothing to cover her nudity. Dr Munkhouse and another man, being in the woods not far from the watering place, discovered six more of the natives, who at first seemed to wait his coming, but as he was going up to them had a dart thrown at him out of a tree which narrowly escaped him; as soon as the fellow had thrown the dart he descended the tree and made off, and with him all the rest, and these were all that were met with in the course of this day.

Sunday 6 May. In the evening the yawl returned from fishing, having caught two sting-rays weighing near 600 pounds. The great quantity of new plants, etc. Mr Banks and Dr Solander collected in this place occasioned my giving it the name of Botany Bay. It is situated in the latitude of 34° 0'S. Longitude 208° 37' west; it is capacious, safe, and commodious . . .

BOSTON TEA PARTY, AMERICA, 16 DECEMBER 1773

John Andrews

To relieve the East India Company of its surplus stocks, the British government enforced the import of cheap tea into its American colony. In protest, a gang of Americans disguised as Indians dumped 300 chests of tea in Boston harbour. The incident helped set in train the American War of Independence.

However precarious our situation may be, yet such is the present calm composure of the people that a stranger would hardly think that ten thousand pounds sterling of the East India Company's tea was destroyed the night, or rather evening, before last, yet it's a serious truth; and if yours, together with the other Southern provinces, should rest satisfied with their quota being stored, poor Boston will feel the whole weight of ministerial vengeance. However, it's the opinion of most people that we stand an equal chance now, whether troops are sent in consequence of it or not; whereas, had it been stored, we should inevitably have had them, to enforce the sale of it.

The affair was transacted with the greatest regularity and despatch. . . . A general muster was assembled, from this and all the neighbouring towns, to the number of five or six thousand, at 10 o'clock Thursday morning in the Old South Meeting House, where they passed a unanimous vote that the Tea should go out of the harbour that afternoon, and sent a committee with Mr. Rotch* to the Customhouse to demand a clearance, which the Collector told them it was not in his power to give, without the duties being first paid. They then sent Mr. Rotch to Milton, to ask a pass from the Governor, who sent for answer, that "consistent with the rules of government and his duty to the King he could not grant one without they produced a previous clearance from the office". By the time he returned with this message the candles were light in the house, and upon reading it, such prodigious shouts were made, that induced me, while drinking tea at home, to go out and know the cause of it. The house was so crowded I could get no farther than the porch, when I found the moderator was just declaring the meeting to be dissolved, which caused another general shout, outdoors and in, and three cheers. What with that,

---

* Owner of one of the tea ships.

and the consequent noise of breaking up the meeting, you'd thought that the inhabitants of the infernal regions had broke loose.

For my part, I went contentedly home and finished my tea, but was soon informed what was going forward; but still not crediting it without ocular demonstration, I went and was satisfied. They mustered, I'm told, upon Fort Hill to the number of about two hundred, and proceeded, two by two, to Griffin's wharf, where *Hall, Bruce*, and *Coffin* lay, each with 114 chests of the ill-fated article on board; the two former with only that article, but the latter, arrived at the wharf only the day before, was freighted with a large quantity of other goods, which they took the greatest care not to injure in the least, and before nine o'clock in the evening every chest from on board the three vessels was knocked to pieces and flung over the sides.

They say the actors were Indians from Narragansett. Whether they were or not, to a transient observer they appeared as such, being clothed in blankets with the heads muffled, and copper-coloured countenances, being each armed with a hatchet or axe, and pair pistols, nor was their dialect different from what I conceive these geniuses to speak, as their jargon was unintelligible to all but themselves. Not the least insult was offered to any person, save one Captain Connor, a letter of horses in this place, not many years since removed from dear Ireland, who had ripped up the lining of his coat and waistcoat under the arms, and watching his opportunity had nearly filled them with tea, but being detected, was handled pretty roughly. They not only stripped him of his clothes, but gave him a coat of mud, with a severe bruising into the bargain; and nothing but their utter aversion to make any disturbance prevented his being tarred and feathered.

Should not have troubled you with this, by this post, hadn't I thought you would be glad of a more particular account of so important a transaction than you could have obtained by common report; and if it affords my brother but a temporary amusement, I shall be more than repaid for the trouble of writing it.

THE AMERICAN WAR OF INDEPENDENCE: IN ACTION AGAINST THE BRITISH AT BUNKER HILL, 16–17 JUNE 1775

Israel R. Potter

By the break of day Monday morning I swung my knapsack, shouldered my musket, and with the company commenced my march with a quick step for Charleston, where we arrived about sunset and remained encamped in the vicinity until about noon on the 16th June; when, having been previously joined by the remainder of the regiment from Rhode Island, to which our company was attached, we received orders to proceed and join a detachment of about 1000 American troops; which had that morning taken possession of Bunker Hill and which we had orders immediately to fortify, in the best manner that circumstances would admit of. We laboured all night without cessation and with very little refreshment, and by the dawn of day succeeded in throwing up a redoubt of eight or nine rods square. As soon as our works were discovered by the British in the morning, they commenced a heavy fire upon us, which was supported by a fort on Copp's hill; we however (under the command of the intrepid Putnam) continued to labour like beavers until our breast work was completed.

About noon, a number of the enemy's boats and barges, filled with troops, landed at Charlestown, and commenced a deliberate march to attack us – we were now harangued by Gen. Putnam, who remained us, that exhausted as we were, by our incessant labour through the preceding night, the most important part of our duty was yet to be performed, and that much would be expected from so great a number of excellent marksmen – he charged us to be cool, and to reserve our fire until the enemy approached so near as to enable us to see the white of their eyes – when within about ten rods of our works we gave them the contents of our muskets, and which were aimed with so good effect, as soon to cause them to turn their backs and to retreat with a much quicker step than with what they approached us. We were now again harangued by "old General Put," as he was termed, and requested by him to aim at the officers, should be enemy renew the attack – which they did in a few moments, with a reinforcement – their approach was with a slow step, which gave us an excellent opportunity to obey the commands of our General in bringing down their officers. I feel but little disposed to boast of my own performances on this occasion and will only say, that after devoting so many months in hunting the wild animals of the wilderness, while an inhabitant of New Hampshire, the reader will not suppose me a bad or inexperienced marksman, and that such were the fare shots which the epauletted red coats presented in the two attacks, that every shot which they received from me, I am confident on another occasion would have produced me a deer skin.

So warm was the reception that the enemy met with in their second attack, that they again found it necessary to retreat, but soon after receiving a fresh reinforcement, a third assault was made, in which, in consequence of our ammunition failing, they too well succeeded – a close and bloody engagement now ensued – to fight our way through a very considerable body of the enemy, with clubbed muskets (for there were not one in twenty of us provided with bayonets) were now the only means left us to escape the conflict, which was a sharp and severe one, is still fresh in my memory, and cannot be forgotten by me while the scars of the wounds which I then received, remain to remind me of it! Fortunately for me, at this critical moment, I was armed with a cutlass, which although without an edge, and much rust-eaten, I found of infinite more service to me than my musket – in one instance I am certain it was the means of saving my life – a blow with a cutlass was aimed at my head by a British officer, which I parried and received only a slight cut with the point on my right arm near the elbow, which I was then unconscious of, but this slight wound cost my antagonist at the moment a much more serious one, which effectually *dis-armed* him, for with one well-directed stroke I deprived him of the power of very soon again measuring swords with a "yankee rebel!" We finally however should have been mostly cut off, and compelled to yield to a superior and better equipped force, had not a body of three or four hundred Connecticut men formed a temporary breast work, with rails &c. and by which means held the enemy at bay until our main body had time to ascend the heights, and retreat across the neck; – in this retreat I was less fortunate than many of my comrades – I received two musket ball wounds, one in my hip and the other near the ankle of my left leg. I succeeded however without any assistance in reaching Prospect Hill, where the main body of the Americans had made a stand and commenced fortifying – from thence I was soon after conveyed to the Hospital in Cambridge, where my wounds were dressed and the bullet extracted from my hip by one of the Surgeons; the house was nearly filled with the poor fellows who like myself had received wounds in the late engagement, and presented a melancholy spectacle.

Bunker Hill fight proved a sore thing for the British, and will I doubt not be long remembered by them; while in London I heard it frequently spoken of by many who had taken an active part therein, some of whom were pensioners, and bore indelible proofs of American bravery – by them the Yankees, by whom they were opposed, were not infrequently represented as a set of infuriated beings, whom nothing could daunt or intimidate: and who, after their ammunition failed, disputed the ground, inch by inch, for a full hour with clubbed muskets, rusty swords, pitchforks and billets of wood, against the British bayonets.

HAWAIIAN ISLANDERS KILL CAPTAIN COOK, 14 FEBRUARY 1779

Captain James King

During our absence, a difference, of a more serious and unpleasant nature, had happened. The officer, who had been sent in the small boat, and was returning on board, with the goods which had been restored, observing Captain Cook and me engaged in the pursuit of the offenders, thought it his duty to seize the canoe, which was left drawn up on the shore. Unfortunately, this canoe belonged to Pareea, who, arriving at the same moment from on board the *Discovery*, claimed his property, with many protestations of his innocence. The officer refusing to give it up, and being joined by the crew of the pinnace, which was waiting for Captain Cook, a scuffle ensued, in which Pareea was knocked down, by a violent blow on the head, with an oar. The natives, who were collected about the spot and had hitherto been peaceable spectators, immediately attacked our people with such a shower of stones as forced them to retreat, with great precipitation, and swim off to a rock at some distance from the shore. The pinnace was immediately ransacked by the islanders and, but for the timely interposition of Pareea, who seemed to have recovered from the blow, and forgot it at the same instant, would soon have been entirely demolished. Having driven away the crowd, he made signs to our people that they might come and take possession of the pinnace, and that he would endeavour to get back the things which had been taken out of it. After their departure, he followed them in his canoe, with a midshipman's cap, and some other trifling articles of the plunder, and, with much apparent concern at what had happened, asked if the *Orono* would kill him, and whether he would permit him to come on board the next day? On being assured, that he should be well received, he joined noses (as their custom is) with the officers, in token of friendship, and paddled over to the village of Kowrowa.

When Captain Cook was informed of what had passed, he expressed much uneasiness at it, and as we were returning on board, "I am afraid", said he, "that these people will oblige me to use some violent measures; for", he added, "they must not be left to imagine that they have gained an advantage over us." However, as it was too late to take any steps this evening, he contented himself with giving orders that every man and woman on board should be immediately turned out of the ship. As soon as this order was executed, I returned on shore; and our former confidence in the natives being now much abated by the events of the day, I posted a double guard on the *Morai*, with orders to call me if they saw any men lurking about the beach. At about eleven o'clock, five islanders were observed, creeping round the bottom of the *Morai*; they seemed very cautious in approaching us, and, at last, finding themselves discovered retired out of sight. About midnight, one of them venturing up close to the observatory, the sentinel fired over him; on which the men fled, and we passed the remainder of the night without further disturbance. Next morning, at daylight, I went on board the *Resolution* for the time-keeper, and, in my way, was hailed by the *Discovery* and informed that their cutter had been stolen during the night from the buoy where it was moored.

When I arrived on board I found the marines arming, and Captain Cook loading his double-barrelled gun. Whilst I was relating to him what had happened to us in the night, he interrupted me, with some eagerness, and acquainted me with the loss of the *Discovery's* cutter, and with the preparations he was making for its recovery. It had been his usual practice, whenever anything of consequence was lost at any of the islands in this ocean, to get the king, or some of the principal *Erees*, on board, and to keep them as hostages till it was restored. This method, which had been always attended with success, he meant to pursue on the present occasion; and at the same time had given orders to stop all the canoes that should attempt to leave the bay, with an intention of seizing and destroying them, if he could not recover the cutter by peaceable means. Accordingly, the boats of both ships, well manned and armed, were stationed across the bay; and, before I left the ship, some great guns had been fired at two large canoes, that were attempting to make their escape.

It was between seven and eight o'clock when we quitted the ship together: Captain Cook in the pinnace, having Mr Phillips and nine marines with him, and myself in the small boat. The last orders I received form him were to quiet the minds of the natives, on our side of the bay, by assuring them they should not be hurt: to keep my people together; and to be on my guard. We then parted; the Captain went toward Kowrowa, where the king resided; and I proceeded to the beach. My first care, on going ashore, was to give strict orders to the marines to remain within the tent, to load their pieces with ball, and not to quit their arms. Afterward I took a walk to the huts of old Kaoo and the priests, and explained to them as well as I could the object of the hostile preparations, which had exceedingly alarmed them. I found that they had already heard of the cutter's being stolen, and I assured them that, though Captain Cook was resolved to recover it and to punish the authors of the theft, yet that they and the people of the village on our side need not be under the smallest apprehension of suffering any evil from us. I desired the priests to explain this to the people, and to tell them not to be alarmed, but to continue peaceable and quiet. Kaoo asked me, with great earnestness, if Terreeoboo was to be hurt? I assured him, he was not; and both he and the rest of his brethren seemed much satisfied with this assurance.

In the mean time, Captain Cook, having called off the launch, which was stationed at the north point of the bay, and taken it along with him, proceeded to Kowrowa and landed with the Lieutenant and nine marines. He immediately marched into the village, where he was received with the usual marks of respect; the people prostrating themselves before him and bringing their accustomed offerings of small hogs. Finding that there was no suspicion of his design, his next step was, to enquire for Terreeoboo, and the two boys, his sons, who had been his constant guests on board the *Resolution*. In a short time the boys returned along with the natives who had been sent in search of them, and immediately led Captain Cook to the house where the king had slept. They found the old man just awoke from sleep; and, after a short conversation about the loss of the cutter, from which Captain Cook was convinced that he was in no wise privy to it, he invited him to return in the boat, and spend the day on board the *Resolution*. To this proposal the king readily consented, and immediately got up to accompany him.

Things were in this prosperous train, the two boys being already in the pinnace, and the rest of the party having advanced near the waterside, when an elderly woman called Kanee-kabareea, the mother of the boys and one of the king's favourite wives, came after him and, with many tears and entreaties, besought him not go on board. At the same time two chiefs, who came along with her, laid hold of him and, insisting that he should go no further, forced him to sit down. The natives, who were collecting in prodigious numbers along the shore, and had probably been alarmed by the firing of the great guns, and the appearances of hostility in the bay, began to throng round Captain Cook and their king. In this situation, the Lieutenant of marines, observing that his men were huddled close together in the crowd, and thus incapable of using their arms if any occasion should require it, proposed to the Captain to draw them up along the rocks, close to the water's edge; and the crowd readily making way for them to pass, they were drawn up in a line, at the distance of about thirty yards from the place where the king was sitting.

All this time the old king remained on the ground, with the strongest marks of terror and dejection in his countenance; Captain Cook, not willing to abandon the object for which he had come on shore, continued to urge him, in the most pressing manner, to proceed; whilst, on the other hand, whenever the king appeared inclined to follow him, the chiefs who stood round him interposed, at first with prayers and entreaties, but afterward having recourse to force and violence, and insisted on his staying where he was. Captain Cook, therefore, finding that the alarm had spread too generally, and that it was in vain to think any longer of getting him off without bloodshed, at last gave up the point; observing to Mr Phillips that it would be impossible to compel him to go on board without the risk of killing a great number of the inhabitants.

Though the enterprise which had carried Captain Cook on shore had now failed, and was abandoned, yet his person did not appear to have been in the least danger, till an accident happened, which gave a fatal turn to the affair. The boats which had been stationed across the bay, having fired at some canoes that were attempting to get out, unfortunately had killed a chief of the first rank. The news of his death arrived at the village where Captain Cook was, just as he had left the king and was walking slowly toward the shore. The ferment it occasioned was very conspicuous; the women and children were immediately sent off; and the men put on their war-mats, and armed themselves with spears and stones. One of the natives, having in his hands a stone and a long iron spike (which they call a *pahooa*) came up to the Captain, flourishing his weapon, by way of defiance, and threatening to throw the stone. The Captain desired him to desist; but the man persisting in his insolence, he was at length provoked to fire a load of small-shot. The man having his mat on, which the shot were not able to penetrate, this had no other effect than to irritate and encourage them. Several stones were thrown at the marines; and one of the *Erees* attempted to stab Mr Phillips with his *pahooa*; but failed in the attempt, and received from him a blow with the butt end of his musket.

Captain Cook now fired his second barrel, loaded with ball, and killed one of the foremost of the natives. A general attack with stones immediately followed, which was answered by a discharge of musquetry from the marines, and the people in the boats. The islanders, contrary to the expectations of everyone, stood the fire with great firmness; and before the marines had time to reload, they broke in upon them with dreadful shouts and yells. What followed was a scene of the utmost horror and confusion.

Our unfortunate Commander, the last time he was seen distinctly, was standing at the water's edge and calling out to the boats to cease firing and to pull in. If it be true, as some of those who were present have imagined, that the marines and boatmen had fired without his orders, and that he was desirous of preventing any further bloodshed, it is not improbable that his humanity, on this occasion, proved fatal to him. For it was remarked that, whilst he faced the natives, none of them had offered him any violence, but that, having turned about to give his orders to the boats, he was stabbed in the back, and fell with his face into the water. On seeing him fall the islanders set up a great shout, and his body was immediately dragged on shore and surrounded by the enemy who, snatching the dagger out of each other's hands, showed a savage eagerness to have a share in his destruction.

Thus fell our great and excellent Commander! After a life of so much distinguished and successful enterprise, his death, as far as regards himself, cannot be reckoned premature; since he lived to finish the great work for which he seems to have been designed; and was rather removed from the enjoyment than cut off from the acquisition of glory.

THE INDUSTRIAL REVOLUTION: THE MOB DESTROY THE MACHINES, ENGLAND, OCTOBER 1779

Thomas Bentley

The introduction of technology, widely believed to cause unemployment, was often met by "wrecking", a movement which reached its British apogee in the Luddism of the early nineteenth century.

I wrote to my dear friend last from Bolton, and I mention'd the mob which had assembled in that neighbourhood; but they had not done much mischief; they only destroyed a small engine or two near Chowbent. We met them on Saturday morning, but I apprehend what we saw were not the main body; for on the same day, in the afternoon, a capital engine or mill, in the manner of Arcrites, and in which he is a partner, near Chorley, was attacked; but from its peculiar situation they could approach to it by one passage only; and this circumstance enabled the owner, with the assistance of a few neighbours, to repulse the enemy and preserve the mill for that time. Two of the mob were shot dead upon the spot, one drowned, and several wounded. The mob had no fire-arms, and did not expect so warm a reception. They were greatly exasperated, and vowed revenge; accordingly they spent all Sunday and Monday morning in collecting fire-arms and ammunition and melting their pewter dishes into bullets. They were now join'd by the Duke of Bridgewater's colliers and others, to the number, we are told, of eight thousand, and march'd by beat of drum and with colours flying to the mill, where they met with a repulse on Saturday. They found Sir Richard Clayton guarding the place with fifty Invalids armed, but this handful were by no means a match for enraged thousands; they (the Invalids) therefore contented themselves with looking on, while the mob completely destroyed a set of mills valued at 10,000*l*.

This was Monday's employment. On Tuesday morning we heard their drum at about two miles distance from Bolton, a little, before we left the place, and their professed design was to take Bolton, Manchester, and Stockport on their way to Crumford, and to destroy all the engines not only on these places, but throughout all England. How far they will be able to put their threats into execution time alone can discover.

INVENTION OF THE POWER LOOM, 1784
Edmund Cartwright

The power loom, the first machine for the weaving of yarn, revolutionised the textile industry. The Reverend Edmund Cartwright was its inventor.

Happening to be at Matlock in the summer of 1784, I fell in company with some gentlemen of Manchester, when the conversation turned on Arkwright's spinning machinery. One of the company observed, that as soon as Arkwright's patent expired so many mills would be erected, and so much cotton spun that hands never could be found to weave it. To this observation I replied that Arkwright must then set his wits to work to invent a weaving mill. This brought on a conversation on the subject, in which the Manchester gentlemen unanimously agreed that the thing was impracticable, and in defence of their opinion, they adduced arguments which I certainly was incompetent to answer, or even to comprehend, being totally ignorant of the subject, having never at that time seen a person weave. I controverted, however, the impracticability of the thing by remarking that there had lately been exhibited in London an automaton figure which played at chess. Now you will not assert, gentlemen, said I, that it is more difficult to construct a machine that shall weave than one which shall make all the variety of moves which are required in that complicated game.

Some little time afterwards, a particular circumstance recalling this conversation to my mind, it struck me that, as in plain weaving, according to the conception I then had of the business, there could only be three movements which were to follow each other in succession, there would be little difficulty in producing and repeating them. Full of these ideas, I immediately employed a carpenter and smith to carry them into effect. As soon as the machine was finished I got a weaver to put in the warp, which was of such material as sail cloth is usually made of. To my great delight, a piece of cloth, such as it was, was the product. As I had never before turned my thoughts to anything mechanical, either in theory or practice, nor had ever seen a loom at work, or known anything of its construction, you will readily suppose that my first loom was a most rude piece of machinery. The warp was placed perpendicularly, the reed fell with the weight of at least half a hundred weight, and the springs which threw the shuttle were strong enough to have thrown a congreve rocket. In short, it required the strength of two powerful men to work the machine at a slow rate, and only for a short time. Conceiving, in my great simplicity, that I had accomplished all that was required, I then secured what I thought a most valuable property by a patent, 4th of April, 1785.

This being done, I then condescended to see how other people wove: and you will guess my astonishment when I compared their easy modes of operation with mine. Availing myself, however, of what I then saw, I made a loom, in its general principles nearly as they are now made. But it was not till the year 1787 that I completed my invention, when I took out my last weaving patent, August 1st of that year . . .

THE FIRST AERIAL VOYAGE IN ENGLAND, LONDON, 15 SEPTEMBER 1784

Vincent Lunardi

A little before two o'clock on Wednesday, Mr Biggin and myself were prepared for our expedition. His attention was allotted to the philosophical experiments and observations, mine to the conduct of the Machine, and the use of the vertical cars, in depressing the Balloon at pleasure.

The impatience of the multitude made it unadvisable to proceed in filling the Balloon so as to give it the force it was intended to have: the process being therefore stopped, I retired for a few minutes to recollect and refresh myself previous to my departure, when a servant brought me a sudden account that by the falling of one of the masts which had been erected for the purpose of suspending the Balloon while filling, it had received a material injury which might possibly retard, if not prevent my voyage. I hastened instantaneously from the Armory House, where I then was, and though I was happy to find that the accident was prevented by giving the falling fixture an opposite direction, yet I was so extremely shocked at the danger that menaced me, and the word I had received, that I did not possess myself or recover the effect of my apprehension during the remainder of my stay on the earth. The consequence was, that in the convulsion of my ideas, I forgot to supply myself with those instruments of observation which had been appointed for the voyage. On balancing the rising force of the Balloon, it was supposed incapable of taking up Mr Biggin with me, (whether he felt the most regret in relinquishing his design, or I in being deprived of his company it may be difficult to determine) but we were before a Tribunal, where an immediate decision was necessary, for hesitation and delay would have been construed into guilt, and the displeasure impending over us would have been fatal, if in one moment he had not the heroism to leave the gallery, and I the resolution to go alone. I now determined on my immediate ascension, being assured by the dread of any accident which might consign me and my Balloon to the fury of the populace, whose impatience had wrought them up to a degree of ferment. An affecting, because unpremeditated testimony of approbation and interest in my fate, was here given. The Prince of Wales, and the whole surrounding assembly, almost at one instant, took off hats, hailed my resolution, and expressed the kindest and most cordial wishes for my safety and success. At five minutes after two, the last gun was fired, the cords divided, and the Balloon rose, the company returning my signals of adieu with the most unfeigned acclamations and applauses. The effect was, that of a miracle, on the multitudes which surrounded the place; and they passed from incredulity and menace, into the most extravagant expressions of approbation and joy.

At the height of twenty yards, the Balloon was a little depressed by the wind, which had a fine effect; it held me over the ground for a few seconds, and seemed to pause majestically before its departure.

On discharging a part of the ballast, it ascended to the height of two hundred yards. As a multitude lay before me of a hundred and fifty thousand people, who had not seen my ascent from the ground, I had recourse to every stratagem to let them know I was in the gallery, and they literally rent the air with their acclamations and applause, in these stratagems I devoted my flag, and worked my oars, one of which was immediately broken, and fell from me, a pidgeon too escaped, which, with a dog, and cat, were the only companions of my excursions.

When the thermometer had fallen from 68° to 61° I perceived a great difference in the temperature of the air. I became very cold and found it necessary to take a few glasses of wine. I likewise ate the leg of a chicken, but my bread and other provisions had been rendered useless, by being mixed with the sand, which I carried as ballast.

When the thermometer was at fifty, the effect of the atmosphere and the combination of circumstances around, produced a calm delight, which is inexpressible, and which no situation on earth could give. The stillness, extent, and magnificence of the scene, rendered it highly awful. My horizon seemed a perfect circle; the terminating line several hundred miles in circumference. This I conjectured from the view of London; the extreme points of which, formed an angle of only a few degrees. It was so reduced on the great scale before me, that I can find no simile to convey an idea of it. I could distinguish Saint Paul's and other churches, from the houses. I saw the streets as lines, all animated with beings, whom I knew to be men and women, but which I should otherwise have had a difficulty in describing. It was an enormous bee-hive, but the industry of it was suspended. All the moving mass seemed to have no object but myself, and the transition from the suspicion, and perhaps contempt of the preceding hour, to the affectionate transport, admiration and glory of the present moment, was not without its effect on my mind. I recollected the puns on my name, and was glad to find myself calm. I had soared from the apprehensions and anxieties of the Artillery Ground, and felt as if I had left behind me all the cares and passions that molest mankind.

WOMEN CONVICTS, PORT JACKSON, AUSTRALIA, 14 NOVEMBER 1788

Anon

After losing its American colonies, Britain determined to transport its convicts to Australia. The first penal settlement was founded at Port Jackson in 1788; it was another eighty years before transportation to

Australia was ended. The letter below was written by a woman convict to her family in Worcestershire.

I take the first opportunity that has been given us, to acquaint you with our disconsolate situation in this solitary waste of the creation. Our passage, you may have heard by the first ships, was tolerably favourable; but the inconveniences since suffered for want of shelter, bedding &c. are not to be imagined by any stranger. However, we have now two streets, if four rows of the most miserable huts you can possibly conceive of, deserve that name: windows they have none, as from the Governor's house, &c. now nearly finished, no glass could be spared; so that lattices of twigs are made by our people to supply their places. At the extremity of the lines, where, since our arrival, the dead are buried there is a place called the church-yard, but we hear as soon as a sufficient quantity of bricks can be made, a church is to be built, and named St. Philip, after the Governor. Notwithstanding all our presents, the savages continue to do us all the injury they can, which makes the soldiers' duty very hard, and much disaffection among the officers. I know not how many of our people have been killed. As for the distresses of the women, they are past description, as they are deprived of tea and other things they were indulged in, in the voyage, by the seamen: and as they are all totally unprovided with clothes, those who have young children are quite wretched. Besides this, though a number of marriages have taken place, several women who became pregnant on the voyage, and are since left by their partners, who have returned to England, are not likely even here to form any fresh connections. We are comforted with the hopes of a supply of tea from China, and flattered with getting riches when the settlement is complete, and the hemp which the place produces is brought to perfection. Our kangaroo cats are like mutton, but much leaner; and here is a kind of chickweed so much in taste like our spinage, that no difference can be discerned. Something like ground ivy is used for tea; but a scarcity of salt and sugar makes our best meals insipid. The separation of several of us to an uninhabited island was like a second transportation. In short, everyone is so taken up with their own misfortunes, that they have no pity to bestow upon others. All our letters are examined by an officer; but a friend takes this for me privately. The ships sail tonight.

A MEETING WITH MAD KING GEORGE, 2 FEBRUARY 1789

Fanny Burney

George III suffered from insanity, probably caused by porphyria, which eventually resulted in complete incapacity.

Kew Palace

What an adventure had I this morning! one that has occasioned me the severest personal terror I ever experienced in my life.

Sir Lucas Pepys still persisting that exercise and air were absolutely necessary to save me from illness, I have continued my walks, varying my gardens from Richmond to Kew, according to the accounts I received of the movements of the King. For this I had her Majesty's permission, on the representation of Sir Lucas.

This morning, when I received my intelligence of the King from Dr. John Willis, I begged to know where I might walk in safety. "In Kew Gardens," he said, "as the King would be in Richmond."

"Should any unfortunate circumstance," I cried, "at any time, occasion my being seen by his Majesty, do not mention my name, but let me run off without call or notice."

This he promised. Everybody, indeed, is ordered to keep out of sight.

Taking, therefore, the time I had most at command, I strolled into the gardens. I had proceeded, in my quick way, nearly half the round, when I suddenly perceived through some trees, two or three figures. Relying on the instructions of Dr. John, I concluded them to be workmen and gardeners; yet tried to look sharp, and in so doing, as they were less shaded, I thought I saw the person of his Majesty!

Alarmed past all possible expression, I waited not to know more, but turning back, ran off with all my might. But what was my terror to hear myself pursued! – to hear the voice of the King himself loudly and hoarsely calling after me, "Miss Burney! Miss Burney!"

I protest I was ready to die. I knew not in what state he might be at the time; I only knew the orders to keep out of his way were universal; that the Queen would highly disapprove any un-authorised meeting, and that the very action of my running away might deeply, in his present irritable state, offend him. Never-theless, on I ran, too terrified to stop, and in search of some short passage, for the garden is full of little labyrinths, by which I might escape.

The steps still pursued me, and still the poor hoarse and altered voice rang in my ears: – more and more footsteps resounded frightfully behind me, – the attendants all running, to catch their eager master, and the voices of the two Doctor Willises loudly exhorting him not to heat himself so unmercifully.

Heavens, how I ran! I do not think I should have felt the hot lava from Vesuvius – at least not the hot cinders – had I so run during its eruption. My feet were not sensible that they even touched the ground.

Soon after, I heard other voices, shriller, though less nervous, call out "Stop! Stop! Stop!"

I could by no means consent: I knew not what was purposed, but I recollected fully my agreement with Dr. John that very morning, that I should decamp if surprised, and not be named.

My own fears and repugnance, also, after a flight and disobedience like this, were doubled in the thought of not escaping: I knew not to what I might be exposed, should the malady be then high, and take the turn of resentment. Still, therefore, on I flew; and such was my speed, so almost incredible to relate or recollect, that I fairly believe no one of the whole party could have overtaken me, if these words, from one of the attendants, had not reached me, "Doctor Willis begs you to stop!"

"I cannot! I cannot!" I answered, still flying on, when he called out, "You must, ma'am; it hurts the King to run."

Then, indeed, I stopped – in a state of fear really amounting to agony. I turned round, I saw the two Doctors had got the King between them, and three attendants of Dr. Willis's were hovering about. They all slackened their pace, as they saw me stand still; but such was the excess of my alarm, that I was wholly insensible to the effects of a race which, at any other time, would have required an hour's recruit.

As they approached, some little presence of mind happily came to my command: it occurred to me that, to appease the wrath of my flight, I must now show some confidence: I therefore faced them as undauntedly as I was able, only charging the nearest of the attendants to stand by my side.

When they were within a few yards of me, the King called out, "Why did you run away?"

Shocked at a question impossible to answer, yet a little assured by the mild tone of his voice, I instantly forced myself forward, to meet him, though the internal sensation, which satisfied me this was a step the most proper to appease his suspicions and displeasure, was so violently combated by the tremor of my nerves, that I fairly think I may reckon it the greatest effort of personal courage I have ever made.

The effort answered: I looked up, and met all his wonted benignity of countenance, though something still of wildness in his eyes. Think, however, of my surprise, to feel him put both his hands round my two shoulders, and then kiss my cheek!

I wonder I did not really sink, so exquisite was my affright when I saw him spread out his arms! Involuntarily, I concluded he meant to crush me: but the Willises, who have never seen him till this fatal illness, not knowing how very extraordinary an action this was from him, simply smiled and looked pleased, supposing, perhaps, it was his customary salutation!

I believe, however, it was but the joy of a heart unbridled, now, by the forms and proprieties of established custom and sober reason. To see any of his household thus by accident, seemed such a near approach to liberty and recovery, that who can wonder it should serve rather to elate than lessen what yet remains of his disorder!

He now spoke in such terms of his pleasure in seeing me, that I soon lost the whole of my terror; astonishment to find him so nearly well, and gratification to see him so pleased, removed every uneasy feeling, and the joy that succeeded, in my conviction of his recovery, made me ready to throw myself at his feet to express it.

What a conversation followed! When he saw me fearless, he grew more and more alive, and made me walk close by his side, away from the attendants, and even the Willises themselves, who, to indulge him, retreated. I own myself not completely composed, but alarm I could entertain no more.

Everything that came uppermost in his mind he mentioned; he seemed to have just such remains of his flightiness as heated his imagination without deranging his reason, and robbed him of all control over his speech, though nearly in his perfect state of mind as to his opinions.

What did he not say! He opened his whole heart to me, — expounded all his sentiments, and acquainted me with all his intentions.

The heads of his discourse I must give you briefly, as I am sure you will be highly curious to hear them, and as no accident can render of much consequence what a man says in such a state of physical intoxication.

He assured me he was quite well – as well as he had ever been in his life; and then inquired how I did, and how I went on? and whether I was more comfortable?

If these questions, in their implication, surprised me, imagine how that surprise must increase when he proceeded to explain them! He asked after the coadjutrix, laughing, and saying, "Never mind her! – don't be oppressed – I am your friend! don't let her cast you down! – I know you have a hard time of it – but don't mind her!"

Almost thunderstruck with astonishment, I merely curt-seyed to his kind "I am your friend," and said nothing.

Then presently he added, "Stick to your father – stick to your own family – let them be your objects."

How readily I assented!

Again he repeated all I have just written, nearly in the same words, but ended it more seriously: he suddenly stopped, and held me to stop too, and putting his hand on his breast, in the most solemn manner, he gravely and slowly said, "I will protect you! – I promise you that – and therefore depend upon me!"

I thanked him; and the Willises, thinking him rather too elevated, came to propose my walking on. "No, no, no," he cried, a hundred times in a breath; and their good humour prevailed, and they let him again walk on with his new companion.

He then gave me a history of his pages, animating almost into a rage, as he related his subjects of displeasure with them, particularly with Mr. Ernst, who, he told me, had been brought up by himself. I hope his ideas upon these men are the result of the mistakes of his malady.

Then he asked me some questions that very greatly distressed me, relating to information given him in his illness, from various motives, but which he suspected to be false, and which I knew he had reason to suspect: yet was it most dangerous to set anything right, as I was not aware what might be the view of their having been stated wrong. I was as discreet as I knew how to be, and I hope I did no mischief; but this was the worst part of the dialogue.

He next talked to me a great deal of my dear father, and made a thousand inquiries concerning his "History of Music." This brought him to his favourite theme, Handel; and he told me innumerable anecdotes of him, and particularly that celebrated tale of Handel's saying of himself, when a boy, "While that boy lives, my music will never want a protector." And this, he said, I might relate to my father.

Then he ran over most of his oratorios, attempting to sing the subjects of several airs and choruses, but so dreadfully hoarse that the sound was terrible.

Dr. Willis, quite alarmed at this exertion, feared he would do himself harm, and again proposed a separation. "No! No! No!" he exclaimed, "not yet; I have something I must just mention first."

Dr. Willis, delighted to comply, even when uneasy at compliance, again gave way.

The good King then greatly affected me. He began upon my revered old friend, Mrs. Delany; and he spoke of her with such warmth – such kindness! "She was my friend," he cried, "and I loved her as a friend! I have made a memorandum when I lost her – I will show it you."

He pulled out a pocket-book, and rummaged some time, but to no purpose.

The tears stood in his eyes – he wiped them, and Dr. Willis again became very anxious. "Come, sir," he cried, "now do you come in and let the lady go on her walk – come, now, you have talked a long while, – so we'll go in – if your Majesty pleases."

"No, no!" he cried, "I want to ask her a few questions; – I have lived so long out of the world, I know nothing!"

This touched me to the heart. We walked on together, and he inquired after various persons, particularly Mrs. Boscawen, because she was Mrs. Delany's friend! Then, for the same reason, after Mr. Frederick Montagu, of whom he kindly said, "I know he has a great regard for me, for all he joined the opposition." Lord Grey de Wilton, Sir Watkin Wynn, the Duke of Beaufort, and various others, followed.

He then told me he was very much dissatisfied with several of his state officers, and meant to form an entire new establishment. He took a paper out of his pocket-book, and showed me his new list.

This was the wildest thing that passed; and Dr. John Willis now seriously urged our separating; but he would not consent; he had only three more words to say, he declared, and again he conquered.

He now spoke of my father, with still more kindness, and told me he ought to have had the post of Master of the Band, and not that little poor musician Parsons, who was not fit for it: "But Lord Salisbury," he cried, "used your father very ill in that business, and so he did me! However, I have dashed out his name, and I shall put your father's in, – as soon as I get loose again!"

This again – how affecting was this!

"And what," cried he, "has your father got, at last? nothing but that poor thing at Chelsea? O fie! fie! fie! But never mind! I will take care of him! I will do it myself!"

Then presently he added, "As to Lord Salisbury, he is out already, as this memorandum will show you, and so are many more. I shall be much better served; and when once I get away, I shall rule with a rod of iron!"

This was very unlike himself, and startled the two good doctors, who could not bear to cross him, and were exulting at my seeing his great amendment, but yet grew quite uneasy at his earnestness and volubility.

Finding we now must part, he stopped to take leave, and renewed again his charges about the coadjutrix. "Never mind her!" he cried, "depend upon me! I will be your friend as long as I live! I here pledge myself to be your friend!" And then he saluted me again just as at the meeting, and suffered me to go on.

What a scene! how variously was I affected by it! but, upon the whole, how inexpressibly thankful to see him so nearly himself – so little removed from recovery!

MUTINY ON THE *BOUNTY*, SOUTH PACIFIC, 1789

William Bligh

Lieutenant Bligh, commander of HMS *Bounty*, was tasked with procuring bread fruit trees from the South Pacific and shipping them to the West Indies; his crew, led by Fletcher Christian, mutinied to stay in the Paradise of Tahiti.

Just before sun-rising, while I was yet asleep, Mr Christian, with the master-at-arms, gunner's mate, and Thomas Burkitt, seaman, came into my cabin, and, seizing me, tied my hands with a cord behind my back, threatening me with instant death if I spoke or made the least noise. I, however, called as loud as I could in hopes of assistance; but they had already secured the officers who were not of their party, by placing sentinels at their doors. There were three men at my cabin door, besides the four within; Christian had only a cutlass in his hand, the others had muskets and bayonets. I was hauled out of bed and forced on deck in my shirt, suffering great pain from the tightness with which they had tied my hands. I demanded the reason of such violence, but received no other answer than abuse for not holding my tongue. The master, the gunner, the surgeon, Mr Elphinstone, master's mate, and Nelson, were kept confined below, and the forehatchway was guarded by sentinels. The boatswain and carpenter, and also the clerk, Mr Samuel, were allowed to come upon deck, where they saw me standing abaft the mizen-mast, with my hands tied behind my back, under a guard, with Christian at their head. The boatswain was ordered to hoist the launch out, with a threat, if he did not do it instantly, *to take care of himself.*

When the boat was out, Mr Hayward and Mr Haller, two of the midshipmen, and Mr Samuel, were ordered into it. I demanded what their intention was in giving this order, and endeavoured to persuade the people near me not to persist in such acts of violence; but it was to no effect. "Hold your tongue, sir, or you are dead this instant," was constantly repeated to me.

I continued my endeavours to turn the tide of affairs, when Christian changed the cutlass which he had in his hand for a bayonet that was brought to him, and holding me with a strong gripe by the cord that tied my hands, he with many oaths threatened to kill me immediately, if I would not be quiet; the villains round me had their pieces cocked and bayonets fixed. Particular people were called on to go into the boat, and were hurried over the side, whence I concluded that with these people I was to be set adrift. I therefore made another effort to bring about a change, but with no other effect than to be threatened with having my brains blown out.

The mutineers having forced those of the seamen whom they meant to get rid of into the boat, Christian directed a dram to be served to each of his own crew. I then unhappily saw that nothing could be done to effect the recovery of the ship: there was no one to assist me, and every endeavour on my part was answered with threats of death.

Cast off in a small boat with 18 men, Bligh navigated 3600 miles to Timor and survival. Of the mutineers, some established a colony on Pitcairn Island, where they were murdered (Christian among them) with the exception of John Adams. Ten other mutineers were eventually court-martialled and three hanged.

THE INDUSTRIAL REVOLUTION: A SCIENTIST AGAINST THE MOB, 19 JULY 1791

Joseph Priestley

Priestley was the discoverer of oxygen. The letter below was addressed to "The Inhabitants of Birmingham" after his house there was burnt by a mob, destroying all his scientific apparatus and manuscripts.

My Late Townsmen and Neighbours,

You have destroyed the most truly valuable and useful apparatus of philosophical instruments that perhaps any individual, in this or any other country, was ever possessed of, in my use of which I annually spent large sums with no pecuniary view whatever, but only in the advancement of Science, for the benefit of my country and mankind. You have destroyed the Library corresponding to that apparatus, which no money can re-purchase, except in course of time. But what I feel far more, you have destroyed manuscripts which have been the result of the laborious study of many years, and which I shall never be able to recompense; and this has been done to one who never did, or imagined, you any harm.

In this business we are the sheep and you the wolves. We will preserve our character and hope you will change yours. At all events we return you blessings for curses, and hope that you shall soon return to that industry and those sober manners for which the inhabitants of Birmingham were formerly distinguished.

Your faithfully,

J. Priestley

THE FRENCH REVOLUTIONARY WAR: "THE GLORIOUS FIRST OF JUNE", 1794

Midshipman William Parker

Britain joined the European war against the French Revolution when France invaded the Netherlands and so threatened British maritime security.

Lord Howe always likes to begin in the morning and let us have a whole day at it. The next morning (June 1st) early the signal was made to form the line of battle; we beat to quarters and got up sufficiently of powder and shot to engage the enemy. The enemy also formed their line to leeward. Upon our making observations on the enemy's fleet we found that one of their three-deck ships was missing, but counted twenty-eight sail-of-the-line, which was two more than they had on May 29. We supposed the Isle d'Aix squadron had joined them, and the ship that we had disabled on the 29th had bore up for Brest or sunk, and some thought the *Audacious* must have taken one of them, and took her away from the fleet, as she was missing May 30; but the best joke was that the French Commander-in-Chief had the impudence to say to those ships who joined him that he had thrashed us on the 29th completely, and that he only wanted to have another little dust with us before he should carry us all into Brest. Our fleet was formed, and we only waited to get near enough to the enemy to begin.

At eight the action began, and the firing from the enemy was very smart before we could engage the ship that came to our turn to engage, as every ship is to have one because our line is formed ahead, and theirs is formed also. Suppose their first or leading ship is a 100 guns and ours a 74, our ship must engage her. I believe we were the ninth or tenth ship; our lot fell to an 80-gun ship, so we would not waste our powder and shot by firing at other ships, though I am sorry to say they fired very smartly at us and unluckily killed two men before we fired a gun, which so exasperated our men that they kept singing out, "For God's sake, brave captain, let us fire! Consider, sir, two poor souls are slaughtered already." But Captain Duckworth would not let them fire till we came abreast of the ship we were to engage, when Captain Duckworth cried out, "Fire, my boys, fire!" upon which our enraged boys gave them such an extraordinary warm reception that I really believe it struck the rascals with the panic. The French ever since the 29th (because we so much damaged one of their ships) called us the little devil and the little black ribband, as we have a black streak painted on our side. They made the signal for three or four of their ships to come down and sink us, and if we struck to them to give us no quarter; but all this did not in the least dishearten our ship's company, and we kept up a very smart fire when some of the enemy's masts and yards went over their side, which we gave credit for some of our doing.

The smoke was so thick that we could not at all times see the ships engaging ahead and astern. Our main-topmast and main-yard being carried away by the enemy's shot, the Frenchmen gave three cheers, upon which our ship's company, to show they did not mind it, returned them the three cheers, and after that gave them a furious broadside. About this time a musket ball came and struck Captain Duckworth between the bottom part of his thumb and finger, but very slightly, so that he only wrapped a handkerchief about it, and it is now almost quite well. But to proceed with my account: at about ten the *Queen* broke their line again, and we gave three cheers at our quarters; and now we engaged whichever ship we could best. A ship of 80 guns, which we had poured three or four broadsides into on May 29, we saw drawing ahead on our lee quarter to fire into us, which ship our ship's company had a great desire to have made strike to us on the 29th, and now quite rejoiced at having an opportunity of engaging her again, gave three cheers at their quarters, and began a very smart firing at their former antagonist.

Their firing was not very smart, though she contrived to send a red-hot shot into the captain's cabin where I am quartered, which kept rolling about and burning everybody, when gallant Mears, our first lieutenant, took it up in his speaking-trumpet and threw it overboard. At last being so very close to her we supposed her men had left their quarters, as Frenchmen do not like close quarters. She bore down to leeward of the fleet, being very much disabled. The French fleet then ran away like cowardly rascals and we made all the sail we could.

Lord Howe ordered our ships that were not very much disabled to take the prizes in tow, and our own dismasted ships, who were erecting jury masts as fast as possible. But I forgot to tell you that the ship which struck to us was so much disabled that she could not live much longer upon the water, but gave a dreadful reel and lay down on her broadside. We were afraid to send any boats to help them, because they would have sunk her by too many poor souls getting into her at once. You could plainly perceive the poor wretches climbing over to windward and crying most dreadfully. She then righted a little, and then her head went down gradually, and she sunk. She after that rose again a little and then sunk, so that no more was seen of her. Oh, my dear father! when you consider of five or six hundred souls destroyed in that shocking manner, it will make your very heart relent. Our own men even were a great many of them in tears and groaning, they said God bless them. Oh, that we had come into a thousand engagements sooner than so many poor souls should be at once destroyed in that shocking manner. I really think it would have rent the hardest of hearts . . .

Most of our brave boys have undone all the good they ever did. They contrived to smuggle a great deal of liquor into the ship, and with the joy of the victory, most of the ship's company got so drunk that they mutinied. They said that they would have liberty to go ashore. They released the English prisoners out of irons. Every officer belonging to the ship was sent for. The Captain almost broke his heart about it. Seven of the ringleaders were seized by the officers and twenty others, when they were put in irons; and the next morning, when they were told of their night's proceedings they all cried like children. They punished the twenty with two dozen lashes each, and the seven were kept in irons to be hung, if tried by a Court Martial; but Captain Duckworth came on board today and said that, as he was of a forgiving temper, he gave them into the hands of the ship's company, that he looked up to them with love for the services they had done him . . .

THE FRENCH REVOLUTIONARY WAR: RULES ON EATING FOR THE RICH AND POOR, 23 JULY 1795

The Times

During the war against revolutionary France, there were periodic attempts to introduce food economies (and better behaviour) in Britain.

The Way to Peace and Plenty
Rules for the Rich
1. Abolish gravy soups, and second courses.
2. Buy no starch when wheat is dear.
3. Destroy all useless dogs.
4. Give no dog, or other animal, the smallest bit of bread or meat.
5. Save all your skim-milk carefully, and give it all to the poor, or sell it at a cheap rate.
6. Make broth, rice pudding, &c., for the poor, and teach them to make such things.

7. Go to church yourselves, and take care your servants go constantly.
8. Look into the management of your own families, and visit your poor neighbours.
9. Prefer those poor who keep steadily to their work, and go constantly to church, and give nothing to those who are idle, and riotous, or keep useless dogs.
10. Buy no weighing meat, or gravy beef: if the rich would buy only the prime pieces, the poor could get the others cheap.

Rules for the Poor

1. Keep steadily to your work, and never change masters, if you can help it.
2. Go to no gin-shop, or alehouse: but lay out all your earnings in food, and cloaths, for yourself, and your family: and try to lay up a little for rent and rainy days.
3. Avoid bad company.
4. Keep no dogs: for they rob your children, and your neighbours.
5. Go constantly to church, and carry your wives, and children, with you, and God will bless you.
6. Be civil to your superiors, and they will be kind to you.
7. Learn to make broth, milk pottage, rice-pudding, &c. One pound of meat, in both, will go further than two pounds boiled or roasted.
8. Be quiet, and contented, and never steal, or swear, or you will never thrive.

JENNER EXPERIMENTS WITH VACCINATION, GLOUCESTERSHIRE, 1796

Edward Jenner

A country physician, Jenner made his crowning experiment in vaccination after twenty one years research into the tradition that milkmaids who contracted cowpox never succumbed to smallpox.

During the investigation of the casual Cow Pox, I was struck with the idea that it might be practicable to propagate the disease by inoculation, after the manner of the Small Pox, first from the Cow, and finally from one human being to another. I anxiously waited some time for an opportunity of putting this theory to the test. At length the period arrived. The first experiment was made upon a lad of the name of Phipps, in whose arm a little Vaccine Virus was inserted, taken from the hand of a young woman who had been accidentally infected by a cow. Notwithstanding the resemblance which the pustule, thus excited on the boy's arm, bore to variolous inoculation, yet as the indisposition attending it was barely perceptible, I could scarcely persuade myself the patient was secure from the Small Pox. However, on his being inoculated some months afterwards, it proved that he was secure. This Case inspired me with confidence; and as soon as I could again furnish myself with Virus from the Cow, I made an arrangement for a series of inoculations. A number of children were inoculated in succession, one from the other; and after several months had elapsed, they were exposed to the infection of the Small Pox; some by Inoculation, others by various effluvia and some in both ways; but they all resisted it. The distrust and scepticism which naturally arose in the minds of medical men, on my first announcing so unexpected a discovery has now nearly disappeared. Many hundreds of them, from actual experience, have given their attestations that the inoculated Cow Pox proves a perfect security against the Small Pox; and I shall probably be within compass if I say, thousands are ready to follow their example; for the scope that this inoculation has now taken is immense. An hundred thousand persons, upon the smallest computation, have been inoculated in these realms.

THE NAVAL MUTINY AT SPITHEAD, APRIL 1797

Lieutenant Philip Beaver, HMS Monarch

Occassioned by the barbarity of lower-deck conditions.

. . . You have doubtless heard of the situation of the fleet at Spithead. They have, every ship, refused to go to sea till their pay is increased, unless the French fleet should be out; in which case they are ready and willing to go. The origin of this business I believe to be as follows. After the battle of the 1st June, Lord Howe hinted, if he did not actually promise, that he would endeavour to get the seamen's pay increased. Though he has been lately the nominal commander of the Grand Fleet, Lord Bridport has always gone to sea with the command of it; and during this time several petitions have been sent out from the seamen of the fleet to Lord Howe, requesting this increase of pay. Similar ones were sent by them to the lords of the admiralty, and others I believe to the minister; to none of which have they received any answer; they have all been treated with contemptuous silence.

The other day, on Lord Howe's resignation, Lord Bridport, you know, was appointed admiral of the fleet. When, intending to go to sea, he made the signal to unmoor, every ship's company gave three cheers and refused to go, with the exception before mentioned. They have all, however, excepting one ship only, behaved with great prudence, decency, and moderation (if I may use those terms when speaking of an act of mutiny) in this business; and obey their officers as before in the regular routine of ship's duty – saying that they are not dissatisfied with their officers or the service, but are determined to have an increase of pay, because it has not been increased since the time of Charles the First, and that everything since that period has risen 50 per cent., that no attention had been paid to their petitions, and that on the resignation of Lord Howe they were forced to pursue the present measures.

As an officer, I must condemn their conduct; as a well-wisher to my country, I must regret its being so exceedingly ill-timed; but as a man, I can find many excuses for them. I could say many things to extenuate their conduct, and I cannot but admire their moderation in so daring an exercise of illegal power, and their patriotism in having so studiously prevented our enemies from conceiving they can derive any advantage from it, by declaring that if their fleets appear at sea they are ready to follow them. . . .

FRENCH REVOLUTIONARY WAR: THE ATTACK ON TENERIFE, JULY 1797

Captain T. Troubridge

A report to Rear-Admiral Nelson.

From the darkness of the night, I did not immediately hit the Mole, the spot appointed to land at, but pushed on shore under the enemy's battery, close to the southward of the Citadel. Captain Waller landed at the same instant, and two or three other boats. The surf was so high, many put back: the boats were full of water in an instant, and stove against the rocks, and most of the ammunition in the men's pouches wet. As soon as I had collected a few men, I immediately pushed, with Captain Waller, for the Square, the place of Rendezvous, in hopes of there meeting you and the remainder of the people, and waited about an hour, during which time I sent a Sergeant with two gentlemen of the Town, to summons the Citadel. I fear the Sergeant was shot on his way, as I heard nothing of him afterwards.

The ladders being all lost in the surf, or not to be found, no immediate attempt could be made on the Citadel. I therefore marched to join Captains Hood and Miller, who, I had intelligence, had made good their landing to the S.W. of the place I did, with a body of men. I endeavoured then to procure some intelligence of you, and the rest of the officers, without success. By day-break, we had collected about eighty Marines, eighty Pikemen, and one hundred and eighty small-arm Seamen. These, I found, were all that were alive that had made good their landing. With this force, having procured some ammunition from the Spanish prisoners we had made, we were marching to try what could be done with the Citadel without ladders; but found the whole of the streets commanded by field-pieces, and upwards of eight thousand Spaniards and one hundred French under arms, approaching by every avenue. As the boats were all stove, and I saw no possibility of getting more men on shore – the ammunition wet, and no provisions – I sent Captain Hood with a Flag of Truce to the Governor, to say I was prepared to burn the Town, which I should immediately put in force if he approached one inch further; and, at the same time, I desired Captain Hood to say it would be done with regret, as I had no wish to injure the inhabitants; that if he would come to my terms, I was ready to treat, which he readily agreed to: a copy of which I had the honour to send you by Captain Waller, which, I hope, will meet your approbation, and appear highly honourable.

From the small body of men, and the greater part being pike and small-arm seamen, which can be only called irregulars, with very little ammunition in the pouches but what was wet in the surf at landing, I could not expect to succeed in any attempt upon the enemy, whose superior strength I have before mentioned. The Spanish Officers assure me they expected us, and were perfectly prepared with all the batteries, and the number of men I have before mentioned under arms: with the great disadvantage of a rocky coast, high surf, and in the face of forty pieces of cannon, though we were not successful, will show what an Englishman is equal to.

THE FRENCH REVOLUTIONARY WAR: THE BATTLE OF THE NILE, 1 AUGUST 1798

Captain Sir Edward Berry

The view from HMS *Vanguard*.

The enemy appeared to be moored in a strong and compact Line of Battle, close in with the shore, their line describing an obtuse angle in its form, flanked by numerous Gun-boats, four Frigates, and a battery of guns and mortars, on an Island in their Van. This situation of the enemy seemed to secure to them the most decided advantages, as they had nothing to attend to but their artillery, in their superior skill in the use of which the French so much pride themselves, and to which indeed their splendid series of land victories are in a great measure to be imputed.

The position of the enemy presented the most formidable obstacles; but the Admiral viewed these with the eye of a seaman determined on attack, and it instantly struck his eager and penetrating mind, that where there was room for an enemy's ship to swing, there was room for one of ours to anchor. No further signal was necessary than those which had already been made. The Admiral's designs were as fully known to his whole squadron, as was his determination to conquer or perish in the attempt. The *Goliath* and *Zealous* had the honour to lead inside, and to receive the first fire from the van ships of the enemy . . . These two ships, with the *Orion*, *Audacious* and *Theseus*, took their stations inside of the enemy's line, and were immediately in close action. The *Vanguard* anchored the first on the outer side of the enemy, and was opposed within half pistol-shot to *Le Spartiate*, the third in the enemy's line. In standing in, our leading ships were unavoidably obliged to receive into their bows the whole fire of the broadsides of the French line; until they could take their respective stations . . . At this time the necessary number of our men were employed aloft in furling sails, and on deck, in hauling the braces, etc., preparatory to our casting anchor. As soon as this took place, a most animated fire was opened from the *Vanguard*, which ship covered the approach of those in the rear, which were following in a close line. The *Minotaur*, *Defence*, *Bellerophon*, *Majestic*, *Swiftsure*, and *Alexander*, came up in succession, and passing within hail of the *Vanguard*, took their respective stations opposed to the enemy's line . . . Captain Thompson, of the

Leander, of 50 guns, . . . advanced towards the enemy's line on the outside, and most judiciously dropped his anchor athwart hause of *Le Franklin*, raking her with great success, the shot from the *Leander's* broadside which passed that ship all striking *L'Orient*, the flag-ship of the French Commander-in-Chief.

The action commenced at sun-set which was at thirty-one minutes past six p.m., with an ardour and vigour, which it is impossible to describe. At about seven o'clock total darkness had come on, but the whole hemisphere was, with intervals, illuminated by the fire of the hostile fleets. Our ships, when darkness came on, had all hoisted their distinguishing lights, by a signal from the Admiral. The van ship of the enemy, *Le Guerrier*, was dismasted in less than twelve minutes, and, in ten minutes after, the second ship, *Le Conquérant*, and the third, *Le Spartiate*, very nearly at the same moment were almost dismasted. *L'Aquilon* and *Le Souverain Peuple*, the fourth and fifth ships of the enemy's line, were taken possesèsion of by the British at half-past eight in the evening. Captain Berry, at that hour, sent Lieutenant Galwey, of the *Vanguard*, with a party of marines, to take possession of *Le Spartiate*, and that officer returned by the boat the French captain's sword, which Captain Berry immediately delivered to the Admiral, who was then below, in consequence of the severe wound which he had received in the head during the heat of the attack. At this time it appeared that victory had already declared itself in our favour, for although *L'Orient*, *L'Heureux*, and *Tonnant* were not taken possession of, they were considered as completely in our power, which pleasing intelligence Captain Berry had likewise the satisfaction of communicating in person to the Admiral. At ten minutes after nine, a fire was observed on board *L'Orient*, the French admiral's ship, which seemed to proceed from the after part of the cabin, and which increased with great rapidity, presently involving the whole of the after part of the ship in flames. This circumstance Captain Berry immediately communicated to the Admiral, who, though suffering severely from his wound, came up on deck, where the first consideration that struck his mind was concern for the danger of so many lives, to save as many as possible of whom he ordered Captain Berry to make every practicable exertion. A boat, the only one that could swim, was instantly despatched from the *Vanguard*, and other ships that were in a condition to do so immediately followed the example; by which means, from the best possible information the lives of about seventy

Frenchmen were saved. The light thrown by the fire of *L'Orient* upon the surrounding objects, enabled us to perceive with more certainty the situation of the two fleets, the colours of both being clearly distinguishable. The cannonading was partially kept up to leeward of the centre till about ten o'clock, when *L'Orient* blew up with a most tremendous explosion. An awful pause and death-like silence for about three minutes ensued, when the wreck of the masts, yards etc. which had been carried to a vast height, fell down into the water, and on board the surrounding ships. A port fire from *L'Orient* fell into the main royal of the *Alexander*, the fire occasioned by which was, however, extinguished in about two minutes, by the active exertions of Captain Ball.

After this awful scene, the firing was recommenced with the ships to leeward of the centre, till twenty minutes past ten, when there was a total cessation of firing for about ten minutes, after which it was revived till about three in the morning when it again ceased . . . The whole of the 2nd was employed in securing the French ships that had struck . . . The Admiral, knowing that the wounded of his own ships had been well taken care of, bent his first attention to those of the enemy. He established a truce with the Commandant of Aboukir, and through him made a communication to the Commandant of Alexandria, that it was his intention to allow all the wounded Frenchmen to be taken ashore to proper hospitals.

LAKELAND BEGGARS, 27 MAY 1800

Dorothy Wordsworth

Dorothy Wordsworth was the sister of the lyrical poet William Wordsworth; they had moved to the Lake District in 1799.

On Tuesday, May 27th (1800), a very tall woman, tall much beyond the measure of tall women, called at the door. She had on a very long brown cloak, and a very white cap without bonnet – her face was excessively brown, but it had plainly once been fair. She led a little bare-footed child about two years old by the hand and said her husband who was a tinker was gone before with the other children. I gave her a piece of bread. Afterwards on my road to Ambleside, beside the bridge at Rydale, I saw her husband sitting by the roadside, his two asses feeding beside him and the two young children at play upon the grass. The man did not beg. I passed on and about a quarter of a mile further I saw two boys before me, one about ten, the other about eight years old, at play chasing a butterfly. They were wild figures, not very ragged, but without shoes and stockings; the hat of the elder was wreathed round with yellow flowers; the younger, whose hat was only a rimless crown, had stuck it round with laurel leaves. They continued at play till I drew very near and then they addressed me with the beggars' cant and the whining voice of sorrow. I said: "I served your mother this morning." (The boys were so like the woman who had called at the door that I could not be mistaken.) "Oh," says the elder, "you could not serve my mother, for she's dead and my father's on at the next town – he's a potter." I persisted in my assertion and that I would give them nothing. Says the elder, "Come, let's away," and away they flew like lightning. They had, however, sauntered so long in their road that they did not reach Ambleside before me, and I saw them go up to Matthew Harrison's house with their wallet upon the elder's shoulder, and creeping with a beggar's complaining foot. On my return through Ambleside I met in the street the mother driving her asses; in the two panniers of one of which were the two little children, whom she was chiding and threatening with the wand which she used to drive on her assess, while the little things hung in wantonness over the pannier's edge. The woman had told me in the morning that she was of Scotland, which her accent fully proved, but that she had lived, I think, at Wigton, that they could not keep a house and so they travelled.

MAJESTIC MOUNTAINS, SERENE SKY, SCOUNDREL PEN: COLERIDGE AT KESWICK, 25 JULY 1800

Samuel Taylor Coleridge

Following the example of his lyrical poet collaborator Wordsworth, Samuel Taylor Coleridge also moved to the Lake District.

Friday, July 25, 1800
From the leads on the housetop of Greta Hall,
Keswick, Cumberland, at the present time in the
occupancy and usufruct-possession of S. T. Coleridge,
Esq., Gentleman-poet and Philosopher in a mist.

Yes, my dear Tobin, here I am, with Skiddaw behind my back; the Lake of Bassenthwaite, with its simple and majestic *case* of mountains, on my right hand; on my left, and stretching far away into the fantastic mountains of Borrowdale, the Lake of Derwentwater; straight before me a whole camp of giants' tents, – or is it an ocean rushing in, in billows that, even in the serene sky, reach halfway to heaven? When I look at the feathery top of this scoundrel pen, with which I am making desperate attempts to write. I see (in that slant direction) the sun almost setting, – in ten minutes it will touch the top of the crag; the vale of Keswick lies between us, so much for the topography of the letter; as to the chronology, it is half past seven in the evening.

I left Wordsworth yesterday; he was tolerably well, and meditates more than his side permits him even to attempt. He has a bed for you; but I absolutely stipulate that you shall be half the time at Keswick. We have house-room enough, and I am sure I need say nothing of anything else. What should prevent you from coming and spending the next brace of months here? I will suppose you to set off in the second week of August, and Davy will be here in the first week of September at the farthest; and then, my dear fellow, for physiopathy and phileleutherism – sympathy lemonaded with a little argument – punning and green peas with bacon, or *very ham*; rowing and sailing on the lake (there is a nice boat obsequious to my purposes). Then, as to chemistry, there will be Davy with us. We shall be as rich with reflected light as you cloud which the sun has taken to his very bosom!

When you come. I pray you do not forget to bring Bartram's Travels with you. Where is John Pinny? He talked of accompanying you. Wordsworth builds on his coming down this autumn; if I knew his present address. I would write to him. Wordworth remains at Grasmere till next summer (perhaps longer). His cottage is indeed in every respect so delightful a residence, the walks so dry after the longest rains, the heath and a silky kind of fern so luxurious a bedding on every hilltop, and the whole vicinity so tossed about on those little hills at the feet of the majestic mountains, that he moves in an eddy; he cannot get out of it.

In the way of books, we are extraordinarily well off for a country place. My landlord has a respectable library, full of dictionaries and useful modern things; *ex., gr.*, the Scotch Encyclopaedia, the authors of which may the devil scotch, for toothless serpents that poison with dribble! But there is at some distance Sir Wilfred

Lawson's magnificent library, and Sir Wilfred talks of calling upon me, and of course I keep the man in good humor with me, and gain the use of his books.

Hartley* returns his love to you; he talks often about you. I hear his voice at this moment distinctly; he is below in the garden, shouting to some foxgloves and fern, which he has transplanted, and telling them what he will do for them if they grow like good boys! This afternoon I sent him naked into a shallow of the river Greta; he trembled with the novelty, yet you cannot conceive his raptures.

God bless you!

I remain, with affectionate esteem,
Yours sincerely,
S. T. Coleridge.

I open the letter, and make a new fold, to tell you that I have bit the wafer [seal] into the very shape of the young moon that is just above the opposite hill.

Coleridge's happiness did not last. His opium habit precipitated a moral collapse of some years duration.

WELLINGTON MEETS NELSON, 10 SEPTEMBER 1805

Arthur Wellesley, 1st Duke of Wellington

I went to the Colonial Office in Downing Street and there I was shown into the little waiting-room on the right hand, where I found, also waiting to see the Secretary of State, a gentleman whom, from his likeness to his pictures and the loss of an arm, I immediately recognised as Lord Nelson. He could not know who I was, but he entered at once into conversation with me, if I can call it conversation, for it was almost all on his side and all about himself, and in, really, a style so vain and so silly as to surprise and almost disgust me. I suppose something that I happened to say may have made him guess that I was *somebody*, and he went out of the room for a moment, I have no doubt to ask the office-keeper who I was, for when he came back he was altogether a different

* STC's son.

man, both in manner and matter. All that I had thought a charlaton style had vanished, and he talked of the state of this country, and of the aspect and probabilities of affairs on the Continent with a good sense, and a knowledge of subjects both at home and abroad that surprised me . . . in fact he talked like an officer and a statesman. The Secretary of State kept us long waiting, and certainly, for the last half or three-quarters of an hour, I don't know that I ever had a conversation that interested me more. Now, if the Secretary of State had been punctual, and admitted Lord Nelson in the first quarter of an hour I should have had the same impression of a light and trivial character that other people have had.

FATAL DUEL, PLYMOUTH, 12 OCTOBER 1806

Naval Chronicle

Sunday Morning, 12 October, a duel was fought near the obelisk, Mount Edgecombe, by a Mr Armstrong, Midshipman of His Majesty's ship *Prince of Wales* and a Mr Long of the *Resistance* frigate, which lately sailed from Plymouth. His antagonist's ball entered Mr Long's right side and it is thought lodged in his left shoulder. This circumstance took place at half past eight o'clock in the morning, and was not made known until three in the afternoon when the Port Admiral ordered search for the deceased. He was found lying on his back, his hat on, his pockets turned out, and a cane lying across his arm. His second, Mr ——, Midshipman of the *Monarch* had left him immediately after the fatal ball was fired and returned to Dock with Mr Armstrong and Mr Wells of the *Prince of Wales*, his second.

The dispute originated in a common hop in Pembroke Street, where Armstrong wanted to put out the lights while the deceased was dancing with his girl. High words arose, and they immediately adjourned to an inn where the challenge was settled. Mr Long was a youth of engaging manners, about 18 years old, and, it is said, related to the Duke of Montrose. A strict search is making after the parties who, it is supposed, have gone on board their respective ships.

TRAFALGAR: THE VIEW FROM THE LOWER-DECK, 21 OCTOBER 1805

Sam

Trafalgar, off the port of Cadiz in Spain, was the decisive naval battle of the Napoleonic Wars. The author served aboard the *Royal Sovereign*.

Honoured Father,

This comes to tell you I am alive and hearty except three fingers; but that's not much, it might have been my head. I told brother Tom I should like to see a greadly battle, and I have seen one, and we have peppered the Combined rarely; and for the matter of that, they fought us pretty tightish for French and Spanish. Three of our mess are killed, and four more of us winged. But to tell you the truth of it, when the game began, I wished myself at Warnborough with my plough again; but when they had given us one duster, and I found myself snug and tight, I set to in good earnest, and thought no more about being killed than if I were at Murrell Green Fair, and I was presently as busy and as black as a collier. How my fingers got knocked overboard I don't know, but off they are, and I never missed them till I wanted them. You see, by my writing, it was my left hand, so I can write to you and fight for my King yet. We have taken a rare parcel of ships, but the wind is so rough we cannot bring them home, else I should roll in money, so we are busy smashing 'em, and blowing 'em up wholesale.

Our dear Admiral Nelson is killed! so we have paid pretty sharply for licking 'em. I never sat eyes on him, for which I am both sorry and glad; for, to be sure, I should like to have seen him – but then, all the men in our ship who have seen him are such soft toads, they have done nothing but blast their eyes, and cry, ever since he was killed. God bless you! chaps that fought like the devil, sit down and cry like a wench. I am still in the *Royal Sovereign*, but the Admiral (Collingwood) has left her, for she is like a horse without a bridle, so he is in a frigate that he may be here and there and everywhere, for he's as *cute* as here and there one, and as bold as a lion, for all he can cry! – I saw his tears with my own eyes, when the boat hailed and said my lord was dead. So no more at present from your dutiful son,

SAM.

TRAFALGAR: THE DEATH OF NELSON, 21 OCTOBER 1805

Dr William Beatty

Britain's victory over the combined French and Spanish fleet came at the cost of the life of Admiral Lord Nelson. Beatty was the *Victory*'s surgeon.

About half an hour before the enemy opened their fire, the memorable telegraphic signal was made, that "ENGLAND EXPECTS EVERY MAN WILL DO HIS DUTY," which was spread and received throughout the fleet with enthusiasm. It is impossible adequately to describe by any language the lively emotions excited in the crew of the *Victory* when this propitious communication was made known to them: confidence and resolution were strongly portrayed in the countenance of all; and the sentiment generally expressed to each other was that they would prove to their country that day how well British seamen *could* "do their duty" when led to battle by their revered admiral.

At fifty minutes past eleven, the enemy opened their fire on the commander in chief. They shewed great coolness in the commencement of the battle; for as the *Victory* approached their line, their ships lying immediately ahead of her and across her bows fired only one gun at a time, to ascertain whether she was yet within their range. This was frequently repeated by eight or nine of their ships, till at length a shot passed through the *Victory*'s main topgallant sail; the hole in which being discovered by the enemy, they immediately opened their broadsides, supporting an awful and tremendous fire.

In a very short time afterwards, Mr Scott, public secretary to the commander in chief, was killed by a cannon shot while in conversation with Captain Hardy. Lord Nelson being then near them; Captain Adair of the marines, with the assistance of a seaman, endeavoured to remove the body from his Lordship's sight: but he had already observed the fall of his secretary; and now said with anxiety, "Is that poor Scott that is gone?" and on being answered in the affirmative by Captain Adair, he replied, "Poor fellow!"

Lord Nelson and Captain Hardy walked the quarter deck in conversation for some time after this, while the enemy kept up an incessant raking fire.

A double-headed shot struck one of the parties of marines drawn up on the poop, and killed eight of them; when his Lordship, perceiving this, ordered Captain Adair to disperse his men round the ship, that they might not suffer so much from being together.

In a few minutes afterwards a shot struck the fore brace bits on the quarter deck, and passed between Lord Nelson and Captain Hardy; a splinter from the bits bruising Captain Hardy's foot, and tearing the buckle from his shoe. They both instantly stopped; and were observed by the officers on deck to survey each other with inquiring looks, each supposing the other to be wounded. His Lordship then smiled, and said: "This is too warm work, Hardy, to last long"; and declared that "through all the battles he had been in, he had never witnessed more cool courage than was displayed by the *Victory*'s crew on this occasion."

The *Victory* by this time, having approached close to the enemy's van, had suffered very severely without firing a single gun: she had lost about twenty men killed, and had about thirty wounded. Her mizzen topmast, and all her studding sails and their booms on both sides were shot away; the enemy's fire being chiefly directed at her rigging, with a view to disable her before she could close with them.

At four minutes past twelve o'clock, she opened her fire, from both sides of her decks, upon the enemy; when Captain Hardy represented to his Lordship, that "it appeared impracticable to pass through the enemy's line without going on board some one of their ships."

Lord Nelson answered, "I cannot help it: it does not signify which we run on board of; go on board which you please; take your choice."

At twenty minutes past twelve, the tiller ropes being shot away: Mr Atkinson, the master, was ordered below to get the helm put to port; which being done, the *Victory* was soon run on board the *Redoubtable* of seventy-four guns.

On coming alongside and nearly on board of her, that ship fired her broadside into the *Victory*, and immediately let down her lower deck ports; which, as has been since learnt, was done to prevent her from being boarded through them by the *Victory*'s crew. She never fired a great gun after this single broadside.

A few minutes after this, the *Téméraire* fell likewise on board of the *Redoubtable*, on the side opposite to the *Victory*; having also an enemy's ship, said to be *La Fougueux*, on board of *her* on her other side: so that the extraordinary and unprecedented circumstance occurred here, of *four* ships of the line being *on board of each other* in the heat of battle; forming as compact a tier as if they had been moored together, their heads lying all the same way. The *Téméraire*, as was just before mentioned, was between the *Redoubtable* and *La Fougueux*.

The *Redoubtable* commenced a heavy fire of musketry from the tops, which was continued for a considerable time with destructive effect to the *Victory*'s crew: her great guns however being silent, it was supposed at different times that she had surrendered; and in consequence of this opinion, the *Victory* twice ceased firing upon her by orders transmitted from the quarter deck.

At this period, scarcely a person in the *Victory* escaped unhurt who was exposed to the enemy's musketry; but there were frequent huzzas and cheers heard from between the decks, in token of the surrender of different of the enemy's ships. An incessant fire was kept up from both sides of the *Victory*: her larboard guns played upon the *Santissima Trinidada* and the *Bucentaur*; and the starboard guns of the middle and lower decks were depressed, and fired with a diminished charge of powder, and three shot each, into the *Redoubtable*. This mode of firing was adopted by Lieutenants Williams, King, Yule, and Brown, to obviate the danger of the *Téméraire*'s suffering from the *Victory*'s shot passing through the *Redoubtable*; which must have been the case if the usual quantity of powder, and the common elevation, had been given to the guns.

A circumstance occurred in this situation which showed in a most striking manner the cool intrepidity of the officers and men stationed on the lower deck of the *Victory*. When the guns on this deck were run out, their muzzles came into contact with the *Redoubtable*'s side; and consequently at every discharge there was reason to fear that the enemy would take fire, and both the *Victory* and the *Téméraire* be involved in her flames. Here then was seen the astonishing spectacle of the fireman of each gun standing ready with a bucket full of water, which as soon as his gun was discharged he dashed into the enemy through the holes made in her side by the shot.

It was from this ship (the *Redoubtable*) that Lord Nelson received his mortal wound. About fifteen minutes past one o'clock, which was in the heat of the engagement, he was walking the middle of the quarterdeck with Captain Hardy, and in the act of turning near the hatchway with his face towards the stern of the *Victory*, when the fatal ball was fired from the enemy's mizen-top; which, from the situation of the two ships (lying on board of each other), was brought just abaft, and rather below, the *Victory's* main-yard, and of course not more than fifteen yards distant from that part of the deck where his Lordship stood. The ball struck the epaulette on his left shoulder, and penetrated his chest. He fell with his face on the deck. Captain Hardy, who was on his right (the side furthest from the enemy) and advanced some steps before his Lordship, on turning round, saw the Sergeant-Major (Secker) of Marines with two seamen raising him from the deck; where he had fallen on the same spot on which, a little before, his secretary had breathed his last, with whose blood his Lordship's clothes were much soiled. Captain Hardy expressed a hope that he was not severely wounded; to which the gallant Chief replied: "They have done for me at last, Hardy." "I hope not," answered Captain Hardy. "Yes," replied his Lordship, "my backbone is shot through."

Captain Hardy ordered the seamen to carry the Admiral to the cockpit; and now two incidents occurred strikingly characteristic of this great man, and strongly marking that energy and reflection which in his heroic mind rose superior even to the immediate consideration of his present awful condition. While the men were carrying him down the ladder from the middle deck, his Lordship observed that the tiller ropes were not yet replaced; and desired one of the midshipmen stationed there to go up on the quarterdeck and remind Captain Hardy of that circumstance, and request that new ones should be immediately rove. Having delivered this order, he took his handkerchief from his pocket and covered his face with it, that he might be conveyed to the cockpit at this crisis unnoticed by the crew . . .

The *Victory's* crew cheered whenever they observed an enemy's ship surrender. On one of these occasions, Lord Nelson anxiously inquired what was the cause of it; when Lieutenant Pasco, who lay wounded at some distance from his Lordship, raised himself up, and told him that another ship had struck: which appeared to give him much satisfaction. He now felt an ardent thirst; and frequently called for drink, and to be fanned with paper, making use of these words: "Fan, fan," and "Drink, drink." This he continued to repeat, when he wished for drink or the refreshment of cool air, till a very few minutes before he expired . . .

His Lordship now requested the surgeon, who had been previously absent a short time attending Mr Rivers to return to the wounded, and give his assistance to such of them as he could be useful to; "for," said he, "you can do nothing for me." The surgeon assured him that the assistant surgeons were doing everything that could be effected for those unfortunate men; but on his Lordship's several times repeating his injunctions to that purpose, he left him, surrounded by Doctor Scott, Mr Burke and two of his Lordship's domestics. After the surgeon had been absent a few minutes attending Lieutenants Peake and Reeves of the Marines, who were wounded, he was called by Doctor Scott to his Lordship, who said: "Ah, Mr Beatty! I have sent for you to say, what I forgot to tell you before, that all power of motion and feeling below my breast are gone; and *you*," continued he, "very well *know* I can live but a short time." The emphatic manner in which he pronounced these last words left no doubt in the surgeon's mind, that he adverted to the case of a man who had some months before received a mortal injury of the spine on board the *Victory*, and had laboured under similar privations of sense and muscular motion. The case had made a great impression on Lord Nelson: he was accordingly explained to him; and he now appeared to apply the situation and fate of this man to himself. The surgeon answered, "My Lord, you told me so before": but he now examined the extremities, to ascertain the fact; when his Lordship said, "Ah, Beatty! I am too certain of it: Scott and Burke have tried it already. *You know* I am gone." The surgeon replied: "My Lord, unhappily for our country, nothing can be done for you", and having made this declaration he was so much affected, that he turned round and withdrew a few steps to conceal his emotions. His Lordship said: "I know it. I feel something rising in my breast," putting his hand on his left side, "which tells me I am gone." Drink was recommended liberally, and Doctor Scott and Mr Burke fanned him with paper. He often exclaimed, "God be praised, I have done my duty": and upon the surgeon's inquiring whether his pain was still very great, he declared, it continued so very severe, that he wished he was dead. "Yet," said he in a lower voice, "one would like to live a little longer, too": and after a pause of a few minutes, he added in the same tone, "What would become of poor Lady Hamilton (Nelson's mistress), if she knew my situation!" . . .

Captain Hardy now came to the cockpit to see his Lordship a second time, which was after an interval of about fifty minutes from the conclusion of his first visit. Before he quitted the deck, he sent Lieutenant Hills to acquaint Admiral Collingwood with the lamentable circumstance of Lord Nelson's being wounded. Lord Nelson and Captain Hardy shook hands again: and while the Captain retained his Lordship's hand, he congratulated him, even in the arms of death, on his brilliant victory; "which," said he, "was complete"; though he did not know how many of the enemy were captured, as it was impossible to perceive every ship distinctly. He was certain however of fourteen or fifteen having surrendered. His Lordship answered, "That is well, but I bargained for twenty": and then emphatically exclaimed, "*Anchor*, Hardy, *anchor*!" To this the Captain replied: "I suppose, my Lord, Admiral Collingwood will now take upon himself the direction of affairs." "Not while I live, I hope, Hardy!" cried the dying chief; and at that moment endeavoured ineffectually to raise himself from the bed. "No," added he; "do *you* anchor, Hardy." Captain Hardy then said: "Shall *we* make the signal, sir?" "Yes," answered his Lordship, "for if I live, I'll anchor." The energetic manner in which he uttered these his last orders to Captain Hardy, accompanied with his efforts to raise himself, evinced his determination never to resign the command while he retained the exercise of his transcendent faculties, and that he expected Captain Hardy still to carry into effect the suggestions of his exalted mind; a sense of his duty overcoming the pains of death. He then told Captain Hardy, he felt that in a few minutes he should be no more; adding in a low tone, "Don't throw me overboard, Hardy." The Captain answered: "Oh! no, certainly not", "Then," replied his Lordship, "You know what to do: and", continued he, "take care of my dear Lady Hamilton, Hardy: take care of poor Lady Hamilton. Kiss me, Hardy." The Captain now knelt down, and kissed his cheek; when his Lordship said, "Now I am satisfied. Thank God, I have done my duty." Captain Hardy stood for a minute or two in silent contemplation: he knelt down again, and kissed his Lordship's forehead. His Lordship said: "Who is that?" The Captain answered: "It is Hardy"; to which his Lordship replied, "God bless you, Hardy!" . . . His thirst now increased; and he called for "drink, drink," "fan, fan," and "rub, rub," addressing himself in the last case to Doctor Scott, who had been rubbing his Lordship's breast with his hand, from which he found some relief. These words he spoke in a very rapid manner, which rendered his articulation difficult: but he every now and then, with evident increase of pain, made a greater effort with his vocal powers, and pronounced distinctly these last words: "Thank God, I have done my duty";

and this great sentiment he continued to repeat as long as he was able to give it utterance.

PLUNDERING A DEAD FRENCH SOLDIER, VIMEIRO, 21 AUGUST 1808

Rifleman Harris

An incident from the Peninsular War. Robbing the battlefield dead was almost an occupational perk for the 19th century soldier.

After the battle I strolled about the field in order to see if there was anything to be found worth picking up amongst the dead. The first thing I saw was a three-pronged silver fork, which, as it lay by itself, had most likely been dropped by some person who had been on the look-out before me. A little further on I saw a French soldier sitting against a small rise in the ground or bank. He was wounded in the throat, and appeared very faint, the bosom of his coat being saturated with the blood which had flowed down. By his side lay his cap, and close to that was a bundle containing a quantity of gold and silver crosses, which I concluded he had plundered from some convent or church. He looked the picture of a sacrilegious thief, dying hopelessly, and overtaken by Divine wrath. I kicked over his cap, which was also full of plunder, but I declined taking anything from him. I felt fearful of incurring the wrath of Heaven for the like offence, so I left him, and passed on. A little further off lay an officer of the 50th regiment. I knew him by sight, and recognised him as he lay. He was quite dead, and lying on his back. He had been plundered, and his clothes were torn open. Three bullet-holes were close together in the pit of his stomach: beside him lay an empty pocket-book, and his epaulette had been pulled from his shoulder.

I had moved on but a few paces when I recollected that perhaps the officer's shoes might serve me, my own being considerably the worse for wear, so I returned again, went back, pulled one of his shoes off, and knelt down on one knee to try it on. It was not much better than my own; however, I determined on the exchange, and proceeded to take off its fellow. As I did so I was startled by the sharp report of a firelock, and, at the same moment, a bullet whistled close by my head. Instantly starting up, I turned, and looked in the direction whence the shot had come. There was no person near me in this part of the field. The dead and the dying lay thickly all around; but nothing else could I see. I looked to the priming of my rifle, and again turned to the dead officer of the 50th. It was evident that some plundering scoundrel had taken a shot at me, and the fact of his doing so proclaimed him one of the enemy. To distinguish him amongst the bodies strewn about was impossible; perhaps he might himself be one of the wounded. Hardly had I effected the exchange, put on the dead officer's shoes, and resumed my rifle, when another shot took place, and a second ball whistled past me. This time I was ready, and turning quickly, I saw my man: he was just about to squat down behind a small mound, about twenty paces from me. I took a haphazard shot at him, and instantly knocked him over. I immediately ran up to him; he had fallen on his face, and I heaved him over on his back, bestrode his body, and drew my sword-bayonet. There was, however, no occasion for the precaution as he was even then in the agonies of death.

It was a relief to me to find I had not been mistaken. He was a French light-infantry man, and I therefore took it quite in the way of business – he had attempted my life, and lost his own. It was the fortune of war; so, stooping down, with my sword I cut the green string that sustained his calibash, and took a hearty pull to quench my thirst.

After I had shot the French light-infantry man, and quenched my thirst from his calibash, finding he was quite dead, I proceeded to search him. Whilst I turned him about in the endeavour at finding the booty I felt pretty certain he had gathered from the slain, an officer of the 60th approached, and accosted me.

"What! looking for money, my lad," said he, "eh?"

"I am, sir," I answered; "but I cannot discover where this fellow has hid his hoard."

"You knocked him over, my man," he said, "in good style, and deserve something for the shot. Here," he continued, stooping down and feeling in the lining of the Frenchman's coat, "this is the place where these rascals generally carry their coin. Rip up the lining of his coat, and then search in his stock. I know them better than you seem to do."

Thanking the officer for his courtesy, I proceeded to cut open the lining of his jacket with my sword-bayonet, and was quickly rewarded for my labour by finding a yellow silk purse, wrapped up in an old black silk handkerchief. The purse contained several doubloons, three or four napoleons, and a few dollars. Whilst I was counting the money, the value of which, except the dollars, I did not then know, I heard the bugle of the Rifles sound out the assembly, so I touched my cap to the officer, and returned towards them.

The men were standing at ease, with the officers in front. As I approached them, Major Travers, who was in command of the four companies, called me to him.

"What have you got there, sir?" he said. "Show me."

I handed him the purse, expecting a reprimand for my pains. He, however, only laughed as he examined it, and, turning, showed it to his brother officers.

"You did that well, Harris," he said, "and I am sorry the purse is not better filled. Fall in." In saying this, he handed me back the purse, and I joined my company. Soon afterwards, the roll being called, we were all ordered to lie down and gain a little rest after our day's work.

LONDON ON SATURDAY NIGHT (AFTER THE PARTAKING OF OPIUM), c. 1812

Thomas De Quincey

From De Quincey's *Confessions of an English Opium-Eater*.

. . . I used often, on Saturday nights, after I had taken opium, to wander forth, without much regarding the direction or the distance, to all the markets, and other parts of London, whither the poor resort on a Saturday night, for laying out their wages. Many a family party, consisting of a man, his wife, and sometimes one or two of their children, have I listened to, as they stood consulting on their ways and means, or the strength of their exchequer, or the price of household articles. Gradually I became familiar with their wishes, their difficulties, and their opinions. Sometimes there might be heard murmurs of discontent; but far oftener expressions on the countenance, or uttered in words, of patience, of hope, and of reconciliation to their lot. Generally speaking, the impression left upon my mind was, that the poor are practically more philosophic than the rich; that they show a more ready and cheerful submission to what they consider as irremediable evils or irreparable losses. Whenever I saw occasion, or could do it without appearing to be intrusive, I joined their parties, and gave my opinion upon the matter in discussion, which, if not always judicious, was always received indulgently. If wages were a little higher, or were expected to be so – if the quartern loaf were a little lower, or it was reported that onions and butter were falling, I was glad; yet, if the contrary were true, I drew from opium some means of consolation. For opium (like the bee, that extracts its materials indiscriminately from roses and from the soot of chimneys) can overrule all feelings into a compliance with the master-key. Some of these rambles led me to great distances; for an opium-eater is too happy to observe the motion of time. And sometimes, in my attempts to steer homewards, upon nautical principles, by fixing my eye on the pole-star, and seeking ambitiously for a north-west passage, instead of circumnavigating all the capes and headlands I had doubled in my outward voyage, I came suddenly upon such knotty problems of alleys, alleys without soundings, such enigmatical entries, and such sphinx's riddles of streets, without obvious outlets or thoroughfares, as must baffle the audacity of porters, and confound the intellects of hackney coachmen. I could almost have believed, at times, that I must be the first discoverer of some of these *terrae incognitae*, and doubted whether they had yet been laid down in the modern charts of London. Positively, in one line of communication to the south of Holborn, for foot passengers (known, I doubt not, to many of my London readers), the road lay through a man's kitchen; and as it was a small kitchen, you needed to steer cautiously, or else you might run foul of the dripping-pan.

STORMING BADAJOZ, 6 APRIL 1812

Lieutenant William Grattan

Although Britannia ruled the waves in the Napoleonic Wars (1803–1815), her military interventions on land tended to be inglorious affairs on the edge of matters. The exceptions were Waterloo in 1815 and before that Wellington's determined campaign in Iberia.

There is a solemnity of feeling which accompanies the expectation of every great event in our lives, and the man who can be altogether dead to such feeling is little, if anything, better than a brute. The present moment was one that was well calculated to fill every bosom throughout the army; for, mixed with expectation, hope, and suspense, it was rendered still more touching to the heart by the music of some of the regiments, which played at the head of

THE AGE OF EMPIRE 343

each battalion as the soldiers sauntered about to beguile the last hour many of them were destined to live. The band of my corps, the 88th, all Irish, played several airs which exclusively belong to their country, and it is impossible to describe the effect it had upon us all; such an air as "Savourneen Deelish" is sufficient, at any time, to inspire a feeling of melancholy, but on an occasion like the present it acted powerfully on the feelings of the men: they thought of their distant homes, of their friends, and of bygone days. It was Easter Sunday, and the contrast which their present position presented to what it would have been were they in their native land afforded ample food for the occupation of their minds; but they were not allowed time for much longer reflection. The approach of General Kempt, accompanied by his staff, was the signal for the formation of the column of attack; and almost immediately the men were ordered to stand to their arms. Little, if any, directions were given; indeed, they were unnecessary, because the men, from long service, were so conversant with the duty they had to perform, that it would have been but a waste of words and time to say what was required of them.

All was now in readiness. It was twenty-five minutes past nine; the soldiers, unencumbered with their knapsacks – their stocks off – their shirt-collars unbuttoned – their trousers tucked up to the knee – their tattered jackets, so worn out as to render the regiment they belonged to barely recognisable – their huge whiskers and bronzed faces, which several hard-fought campaigns had changed from their natural hue – but, above all, their self-confidence, devoid of boast or bravado, gave them the appearance of what they in reality were – an invincible host.

The division now moved forward in one solid mass – the 45th leading, followed closely by the 88th and 74th; the brigade of Portuguese, consisting of the 9th and 21st Regiments of the line, under Colonel de Champlemond, were next; while the 5th, 77th, 83rd, and 94th, under Colonel Campbell, brought up the rear. Their advance was undisturbed until they reached the Rivillas; but at this spot some fire-balls, which the enemy threw out, caused a great light, and the 3rd Division, four thousand strong, was to be seen from the ramparts of the castle. The soldiers, finding they were discovered, raised a shout of defiance, which was responded to by the garrison, and in a moment afterwards every gun that could be brought to bear against them was in action; but, no way daunted by the havoc made in his ranks, Picton, who just then joined his soldiers, forded the Rivillas, knee-deep, and soon gained the foot of the castle wall, and here he saw the work that was cut out for him, for he no longer fought in darkness. The vast quantity of combustible matter which out-topped this stupendous defence was in a blaze, and the flames which issued forth on every side lighted not only the ramparts and the ditch, but the plain that intervened between them and the Rivillas. A host of veterans crowned the wall, all armed in a manner as imposing as novel; each man had beside him eight loaded firelocks; while at intervals, and proportionably distributed, were pikes of an enormous length, with crooks attached to them, for the purpose of grappling with the ladders. The top of the wall was covered with rocks of ponderous size, only requiring a slight push to hurl them upon the heads of our soldiers, and there was a sufficiency of hand-grenades and small shells at the disposal of the men that defended this point to have destroyed the entire of the besieging army; while on the flanks of each curtain, batteries, charged to the muzzle with grape and case shot, either swept away entire sections or disorganised the ladders as they were about to be placed, and an incessant storm of musketry, at the distance of fifteen yards, completed the resources the enemy brought into play, which, as may be seen, were of vast formidableness.

To oppose this mass of warriors and heterogeneous congregation of missiles Picton had nothing to depend upon for success but his tried and invincible old soldiers – he relied firmly upon their devoted courage, and he was not disappointed. The terrible aspect of the rugged wall, thirty feet in height, in no way intimidated them; and, under a frightful fire of small arms and artillery, the ponderous ladders were dragged into the ditch and, with a degree of hardihood that augured well for the issue, were planted against the lofty battlements that domineered above his soldiers' heads: but this was only the commencement of one of the most terrific struggles recorded during this hardfought night. Each ladder, so soon as placed upright, was speedily mounted and crowded from the top round to the bottom one; but those who escaped the pike-thrusts were shattered to atoms by the heavy cross-fire from the bastions, and the soldiers who occupied them, impaled upon the bayonets of their comrades in the ditch, died at the foot of those ladders which they had carried such a distance and with so much labour.

An hour had now passed over. No impression had been made

upon the castle, and the affair began to have a very doubtful appearance, for already well nigh half of the 3rd Division had been cut off. General Kempt, commanding the right brigade, fell wounded, early in the night; and the 88th Regiment alone, the strongest in the division, lost more than half their officers and men, while the other regiments were scarcely in a better condition. Picton, seeing the frightful situation in which he was placed, became uneasy; but the goodwill with which his brave companions exposed and laid down their lives reassured him; he called out to his men – told them they had never been defeated, and that now was the moment to conquer or die. Picton, although not loved by his soldiers, was respected by them; and his appeal, as well as his unshaken front, did wonders in changing the desperate state of the division. Major Ridge of the 5th, by his personal exertions, caused two ladders to be placed upright, and he himself led the way to the top of one, while Canch, a Grenadier officer of the 5th, mounted the other. A few men at last got footing on the top of the wall; at the same time Lieutenant William Mackie of the 88th – he who led the forlorn hope at Rodrigo (unnoticed! – still a lieutenant!!) – and Mr Richard Martin (son of the member for Galway, who acted as a volunteer with the 88th during the siege) succeeding in mounting another. Mackie – ever foremost in the fight – soon established his men on the battlements, himself unhurt; but Martin fell desperately wounded. A general rush to the ladders now took place, and the dead and wounded that lay in the ditch were indiscriminately trampled upon, for humanity was nowhere to be found. A frightful butchery followed this success; and the shouts of our soldiery, mingled with the cries of the Frenchmen, supplicating for mercy or in the agonies of death, were heard at a great distance. But few prisoners were made; and the division occupied, with much regularity, the different points allotted to each regiment. Meanwhile the ravelin of San Roque was carried by the gorge, by a detachment drawn from the trenches, under the command of Major Wilson of the 48th; and the engineers were directed to blow up the dam and sluice that caused the inundation of the Rivillas, by which means the passage of that river between La Picurina and the breaches could be more easily effected. One entire regiment of Germans, called the regiment of Hesse Darmstadt, that defended the ravelin were put to death.

While all this was taking place at the castle and San Roque, a fearful scene was acting at the breaches. The Light and 4th

Divisions, ten thousand strong, advanced to the glacis undiscovered – a general silence pervading the whole, as the spirits of the men settled into that deep sobriety which denotes much determination of purpose; but at this spot their footsteps were heard, and, "perhaps since the invention of gunpowder," its effects were never more powerfully brought into action. In a moment the different materials which the enemy had arranged in the neighbourhood of the breaches were lighted up – darkness was converted into light – torches blazed along the battlements – and a spectator, at a short distance from the walls, could distinguish the features of the contending parties. A battery of mortars, doubly loaded with grenades, and a blaze of musketry, unlike anything hitherto witnessed by the oldest soldier, opened a murderous fire against the two divisions; but, unshaken by its effects, they pressed onward and jumped into the ditch. The 4th Division, destined to carry the breach to the right, met with a frightful catastrophe at the onset. The leading platoons, consisting of the fusilier brigade, sprang into that part of the ditch that had been filled by the inundation of the Rivillas, and were seen no more; but the bubbles that rose on the surface of the water were a terrible assurance of the struggles which those devoted soldiers – the men of Albuera – ineffectually made to extricate themselves from the deadly grasp of each other, and from so unworthy an end.

Warned by the fate of their companions, the remainder turned to the left, and following the footsteps of the Light Division, pressed onwards in one mingled mass to the breaches of the curtain and La Trinidad. Arrived here, they encountered a series of obstacles that it was impossible to surmount, and which I find great difficulty in describing. Planks, of a sufficient length and breadth to embrace the entire face of the breaches, studded with spikes a foot long, were to be surmounted ere they reached the top of the breach; yet some there were – the brave Colonel Macleod, of the 43rd, amongst the number – who succeeded so far, but on gaining the top, *chevaux de frise*, formed of long swordblades firmly fixed in the trunks of trees of a great size, and chained, boom-like, across the breach, were still to be passed; while at each side, and behind the *chevaux de frise*, trenches were cut, sufficiently extensive for the accommodation of three thousand men, who stood in an amphitheatrical manner – each tier above the other – and armed with eight muskets each, like their companions at the castle, awaited the attack so soon as the planks on the face, and the *chevaux de frise* on

the top of the breach were surmounted; but they might have
waited until doomsday for that event, because it was morally
impossible.

The vast glare of light caused by the different explosions, and the
fire of cannon and musketry, gave to the breaches the appearance
of a volcano vomiting forth fire in the midst of the army: the
ground shook – meteors shone forth in every direction – and when
for a moment the roar of battle ceased, it was succeeded by cries of
agony, or the furious exultation of the imperial soldiers. To stand
before such a storm of fire, much less endeavour to overcome a
barrier so impregnable, required men whose minds, as well as
frames, were cast in a mould not human; but, nevertheless, so it
was. The gallant Light and 4th Divisions boldly braved every
danger, and with a good will, rarely to be found, prolonged a
struggle, the very failure of which, taking into account the nature
of the obstacles opposed to them, and their immense losses, was
sufficient to immortalise them. At length, after a dreadful sacrifice
of lives – all the generals, and most of the colonels, being either
killed or wounded – they were driven from the breaches, while the
Frenchmen, securely entrenched behind them, might be seen
waving their caps in token of defiance. This was too galling for
men who had never known defeat – and they ran back headlong to
the attack, and destruction. But for what end? To judge from the
past, when their numbers were more numerous, they had failed;
they were now reduced to less than half, while the resources of the
enemy were unimpaired, and the prospect before them was
hideous. Again did they attempt to pass this terrible gulf of steel
and flame – and again were they driven back – cut down –
annihilated. Hundreds of brave soldiers lay in piles upon each
other, weltering in blood, and trodden down by their own companions. The 43rd left twenty-two officers and three hundred men
on the breach; four companies of the 52nd were blown to atoms by
an explosion; and the 95th, as indeed every other regiment engaged, suffered in proportion. Our batteries, from whence a clear
view of all that was passing could be distinguished, maddened by
the havoc at the breaches, poured in a torrent of shot; and, in the
excitement of the moment, killed friends as well as foes. Finally, the
remnant of the two divisions retired; and, with a valour bordering
upon desperation, prepared for a third trial; but the success of
Picton's attack was by this time whispered amongst them, and the
evacuation of the breaches soon after confirmed the rumour.

While the attack of the castle and breaches was in progress, the 5th Division, under General Leith, maintained a fierce and dangerous struggle on the other side of the city beyond the Pardeleras fort; but the resistance at those points was feeble, as compared with the other two. In some instances the French troops deserted the walls before they were carried; and it is worthy of remark, that while the 38th Regiment were mounting the ladders, the imperial soldiers were scrambling down them at the reverse side – in many instances treading upon the fingers of our own men! The few men of Leith's division, thus established on the ramparts, boldly pressed on in the hope of causing a change in favour of the men at the breaches; but the multitude that had fled before this handful of troops became reassured when they beheld the scantiness of their numbers, and, returning to the fight, forced them up a street leading to the ramparts. Leith's men became panic-struck by this unexpected burst, and retraced their steps in confusion; many were killed ere they reached the wall; and some, infected by the contagion of the moment, jumped over the battlements, and were dashed to pieces in their fall. One, an officer, bearing the flag of his regiment, fearing it might be captured, flung himself from the wall, and falling into a part of the ditch that was filled with the slime of the river, escaped unhurt. At this critical moment General Walker reached the spot with a fresh body of troops, and driving back the French with ruinous disorder, established his men at this point; and from that moment the fate of Badajoz was sealed. The enemy fled in every direction towards the bridge leading to San Christoval; and the remnant of the ill-fated Light and 4th Divisions with difficulty entered the town by the breaches, although unopposed.

It was now half-past two o'clock in the morning, and the fighting had continued, without cessation, from ten the preceding night. More than three hundred and fifty officers and four thousand men had fallen on our side; yet the enemy's loss was but small in proportion; because, with the exception of the castle, where the 3rd Division got fairly amongst them, the French, with that tact for which they are so remarkable, got away the moment they found themselves out-matched.

British casualties in the assault were 34,000. Afterwards, British troops vented their fury in a drunken, bloody orgy and for 29 hours Wellington was unable to gain control of the "scum of the earth".

THE WAR OF 1812: A RELUCTANT FUSILIER AT NEW ORLEANS, 8 JANUARY 1815

Sergeant John Spencer Cooper

The US Congress declared war on Britain in 1812 after the latter's repeated violations of American maritime rights. A less honourable cause of the war was American desire to assimilate parts of British Canada.

After landing, we marched towards New Orleans, each man carrying a cannon ball in his haversack, as we had no baggage animals. Now two balls would have been more easily carried than one, because they would have poised each other.

'Tis said "Delays are dangerous." So we proved it. The troops that had preceded us had been on shore about three weeks; but not being strong enough to meet the enemy, they had not advanced far from the sea.

As the fleet could not approach within about forty miles of the position, all the artillery, ammunition, and provisions, etc., had to be brought to us in boats. While all went on so tardily, the Americans were cutting trenches, mounting cannon, etc., across a narrow plain, which had the mighty Mississippi on the right, and a marshy dense wood on the left. A frigate also was posted on the river in such a situation that it could rake the whole line. Batteries were also planted on the right or farther bank of the river.

The force which the Americans had to defend this narrow front was said to be about 14,000. A deep wide ditch, in front of high breastworks, ran along the whole line of defence. Our whole force for attacking this formidable work, did not exceed 7,000 including several hundred sailors sent from the fleet.

The front of our position was perfectly flat, on which three small guns were planted; but these were of little use, being only six pounders.

On the day before the battle, I, with three or four more, was selected to join my old comrades in the Light Company, from which I had been transferred when made sergeant; but the captain would not let me go back. This probably saved my life, for the Light Company, with a company of the 43rd, and one of the 85th, stormed the right redoubt next day, and would have established themselves there, had they been supported.

The same evening, hearing that we were to storm the enemy's works in the morning, several of us went to the colonel's tent, and reminded him that we should have been discharged at Portsmouth and sent home, according to orders from the Duke of York, then Commander-in-Chief. He said it could not be helped. This did not satisfy us, so we hurried to Head Quarters, to speak to Sir Edward Pakenham, but he was out viewing the enemy's defences.

Early in the morning of January 8th, 1815, we were assembled within cannon shot of the American entrenchments, as the reserve or second line. This was certainly a grand mistake, for the troops in front were composed of two black West India regiments, and other corps that had not been employed in sieges, etc., as we had in Spain.

Just as the day was breaking, a rocket whizzed aloft. All stood ready for the assault. At the word "Forward!" the two lines approached the ditch under a murderous discharge of musketry; but crossing the ditch and scaling the parapet were found impossible without ladders. These had been prepared, but the regiment that should have carried them left them behind, and thereby caused, in a few minutes, a dreadful loss of men and officers; while the enemy suffered little, being ensconced behind the parapet. The front line now fell into great confusion, and retreated behind us, leaving numerous killed and wounded. We then advanced to within musket shot; but the balls flew so thickly that we were ordered to lie down to avoid the shower.

In the meantime our Light Company, and the two companies before mentioned, had gained a footing on the right of the American works; but having no support at hand, the enemy returned in force, and drove them into the ditch, where they were exposed to a plunging fire from above, and a flank fire from the frigate. One of the officers in the ditch vented his spleen at the enemy above by throwing stones. At last, the companies bolted from the ditch and ran off stoopingly in different directions. One of them, named Henry Axhorn, a smart young fellow, received a ball above his hip, which ran up his body, and stuck near his eye. It was extracted in a hospital at New Orleans. He joined us again after the peace, much altered in shape, and not fit for further service. Our Light Company went into this action sixty-four strong, and returned sixteen-having lost forty-eight.

That part of our force which was despatched to storm the enemy's works on the other side of the river, pushed off when the rocket was fired; but being few in number, they effected nothing of importance.

On our part, just before the order was given to lie down, my right hand man received a bullet in his forehead, and fell dead across my feet. This man was drunk the night before, and cursing the seven years' men for wishing to be discharged. Poor Fitzpatrick had been considered an honest man; but his knapsack, when opened, showed him to have been a sly thief.

Another man, about ten or twelve files on my right, was smashed to pieces by a cannon ball. I felt something strike my cap; I took it off, and found sticking to it a portion of his brains, about the size of a marble. A young man on my left got a wound on the top of his head, and ran to the surgeon behind us; he was dressed and sent into his place again. Close to him, another man had his arm so badly fractured near the shoulder that it was taken out of the cup. A few yards behind sat a black man, with all the lower part of his face shot away; his eyes were gone, and the bones of his brow all jagged, and dripping blood. Near him, in a ditch, lay one of the 43rd, trying to hold in his bowels.

The enemy kept pounding away at us all day; during which a shower of grape came whizzing like a flock of partridges, and struck Major King dead.

We lay on the ground under the enemy's fire until dusk, when we retired four or five hundred yards, and took up our quarters in some huts made of sugar canes. Here, without a single breastwork, battery, or ditch, we remained ten days; while the enemy threw shot and shell into our lines day and night. However, they took care not to leave their works.

The day after the battle, a truce for six hours being agreed upon, a party of us was sent to bury the dead. In this sad duty, the Americans brought ours to a ditch between our lines and theirs, and laid the bodies in rows. We then took them and threw them into ditches. While this was being done, an American officer strutted about, sword in hand, on his side of the ditch, to our great amusement. An American soldier, looking at the long rows of the slain, exclaimed, "I never saw the like of that!" One of our party sneeringly said. "That's nowt, man; if you'd been wi' us in Spain, you would ha' seen summat far war!"

While removing the bodies, I stripped two poor fellows of their shirts; they were bloody enough, but I wanted them sadly.

The funeral being over, and the truce having expired, we retired to our huts in haste, and then the game of cannonading began again.

The Americans were highly elated at having beaten the Brit-ishers, and I believe they boast of it to this day. But all things considered, they had little reason. Let us recapitulate-they were in number about 14,000, behind strong breast works, and a deep ditch; a frigate protected their right flank, a wood and morass their left. Cannon were plentiful all along their front.

Our force numbered about 7,000 including perhaps 1,000 sailors. We had no works, no ditch and only three small guns. Shelter we had none, for the ground in front of the enemy's works for about a mile was as flat as a bowling green.

Of the 1,200 that should have crossed the river, no more than three or four hundred could be supplied with boats. But the chief cause of our failure was the want of ladders, which a certain regiment should have carried, but did not. Had Wellington been there, the Americans would have had less to boast of.

British losses were 2000 killed, wounded or captured. American losses were eight dead.

WATERLOO, BELGIUM, 18 JUNE 1815

Ensign Edmund Wheatley, the King's German Legion

The armies of Napoleon and the Duke of Wellington that met at Water-loo, a village in Belgium, were of similar size, at around 70,000 men apiece.

About ten o'clock, the order came to clean out the muskets and fresh load them. Half an allowance of rum was then issued, and we descended into the plain, and took our position in solid Squares. When this was arranged as per order, we were ordered to remain in our position but, if we like, to lay down, which the battalion did [as well as] the officers in the rere.

I took this opportunity of surveying our situation. It was singular to perceive the shoals of Cavalry and artillery suddenly in our rere all arranged in excellent order as if by a magic wand. The whole of the horse Guards stood behind us. For my part I thought they were at Knightsbridge barracks or prancing on St James's Street.

A Ball whizzed in the air. Up we started simultaneously. I looked at my watch. It was just eleven o'clock, Sunday . . . morning. In five minutes a stunning noise took place and a shocking havock commenced.

One could almost feel the undulation of the air from the multitude of cannon shot. The first man who fell was five files on my left. With the utmost distortion of feature he lay on his side and shrivelling up every muscle of the body he twirled his elbow round and round in acute agony, then dropped lifeless, dying as it's called a death of glory, heaving his last breath on the field of fame. *Dieu m'engarde!*

A black consolidated body was soon seen approaching and we distinguished by sudden flashes of light from the sun's rays, the iron-cased cavalry of the enemy. Shouts of "Stand firm!" "Stand fast!" were heard from the little squares around and very quickly these gigantic fellows were upon us.

No words can convey the sensation we felt on seeing these heavy-armed bodies advancing at full gallop against us, flourishing their sabres in the air, striking their armour with the handles, the sun gleaming on the steel. The long horse hair, dishevelled by the wind, bore an appearance confounding the senses to an astonishing disorder. But we dashed them back as coolly as the sturdy rock repels the ocean's foam. The sharp-toothed bayonet bit many an adventurous fool, and on all sides we presented our bristly points like the peevish porcupines assailed by clamorous dogs.

The horse Guards then came up and drove them back; and although the sight is shocking 'tis beautiful to see the skirmish of Cavalry.

The French made repeated attacks of this kind. But we stood firm as the ground we stood on, and two long hours were employed in these successive attacks.

About two o'clock the cavalry ceased annoying and the warfare took a new turn. In order to destroy our squares, the enemy filled the air with shells, howitzers and bombs, so that every five or six minutes, the whole Battalion lay on its face then sprang up again when the danger was over.

The Prince of Orange gallop'd by, screaming out like a new born infant, "Form into line! Form into line!" And we obeyed.

About this time the battle grew faint and a mutual cannonade with musketry amused us for one and a half hours, during which time I walked up and down chatting and joking with the young officers who had not until then smelt powder.

An ammunition cart blew up near us, smashing men and horses. I took a calm survey of the field around and felt shocked at the sight of broken armour, lifeless bodies, murdered horses, shattered wheels, caps, helmets, swords, muskets, pistols, still and silent. Here and there a frightened horse would rush across the plain trampling on the dying and the dead. Three or four poor wounded animals standing on three legs, the other dangling before them. We killed several of these unfortunate beasts and it would have been an equal Charity to have perform'd the same operation on the wriggling, feverish, mortally lacerated soldiers as they rolled on the ground.

About four o'clock the battle was renewed with uncommon ardour. We still stood in line. The carnage was frightful. The balls which missed us mowed down the Dutch behind us, and swept away many of the closely embattled Cavalry behind them.

I saw a cannon ball take away a Colonel of the Nassau Regiment so cleanly that the horse never moved from under him. While I was busy in keeping the men firm in their ranks, closing up the vacuities as the balls swept off the men, inspecting the fallen to detect deception or subterfuge, a regiment of Cuirassiers darted like a thunderbolt among us. At the instant a squadron of horse Guards dashed up to our rescue. In the confusion of the moment I made for the Colors to defend them. And we succeeded with infinite difficulty in rallying the men again.

I parried with great good fortune a back stroke from a horseman as he flew by me and Captain Sander had a deep slice from the same fellow on the head the instant after.

The battalion once more formed into a solid square, in which we remained the whole afternoon.

I felt the ardor of the fight increase very much within me, from the uncommon fury of the engagement.

Just then I fired a slain soldier's musket until my shoulder was nearly jellied and my mouth was begrimed with gunpowder to such a degree that I champed the gritty composition unknowingly.

Nothing could equal the splendor and terror of the scene. Charge after charge succeeded in constant succession. The clashing of swords, the clattering of musketry, the hissing of balls, and shouts and clamours produced a sound, jarring and confounding the senses, as if hell and the Devil were in evil contention.

About this time I saw the Duke of Wellington running from a charge of Cavalry towards the Horse-Guards, waving his hat to beckon them to the encounter.

All our artillery in front fell into the French power, the bombardiers skulking under the carriages. But five minutes put them again into our hands and the men creeping out applied the match and sent confusion and dismay into the retreating enemy.

Several times were these charges renewed and as often defeated. Charge met charge and all was pellmell. The rays of the sun glittered on the clashing swords as the two opposing bodies closed in fearful combat and our balls clattered on the shining breastplates like a hail shower.

As I stood in the square I looked down, I recollect, to take a pinch of snuff and thought of the old ballad, which I had seen somewhere, of the aged Nurse who describes the glorious battles of Marlborough to the child. After each relation of valor and victory, the infant says:

> "Ten thousand slain you say and more?
> What did they kill each other for?"
> "Indeed I cannot tell," said she,
> "But 'twas a famous victory."

The field was now thickened with heaps of bodies and shattered instruments. Carcases of men and beasts lay promiscuously entwined. Aide-de-Camps scoured across with inconceivable velocity. All was hurry and indefatigable exertion. The small squares on our right kept up incessant firings and the fight was as obstinate as at the commencement.

The Duke of Wellington passed us twice, slowly and coolly.

No advantage as yet was discernible on either side. The French Cavalry were less annoying. Their brave, repeated assaults had cost them very dear.

About six o'clock a passe-parole ran down the line – not to be disheartened, as the Prussians were coming up to our left, which news we received with loud cheers. And on looking to the left I perceived at some distance a dark swarm moving out of a thick wood. In twenty minutes a fresh cannonading began as if in rere of the French and the battle ragad with increased vehemence.

A French Regiment of Infantry before us opposite the Farm house called the holy hedge (La Haye Sainte) advanced considerably just then and poured a destructive fire into our Battalion.

Colonel Ompteda ordered us instantly into line to charge, with a strong injunction to "walk" forward, until he gave the word. When within sixty yards he cried "Charge", we ran forward huzzaing. The trumpet sounded and no one but a soldier can describe the thrill one instantly feels in such an awful moment. At the bugle sound the French stood until we just reached them. I ran by Colonel Ompteda who cried out, "That's right, Wheatley!"

I found myself in contact with a French officer but ere we could decide, he fell by an unknown hand. I then ran at a drummer, but he leaped over a ditch through a hedge in which he stuck fast. I heard a cry of, "The Cavalry! The Cavalry!" But so eager was I that I did not mind it at the moment, and when on the eve of dragging the Frenchman back (his iron-bound hat having saved him from a Cut) I recollect no more. On recovering my senses, I look'd up and found myself, bareheaded, in a clay ditch with a violent head-ache. Close by me lay Colonel Ompteda on his back, his head stretched back with his mouth open, and a hole in his throat. A Frenchman's arm across my leg.

So confused was I that I did not remember I was on the field of Battle at the moment. Lifting up a little, I look'd over the edge of the ditch and saw the backs of a French Regiment and all the day's employment instantly suggested itself to my mind. Suddenly I distinguished some voices and heard one say *"En voici! En voici!"*

I lay down as dead, retaining my breath, and fancied I was shot in the back of my head. Presently a fellow cries, *"Voici un autre b."* And a tug at my epaulette bespoke his commission. A thought struck me – he would turn me round to rifle my pockets. So starting up, I leaped up the ditch; but a swimming seized me and I was half on the ground when the fellow thrust his hand in my collar, grinning, *"Ou va's tu, chien?"* I begged of him to let me pick up my cap and he dragged me into the house.

The inside of La Haye Sainte I found completely destroyed, nothing but the rafters and props remaining. The floor, covered with mortar bricks and straw, was strewed with bodies of the German Infantry and French Tirailleurs. A Major in Green lay by the door. The carnage had been very great in this place.

I was taken over these bodies out of a door on the right, through a garden to the back of the house where I found several Officers and men standing. They instantly crowded round me. One of my wings was on and the other half off. My oil skin haversac was across my shoulder, and my cap fastened to my waist, by running my sash through the internal lining.

A multitude of questions was put to me by the men and Officers while I fastened on my Cap: *"Vous êtes Chef de Battalion, Monsieur?"* . . .

Wheatley was unlucky to be captured for, within the hour, Wellington would begin the advance which would drive the French from the field.

CLIMBING BOYS, 1817

John Cook

The use of climbing boys to clean chimneys was banned by legislation in 1788, but was standardly ignored. Cook was a master sweep called to give evidence before an 1817 Select Committee on Climbing Boys.

Is it not the practice of some masters to advertise themselves as being in possession of small boys for the purpose of ascending flues? – Almost every one has got it in their bills, that they keep small boys for register stoves, and such like as that; I do not recollect ever seeing it in the newspapers, but they do it in their bills.

How do you ascertain the age of the boy when he is offered to you as an apprentice; do you take the parents' word for it? – The parents will often say that he is older than what he is.

Are you in the habit of getting any other evidence of their ages than the parents' own words? – No.

Are the boys ever washed? – Yes, I wash mine regularly; but some of the lower class are not washed for six months.

Do they receive any education? – Many do not.

Is it a general practice to attend divine worship? – Great numbers are neither washed nor attend on the Sunday.

Are not climbing boys subject to sores and bruises, and wounds and burns on their thighs and knees, in consequence of ascending chimneys? – Yes, because learning very fresh boys makes their knees and elbows very sore, but when they have properly learnt their trade these parts get very hard, and they very seldom get sore again unless they meet with an accident; sometimes they get burnt by chimneys partly on fire.

The committee understand, by use, that the extremities of the elbows and of the knees become as hard as the heel of the foot of a person who walks without shoes? – Yes, it does.

What time does it take before those parts get cartilaginous? – Six months.

Do you find many boys show great repugnance to go up at first? – Yes, most of them do.

And if they resist and reject, in what way do you force them up? – By telling them we must take them back again to their father and mother, and give them up again; and their parents are generally people who cannot maintain them.

So that they are afraid of going back to their parents for fear of being starved? – Yes; they go through a deal of hardship before they come to our trade.

Do you use any more violent means? – Sometimes a rod. When I was an apprentice, journeymen often used to keep a cat, made of rope, hard at each end and as thick as your thumb, in their pocket to flog the boys; and I think it is sometimes used now.

Have you ever known a journeyman ill-use any of the children? – Yes, for very little faults they will frequently kick them and smack them about; the boys are more afraid of them than of their masters.

You said that the elbows and knees of the boys, when they first begin the business, become very sore, and afterwards get callous; are those boys employed in sweeping chimneys during the soreness of those parts? – It depends upon the sort of the master they have got; you must keep them a little at it, or they will never learn their business, even during the sores.

PETERLOO, MANCHESTER, 16 APRIL 1819

Samuel Bamford

A peaceful demonstration for universal suffrage was, on the orders of local magistrates, attacked by troops of the Cheshire Volunteers, the Manchester Yeomanry and 15th Hussars. Eleven protesters were killed.

In about half an hour after our arrival the sounds of music and reiterated shouts proclaimed the near approach of Mr Hunt and his party; and in a minute or two they were seen coming from Deansgate, preceded by a band of music and several flags. On the driving seat of a barouche sat a neatly dressed female, supporting a small flag, on which were some emblematical drawings and an inscription. Within the carriage were Mr Hunt, who stood up, Mr Johnson, of Smedley Cottage; Mr Moorhouse, of Stockport; Mr Carlile, of London; Mr John Knight, of Manchester; and Mr Saxton, a sub-editor of the *Manchester Observer*. Their approach was hailed by one universal shout from probably eighty thousand persons. They threaded their way slowly past us and through the crowd, which Hunt eyed, I thought, with almost as much of astonishment as satisfaction. This spectacle could not be otherwise in his view than solemnly impressive. Such a mass of human beings he had not beheld till then. His responsibility must weigh on his mind. Their power for good or evil was irresistible, and who should direct that power? Himself alone who had called it forth. The task was great, and not without its peril. The meeting was a tremendous one. He mounted the hustings; the music ceased; Mr Johnson proposed that Mr Hunt should take the chair; it was seconded, and carried with acclamation; and Mr Hunt, stepping towards the front of the stage, took off his white hat, and addressed the people.

Whilst he was doing so, I proposed to an acquaintance that, as the speeches and resolutions were not likely to contain anything new to us, and as we could see them in the papers, we should retire awhile and get some refreshment, of which I stood much in need, being not in very robust health. He assented, and we had got to nearly the outside of the crowd, when a noise and strange murmur arose towards the church. Some persons said it was the Blackburn people coming, and I stood on tip-toe and looked in the direction whence the noise proceeded, and saw a party of cavalry in blue and white uniform come trotting, sword in hand, round the corner of the garden-wall, and to the front of a row of new houses, where they reined up in a line.

"The soldiers are here," I said; "we must go back and see what this means." "Oh," some one made reply, "they are only come to be ready if there should be any disturbance in the meeting." "Well, let us go back," I said, and we forced our way towards the colours.

On the cavalry drawing up they were received with a shout of good-will, as I understood it. They shouted again, waving their sabres over their heads; and then, slackening rein, and striking spur into their steeds, they dashed forward and began cutting the people.

"Stand fast," I said, "they are riding upon us; stand fast." And there was a general cry in our quarter of "Stand fast." The cavalry were in confusion: they evidently could not, with all the weight of man and horse, penetrate that compact mass of human beings; and their sabres were plied to hew a way through naked held-up hands and defenceless heads; and then chopped limbs and wound-gaping skulls were seen; and groans and cries were mingled with the din of that horrid confusion. "Ah! Ah!" "for shame! for shame!" was shouted. Then, "Break! break! they are killing them in front, and they cannot get away"; and there was a general cry of "break! break!" For a moment of the crowd held back as in a pause; then was a rush, heavy and resistless as a headlong sea, and a sound like low thunder, with screams, prayers, and imprecations from the crowd moiled and sabre-doomed who could not escape.

By this time Hunt and his companions had disappeared from the hustings, and some of the yeomanry, perhaps less sanguinarily disposed than others, were busied in cutting down the flag-staves and demolishing the flags at the hustings.

On the breaking of the crowd the yeomanry wheeled, and, dashing whenever there was an opening, they followed, pressing and wounding. Many females appeared as the crowd opened; and striplings of mere youths also were found. Their cries were piteous and heart-rending, and would, one might have supposed, have disarmed any human resentment: but here their appeals were in vain. Women, white-vested maids, and tender youths, were indiscriminately sabred or trampled; and we have reason for believing that few were the instances in which that forbearance was vouchsafed which they so earnestly implored.

In ten minutes from the commencement of the havoc the field was an open and almost deserted space. The sun looked down through a sultry and motionless air. The curtains and blinds of the windows within view were all closed. A gentleman or two might occasionally be seen looking out from one of the new houses before mentioned, near the door of which a group of persons (special constables) were collected, and apparently in conversation; others were assisting the wounded or carrying off the dead. The hustings remained, with a few broken and hewed flag-staves erect, and a torn and gashed banner or two dropping; whilst over the whole field were strewed caps, bonnets, hats, shawls, and shoes, and other parts of male and female dress, trampled, torn, and bloody. The yeomanry had dismounted – some were easing their horses' girths, others adjusting their accoutrements, and some were wiping their sabres. Several mounds of human beings still remained where they had fallen, crushed down and smothered. Some of these, still groaning, others with staring eyes, were gasping for breath, and others would never breathe more. All was silent save those low sounds, and the occasional snorting and pawing of steeds. Persons might sometimes be noticed peeping from attics and over the tall ridgings of houses, but they quickly withdrew, as if fearful of being observed, or unable to sustain the full gaze of a scene so hideous and abhorrent.

BILL NEATE V THE GAS-MAN, 1822

William Hazlitt

The *swells* were parading in their white box-coats, the outer ring
was cleared with some bruises on the heads and shins of the rustic
assembly (for the *cockneys* had been distanced by the sixty-six
miles); the time drew near; I had got a good stand; a bustle, a
buzz, ran through the crowd; and from the opposite side entered
Neate, between his second and bottle-holder. He rolled along,
swathed in his loose great coat, his knock-knees bending under his
huge bulk; and, with a modest cheerful air, threw his hat into the
ring. He then just looked round, and began quietly to undress;
when from the other side there was a similar rush and an opening
made, and the Gas-man (*Thomas Hickman*) came forward with a
conscious air of anticipated triumph, too much like the cock-of-
the-walk. He strutted about more than became a hero, sucked
oranges with a supercilious air, and threw away the skin with a
toss of his head, and went up and looked at Neate, which was an
act of supererogation. The only sensible thing he did was, as he
strode away from the modern Ajax, to fling out his arms, as if he
wanted to try whether they would do their work that day. By this
time they had stripped, and presented a strong contrast in
appearance. If Neate was like Ajax, "with Atlantean shoulders,
fit to bear" the pugilistic reputation of all Bristol, Hickman might
be compared to Diomed, light, vigorous, elastic, and his back
glistened in the sun, as he moved about, like a panther's hide.
There was now a dead pause – attention was awe-struck. Who at
that moment, big with a great event, did not draw his breath
short – did not feel his heart throb? All was ready. They tossed up
for the sun, and the Gas-man won. They were led up to the *scratch*
– shook hands, and went at it.

In the first round everyone thought it was all over. After
making play a short time, the Gas-man flew at his adversary
like a tiger, struck five blows in as many seconds, three first, and
then following him as he staggered back, two more, right and left,
and down he fell, a mighty ruin. There was a shout, and I said,
"There is no standing this." Neate seemed like a lifeless lump of
flesh and bone, round which the Gasman's blows played with the
rapidity of electricity or lightning, and you imagined he would
only be lifted up to be knocked down again. It was as if Hickman

held a sword or a fire in that right hand of his, and directed it against an unarmed body. They met again, and Neate seemed, not cowed, but particularly cautious. I saw his teeth clenched together and his brows knit close against the sun. He held out both his arms at full length straight before him, like two sledge-hammers, and raised his left an inch or two higher. The Gas-man could not get over this guard – they struck mutually and fell, but without advantage on either side. It was the same in the next round; but the balance of power was thus restored – the fate of the battle was suspended. No one could tell how it would end. This was the only moment in which opinion was divided; for, in the next, the Gas-man aiming a mortal blow at his adversary's neck, with his right hand, and failing from the length he had to reach, the other returned it with his left at full swing, planted a tremendous blow on his cheek-bone and eye-brow, and made a red ruin of that side of his face. The Gas-man went down, and there was another shout – a roar of triumph as the waves of fortune rolled tumultuously from side to side. This was a settler. Hickman got up, and "grinned horrible a ghastly smile", yet he was evidently dashed in his opinion of himself; it was the first time he had ever been so punished; all one side of his face was perfect scarlet, and his right eye was closed in dingy blackness, as he advanced to the fight, less confident, but still determined. After one or two rounds, not receiving another such remembrancer, he rallied and went at it with his former inspetuosity. But in vain. His strength had been weakened, – his blows could not tell at such a distance, – he was obliged to fling himself at his adversary, and could not strike from his feet; and almost as regularly as he flew at him with his right hand, Neate warded the blow, or drew back out of its reach, and felled him with the return of his left. There was little cautious sparring – no half-hits – no tapping and trifling, none of the *petit-maitreship* of the art – they were almost all knock-down blows:— the fight was a good stand-up fight. The wonder was the half-minute time. If there had been a minute or more allowed between each round, it would have been intelligible how they should by degrees recover strength and resolution; but to see two men smashed to the ground, smeared with gore, stunned, senseless, the breath beaten out of their bodies; and then, before you recover from the shock, to see them rise up with new strength and courage, stand ready to inflict or receive mortal offence, and rush upon each other "like two clouds over the

Caspian" – this is the most astonishing thing of all: – this is the high and heroic state of man! From this time forward the event became more certain every round; and about the twelfth it seemed as if it must have been over. Hickman generally stood with his back to me; but in the scuffle, he had changed positions, and Neate just then made a tremendous lunge at him, and hit him full in the face. It was doubtful whether he would fall backwards or forwards; he hung suspended for a second or two, and then fell back, throwing his hands in the air, and with his face lifted up to the sky. I never saw any thing more terrific than his aspect just before he fell. All traces of life, of natural expression, were gone from him. His face was like a human skull, a death's head, spouting blood. The eyes were filled with blood, the nose streamed with blood, the mouth gaped blood. He was not like an actual man, but like a preternatural, spectral appearance, or like one of the figures in Dante's *Inferno*. Yet he fought on after this for several rounds, still striking the first desperate blow, and Neate standing on the defensive, and using the same cautious guard to the last, as if he had still all his work to do; and it was not till the Gas-man was so stunned in the seventeenth or eighteenth round, that his senses forsook him, and he could not come to time, that the battle was declared over. Ye who despise the Fancy, do something to shew as much *pluck*, or as much self-possession as this, before you assume a superiority which you have never given a single proof of by any one action in the whole course of your lives! – When the Gas-man came to himself, the first words he uttered were, "Where am I? What is the matter?" – "Nothing is the matter, Tom, – you have lost the battle, but you are the bravest man alive." And Jackson whispered to him, "I am collecting a purse for you, Tom." Vain sounds, and unheard at that moment! Neate instantly went up and shook him cordially by the hand, and seeing some old acquaintance, began to flourish with his fists, calling out, "Ah! you always said I couldn't fight – What do you think now?" But all in good humour, and without any appearance of arrogance; only it was evident Bill Neate was pleased that he had won the fight. When it was over, I asked Cribb if he did not think it was a good one. He said, "*Pretty well!*" The carrier-pigeons now mounted into the air, and one of them flew with the news of her husband's victory to the bosom of Mrs Neate. Alas, for Mrs Hickman!

THE CREMATION OF SHELLEY, VIAREGGIO, ITALY, 15 AUGUST 1822

Edward Trelawney

The émigré poet Percy Bysshe Shelley was drowned in a boating accident off Livorno.

Three white wands had been stuck in the sand to mark the Poet's grave, but as they were at some distance from each other, we had to cut a trench thirty yards in length, in the line of the sticks, to ascertain the exact spot, and it was nearly an hour before we came upon the grave.

In the meantime Byron and Leigh Hunt arrived in the carriage, attended by soldiers, and the Health Officer, as before (i.e. when the body of Edward Williams, drowned with Shelley, was cremated). The lonely and grand scenery that surrounded us so exactly harmonized with Shelley's genius, that I could imagine his spirit soaring over us. The sea, with the islands of Gorgona, Capraji, and Elba, was before us; old battlemented watchtowers stretched along the coast, backed by the marble-crested Apennines glistening in the sun, picturesque from their diversified outlines, and not a human dwelling was in sight. As I thought of the delight Shelley felt in such scenes of loneliness and grandeur whilst living, I felt we were no better than a herd of wolves or a pack of wild dogs, in tearing out his battered and naked body from the pure yellow sand that lay so lightly over it, to drag him back to the light of day; but the dead have no voice, nor had I power to check the sacrilege – the work went on silently in the deep and unresisting sand, not a word was spoken, for the Italians have a touch of sentiment, and their feelings are easily excited into sympathy. Even Byron was silent and thoughtful. We were startled and drawn together by a dull hollow sound that followed the blow of a mattock; the iron had struck a skull, and the body was soon uncovered. Lime had been strewn on it; this, or decomposition, had the effect of staining it of a dark and ghastly indigo colour. Byron asked me to preserve the skull for him; but remembering that he had formerly used one as a drinking-cup, I was determined Shelley's should not be so profaned. The limbs did not separate from the trunk, as in the case of Williams's body, so that the corpse was removed entire into the furnace. I had taken the precaution of having more and larger pieces of timber, in consequence of my experience of the day before of the difficulty of consuming a corpse in the open air with our apparatus. After the fire was well kindled we repeated the ceremony of the previous day; and more wine was poured over Shelley's dead body than he had consumed during his life. This with the oil and salt made the yellow flames glisten and quiver. The heat from the sun and fire was so intense that the atmosphere was tremulous and wavy. The corpse fell open and the heart was laid bare. The frontal bone of the skull, where it had been struck with the mattock, fell off; and, as the back of the head rested on the red-hot bottom bars of the furnace, the brains literally seethed, bubbled, and boiled as in a cauldron, for a very long time.

Byron could not face this scene, he withdrew to the beach and swam off to the *Bolivar*. Leigh Hunt remained in the carriage. The fire was so fierce as to produce a white heat on the iron, and to reduce its contents to grey ashes. The only portions that were not consumed were some fragments of bones, the jaw, and the skull, but what surprised us all, was that the heart remained entire. In snatching this relic from the fiery furnace, my hand was severely burnt; and had anyone seen me do the act I should have been put into quarantine.

THE QUALITIES OF A POLICEMAN, 10 OCTOBER 1829

Sir Robert Peel

Peel's establishment of the Metropolitan Police Force (quickly nicknamed "Peelers") was part of a reform of the prison and criminal systems he undertook as Tory Home Secretary.

My dear Croker,

Thanks for your suggestions in regard to the Metropolitan Police.

When I fixed the present rate of pay, I fixed it under an impression that it might be necessary to raise it, but I felt quite sure that it would be much easier to raise than to reduce the rate of pay. I cannot say that the short experience I have hitherto had has confirmed my first impression. I will not as yet speak decidedly on the point, but I am very far from being prepared to admit that the improvement of the situation of a common police constable by the giving him more money, would increase the efficiency of the establishment.

I have above 2000 applications for the appointment at the present rate of pay (this no doubt is a very bad test, if it were the only one). Every man who has been dismissed or has resigned, has with scarcely an exception petitioned for reinstatement. I do not again rely much upon this.

I must first consider what is the class of man I want; and secondly, will the rate of pay maintain the proper respectability of that class?

No doubt three shillings a day will not give me all the virtues under heaven, but I do not want them. Angels would be far above my work. Looking at the duties I want to be performed, I am not at all sure whether (all considerations of expense being put out of the question) three or four shillings a day will not ensure their performance in a much better manner than ten or twelve would. I have refused to employ gentlemen – commissioned officers, for instance – as superintendents and inspectors, because I am certain they would be above their work. They would refuse to associate with other persons holding the same offices who were not of equal rank, and they would therefore degrade the latter in the eyes of men.

A sergeant of the Guards at £200 a year is a better man for my purpose than a captain of high military reputation if he would serve for nothing, or if I could give him a thousand a year without entailing a fresh charge. For somewhat similar reasons, a three shilling a day man is better than a five shilling a day man.

After all, however, the real question is – how will three shillings a day support a man? I speak as yet hesitatingly; but I have good reasons for thinking that one of my police constables, if a single man, can find out of his pay of a guinea a week: (1) lodgings, (2) medical attendance, (3) very comfortable subsistence at his mess, (4) clothing; and can, after finding these, save out of his pay ten shillings a week.

Now, I think the policy of enabling him to save more is questionable. However, the impressions under which I am at present writing are liable to be varied by further experience.

I must add to the number of the police for the present district. I must say that it has worked much better in the first fortnight than I could have expected.

Ever most faithfully yours,
ROBERT PEEL.

THE INDUSTRIAL REVOLUTION: THE BLACK COUNTRY, ENGLAND, 1830

James Nasmyth

On leaving Coalbrookdale I trudged my way towards Wolverhampton. I rested at Shiffinal for the night. Next day I was in the middle of the Black Country. I had no letters of introduction to employers in Wolverhampton; so that, without stopping there, I proceeded at once to Dudley. The Black Country is anything but picturesque. The earth seems to have been turned inside out. Its entrails are strewn about; nearly the entire surface of the ground is covered with cinder-heaps and mounds of scoriae. The coal, which has been drawn from below ground, is blazing on the surface. The district is crowded with iron furnaces, puddling furnaces and coalpit engine furnaces. By day and by night the country is glowing with fire, and the smoke of the ironworks hovers over it. There is a rumbling and clanking of iron forges and rolling mills. Workmen covered with smut, and with fierce white eyes, are seen moving about amongst the glowing iron and dull thud of forge-hammers.

Amidst these flaming, smoky, clanging works, I beheld the remains of what had once been happy farmhouses, now ruined and deserted. The ground underneath them had sunk by the working out of the coal, and they were falling to pieces. They had in former times been surrounded by clumps of trees but only the skeletons of them remained, dilapidated, black, and lifeless. The grass had been parched and killed by the vapours of sulphureous acid thrown out by the chimneys; and every herbaceous object was of a ghastly gray – the emblem of vegetable death in its saddest aspect. Vulcan had driven out Ceres. In some places I heard a sort of chirruping sound, as of some forlorn bird haunting the ruins of the old farmsteads. But no! the chirrup was a vile delusion. It proceeded from the shrill creaking of the coal-winding chains, which were placed in small tunnels beneath the hedgeless road.

I went into some of the forges to see the workmen at their labours. There was no need of introduction; the works were open to all, for they were unsurrounded by walls. I saw the white-hot iron run out from the furnace; I saw it spun, as it were, into bars and iron ribbands, with an ease and rapidity which seemed marvellous. There were also the ponderous hammers and clanking rolling-mills. I wandered from one to another without restraint. I lingered among the blast furnaces, seeing the flood of molten iron run out from time to time, and remained there until it was late. When it became dark the scene was still more impressive. The workmen within seemed to be running about amidst the flames as in a pandemonium; while around and outside the horizon was a glowing belt of fire, making even the stars look pale and feeble. At last I came away with reluctance, and made my way towards Dudley. I reached the town at a late hour. I was exhausted in mind and body, yet the day had been most interesting and exciting. A sound sleep refreshed me, and I was up in the morning early, to recommence my journey of inquiry.

I made my way to the impressive ruins of Dudley Castle, the remnant of a very ancient stronghold, originally built by Dud, the Saxon. The castle is situated on a finely wooded hill; it is so extensive that it more resembles the ruins of a town than of a single building. You enter through a treble gateway, and see the remnants of the moat, the court, and the keep. Here are the central hall, the guard-rooms and the chapel. It must have been a magnificent structure. In the Midlands it was known as the "Castle of the Woods". Now it is abandoned by its owners, and surrounded by the Black Country. It is undermined by collieries, and even penetrated by a canal. The castle walls sometimes tremble when a blast occurs in the bowels of the mountain beneath. The town of Dudley lies quite close to the castle, and was doubtless protected by it in ancient times.

The architectural remains are of various degrees of antiquity, and are well worthy of study, as embodying the successive periods which they represent. Their melancholy grandeur is rendered all the more impressive by the coal and iron works with which they are surrounded – the olden type of buildings confronting the modern. The venerable trees struggle for existence under the destroying influence of sulphureous acid; while the grass is withered and the vegetation everywhere blighted. I sat down on an elevated part of the ruins, and looking down upon the extensive district, with its roaring and blazing furnaces, the smoke of which blackened the country as far as eye could reach; and as I watched the decaying trees I thought of the price we had to pay for our vaunted supremacy in the manufacture of iron. We may fill our purses, but we pay a heavy price for it in the loss of picturesqueness and beauty.

FIRST EXCURSION ON THE LIVERPOOL–MANCHESTER RAILWAY, 25 AUGUST 1830

Fanny Kemble

A party of sixteen persons was ushered into a large court-yard, where, under cover, stood several carriages of a peculiar construction, one of which was prepared for our reception. It was a long-bodied vehicle with seats placed across it, back to back; the one we were in had six of these benches, and was a sort of uncovered *char à banc*. The wheels were placed upon two iron bands, which formed the road, and to which they are fitted, being so constructed as to slide along without any danger of hitching or becoming displaced, on the same principle as a thing sliding on a concave groove. The carriage was set in motion by a mere push, and, having received this impetus, rolled with us down an inclined plane into a tunnel, which forms the entrance to the railroad. This tunnel is four hundred yards long (I believe), and will be lighted by gas. At the end of it we emerged from darkness, and, the ground becoming level, we stopped. There is another tunnel parallel with this, only much wider and longer, for it extends from the place which we had now reached, and where the steam-carriages start, and which is quite out of Liverpool, the whole way under the town, to the docks. This tunnel is for waggons and other heavy carriages; and as the engines which are to draw the trains along the railroad do not enter these tunnels, there is a large building at this entrance which is to be inhabited by steam-engines of a stationary turn of mind, and different constitution from the travelling ones, which are to propel the trains through the tunnels to the terminus in the town, without going out of their houses themselves. The length of the tunnel parallel to the one we passed through is (I believe) two thousand two hundred yards. I wonder if you are understanding one word I am saying all this while! We were introduced to the little engine which was to drag us along the rails. She (for they make these curious little fire-horses all mares) consisted of a boiler, a stove, a small platform, a bench, and behind the bench a barrel containing enough water to prevent her being thirsty for fifteen miles, – the whole machine not bigger than a common fire-engine. She goes upon two wheels, which are her feet, and are moved by bright steel legs called pistons; these are propelled by steam, and in proportion as more steam is applied to the upper extremities (the hip-joints, I suppose) of these pistons, the faster they move the wheels; and when it is desirable to diminish the speed, the steam, which unless suffered to escape would burst the boiler, evaporates through a safety-valve into the air. The reins, bit, and bridle of this wonderful beast is a small steel handle, which applies or withdraws the steam from its legs or pistons, so that a child might manage it. The coals, which are its oats, were under the bench, and there was a small glass tube affixed to the boiler, with water in it, which indicates by its fulness or emptiness when the creature wants water, which is immediately conveyed to it from its reservoirs. There is a chimney to the stove, but as they burn coke there is none of that dreadful black smoke which accompanies the progress of a steam-vessel. This snorting little animal, which I felt rather inclined to pat, was then harnessed to our carriage, and Mr Stephenson having taken me on the bench of the engine with him, we started at about ten miles an hour. The steam-horse being ill adapted for going up and down hill, the road was kept at a certain level, and appeared sometimes to sink below the surface of the earth, and sometimes to rise above it. Almost at starting it was cut through the solid rock, which formed a wall on either side of it, about sixty feet high. You can't imagine how strange it seemed to be journeying on thus, without any visible cause of progress other than the magical machine, with its flying white breath and rhythmical, unvarying pace, between these rocky walls, which are already clothed with moss and ferns and grasses; and when I reflected that these great masses of stone had been cut asunder to allow our passage thus far below the surface of the earth, I felt as if no fairy tale was ever half so wonderful as what I saw. Bridges were thrown from side to side across the top of these cliffs, and the people looking down upon us from them seemed like pigmies standing in the sky. I must be more concise, or I shall want room. We were to go only fifteen miles, that distance being sufficient to show the speed of the engine, and to take us on to the most beautiful and wonderful object on the road. After proceeding through this rocky defile, we presently found ourselves raised upon embankments ten or twelve feet high; we then came to a moss, or swamp of considerable extent, on which no human foot could tread without sinking, and yet it bore the road which bore us. This had been the great stumbling-block in the minds of the committee of the House of

Commons; but Mr Stephenson has succeeded in overcoming it. A foundation of hurdles, or as he called it, basket-work, was thrown over the morass, and the interstices were filled with moss and other elastic matter. Upon this the clay and soil were laid down, and the road *does* float, for we passed over it at the rate of five and twenty miles an hour, and saw the stagnant swamp water trembling on the surface of the soil on either side of us. I hope you understand me. The embankment had gradually been rising higher and higher, and in one place, where the soil was not settled enough to form banks, Stephenson had constructed artificial ones of wood-work, over which the mounds of earth were heaped, for he calculated that though the wood-work would rot, before it did so the banks of earth which covered it would have been sufficiently consolidated to support the road.

We had now come fifteen miles, and stopped where the road traversed a wide and deep valley. Stephenson made me alight and led me down to the bottom of this ravine, over which, in order to keep his road level, he has thrown a magnificent viaduct of nine arches, the middle one of which is seventy feet high, through which we saw the whole of this beautiful little valley. It was lovely and wonderful beyond all words. He here told me many curious things respecting this ravine: how he believed the Mersey had once rolled through it; how the soil had proved so unfavourable for the foundation of his bridge that it was built upon piles, which had been driven into the earth to an enormous depth; how, while, digging for a foundation, he had come to a tree bedded in the earth fourteen feet below the surface of the ground; how tides are caused, and how another flood might be caused; all of which I have remembered and noted down at much greater length than I can enter upon it here. He explained to me the whole construction of the steam-engine, and said he could soon make a famous engineer of me, which, considering the wonderful things he *has* achieved, I dare not say is impossible. His way of explaining himself is peculiar, but very striking, and I understood, without difficulty, all that he said to me. We then rejoined the rest of the party, and the engine having received its supply of water, the carriage was placed behind it, for it cannot turn, and was set off at its utmost speed, thirty-five miles an hour, swifter than a bird flies (for they tried the experiment with a snipe). You cannot conceive what that sensation of cutting the air was; the motion is as smooth as possible, too. I could either have read or written; and as it was, I stood up, and with my bonnet off "drank the air before me." The wind, which was strong, or perhaps the force of our thrusting against it, absolutely weighed my eyelids down. When I closed my eyes this sensation of flying was quite delightful, and strange beyond description; yet, strange as it was, I had a perfect sense of security, and not the slightest fear. At one time, to exhibit the power of the engine, having met another steam-carriage which was unsupplied with water, Mr Stephenson caused it to be fastened in front of ours; moreover, a waggon laden with timber was also chained to us, and thus propelling the idle steam-engine, and dragging the loaded waggon which was beside it, and our own carriage full of people behind, this brave little she-dragon of ours flew on. Farther on she met three carts, which being fastened in front of her, she pushed on before her without the slightest delay or difficulty; when I add that this pretty little creature can run with equal facility either backwards or forwards, I believe I have given you an account of all her capacities.

THE INDUSTRIAL REVOLUTION: CHILD LABOUR IN ENGLAND, 1833

Ellen Hootton

Evidence given before the Parliamentary Commission inquiry into child labour in mines and manufactories.

How old are you?
I shall be ten on the 4th August.
How old were you when you began to work in Eccles' factory [at Wigan]?
I wasn't quite eight. Worked there above a year.
Were you beaten and scolded at Eccles'?
Yes.
Who by?
William Swanton.
What for?
For having my ends down.
How often were you beaten by him?
Twice a week.
What with?
His hands.
Did he hurt you much?
No; but it made my head sore with his hands.

Did Mr Swanton ever tie a weight to you?

Yes, to my back.

What was it tied with, a string?

Yes, it was tied with one string round my neck, one round my shoulders, and one round my middle.

How heavy was it?

I don't know. It was a great piece of iron, and two more beside.

How big were they?

One was as big as this book (pointing to the Lords' Report of 1818).

Was it as thick?

No; it was thicker. (Pointing to an unbound octavo book of 419 pages.) As thick as that.

What time of the day was it?

It was after breakfast.

How long was it kept on you?

About half an hour.

What did you do?

I walked up and down the room.

What did you walk up and down the room for?

He made me.

Was it that other children might see you with it?

Yes.

Did you ever see such weights tied to other children?

Yes; there was one other that had them tied to his legs.

Was there more than one?

Yes, there was two beside him.

How long did they wear it?

About an hour.

Did they walk up and down the room too?

Yes.

Now mind and don't tell a lie; what had you done?

I did nothing but run away because he beat me.

Had you stolen any thing?

No.

Did you tell your mother of it?

Yes. She said nothing.

Is your father dead?

I have no father.

INITIATION INTO THE TOLL PUDDLE UNION, DORSET, JANUARY 1834

John Lock

Trade unions were legalised in Britain in 1824 but their use of secret initiation ceremonies alarmed the authorities and gave the farmers and magistrates of Toll Puddle, Dorset, a pretext for suppressing the local Friendly Society of Agricultural Labourers. John Lock testified against his fellow trade unionists at their trial for administering "illegal oaths" in March 1834.

I live at Half Puddle. I went to Toll Puddle a fortnight before Christmas. I know the prisoner James Brine. I saw him that evening at John Woolley's. He called me out and I went with him. He took me to Thomas Stanfield's, and asked me if I would go in with him. I refused and went away. I saw him in about a fortnight afterwards in a barn. He asked me if I would go to Toll Puddle with him. I agreed to do so. James Hammet was then with him. Edward Legg, Richard Peary, Henry Courtney, and Elias Riggs were with us. They joined us as we were going along. One of them asked if there would not be something to pay, and one said there would be 1 shilling to pay on entering, and 1d. a week after. We all went into Thomas Stanfield's house into a room upstairs. John Stanfield came to the door of the room. I saw James Lovelace and George Lovelace go along the passage. One of the men asked if we were ready. We said, yes. One of them said, "Then bind your eyes", and we took out handkerchiefs and bound over our eyes. They then led us into another room on the same floor. Someone then read a paper, but I don't know what the meaning of it was. After that we were asked to kneel down, which we did. Then there was some more reading; I don't know what it was about. It seemed to be out of some part of the Bible. Then we got up and took off the bandages from our eyes. I had then seen James Lovelace and John Stanfield in the room. Some one read again, but I don't know what it was, and then we were told to kiss the book, when our eyes were unblinded, and I saw the book, which looked like a little Bible. I then saw all the prisoners there. James Lovelace had on a white dress, it was not a smock-frock. They told us the rules, that we should have to pay 1 shilling then, and a 1d. a week afterwards, to support the men when they were standing out from their work. They said we were as brothers; that when we were to stop for wages we should not tell our masters ourselves, but that the masters would have a note or a letter sent to them.

Six labourers were convicted and sentenced to transportation for seven years. Widespread protest and petitioning saw the sentence of the "Toll Puddle Martyrs" remitted in 1836.

DARWIN IN THE GALAPAGOS, 1835

Charles Darwin

Before Darwin it was scientific orthodoxy that the Creator had designed every organism; after Darwin's *Origin of Species*, 1859, it was allowed that Evolution, principally natural selection, had some hand in the development of the living world. Darwin attributed the breakthrough in his thought to a visit he paid to the Galapagos Archipelago in 1835, when he was the naturalist aboard HMS *Beagle*.

. . . The natural history of these islands is eminently curious, and well deserves attention. Most of the organic productions are aboriginal creations, found nowhere else; there is even a difference between the inhabitants of the different islands; yet all show a marked relationship with those of America, though separated from that continent by an open space of ocean between 500 and 600 miles in width. The archipelago is a little world within itself, or rather, a satellite attached to America, whence it has derived a few stray colonists, and has received the general character of its indigenous productions. Considering the small size of these islands, we feel the more astonished at the number of their aboriginal beings, and at their confined range. Seeing every height crowned with its crater, and the boundaries of most of the lava-streams still distinct, we are led to believe that within a period geologically recent the unbroken ocean was here spread out. Hence, both in space and time, we seem to be brought somewhat near to that great fact – that mystery of mysteries – the first appearance of new beings on this earth. . . .

Of land-birds I obtained twenty-six kinds, all peculiar to the group and found nowhere else, with the exception of one lark-like finch from North America. . . . The other twenty-five birds consist, firstly, of a hawk, curiously intermediate in structure between a buzzard and the American group of carrion-feeding Polybori. . . . Secondly, there are two owls, representing the short-eared and white barn-owls of Europe. Thirdly, a wren, three tyrant-flycatchers . . ., and a dove – all analogous to, but distinct from, American species. Fourthly, a swallow . . . Fifthly, there are three species of mocking thrush. . . . The remaining land-birds form a most singular group of finches, related to each other in the structure of their beaks, short tails, form of body and plumage: there are thirteen species . . . all . . . peculiar to this archipelago. . . . The most curious fact is the perfect gradation in the size of the beaks in the different species of Geospiza, from one as large as that of a hawfinch to that of a chaffinch, and . . . even to that of a warbler. [The *Journal* is illustrated at this point with drawings of the beaks of the finches.]. . . . Seeing this gradation and diversity of structure in one small, intimately related group of birds, one might really fancy that from an original paucity of birds in this archipelago, one species had been taken and modified for different ends. . . .

I have not as yet noticed by far the most remarkable feature in the natural history of this archipelago; it is, that the different islands to a considerable extent are inhabited by a different set of beings. My attention was first called to this fact by the Vice-Governor, Mr. Lawson, declaring that the tortoises differed from the different islands, and that he could with certainty tell from which island any one was brought. I did not for some time pay sufficient attention to this statement, and I had already partially mingled together the collections from two of the islands. I never dreamed that islands, about 50 or 60 miles apart, and most of them in sight of each other, formed of precisely the same rocks, placed under a quite similar climate, rising to a nearly equal height, would have been differently tenanted; but we shall soon see that this is the case. It is the fate of most voyagers no sooner to discover what is most interesting in any locality, than they are hurried from it; but I ought, perhaps, to be thankful that I obtained sufficient materials to establish this most remarkable fact in the distribution of organic beings. . . .

PRINCESS VICTORIA BECOMES QUEEN, 20 JUNE 1837

Queen Victoria

Victoria was born in 1819.

I was awoke at 6 o'clock by Mamma, who told me that the Archbishop of Canterbury and Lord Conyngham were here, and wished to see me. I got out of bed and went into my sitting-room (only in my dressing-gown) and *alone*, and saw them, Lord Conyngham (the Lord Chamberlain) then acquainted me that my poor Uncle, the King,* was no more, and had expired at 12 minutes past 2 this morning, and consequently that I am *Queen*. Lord Conyngham knelt down and kissed my hand, at the same time delivering to me the official announcement of the poor King's demise. The Archbishop then told me that the Queen was desirous that he should come and tell me the details of the last moments of my poor good uncle; he said that he had directed his mind to religion, and had died in a perfectly happy, quiet state of mind, and was quite prepared for his death, . . . Lord Conyngham, whom I charged to express my feelings of condolence and sorrow to the poor Queen, returned directly to Windsor. I then went to my room and dressed.

Since it has pleased Providence to place me in this station, I shall do my utmost to fulfil my duty towards my country; I am very young and perhaps in many, though not in all things, inexperienced, but I am sure that very few have more real goodwill and more real desire to do what is fit and right than I have.

THE CORONATION OF QUEEN VICTORIA, 28 JUNE 1838

Queen Victoria

I was awoke at four o'clock by the guns in the Park, and could not get much sleep afterwards on account of the noise of the people, bands, etc. Got up at seven, feeling strong and well. . . . I dressed, having taken a little breakfast before I dressed, and a little after. . . . At 10 I got into the State Coach with the Duchess of Sutherland and Lord Albemarle and we began our Progress. . . . It was a fine day, and the crowds of people exceeded what I have ever seen. . . . Their good humour and excessive loyalty was beyond everything, and I really cannot say *how* proud I feel to be the Queen of *such* a nation. I was alarmed at times for fear that the people would be crushed and squeezed on account of the tremendous rush and pressure.

I reached the Abbey amid deafening cheers at a little after half-past eleven. [H.M. describes the ceremony, and then goes on.]

* William IV, whose legitimate issue had died in infancy.

Then followed all the various things; and last (of those things) the Crown being placed on my head – which was, I must own, a most beautiful impressive moment; all the Peers and Peeresses put on their coronets at the same moment.

My excellent Lord Melbourne, who stood very close to me throughout the whole ceremony, was *completely* overcome at this moment, and very much affected; he gave me *such* a kind, and I may say *fatherly* look. The shouts, which were very great, the drums, the trumpets, the firing of the guns, all at the same instant, rendered the spectacle most imposing.

The Enthronisation and the Homage of, first, all the Bishops, and then my Uncles, and lastly of all the Peers, in their respective order was very fine. . . . Poor old Lord Rolle, who is 82, and dreadfully infirm, in attempting to ascend the steps fell and rolled quite down, but was not the least hurt; when he attempted to re-ascend them I got up and advanced to the end of the steps, in order to prevent another fall. When Lord Melbourne's turn to do Homage came, there was loud cheering; they also cheered Lord Grey and the Duke of Wellington. . . . I then again descended from the throne and repaired with all the Peers bearing the Regalia, my Ladies and Train-bearers, to St. Edward's Chapel, as it is called; but which, as Lord Melbourne said, was more *un*like a Chapel than anything he had ever seen; for what was *called* an *Altar* was covered with sandwiches, bottles of wine, etc. The Archbishop came in and *ought* to have delivered the Orb to me, but I had already got it, and he (as usual) was *so* confused and puzzled and knew nothing, and – went away. Here we waited some minutes. Lord Melbourne took a glass of wine, for he seemed completely tired. The Procession being formed, I replaced my Crown (which I had taken off for a few minutes), took the Orb in my left hand and the Sceptre in my right, and thus *loaded*, proceeded through the Abbey – which resounded with cheers, to the first robing-room. . . . The Archbishop had (most awk-wardly) put the ring on the wrong finger, and the consequence was that I had the greatest difficulty to take it off again, which I at last did with great pain. . . . At about half-past four I re-entered my carriage, the Crown on my head, and the Sceptre and Orb in my hands, and we proceeded the same way as we came – the crowds if possible having increased. The enthusiasm, affection, and loyalty were really touching, and I shall ever remember this day as the *proudest* of my life!

PROSTITUTES, PIMPS AND PEERS: SCENES FROM LONDON'S DEMI-MONDE, 1839

Flora Tristan

A French socialist, Tristan made several explorations in darkest England.

Between seven and eight o'clock one evening, accompanied by two friends armed with canes, I went to take a look at the new suburb which lies on either side of the long broad thoroughfare called Waterloo Road at the end of Waterloo Bridge. This neighbourhood is almost entirely inhabited by prostitutes and people who live off prostitution; it is courting danger to go there alone at night. It was a hot summer evening; in every window and doorway women were laughing and joking with their protectors. Half-dressed, some of them *naked to the waist*, they were a revolting sight, and the criminal, cynical expressions of their companions filled me with apprehension. These men are for the most part very good-looking – young, vigorous and well made – but their coarse and common air marks them as animals whose sole instinct is to satisfy their appetites.

Several of them accosted us and asked if we wanted a room. When we answered in the negative, one bolder than the rest demanded in a threatening tone, "What are you doing here then, if you don't want a room for you and your lady friend?" I must confess I would not have liked to find myself alone with that man.

We went on our way and explored all the streets in the vicinity of Waterloo Road, then we sat upon the bridge to watch the women of the neighbourhood flock past, as they do every evening between the hours of eight and nine, on their way to the West End, where they ply their trade all through the night and return home between eight and nine in the morning. They infest the promenades and any other place where people gather, such as the approaches to the Stock Exchange, the various public buildings and the theatres, which they invade as soon as entry is reduced to half-price, turning all the corridors and foyers into their receiving-rooms. After the play they move on to the "finishes"; these are squalid taverns or vast resplendent gin-palaces where people go to spend what remains of the night.

The "finish" is as much a part of life in England as the beer-cellar in Germany or the elegant café in France. In the tavern the clerk and the shop assistant drink ale, smoke cheap tobacco and get drunk with tawdrily dressed women; in the gin-palace, fashionable gentlemen drink Cognac, punch, sherry, port, and French and Rhenish wines, smoke excellent Havana cigars, and flirt with beautiful young girls in splendid gowns. But in both places scenes of orgy are acted out in all their brutality and horror.

I had heard descriptions of the debauchery to be seen at finishes, but could never bring myself to believe them. Now I was in London for the fourth time with the firm resolve to discover everything for myself. I determined to overcome my repugnance and go in person to one of these finishes, so that I might judge for myself how far I could trust the various accounts I had been given. The same friends who had accompanied me to the Waterloo Road again offered to be my guides.

What goes on in these places ought to be seen, for it reveals the moral state of England better than any words could express. These splendid pleasure-houses have an appearance all their own. Those who frequent them seem to be dedicated to the night; they go to bed when the sun begins to light the horizon and awaken after it has set. From the outside, these "gin-palaces" with their carefully fastened shutters seem to be quietly slumbering; but no sooner has the doorkeeper admitted you by the little door reserved for initiates than you are dazzled by the light of a thousand gas lamps. Upstairs there is a spacious salon divided down the middle; in one half there is a row of tables separated one from the other by wooden screens, as in all English restaurants, with upholstered seats like sofas on each side of the tables. In the other half there is a dais where the prostitutes parade in all their finery, seeking to arouse the men with their glances and remarks; when a gallant gentleman responds, they lead him off to one of the tables loaded with cold meats, hams, poultry, pastries and every manner of wines and spirits.

The finishes are the temples which English materialism raises to its gods; the servants who minister in them are dressed in rich liveries, and the capitalist owners reverently greet the male guests who come to exchange their gold for debauchery.

Towards midnight the regular clients begin to arrive; several finishes are frequented by men in high society, and this is where the cream of the aristocracy gather. At first the young noblemen recline on the sofas, smoking and exchanging pleasantries with the women; then, when they have drunk enough for the fumes of champagne and Maderia to go to their heads, the illustrious scions of the English nobility, the very honourable members of Parliament, remove their coats, untie their cravats, take off their waistcoats and braces, and proceed to set up their private boudoir in a public place. Why not make themselves at home, since they are paying out so much money for the right to display their contempt? As for any contempt *they* might inspire, they do not care in the least. The orgy rises to a crescendo; between four and five o'clock in the morning it reaches its height.

At this point it takes a good deal of courage to remain in one's seat, a mute spectator of all that takes place. What a worthy use these English lords make of their immense fortunes! How fine and generous they are when they have lost the use of their reason and offer fifty, even a hundred, guineas to a prostitute if she will lend herself to all the obscenities that drunkenness engenders.

For in a finish there is no lack of entertainment. One of the favourite sports is to *ply a woman with drink* until she falls dead drunk upon the floor, then to make her swallow a draught compounded of *vinegar, mustard*, and *pepper*, this invariably throws the poor creature into horrible convulsions, and her spasms and contortions provoke the *honourable company* to gales of laughter and infinite amusement. Another diversion much appreciated at these fashionable gatherings is to empty the contents of the nearest glass upon the women as they lie insensible on the ground. I have seen satin dresses of no recognizable colour, only a confused mass of stains: wine, brandy, beer, tea, coffee, cream, etc., daubed all over them in a thousand fantastic shapes – the handiwork of debauchery!

WOMEN PRISONERS IN NEWGATE, 1841

Flora Tristan

There is no fresh air or daylight; the prisoner can still hear the noise of the street outside, and beneath the door he can still see the sunlight shining in the square. What a dreadful contrast, and how he regrets the loss of his liberty! But once past the lodge he hears nothing more; the atmosphere is as cold, damp and heavy as in a cellar; most of the passages are narrow, and so are the stairs leading to the upper wards.

First I was taken to see the women's wing. Over the past few years several changes have been made at Newgate and now it houses only prisoners awaiting trial, not convicted prisoners; in this respect it corresponds to the Conciergerie in Paris. It is here too that most executions take place.

The governor was kind enough to accompany me over the prison; he told me that thanks to the writings of philanthropists and the constant complaints of humanitarians, Newgate had undergone all the improvements of which it was capable. Mr Cox was particularly happy that prisoners were now divided into different classes, whereas formerly they had all been confined together.

The internal arrangement of the prison is not very satisfactory and there is not enough space for individual cells. In each ward the beds, wooden constructions six feet long and two feet wide, are arranged in two or three tiers like berths on board a ship. There is a large table in the middle with wooden benches all round it; this is where the prisoners eat, work, read and write. On close examination I found the wards very clean and well-kept, but as they are dark and poorly ventilated and the floors are very uneven, their general appearance is unpleasing.

Nearly all the women I saw there were of the lowest class; prostitutes, servants or country girls accused of theft. Four were on charges carrying the death penalty for crimes classified as felonies under English law. Most of them seemed to be of low intelligence, but I noticed several whose tight thin lips, pointed nose, sharp chin, deep-set eyes and sly look I took as signs of exceptional depravity. I saw only one woman there who aroused my interest. She was confined with six others in a dark, damp low-ceilinged cell; when we entered they all rose and made us the customary servile curtsey which had embarrassed and irritated me from the moment I set foot in the prison. One alone refrained and it was this sign of independence which attracted my attention. Picture a young woman of twenty-four, small, well-made and tastefully dressed, standing with head held high to reveal a perfect profile, graceful neck. My eyes filled with tears and only the presence of the governor prevented me from going up to her and taking her hand so that she might understand my interest in her fate and so that my sympathy might calm for a few moments the sufferings of her heart.

Beauty can only be supreme when it reflects the noblest qualities of the soul. Without that inner radiance even the most beautiful woman in that sad place would have left me unmoved; but there was such dignity in this beauty which bore the depths of misfortune with pride and courage.

A CHARTIST SPEAKS, 1842

Thomas Cooper

Named for *The People's Charter* of 1838, Chartism advanced universal male suffrage and annual parliaments. It also expressed working class resentment at economic distress and the Poor Law.

On Sunday morning, in company with these Chartist friends, I went and spoke in the open air at Fenton, and in the afternoon at Longton. In the evening I addressed an immense crowd at Hanley, standing on a chair in front of the Crown Inn: such ground being called the Crown Bank by the natives. I took for a text the sixth commandment: "Thou shalt do no murder" – after we had sung Bramwich's hymn, "Britannia's sons, though slaves ye be," and I had offered up a short prayer.

I showed how kings, in all ages, had enslaved the people, and spilt their blood in wars of conquest, thus violating the precept, "Thou shalt do no murder."

I described how the conquerors of America had nearly exterminated the native races, and thus violated the precept, "Thou shalt do no murder."

I recounted how English and French and Spanish and German wars, in modern history, had swollen the list of the slaughtered and had violated the precept, "Thou shalt do no murder."

I described our own guilty Colonial rule, and still guiltier rule of ireland; and asserted that British rulers had most awfully violated the precept, "Thou shalt do no murder."

I showed how the immense taxation we were forced to endure, to enable our rulers to maintain the long and ruinous war with France and Napoleon, had entailed indescribable suffering on millions, and that thus had been violated the precept, "Thou shalt do no murder."

I asserted that the imposition of the Bread Tax was a violation of the same precept; and that such was the enactment of the Game Laws; that such was the custom of primogeniture and keeping of land in the possession of the privileged classes; and that such was the enactment of the infamous new Poor Law.

The general murmur of applause now began to swell into loud cries; and these were mingled with execrations of the authors of the Poor Law. I went on.

THE INDUSTRIAL REVOLUTION: THE SLUMS OF MANCHESTER, ENGLAND, 1844

Friedrich Engels

The south bank of the Irk is here very steep and between fifteen and thirty feet high. On this declivitous hillside there are planted three rows of houses, of which the lowest rise directly out of the river, while the front walls of the highest stand on the crest of the hill in Long Millgate. Among them are mills on the river, in short, the method of construction is as crowded and disorderly here as in the lower part of Long Millgate. Right and left a multitude of covered passages lead from the main street into numerous courts, and he who turns in thither gets into a filth and disgusting grime, the equal of which is not be found – especially in the courts which lead down to the Irk, and which contain unqualifiedly the most horrible dwellings which I have yet beheld. In one of these courts there stands directly at the entrance, at the end of the covered passage, a privy without a door, so dirty that the inhabitants can pass into and out of the court only by passing through foul pools of stagnant urine and excrement. This is the first court on the Irk above Ducie Bridge – in case any one should care to look into it. Below it on the river there are several tanneries which fill the whole neighborhood with the stench of animal putrefaction. Below Ducie Bridge the only entrance to most of the houses is by means of narrow, dirty stairs and over heaps of refuse and filth. The first court below Ducie Bridge, known as Allen's Court, was in such a state at the time of the cholera that the sanitary police ordered it evacuated, swept and disinfected with chloride of lime. Dr Kay gives a terrible description of the state of this court at that time. Since then, it seems to have been partially torn away and rebuilt; at least looking down from Ducie Bridge, the passer-by sees several ruined walls and heaps of *débris* with some newer houses. The view from this bridge, mercifully concealed from mortals of small stature by a parapet as high as a man, is characteristic for the whole district. At the bottom flows, or rather stagnates, the Irk, a narrow, coal-black, foul-smelling stream, full of *débris* and refuse, which it deposits on the shallower right bank. In dry weather, a long string of the most disgusting blackish-green slime pools are left standing on this bank, from the depths of which bubbles of miasmatic gas constantly arise and give forth a stench unendurable even on the bridge forty of fifty feet above the surface of the stream. But besides this, the stream itself is checked every few paces by high weirs, behind which slime and refuse accumulate and rot in thick masses. Above the bridge are tanneries, bonemills, and gasworks, from which all drains and refuse find their way into the Irk, which receives further the contents of all the neighbouring sewers and privies. It may be easily imagined, therefore, what sort of residue the stream deposits. Below the bridge you look upon the piles of *débris*, the refuse, filth, and offal from the courts on the steep left bank; here each house is packed close behind its neighbour and a piece of each is visible, all black, smoky, crumbling, ancient, with broken panes and window-frames. The background is furnished by old barrack-like factory buildings. On the lower right bank stands a long row of houses and mills; the second house being a ruin without a roof, piled with *débris*; the third stands so low that the lowest floor is uninhabitable, and therefore without windows or doors. Here the background embraces the pauper burial-ground, the station of the Liverpool and Leeds railway, and, in the rear of this, the Workhouse, the "Poor-Law Bastille" of Manchester, which, like a citadel, looks threateningly down from behind its high walls and parapets on the hilltop, upon the working-people's quarter below.

Above Ducie Bridge, the left bank grows more flat and the right bank steeper, but the condition of the dwellings on both banks grows worse rather than better. He who turns to the left here from the main street, Long Millgate, is lost; he wanders from one court to another, turns countless corners, passes nothing but narrow, filthy nooks and alleys, until after a few minutes he has lost all clue, and knows not whither to turn. Everywhere half or wholly ruined buildings, some of them actually uninhabited, which means a great deal here; rarely a wooden or stone floor to be seen in the houses, almost uniformly broken, ill-fitting windows and doors, and a state of filth! Everywhere heaps of *débris*, refuse, and offal; standing pools for gutters, and a stench which alone would make it impossible for a human being in any degree civilised to live in such a district. The newly-built extension of the Leeds railway, which crosses the Irk here, has swept away some of these courts and lanes, laying others completely open to view. Immediately under the railway bridge there stands a court, the filth and horrors of which surpass all the others by far, just because it was hitherto so shut off, so secluded that the way to it could not be found without a good deal of trouble. I should never have discovered it myself, without the breaks made by the railway, though I thought I knew this whole region thoroughly. Passing along a rough bank, among stakes and washing-lines, one penetrates into this chaos of small one-storied, one-roomed huts, in most of which there is no artificial floor; kitchen, living and sleeping-room all in one. In such a hole, scarcely five feet long by six broad, I found two beds – and such bedsteads and beds! – which, with a staircase and chimney-place, exactly filled the room. In several others I found absolutely nothing, while the door stood open, and the inhabitants leaned against it. Everywhere before the doors refuse and offal; that any sort of pavement lay underneath could not be seen but only felt, here and there, with the feet. This whole collection of cattle-sheds for human beings was surrounded on two sides by houses and a factory, and on the third by the river, and besides the narrow stair up the bank, a narrow doorway alone led out into another almost equally ill-built, ill-kept labyrinth of dwellings.

Enough! The whole side of the Irk is built in this way, a planless, knotted chaos of houses, more or less on the verge of uninhabitableness, whose unclean interiors fully correspond with their filthy external surroundings. And how could the people be clean with no proper opportunity for satisfying the most natural and ordinary wants? Privies are so rare here that they are either filled up every day, or are too remote for most of the inhabitants to use. How can people wash when they have only the dirty Irk water at hand, while pumps and water pipes can be found in decent parts of the city alone? In truth, it cannot be charged to the account of these helots of modern society if their dwellings are not more clean than the pig sties which are here and there to be seen among them. The landlords are not ashamed to let dwellings like the six or seven cellars on the quay directly below Scotland Bridge, the floors of which stand at least two feet below the low-water level of the Irk that flows not six feet away from them; or like the upper floor of the corner-house on the opposite shore directly above the bridge, where the ground-floor, utterly uninhabitable, stands deprived of all fittings for doors and windows, a case by no means rare in this region, when this open ground-floor is used as a privy by the whole neighbourhood for want of other facilities!

If we leave the Irk and penetrate once more on the opposite side from Long Millgate into the midst of the working-men's dwellings, we shall come into a somewhat newer quarter, which stretches from St Michael's Church to Withy Grove and Shude Hill. Here there is somewhat better order. In place of the chaos of buildings, we find at least long straight lanes and alleys or courts, built according to a plan and usually square. But if, in the former case, every house was built according to caprice, here each lane and court is so built, without reference to the situation of the adjoining ones. The lanes run now in this direction, now in that, while every two minutes the wanderer gets into a blind alley, or on turning a corner, finds himself back where he started from; certainly no one who has not lived a considerable time in this labyrinth can find his way through it.

If I may use the word at all in speaking of this district, the ventilation of these streets and courts is, in consequence of this confusion, quite as imperfect as in the Irk region; and if this quarter may, nevertheless, be said to have some advantage over that of the Irk, the houses being newer and the streets occasionally having gutters, nearly every house has, on the other hand, a cellar dwelling, which is rarely found in the Irk district, by reason of the greater age and more careless construction of the houses. As for the rest, the filth, *débris*, and offal heaps, and the pools in the streets are common to both quarters, and in the district now under discussion, another feature most injurious to the cleanliness of the inhabitants, is the multitude of pigs walking about in all the alleys, rooting into the offal heaps, or kept imprisoned in small pens. Here, as in most of the working-men's quarters of Manchester, the pork-raisers rent the courts and build pig-pens in them. In almost every court one or even several such pens may be found, into which the inhabitants of the court throw all refuse and offal, whence the swine grow fat; and the atmosphere, confined on all four sides, is utterly corrupted by putrefying animal and vegetable substances. Through this quarter, a broad and measurably decent street has been cut, Millers Street, and the background has been pretty successfully concealed. But if any one should be led by curiosity to pass through one of the numerous passages which lead into the courts, he will find this piggery repeated at every twenty paces.

THE IRISH POTATO FAMINE, 1847

William Forster

In 1845 blight ruined the potato crop, the staple diet of Ireland. Government relief was reluctant and inadequate, and about one million Irish people died from disease and starvation; another million emigrated, most to America. Forster was an English Quaker on a fact finding mission to Ireland.

I left Dublin by mail on the 17th of First-month, 1847, and joined my father and his companions at Westport on the following evening.

The next day we left Westport, on our way to Connemara, after a morning of much pressure; applications for aid coming in from all sides, especially from Louisburgh, a populous and most distressed parish along the coast to the south; the surgeon of the dispensary there describing the people as swept off by dysentery, the most usual form of the famine-plague, by ten to twenty a day. The town of Westport was in itself a strange and fearful sight, like what we read of in beleaguered cities, its streets crowded with gaunt wanderers sauntering to and fro with hopeless air and hunger-struck look; a mob of starved, almost naked women, around the poor-house, clamouring for soup-tickets; our inn, the head-quarters of the road-engineer and pay clerks beset by a crowd of beggars for work.

Early next morning, we proceeded to the small village of Leenane, where we found a large body of men engaged in making a pier under the Labour-rate Act. This village appeared to me, comparatively speaking, well off, having had in it public works for some weeks, and the wages of pier-making being rather better than those earned on the roads. Still, even here, the men were weak, evidently wasting away for want of sufficient food.

Bundorragha, the village of which we had heard so bad an account the previous evening, being on the other side of the harbour, I took a boat to it, and was much struck by the pale, spiritless look and air of the boatmen, so different from their wild Irish fun when I had made the same excursion before. Having lately walked through all this district of Connemara, I had an opportunity of comparing its present with its then aspect, and of noting the effects produced on it by the famine: in this village of Bundorragha, the change was peculiarly striking. In my previous visit, it struck me even then as a very poor place; the dark thunder-cloud was brooding over it, but as yet the tempest had not broken. The small cottiers, then gathering in their few potatoes, were in great fear: they saw the quick, sure approach of famine: death stared them in the face, but as yet his hand was stayed. One poor woman, whose cabin I visited, said, "There will be nothing for us but to lie down and die." I tried to give her hope of English aid, but, alas! her prophecy has been but too true. Out of a population of 240, I found 13 already dead from want. The survivors were like walking skeletons; the men stamped with the livid mark of hunger; the children crying with pain; the women in some of the cabins too weak to stand. When there before, I had seen cows at almost every cabin, and there were, besides, many sheep and pigs owned in the village. But now all the sheep were gone; all the cows, all the poultry killed; only one pig left; the very dogs which had barked at me before had disappeared; no potatoes, no oats. We ordered a ton of meal to be sent there from Westport, but it could not arrive for some time. I tried to get some immediate help for those who were actually starving; there was hardly enough of meal in the village to fill my pockets, and I was compelled to send a boat four miles to Leenane, to buy a small quantity there.

I here met with a striking instance of the patience of these sufferers. The Bundorragha men had been at work for three weeks on the roads, and the men at a neighbouring village for five weeks; owing to the negligence or mistake of some officers of the works, with the exception of two of the gangsmen, who had gone themselves to Westport the end of the previous week, no wages had until this morning been received. While I was there, the pay clerk sent a messenger over; but still only with wages for a few; and it was wonderful, but yet most touching, to see the patient, quiet look of despair with which the others received the news that they were still left unpaid. I doubt whether it would have been easy to find a man who would have dared to bear the like announcement to starving Englishmen.

On recrossing the water, I found my father waiting for me on a car, on which we proceeded to Clifden, which we did not reach till after night-fall. Near the Kylemore Lake, under that grand chain of mountains, the Twelve Pins, we found full a hundred men making a new road. After long cross-questioning, we learned that their wages did not average, taking one week with another, and allowing for broken days, more than four shillings and sixpence per week per head: and this we found confirmed by our enquiries in other districts; in fact, for the most distressed localities in Mayo and Galway, I should consider this too high an average. To get to their work, many of the men have to walk five, or even seven, Irish miles.

Galway, 25th of First-month, 1847.

The next day we spent chiefly in interviews with different gentlemen, especially the Protestant and Roman Catholic clergymen, who showed great zeal in their efforts to give relief in their town and neighbourhood. We found deep distress, resulting in greatly increased mortality in this town, especially in the Claddagh, the quarter in which the fishermen chiefly reside; but we were glad to have reason to believe that the more wealthy inhabitants were grappling with the evil according to their ability; and it was comforting to observe how cordially Roman Catholics and Protestants, both lay and clerical, were uniting together in common efforts to save their poor neighbours.

Among other callers at our hotel, was the clergyman of the district on the northern side of Galway Bay, including Spiddal and Lettermore, and also the isles of Arran. This parish, or rather portion of a parish, comprised, he stated, a population of at least 15,000 in great distress, especially the inhabitants of the main land, and of Lettermore and its adjoining group of islands.

There are in this wide tract, so thickly peopled in proportion to its cultivation, scarcely any resident land-owners, and no store for the sale of provisions; and many of his parishioners had, this gentleman told us, to make a journey of thirty miles to Galway, to buy a stone of meal. This was one among many cases, in which was brought home to us the great need for the establishment of small depots for provisions, or retail stores. In many of the more remote and distressed, because neglected districts, where the inhabitants have hitherto subsisted upon potatoes, a retail trade in provisions is altogether novel to their habits; and so complete is the absence of capital, that there is no probability (at least this year) of its overtaking the demand. Often the poor people have, after earning their wretched pittance at the public works, to walk ten, twenty, or even thirty miles to the nearest store, to get a stone of meal; or to buy it from the small hucksters, at an advance of as much as thirty per cent above the market price.

. . . The impression made on me by this short tour can never be effaced. Bad as were my expectations, the reality far exceeded them. There is a prevailing idea in England, that the newspaper accounts are exaggerated. Particular cases may or may not be coloured, but no colouring can deepen the blackness of the truth.

THE GREAT EXHIBITION AT CRYSTAL PALACE, LONDON, 7 JUNE 1851

Charlotte Brontë

Yesterday I went for the second time to the Crystal Palace. We remained in it about three hours, and I must say I was more struck with it on this occasion than at my first visit. It is a wonderful place – vast, strange, new, and impossible to describe. Its grandeur does not consist in *one* thing, but in the unique assemblage of *all* things. Whatever human industry has created you find there, from the great compartments filled with railway engines and boilers, with mill machinery in full work, with splendid carriages of all kinds, with harness of every description, to the glass-covered and velvet spread stands loaded with the most gorgeous work of the goldsmith and silversmith, and the carefully guarded caskets full of real diamonds and pearls worth hundreds of thousands of pounds. It may be called a bazaar or a fair, but it is such a bazaar or fair as Eastern genii might have created. It seems as if only magic could have gathered this mass of wealth from all the ends of the earth – as if none but supernatural hands could have arranged it thus, with such a blaze and contrast of colours and marvellous power of effect. The multitude filling the great aisles seems ruled and subdued by some invisible influence. Amongst the thirty thousand souls that peopled it the day I was there not one loud noise was to be heard, not one irregular movement seen; the living tide rolls on quietly, with a deep hum like the sea heard from the distance.

AN AERIAL VIEW OF LONDON, 13 SEPTEMBER 1852

Henry Mayhew and John Binny

It was late in the evening (a fine autumn one) when the gun was fired that was the signal for the great gas-bag to be loosened from the ropes that held it down to the soil; and immediately the buoyant machine bounded, like a big ball, into the air. Or, rather let us say, *the earth seemed to sink* suddenly down as if the spot of ground to which it had been previously fastened had been constructed upon the same principle as the Adelphi stage, and admitted of being lowered at a moment's notice. Indeed, no sooner did the report of the gun clatter in the air, than the people, who had before been grouped about the car, appeared to fall from a level with the eye; and, instantaneously, there was seen a multitude of flat, upturned faces in the gardens below, with a dense chevaux de frise of arms extended above them, and some hundreds of outstretched hands fluttering farewell to us.

The moment after this, the balloon vaulted over the trees, and we saw the roadway outside the gardens stuck all over with mobs of little black Lilliputian people, while the hubbub of the voices below, and the cries of "Ah *bal*-loon!" from the boys, rose to the ear like the sound of a distant school let loose to play.

Now began that peculiar panoramic effect which is the distinguishing feature of the first portion of a view from a balloon, and which arises from the utter absence of all sense of motion in the machine itself, and the consequent transference of the movement to the ground beneath. The earth, as the aeronautic vessel glided over it, seemed positively to consist of a continuous series of scenes which were being drawn along underneath us, as if it were some diorama laid flat upon the ground, and almost gave one the notion that the world was an endless landscape stretched up on rollers, which some invisible sprites below were busy revolving for our especial amusement.

Then, as we floated along above the fields, in a line with the Thames towards Richmond, and looked over the edge of the car in which we were standing (and which, by the bye, was like a big "buck basket", reaching to one's breast), the sight was the most exquisite visual delight ever experienced. The houses directly underneath us looked like the tiny wooden things out of a child's box of toys, and the streets as if they were ruts in the ground; and we could hear the hum of the voices from every spot we passed over, faint as the buzzing of so many bees.

Far beneath, in the direction we were sailing, lay the suburban fields; and here the earth, with its tiny hills and plains and streams, assumed the appearance of the little coloured plaster models of countries. The roadways striping the land were like narrow brown ribbons, and the river, which we could see winding far away, resembled a long, gray metallic-looking snake, creeping through the fields. The bridges over the Thames were positively like planks; and the tiny black barges, as they floated along the stream, seemed no bigger than summer insects on the water. The largest meadows were about the size of green-baize table covers; and across these we could just trace the line of the South-Western Railway, with the little whiff of white steam issuing from some passing engine, and no greater in volume than the jet of vapour from an ordinary tea-kettle.

Then, as the dusk of evening descended, and the gas-lights along the different lines of road started into light, one after another, the ground seemed to be covered with little illumination lamps, such as are hung on Christmas-trees, and reminding one of those that are occasionally placed, at intervals, along the grass at the edge of the gravel-walks in suburban tea-gardens; whilst the clusters of little lights at the spots where the hamlets were scattered over the scene, appeared like knots of fire-flies in the air; and in the midst of these the eye could, here and there, distinguish the tiny crimson speck of some railway signal.

In the opposite direction to that in which the wind was insensibly wafting the balloon, lay the leviathan Metropolis, with a dense canopy of smoke hanging over it, and reminding one of the fog of vapour that is often seen steaming up from the fields at early morning. It was impossible to tell where the monster city began or ended, for the buildings stretched not only to the horizon on either side, but far away into the distance, where, owing to the coming shades of evening and the dense fumes from the million chimneys, the town seemed to blend into the sky, so that there was no distinguishing earth from heaven. The multitude of roofs that extended back from the fore-ground was positively like a dingy red sea, heaving in bricken billows, and the seeming waves rising up one after the other till the eye grew wearied with following them. Here and there we could distinguish little bare green patches of parks, and occasionally make out the tiny circular enclosures of the principal squares, though, from the height, these appeared scarcely bigger than wafers. Further, the fog of smoke that over-shadowed the giant town was pierced with a thousand steeples and pin-like factory-chimneys.

That little building, no bigger than one of the small china houses that are used for burning pastilles in, is Buckingham Palace – with St James's Park, dwindled to the size of a card-table, stretched out before it. Yonder is Bethlehem Hospital, with its dome, now about the same dimensions as a bell.

Then the little mites of men, crossing the bridges, seemed to have no more motion in them than the animalcules in cheese; while the streets appeared more like cracks in the soil than highways, and the tiny steamers on the river were only to be distinguished by the thin black thread of smoke trailing after them.

Indeed, it was a most wonderful sight to behold that vast bricken mass of churches and hospitals, banks and prisons, palaces and workhouses, docks and refuges for the destitute, parks and squares, and courts and alleys, which make up London – all blent into one immense black spot – to look down upon the whole as the birds of the air look down upon it, and see it dwindled into a mere rubbish heap – to contemplate from afar that strange conglomeration of vice, avarice, and low cunning, of noble aspirations and humble heroism, and to grasp it in the eye, in all its incongruous integrity, at one single glance – to take, as it were, an angel's view of that huge town where, perhaps, there is more virtue and more iniquity, more wealth and more want, brought together into one dense focus than in any other part of the earth – to hear the hubbub of the restless sea of life and emotion below, and hear it, like the ocean in a shell, whispering of the incessant strugglings and chafings of the distant tide – to swing in the air high above all the petty jealousies and heart-burnings, small ambitions and vain parade of "polite" society, and feel, for once, tranquil as a babe in a cot, and that you are hardly of the earth, earthy, as, Jacob-like, you mount the aerial ladder, and half lose sight of the "great commercial world" beneath, where men are regarded as mere counters to play with, and where to do your neighbour as your neighbour would do you constitutes the first principle in the religion of trade – to feel yourself floating through the endless realms of space, and drinking in the pure thin air of the skies, as you go sailing along almost among the stars, free as "the lark at heaven's gate", and enjoying, for a brief half hour, at least, a foretaste of that Elysian destiny which is the ultimate hope of all.

Such is the scene we behold, and such the thoughts that stir the brain on contemplating London from the car of a balloon.

THE BATTLE OF BALACLAVA: THE CHARGE OF THE LIGHT BRIGADE, CRIMEA, 25 OCTOBER 1854

William Howard Russell

Russell was the war correspondent for the London *Times*.

If the exhibition of the most brilliant valour, of the excess of courage, and of a daring which would have reflected lustre on the best days of chivalry can afford full consolation for the disaster of today, we can have no reason to regret the melancholy loss which we sustained in a contest with a savage and barbarian enemy.

I shall proceed to describe, to the best of my power, what occurred under my own eyes, and to state the facts which I have heard from men whose veracity is unimpeachable, reserving to myself the exercise of the right of private judgement in making public and in suppressing the details of what occurred on this memorable day . . .

It will be remembered that in a letter sent by last mail from this place it was mentioned that eleven battalions of Russian infantry had crossed the Tchernaya, and that they threatened the rear of our position and our communication with Balaclava. Their bands could be heard playing at night by travellers along the Balaclava road to the camp, but they "showed" but little during the day and kept up among the gorges and mountain passes through which the roads to Inkermann, Simpheropol, and the south-east of the Crimea wind towards the interior. It will be recollected also that the position we occupied in reference to Balaclava was supposed by most people to be very strong – even impregnable. Our lines were formed by natural mountain slopes in the rear, along which the French had made very formidable intrenchments. Below those intrenchments, and very nearly in a right line across the valley beneath, are four conical hillocks, one rising above the other as they recede from our lines . . . On the top of each of these hills the Turks had thrown up earthen redoubts, defended by 250 men each, and armed with two or three guns – some heavy ship guns – lent by us to them, with one artilleryman in each redoubt to look after them. These hills cross the valley of Balaclava at the distance of about two and a half miles from the town. Supposing the spectator then to take his stand on one of the heights forming the rear of our camp before Sebastopol, he would see the town of Balaclava, with its scanty shipping, its narrow strip of water, and its old forts on his right hand; immediately below he would behold the valley and plain of coarse meadowland, occupied by our cavalry tents, and stretching from the base of the ridge on which he stood to the foot of the formidable heights on the other side; he would see the French trenches lined with Zouaves a few feet beneath, and distant from him, on the slope of the hill; a Turkish redoubt lower down, then another in the valley, then in a line with it some angular earthworks, then, in succession, the other two redoubts up Canrobert's Hill.

At the distance of two or two and a half miles across the valley there is an abrupt rocky mountain range of most irregular and picturesque formation, covered with scanty brushwood here and there, or rising into barren pinnacles and plateaux of rock. In outline and appearance, this position of the landscape is wonderfully like the Trossachs. A patch of blue sea is caught in between the overhanging cliffs of Balaclava as they close in the entrance to the harbour on the right. The camp of the Marines pitched on the hillsides more than one thousand feet above the level of the sea is opposite to you as your back is turned to Sebastopol and your right side towards Balaclava. On the road leading up the valley, close to the entrance of the town and beneath these hills, is the encampment of the 93rd Highlanders.

The cavalry lines are nearer to you below, and are some way in advance of the Highlanders, and nearer to the town than the Turkish redoubts. The valley is crossed here and there by small waves of land. On your left the hills and rocky mountain ranges gradually close in toward the course of the Tchernaya, till at three or four miles' distance from Balaclava the valley is swallowed up in a mountain gorge and deep ravines, above which rise tier after tier of desolate whitish rock garnished now and then by bits of scanty herbage, and spreading away towards the east and south, where they attain the alpine dimensions of Tschatir Dagh. It is very easy for an enemy at the Belbek, or in command of the road of Mackenzie's Farm, Inkermann, Simpheropol, or Bakhchisarai, to debouch through these gorges at any time upon this plain from the neck of the valley, or to march from Sebastopol by the Tchernaya and to advance along it towards Balaclava, till checked by the Turkish redoubts on the southern side or by the fire from the French works on the northern side, i.e., the side which in relation to the valley of Balaclava forms the rear of our position.

At half past seven o'clock this morning an orderly came galloping in to the headquarters camp from Balaclava, with the news that at dawn a strong corps of Russian horse supported by guns and battalions of infantry had marched into the valley, and had already nearly dispossessed the Turks of the redoubt No. 1 (that on Canrobert's Hill, which is farthest from our lines) and that they were opening fire on the redoubts Nos. 2, 3 and 4, which would speedily be in their hands unless the Turks offered a stouter resistance than they had done already.

Orders were dispatched to Sir George Cathcart and to HRH the Duke of Cambridge to put their respective divisions, the 4th and 1st, in motion for the scene of action, and intelligence of the advance of the Russians was also furnished to General Canrobert. Immediately on receipt of the news the General commanded General Bosquet to get the Third Division under arms, and sent a strong body of artillery and some 200 Chasseurs d'Afrique to assist us in holding the valley. Sir Colin Campbell, who was in command of Balaclava, had drawn up the 93rd Highlanders a little in front of the road to the town at the first news of the advance of the enemy. The marines on the heights got under arms; the seamen's batteries and marines' batteries on the heights close to the town were manned, and the French artillerymen and the Zouaves prepared for action along their lines. Lord Lucan's little camp was the scene of great excitement. The men had not had time to water their horses; they had not broken their fast from the evening of the day before, and had barely saddled at the first blast of the trumpet, when they were drawn up on the slope behind the redoubts in front of the camp to operate on the enemy's squadrons. It was soon evident that no reliance was to be placed on the Turkish infantrymen or artillerymen. All the stories we had heard about their bravery behind stone walls and earthworks proved how differently the same or similar people fight under different circumstances. When the Russians advanced the Turks fired a few rounds at them, got frightened at the distance of their supports in the rear, looked round, received a few shots and shell, and then "bolted", and fled with an agility quite at variance with the commonplace notions of oriental deportment on the battlefield. But Turks on the Danube are very different beings from Turks in the Crimea, as it appears that the Russians of Sebastopol are not at all like the Russians of Silistria.

Soon after eight Lord Raglan and his staff turned out and cantered towards the rear of our position. The booming of artillery, the spattering roll of musketry, were heard rising from the valley, drowning the roar of the siege guns in front before Sebastopol. As I rode in the direction of the firing over the thistles and large stones which cover the undulating plain which stretches away towards Balaclava, on a level with the summit of the ridges above it, I observed a French light infantry regiment (the 27th, I think) advancing with admirable care and celerity from our right towards the ridge near the telegraph house, which was already lined with companies of French infantry, while mounted officers scampered along its broken outline in every direction.

General Bosquet, a stout soldierlike-looking man, who reminds one of the old *genre* of French generals as depicted at Versailles, followed, with his staff and small escort of Hussars, at a gallop. Faint white clouds rose here and there above the hill from the cannonade below. Never did the painter's eye rest upon a more beautiful scene than I beheld from the ridge. The fleecy vapours still hung around the mountain tops and mingled with the ascending volumes of smoke; the patch of sea sparkled freshly in the rays of the morning sun, but its light was eclipsed by the flashes which gleamed from the masses of armed men below.

Looking to the left towards the gorge we beheld six compact masses of Russian infantry which had just debouched from the mountain passes near the Tchernaya, and were slowly advancing with solemn stateliness up the valley. Immediately in their front was a regular line of artillery, of at least twenty pieces strong. Two batteries of light guns were already a mile in advance of them, and were playing with energy on the redoubts, from which feeble puffs of smoke came at long intervals. Behind the guns, in front of the infantry, were enormous bodies of cavalry. They were in six compact squares, three on each flank, moving down *en échelon* towards us, and the valley was lit up with the blaze of their sabres and lance points and gay accoutrements. In their front, and extending along the intervals between each battery of guns, were clouds of mounted skirmishers, wheeling and whirling in the front of their march like autumn leaves tossed by the wind. The Zouaves close to us were lying like tigers at the spring, with ready rifles in hand, hidden chin deep by the earthworks which run along the line of these ridges on our rear, but the quick-eyed Russians were manoeuvring on the other side of the valley, and did not expose their columns to attack. Below the Zouaves we could see the Turkish gunners in the redoubts, all in confusion as the shells burst over them. Just as I came up the Russians had carried No. 1 redoubt, the farthest and most elevated of all, and their horsemen were chasing the Turks across the interval which lay between it and redoubt No. 2. At that moment the cavalry, under Lord Lucan, were formed in glittering masses – the Light Brigade, under Lord Cardigan, in advance of the Heavy Brigade, under Brigadier-General Scarlett, in reserve. They were drawn up just in front of their encampment, and were concealed from the view of the enemy by a slight "wave" in the plain. Considerably to the rear of their right, the 93rd Highlanders were drawn up in line, in front of the approach to Balaclava. Above and behind them on the heights, the marines were visible through the glass, drawn up under arms, and the gunners could be seen ready in the earthworks, in which were placed the heavy ships' guns. The 93rd had originally been advanced somewhat more into the plain, but the instant the Russians got possession of the first redoubt they opened fire on them from our own guns, which inflicted some injury, and Sir Colin Campbell "retired" his men to a better position. Meantime the enemy advanced his cavalry rapidly. To our inexpressible disgust we saw the Turks in redoubt No. 2 fly at their approach. They ran in scattered groups across towards redoubt No. 3, and towards Balaclava, but the horse-hoof of the Cossacks was too quick for them, and sword and lance were busily plied among the retreating band. The yells of the pursuers and pursued were plainly audible. As the Lancers and Light Cavalry of the Russians advanced they gathered up their skirmishers with great speed and in excellent order – the shifting trails of men, which played all over the valley like moonlight on water, contracted, gathered up, and the little *peloton* in a few moments became a solid column. Then up came their guns, in rushed their gunners to the abandoned redoubt, and the guns of No. 2 redoubt soon played with deadly effect upon the dispirited defenders of No. 3 redoubt. Two or three shots in return from the earthworks, and all is silent. The Turks swarm over the earthworks and run in confusion towards the town, firing their muskets at the enemy as they run. Again the solid column of cavalry opens like a fan, and resolves itself into the "long spray" of skirmishers. It laps the flying Turks, steel flashes in the air, and down go the poor Muslim quivering on the plain, split through fez and musket-guard to the chin and breast-belt. There is no support for them. It is evident the Russians have been too quick for us. The Turks have been too quick also, for they have not held their redoubts long enough to enable us to bring them help. In vain the naval guns on the heights fire on the Russian cavalry; the distance is too great for shot or shell to reach. In vain the Turkish gunners in the earthen batteries which are placed along the French intrenchments strive to protect their flying countrymen; their shots fly wide and short of the swarming masses. The Turks betake themselves towards the Highlanders, where they check their flight and form into companies on the flanks of the Highlanders.

As the Russian cavalry on the left of their line crown the hill, across the valley they perceive the Highlanders drawn up at the distance of some half-mile, calmly awaiting their approach. They halt, and squadron after squadron flies up from the rear, till they have a body of some 1500 men along the ridge – Lancers and Dragoons and Hussars. Then they move *en échelon* in two bodies, with another in reserve. The cavalry who have been pursuing the Turks on the right are coming up the ridge beneath us, which conceals our cavalry from view. The heavy brigade in advance is drawn up in two columns. The first column consists of the Scots Greys and of their old companions in glory, the Enniskillens; the second of the 4th Royal Irish, of the 5th Dragoon Guards, and of the 1st Royal Dragoons. The Light Cavalry Brigade is on their left in two lines also. The silence is oppressive; between the cannon bursts, one can hear the champing of bits and the clink of sabres in the valley below. The Russians on their left drew breath for a moment, and then in one grand line dashed at the Highlanders. The ground flies beneath their horses' feet – gathering speed at every stride they dash on towards that thin red streak topped with a line of steel. The Turks fire a volley at 800 yards, and run. As the Russians come within 600 yards, down goes that line of steel in front, and out rings a rolling volley of Minié musketry. The distance is too great. The Russians are not checked, but still sweep onwards with the whole force of horse and man, through the smoke, here and there knocked over by the shot of our batteries above. With breathless suspense everyone awaits the bursting of the wave upon the line of Gaelic rock; but ere they came within 150 yards, another deadly volley flashes from the levelled rifles, and carries death and terror into the Russians. They wheel about, open files right and left, and fly back faster than they came.

"Bravo Highlanders! well done!" shout the excited spectators; but events thicken. The Highlanders and their splendid front are soon forgotten. Men scarcely have a moment to think of this fact that the 93rd never altered their formation to receive that tide of horsemen.

"No," said Sir Colin Campbell, "I did not think it worth while to form them even four deep!"

The ordinary British line, two deep, was quite sufficient to repel the attack of these Muscovite chevaliers. Our eyes were, however, turned in a moment on our own cavalry. We saw

Brigadier-General Scarlett ride along in front of his massive squadrons. The Russians – evidently *corps d'élite* – their light-blue jackets embroidered with silver lace, were advancing on their left at an easy gallop, towards the brow of the hill. A forest of lances glistened in their rear, and several squadrons of grey-coated dragoons moved up quickly to support them as they reached the summit. The instant they came in sight the trumpets of our cavalry gave out the warning blast which told us all that in another moment we would see the shock of battle beneath our very eyes. Lord Raglan, all his staff and escort, and groups of officers, the Zouaves, the French generals and officers, and bodies of French infantry on the height, were spectators of the scene as though they were looking on the stage from the boxes of a theatre. Nearly everyone dismounted and sat down, and not a word was said.

The Russians advanced down the hill at a slow canter, which they changed to a trot and at last nearly halted. The first line was at least double the length of ours – it was three times as deep. Behind them was a similar line, equally strong and compact. They evidently despised their insignificant-looking enemy, but their time was come.

The trumpets rang out through the valley, and the Greys and Enniskillens went right at the centre of the Russian cavalry. The space between them was only a few hundred yards; it was scarce enough to let the horses "gather way", nor had the men quite space sufficient for the full play of their sword arms. The Russian line brings forward each wing as our cavalry advance and threaten to annihilate them as they pass on. Turning a little to their left, so as to meet the Russians' right, the Greys rush on with a cheer that thrills to every heart – the wild shout of the Enniskillens rises through the air at the same moment. As lightning flashes through a cloud the Greys and Enniskillens pierced through the dark masses of the Russians. The shock was but for a moment. There was a clash of steel and a light play of sword blades in the air, and then the Greys and the redcoats disappear in the midst of the shaken and quivering columns. In another moment we see them merging and dashing on with diminished numbers, and in broken order, against the second line, which is advancing against them to retrieve the fortune of the charge.

It was a terrible moment. "God help them! They are lost!" was the exclamation of more than one man, and the thought of many.

With unabated fire the noble hearts dashed at their enemy – it was a fight of heroes. The first line of Russians which had been smashed utterly by our charge, and had fled off at one flank and towards the centre, were coming back to swallow up our handful of men. By sheer steel and sheer courage Enniskillen and Scot were winning their desperate way right through the enemy's squadrons, and already grey horses and redcoats had appeared right at the rear of the second mass, when, with irresistible force, like one bolt from a bow, the 1st Royals, the 4th Dragoon Guards, and the 5th Dragoon Guards rushed at the remnants of the first line of the enemy, went through it as though it were made of pasteboard, and dashing on the second body of Russians, as they were still disordered by the terrible assault of the Greys and their companions, put them to utter rout. This Russian horse in less than five minutes after it met our dragoons was flying with all its speed before a force certainly not half its strength.

A cheer burst from every lip – in the enthusiasm officers and men took off their caps and shouted with delight, and thus keeping up the scenic character of their position, they clapped their hands again and again . . .

And now occurred the melancholy catastrophe which fills us all with sorrow. It appears that the Quartermaster General, Brigadier Airey, thinking that the Light Cavalry had not gone far enough in front when the enemy's horse had fled, gave an order in writing to Captain Nolan, 15th Hussars, to take to Lord Lucan, directing His Lordship "to advance" his cavalry nearer to the enemy. A braver soldier than Captain Nolan the army did not possess. He was known to all his arm of the service for his entire devotion to his profession, and his name must be familiar to all who take interest in our cavalry for his excellent work published a year ago on our drill and system of remount and breaking horses. I had the pleasure of his acquaintance, and I know he entertained the most exalted opinions respecting the capabilities of the English horse soldier. Properly led, the British Hussar and Dragoon could in his mind break square, take batteries, ride over columns of infantry, and pierce any other cavalry in the world, as if they were made of straw. He thought they had not had the opportunity of doing all that was in their power, and that they had missed even such chances as they had offered to them – that, in fact, they were in some measure disgraced. A matchless rider and a first-rate swordsman, he held in contempt, I am afraid, even grape and canister.

He rode off with his orders to Lord Lucan. He is now dead and gone.

God forbid I should cast a shade on the brightness of his honour, but I am bound to state what I am told occurred when he reached His Lordship. I should premise that, as the Russian cavalry retired, their infantry fell back towards the head of the valley, leaving men in three of the redoubts they had taken and abandoning the fourth. They had also placed some guns on the heights over their position, on the left of the gorge. Their cavalry joined the reserves, and drew up in six solid divisions, in an oblique line, across the entrance to the gorge. Six battalions of infantry were placed behind them, and about thirty guns were drawn up along their line, while masses of infantry were also collected on the hills behind the redoubts on our right. Our cavalry had moved up to the ridge across the valley, on our left, as the ground was broken in front, and had halted in the order I have already mentioned.

When Lord Lucan received the order from Captain Nolan and had read it, he asked, we are told, "Where are we to advance to?"

Captain Nolan pointed with his finger to the line of the Russians, and said, "There are the enemy, and there are the guns, sir, before them. It is your duty to take them," or words to that effect, according to the statements made since his death.

Lord Lucan with reluctance gave the order to Lord Cardigan to advance upon the guns, conceiving that his orders compelled him to do so. The noble Earl, though he did not shrink, also saw the fearful odds against him. Don Quixote in his tilt against the windmill was not near so rash and reckless as the gallant fellows who prepared without a thought to rush on almost certain death.

It is a maxim of war that "cavalry never act without support", that "infantry should be close at hand when cavalry carry guns, as the effect is only instantaneous", and that it is necessary to have on the flank of a line of cavalry some squadrons in column, the attack on the flank being most dangerous. The only support our Light Cavalry had was the reserve of Heavy Cavalry at a great distance behind them – the infantry and guns being far in the rear. There were no squadrons in column at all, and there was a plain to charge over before the enemy's guns were reached of a mile and a half in length.

At ten past eleven our Light Cavalry Brigade rushed to the front. They numbered as follows, as well as I could ascertain:

	MEN
4th Light Dragoons	118
8th Irish Hussars	104
11th Prince Albert's Hussars	110
13th Light Dragoons	130
17th Lancers	145

Total 607 sabres

The whole brigade scarcely made one effective regiment, according to the numbers of continental armies; and yet it was more than we could spare. As they passed towards the front, the Russians opened on them from the guns in the redoubts on the right, with volleys of musketry and rifles.

They swept proudly past, glittering in the morning sun in all the pride and splendour of war. We could hardly believe the evidence of our senses! Surely that handful of men were not going to charge an army in position? Alas! it was but too true – their desperate valour knew no bounds, and far indeed was it removed from its so-called better part – discretion. They advanced in two lines, quickening their pace as they closed towards the enemy. A more fearful spectacle was never witnessed than by those who, without the power to aid, beheld their heroic countrymen rushing to the arms of death. At the distance of 1200 yards the whole line of the enemy belched forth, from thirty iron mouths, a flood of smoke and flame, through which hissed the deadly balls. Their flight was marked by instant gaps in our ranks, by dead men and horses, by steeds flying wounded or riderless across the plain. The first line was broken – it was joined by the second, they never halted or checked their speed an instant. With diminished ranks, thinned by those thirty guns, which the Russians had laid with the most deadly accuracy, with a halo of flashing steel above their heads, and with a cheer which was many a noble fellow's death cry, they flew into the smoke of the batteries; but ere they were lost from view, the plain was strewed with their bodies and with the carcasses of horses. They were exposed to an oblique fire from the batteries on the hills on both sides, as well as to a direct fire of musketry.

Through the clouds of smoke we could see their sabres flashing as they rode up to the guns and dashed between them, cutting down the gunners as they stood. The blaze of their steel, as an officer standing near me said, was "like the turn of a shoal of mackerel". We saw them riding through the guns, as I have said; to our delight we saw them returning, after breaking through a column of Russian infantry, and scattering them like chaff, when the flank fire of the battery on the hill swept them down, scattered and broken as they were. Wounded men and dismounted troopers flying towards us told the sad tale – demigods could not have done what they had failed to do. At the very moment when they were about to retreat, an enormous mass of lancers was hurled upon their flank. Colonel Shewell, of the 8th Hussars, saw the danger, and rode his few men straight at them, cutting his way through with fearful loss. The other regiments turned and engaged in a desperate encounter. With courage too great almost for credence, they were breaking their way through the columns which enveloped them, when there took place an act of atrocity without parallel in the modern warfare of civilized nations. The Russian gunners, when the storm of cavalry passed, returned to their guns. They saw their own cavalry mingled with the troopers who had just ridden over them, and to the eternal disgrace of the Russian name the miscreants poured a murderous volley of grape and canister on the mass of struggling men and horses, mingling friend and foe in one common ruin. It was as much as our Heavy Cavalry Brigade could do to cover the retreat of the miserable remnants of that band of heroes as they returned to the place they had so lately quitted in all the pride of life.

At twenty-five to twelve not a British soldier, except the dead and dying, was left in front of these bloody Muscovite guns. Our loss, as far as it could be ascertained in killed, wounded, and missing at two o'clock today, was as follows:

	WENT INTO ACTION STRONG	RETURNED FROM ACTION	LOSS
4th Light Dragoons	118	39	79
8th Hussars	104	38	66
11th Hussars	110	25	85
13th Light Dragoons	130	61	69
17th Lancers	145	35	110
	607	198	409

DISCOVERING THE VICTORIA FALLS, AFRICA, 1856

Dr David Livingstone

Dr Livingstone was a Scottish explorer and missionary.

I resolved on the following day to visit the falls of Victoria, called by the natives Mosioatunya, or more anciently Shongwe. Of these we had often heard since we came into the country: indeed one of the questions asked by Sebituane was, "Have you smoke that sounds in your country?" They did not go near enough to examine them, but, viewing them with awe at a distance, said, in reference to the vapour and noise, "Mosi oa tunya" (smoke does sound there). It was previously called Shongwe, the meaning of which I could not ascertain. The word for a "pot" resembles this, and it may mean a seething cauldron; but I am not certain of it. Being persuaded that Mr Oswell and myself were the very first Europeans who ever visited the Zambesi in the centre of the country, and that this is the connecting link between the known and unknown portions of that river, I decided to use the same liberty as the Makololo did, and gave the only English name I have affixed to any part of the country . . .

Sekeletu intended to accompany me, but, one canoe only having come instead of the two he had ordered, he resigned it to me. After twenty minutes' sail from Kalai, we came in sight, for the first time, of the columns of vapour, appropriately called "smoke", rising at a distance of five or six miles, exactly as when large tracts of grass are burned in Africa. Five columns now arose, and bending in the direction of the wind, they seemed placed against a low ridge covered with trees; the tops of the columns at this distance appeared to mingle with the clouds. They were white below, and higher up became dark, so as to simulate smoke very closely. The whole scene was extremely beautiful; the banks and islands dotted over the river are adorned with sylvan vegetation of great variety of colour and form. At the period of our visit several trees were spangled over with blossoms. Trees have each their own physiognomy. There, towering over all, stands the great burly baobab, each of whose enormous arms would form the trunk of a large tree, beside groups of graceful palms, which, with their feathery-shaped leaves depicted on the sky, lend their beauty to the scene. As a hieroglyphic they always

mean "far from home", for one can never get over their foreign
air in a picture or landscape. The silvery mohonono, which in the
tropics is in form like the cedar of Lebanon, stands in pleasing
contrast with the dark colour of the motsouri, whose cypress-form
is dotted over at present with its pleasant scarlet fruit. Some trees
resemble the great spreading oak, others assume the character of
our own elms and chestnuts; but no one can imagine the beauty
of the view from anything witnessed in England. It had never
been seen before by European eyes; but scenes so lovely must
have been gazed upon by angels in their flight. The only want felt
is that of mountains in the background. The falls are bounded on
three sides by ridges 300 or 400 feet in height, which are covered
with forest, with the red soil appearing among the trees. When
about half a mile from the falls, I left the canoe by which we had
come thus far, and embarked in a lighter one, with men well
acquainted with the rapids, who, by passing down the centre of
the stream in the eddies and still places caused by many jutting
rocks, brought me to an island situated in the middle of the river,
and on the edge of the lip over which the water rolls. In coming
hither, there was danger of being swept down by the streams
which rushed along on each side of the island; but the river was
now low, and we sailed where it is totally impossible to go when
the water is high. But though we had reached the island, and
were within a few yards of the spot, a view from which would
solve the whole problem, I believe that no one could perceive
where the vast body of water went; it seemed to lose itself in the
earth, the opposite lip of the fissure into which it disappeared
being only 80 feet distant. At least I did not comprehend it until,
creeping with awe to the verge, I peered down into a large rent
which had been made from bank to bank of the broad Zambesi,
and saw that a stream of a thousand yards broad leaped down a
hundred feet and then became suddenly compressed into a space
of fifteen or twenty yards. The entire falls are simply a crack
made in a hard basaltic rock from the right to the left bank of the
Zambesi, and then prolonged from the left bank away through
thirty or forty miles of hills. If one imagines the Thames filled
with low, tree-covered hills immediately beyond the tunnel,
extending as far as Gravesend; the bed of black basaltic rock
instead of London mud; and a fissure made therein from one end
of the tunnel to the other, down through the keystones of the
arch, and prolonged from the left end of the tunnel through thirty

miles of hills; the pathway being 100 feet down from the bed of the river instead of what it is, with the lips of the fissure from 80 to 100 feet apart; then fancy the Thames leaping bodily into the gulf; and forced there to change its direction, and flow from the right to the left bank; and then rush boiling and roaring through the hills – one may have some idea of what takes place at this the most wonderful sight I have witnessed in Africa.

INDIAN MUTINY: CAWNPORE AFTER THE MASSACRE, OCTOBER 1857

Richard Barter

The Indian Mutiny against British rule began in Meerut and Delhi, but quickly spread to the entire Ganges Valley. Among the victims were 200 British women and children, hacked to death in a Cawnpore house called the Bibigrah.

The inside of the house was of course bare of furniture and there was no matting or carpet on the floor, but instead blood, thick clotted blood looking like Russia leather, with which the walls also for three or four feet from the ground were spattered, and in some places smeared as if a great spout of it had gushed out on them, while here and there were marks where the murderers had dried their bloody hands by rubbing them against the walls in which were also deep sword cuts, as if some poor victim had dodged aside from the blow. There were also several pencil inscriptions, noting the date of arrival there, and memoranda of deaths of friends or relatives, or short prayers for help. Bonnets, slippers, hats, stays and various other articles of female clothing, with tresses and plaits of hair were scattered about with fragments of books, most, if not all of them Bibles and prayer books. Some of the bonnets and hats were hanging from the beams in the back verandah, which as well as the back yard was covered thick with clotted blood. All the way to the well was marked by a regular track along which the bodies had been dragged and the thorny bushes had entangled in them scraps of clothing and long hairs. One of the large trees to the left of this track going to the well had evidently had children's brains dashed out against its trunk for it was covered thick with blood and children's hair matted into the coarse bark, and an eye, glazed and withered could be plainly made out pasted into the trunk. A few paces on and you stood by the well itself, now the receptacle of all

these poor mangled bodies. It looked old and going fast to decay
for the bricks and mortar had given way and crumbled in many
places round the low edge. I think it must have been dry or very
nearly so. After peering into it for some time until the eyes had
become accustomed to the gloom, you could see members of
human bodies, legs and arms sticking up browned and withered
like those of a mummy. But there was no putrid smell or anything
of that kind that I could perceive. Those dead arms of our
murdered country people seemed to be making a mute appeal
to us from the darkness below; far more eloquent than words they
called to Heaven for vengeance on the ruthless perpetrators of
untold atrocities, and many a vow was registered over that well
never to spare should they be met with hand to hand in the
approaching struggle for the Relief of Lucknow, but four short
marches now lay between us and that city where we knew the
garrison with a crowd of women and children, were daily subject
to the attacks of the Cawnpore, and thousands of similar ruffians
all eager to repeat the horrors of the place where we now stood; but
we had to curb our impatience to go to their relief and had days
still to wait the coming of Sir Colin Campbell, the new Commander-in-Chief, who with a large force was now pushing up country.

EXPLOSION ABOARD THE SS *GREAT EASTERN*, 12 SEPTEMBER 1859

George Augustus Sala

IK Brunel's liner the *Great Eastern* was, until 1899, the largest vessel ever
constructed. Salva was a *Daily Telegraph* journalist sent to cover her trials.

We had dined. It was six o'clock, and we were off Hastings, at
about seven miles' distance from the shore. The majority of the
passengers, having finished their repast, had gone on deck. The
ladies had retired, and, as we conjectured, according to their usual
custom, to their boudoir. The dining saloon was deserted, save by a
small knot of joyous guests, all known to each other, who had
gathered round the most popular of the directors, Mr Ingram.
That gentleman, his hand on the shoulder of his young son, was
listening, not apparently unpleased, to the eloquence of a friend,
who was decanting on his merits while proposing his health. The
glasses were charged; the orator's peroration had culminated; the
revellers were upstanding; when – as if the fingers of a man's hand

had come out against the cabin wall, and written, as in sand, that the Medes and Persians were at the gate, the verberation of a tremendous explosion was heard. The reverberation followed. Then came – to our ears, who were in the dining room – a tremendous crash, not hollow, as of thunder, but solid, as of objects that offered resistance. Then a sweeping, rolling, swooping, rumbling sound, as of cannon balls scudding along the deck above. Remember, I am only describing *now* my personal experience and sensations. The rumbling noise was followed by the smash of the dining saloon skylights, and the irruption of a mass of fragments of wood and iron, followed by a thick cloud of powdered glass, and then by coaldust. My garments are full of the first, my hair and eyebrows of the last, now. There was but one impulse, one question – to go on deck; to ask, "What can it be?" To me, the crash was greater than the explosion; and I thought more of a collision, or of the fall of one of the huge yards, than of an explosion; but my next neighbour cried out, "The boiler has burst!" On gaining the deck I could at first see nothing but billows of steam rolling towards us. Then along the deck I saw the engine hose rapidly drawn along, and in another moment dozens of men were seizing it and carrying it forward. The wind was blowing tolerably strong, and when the steam cleared away a little in my immediate vicinity, there came an eddying shower of splinters, fragments of gilt moulding, shreds of ornamental paper, and tatters of crimson curtains. Several gentlemen now exerted themselves in the most praiseworthy manner to get the passengers aft; the danger was evidently forward; a thick cloud of steam there concealed all objects; but there was smoke as well as vapour, and I thought the ship was on fire. As men and passengers came rushing by I heard ejaculations of "Fire", "The boilers", "The donkey engine has burst"; but these were more matters of question and answer than evidences of terror. There seemed to be amazement and curiosity, but – among the passengers at least – not the slightest panic. The Great Ship Company's guests requited the hospitality of the directors by rendering every assistance in their power to the officers by setting an example of quietude and cheerfulness, and by endeavouring to inspire confidence. It was a noble sight afterwards to see the young Marquis of Stafford, his sleeves tucked up, his hands and face grimed to the similitude of a chimneysweep, panting with his exertions in working at the hose and clearing away rubbish. There was another nobleman, who passed the ensuing night anointing the scarified limbs of tortured men with oil, and cheering them up with kindly words. There was *another*, who, the moment the accident occurred, derogated slightly from the dignity of his pilot coat and "Jack Tar" manners, wanted a boat to be lowered for his conveyance on shore, and vehemently expressed his opinion that the conduct of the Captain, in not making immediately for Dungeness, was "unjustifiable". But let this pass. I went forward and then had the first glimpse of the Ruin that had blasted a large portion of the ship. The "very forward" funnel and its flange, which last should have been dozens of feet below, were lying aslant on the raised centre of the foredeck; and forward of the grand saloon staircase the hoses were playing fast and furiously down through the cavity where the funnel should have been, down down into a hideous pit of Flame. The ship, thank god! was not on fire; but, by the abolition of the upward draught caused by the loss of the funnel – which had shot upwards through three tiers of deck like a skyrocket, and had been projected, some say ten, some say twenty, some say thirty feet into the air – the flames of the now unconfined furnace were spreading outwards below in a hundred myriad tongues of fire. Once for all, let me assure you that, although the danger was imminent, the *Great Eastern* was never on fire. Objects were blown up and away; but of the planks, and beams, and girders, I saw afterwards among the *debris*, I could not discern so much as a batten that, shattered and splintered as it may have been, was charred or even scorched.

The effects of the catastrophe soon became lamentably apparent. One by one, borne on the shoulders or in the arms of their comrades, or, in one or two cases, staggering past, came by the unfortunate men who had been scalded in the stokehole. The face of one was utterly without human semblance, and looked simply like a mass of raw beef-steak. Another was so horribly scalded about the groin, that the two hands might be laid in the raw cavity, and scraps of his woolen undergarment were mixed up with hanks of boiled flesh. Another I saw had his trousers scalded away from the mid-thigh; his two legs, bare from thigh to heel, were continuous scalds, the skin and flesh hanging here and there. As they raised another man, the flesh of his hands came away in the grasp of those who held him, and he looked as though he had two bloody gloves on. There were some cases of severe contusions, and cuts from fractured glass; but curiously enough, not one instance of broken limbs. Some of the sufferers were hysterical, laughing and crying in a pitiable manner. When in the hospital, or sick bay, the agony of some was so intolerable that – all gently and soothingly as it was done – they had to be held down. The remedies applied were linseed oil and cotton-wool, continuously renewed.

Descending to the lower deck, the scene irresistibly reminded one of the interior of the area of Convent Garden Theatre after the fire of 1856. The vast expanse between decks was one heap of fragments. You trod upon one vast sultry mass of ruin and desolation. The nests of sleeping berths, the corridors and stair-cases were all (save the main one) gone. The cabin which with two friends I had occupied no longer existed. With all in the same block it had been blown entirely away. A portmanteau belonging to your correspondent was subsequently recovered from the *débâcle*; but my two companions lost everything they possessed on board. Forward, in this lower deck, you saw the great, gaping pit, which had vomited forth the fruits of the "collapse". It was an infernal region, that horrible hole. The bed of the accursed "jacket", with torn and jagged ends, was still visible. In the hole, were beams and girders, planks and rails, and gigantic steampipes twisted double like disused speaking trumpets. The huge iron plates at the root of the funnel were torn or crumpled up like writing paper. The great wrought iron girders supporting the lower deck were curved and bent; the flooring of the deck itself was, in part, upheaved, and disclosed ominous gaps. The boilers had sustained no injury. Weeks' time and thousands of pounds in expenditure, must be consumed ere the *Great Eastern*'s proprietors will be able to repair the damage done to her "main cabin fittings".

Neither ship – as a ship – nor paddles, nor screw, were injured. At first there was an expressed intention to put into the nearest haven; but this idea was abandoned, and the *Great Eastern* pro-ceeded on her voyage to Portland.

BELOW STAIRS, 1864

Hannah Cullwick

Cullwick entered "service" at the age of eight. At the time of the extract below she worked as a servant in a boarding-house.

I often thought of Myself & them, all they ladies sitting up stairs & talking & sewing & playing games & pleasing themselves, all so smart & delicate to what i am, though they was not real ladies the missis told me – & then *me* by myself in that kitchen, drudging all day in my dirt, & ready to do any thing for 'em whenever they rung for me – it seems like been a different kind o creature to them, but it's always so with ladies & servants & of course there is a difference cause their bringing up is so different – servants may feel it sharply & do sometimes i believe, but it's best not to be delicate, nor mind what work we do so as it's honest. i mean it's best to be really strong in body & ready for any sort o rough work that's useful: but keeping a soft & tender heart all while & capable o *feeling*. How shamed ladies'd be to have hands & arms like mine, & how weak they'd be to do my work, & how shock'd to touch the dirty things even, what i black my whole hands with every day – yet such things must be done, & the lady's'd be the first to cry out if they was to find nobody to do for 'em – so the lowest work i think is honourable in itself & the poor drudge is honourable too providing her mind isn't as coarse & low as her work is, & yet loving her dirty work too – both cause it's useful & for been content wi the station she is placed in. But how often poor servants have to bear the scorn & harsh words & proud looks from them above her which to my mind is very wicked & unkind & certainly most disheartening to a young wench. A good hard day's work of cleaning with a pleasant work & look from the Missis is to my mind the greatest pleasure of a servants life. There was two Miss Knights, & one was always in bed, & couldn't bear a bit o noise, so it was tiresome often to be stopp'd doing a job when i was doing it as quiet as ever i could, but i bore it patient knowing she was ill & that it vex'd the Missis so to have her disturb'd, & Miss Julia (the Missis) was the first real lady that ever talk'd to me, & she doing all the light part o cooking was a good deal wi me in the kitchen – she lent me a very nice book (The Footsteps o St. Paul), & said she was sure i shd not dirty it & I read it through wi a bit of paper under my thumb & give it her back as clean as when she give it me. She used to tell me things too about the moon & stars & fire & earth & about history that I knew not of & it surprised me, & she advised me to read the Bible now i was got older for that i may understand better than when i was younger – But she said it was difficult in some parts even to her & she'd study'd a great deal having bin a governess – And so I enjoy'd Miss Knight's company in the Kitchen & she sat one day ever so long seen me clean the paint, & she said she could watch me all day, there was something so very interesting in cleaning & that i seem'd to do it so hearty & i said i was really fond of it. But the poor

thing couldn't wash a plate or a saucepan or peel a tato, nor even
draw a cork of a bottle, which was unlucky for her, been so poor in
pocket – & she *did* wish she could afford to give me more wages.

EASTER SUNDAY IN THE COUNTRY, CLYRO, WALES, 17 APRIL 1870

Reverend Francis Kilvert

Diary: The happiest, brightest, most beautiful Easter I have ever
spent. I woke early and looked out. As I had hoped the day was
cloudless, a glorious morning. My first thought was "Christ is
Risen". It is not well to lie in bed on Easter morning, indeed it is
thought very unlucky. I got up between five and six and was out
soon after six. There had been a frost and the air was rimy with a
heavy thick white dew on hedge, bank and turf, but the morning
was not cold. There was a heavy white dew with a touch of hoar
frost on the meadows, and as I leaned over the wicket gate by the
mill pond looking to see if there were any primroses in the banks
but not liking to venture into the dripping grass suddenly I heard
the cuckoo for the first time this year. He was near Peter's Pool and
he called three times quickly one after another. It is very well to
hear the cuckoo for the first time on Easter Sunday morning. I
loitered up the lane again gathering primroses.

The village lay quiet and peaceful in the morning sunshine, but
by the time I came back from primrosing there was some little stir
and people were beginning to open their doors and look out into
the fresh fragrant splendid morning.

There was a very large congregation at morning church, the
largest I have seen for some time, attracted by Easter and the
splendour of the day, for they have here an immense reverence for
Easter Sunday. The anthem went very well and Mr Baskerville
complimented Mr Evans after church about it, saying that it was
sung in good tune and time and had been a great treat. There were
more communicants than usual: 29. This is the fifth time I have
received the Sacrament within four days. After morning service I
took Mr V. round the churchyard and showed him the crosses on
his mother's, wife's, and brother's graves. He was quite taken by
surprise and very much gratified. I am glad to see that our
primrose crosses seem to be having some effect for I think I notice
this Easter some attempt to copy them and an advance towards the

form of the cross in some of the decorations of the graves. I wish we could get the people to adopt some little design in the disposition of the flowers upon the graves instead of sticking sprigs into the turf aimlessly anywhere, anyhow and with no meaning at all. But one does not like to interfere too much with their artless, natural way of showing their respect and love for the dead. I am thankful to find this beautiful custom on the increase, and observed more and more every year. Some years ago it was on the decline and nearly discontinued. On Easter Day all the young people come out in something new and bright like butterflies. It is almost part of their religion to wear something new on this day. It was an old saying that if you don't wear something new on Easter Day, the crows will spoil everything you have on.

Between the services a great many people were in the church-yard looking at the graves. I went to Bettws Chapel in the afternoon. It was burning hot and as I climbed the hill the perspiration rolled off my forehead from under my hat and fell in drops on the dusty road. Lucretia Wall was in chapel looking pale and pretty after her illness. Coming down the hill it was delightful, cool and pleasant. The sweet suspicion of spring strengthens, deepens and grows more sweet every day. Mrs Pring gave us lamb and asparagus at dinner.

MEETING LIVINGSTONE, UJIJI, AFRICA, 10 NOVEMBER 1871

Sir Henry Morton Stanley

Dr Livingstone went missing during a search for the headwaters of the River Nile. The *New York Herald* sent Henry M. Stanley to find him.

We push on rapidly, lest the news of our coming might reach the people of Bunder Ujiji before we come in sight, and are ready for them. We halt at a little brook, then ascend the long slope of a naked ridge, the very last of the myriads we have crossed. This alone prevents us from seeing the lake in all its vastness. We arrive at the summit, travel across and arrive at its western rim, and pause, reader – the port of Ujiji is below us, embowered in the palms, only five hundred yards from us! At this grand moment we do not think of the hundreds of miles we have marched, of the hundreds of hills that we have ascended and descended, of the many forests we have traversed, of the jungles and thickets that annoyed us, of the fervid salt plains that blistered our feet, of the hot suns that scorched us, nor the dangers and difficulties, now happily surmounted. At last the sublime hour has arrived! – our dreams, our hopes, and anticipations are now about to be realized! Our hearts and our feelings are with our eyes as we peer into the palms and try to make out in which hut or house lives the white man with the grey beard we heard about on the Malagarazi.

We were now about three hundred yards from the village of Ujiji and the crowds are dense about me. Suddenly I hear a voice on my right side.

"Good morning, sir!"

Startled at hearing this greeting in the midst of such a crowd of black people, I turn sharply around in search of the man, and see him at my side, with the blackest of faces, but animated and joyous – a man dressed in a long white shirt, with a turban of American sheeting around his woolly head, and I ask:

"Who the mischief are you?"

"I am Susi, the servant of Dr Livingstone," said he, smiling, and showing a gleaming row of teeth.

"What! Is Dr Livingstone here?"

"Yes, sir."

"In this village?"

"Yes, sir."

"Are you sure?"

"Sure, sure, sir. Why, I leave him just now." . . .

"Now, you Susi, run, and tell the Doctor I am coming."

"Yes, sir," and off he darted like a madman . . .

Soon Susi came running back, and asked me my name; he had told the Doctor that I was coming, but the Doctor was too surprised to believe him, and, when the Doctor asked him my name, Susi was rather staggered.

But, during Susi's absence, the news had been conveyed to the Doctor that it was surely a white man that was coming, whose guns were firing and whose flag could be seen; and the great Arab magnates of Ujiji – Mohammed bin Sali, Sayd bin Majid, Abid bin Suleiman, Mohammed bin Gharib, and others – had gathered together before the Doctor's house, and the Doctor had come out from his veranda to discuss the matter and await my arrival.

In the meantime, the head of the Expedition had halted, and the *kirangozi* was out of the ranks, holding his flag aloft, and Selim said to me, "I see the Doctor, sir. Oh, what an old man! He has got a white beard." And I – what would I not have given for a bit of friendly wilderness, where, unseen, I might vent my joy in some mad freak, such as idiotically biting my hand, turning a somer-sault, or slashing at trees, in order to allay those exciting feelings that were well-nigh uncontrollable. My heart beats fast, but I must not let my face betray my emotions, lest it shall detract from the dignity of a white man appearing under such extraordinary circumstances.

So I did that which I thought was most dignified. I pushed back the crowds and, passing from the rear, walked down a living avenue of people, until I came in front of the semicircle of Arabs, in the front of which stood the white man with the grey beard. As I advanced slowly towards him I noticed he was pale, looked wearied, had a grey beard, wore a bluish cap with a faded gold band round it, had on a red sleeved waistcoat, and a pair of grey tweed trousers. I would have run to him, only I was a coward in the presence of such a mob – would have embraced him, only, he being an Englishman I did not know how he would receive me; so I did what cowardice and false pride suggested was the best thing – walked deliberately to him, took off my hat, and said:

"Dr Livingstone, I presume?"

"YES," said he, with a kind smile, lifting his cap slightly.

I replace my hat on my head, and he puts on his cap, and we both grasp hands, and I then say aloud.

"I thank God, Doctor, I have been permitted to see you."

He answered, "I feel thankful that I am here to welcome you."

I turn to the Arabs, take off my hat to them in response to the saluting chorus of "Yambos" I receive, and the Doctor introduces them to me by name. Then, oblivious of the crowds, oblivious of the men who shared with me my dangers, we – Livingstone and I – turn our faces towards his *tembe*. He points to the veranda, or, rather, mud platform, under the broad overhanging eaves; he points to his own particular seat, which I see his age and experience in Africa has suggested, namely, a straw mat, with a goatskin over it, and another skin nailed against the wall to protect his back from contact with the cold mud. I protest against taking this seat, which so much more befits him than me, but the Doctor will not yield: I must take it.

We are seated – the Doctor and I – with our backs to the wall. The Arabs take seats on our left. More than a thousand natives are in our front, filling the whole square densely, indulging their curiosity, and discussing the fact of two white men meeting at

Ujiji – one just come from Manyuema, in the west, the other from Unyanyembe, in the east.

CAPTAIN WEBB'S CHANNEL SWIM, 25 AUGUST 1875

Anon

At 3.22 a.m. he declined any refreshment, and half an hour later there was light enough to dowse lanterns . . . The breeze then produced a nasty bobble, but as the tide was at present setting to leeward it was not so bad as it might have been . . . Two bells found it very hazy over the land, but he still seemed in as good spirits as ever, and even had a little personal chaff with us. He did not seem strong enough, however, to make much way across the tide, and . . . it was a touch-and-go matter whether he would not be drifted too far to the eastward, and have to await another tide to fetch in . . . Some beef tea and a top-up of brandy were called for at 5.25 a.m., when his voice seemed faltering a bit. By four bells the lop had become really serious, but he declined to wear his spectacles. All hope of fetching in off Sangatte had to be abandoned. For the next hour he made literally no in shore progress, although both the row boats were kept on his weather side, to ward off the sea as much as possible . . . at 7.25 the poor fellow complained bitterly of the sea, which of course increased greatly in crossing the broken water of the Ridens. It was cruel to think that this might be the cause of defeat when within actual hail of port, and nothing but unflinching bulldog pluck now kept the man going . . . At eight bells we sounded in ten fathoms, and had all but opened the entrance to Calais harbour. Luckily, however, the tide had by this time eased considerably, and he was enabled to get almost slack water and make a little headway for the shore instead of getting drifted to the eastward of Calais.

At 8.23 a.m. he took some brandy, and said he was "as right as a bird, bar the sea." He was swimming a quicker but shorter stroke of twenty-two to the minute . . . At 9.20 a.m. Capt. Dane was sighted coming out of Calais harbour in his gig, with all possible speed; and this was the best bit of luck we had met with since the same gallant skipper had left us at sea just before midnight. By 9.25 a.m. he had placed his gig in a capital position on Webb's weather side, where such a large craft made a far more effectual breakwater than our own two cockleshells of row boats. At 9.34 he seemed quite lively when Capt. Dane told him there was a grand reception waiting him ashore. Now, however, the S.W. stream had begun to make and the tide was going aweather, which further increased the brave swimmer's difficulties. At 9.40 a.m. we timed him at twenty-six strokes to the minute but they were short indeed compared to those of the first eighteen hours or so. However, the gig mended matters, somewhat, and her crew cheered him repeatedly in true British Jack Tar fashion . . . At 10.30 he laughingly hoped that "the Frenchmen would give him some good grub ashore." As a proof of how keen his intellect had remained throughout, he promptly requested us by name to immediately take in two or three feet of rope which had accidentally got overboard as he wished to take no unfair advantage. After a few more strokes the brave Matthew Webb stood upright in five feet of water on Calais sands abreast of the bathing establishment and half a mile to the westward of Calais pier at 10.40.15 a.m. English time on Wednesday, 25 August 1875, after having been in the water twenty-one hours forty-four minutes and fifty-five seconds without touching artificial support of any kind, and having swum as nearly as possible over thirty-nine miles and a half of ground.

Capt. Webb was assisted into a trap, driven to the Hotel de Paris, and at once put to bed, a medical man being in attendance. His pulse was at 72, and after three hours' sleep he woke up all right, bar weakness and hunger. At 10 p.m. he again turned in and slept soundly for twelve hours.

RORKE'S DRIFT, 21 JANUARY 1879

Henry Hook

The day of 21 January 1879 saw the British Army in tragedy and triumph; a force of 10,000 Zulus under Cetewayo attacked a British camp at Isandhlawana, utterly annihilating it. The Zulus then advanced on the hospital and garrison at Rorke's Drift, manned by 120 soldiers including the sick. Fighting continued all night, and six times the Zulus attacked, and six times they were repulsed. They withdrew the next morning, leaving 350 dead. The Victoria Cross was awarded to eleven soldiers – more than for any other single engagement – at Rorke's Drift, including Henry Hook.

. . . there was a commotion in the camp, and we saw two men galloping towards us from the other side of the river, which was

Zululand. Lieutenant Chard of the Engineers was protecting the ponts over the river and, as senior officer, was in command at the drift. The ponts were very simple affairs, one of them being supported on big barrels, and the other on boats. Lieutenant Bromhead was in the camp itself. The horsemen shouted and were brought across the river, and then we knew what had happened to our comrades. They had been butchered to a man. That was awful enough news, but worse was to follow, for we were told that the Zulus were coming straight on from Isandhlwana to attack us. At the same time a note was received by Lieutenant Bromhead from the Column to say that the enemy was coming on, and that the post was to be held at all costs.

For some time we were all stunned, then everything changed from perfect quietness to intense excitement and energy. There was a general feeling that the only safe thing was to retire and try and join the troops at Helpmakaar. The horsemen had said that the Zulus would be up in two or three minutes; but luckily for us they did not show themselves for more than an hour. Lieutenant Chard rushed up from the river, about a quarter of a mile away, and saw Lieutenant Bromhead.

Orders were given to strike the camp and make ready to go, and we actually loaded up two waggons. Then Mr Dalton, of the Commissariat Department, came up and said that if we left the drift every man was certain to be killed. He had formerly been a sergeant-major in a line regiment and was one of the bravest men that ever lived. Lieutenants Chard and Bromhead held a consultation, short and earnest, and orders were given that we were to get the hospital and storehouse ready for defence, and that we were never to say die or surrender.

Not a minute was lost. Lieutenant Bromhead superintended the loop-holing and barricading of the hospital and storehouse, and the making of a connection of the defences between the two buildings with walls of mealie-bags and waggons. The mealie bags were good big heavy things, weighing about 200 pounds each, and during the fight many of them were burst open by assegais and bullets, and the mealies (Indian corn) were thickly spread about the ground.

The biscuit boxes contained ordinary biscuit. They were big, square, wooden boxes, weighing about a hundred-weight each. The meat boxes, too, were very heavy, as they contained tinned meat. They were smaller than the biscuit boxes. While these preparations were being made, Lieutenant Chard went down to the river and brought in the pont guard of a sergeant and half-a-dozen men, with the waggons and gear. The two officers saw that every soldier was at his post, then we were ready for the Zulus when they cared to come.

They were not long. Just before half past four we heard firing behind the conical hill at the back of the drift, called Oskarsberg Hill, and suddenly about five or six hundred Zulus swept around, coming for us at a run. Instantly the natives – Kaffirs who had been very useful in making the barricade of waggons, mealie-bags and biscuit boxes around the camp – bolted towards Helpmakaar, and what was worse their officer and a European sergeant went with them. To see them deserting like that was too much for some of us, and we fired after them. The sergeant was struck and killed. Half-a-dozen of us were stationed in the hospital, with orders to hold it and guard the sick. The ends of the building were of stone, the side walls of ordinary bricks, and the inside walls or partitions of sun-dried bricks of mud. These shoddy inside bricks proved our salvation, as you will see. It was a queer little one-storeyed building, which it is almost impossible to describe; but we were pinned like rats in a hole, because all the doorways except one had been barricaded with mealie-bags and we had done the same with the windows. The interior was divided by means of partition walls into which were fitted some very slight doors. The patients' beds were simple rough affairs of boards, raised only about half a foot above the floor. To talk of hospitals and beds gives the idea of a big building, but as a matter of fact this hospital was a mere little shed or bungalow, divided up into rooms so small that you could hardly swing a bayonet in them. There were about nine men who could not move, but altogether there were about thirty. Most of these, however could not help to defend themselves.

As soon as our Kaffirs bolted, it was seen that the fort as we had first made it was too big to be held, so Lieutenant Chard instantly reduced the space by having a row of biscuit-boxes drawn across the middle, about four feet high. This was our inner entrenchment, and proved very valuable. The Zulus came on at a wild rush, and although many of them were shot down they got to within about fifty yards of our south wall of mealie-bags and biscuit boxes and waggons. They were caught between two fires, that from the hospital and that from the storehouse, and were checked; but they gained the shelter of the cookhouse and ovens, and gave us many heavy volleys. During the fight they took advantage of every bit of cover there was, anthills, a tract of bush that we had not had time to clear away, a garden or sort of orchard which was near us, and a ledge of rock and some caves (on the Oscarsberg) which were only about a hundred yards away. They neglected nothing, and while they went on firing, large bodies kept hurling themselves against our slender breastworks.

But it was the hospital they assaulted most fiercely. I had charge with a man that we called Old King Cole of a small room with only one patient in it. Cole kept with me for some time after the fight began, then he said he was not going to stay. He went outside and was instantly killed by the Zulus, so that I was left alone with the patient, a native whose leg was broken and who kept crying out, "Take my bandage off, so that I can come." But it was impossible to do anything except fight, and I blazed away as hard as I could. By this time I was the only defender of my room. Poor Old King Cole was lying dead outside and the helpless patient was crying and groaning near me. The Zulus were swarming around us, and there was an extraordinary rattle as the bullets struck the biscuit boxes, and queer thuds as they plumped into the bags of mealies. Then there was the whizz and rip of the assegais, of which I had experience during the Kaffir Campaign of 1877–8. We had plenty of ammunition, but we were told to save it and so we took careful aim at every shot, and hardly a cartridge was wasted. Private Dunbar, shot no fewer than nine Zulus, one of them being a Chief.

From the very first the enemy tried to rush the hospital, and at last they managed to set fire to the thick grass which formed the roof. This put us in a terrible plight, because it meant that we were either to be massacred or burned alive, or get out of the building.

All this time the Zulus were trying to get into the room. Their assegais kept whizzing towards us, and one struck me in front of the helmet. We were wearing the white tropical helmets then. But the helmet tilted back under the blow and made the spear lose its power, so that I escaped with a scalp wound which did not trouble me much then, although it has often caused me illness since. Only one man at a time could get in at the door. A big Zulu sprang forward and seized my rifle, but I tore it free and, slipping a cartridge in, I shot him point-blank. Time after time the Zulus gripped the muzzle and tried to tear the rifle from my grasp, and time after time I wrenched it back, because I had a better grip than they had. All this time Williams was getting the sick through the hole into the next room, all except one, a soldier of the 24th named Conley, who could not move because of a broken leg. Watching for my chance I dashed from the doorway, and grabbing Conley I pulled him after me through the hole. His leg got broken again, but there was no help for it. As soon as we left the room the Zulus burst in with furious cries of disappointment and rage.

Now there was a repetition of the work of holding the doorway, except that I had to stand by a hole instead of a door, while Williams picked away at the far wall to make an opening for escape into the next room. There was more desperate and almost hopeless fighting, as it seemed, but most of the poor fellows were got through the hole.

. . . All this time, of course, the storehouse was being valiantly defended by the rest of the garrison. When we got into the inner fort, I took my post at a place where two men had been shot. While I was there another man was shot in the neck, I think by a bullet which came through the space between two biscuit boxes that were not quite close together. This was at about six o'clock in the evening, nearly two hours after the opening shot of the battle had been fired. Every now and then the Zulus would make a rush for it and get in. We had to charge them out. By this time it was dark, and the hospital was all in flames, but this gave us a splendid light to fight by. I believe it was this light that saved us. We could see them coming, and they could not rush us and take us by surprise from any point. They could not get at us, and so they went away and had ten or fifteen minutes of a war-dance. This roused them up again, and their excitement was so intense that the ground fairly seemed to shake. Then, when they were goaded to the highest pitch, they would hurl themselves at us again. We could sometimes, by the light of the flames, keep them well in sight, so well that we could take aim and fire coolly. When we could do this they never advanced as far as the barricade, because we shot them down as they ran in on us. But every now and then one or two managed to crawl in and climb over the top of the sacks. They were bayoneted off.

All this time the sick and wounded were crying for water. We had the water-cart full of water, but it was just by the deserted hospital, and we could not hope to get at it until the day broke, when the Zulus might begin to lose heart and to stop their mad rushes. But we could not bear the cries any longer, and three or four of us jumped over the boxes and ran and fetched some water in.

The long night passed and the day broke. Then we looked

around us to see what had happened, and there was not a living soul who was not thankful to find that the Zulus had had enough of it and were disappearing over the hill to the south-west. Orders were given to patrol the ground, collect the arms of the dead blacks, and make our positions as strong as possible in case of fresh attacks.

THE 1882 CUP FINAL
The Blackburn Times

Over the course of British history, football evolved from a medieval brawl (see p. 182) into a game of skill and rules. The Football Association Cup was instituted in 1871. Initially dominated by public school teams, the FA Cup was taken up with a vengeance by the new clubs of industrial Britain. Eton won in 1882, but the future belonged to Blackburn Rovers.

With fine weather and the prospect of an exciting contest, it was to be expected that a large number of persons would be attracted to Kennington Oval, on Saturday afternoon, and the expectation was realised, as the attendance was swollen to 6,000 about three o'clock. There was a considerable body of the Rovers' supporters in attendance, the two special trains from East Lancashire in the early hours of the morning having brought about 700 persons, while 200 others had made the journey on the previous day. Amongst them were many Blackburn gentlemen and tradesmen, and, clustered on the grandstand in front of the pavilion of the Surrey Cricket Club, they gave a hearty welcome to their Parliamentary representatives, Mr. W. E. Briggs and Mr. W. Coddington. Another well-known Blackburnian, Major-General Feilden, C.M.G., of Witton Park, lord of the manor, and junior member for the northern division of the county palatine, was also present to view the contest. The section of the ground in front of the pavilion, only once or twice previously used for football purposes, was enclosed for the match, and it was in splendid condition, as rain had not fallen there the previous day. The sunshine was not so glaring as to greatly dazzle the eyes of the players who had to face it, but during more than half the game a strong wind blew from goal to goal.

Some of the Old Etonians first appeared within the enclosure, and were soon followed by the main body of the Rovers, while the majority of the Eton men, followed by the two captains, did not leave the dressing room until some minutes later. The appearance of the Rovers was somewhat disappointing, for the familiar jerseys had been for the time discarded, and dark blue jerseys with white stripes donned in their stead. In the evening one member of the team jestingly attributed the result of the match to the change of jerseys, and affirmed that he had in one instance passed the ball to an opponent instead of to his partner. An alteration was requisite, however, as the jerseys of the opposing teams were similar in style and the Rovers, as the younger organisation, had to give way in the matter. There was a marked contrast in the style of play of the rival teams and to Blackburn spectators the game revealed features unusual in the north. While the Rovers worked their way towards their opponents' goal by passing, the Etonians did so by rushes, the player securing the ball at the start retaining possession of it until robbed or checked, and his partner bearing him company to render assistance when opposition appeared. The Etonians indulged in none of the dribbling or dodging which forms an interesting and pleasing part of the famous Lancashire team's play, reliance being placed instead on the weight and speed of the forwards. A still greater contrast was afforded in the kicking of the ball when running. While the Rovers sent the leather forward so little raised above the ground as almost to touch it in skimming along, their opponents kicked the ball much higher, and springing up at it while dashing along delivered the kick frequently with both feet off the ground. The spring was made whether or not an opponent was close to the ball when it bounded, and the Rovers, unaccustomed to this practice, were badly kicked, particularly towards the finish when the play was mainly in close quarters. To the same fact was probably due the entire absence, or nearly so, of the scrimmages almost on the goal-line that are often seen on northern football fields, and while the Rovers used heads, chests, and knees as well as feet in manipulating the ball, the Old Boys relied entirely on kicking.

When the cheering which greeted the advent of the rival captains had subsided, the toss for choice of goals was made, and the Rovers' chief was unfortunate in losing. The Etonians chose to play with the wind in their favour and the sun at their backs. The ball was "kicked off" by Strachan at eight minutes past three. A light touch to the left gave the leather to Brown, who sent it forward, but it was instantly returned, and the Etonians rushed along and in a few seconds Chevallier made a couple of corner kicks but each was followed by a kick from the goal. Of the Rovers forwards the right wing pair first became prominent. Heading back the leather, J. Hargreaves, aided by Avery, made a good run, but when the other goal was almost reached Macauley intervened and sent it back again. Suter twice relieved his goal cleverly, but Howorth was compelled to use his hands, and then the besiegers had another corner kick, which like its predecessors, proved fruitless. A free kick awarded for a handling of the ball enabled Suter to place it well to the right wing forwards, and the first kick from the corner flag for the Rovers was immediately afterwards made by Douglas. The ball was missed by all the players in the mouth of the goal, but was promptly sent in by the Rovers captain. Kinnaird relieved his side, and Macauley made a run, in which he was aided by Dunn, who passed to Anderson, and that player by a side shot scored a goal at the end of the first eight minutes' play.

Suter and McIntyre in turn interposed with good effect, and enabled Strachan, Douglas, and Duckworth to make an attack upon the Eton citadel. The leather was sent into the hands of Rawlinson, who threw it away before he could be charged through the goal. A free kick from close to the goal enabled the Etonians to return to the attack, but they were unsuccessful, a tremendous kick from Macauley sending the ball some yards above the top bar. Subsequently the ball was thrown right into the mouth of goal by Anderson, and Howorth's charge was seriously imperilled for a time.

For a breach of rule, which forbids handling, a free kick was awarded against the Etonians in their quarters, but McIntyre missed the ball when it was lightly sent to him by Fred Hargreaves and, as the penalty, the opposing forwards rushed along the ground, and Dunn by a good kick sent the leather into the hands of Howorth.

Another rush was frustrated by McIntyre and Fred Hargreaves, and Avery secured possession of the ball. Foley interposed to bar his progress, and, jumping at the ball, gave Avery a tremendous kick on the thigh, which placed him "hors de combat" for some minutes, and partially disabled him during the remainder of the game.

Drs. Porteus and Morley attended him on the grass outside the bounds of play, and soon reported that no serious injury had been sustained.

Play was transferred to the Etonians' quarters, and kept there for a few minutes, during which J. Hargreaves, Avery, and Douglas appeared to advantage, but eventually the ball was again sent over the goal line. The ball, thrown in by Anderson, was headed back from the goal mouth by Suter just as the whistle sounded "half-time". Play this far had been remarkably fast, and, with the strong wind against them, the Rovers could not invade their opponents' territory very often, but their defence was good, and in the circumstances they had done exceedingly well to prevent the scoring of more than one goal against them.

With the score so low the Rovers' supporters hopefully awaited the result. At four minutes to four Goodhart started the ball from the centre, but he was instantly robbed by Strachan, who passed it to the left wing, along which it was taken by J. Hargreaves and Avery. Their progress was barred, and the Etonian forwards returned, but a strong kick sent the ball considerably in advance of them, and Howorth ran out from the goal to kick the ball back. A free kick by Kinnaird was rendered of non-effect by the interposition of the head of Strachan, who played exceedingly well throughout, and the Eton quarters were again invaded.

Some combined play by the Etonian forwards enabled them to approach the Rovers' goal, but they were speedily driven back, and Douglas and Duckworth again came into prominence. The goalkeeper was forced to use his hands, but he had a place kick immediately afterwards, and Fred Hargreaves missing the ball, the Etonian forwards secured a chance which they promptly utilised, to break away, and Chevallier shot the leather behind the goal.

Macauley subsequently made a better attempt to score, but Howorth stopped the ball with his hands, while when Duckworth a few seconds later gave Douglas an opportunity he shot the leather over the bar of the Etonian citadel, and on a second attempt he sent it over the line. As the time for play gradually shortened, the supporters of the Rovers became less confident, and there were shouts from the grand stand of "Play up Black-burn", to which admirers of their opponents responded by cries of "E-e-ton". But there was ominous silence amongst the Lancashire spectators. For nearly twenty minutes before the close the Etonians were practically penned in their own quarters, and the Rovers were constantly striving to score, but only to be disappointed by seeing the ball go over the line, on the wrong side of the posts or to be stopped by the goalkeeper. All the shots were high, however, and there was no opportunity of judging of Rawlinson's power with his feet. The desperate struggle was continued until the referee's whistle signalled the expiration of time, and the Etonians were hailed the victors by one goal to none. Suter played magnificently, Strachan and Duckworth did remarkably well; McIntyre rendered good service; and the other members played well, but on the whole the team did not quite reach its most brilliant form. Of the Old Etonians the captain and Foley were best, while both backs played well; Rawlinson far exceeded expectations as goalkeeper and elicited many complimentary comments; and Macauley, Dunn, Novelli, and Anderson were the pick of the forward division.

The teams were composed as follows:

Rovers: R. Howorth, goal; H. McIntyre and F. Suter, backs; H. Sharples and F. W. Hargreaves (captain), half backs; J. Duckworth and J. Douglas, right wing; J. Hargreaves and G. Avery, left wing; T. Strachan and J. Brown, centre.

Old Etonians: J. F. P. Rawlinson, goal; T. H. French and P. J. de Paravicini, backs; Hon. A. F. Kinnaird (captain) and C. W. Foley, half backs; W. J. Anderson and J. B. Chevallier, right wing; P. C. Novelli and A. T. R. Dunn, left wing; R. H. Macauley and H. C. Goodhart, centre.

The umpires were Mr. C. H. R. Wollaston (Wanderers), and member of the committee of the Football Association; and Mr. C. Crump, president of the Birmingham Association; and the referee, Mr. J. C. Clegg, vice president of the Sheffield Association. All had been appointed by the Association committee.

WILDE ROMPS WITH HIS CHILDREN, c. 1892

Vyvyan Holland

Holland was the son of the poet, playwright and wit Oscar Wilde.

. . . he had so much of the child in his own nature that he delighted in playing our games. He would go down on all fours on the nursery floor, being in turn a lion, a wolf, a horse, caring nothing for his usually immaculate appearance. And there was nothing halfhearted in his methods of play. One day he arrived with a toy milkcart drawn by a horse with real hair on it. All the harness undid and took off, and the churns with which the cart was filled could be removed and opened. When my father discovered this he immediately went downstairs and came back with a jug of milk with which he proceeded to fill the churns. We then all tore round the nursery table, slopping milk all over the place, until the arrival of our nurse put an end to that game.

Like other fathers, he mended our toys; he spent most of one afternoon repairing a wooden fort that had come to pieces in the course of various wars, and when he had finished he insisted upon everyone in the house coming to see how well he had done it and to give him a little praise. He also played with us a great deal in the dining-room, which was in some ways more suited to romping than the nursery, as there were more chairs and tables and sideboards to dodge through, and more room to clamber over Papa as well.

When he grew tired of playing he would keep us quiet by telling us fairy stories, or tales of adventure, of which he had a never-ending supply. He was a great admirer of Jules Verne and Stevenson, and of Kipling in his more imaginative vein. The last present he gave me was *The Jungle Book*; he had already given me *Treasure Island* and Jules Verne's *Five Weeks in a Balloon*, which were the first books I read through entirely by myself. He told us all his own written fairy stories suitably adapted for our young minds, and a great many others as well. There was one about the fairies who lived in the great bottles of coloured water that chemists used to put in their windows, with lights behind them that made them take on all kinds of different shapes. The fairies came down from their bottles at night and played and danced and made pills in the empty shop. Cyril once asked him why he had tears in his eyes when he told us the story of *The Selfish Giant*, and he replied that really beautiful things always made him cry.

THE DIAMOND JUBILEE, 1897

Queen Victoria

A defining moment in the Victorian era.

22nd June. A never-to-be-forgotten day. No one ever, I believe, has met with such an ovation as was given to me, passing through those six miles of streets, including Constitution Hill. The crowds were quite indescribable, and their enthusiasm truly marvellous and deeply touching. The cheering was quite deafening, and every face seemed to be filled with real joy. I was much moved and gratified.

. . . At a quarter-past eleven, the others being seated in their carriages long before, and having preceded me a short distance, I started from the State entrance in an open State landau, drawn by eight creams, dear Alix,[1] looking very pretty in lilac, and Lenchen[2] sitting opposite me. I felt a good deal agitated, and had been so all these days, for fear anything might be forgotten or go wrong. Bertie[3] and George C.[4] rode one on each side of the carriage, Arthur[5] (who had charge of the whole military arrangements) a little in the rear. My escort was formed from the 2nd Life Guards and officers of the native Indian regiments, these latter riding immediately in front of my carriage. Guard of Honour of Blue-jackets, the Guards, and the 2nd Surrey Regiment (Queen's) were mounted in the Quadrangle and outside the Palace.

Before leaving I touched an electric button, by which I started a message which was telegraphed throughout the whole Empire. It was the following: "From my heart I thank my beloved people. May God bless them!" At this time the sun burst out. Vicky[6] was in the carriage nearest me, not being able to go in mine, as her rank as Empress prevented her sitting with her back to the horses, for I had to sit alone. Her carriage was drawn by four blacks, richly caparisoned in red. We went up Constitution Hill and Piccadilly, and there were seats right along the former, where my own servants and personal attendants, and members of the other Royal Households, the Chelsea Pensioners, and the children of the Duke of York's and Greenwich schools had seats. St. James's Street was beautifully decorated. . . . Trafalgar Square was very striking. . . . The denseness of the crowds was immense, but the order maintained wonderful. The streets in the Strand are now quite wide, but one misses Temple Bar. Here the Lord Mayor received me and presented the sword, which I touched. . . . As we neared St. Paul's the procession was often stopped, and the crowds broke out into singing God Save the Queen. . . .

In front of the Cathedral the scene was most impressive. All the Colonial troops, on foot, were drawn up round the Square. My carriage, surrounded by all the Royal Princes, was drawn up close to the steps, where the Clergy were assembled, the Bishops in rich copes, with their croziers, the Archbishop of Canterbury and the Bishop of London each holding a very fine one. A Te Deum was sung. . . .

1 The future Queen Alexandra.
2 Princess Helena.
3 The Prince of Wales: the future King Edward VII.
4 George, 2nd Duke of Cambridge.
5 Arthur, Duke of Connaught.
6 Princess Victoria, The Princess Royal.

I stopped in front of the Mansion House, where the Lady Mayoress presented me with a beautiful silver basket full of orchids. Here I took leave of the Lord Mayor. Both he and the Lady Mayoress were quite *émus*. We proceeded over London Bridge, where no spectators were allowed, only troops, and then along the Borough Road, where there is a very poor population, but just as enthusiastic and orderly as elsewhere. The decorations there were very pretty. . . . Crossed the river again over Westminster Bridge. . . . The heat during the last hour was very great, and poor Lord Howe, who was riding as Gold Stick, fainted and had a bad fall, but was not seriously hurt.

Got home at a quarter to two. . . . Had a quiet luncheon with Vicky, Beatrice,[7] and her three children. Troops continually passing by. Then rested and later had tea in the garden with Lenchen. There was a large dinner in the supper-room. . . . I walked into the Ball-room afterwards, and sat down in front of the dais. Felt very tired, but tried to speak to most of the Princes and Princesses. . . . In the morning I wore a dress of black silk trimmed with panels of grey satin veiled with black net and steel embroideries, and some black lace, my lovely diamond chain, given me by my younger children, round my neck. My bonnet was trimmed with creamy white flowers, and white aigrette and some black lace.

OMDURMAN, 2 SEPTEMBER 1898

George Warrington Steevens

The death of General Gordon at the hands of Pan-Islamic Mahdists at Khartoum in 1895 was viewed in Britain as a national disgrace. Victorian pride and geo-politics (the threat posed to the Suez, the empire's lifeline to India) required the suppression of the Mahdi and reconquest of Sudan. This was accomplished by Major-General Horatio Kitchener. The last day of Mahdism came at the battle of Omdurman. George Warrington Steevens was war correspondent for the *Daily Mail*, and an authentically jingoist voice in imperial times.

A trooper rose out of the dimness from behind the shoulder of Gebel Surgham, grew larger and plainer, spurred violently up to the line and inside. A couple more were silhouetted across our front. Then the electric whisper came racing down the line; they

7 Daughter of Queen Victoria.

were coming. The lancers came in on the left; the Egyptian mounted troops drew like a curtain across us from left to right. As they passed a flicker of white flags began to extend and fill the front in their place. The noise of something began to creep in upon us; it cleared and divided into the tap of drums and the far-away surf of raucous war-cries. A shiver of expectancy thrilled along our army, and then a sigh of content. They were coming on. Allah help them! they were coming on.

It was now half-past six. The flags seemed very distant, the roar very faint, and the thud of our first gun was almost startling. It may have startled them too, but it startled them into life. The line of flags swung forward and a mass of white flying linen swung forward with it too. They came very fast, and they came very straight; and then presently they came no farther. With a crash the bullets leaped out of the British rifles. It began with the Guards and Warwicks – section volleys at 2,000 yards; then, as the Dervishes edged rightward, it ran along to the Highlanders, the Lincolns, and to Maxwell's Brigade. The British stood up in double rank behind their zariba; the blacks lay down in their shelter-trench; both poured out death as fast as they could load and press trigger. Shrapnel whistled and Maxims growled savagely. From all the line came perpetual fire, fire, fire, and shrieked forth in great gusts of destruction.

And the enemy? No white troops would have faced that torrent of death for five minutes. It was the last day of Mahdism, and the greatest. They could never get near, and they refused to hold back. By now the ground before us was all white with dead men's drapery. Rifles grew red-hot; the soldiers seized them by the slings and dragged them back to the reserve to change for cool ones. It was not a battle, but an execution . . . and then the sudden bugle called us to our feet. "Advance," it cried; "To Omdurman!" added we. Slowly the force broke up and expanded. The evident intention was to march in echelon of brigades. Movement was slow, since the leading brigades had to wait till the others had gone far enough inland to take their positions. We passed over a corner of the field of fire, and saw for certain what awful slaughter we had done. The bodies were not in heaps – bodies hardly ever are; but they spread evenly over acres and acres. Some lay very composedly, with their slippers placed under their heads for a last pillow; some knelt, cut short in the middle of a last prayer. Others were torn to pieces, vermilion blood already drying on brown skin, killed instantly beyond doubt. Others, again, seemingly as dead as these, sprang up as we approached, and rushed savagely, hurling spears at the nearest enemy. They were bayoneted or shot . . .

It was over. The Khalifa and the Sheikh-ed-Din had galloped back to Omdurman. Yakub lay dead under his brother's-banner. There now came only death-enamoured desperadoes, strolling one by one towards the rifles, pausing to shake a spear, turning aside to recognise a corpse, then caught by a sudden jet of fury, bounding forward, checking, sinking limply to the ground. Now under the black flag in a ring of bodies stood only three men. They folded their arms about the staff and gazed steadily forward. Two fell. The last Dervish stood up and filled his chest; he shouted the name of his God and hurled his spear. Then he stood quite still, waiting. It took him full; he quivered, gave at the knees, and toppled with his head on his arms and his face towards the legions of his conquerors.

"AFTER THE MANNER OF HIS RACE": THE FUNERAL OF GORDON, KHARTOUM, SEPTEMBER 1898

George Warrington Steevens

After Omdurman, British troops entered Khartoum where they disinterred the bones of Gordon and gave them a Christian burial.

The troops formed up before the palace in three sides of a rectangle – Egyptians to our left as we looked from the river, British to the right. The Sirdar, the generals of division and brigade, and the staff stood in the open space facing the palace. Then on the roof – almost on the very spot where Gordon fell, though the steps by which the butchers mounted have long since vanished – we were aware of two flagstaves. By the right-hand halliards stood Lieutenant Staveley, RN, and Captain Watson, KRR; by the left hand Bimbashi Mitford and his Excellency's Egyptian ADC.

The Sirdar raised his hand. A pull on the halliards: up ran, out flew, the Union Jack, tugging eagerly at his reins, dazzling gloriously in the sun, rejoicing in his strength and his freedom. "Bang!" went the "Melik's" 12½-pounder, and the boat quivered to her backbone. "God Save our Gracious Queen" hymned the Guards' band – "bang!" from the "Melik" – and Sirdar and private stood stiff – "bang!" – to attention, every hand at the helmet peak in – "bang!" – salute. The Egyptian flag had gone up at the same instant; and now, the same ear-smashing, soul-uplifting bangs marking time, the band of the 11th Sudanese was playing the Khedivial hymn. "Three cheers for the Queen!" cried the Sirdar: helmets leaped in the air, and the melancholy ruins woke to the first wholesome shout of all these years. Then the same for the Khedive. The comrade flags stretched themselves lustily, enjoying their own again; the bands pealed forth the pride of country; the twenty-one guns banged forth the strength of war. Thus, white men and black, Christian and Moslem, Anglo-Egypt set her seal once more, for ever, on Khartum (Khartoum).

Before we had time to think such thoughts over to ourselves, the Guards were playing the Dead March in "Saul". Then the black band was playing the march from Handel's "Scipio", which in England generally goes with "Toll for the Brave"; this was in memory of those loyal men among the Khedive's subjects who could have saved themselves by treachery, but preferred to die with Gordon. Next fell a deeper hush than ever, except for the solemn minute guns that had followed the fierce salute. Four chaplains – Catholic, Anglican, Presbyterian, and Methodist – came slowly forward and ranged themselves, with their backs to the palace, just before the Sirdar. The Presbyterian read the Fifteenth Psalm. The Anglican led the rustling whisper of the Lord's Prayer. Snow-haired Father Brindle, best beloved of priests, laid his helmet at his feet, and read a memorial prayer bareheaded in the sun. Then came forward the pipers and wailed a dirge, and the Sudanese played "Abide with me". Perhaps lips did twitch just a little to see the ebony heathens fervently blowing out Gordon's favourite hymn; but the most irrestible incongruity would hardly have made us laugh at that moment. And there were those who said the cold Sirdar himself could hardly speak or see, as General Hunter and the rest stepped out according to their rank and shook his hand. What wonder? He has trodden this road to Khartum for fourteen years, and he stood at the goal at last.

Thus with Maxim-Nordenfeldt and Bible we buried Gordon after the manner of his race. The parade was over, the troops were dismissed, and for a short space we walked in Gordon's garden. Gordon has become a legend with his countrymen, and they all but deify him dead who would never have heard of him had he lived. But in this garden you somehow came to know Gordon the man, not the myth, and to feel near to him. Here was an Englishman doing his duty, alone and at the instant peril of his life; yet still he loved his garden. The garden was a yet more pathetic ruin than the palace. The palace accepted its doom mutely; the garden strove against it. Untrimmed, unwatered, the oranges and citrons still struggled to bear their little, hard, green knobs, as if they had been full ripe fruit. The pomegranates put out their vermilion starflowers, but the fruit was small and woody and juiceless. The figs bore better, but they, too, were small and without vigour. Rankly overgrown with dhurra, a vine still trailed over a low roof its pale leaves and limp tendrils, but yielded not a sign of grapes. It was all green, and so far vivid and refreshing after Omdurman. But it was the green of nature, not of cultivation: leaves grew large and fruit grew small, and dwindled away. Reluctantly, despairingly, Gordon's garden was dropping back to wilderness. And in the middle of the defeated fruit-trees grew rankly the hateful Sodom apple, the poisonous herald of desolation.

The bugle broke in upon us; we went back to the boats. We were quicker steaming back than steaming up. We were not a whit less chastened, but every man felt lighter. We came with a sigh of shame: we went away with a sigh of relief. The long-delayed duty was done. The bones of our countrymen were shattered and scattered abroad, and no man knows their place; none the less Gordon had his due burial at last. So we steamed away to the roaring camp and left him alone again. Yet not one nor two looked back at the mouldering palace and the tangled garden with a new and a great contentment. We left Gordon alone again – but alone in majesty under the conquering ensign of his own people.

Part Five

Modern Times
1900–2001

". . . we shall defend our island, whatever the cost may be. We shall fight on the beaches, we shall fight on the landing grounds, we shall fight in the fields and in the streets, we shall fight in the hills; we shall never surrender . . ."

Winston Churchill, 4 June 1940

INTRODUCTION

A man walks on the moon. To the crowds that gathered in London to see in the new century on the winter's evening of 31 December 1899, such an event was the stuff of the wildest fantasy. The aeroplane itself was still on the drawing board of an obscure duo of American brothers, Orville and Wilbur Wright. Yet humankind's ability to escape from the confining gravity of Earth is neatly symbolic of how far the frontiers of technology and knowledge have been conquered in the twentieth century. The fact that many millions could watch the 1969 moon landing live at home through the medium of television only proves the point that this has been, without doubt, the most changeful century in history.

It has also been the most turbulent. On the eve of 1900 about a quarter of the world's population looked to Britain as their ruling nation. The Empire on which the "sun never sets" stretched from Cardiff to Calcutta. Yet, even as the new century dawned, Britain's imperial grip was starting to slacken. The most prescient of the revellers in Trafalgar Square may have realized the future belonged to others; a portent of this was the surprising trouble the British were having in winning the then recent, remote war against uppity Dutch settlers in South Africa.

Any economists among the revellers might, meanwhile, have noted an even more disturbing omen. Britain's economy had already been eclipsed by that of the USA, while Germany was catching up fast. In the year 1900 Great Britain's share of world manufacturing output was 18.5 per cent; America's was 23 per cent; Germany's 13.2 per cent. The relative decline of the British economy would continue almost uninterrupted until the end of the millennium, and almost everything the nation would and could do was palled by its shadow.

Paradoxically, though, the events which truly finished off Britain as the world's premier power (after all money isn't everything) were the two she "won"; the World Wars of 1914–18 and 1939–45. The slaughter in the trenches in the First World War caused the rise of nationalism everywhere – including Britannia's own empire. The Second World War against Nazi Germany continued the process; after all, if the Allied war effort was a "crusade for liberty", Britain could hardly justify keeping vassal states. Slowly and surely, the Empire slipped away in the "winds of change" until nothing was left but small dots of islands, and Britain herself had fallen well down the super power league. The final ignominy came in 1956 with the Suez crisis when the USA and USSR virtually instructed Britain to leave Port Said and go home. Although Britain has played a role in most world "policing" events since, she has done so as a constable not the sergeant.

The Empire gone, Britain found itself once more a place off the mainland of Europe. How to relate to the neighbours has dominated modern foreign politics in the UK: to enter the Common Market or not? Monetary union or not? ECUs anybody?

Domestic politics, meanwhile, continued age old trends but were amplified by the industrial and political struggles of the years before and after the First World War. The Great War itself, like the Second World War, caused sharp leftwards moves in the electorate (universal suffrage for men was introduced in 1918; for women in 1928). It was for fear that the workers might turn militant as well as for honourable altruism, that governments built homes "fit for heroes" and established a welfare state. But established it was. Since World War II, the people of this "sceptr'd isle" have never had it so good.

Except for the weather.

THE BOER WAR: SKIRMISH AT KARI SIDING, 29 MARCH 1900

Rudyard Kipling

For the British the new century began as the old ended – fighting the Boer War (1899–1902) in South Africa. The war had initially been prompted by the discovery of vast quantities of diamonds and gold in a territory of South Africa that was outside Britain's jurisdiction. Although the British army outnumbered the Boers by more than five to one, the country in which they were fighting was difficult and hostile. The British campaign against the Afrikaner nationalists had been initially an exercise in humiliation, but the arrival of Generals Robert and Kitchener in January 1900 began to see the tide of war turn in imperial favour, with victories such as that at Kari Siding. At the time of the skirmish, the novelist Rudyard Kipling was working as a correspondent for the *Friend*, a newspaper for British soldiers.

So there had to be a battle, which was called the Battle of Kari Siding. All the staff of the Bloemfontein *Friend* attended. I was put in a Cape cart, with native driver, containing most of the drinks, and with me was a well-known war correspondent. The enormous pale landscape swallowed up 7,000 troops without a sign, along a front of seven miles. On our way we passed a collection of neat, deep and empty trenches well undercut for shelter on the shrapnel side. A young Guards officer, recently promoted to *Brevet-Major* – and rather sore with the paper that we had printed it *Branch* – studied them interestedly. They were the first dim lines of the dugout, but his and our eyes were held. The Hun had designed them *secundum artem*, but the Boer had preferred the open within reach of his pony. At last we came to a lone farmhouse in a vale adorned with no less than five white flags. Beyond the ridge was a sputter of musketry and now and then the whoop of a field-piece. "Here," said my guide and guardian, "we get out and walk. Our driver will wait for us at the farmhouse." But the driver loudly objected. "No, sar. They shoot. They shoot me." "But they are white-flagged all over," we said. "Yess, sar. That *why*," was his answer, and he preferred to take his mules down into a decently remote donga and wait our return.

The farmhouse held two men and, I think, two women, who received us disinterestedly. We went on into a vacant world of sunshine and distances, where now and again a single bullet sang to himself. What I most objected to was the sensation of being under aimed fire – being, as it were, required as a head. "What are they doing this for?" I asked my friend. "Because they think we are the Something Light Horse. They ought to be just under this slope." I prayed that the particularly Something Light Horse would go elsewhere, which they presently did, for the aimed fire slackened and a wandering Colonial, bored to extinction, turned up with news from a far flank. "No; nothing doing and no one to see." Then more cracklings and a most cautious move forward to the lip of a large hollow where sheep were grazing. Some of them began to drop and kick. "That's both sides trying sighting-shots," said my companion. "What range do you make it?" I asked. "Eight hundred, at the nearest. That's close quarters nowadays. You'll never see anything closer than this. Modern rifles make it impossible. We're hung up till something cracks somewhere." There was a decent lull for meals on both sides, interrupted now and again by sputters. Then one indubitable shell – ridiculously like a pipsqueak in that vastness but throwing up much dirt. "Krupp! Four or six pounder at extreme range," said the expert. "They still think we're the— Light Horse. They'll come to be fairly regular from now on." Sure enough, every twenty minutes or so, one judgmatic shell pitched on our slope. We waited, seeing nothing in the emptiness, and hearing only a faint murmur as of wind along gas-jets, running in and out of the unconcerned hills.

Then pom-poms opened. These were nasty little one-pounders, ten in a belt (which usually jammed about the sixth round). On soft ground they merely thudded. On rock-face the shell breaks up and yowls like a cat. My friend for the first time seemed interested. "If these are *their* pom-poms, it's Pretoria for us," was his diagnosis. I looked behind me – the whole length of South Africa down to Cape Town – and it seemed very far. I felt that I could have covered it in five minutes under fair conditions – but *not* with those aimed shots up my back. The pom-poms opened again at a bare rock-reef that gave the shells full value. For about two minutes a file of racing ponies, their tails and their riders' heads well down, showed and vanished northward. "Our pom-poms," said the correspondent. "Le Gallais, I expect. *Now* we shan't be long." All this time the absurd Krupp was faithfully feeling for us, *vice*— Light Horse, and, given a few more hours, might perhaps hit one of us. Then to the left, almost under us, a small piece of hanging woodland filled and fumed with our shrapnel much as a man's moustache fills with cigarette-smoke. It was most impressive and lasted for quite twenty minutes. Then silence; then a movement of men and horses from our side up the slope, and the hangar our guns had been hammering spat steady fire at them. More Boer ponies on more skylines; a flurry of pom-poms on the right and a little frieze of far-off meek-tailed ponies, already out of rifle range.

"*Maffeesh*," said the correspondent, and fell to writing on his knee. "We've shifted 'em."

Leaving our infantry to follow men on ponyback towards the Equator, we returned to the farmhouse. In the donga where he was waiting someone squibbed off a rifle just after we took our seats, and our driver flogged out over the rocks to the danger of our sacred bottles.

Then Bloemfontein, and Gwynne storming in late with his accounts complete – 125 casualties, and the general opinion that "French was a bit of a butcher" and a tale of the General commanding the cavalry who absolutely refused to break up his horses by galloping them across raw rock – "not for any dam' Boer'.

THE BOER WAR: THE SIEGE OF MAFEKING, CAPE PROVINCE, SOUTH AFRICA, APRIL–MAY 1900

J. E. Neilly

Besieged by the Boers from October 1899, the British garrison and the civilian population at Mafeking was reduced to starvation levels by spring 1900.

Words could not portray the scene of misery. The best thing I can do is ask you to fancy 500–600 human frameworks of both sexes and all ages, from the tender infant upwards, dressed in the remains of tattered rags, standing in lines, each holding an old blackened can or beef tin, awaiting turn to crawl painfully up to the kitchen where the food was distributed. Having obtained the horse soup, fancy them tottering off a few yards and sitting down to wolf up the life-fastening mess, and lick the tins when they had finished. It was one of the most heart-rending sights I ever witnessed, and I have seen many . . .

When a flight of locusts came it was regarded as a godsend – this visitation that is looked upon by farmer as hardly less of a curse than the rinderpest or drought. The starving ones gathered the insects up in thousands, stripped them of their heads, legs, and wings, and ate the bodies. They picked up meat-tins and licked them; they fed like outcast curs. They went further than the mongrel. When a dog gets a bone he polishes it white and leaves it there. Day after day I heard outside my door continuous thumping sounds. They were caused by the living skeletons who, having eaten all that was outside the bones, smashed them up with stones and devoured what marrow they could find. They looked for bones on the dust-heaps, on the roads everywhere, and I pledge my word that I saw one poor fellow weakly follow a dog with a stone and with unerring aim strike him on the ribs, which caused the lean and hungry brute to drop a bone, which the Kaffir carried off in triumph to the kerb, where he smashed it and got what comfort he could from it.

QUEEN VICTORIA'S FUNERAL CORTÈGE, 1 FEBRUARY 1901

Countess of Denbigh

The death of Victoria, Queen of Great Britain and Ireland, Empress of India, on 22 January 1901 at Osborne on the Isle of Wight, truly marked the end of the old century. Her reign of almost sixty-four years had been the longest in British history, and she had spent the last forty years of it in mourning for her late husband, Prince Albert. She had imprinted her personality upon a whole era.

I think you will like to hear of my going down to Southampton to see the passing of our dear Queen from Osborne to Portsmouth.

I went on the *Scot*, where both Houses were embarked. We steamed out, and took up our position between the last British ship and the first foreign ships of war, on the south side of the double line down which the procession was to pass. The day was one of glorious sunshine, with the smoothest and bluest of seas. After a while a black torpedo destroyer came dashing down the line signalling that the *Alberta* was leaving Osborne and from every ship, both British and foreign, boomed out the minute guns for close on an hour before the procession reached us. The sun was now (three p.m.) beginning to sink, and a wonderful golden pink appeared in the sky and as the smoke slowly rose from the guns it settled in one long festoon behind them, over Haslar, a purple festoon like the purple hangings ordered by the King.

Then slowly down the long line of battleships came eight torpedo destroyers, dark gliding forms, and after them the white *Alberta* looking very small and frail next the towering battleships. We could see the motionless figures standing round the white pall which, with the crown and orb and sceptre, lay upon the coffin.

Solemnly and slowly, it glided over the calm blue water, followed by the other three vessels, giving one a strange choke, and a catch in one's heart as memory flew back to her triumphal passage down her fleet in the last Jubilee review. As slowly and as silently as it came the cortège passed away into the haze: with the solemn booming of the guns continuing every minute till Portsmouth was reached. A wonderful scene and marvellously impressive, leaving behind it a memory of peace and beauty and sadness which it is impossible to forget.

THE FIRST RADIO SIGNAL ACROSS THE ATLANTIC, CANADA, 12 DECEMBER 1901

Guglielmo Marconi

Marconi awaited the signal transmitted from Poldhu in Cornwall in a hut on the cliffs of Newfoundland. Until this time few scientists had believed that radio signals could follow the curvature of the earth for more than a hundred miles or so. Marconi's achievement created a sensation worldwide, and paved the way for the revolutionary development in radio communications and broadcasting.

Shortly before midday I placed the single earphone to my ear and I started listening. The receiver on the table before me was very crude – a few coils and condensers and a coherer – no valves, no amplifiers, not even a crystal. But I was at last on the point of putting the correctness of all my beliefs to test. The answer came at twelve-thirty when I heard, faintly but distinctly, *pip-pip-pip*. I handed the phone to Kemp: "Can you hear anything?" I asked. "Yes," he said, "the letter S" – he could hear it. I knew then that all my anticipations had been justified. The electric waves sent out into space from Poldhu had traversed the Atlantic – the distance, enormous as it seemed then, of 1,700 miles – unimpeded by the curvature of the earth. The result meant much more to me than the mere successful realization of an experiment. As Sir Oliver Lodge has stated, it was an epoch in history. I now felt for the first time absolutely certain that the day would come when mankind would be able to send messages without wires not only across the Atlantic but between the farthermost ends of the earth.

HOME SWEET HOME, SALFORD, c. 1907

Robert Roberts

The Edwardian slum child, like his forebears, felt an attachment to family life that a later age may find hard to understand. Home, however poor, was the focus of his love and interests, a sure fortress against a hostile world. Songs about its beauties were ever on people's lips. "Home, sweet home", first heard in the 1870s, had become "almost a second national anthem". Few walls in lower working-class houses lacked "mottoes" – coloured strips of paper, about nine inches wide and eighteen inches in length, attesting to domestic joys: EAST, WEST, HOME'S BEST; BLESS OUR HOME; GOD IS MASTER OF THIS HOUSE; . . . HOME IS THE NEST WHERE ALL IS BEST. To hear of a teenager leaving or being turned out of it struck dark fear in a child's mind. He could hardly imagine a fate more awful.

BLÉRIOT FLIES THE CHANNEL, 25 JULY 1909

Louis Blériot

In 1909, the London *Daily Mail* offered a prize of £1,000 to the first aviator to fly the English Channel. The prize was won by the Frenchman Louis Blériot who achieved the crossing in a 28 hp monoplane. It took a little over forty minutes.

At four-thirty we could see all around: daylight had come. M. Le Blanc endeavoured to see the coast of England, but could not. A light breeze from the south-west was blowing. The air was clear.

Everything was prepared. I was dressed, as I am at this moment, in a khaki jacket lined with wool for warmth over my tweed clothes and beneath an engineer's suit of blue cotton overalls. My close-fitting cap was fastened over my head and ears. I had neither eaten nor drunk anything since I rose. My thoughts were only upon the flight, and my determination to accomplish it this morning.

Four-thirty five! *Tout est prêt!* Le Blanc gives the signal and in an instant I am in the air, my engine making 1,200 revolutions – almost its highest speed – in order that I may get quickly over the telegraph wires along the edge of the cliff. As soon as I am over the cliff I reduce my speed. There is now no need to force my engine.

I begin my flight, steady and sure, towards the coast of England. I have no apprehensions, no sensations, *pas du tout*.

The *Escopette* has seen me. She is driving ahead at full speed. She makes perhaps 42 kilometres (about 26 miles per hour). What matters? I am making at least 68 kilometres (42 miles per hour).

Rapidly I overtake her, travelling at a height of 80 metres (about 260 feet).

The moment is supreme, yet I surprise myself by feeling no exultation. Below me is the sea, the surface disturbed by the wind, which is now freshening. The motion of the waves beneath me is not pleasant. I drive on.

Ten minutes have gone. I have passed the destroyer, and I turn my head to see whether I am proceeding in the right direction. I am amazed. There is nothing to be seen, neither the torpedo-destroyer, nor France, nor England. I am alone. I can see nothing at all – *rien du tout*!

For ten minutes I am lost. It is a strange position, to be alone, unguided, without compass, in the air over the middle of the Channel.

I touch nothing. My hands and feet rest lightly on the levers. I let the aeroplane take its own course. I care not whither it goes.

For ten minutes I continue, neither rising nor falling, nor turning. And then, twenty minutes after I have left the French coast, I see the green cliffs of Dover, the castle, and away to the west the spot where I intended to land.

What can I do? It is evident that the wind has taken me out of my course. I am almost at St Margaret's Bay and going in the direction of the Goodwin Sands.

Now it is time to attend to the steering. I press the lever with my foot and turn easily towards the west, reversing the direction in which I am travelling. Now, indeed, I am in difficulties, for the wind here by the cliffs is much stronger, and my speed is reduced as I fight against it. Yet my beautiful aeroplane responds. Still I fly westwards, hoping to cross the harbour and reach the Shakespear Cliff. Again the wind blows. I see an opening in the cliff.

Although I am confident that I can continue for an hour and a half, that I might indeed return to Calais, I cannot resist the opportunity to make a landing upon this green spot.

Once more I turn my aeroplane, and, describing a half-circle, I enter the opening and find myself again over dry land. Avoiding the red buildings on my right, I attempt a landing; but the wind catches me and whirls me round two or three times.

At once I stop my motor, and instantly my machine falls straight upon the land from a height of twenty metres (65 ft). In two or three seconds I am safe.

Soldiers in khaki run up, and a policeman. Two of my compatriots are on the spot. They kiss my cheeks. The conclusion of my flight overwhelms me. I have nothing to say, but accept the congratulations of the representatives of the *Daily Mail* and accompany them to the Lord Warden Hotel.

Thus ended my flight across the Channel. The flight could be easily done again. Shall I do it? I think not. I have promised my wife that after a race for which I have entered I will fly no more.

FORCE-FEEDING OF A SUFFRAGETTE, WALTON, 18 JANUARY 1910

Lady Constance Lytton

The civil disobedience tactics of the Women's Suffrage Movement saw numerous supporters sent to jail, where they frequently resorted to hunger strikes. In response, the authorities force-fed them.

I was visited again by the Senior Medical Officer, who asked me how long I had been without food. I said I had eaten a buttered scone and a banana sent in by friends to the police station on Friday at about midnight. He said, "Oh, then, this is the fourth day; that is too long, I shall feed you, I must feed you at once," but he went out and nothing happened till about six o'clock in the evening, when he returned with, I think, five wardresses and the feeding apparatus. He urged me to take food voluntarily. I told him that was absolutely out of the question, that when our legislators ceased to resist enfranchising women then I should cease to resist taking food in prison. He did not examine my heart nor feel my pulse; he did not ask to do so, nor did I say anything which could possibly induce him to think I would refuse to be examined. I offered no resistance to being placed in position, but lay down voluntarily on the plank bed. Two of the wardresses took hold of my arms, one held my head and one my feet. One wardress helped to pour the food. The doctor leant on my knees as he stooped over my chest to get at my mouth. I shut my mouth and clenched my teeth. I had looked forward to this moment with so much anxiety lest my identity should be discovered beforehand, that I felt positively glad when the time had come. The sense of being overpowered by more force than I could possibly resist was complete, but I resisted nothing except with my mouth. The doctor offered me the choice of a wooden or steel gag; he explained elaborately, as he did on most subsequent occasions, that the steel gag would hurt and the wooden one not, and he urged me not to force him to use the steel gag. But I did not speak nor open my mouth, so that after playing about for a moment or two with the wooden one he finally had recourse to the steel. He seemed annoyed at my resistance and he broke into a temper as he plied my teeth with the steel implement. He found that on either side at the back I had false teeth mounted on a bridge which did not take out. The superintending wardress asked if I had any false teeth, if so, that they must be taken out; I made no answer and the process went on. He dug his instrument down on to the sham tooth, it pressed fearfully on the gum. He said if I resisted so much with my teeth, he would have to feed me through the nose. The pain of it was intense and at last I must have given way for he got the gag between my teeth, when he proceeded to turn it much more than necessary until my jaws were fastened wide apart, far more than they could go naturally. Then he put down my throat a tube which seemed to me much too wide and was something like four feet in length. The irritation of the tube was excessive. I choked the moment it touched my throat until it had got down. Then the food was poured in quickly; it made me sick a few seconds after it was down and the action of the sickness made my body and legs double up, but the wardresses instantly pressed back my head and the doctor leant on my knees. The horror of it was more than I can describe.

THE ARREST OF DR H. H. CRIPPEN, 31 JULY 1910

Captain H. G. Kendall

After murdering his wife – with the exotic poison, hyoscine – Crippen tried to flee to Canada with his paramour, Ethel LeNeve, but became the first criminal to be caught by use of the wireless. Captain Kendall was the master of the steamship *Montrose*.

The *Montrose* was in port at Antwerp when I read in the *Continental Daily Mail* that a warrant had been issued for Crippen and LeNeve. They were reported to have been traced to a hotel in Brussels but had then vanished again.

Soon after we sailed for Quebec I happened to glance through the porthole of my cabin and behind a lifeboat I saw two men. One was squeezing the other's hand. I walked along the boat deck and got into conversation with the elder man. I noticed that there was a mark on the bridge of his nose through wearing spectacles, that he had recently shaved off a moustache, and that he was growing a beard. The young fellow was very reserved, and I remarked about his cough.

"Yes," said the elder man, "my boy has a weak chest, and I'm taking him to California for his health."

I returned to my cabin and had another look at the *Daily Mail*. I studied the description and photographs issued by Scotland Yard. Crippen was fifty years of age, 5 ft 4 ins high, wearing spectacles and a moustache; Miss LeNeve was twenty-seven, 5 ft 5 ins, slim, with pale complexion. I then examined the passenger list and ascertained that the two passengers were travelling as "Mr Robinson and son". I arranged for them to take meals at my table.

When the bell went for lunch I tarried until the coast was clear, then slipped into the Robinsons' cabin unobserved, where I noticed two things: that the boy's felt hat was packed round the rim to make it fit, and that he had been using a piece of a woman's bodice as a face flannel. That satisfied me. I went down to the dining saloon and kept my eyes open. The boy's manners at table were ladylike. Later, when they were promenading the saloon deck, I went out and walked behind them, and called out, "Mr Robinson!" I had to shout the name several times before the man turned and said to me, "I'm sorry, Captain, I didn't hear you – this cold wind is making me deaf."

In the next two days we developed our acquaintance. Mr Robinson was the acme of politeness, quiet-mannered, a non-smoker; at night he went on deck and roamed about on his own. Once the wind blew up his coat tails and in his hip pocket I saw a revolver. After that I also carried a revolver, and we often had pleasant little tea parties together in my cabin, discussing the book he was reading, which was *The Four Just Men*, a murder mystery by Edgar Wallace – and when that little fact was wirelessed to London and published it made Edgar Wallace's name ring, so agog was everybody in England over the Crippen case.

That brings me to the wireless. On the third day out I gave my wireless operator a message for Liverpool: *One hundred and thirty miles west of Lizard . . . have strong suspicions that Crippen London cellar murderer and accomplice are among saloon passengers . . . Accomplice dressed as boy; voice, manner, and build undoubtedly a girl.*

I remember Mr Robinson sitting in a deckchair, looking at the wireless aerials and listening to the crackling of our crude spark-transmitter, and remarking to me what a wonderful invention it was.

I sent several more reports, but our weak transmitting apparatus was soon out of communication with land. We could hear other ships at a great distance, however, and you may imagine my excitement when my operator brought me a message he had intercepted from a London newspaper to its representative aboard the White Star liner *Laurentic* which was also heading westward across the Atlantic: *What is Inspector Dew doing? Is he sending and receiving wireless messages? Is he playing games with passengers? Are passengers excited over chase? Rush reply.*

This was the first I knew that my message to Liverpool had caused Inspector Dew to catch the first boat out – the *Laurentic*. With her superior speed, I knew she would reach the Newfoundland coast before me. I hoped that if she had any news for me the *Laurentic* would leave it at the Belle Island station to be transmitted to me as soon as I passed that point on my approach to Canada.

She had news indeed: *Will board you at Father Point . . . strictly confidential . . . from Inspector Dew, Scotland Yard, on board Laurentic.*

I replied: *Shall arrive Father Point about 6 a.m. tomorrow . . . should advise you to come off in small boat with pilot, disguised as pilot . . .*

This was confirmed. The last night was dreary and anxious, the sound of our fog-horn every few minutes adding to the monotony. The hours dragged on as I paced the bridge; now and then I could see Mr Robinson strolling about the deck. I had invited him to get up early to see the "pilots" come aboard at Father Point in the River St Lawrence. When they did so they came straight to my cabin. I sent for Mr Robinson. When he entered I stood with the detective facing the door, holding my revolver inside my coat pocket. As he came in, I said, "Let me introduce you."

Mr Robinson put out his hand; the detective grabbed it, at the same time removing his pilot's cap, and said, "Good morning, Dr Crippen. Do you know me? I'm Inspector Dew, from Scotland Yard."

Crippen quivered. Surprise struck him dumb. Then he said, "Thank God it's over. The suspense has been too great. I couldn't stand it any longer."

Ethel LeNeve was acquitted of aiding Crippen in the murder of his wife. The doctor, however, was found guilty and sentenced to be hanged at Pentonville Prison.

THE TONYPANDY RIOT, SOUTH WALES, NOVEMBER 1910

J. V. Radcliffe

Churchill has often been blamed for the escalating violence of the Tonypandy riots when coal miners on strike clashed with the police and military. In fact, he had ordered that the troops "should not come into direct contact with rioters unless and until action had been taken by the police". However, as this eye-witness account reveals, his message arrived too late for strike leaders to calm the situation.

The centre stretch of the Rhondda Valley, where it lies deep between mountain slopes all autumn brown and ashen grey, was in wild turmoil late last night and early this morning. Strikers and policemen were in furious conflict, stones were thrown in showers, truncheons were drawn and vigorously used, colliery property was smashed, and more than a hundred strikers and six or seven policemen were injured, some of them badly. What set the bad spirit abroad cannot be known. It seemed to fall with the gathering darkness. High above the Llwynypia pit is a frowning head of rock, which the clouds wrapped round last night in sullen gloom, and if they had distilled riot and fury down its threatening front the effect in the valley could scarcely have been more sombre and wild. The first mutterings of trouble were heard about nine o'clock. Four thousand men marched to the pit and halted at its gate. This was a repetition so far of the morning and midday marches, but the temper of the men underwent a sudden change. Some youths showed the first symptoms of what was stirring. They made a rush towards the gates, where the police kept guard. It was not a formidable movement, and the police withstood the shock without a tremor, but the repulse set more evil designs on foot. A sober-minded collier very bravely ventured to set himself against the current of feeling. Climbing a bank, he began a speech of counsel to his fellow workmen to act humanely and justly. The counsel was too quiet for distempered minds, and if it had any effect at all it was only to divert attention from the colliery gates and their police guard to the long line of palisading that shuts off the pit yard from the road.

One common motive actuated the thousands of men massed together. It was to get to the electric power-house, to drive out the men in charge and stop the machinery. The power-house since Sunday has been manned by under-managers and other officials of the Glamorgan Colliery Company, with Mr Llewellyn, the general manager, at their head. The regular enginemen and stokers have been frightened away. The power station is the citadel of the situation so far as the Glamorgan Company is concerned. It supplies the power for pumping and ventilating five pits. The pits, at any rate, will be in danger of flooding, the ventilation has already ceased, and as a consequence the fate of hundreds of horses is only a matter of hours. To stop every bit of work at the collieries, to stop the pumping as well as the ventilating, was what one man called the trump card that the strikers were now to play. They rushed at the palisading to tear it down. They dare not push it before them lest they should fall with it on the railway below. It had to come down on the road. Thick stumps were snapped and props and stays torn up by the pulling of thousands of hands, and the men began to swarm into the pit yard. The brightly lighted power-station was in front of them, and to hinder their advance only the railway, a line of trucks, and a score or two of policemen advancing in scouting order. Not one of the strikers got behind the line of trucks. Big, active men more than their match physically drove them violently back, and they did not try that way any more. Worse things were in store. Stone-throwing began. The road that skirts the colliery is cut low down on the hillside. Another road descends the hill to join it fast by the colliery, and for 150 yards it overlooks the colliery entrance. A band of strikers had taken up places here as well as on the slope between the two highways. Stones were plentiful, and big and small, just as they came to hand, they were hurled at the policemen at the gates.

The policemen were unfortunately conspicuous. The light from the power station, without which the men there could not work, shone on the silver facings of their helmets and made them an easy mark. Man after man was hit, and when the line was weakened and another attempt was made to carry the pit by storm the policemen gave way, and the strikers were already within the gates when reinforcements came from another part of the yard. These men had their truncheons drawn, and laying freely about them they drove the crowd beyond the gates and some distance along the lower road. The men on the higher road were at the moment beyond reach, but when the stone-throwing commenced Captain Lionel Lindsay, Chief Constable of the county, called his men together and led them in a charge up the hill. The attacking force consisted of 118 men, every one of them 6 ft tall or thereabouts. With their truncheons in their hands they advanced with long swinging strides. The colliers did not wait. They preferred throwing stones from a distance to a personal encounter, in which, indeed, they would have been completely overmatched. They scuttled off as fast as their legs would carry them, but not fast enough for all to escape the horrid thud of truncheons on their heads and shoulders. It was a wild, headlong flight for safety, only limited by the necessity for the policemen to remain in touch with their base. Even after this there was no quietness. The strikers re-formed once and again, and other though minor charges were made. The night passed into morning, and still the road was in turmoil. About four o'clock there was a second but this time half-hearted attempt to storm the power-house. It was easily defeated.

Daylight revealed in a striking manner the part of the conflict that darkness had hidden. Most fearful-looking of the wreckage was the litter of stones, half-bricks, and bits of rock that lay all about the colliery gate. It was appalling to think of enduring that merciless, invisible hail. In less profusion, the missiles lay a considerable distance along the road, and a walk up to the hill showed where the supply had come from and the commanding position the throwers held. The best-placed would be thirty or forty feet above the heads of the police and scarcely more than a street's width from them. Standing in a body, as they were obliged to do, and picked out by the colliery lights, the police were completely exposed, a mark for any coward who chose to aim from a distance.

The power-house itself, though it stands well back from the road, had not escaped scot-free. A number of its windows were perforated by stones, but no one inside was hurt. Those of its garrison who were struck were hit while passing to and from the boilers. Twenty men who are really prisoners in this building are waging a hard, unresting struggle against a flood of water in the mine. Amateurs at stoking as they are, they find it almost beyond their power to keep a sufficient head of steam to run the pumping machinery. None of them has slept since Sunday night, and weariness compels them to lie down sometimes on the hard concrete floor, but the rest is brief. They are doing all that men can do to save the pits, and are just keeping the water down. If it overflows the dam it will invade the steam coal pit, and incalculable damage may be done and some 300 horses drowned. As it is three fates threaten the horses – by starvation, asphyxiation, or drowning – and one can scarcely tell which is coming fastest.

I was permitted this morning to enter the power-house. I found its occupants as eager to gain news from outside as I was to know what had happened within. We therefore exchanged information. Their great physical needs, I ascertained, were first sleep and second cigarettes. The strain of the past thirty hours' vigil and the constant exertion were marked in weary lines on their faces. Some of them were on duty and alert, and the remainder were getting some relief in the easiest attitudes they could assume on the floor. There was not a chair or a form in the place.

There was hope for a time during the afternoon that troops would not be necessary to enforce order in the Valley. The morning had passed quietly, and the afternoon was occupied chiefly, so far as the strikers were concerned, with a mass meeting at which 10,000 were present, and a huge parade round the district. The long delay in the arrival of troops known to have started for the coalfield caused wonder and surprise, and the explanation came later in the afternoon. The strike leaders received a telegram from Mr Winston Churchill inviting them to meet him in London tomorrow. The Home Secretary's telegram added (according to a statement made by the strike leaders) that he was reluctant to have troops quartered in the Valley, and that if quietness were maintained the troops on the way would not be sent to their destination. It was extremely unfortunate that this telegram had not arrived in time to be read at the mass meeting. The strike leaders met immediately afterwards to consider what reply they should send, and decided to accept Mr Churchill's offer and to advise the men to keep the peace.

There were, however, no effective means of promulgating their decision, and tonight Tonypandy has been the scene for hours of a terrible uproar. Rioting broke out again as soon as twilight fell. It began down at the Llwynypia (Glamorgan Colliery) pit. The police in strong force were again on duty at the gates and in the yard concentrating their force so as to defend the power-house. A great crowd drew up in the road. All at once stones began to hurtle through the air. Another attack was made on the palisading, and the wreckage of last night was piled up in the road to prevent the mounted police from charging. The fusilade on the police was unendurable. The Chief Constable took advantage of a temporary cessation of the onslaught to make a last appeal for order. The reply was another volley of stones.

The Chief Constable himself was hit and knocked to the ground. There was a menacing rush to the gates, and the police replied by drawing their staves and charging. They drove the men before them until they had cleared a good space, and just the same as last night it was necessary to clear the higher road with truncheons. This space the police resolved to defend. Their line was weakened by being extended, but they were in a less vulnerable position. On each side of them was a desperate crowd, but for a time they won a breathing space. The tale of the injured has yet to be told, however. Nobody knows how many are injured, but news comes from the pit that nine constables are lying there in a serious condition. The riot is spreading throughout the town, and it is unsafe to venture into the street. A fellow-journalist has just come in bleeding from a wound in the head, inflicted by a stone. He was a stranger, and that alone seems to account for the attack. A reckless crowd is marching through the streets. There seem to be no police about. The rioters swarm down the main street.

A number of men started a short time ago on a mission of wanton destruction bringing half bricks with them. They hurled them right and left into the shop windows. I followed safely in their tracks and saw the damage they had done. Some shops have not a particle of glass left in their fronts, and it is impossible to say how many windows are smashed. There has also been unrestricted looting. In the central square of the town a dozen shops have had their fronts completely broken out, and the goods that filled the windows three hours ago are now lying in the street. Companies of strikers have climbed to the upper floors and are rifling the stores, throwing them out of the windows to the people below, who are bearing them away in armfuls. The square is littered with clothing, millinery, groceries, confectionery, and chemists' wares. It is an amazing sight and quite indescribable.

The scene in the centre of the town is one of utter confusion. People stand about in small groups, either silent or discussing under their breath the events of the past few hours. The looting of shops is still going on. I have just seen a man standing behind the broken glass of a clothier's window emptying a broken bale of goods. He called out, "Who wants a waistcoat?" and handed one to the man who first spoke; then a pair of trousers, then a coat; in this way the goods were distributed until the bale was empty. To assist the distribution the gas in the shop window had been lighted. Everything was done openly. There are no police about. Carpenters are already at work boarding up the broken windows.

Tonypandy, Wednesday 9 November. The town was awake all night. Excitement and fear kept many out of bed, and only the dawn scattered the prevailing alarm. All night long men were boarding up the shattered shop fronts and carts were going round for the sweepings of plate glass that littered the main street for three quarters of a mile. Now and again there was the heavy tramp of large bodies of police going or returning from the Glamorgan pit at Llwynypia, but nothing occurred to remove or increase the anxious suspense. Today is also full of fear. The few shops that escaped damage yesterday are being barricaded today, and the night is awaited with dread. Soldiers have arrived. A squadron of the 18th Hussars reached Pontypridd early this morning, and after a rest a troop came here by road, a distance of seven miles, while the other troop went to Aberdare. Their places at Pontypridd were taken by another squadron brought from Cardiff, where they had been overnight. The troop here rode through the town about one o'clock to their quarters at the New Colliery offices. The Metropolitan Mounted Constablary have also arrived. Superficially there is nothing but curiosity in the minds of the slow-moving crowds that are in the streets, but the same could have been said yesterday, and those who know the temper of the Rhondda miners predict more trouble. Let us hope the prophets of evil are wrong.

Ten o'clock. Tonypandy tonight and Tonypandy last night are not like the same town. Even within the past two hours there has been a great change. There is not even a crowd about except in the square, where the number of people is perhaps large enough to be called a crowd. At first the disappearance of the strikers caused misgiving. It seemed as if they had acted on a common understanding, and the fear was that they might be congregating elsewhere. A good effect was produced by a proclamation in the square inviting all well-disposed persons to avoid associating themselves with riotous assemblies. I have walked to Llwynypia and as far as the grounds of Mr Llewellyn's house. There are only curious sightseers about. The colliery is brightly lighted, and the loud hum of the machinery in the power-house shows that it is running at full speed. The police, chilled by the cold night air, are stamping up and down to keep themselves warm. Mr Llewellyn's house looks as secure as Buckingham Palace. No doubt there are many police guarding it, but they are all sudden by the darkness, and it has not been thought necessary to secure the gates.

ANTARCTIC EXPEDITION: THE FINAL DIARIES AND LETTERS OF CAPTAIN R. F. SCOTT, JANUARY 1912

Captain Scott

Scott had set out for the South Pole with eleven others on 24 October, only to find that Amundsen's Norwegians had arrived first. On their return journey, in 1912, Scott and his companions all perished. Their bodies were found by searchers later that year on 12 November. This diary entry leaves some confusion as to the date of his actual death, but it is now generally assumed that he mistakenly wrote "March" for "January".

It is wonderful to think that two long marches would land us at the Pole. We left our depot today with nine days' provisions, so that it ought to be a certain thing now, and the only appalling possibility the sight of the Norwegian flag forestalling ours. Little Bowers continues his indefatigable efforts to get good sights, and it is wonderful how he works them up in his sleeping-bag in our congested tent. (Minimum for night –27.5°.) Only 27 miles from the Pole. We *ought* to do it now.

Tuesday, 16 January . . . The worst has happened, or nearly, the worst . . . About the second hour of the march Bowers' sharp eyes detected what he thought was a cairn; he was uneasy about it, but argued that it must be a sastrugus. Half an hour later he detected a black speck ahead. Soon we knew that this could not be a natural snow feature. We marched on, found that it was a black flag tied to a sledge bearer; near by the remains of a camp; sledge tracks and ski tracks going and coming and the clear trace of dogs' paws – many dogs. This told us the whole story. The Norwegians have forestalled us and are first at the Pole. It is a terrible disappointment; and I am very sorry for my loyal companions. Many thoughts come and much discussion have we had. Tomorrow we must march on to the Pole and then hasten home with all the speed we can compass. All the day-dreams must go; it will be a wearisome return. We are descending in altitude – certainly also the Norwegians found an easy way up.

Wednesday, 17 January . . . The Pole. Yes, but under very different circumstances from those expected. We have had a horrible day – add to our disappointment a head wind 4 to 5, with a temperature –22°, and companions labouring on with cold feet and hands.

We started at 7.30, none of us having slept much after the shock of our discovery. We followed the Norwegian sledge tracks for some way; as far as we make out there are only two men. In about three miles we passed two small cairns. Then the weather overcast, and the tracks being increasingly drifted up and obviously going too far to the west, we decided to make straight for the Pole according to our calculations . . . Great God! this is an awful place and terrible enough for us to have laboured to it without the reward of priority. Well, it is something to have got here, and the wind may be our friend tomorrow. We have had a fat Polar hoosh in spite of our chagrin, and feel comfortable inside – added a small stick of chocolate and the queer taste of a cigarette brought by Wilson. Now for the run home and a desperate struggle. I wonder if we can do it.

Thursday morning, 18 January . . . We have just arrived at this tent, 2 miles from our camp, therefore about 1½ miles from the Pole. In the tent we find a record of five Norwegians having been here, as follows: "Roald Amundsen, Olav Olavson Bjaaland, Hilmer Hanssen, Sverre H. Hassel, Oscar Wisting; 16 Dec. 1911". The tent is fine – a small, compact affair supported by a single bamboo. A note from Amundsen, which I keep, asks me to forward a letter to King Haakon!

The following articles have been left in the tent: three half-bags of reindeer containing a miscellaneous assortment of mitts and sleeping socks, very various in description, a sextant, a Norwegian artificial horizon and a hypsometer without boiling-point thermometers, a sextant and hypsometer of English make. Left a note to say I had visited the tent with companions . . .

This morning started with southerly breeze, set sail and passed another cairn at good speed; half-way, however, the wind shifted to W by S or WSW, blew through our wind clothes and into our mitts. Poor Wilson horribly cold, could not get off ski for some time. Bowers and I practically made camp, and when we got into the tent at last we were all deadly cold. Then temp now midday down –43° and the wind strong. We *must* go on, but now the making of every camp must be more difficult and dangerous. It must be near the end, but a pretty merciful end. Poor Oates got it again in the foot. I shudder to think what it will be like tomorrow. It is only with greatest pains rest of us keep off frostbites. No idea there could be temperatures like this at this time of year with such winds. Truly awful outside the tent. Must fight it out to the last biscuit, but can't reduce rations.

Friday, 16 March or Saturday 17. Lost track of dates, but think the last correct. Tragedy all along the line. At lunch, the day before yesterday, poor Titus Oates said he couldn't go on; he proposed we should leave him in his sleeping-bag. That we could not do, and induced him to come on, on the afternoon march. In spite of its awful nature for him he struggled on and we made a few miles. At night he was worse and we knew the end had come.

Should this be found I want these facts recorded. Oates' last thoughts were of his mother, but immediately before he took pride in thinking that his regiment would be pleased with the bold way in which he met his death. We can testify to his bravery. He has borne intense suffering for weeks without complaint, and to the very last was able and willing to discuss outside subjects. He did not – would not – give up hope to the very end. He was a brave soul. This was the end. He slept through the night before last, hoping not to wake; but he woke in the morning – yesterday. It was blowing a blizzard. He said, "I am just going outside and may be some time." He went out into the blizzard and we have not seen him since.

I take this opportunity of saying that we have stuck to our sick companions to the last. In case of Edgar Evans, when absolutely out of food and he lay insensible, the safety of the remainder seemed to demand his abandonment, but Providence mercifully removed him at this critical moment. He died a natural death, and we did not leave him till two hours after his death. We knew that

poor Oates was walking to his death, but though we tried to
dissuade him, we knew it was the act of a brave man and an
English gentleman. We all hope to meet the end with a similar
spirit, and assuredly the end is not far.

I can only write at lunch and then only occasionally. The cold is
intense, −40° at midday. My companions are unendingly cheerful,
but we are all on the verge of serious frostbites, and though we
constantly talk of fetching through I don't think any one of us
believes it in his heart.

We are cold on the march now, and at all times except meals.
Yesterday we had to lay up for a blizzard and today we move
dreadfully slowly. We are at No. 14 pony camp, only two pony
marches from One Ton Depot. We leave here our theodolite, a
camera, and Oates' sleeping-bags. Diaries, etc., and geological
specimens carried at Wilson's special request, will be found with us
or on our sledge.

Sunday, 18 March. Today, lunch, we are 21 miles from the depot.
Ill fortune presses, but better may come. We have had more wind
and drift from ahead yesterday; had to stop marching; wind NW,
force 4, temp. −35°. No human being could face it, and we are
worn out *nearly*.

My right foot has gone, nearly all the toes − two days ago I was
proud possessor of best feet. These are the steps of my downfall.
Like an ass I mixed a small spoonful of curry powder with my
melted pemmican − it gave me violent indigestion. I lay awake
and in pain all night; woke and felt done on the march; foot went
and I didn't know it. A very small measure of neglect and have a
foot which is not pleasant to contemplate. Bowers takes first place
in condition, but there is not much to choose after all. The others
are still confident of getting through − or pretend to be − I don't
know! We have the last *half* fill of oil in our primus and a very
small quantity of spirit − this alone between us and thirst. The
wind is fair for the moment, and that is perhaps a fact to help.
The mileage would have seemed ridiculously small on our outward journey.

Monday, 19 March. Lunch. We camped with difficulty last night
and were dreadfully cold till after our supper of cold pemmican
and biscuit and a half a pannikin of cocoa cooked over the spirit.
Then, contrary to expectation, we got warm and all slept well.
Today we started in the usual dragging manner. Sledge dreadfully
heavy. We are 15½ miles from the depot and ought to get there in

three days. What progress! We have two days' food but barely a day's fuel. All our feet are getting bad – Wilson's best, my right foot worst, left all right. There is no chance to nurse one's feet till we can get hot food into us. Amputation is the least I can hope for now, but will the trouble spread? That is the serious question. The weather doesn't give us a chance – the wind from N to NW and –40° temp. today.

Wednesday, 21 March. Got within 11 miles of depot Monday night; had to lay up all yesterday in severe blizzard. Today forlorn hope, Wilson and Bowers going to depot for fuel.

Thursday, 22 and 23 March. Blizzard bad as ever – Wilson and Bowers unable to start – tomorrow last chance – no fuel and only one or two of food left – must be near the end. Have decided it shall be natural – we shall march for the depot with or without our effects and die in our tracks.

Thursday, 29 March. Since the 21st we have had a continuous gale from WSW and SW. We had fuel to make two cups of tea apiece and bare food for two days on the 20th. Every day we have been ready to start for our depot *11 miles* away, but outside the door of the tent it remains a scene of whirling drift. I do not think we can hope for any better things now. We shall stick it out to the end, but we are getting weaker, of course, and the end cannot be far.

It seems a pity, but I do not think I can write more.

R. SCOTT

For God's sake look after our people.

THE *TITANIC* SINKS, 15 APRIL 1912

Harold Bride

Hailed by its builders and owners as "unsinkable", the liner *Titanic* had a total complement of 2,224 passengers and crew but it transpired there was room for only 1,178 passengers in its lifeboats when it struck an iceberg in the Atlantic on its maiden voyage. A total of 1,513 lives were lost. Harold Bride was a *Titanic* wireless operator.

From aft came the tunes of the band. It was a ragtime tune. I don't know what. Then there was "Autumn" . . . I went to the place I had seen the collapsible boat on the boat deck, and to my surprise I saw the boat, and the men still trying to push it off. I guess there wasn't a sailor in the crowd. They couldn't do it. I went up to them and was just lending a hand when a large wave came awash of the deck. The big wave carried the boat off. I had hold of an oarlock and I went with it. The next I knew I was in the boat. But that was not all. I was in the boat and the boat was upside-down, and I was under it. And I remember realizing I was wet through and that whatever happened I must not breathe, for I was under water. I knew I had to fight for it, and I did. How I got out from under the boat I do not know but I felt a breath of air at last. There were men all around me – hundreds of them. The sea was dotted with them, all depending on their lifebelts. I felt I simply had to get away from the ship. She was a beautiful sight then. Smoke and sparks were rushing out of her funnel. There must have been an explosion, but we heard none. We only saw the big stream of sparks. The ship was turning gradually on her nose – just like a duck that goes for a dive. I had only one thing on my mind – to get away from the suction. The band was still playing. I guess all of them went down. They were playing "Autumn" then. I swam with all my might. I suppose I was 150 feet away when the *Titanic*, on her nose, with her after-quarter sticking straight up in the air, began to settle – slowly.

When at last the waves washed over her rudder there wasn't the least bit of suction I could feel. She must have kept going just so slowly as she had been . . . I felt after a little while like sinking. I was very cold. I saw a boat of some kind near me, and put all my strength into an effort to swim to it. It was hard work. I was all done when a hand reached out from the boat and pulled me aboard. It was our same collapsible. The same crowd was on it. There was just room for me to roll on the edge. I lay there not caring what happened. Somebody sat on my legs. They were wedged in between slats and were being wrenched. I had not the heart left to ask the man to move. It was a terrible sight all around – men swimming and sinking.

I lay where I was, letting the man wrench my feet out of shape. Others came near. Nobody gave them a hand. The bottom-up boat already had more men than it would hold, and it was sinking. At first the larger waves splashed over my clothing. Then they began to splash over my head, and I had to breathe when I could. As we floated around on our capsized boat and I kept straining my eyes for a ship's lights, somebody said, "Don't the rest of you think we ought to pray?" The man who made the suggestion asked what the religion of the others was. Each man called out his religion. One was a Catholic, one a Methodist, one a Presbyterian. It was decided the most appropriate prayer for all was the Lord's Prayer. We spoke it over in chorus with the man who first suggested that we pray as the leader. Some splendid people saved us. They had a right-side-up boat and it was full to capacity. Yet they came to us and loaded us all into it. I saw some lights off in the distance and knew a steamship was coming to our aid.

A SUFFRAGETTE COMMITS SUICIDE AT THE DERBY, ENGLAND, 1913

Anon

They had just got round the Corner, and all had passed but the King's horse, when a woman squeezed through the railings and ran out into the course. She made straight for Anmer, and made a sort of leap for the reins. I think she got hold of them, but it was impossible to say. Anyway the horse knocked her over, and then they all came down in a bunch. They were all rolling together on the ground. The jockey fell with the horse, and struck the ground with one foot in the stirrup, but he rolled free. Those fellows know how to tumble. The horse fell on the woman and kicked out furiously, and it was sickening to see his hoofs strike her repeatedly. It all happened in a flash. Before we had time to realize it was over. The horse struggled to its feet – I don't think it was hurt – but the jockey and the woman lay on the ground.

The ambulance men came running up, put them on stretchers, and carried them away. Most of the other jockeys saw nothing of it. They were far ahead. It was a terrible thing.

The woman who died was Emily Wilding, a well-known activist in the cause of women's suffrage.

BRITAIN DECLARES WAR, 4 AUGUST 1914

King George V

Great Britain entered the First World War on 4 August 1914 after Germany refused to respect Belgian neutrality.

I held a council at 10.45 to declare war with Germany. It is a terrible catastrophe but it is not our fault. An enormous crowd collected outside the Palace; we went on the balcony both before and after dinner. When they heard that war had been declared, the excitement increased and May and I with David went on to the balcony; the cheering was terrific. Please to God it may soon be over and that He will protect dear Bertie's life.

King George V

JOINING UP, AUTUMN 1914

Arthur Conan Doyle

The British author of the *Sherlock Holmes* stories writes a letter to the War-Office.

I have been told that there may be some difficulty in finding officers for the New Army. I think I may say that my name is well-known to the younger men of this country and that if I were to take a commission at my age it might be of help. I can drill a company – I do so every evening. I have seen something of campaigning, having served as a surgeon in South Africa. I am fifty-five but I am very strong and hardy, and can make my voice audible at great distances which is useful at drill. Should you entertain my application, I should prefer a regiment which was drawn from the South of England – Sussex for choice.

Robert Graves

At the time of writing Robert Graves was a student. He later joined the Royal Welch Fusiliers, and wrote one of the classic memoirs of the conflict, *Goodbye to All That*.

I had just finished with Charterhouse and gone up to Harlech, when England declared war on Germany. A day or two later I decided to enlist. In the first place, though the papers predicted only a very short war – over by Christmas at the outside – I hoped that it might last long enough to delay my going to Oxford in October, which I dreaded. Nor did I work out the possibilities of getting actively engaged in the fighting, expecting garrison service at home, while the regular forces were away. In the second place, I was outraged to read of the Germans' cynical violation of Belgian neutrality. Though I discounted perhaps twenty per cent of the atrocity details as wartime exaggeration, that was not, of course, sufficient.

"THE TOMMY"

The marching song of the Regular Army in 1914:

> "Send out the Army and the *NAVY*
> Send out the rank and file.
> (Have a banana!)
> Send out the brave Territorials,
> They'll face the danger with a smile.
> (I don't think!)
> Send out the boys of the girls' brigade,
> They will keep old England free;
> Send out my mother, my sister and my brother,
> But for Gawd's sake don't send me!"

CHRISTMAS IN THE TRENCHES, WESTERN FRONT, 1914

Private Frank Richards

On Christmas morning we stuck up a board with "A Merry Christmas" on it. The enemy had stuck up a similar one. Platoons would sometimes go out for twenty-four hours' rest – it was a day at least out of the trench and relieved the monotony a bit – and my platoon had gone out in this way the night before, but a few of us stayed behind, to see what would happen. Two of our men then threw their equipment off and jumped on the parapet with their hands above their heads. Two of the Germans done the same and commenced to walk up the river bank, our two men going to meet them. They met and shook hands and then we all got out of the trench. Buffalo Bill rushed into the trench and endeavoured to prevent it, but he was too late: the whole of the Company were now out, and so were the Germans. He had to accept the situation, so soon he and the other company officers climbed out too. We and the Germans met in the middle of no-man's-land. Their officers was also now out. Our officers exchanged greetings with them. One of the German officers said that he wished he had a camera to take a snapshot, but they were not allowed to carry cameras. Neither were our officers.

We mucked in all day with one another. They were Saxons and some of them could speak English. By the look of them their trenches were in as bad a state as our own. One of their men, speaking in English, mentioned that he had worked in Brighton for some years and that he was fed up to the neck with this damned war and would be glad when it was all over. We told him that he wasn't the only one that was fed up with it. We did not allow them in our trench and they did not allow us in theirs. The German Company-Commander asked Buffalo Bill if he would accept a couple of barrels of beer and assured him that they would not make his men drunk. They had plenty of it in the brewery. He accepted the offer with thanks and a couple of their men rolled the barrels over and we took them into our trench. The German officer sent one of his men back to the trench, who appeared shortly after carrying a tray with bottles and glasses on it. Officers of both sides clinked glasses and drunk one another's health. Buffalo Bill had presented them with a plum pudding just before. The officers came to an understanding that the unofficial truce would end at midnight. At dusk we went back to our respective trenches.

We had a decent Christmas dinner. Each man had a tin of Maconochie's and a decent portion of plum pudding. A tin of Maconochie's consisted of meat, potatoes, beans and other vegetables and could be eaten cold, but we generally used to fry them up in the tin on a fire. I don't remember any man ever suffering from tin or lead poisoning through doing them in this way. The best firms that supplied them were Maconochie's and Moir Wilson's and we could always depend on having a tasty dinner when we opened one of their tins. But another firm that supplied them at this time must have made enormous profits out of the British Government. Before ever we opened the first tins that were supplied by them we smelt a rat. The name of the firm made us suspicious. When we opened them our suspicions were well founded. There was nothing inside but a rotten piece of meat and some boiled rice. The head of that firm should have been put against the wall and shot for the way they sharked us troops. The two barrels of beer were drunk, and the German officer was right: if it was possible for a man to have drunk the two barrels himself he would have bursted before he had got drunk. French beer was rotten stuff.

Just before midnight we all made it up not to commence firing before they did. At night there was always plenty of firing by both sides if there were no working parties or patrols out. Mr Richardson, a young officer who had just joined the Battalion and was now a platoon officer in my company wrote a poem during the night about the Briton and the Bosche meeting in no-man's-land on Christmas Day, which he read out to us. A few days later it was published in *The Times* or *Morning Post*, I believe. During the whole of Boxing Day we never fired a shot, and they the same, each side seemed to be waiting for the other to set the ball a-rolling. One of their men shouted across in English and inquired how we had enjoyed the beer. We shouted back and told him it was very weak but that we were very grateful for it. We were conversing off and on during the whole of the day. We were relieved that evening at dusk by a battalion of another brigade. We were mighty surprised as we had no whisper of any relief during the day. We told the men who relieved us how we had spent the last couple of days with the enemy, and they told us that by what they had been told the whole of the British troops in the line, with one or two exceptions, had mucked in with the enemy. They had only been out of action themselves forty-eight hours after being twenty-eight days in the front-line trenches. They also told us that the French people had heard how we had spent Christmas Day and were saying all manner of nasty things about the British Army.

ZEPPELIN RAID ON LONDON, SUMMER 1915

Freiharr Treusch von Buttlar Brandenfels

We were flying at a height of 15,000 feet. Suddenly the steersman called out to me: "Searchlights on our starboard bow!" Then the whole car became alive, and with our binoculars to our eyes we leant out of the control car down to our waists.

What a magnificent sight! How wonderful to see the beams of the searchlights exploring the heavens inch by inch, intersecting one another, then collecting into groups of three, four and five from different directions, and cutting each other again, and at last, at the point where they intersected, possibly finding a Zeppelin hanging like a huge incandescent cigar in the sky!

In a moment red lights were scattered through the blackness. They were the shrapnel-bursts.

Soon corresponding red lights appeared below on the ground. They were our own bombs.

There could not be the slightest doubt that our ship, too, was now quite close to the English coast.

Suddenly I staggered and was enveloped in blackness. In the heat of the fight I had lost my liquid-air pipe. It had dropped off the mouthpiece. It grew darker and darker. I felt I was going to be sick. I groped madly about the floor and seized hold of legs, cables, machine-gun belts. At last, just as I felt I should faint from the leaden weight on my head, I found the pipe!

It was marvellous. The moment I was able to breathe in the liquid air again I felt I could have knocked down whole barricades of brick walls, or lifted our tender with my little finger, or juggled with the machine-gun as though it were a billiard-cue, so elemental and powerful is the sudden fresh breath of life that is breathed into one!

"Climb to 18,000 feet!"

Minus twenty-one degrees, thirty degrees, thirty-five degrees Centigrade! Splendid! We met with no inversion. On the contrary, the temperature decreased appreciably the higher we rose.

A quarter of an hour later we had made the coast. We could see the lights of towns and villages, and of railways with their red and green signals, quite plainly. Suddenly everything below went black again. The district was certainly very skilful at putting out or concealing lights. It knew all about airship raids!

Ahead of us, I should say about ten miles away, one of our ships was attacking, and it immediately occurred to me that I ought to keep a more southerly course. So I changed my direction, intending, as soon as I had the attacking ship on my starboard beam, to course about and, flying north-east, to attack the same objective.

Everything depended on our reaching our objective unobserved. We were lucky. It was not long before we located the brightly illumined ship four points abaft the starboard beam, and I gave the order to steer north-east with rudder hard aport. The attack could begin.

The trap-doors for the bombs, which were in the catwalk, could be opened by the *Wachoffizier* by simply pressing a button. We were on the western edge of our objective. I gave the order for action!

Schiller pressed the first button and the first ten-pounder bomb whistled down to the depths. In spite of the buzz of the engines we could hear it whizzing through the air. The whole thing happened in a flash; the next bomb followed, then the third and fourth.

The bombs were plainly visible. A tiny blob of light appeared

18,000 feet below us, a few seconds later we heard the dull thud above the hum of the engines.

There could be no doubt that we were well over our objective, so the heavier fellows, the one-hundred-weight and two-hundred-weight bombs, were also dropped. They were released at regular intervals and crashed down below with a loud whine, followed quite rhythmically by a heavy thud as they reached the ground. The last three bombs were released simultaneously, and a heavy roll of thunder resounded below.

The crew knew what to do. Out with the ammunition!

It was so light that my eyes began to smart. Immediately after the first burst the searchlights had found us. One, two, three, four! We were flying through a cloud of glaring light. I could read the smallest print on the map before me.

How magnificent the huge, dazzlingly bright form of the ship must have looked 18,000 feet up in the sky, as she steered her way across the heavens!

The shrapnel salvoes drew nearer and nearer. At first they burst 3,000 feet below us. Oh, so the man in front of us had been flying at 15,000 feet!

But they corrected their range damnably quickly. Now they were getting very close indeed. We could hear the shells bursting all round and the whine of the splinters as they hurtled through space – high-explosive shells.

Should we climb higher, exhaust our last reserve strength, and, for the sake of 300 feet, risk being brought down by a hit, in which case all would be lost?

Suddenly on our port bow we saw a brilliant light, but no searchlight beam. It was deep and broad, a regular bank of light. The searchlight was penetrating a cloud.

"All engines full throttle." We were saved! Up we climbed into the cloud. The next salvo would certainly have hit the ship if we had not been able to hide.

AN ANZAC AT GALLIPOLI, JULY–AUGUST 1915

Major Oliver Hogue

The landing of Allied troops – predominantly British and Anzac (Australian and New Zealand Army Corps) – at the entrance to the Dardanelles, the straits between the Mediterranean and Sea of Marmara, giving access to Istanbul (Constantinople), was intended to open a front against the Turks, and so lessen the pressure on the Russian Army. At the outset, it was regarded as a highly dangerous and almost unachievable move, and it proved one of the greatest military disasters of the First World War, with the Allies slaughtered as they tried to struggle ashore. Even those that made it found themselves unable to break out of a narrow bridgehead on the rocky, sun-beaten Gallipoli peninsula.

Hogue served with the 14th Australian Light Horse.

3 August, 1915
Ryrie's Post, Anzac

My Bonnie Jean,

You'll be sorry to hear that poor Harry Robson is dead, killed on 24 July by a shrapnel shell. He was one of the patriots, well off, with a wife and family, automobile and everything that makes life worth living. Yet when Britain stepped in to defend Belgium and when Australia offered 20,000 men, Lieutenant Robson heard the Empire call and buckled on his sword. (By the bye, Australia will have sent nearly 250,000 men to the war soon.)

Robson was all over South Africa with Colonel Cox during the South African War and was a splendid transport officer. He could do anything with horses and cattle. On various occasions when the columns were stuck up and bogged in the drifts he managed to improvise some scheme for getting the wagons through. He was a great swordsman and won several prizes at the big tournaments when he went to London with the New South Wales Lancers. We put up a cross with crossed swords over the little shallow grave on Shell Green. May poor old Robbo rest in peace!

Tresilian has gone – top-sergeant Tresilian, whom you met at the camp. He was reckoned quite the best of all the non-coms in our regiment and was generally looked upon as certain for a commission. He was game as a pebble, a regular dare-devil, and he never knew what fear was. He came from down Wagga way originally, but of late had been a station manager in the north-west of New South Wales. He got a bullet in his brain, when looking over the parapet on Holly Ridge, and died without a sound.

Did I tell you about Major Midgley? He is one of the very best officers in our brigade, got the D.S.O. in the Zulu War, went through the South African War, and is a regular little fire-eater. He is in charge of Chatham's Post and is always pulling the Turks' leg. He conceives the most wonderful ruses and tricks to worry the Turks and draw their fire. He sends out fiery arrows and rockets and flares, and by simulating preparations for attack at all times, he has the Turks in the Gaba Tepe zone worried to death.

The other night, however, one of his patrols nearly got cut off. They went out under Lieutenant Bolingbroke to try and snare a prisoner, but as they went south along the beach a strong Turkish patrol tried to sneak in behind them and cut them off from our lines. Our lads streaked back like startled wallabies. The men on the post could not give covering fire for fear of hitting our patrol. However, they all got back safely, and the moment they were in, Chatham's Post opened a hot fire and sent the venturesome patrol about their business. They must have thought that the Post was only lightly held, for some time after midnight a couple of hundred Turks made a dash at the Beach Post. They gave us warning by accidentally kicking the tins we had scattered in the grass. Our chaps were ready and the first Turkish shot was answered by a veritable fusillade from our lines, and after a half-hour's hot firing the enemy drew off.

We have come to the conclusion here that only about 10 per cent of the Turks are good shots and snipers, while about 90 per cent of the Light Horsemen are crack marksmen. This being so, we are able to keep their snipers well in subjection. Lately in front of Ryrie's Post and Chatham's, the Turks cannot show a periscope without having it smashed, and our lads now are actually shooting them through their loopholes and smashing the mud bricks with which the Turks surround their fire recesses.

Several of our snipers are putting up fine records in the matter of bagging Turks. But the champion sniper of them all is Trooper Sing of the 5th Light Horse. He is a champion shot, terrible quick on the up-take (as your mither would say), has keen eyesight, and abundant patience. He has now shot over one hundred Turks; and every one is vouched for by an officer or the sergeant on duty, who sits by Sing all day with a telescope and never gives him credit for a kill unless he actually sees the Turk fall. Some of the infantry on our left are rather inclined to be sceptical as to Sing's performances, but there is not the slightest doubt about it. Major Midgley reckons that Sing must have killed at least one hundred and twenty and wounded thirty more, but he only gives credit for those the observer sees actually fall. But Sing never shoots at a stretcher-bearer. He will wait for hours for a sniper. "There is always tomorrow," he says.

Our sharpshooters always get a bag when a batch of Turkish reinforcements arrive. The newcomers don't know the ropes.

They are always very inquisitive, and will go poking their heads up over the parapets, or round sandbags. They don't know that while they may not be visible in front they are "wide open" from either flank, and with trenches rather zigzagging here and there, well, as Sing says, "It's a shame to take the money." One old Turk yesterday was fixing his overhead cover, when one of the Fifth smashed a brick and the thing toppled down on top of him. He lay quite exposed, kicking and yelling and waving his arms frantically. Sing exclaimed, "I'll put the poor cuss out of his agony", and promptly put a bullet through his brain.

Doesn't all this sound shockingly cruel and callous, my darling? But you made me promise to tell you everything; anyhow I have broken my promise time and time again. I simply can't tell you about the aftermath of battle – the shockingly mangled bodies and the comrades maimed and crippled, and the agonies of those poor wounded fellows left between the two firing lines. Yet we are all erring mortals, when we try to gloss over the horrors of war. It's only when the women of the world realize all war's wickedness and misery that there will be even a faint chance of turning our swords into plough-shares . . . Yet I remember when poor Belgium was trodden beneath the iron heel of the Hun, her shrines desecrated, her citizens butchered and her women outraged, it was the women of Great Britain that gladly sent their men to avenge the wrongs of the plucky little kingdom. And when the Empire called, the women of Australia gladly bade their sons and brothers "Go and God-speed". You, too, are not blameless in this regard, my angel, for if you had lifted your little finger to hold me back, I would have been numbered amongst the shirkers . . .

When will it all end, I wonder? How long, O Lord, how long? Yet I know we cannot sheathe the sword till the Hun is humbled and the spirit of Prussian Militarism quenched for good and all.

As for the poor turbaned and malignant Turk, he's merely the unhappy dupe of the German intriguers. Our Australians don't hate the Turk like they do the Hun. The Turkish prisoners have taken quite a liking to the Australians – but they all voice their fear of the Australian bayonets. They call us the "White Gurkhas".

I'm getting long-winded today. Au revoir.

Yours ever,
J.B.

Allied troops were evacuated from Gallipoli in December 1915.

THE EASTER RISING: THE COMMANDER'S PROCLAMATION, 28 APRIL 1916

James Connolly

The Easter Rebellion in Dublin was led by Sinn Fein and the Irish Volunteers. It was suppressed and fourteen of its leaders, including Connolly, were executed.

Army of the Irish Republic
(Dublin Command)
Headquarters, April 28th, 1916.

To Soldiers,

This is the fifth day of the establishment of the Irish Republic, and the flag of our country still floats from the most important buildings in Dublin, and is gallantly protected by the officers and Irish soldiers in arms throughout the country. Not a day passes without seeing fresh postings of Irish soldiers eager to do battle for the old cause. . . .

Let me remind you of what we have done. For the first time in 700 years the flag of a free Ireland floats triumphantly in Dublin City. The British Army, whose exploits we are for ever having dinned in our ears, which boasts of having stormed the Dardanelles and the German lines on the Marne, behind their artillery and machine guns, are afraid to advance or storm any position held by our forces. . . .

As you know I was twice wounded yesterday, and am unable to move about, but have got my bed moved into the firing line, and with the assistance of your officers, will be just as useful to you as ever. . . .

THE SOMME, JULY 1916

Sergeant Major Ernest Shephard

The Battle of the Somme, which began on 1 July 1916, claimed 60,000 British casualties on the first day alone. By the battle's end in mid-November 1916, 420,000 British and 200,000 French lives had been lost. For all this, the Allies had gained only five miles of ground.

Diary: Saturday, 1 July

A lovely day, intensely hot. Lot of casualties in my trench. The enemy are enfilading us with heavy shell, dropping straight on us. A complete trench mortar battery of men killed by one shell, scores of dead and badly wounded in trench, now one p.m. Every move we make brings intense fire, as trenches so badly battered the enemy can see all our movements. Lot of wounded in front we got in, several were hit again and killed in trench. We put as many wounded as possible in best spots in trench and I sent a lot down, but I had so many of my own men killed and wounded that after a time I could not do this. Sent urgent messages to Brigade asking for RAMC bearers to be sent to evacuate wounded, but none came, although Brigade said they had been dispatched. Meanwhile the enemy deliberately shelled the wounded between the trenches with shrapnel, thus killing, or wounding, again most of them. Our own Regtl stretcher bearers worked like niggers to take cases away. Counted all Dorsets at one p.m. Total 53 all ranks. At three p.m. the Manchesters went through the Russian Sap and made an attack, captured a portion of the Leipzig Redoubt. Brigade sent message to say we would be relieved by 15th HLI as soon as possible. Meanwhile we were to hold tight.

We needed to; literally we were blown from place to place. Men very badly shaken. As far as possible we cleared trenches of debris and dead. These we piled in heaps, enemy shells pitching on them made matters worse.

Wounded suffering agonies. I got them water from bottles of dead, a few managed to crawl away to the Aid Post in wood. At dusk we got more wounded in from the front. Eight p.m. we got shelled intensely, and continued at intervals. I had miraculous escapes. The HLI arrived at midnight. I handed care of wounded to them, and took remnants of B and C Coys, only 10 NCOs and men, back via Mounteagle and Rock St, through Wood Post and over same track (Dumbarton) through Blighty Wood, down the valley to Crucifix Corner. Arrived there at one a.m. on *Sunday 2 July*.

A TANK CHARGE, THE SOMME, 15 SEPTEMBER 1916

Bert Chaney

The menacing rumble of a tank was heard for the first time in warfare when thirty-six British Mark 1's were used in an attack on the Somme on 15 September 1916. The Mark 1 weighed 30 tons and was developed from the agricultural tractor designed by the American engineer Benjamin Holt. Its top speed was 5 mph.

We heard strange throbbing noises, and lumbering slowly towards us came three huge mechanical monsters such as we had never seen before. My first impression was that they looked ready to topple on their noses, but their tails and the two little wheels at the back held them down and kept them level. Big metal things they were, with two sets of caterpillar wheels that went right round the body. There was a bulge on each side with a door in the bulging part, and machine-guns on swivels poked out from either side. The engine, a petrol engine of massive proportions, occupied practically all the inside space. Mounted behind each door was a motorcycle type of saddle seat and there was just about enough room left for the belts of ammunition and the drivers . . .

Instead of going on to the German lines the three tanks assigned to us straddled our front line, stopped and then opened up a murderous machine-gun fire, enfilading us left and right. There they sat, squat monstrous things, noses stuck up in the air, crushing the sides of our trench out of shape with their machine-guns swivelling around and firing like mad.

Everyone dived for cover, except the colonel. He jumped on top to the parapet, shouting at the top of his voice, "Runner, runner, go tell those tanks to stop firing at once. At once, I say." By now the enemy fire had risen to a crescendo but, giving no thought to his own personal safety as he saw the tanks firing on his own men, he ran forward and furiously rained blows with his cane on the side of one of the tanks in an endeavour to attract their attention.

Although, what with the sounds of the engines and the firing in such an enclosed space, no one in the tank could hear him, they finally realized they were on the wrong trench and moved on, frightening the Jerries out of their wits and making them scuttle like frightened rabbits.

OVER THE TOP: HIGH WOOD, 15 SEPTEMBER 1916

Bert Steward

Zero hour, and my corporal made a little gesture at me, and we got out of the ditch and started to walk. I never saw him again.

Imagine us then rather like overladen porters going slow over a shockingly ploughed field in a man-made thunder storm. Hailstones of a lethal kind zipped past our heads. From behind us the bombardment from our own guns, which I had seen massed wheel to wheel, went on. To left and right men were moving forward in uneven lines. My plan was to walk alone and not get bunched up with others. I kept away from them. I soon found this easier. On each side some had disappeared. I saw only one tank – in a ditch with a broken track, like a dying hippopotamus, with shells bursting round it. I kept walking. I walked about half a mile. I reached the shelter of an embankment. With this solid mass between me and the enemy I felt safe.

The next moment was the luckiest of my life. I had walked all the way through a hail of bullets. I had been a slowly-moving target for the machine guns. The bullets had all missed, though narrowly, for parts of my tunic were in ribbons. Then, just as I had reached safety, as I thought, what seemed like a hammer blow hit me on the top of my left shoulder. I opened my tunic. There was a clean round hole right through the shoulder. A bullet! But where from? Then I realised I was getting enfiladed by some machine-gunner to my right, on my side of the embankment. I threw myself down, but not before another bullet struck my right thigh.

In the embankment was the entrance to a dugout. I crawled into it. It was occupied by Germans. None of them spoke. They were all dead.

There was parcels from home strewn about, cigarettes, black bread, eatables, and one huge German, lying face downwards, made a good couch to sit on. Now I was joined by two friends, one less lucky, a young lad from Liverpool, with a bullet through the stomach.

Here we were, in front of our front line. About a hundred yards back I could see tin hats bobbing about. The remnants of the cast-irons were manning an improvised front line among the shellholes. Beyond them. I thought, was England, home and beauty.

I had taken High Wood, almost by myself, it seemed. I had no further territorial ambitions. Indeed, what I now had in mind was to go as quickly as possible in the opposite direction, as soon as possible. Leaving the dugout, I ran for it, zigzagging to escape bullets (two were enough) and so fast that I toppled head-first on top of a rifleman who was almost as scared as I was. After he had recovered he told me how I could work my way along the line of shellholes to a dressing station. I went, keeping my head down; I was taking no chances. I had two bullet holes. If they had been drilled by a surgeon they could not have been located more conveniently. I was incredibly lucky. But another might spoil everything. I crawled along.

The dressing station was a captured German underground hospital, with entrance big enough for an ambulance, built like a fortress, furnished with tiers of wooden bunks. It was crowded with wounded, now being sorted out by our adjutant.

"Those who can run follow me, nobody with a leg wound," he said. "We have to move fast," I was the first to follow. In and out of shellholes we went – a rough but rapid journey in the right direction – until we reached a sunken lane where a horse-drawn hooded cart waited to take a dozen of us an hour's trot nearer home . . .

The Canadian doctor looked like any other in his white coat. He turned out to be a saint. "You've been very lucky," he said in a kindly way. Then he explained that one bullet, almost incredibly, had found a narrow gap between collar-bone and shoulder-blade, and that neither of the two had touched muscle or bone. "How old are you and how long have you been in the trenches?" he asked and, when I told him, he wrote on a card and gave it to the nurse.

Later I looked up at the card pinned to the chart above my bed. It was marked with a big B. What did it mean? A nurse hurrying by answered my question. She smiled as she said – "It means Blighty."

A FIRING SQUAD AT DAWN, WESTERN FRONT, 1917

Brig.-Gen. F. P. Crozier

During the 1914–18 war 307 British soldiers were executed for offences – mainly desertion – against the Army Act.

Now, in peace-time, I and the rest of us would have been very upset indeed at having to shoot a colleague, comrade, call him what you will, at dawn on the morrow. We would not, in ordinary circumstances, have slept. Now the men don't like it, but they have to put up with it. They face their ordeal magnificently. I supervise the preliminary arrangements myself. We put the prisoner in a comfortable warm place. A few yards away we drive in a post, in a back garden, such as exists with any villa residence. I send for a certain junior officer and show him all. "You will be in charge of the firing-party," I say; "the men will be cold, nervous and excited, they may miss their mark. You are to have your revolver ready loaded and cocked; if the medical officer tells you life is not extinct you are to walk up to the victim, place the muzzle of the revolver to his heart and press the trigger. Do you understand?" "Yes, sir," comes the quick reply. "Right," I add, "dine with me at my mess tonight." I want to keep this young fellow engaged under my own supervision until late at night, so as to minimize the chance of his flying to the bottle for support. As for Crocker, he leaves this earth, in so far as knowing anything of his surroundings is concerned, by midnight, for I arrange that enough spirituous liquor is left beside him to sink a ship. In the morning, at dawn, the snow being on the ground, the battalion forms up on the public road. Inside the little garden on the other side of the wall, not ten yards from the centre of the line, the victim is carried to the stake. He is far too drunk to walk. He is out of view save from myself, as I stand on a mound near the wall. As he is produced I see he is practically lifeless and quite unconscious. He has already been bound with ropes. There are hooks on the post; we always do things thoroughly in the Rifles. He is hooked on like dead meat in a butcher's shop. His eyes are bandaged – not that it really matters, for he is already blind. The men of the firing-party pick up their rifles, one of which is unloaded, on a given sign. On another sign they come to the "Present" and, on the lowering of a handkerchief by the officer,

they fire – a volley rings out – a nervous ragged volley it is true,
yet a volley. Before the fatal shots are fired I had called the
battalion to attention. There is a pause, I wait. I see the medical
officer examining the victim. He makes a sign, the subaltern
strides forward, a single shot rings out. Life is now extinct. We
march back to breakfast while the men of a certain company pay
the last tribute at the graveside of an unfortunate comrade. This
is war.

ENTRY INTO DAMASCUS, 1 OCTOBER 1918

T. E. Lawrence (Lawrence of Arabia)

Our war was ended – even though we slept that night in Kiswe, for
the Arabs told us the roads were dangerous, and we had no wish to
die stupidly in the dark at the gate of Damascus . . . I wanted to
sleep, for my work was coming on the morrow; but I could not.
Damascus was the climax of our two years' uncertainty, and my
mind was distracted by tags of all the ideas which had been used or
rejected in that time. Also Kiswe was stifling with the exhalations
of too many trees, too many plants, too many human beings: a
microcosm of the crowded world in front of us.

As the Germans left Damascus they fired the dumps and
ammunition stores, so that every few minutes we were jangled
by explosions, whose first shock set the sky white with flame. At
each such roar the earth seemed to shake; we would lift our eyes to
the north and see the pale sky prick out suddenly in sheaves of
yellow points, as the shells thrown to terrific heights from each
bursting magazine, in their turn burst like clustered rockets. I
turned to Stirling and muttered "Damascus is burning," sick to
think of the great town in ashes as the price of freedom.

When dawn came we drove to the head of the ridge, which stood
over the oasis of the city, afraid to look north for the ruins we
expected: but, instead of ruins, the silent gardens stood blurred
green with river mist, in whose setting shimmered the city,
beautiful as ever, like a pearl in the morning sun. The uproar
of the night had shrunk to a stiff tall column of smoke, which rose in
sullen blackness from the store-yard by Kadem, terminus of the
Hejaz line.

We drove down the straight banked road through the watered
fields, in which the peasants were just beginning their day's work.

A galloping horseman checked at our head-cloths in the car, with a merry salutation, holding out a bunch of yellow grapes. "Good news! Damascus salutes you." He came from Shukri.

Nasir was just beyond us: to him we carried the tidings, that he might have the honourable entry, a privilege of his fifty battles. With Nuri Shaalan beside him, he asked a final gallop from his horse, and vanished down the long road in a cloud of dust, which hung reluctantly in the air between the water splashes. To give him a fair start, Stirling and I found a little stream, cool in the depths of a deep channel. By it we stopped to wash and shave.

Some Indian troopers peered at us and our car and its ragged driver's army shorts and tunic. I was in pure Arab dress; Stirling but for his head covering, was all British staff officer. Their N.C.O., an obtuse and bad-tempered person, thought he had taken prisoners. When delivered from his arrest we judged we might go after Nazir.

Quite quietly we drove up the long street to the Government buildings on the bank of the Barada. The way was packed with people, lined solid on the side-walks, in the road, at the windows and on the balconies or house-tops. Many were crying, a few cheered faintly, some bolder ones cried our names: but mostly they looked and looked, joy shining in their eyes. A movement, like a long sigh from gate to heart of the city, marked our course . . .

When we came in there had been some miles of people greeting us: now there were thousands for every hundred of them. Every man, woman and child in this city of a quarter-million souls seemed in the streets, waiting only the spark of our appearance to ignite their spirits. Damascus went mad with joy. The men tossed up their tarbushes to cheer, the women tore off their veils. Householders threw flowers, hangings, carpets, into the road before us: their wives leaned, screaming with laughter, through the lattices and splashed us with bath-dippers of scent.

ARMISTICE DAY IN LONDON, 11 NOVEMBER 1918

Winston Churchill

It was a few minutes before the eleventh hour of the eleventh day of the eleventh month. I stood at the window of my room looking up

Northumberland Avenue towards Trafalgar Square, waiting for Big Ben to tell that the War was over. My mind strayed back across the scarring years . . .

The minutes passed. I was conscious of reaction rather than elation . . . And then suddenly the first stroke of the chime. I looked again at the broad street beneath me. It was deserted. From the portals of one of the large hotels absorbed by Government Departments darted the slight figure of a girl clerk, distractedly gesticulating while another stroke of Big Ben resounded. Then from all sides men and women came scurrying into the street. Streams of people poured out of all the buildings. The bells of London began to clash. Northumberland Avenue was now so crowded with people in hundreds, nay, thousands, rushing hither and thither in a frantic manner, shouting and screaming with joy. I could see that Trafalgar Square was already swarming. Around me in our very headquarters, in the Hotel Metropole, disorder had broken out. Doors banged. Feet clattered down corridors. Everyone rose from the desk and cast aside pen and paper. All bounds were broken. The tumult grew. It grew like a gale, but from all sides simultaneously. The street was now a seething mass of humanity. Flags appeared as if by magic. Streams of men and women flowed from the Embankment. They mingled with torrents pouring down the Strand on their way to acclaim the King. Almost before the last stroke of the clock had died away, the strict, war-straitened, regulated streets of London had become a triumphant pandemonium.

THE SIGNING OF THE TREATY OF VERSAILLES, 28 JUNE 1919

Harold Nicolson

After the capitulation of Germany on 11 November 1918 she was required by the victorious Allies to sign a punitive peace treaty. The signing took place in the Hall of Mirrors at Versailles Palace – the Hall which had witnessed the humiliation of France and the proclamation of the German Empire in 1871.

La journée de Versailles. Lunch early and leave the Majestic in a car with Headlam Morley. He is a historian, yet he dislikes historical occasions. Apart from that he is a sensitive person and does not rejoice in seeing great nations humbled. I, having none of such acquirements or decencies, am just excited.

There is no crowd at all until we reach Ville d'Avray. But there are poilus at every crossroad waving red flags and stopping all other traffic. When we reach Versailles the crowd thickens. The avenue up to the Château is lined with cavalry in steel-blue helmets. The pennants of their lances flutter red and white in the sun. In the Cour d'Honneur, from which the captured German cannon have tactfully been removed, are further troops. There are Generals, Pétain, Gouraud, Mangin. There are St Cyriens. Very military and orderly. Headlam Morley and I creep out of our car hurriedly. Feeling civilian and grubby. And wholly unimportant. We hurry through the door.

Magnificent upon the staircase stand the Gardes Républicains – two caryatides on every step – their sabres at the salute. This is a great ordeal, but there are other people climbing the stairs with us. Headlam and I have an eye-meet. His thin cigaretted fingers make a gesture of dismissal. He is not a militarist.

We enter the two anterooms, our feet softening on to the thickest of savonnerie carpets. They have ransacked the Garde Meubles for their finest pieces. Never, since the Grand Siècle, has Versailles been more ostentatious or more embossed . . .

We enter the Galerie des Glaces. It is divided into three sections. At the far end are the Press already thickly installed. In the middle there is a horseshoe table for the plenipotentiaries. In front of that, like a guillotine, is the table for the signatures. It is supposed to be raised on a dais but, if so, the dais can be but a few inches high. In the nearer distance are rows and rows of tabourets for the distinguished guests, the deputies, the senators and the members of the delegations. There must be seats for over 1,000 persons. This robs the ceremony of all privilege and therefore of all dignity. It is like the Aeolian Hall.

Clemenceau is already seated under the heavy ceiling as we arrive. "Le roi", runs the scroll above him, "gouverne par lui-meme." He looks small and yellow. A crunched homunculus.

Conversation clatters out among the mixed groups around us, it is, as always on such occasions, like water running into a tin bath. I have never been able to get other people to recognize that similarity. There was a tin bath in my house at Wellington: one turned it on when one had finished and ran upstairs shouting "Baath ready" to one's successor: "Right ho!" he would answer: and then would come the sound of water pouring into the tin bath below, while he hurried into his dressing-gown. It is exactly the sound of people talking in undertones in a closed room. But it is not an analogy which I can get others to accept.

People step over the Aubusson benches and escabeaux to talk to friends. Meanwhile the delegates arrive in little bunches and push up the central aisle slowly. (Woodrow) Wilson and Lloyd George are among the last. They take their seats at the central table. The table is at last full. Clemenceau glances to right and left. People sit down upon their escabeaux but continue chattering. Clemenceau makes a sign to the ushers. They say "Ssh! Ssh! Ssh!" People cease chattering and there is only the sound of occasional coughing and the dry rustle of programmes. The officials of the Protocol of the Foreign Office move up the aisle and say, "Ssh! Ssh!" again. There is then an absolute hush, followed by a sharp military order. The Gardes Républicains at the doorway flash their swords into their scabbards with a loud click. "Faîtes entrer les Allemands," says Clemenceau in the ensuing silence. His voice is distant but harshly penetrating. A hush follows.

Through the door at the end appear two huissiers with silver chains. They march in single file. After them come four officers of France, Great Britain, America and Italy. And then, isolated and pitiable, come the two German delegates Dr Müller, Dr Bell. The silence is terrifying. Their feet upon a strip of parquet between the savonnerie carpets echo hollow and duplicate. They keep their eyes fixed away from those 2,000 staring eyes, fixed upon the ceiling. They are deathly pale. They do not appear as representatives of a brutal militarism. The one is thin and pink-eyelidded: the second fiddle in a Brunswick orchestra. The other is moon-faced and suffering: a privat-dozent. It is all most painful.

They are conducted to their chairs. Clemenceau at once breaks the silence. "Messieurs," he rasps, "la sèance est levée." He adds a few ill-chosen words. "We are here to sign a Treaty of Peace." The Germans leap up anxiously when he has finished, since they know that they are the first to sign. William Martin, as if a theatre manager, motions them petulantly to sit down again. Mantoux translates Clemenceau's words into English. Then St Quentin advances towards the Germans and with the utmost dignity leads them to the little table on which the Treaty is expanded. There is general tension. They sign. There is a general relaxation. Conversation hums again in an undertone. The delegates stand up one by one and pass onwards to the queue which waits by the signature table. Meanwhile people buzz round the main table getting autographs. The single file of plenipotentiaries waiting to approach the table gets thicker. It goes quickly. The officials of the Quai d'Orsay stand round, indicating places to sign, indicating procedure, blotting with neat little pads.

Suddenly from outside comes the crash of guns thundering a salute. It announces to Paris that the second Treaty of Versailles has been signed by Dr Müller and Dr Bell. Through the few open windows comes the sound of distant crowds cheering hoarsely. And still the signature goes on.

We had been warned it might last three hours. Yet almost at once it seemed that the queue was getting thin. Only three, then two, and then one delegate remained to sign. His name had hardly been blotted before the huissiers began again their "Ssh! Ssh!" cutting suddenly short the wide murmur which had again begun. There was a final hush. "La séance est levée," rasped Clemenceau. Not a word more or less.

We kept our seats while the Germans were conducted like prisoners from the dock, their eyes still fixed upon some distant point of the horizon.

THE PUBLICATION OF *ULYSSES*, FEBRUARY 1922

James Joyce

James Joyce conceived the idea for his novel – now regarded by many as the greatest of the century – in 1906, but it was not until 1921 that he wrote the final word, battling desperately against poverty and failing eyesight. But this was not the end of the struggle. Episodes from *Ulysses* published in the United States had been confiscated on grounds of obscenity, and publication both there and in Britain was out of the question. Eventually, Sylvia Beach, who owned a bookshop in Paris, published a limited edition on 2 February 1922 (Joyce's fortieth birthday) – after the book had been reset six times, Joyce having almost entirely rewritten it in proof. It was not published in Britain until 1936.

Rue de l'Université 9, Paris VII
Dear Miss Weaver: Many thanks for your kind telegram. Two copies of *Ulysses* (nos. 901 and 902) reached Paris on 2 February and two further copies (nos. 251 and 252) on 5 February. One copy is on show, the other three were taken by subscribers who were leaving for different parts of the world. Since the announce-

ment that the book was out the shop has been in a state of siege – buyers driving up two or three times a day and no copies to give them. After a great deal of telegraphing and telephoning it seems that 7 copies will come today and 30 tomorrow. A more nerve-racking conclusion to the history of the book could scarcely have been imagined! The first 10 copies of the *edition de luxe* will not be ready before Saturday so that you will not receive your copy (no. 1) before Tuesday of next week at the earliest. I am glad for my own sake (though hardly for yours) that you are advertising an English edition. I hope it will be possible in that event to correct the numerous misprints. [Ezra] Pound says it is . . .

Thanks also for the prompt return of the *Penelope* episode (the name of which by another strange coincidence is your own). It did not arrive too late. Your description of it also coincides with my intention – if the epithet "posthuman" were added. I have rejected the usual interpretation of her as a human apparition – that aspect being better represented by Calypso, Nausikaa and Circe, to say nothing of the pseudo Homeric figures. In conception and technique I tried to depict the earth which is prehuman and presumably posthuman.

With kindest regards

yours very sincerely and to the end importunately.

TUTANKHAMEN'S TOMB IS OPENED, LUXOR, EGYPT, 16 FEBRUARY 1923

The Times

Tutankhamen was born in about 1360 BC and succeeded to the Egyptian throne at the age of twelve. He died six years later.

This has been perhaps the most extraordinary day in the whole history of Egyptian excavation. Whatever anyone may have guessed or imagined of the secret of Tutankhamen's tomb, they surely cannot have dreamed the truth as now revealed. Entrance to-day was made into the sealed chamber, and yet another door opened beyond that. No eyes have yet seen the King, but to a practical certainty we now know that he lies there, close at hand, in all his original state, undisturbed.

Moreover, in addition to the great store of treasures which the tomb has already yielded, to-day has brought to light a new wealth of objects of artistic, historical, and even intrinsic value, which is bewildering. It is such a hoard as the most sanguine excavator can hardly have pictured even in visions in his sleep, and puts Lord Carnarvon's and Mr Carter's discovery in a class by itself above all previous finds.

Though the official opening of the sealed chamber had been fixed for Sunday it was obviously impossible to postpone until then the actual work of breaking in the entrance. This was a job involving some hours of work, because it had to be done with the greatest care, so as to keep intact as many of the seals as possible, and also to avoid injury to any of the objects on the other side which might be caused by the falling of the material dislodged. All this could not be done on Sunday while the official guests were kept waiting in the singularly unpleasant atmosphere of the tomb.

So an agreement was made with the Egyptian Government authorities by which the actual breaking through of the wall should be done in their presence to-day. Consequently, Mr Carter was very busy inside the tomb all the morning with Professor Breasted and Dr Alan Gardiner, whose assistance has been invaluable from the beginning in the work of examining the seals and deciphering and copying inscriptions of all kinds. They had finished by noon, and the tomb was closed till after lunch, at which Lord Carnarvon, Mr Carter and Lady Evelyn Herbert entertained all those invited to be present to-day.

It was after one o'clock when the official party entered the tomb and the operation was begun which was to result in such astounding discoveries. Of what followed I am able to give the following authoritative description.

To-day, between the hours of one and three in the afternoon, the culminating moment in the discovery of Tutankhamen's tomb took place, when Lord Carnarvon and Mr Howard Carter opened the inner sealed doorway in the presence of Lady Evelyn Herbert, Abdel Hamid Suliman Pasha, Under-Secretary of Public Works, M. Pierre Lacau, Director-General of the Antiquities Department, Sir William Garstin, Sir Charles Cust, Mr Lythgoe, Curator of the Metropolitan Museum of Art, New York, Mr Winlock, Director of the Egyptian Expedition of the Metropolitan Museum, Professor Breasted, Dr Alan Gardiner, Messrs Alfred Lucas, Arthur C. Mace, Harry Burton, and R. Callander, the Hon. R. Bethell, and the inspectors of the Museum Department, together with other representative of the Government.

The process of opening this doorway bearing the royal insignia and guarded by protective statues of the King had taken several hours of careful manipulation under intense heat. It finally ended in a wonderful revelation, for before the spectators was the resplendent mausoleum of the King, a spacious, beautiful, decorated chamber, completely occupied by an immense shrine covered with gold inlaid with brilliant blue faïence.

This beautiful wooden construction towers nearly to the ceiling and fills the great sepulchral hall within a short span of its four walls. Its sides are adorned with magnificent religious texts and fearful symbols of the dead, and it is capped with a superb cornice and torus moulding like the propylaea of a temple; in fact, indeed a sacred monument. On the eastern end of this shrine are two immense folding doors closed and bolted.

Within it is yet another shrine, closed and sealed, and bearing the cipher of the royal necropolis. On this inner shrine hangs a funerary pall studded with gold, and by the evidence of the papyrus of Rameses IV there must be a series of these shrines within, covering the remains of the King lying in the sarcophagus. Around the outer canopy on the shrine stand great protective emblems of mystic type, finely carved and gilt, and upon the floor lie the seven oars for the King's use in the waters of the Elysian Fields.

In the farther end of the eastern wall of this sepulchral hall is yet another doorway, open and never closed. It leads to another chamber – the store chamber of the sepulchre. There at the end stands an elaborate and magnificently carved and gilded shrine of indescribable beauty. It is surmounted by tiers of "uraei" (Royal serpents), and its sides are protected by open-armed goddesses of finest workmanship, their pitiful faces turned over their shoulders towards the invader. This is no less than the receptacle for the four canopic jars which should contain the viscera of the King.

Immediately at the entrance to this chamber stands the jackal Anubis, black and gold upon his shrine, which again rests upon a portable sled – strange and resplendent. Behind this, again, is the head of a bull, an emblem of the underworld. Stacked on the south side of the chamber in great numbers are black boxes and shrines of all shapes, all closed and sealed, save one with open doors, in which golden effigies of the King stand upon black leopards.

Similarly at the end of the chamber are more of these cases, including miniature coffins, sealed, but no doubt containing funerary statuettes of the monarch – the servants for the dead in the coming world. On the south side of the deity Anubis is a tier of wonderful ivory and wooden boxes, of every shape and design, studded with

gold and inlaid with faïence, and beside them yet another chariot.
This sight is stupendous, and its magnificence indescribable.

And as the time was fast creeping on and dusk falling in, the
tomb was closed for further action and contemplation.

THE GENERAL STRIKE, MAY 1926

Hugh Gaitskell

The General Strike (4–12 May) was called by the Trades Union Congress
in support of the mineworkers, who had been "locked out" by the
employers as a means of forcing a cut in wages. In the first days of the
General Strike the country came to a standstill, but the TUC had little
real stomach for a constitutional conflict with the government and quickly
backed down. The effectiveness of the strike had also been undermined by
troops and volunteers, especially students, running an emergency transport and supply service.

Gaitskell, an Oxford undergraduate, was unusual in supporting the
strikers. He later became leader of the Labour Party.

. . . For me, as I think for many others, the impact of the Strike
was sharp and sudden, a little like a war, in that everybody's lives
were suddenly affected by a new unprecedented situation, which
forced us to abandon plans for pleasure, to change our values and
adjust our priorities.

Above all we had to make a choice. And how we chose was a
clear test of our political outlook.

The vast majority of undergraduates went off to unload ships
and drive trams or lorries. For me this was out of the question. All
my sympathies were instinctively on the side of the miners, the
unions, the Labour Party, and the Left generally. It was their
cause I wanted to help.

But how to help? Someone . . . must have told me about the
Coles. Anyway I went to their house in Holywell where they had
set up a University Strike Committee which was working with the
Official Oxford City Trade Union Committee and also providing a
kind of unofficial employment exchange for those undergraduates
who wanted to do something to help the strikers.

What could I do? Precious little. Speak at meetings? God forbid!
Organise? Absolutely no experience. Had I got a car? No. Could I
by any chance drive a car? Yes, I had learnt the year before. Then
perhaps I could drive John Dugdale's. I knew him personally; he

was a pupil of Douglas Cole's; but as he was taking his "schools" in a few weeks he could not spare much time. John agreed to let me drive his snub-nosed Morris when he himself was not available. So with this plan and the sponsorship of the Coles, I went off to the Oxford Strike Committee Headquarters, got myself enrolled as a driver and received my instructions. When available I was to take speakers to meetings in the Oxford area. But my main job was to act as driver to Margaret Cole who was the liasion officer between the Oxford Committee and the T.U.C. in London, and to bring back our copies of the *British Worker*, the strike broadsheet, printed on the *Daily Herald* presses. I was then given a Union Card (Printers and Paper-makers), fully paid up, to get me through the pickets and crowds in Fleet Street.

Margaret and I must have driven to London and back three or four times during those ten days. A few incidents stand out clearly in my memory. The car stopping on Huntercombe Hill with the radiator boiling; waiting in Eccleston Square while Margaret was in the T.U.C. offices and hearing an old gentleman mutter as he passed "what a crowd" and add, as he realised where he was, "what a crew!"; giving Will Thorne a lift to the House of Commons and the difficulty of getting his vast bulk in and out of the little Morris; going with Margaret to see the Tawneys in Mecklenburgh Square and being surprised to find the famous socialist wearing his old sergeant's jacket from the first World War; trying vainly to climb into college one night when we arrived back after 12 (later I was to find an easier way) and being in consequence fined £1 despite a fierce verbal protest to the Warden of the College – H. A. L. Fisher – that he was shockingly biased against the strikers and those who were helping them. . . .

After the collapse of the Strike, there followed the long-drawn-out agony of the miners' lock-out. We collected money for them and argued hotly with the more conventional about the merits of striking and the whole system. . . .

I WATCH TELEVISION, LONDON, 1 AUGUST 1928

Sydney Moseley

Diary

. . . I met a pale young man named Bartlett who is Secretary to the new Baird Television Company. *Television!* Anxious to see what it is all about . . . He invited me to go along to Long Acre where the new invention is installed. Now *that's* something! Television!

Met John Logie Baird; a charming man – a shy, quietly spoken Scot. He could serve as a model for the schoolboy's picture of a shock-haired, modest, dreamy, absent-minded inventor. Nevertheless shrewd. We sat and chatted. He told me he is having a bad time with the scoffers and sceptics – including the BBC and part of the technical press – who are trying to ridicule and kill his invention of television at its inception. I told him that if he would let me see what he has actually achieved – well, he would have to risk my damning it – or praising it! If I *were* convinced – I would battle for him. We got on well together and I have arranged to test his remarkable claim.

(Later) Saw television! Baird's partner, a tall, good-looking but highly temperamental Irishman, Captain Oliver George Hutchinson, was nice but very nervous of chancing it with me. He was terribly anxious that I should be impressed. Liked the pair of them, especially Baird, and decided to give my support . . . I think we really have what is called television. And so, once more into the fray!

SIR MALCOLM CAMPBELL BREAKS THE LAND SPEED RECORD, DAYTONA BEACH, 22 FEBRUARY 1933

Daily Express reporter

Campbell's average speed in *Bluebird* was 273 mph.

The beach was full of mist at first and he could not take the car out. Then the mist rose, and there was visibility for a few hundred yards.

The officials suggested that Campbell should give (only) an exhibition run.

But he refused to disappoint the thousands who had come to Daytona for a public holiday – today being Washington's birthday.

Nor was he deterred by the fact that today was the anniversary of the death of an American speed king while racing on these very sands.

Campbell's start had been delayed for three weeks by his own attack of influenza – with a temperature of 102 – and by the weather. And his achievement today was all the greater in that the course had been shortened from eleven miles to nine. It takes some miles to get up speed before passing over the electrical timing wires.

Thousands of people held their breath as the great car – a mere blur – flashed out of the mist half a mile away, zipped past and then was lost in the mist again.

At the end of the first run Campbell, with white overalls over his plus fours, stepped out of the car into a madly cheering throng of American mechanics.

He had a look round, changed tyres, and in half an hour sped off on the return trip.

At the end of the second trip, with the record definitely smashed, he lit a cigarette, examined the canvas stitching through his torn tyres and described his experiences.

Then it was seen that heavy bandaging covered his crippled arm.

"It was terrifying," he said. "I lost all sense of direction. Several times I thought I was heading for the sea on one side or the sand hills on the other. I was bounced around like a pea in a pod.

"It takes a lot to frighten me, but if I did not believe in Bluebird with all my heart I would never have faced that return run. Wobbling at 270 miles an hour is not too pleasant.

"I had to keep for safety to a strip 40 yards wide. That's very little when you're travelling at 146 yards a second. I'd find myself shooting out of some mist heading heaven knows where."

THE GRESFORD COLLIERY DISASTER, WREXHAM, 22 SEPTEMBER 1934

H. R. S. Phillpott

Some 260 miners were killed in the explosion at Gresford.

At regular intervals a bell clangs out dully three times and a hush, already unbearable, seems to become deeper still.

It is like the dreadful repetition of a funeral toll, and it has been going on for seemingly endless hours through the daylight and the darkness.

It is merely the signal that a cage is bringing up a rescue party for rest and food, but it gruesomely completes the knowledge that one is standing at the scene of a vast and terrible burial.

For two days and a night the one, two, three of the bell has been almost the only sound to break into a long and loaded silence.

Occasionally there is the low murmur of voices or the purring of the engine and a motor-ambulance. For the rest the silence continues.

The crowds stand hour after hour motionless, thinking neither of rest nor food waiting, watching, and now hardly hoping.

There is no weeping, no fainting, no audible demonstration of the grief that has cruelly covered a whole community.

The people stand staring straight ahead, seeming to see nothing, but with a look of inexpressible hurt in their dry eyes – a dreadful look that makes one turn away and long never to see such a thing again.

I moved quietly about among them yesterday far into a bitterly cold night, and again to-day.

They told me heartbreaking little stories of why they were there, and their halting, simple sentences etched out and affrighted a picture of the smashed homes in which the echoes of the pit-head bell are being heard.

There was one little group I shall never forget – a group of three, two old men and a boy.

One was John Capper, of Pentre Broughton, a nearby village. He has given his own lifetime to the mine and now his son has given his life.

The old cloth-capped father had to cease work eighteen months ago because of nystagmus. He has tell-tale blue marks on his forehead and around his eyes.

He just looked vacantly ahead, his old eyes fixed on the winding gear, the twitching corners of his mouth giving the only sign of his suffering. This was at midnight.

"Waiting all day," he said. "My son is down there."

That was all, and so he continues his vigil, standing straight as a rod and still staring in that dreadful way at the winding gear.

By his side was a 14½-year-old boy, George Peters, of the neighbouring village of Llay. He told me he is one of a family of nine.

I asked him why he was among the watchers. "My father is down there," he said, and then broke down, making not a sound, but the tears streamed down his face. Young George himself works in another pit. On the other side of him was a little man in a bowler hat. "My son is down there," he said.

That is how they phrase it – "down there".

So I left them waiting there in the cold and the darkness – two old men thinking of their sons, and one young boy thinking of his father.

Before I tell you about the other watchers let me try to picture to you the surface scene.

The Gresford Colliery lies two or three miles outside Wrexham, just over a hedge from the main Chester Road. Smoke flows lazily from the top of a towering chimney stack, red brick buildings cluster round the pit-head.

The winding gear traces its familiar pattern on the sky.

The ambulance station is peopled with the nurses ready for anything – but as yet called on only to receive members of rescue gangs as they come to the surface.

Packed round a black yard are fleets of ambulances, which, like the watchers, just wait.

There are doctors, first aid men and ministers of religion all waiting.

That is the tragedy of it. There is nothing they can do but wait, because the men they are waiting for are still "down there".

The only men who can do anything, and they are working with noble heroism, are the rescue gangs.

They come from miles around. Many of them dashed off on their own account as soon as they heard of the disaster; others have been brought in organized gangs by neighbouring mine managers and other officials.

The rescue men are specially picked. Only half a dozen of them can go "down there" at a time. They wear respirators and are at the foremost point of danger.

They are the fire fighters, and I have talked with them before they had gone down and after they had come up.

To speak with one of them for even a moment or two is both an inspiration and a humiliation.

They do not realize they are doing anything remarkable, they put on their respirators, take their lamp and, wearing a pair of shorts, just go "down there".

They have to go two miles or more before they reach the scene of the fire.

Strung out behind them is a long line of volunteers passing up fire extinguishers and bags of sand, and taking back the empties from hand to hand, backwards and forwards along a great heroic human chain.

The work of rescue thus goes on, and when the respirators are nearing exhaustion the rescue men come up again, run across the yard to preserve their sweating bodies from chill, and into a room where a fire is burning, clothes await them and hot drinks and food are ready.

Two of the first rush rescue parties were killed on Saturday morning, and another is still missing.

There is much wonderment here about why or how this should have been, but here is the story told by Price Beard, a member of the rescue team:

"Five of us went down," he said, "we had gone only about 200 yards off the main road, which is about a mile long, when we were faced with flames and fumes.

"In spite of our masks we began to choke. Dan Hughes, of Llay, and Ben Hughes, of Bradley, fell, and the rest of us were powerless to help them out.

"Captain Jack Williams went over, but I managed to pull him away. Later he was taken to hospital. Jack Lewis is still 'down there'."

Come back, like Price Beard, to the surface, and over there in a small building you will find a team of experts preparing and testing respirators.

They are working with the utmost precision and care for they know that the lives of the rescue men depend on what they are doing.

I asked one of them why rescue men had lost their lives.

"We weren't near them," he said, "I can't say anything."

I asked him if he had any idea. "Maybe I have," he said, "but I am keeping them to myself," and his friends carried on, testing and adjusting the stock of respirators.

The volunteer gangs going down to help them still contain scores of men who escaped from the pit at two o'clock on Saturday morning.

They have had little spells of rest, but back they come, insisting that they shall go again to meet the inferno they so narrowly missed.

Many of them are only sixteen or seventeen years old.

They will tell you little, not because they do not want to, but because they do not realize that they are doing anything heroic or dramatic.

Take two of them as examples. Both were as black as soot, when they came up. One of them told me he was only a volunteer. "Passing the stuff to the rescue teams," he said.

He did not get within a mile of the fire and he thought he had done nothing.

I found that his idea of doing nothing was that he was working while falls of coal were taking place round him, and props were bending and breaking.

The rescue team man was scorched and exhausted. He had been within a few yards of the wall of flame and had stayed the official time limit for his respirator.

All he had to say was that he was going down again presently.

Here are some of the stories of men who escaped alive.

One young man was flung by the explosion several feet along one of the pit roads, landing near an air shaft.

He and his companions were trapped by the tremendous fall on either side, and he knew that the only hope of escape was through the narrow air-shaft.

Vainly he tried to persuade his mates to make the attempt to climb the shaft with him, but they refused, as they feared they would become jammed in the shaft.

Alone he scrambled and climbed inch by inch up the shaft, which was barely wide enough to admit his body.

Finally, after nearly an hour's climb, he succeeded in reaching the top of the shaft and jumped to safety.

The shaft through which he made his perilous climb was about 200 feet high and just over 2 feet wide.

Cyril Challinor, aged twenty-one, of Windsor Road, New Broughton, one of the first to be brought out alive, said:

"There were about six of us, about 300 yards from the clutch, laughing and talking. Suddenly there was a gust of wind.

"An elderly fellow came running up and said: 'You had better get your clothes on and get out of here.'

"About twenty other fellows joined us, and we started making our way to the pit bottom.

"We got to the end of the wind road and then we began to meet gas. All of us fanned hard with our shirts. The gas was getting in our eyes, but we had to face it.

"We took turns in leading so that everyone would have the same risk.

"We now began to meet falls, and we had to scramble over them. I thought the twenty fellows who joined us were following us. I looked round, but could not see them. I do not know what happened to them.

"The gas was getting thicker and choking us, but we kept on fanning, and we got through to the pit bottom, where we met the rescue party."

THE BATTLE OF CABLE STREET, LONDON, 7 OCTOBER 1936

Phil Piratin

Following Mussolini's lead, Sir Oswald Mosley had founded the British Union of Fascists which advocated the abolition of free speech, greater interest in the Commonwealth, and anti-Semitism.

It was obvious that the Fascists and the police would now turn their attention to Cable Street. We were ready. The moment this became apparent the signal was given to put up the barricades. We had prepared three spots. The first was near a yard where there was all kinds of timber and other oddments, and also an old lorry. An arrangement had been made with the owner that this old lorry could be used as a barricade. Instructions had been given about this, but when someone shouted "Get the lorry!" evidently not explaining that it was in the nearby yard, some of the lads, looking up the street, saw a stationary lorry about 200 yards away. They went along, brought it back, and pushed it over on its side before anyone even discovered that it was not the lorry meant to be used. Still it was a lorry, and supplemented by bits of old furniture, mattresses, and every kind of thing you expect to find in box-rooms, it was a barricade which the police did not find it easy to penetrate. As they charged they were met with milk bottles, stones, and marbles. Some of the housewives began to drop milk bottles from the roof tops. A number of police surrendered. This had never happened before, so the lads didn't know what to do, but they took away their batons, and one took a helmet for his son as a souvenir.

Cable Street was a great scene. I have referred to "the lads". Never was there such unity of all sections of the working class as was seen on the barricades at Cable Street. People whose lives were poles apart, though living within a few hundred yards of each other; bearded Orthodox Jews and rough-and-ready Irish Catholic dockers – these were the workers that the Fascists were trying to stir up against each other. The struggle, led by the Communist Party, against the Fascists had brought them together against their common enemies, and their lackeys.

Meanwhile, charges and counter-charges were taking place along "the front" from Tower Hill to Gardner's Corner. Many arrests were made, many were injured. It was the police, however, who were carrying on the battle, while the Fascists lurked in the background, protected by a "fence" of police. Mosley was late. As soon as he arrived, in a motor-car, a brick went clean through the window.

It was later rumoured that Sir Philip Game had been on the telephone to the Home Secretary, and had pleaded with Sir John Simon to forbid the march. Sir John was adamant. Sir Philip Game, however, made up his own mind. He forbade the march and told Mosley to argue it out with Sir John Simon. The Fascists lined up, saluted their leader, and marched through the deserted City to the Embankment, where they dispersed. The working class had won the day.

THE JARROW MARCH, OCTOBER 1936

Roy Chadwick

The march from Jarrow to London was undertaken as a protest against unemployment on Tyneside. Chadwick was a journalist with the *Manchester Guardian*.

Harrogate welcomed the Jarrow marchers to-day as cheerfully as if they were a relief column raising a siege. The music of the mouth-organ band might have been that of the bagpipes so surely did it bring the people flocking, and when the two hundred reached the Concert Rooms there were hundreds of folk drawn up on the slopes around to cheer them. The police were in attendance and there was a big banner raised saying, "Harrogate workers welcome the Jarrow marchers". At the Drill Hall, the headquarters for the night, the crowd was even denser.

It was the same to-day all along the road from Ripon. The villagers of Ripley and Killinghall rushed to their doors to see the marchers pass; motorists waved as they went by; one shouted, "How are you sticking it?" and a woman cried, "Hello, Geordies". And the "Geordies" themselves were in great form, so that every moment I expected the band to change from "Annie Laurie" and "Swanee River" to "Cheer, Boys, Cheer". Contributions to the "kitty" fell in as we went; here it was a pound and there it was a penny, the penny specifically being the offering of an ecstatic little girl who ran across the road to meet us as if no one less than Bonnie Prince Charlie was at our head.

There can be no doubt that as a gesture the march is a bounding success. I fell in with it this morning on the Ripon road. Under its two banners ("Jarrow Crusade"), with its harmonicas, its kettle-drum, and its four hundred feet, it was going strong. The marchers have with them two doctors, a barber, a group of pressmen, a Labrador dog mascot, and for a great deal of the time so far the Mayor of Jarrow (Alderman J.W. Thompson), who keeps travel-ling back to Jarrow to maintain touch with his civic duties and then south again to maintain touch with the marchers. It is an example of civic spirit probably without parallel anywhere else in the country. With him at the head of the procession is its marshal, County Councillor D. F. Riley, the inspirer and organizer of the march.

This is not a hunger-march, but a protest march. The unanimity of the protest that Jarrow is making to the rest of the country is indicated in the fact that the political parties represented on the Jarrow Town Council have agreed to bury the political hatchet to the extent of holding no elections this November. Further, although the town cannot by law spend a farthing of the rate-payers' money on this demonstration, the labours of its Mayor in dispatching about 200,000 letters to other corporations, trade unions, co-operative societies and similar bodies at the expense of the march fund has raised that fund to £850, and it is hoped to have the round £1,000 before the marchers reach the Marble Arch on 31 October.

The more fortunate classes of Jarrow, where not fifteen per cent of the employable population is at work, have contributed, but the bulk of the fund has come from the country at large, and more than money. I, for one, had no conception of the cost of organizing such a march until I heard about the value of the gifts in kind that ease the drain on the march fund so considerably. Take cigarettes, for instance, and calculate the cost of distributing two twopenny packets per day per man to 200 men. I will not vouch that "fags" are among the gifts, but it illustrates the point. Any little article costing sixpence means five pounds when distributed to 200 men, and soap, tobacco, and all sorts of things have been given. Before the men set out they all had their boots soled and heeled, and two pairs of socks and two iodine soles were also issued.

With eggs and salmon and such sandwiches as I saw to-day being consumed on the menu it is emphatically not a hunger-march. The men are doing well on it, and only two of them have fallen out for reasons of health in nearly ninety miles of marching. All the time communication is maintained with Jarrow, and if work turns up for a man on the march back he will go to it.

The organization seems well nigh perfect. It includes a transport wagon – a 'bus bought for £20 and converted – which goes ahead with the sleeping kit, waterproofs for every man worn bandolero fashion, 1s. 6d. pocket-money and two 1½d. stamps a week, medical attention, haircutting (and shaving for the inexpert), cobbling, accommodation at night in drill halls, schools, church institutes, and even town halls, and advance agents in the persons of the Labour agent at Jarrow, Mr Harry Stoddert, and the Conservative agent, Mr R. Suddick, who work together in arranging accommodation and getting halls for meetings.

There is no political aspect to this march. It is simply the town of Jarrow saying "Send us work". In the ranks of the marchers are Labour men, Liberals, Tories, and one or two Communists, but you cannot tell who's who. It has the Church's blessing; in fact, it took the blessing of the Bishop of Ripon (Dr Lunt) and a subscription of £5 from him when it set out to-day. It also had the blessing of the Bishop of Jarrow (Dr Gordon).

With the marchers goes, prominently carried, the Jarrow petition for work, a huge book with about 12,000 signatures, which, after a meeting at the Memorial Hall, London, the previous day, Miss Ellen Wilkinson, M.P. for Jarrow, is to present at the bar of the House of Commons on 4 November. Miss Wilkinson met us outside Killinghall this afternoon and became the only woman in the procession. She had motored from Manchester to-day but had met with petrol trouble and had been delayed. It was interesting to watch motorists who passed us on the road recognize her and lean out of windows as they went by. Like us all she made friends with Paddy, the Labrador dog who accompanied the procession uninvited for five miles from Jarrow before anyone realized that he intended to go all the way. When the marshal's whistle goes he goes too and there is no holding him.

It was interesting, too, to watch men employed on the road rest on their spades to watch men unemployed but also on the road go by. Their eyes spoke their thoughts. Most interesting was the meeting at lunch-time between some of these untravelled men and a real knight of the road who seemed to rejoice in his adventures and who on his way to Ripon told us on our way to Harrogate which were the best casual wards, how bugs make an eightpenny bed unbearable, and what are the duties of a "tramp major". One could write columns about it, but we are at Harrogate, and a meeting is to be held at the Winter Gardens with Miss Ellen Wilkinson as one of the speakers. At every stopping-place there is such a meeting so that the world shall know of Jarrow.

A BRITISH SOCIALIST IN THE SPANISH CIVIL WAR, JANUARY 1937

George Orwell

The writer George Orwell was one of several hundred leftist sympathisers from Britain who volunteered to fight for the Spanish Republic against Franco's fascists. Most joined the International Brigade, but Orwell joined the POUM, a Trotskyist militia.

Barbastro, though a long way from the front line, looked bleak and chipped. Swarms of militiamen in shabby uniforms wandered up and down the streets, trying to keep warm. On a ruinous wall I came upon a poster dating from the previous year and announcing that "six handsome bulls" would be killed in the arena on such and such a date. How forlorn its faded colours looked! Where were the handsome bulls and the handsome bull-fighters now? It appeared that even in Barcelona there were hardly any bullfights nowadays; for some reason all the best matadors were Fascists.

They sent my company by lorry to Sietamo, then westward to Alcubierre, which was just behind the line fronting Zaragoza. Sietamo had been fought over three times before the Anarchists finally took it in October, and parts of it were smashed to pieces by shell-fire and most of the houses pockmarked by rifle-bullets. We were 1500 feet above sea level now. It was beastly cold, with dense mists that came swirling up from nowhere. Between Sietamo and Alcubierre the lorry-driver lost his way (this was one of the regular features of the war) and we were wandering for hours in the mist. It was late at night when we reached Alcubierre. Somebody shepherded us through morasses of mud into a mule-stable where we dug ourselves down into the chaff and promptly fell asleep. Chaff is not bad to sleep in when it is clean, not so good as hay but better than straw. It was only in the morning light that I discovered that the chaff was full of breadcrusts, torn newspapers, bones, dead rats, and jagged milk tins.

We were near the front line now, near enough to smell the characteristic smell of war – in my experience a smell of excrement and decaying food. Alcubierre had never been shelled and was in a better state than most of the villages immediately behind the line. Yet I believe that even in peacetime you could not travel in that part of Spain without being struck by the peculiar squalid misery of the Aragonese villages. They are built like fortresses, a mass of mean little houses of mud and stone huddling round the church, and even in spring you see hardly a flower anywhere; the houses have no gardens, only back-yards where ragged fowls skate over the beds of mule-dung. It was vile weather, with alternate mist and rain. The narrow earth roads had been churned into a sea of mud, in places two feet deep, through which the lorries struggled with racing wheels and the peasants led their clumsy carts which were pulled by strings of mules, sometimes as many as six in a string, always pulling tandem. The constant come-and-go of troops had reduced the village to a state of unspeakable filth. It did not possess and never had possessed such a thing as a lavatory or a drain of any kind, and there was not a square yard anywhere where you could tread without watching your step. The church had long been used as a latrine; so had all the fields for a quarter of a mile round. I never think of my first two months at war without thinking of wintry stubble fields whose edges are crusted with dung.

Two days passed and no rifles were issued to us. When you had been to the Comité de Guerra and inspected the row of holes in the wall – holes made by rifle-volleys, various Fascists having been executed there – you had seen all the sights that Alcubierre contained. Up in the front line things were obviously quiet; very few wounded were coming in. The chief excitement was the arrival of Fascist deserters, who were brought under guard from the front line. Many of the troops opposite us on this part of the line were not Fascists at all, merely wretched conscripts who had been doing their military service at the time when war broke out and were only too anxious to escape. Occasionally small batches of them took the risk of slipping across to our lines. No doubt more would have done so if their relatives had not been in Fascist territory.

These deserters were the first "real" Fascists I had ever seen. It struck me that they were indistinguishable from ourselves, except that they wore khaki overalls. They were always ravenously hungry when they arrived – natural enough after a day or two of dodging about in no man's land, but it was always triumphantly pointed to as a proof that the Fascist troops were starving. I watched one of them being fed in a peasant's house. It was somehow rather a pitiful sight. A tall boy of twenty, deeply windburnt, with his clothes in rags, crouched over the fire shovelling a pannikinful of stew into himself at desperate speed; and all the while his eyes flitted nervously round the ring of militiamen who stood watching him. I think he still half-believed that we were bloodthirsty "Reds" and were going to shoot him as soon as he had finished his meal; the armed man who guarded him kept stroking his shoulder and making reassuring noises. On one memorable day fifteen deserters arrived in a single batch. They were led through the village in triumph with a man riding in front of them on a white horse. I managed to take a rather blurry photograph which was stolen from me later.

On our third morning in Alcubierre the rifles arrived. A sergeant with a coarse dark-yellow face was handing them out in the mule-stable. I got a shock of dismay when I saw the thing they gave me. It was a German Mauser dated 1896 – more than forty years old! It was rusty, the bolt was stiff, the wooden barrel-guard was split; one glance down the muzzle showed that it was corroded and past praying for. Most of the rifles were equally bad, some of them even worse, and no attempt was made to give the best weapons to the men who knew how to use them. The best rifle of the lot, only ten years old, was given to a half-witted little beast of fifteen, known to everyone as the *maricón* (Nancy-boy). The sergeant gave us five minutes' "instruction", which consisted in explaining how you loaded a rifle and how you took the bolt to pieces. Many of the militiamen had never had a gun in their hands before, and very few, I imagine, knew what the sights were for. Cartridges were handed out, fifty to a man, and then the ranks were formed and we strapped our kits on our backs and set out for the front line, about three miles away.

The *centuria*, eighty men and several dogs, wound raggedly up the road. Every militia column had at least one dog attached to it as a mascot. One wretched brute that marched with us had had P.O.U.M. branded on it in huge letters and slunk along as though conscious that there was something wrong with its appearance. At the head of the column, beside the red flag, Georges Kopp, the stout Belgian commandante, was riding a black horse; a little way ahead a youth from the brigand-like militia cavalry pranced to and fro, galloping up every piece of rising ground and posing himself in picturesque attitudes at the summit. The splendid horses of the Spanish cavalry had been captured in large numbers during the revolution and handed over to the militia, who, of course, were busy riding them to death.

The road wound between yellow infertile fields, untouched since last year's harvest. Ahead of us was the low sierra that lies between Alcubierre and Zaragoza. We were getting near the front line now, near the bombs, the machine-guns, and the mud. In secret I was frightened. I knew the line was quiet at present, but unlike most of the men about me I was old enough to remember the Great War, though not old enough to have fought in it. War, to me, meant roaring projectiles and skipping shards of steel; above all it meant mud, lice, hunger, and cold. It is curious, but I dreaded the cold much more than I dreaded the enemy. The thought of it had been haunting me all the time I was in Barcelona; I had even lain awake at nights thinking of the cold in the trenches, the stand-to's in the grisly dawns, the long hours on sentry-go with a frosted rifle, the icy mud that would slop over my boot-tops. I admit, too, that I felt a kind of horror as I looked at the people I was marching among. You cannot possibly conceive what a rabble we looked. We straggled along with far less cohesion than a flock of sheep; before we had gone two miles the rear of the column was out of sight. And quite half of the so-called men were children – but I mean literally children, of sixteen years old at the very most. Yet they were all happy and excited at the prospect of getting to the front at last. As we neared the line the boys round the red flag in front began to utter shouts of "Visca P.O.U.M.!" "Fascistas-maricones!" and so forth – shouts which were meant to be war-like and menacing, but which, from those childish throats, sounded as pathetic as the cries of kittens. It seemed dreadful that the defenders of the Republic should be this mob of ragged children carrying worn-out rifles which they did not know how to use. I remember wondering what would happen if a Fascist aeroplane passed our way – whether the airman would even bother to dive down and give us a burst from his machine-gun. Surely even from the air he could see that we were not real soldiers?

As the road struck into the sierra we branched off to the right and climbed a narrow mule-track that wound round the mountain-side. The hills in that part of Spain are of a queer formation, horseshoe-shaped with flattish tops and very steep sides running down into immense ravines. On the higher slopes nothing grows except stunted shrubs and heath, with the white bones of the limestone sticking out everywhere. The front line here was not a continuous line of trenches, which would have been impossible in such mountainous country; it was simply a chain of fortified posts, always known as "positions", perched on each hill-top. In the distance you could see our "position" at the crown of the horseshoe; a ragged barricade of sand-bags, a red flag fluttering, the smoke of dug-out fires. A little nearer, and you could smell a sickening sweetish stink that lived in my nostrils for weeks afterwards. Into the cleft immediately behind the position all the refuse of months had been tipped – a deep festering bed of breadcrusts, excrement, and rusty tins.

The company we were relieving were getting their kits together. They had been three months in the line; their uniforms were caked with mud, their boots falling to pieces, their faces mostly bearded. The captain commanding the position, Levinski by name, but known to everyone as Benjamin, and by birth a Polish Jew, but speaking French as his native language, crawled out of his dug-out and greeted us. He was a short youth of about twenty-five, with stiff black hair and a pale eager face which at this period of the war was always very dirty. A few stray bullets were cracking high overhead. The position was a semi-circular enclosure about fifty yards across, with a parapet that was partly sand-bags and partly lumps of limestone. There were thirty or forty dug-outs running into the ground like rat-holes. Williams, myself, and Williams's Spanish brother-in-law made a swift dive for the nearest unoccupied dug-out that looked habitable. Somewhere in front an occasional rifle banged, making queer rolling echoes among the stony hills. We had just dumped our kits and were crawling out of the dug-out when there was another bang and one of the children of our company rushed back from the parapet with his face pouring blood. He had fired his rifle and had somehow managed to blow out the bolt; his scalp was torn to ribbons by the splinters of the burst cartridge-case. It was our first casualty, and, characteristically, self-inflicted.

In the afternoon we did our first guard and Benjamin showed us round the position. In front of the parapet there ran a system of narrow trenches hewn out of the rock, with extremely primitive loopholes made of piles of limestone. There were twelve sentries, placed at various points in the trench and behind the inner parapet. In front of the trench was the barbed wire, and then the hillside slid down into a seemingly bottomless ravine; opposite were naked hills, in places mere cliffs of rock, all grey and wintry, with no life anywhere, not even a bird. I peered cautiously through a loophole, trying to find the Fascist trench.

"Where are the enemy?"

Benjamin waved his hand expansively. "Over zere." (Benjamin spoke English – terrible English.)

"But *where*?"

According to my ideas of trench warfare the Fascists would be fifty or a hundred yards away. I could see nothing – seemingly their trenches were very well concealed. Then with a shock of dismay I saw where Benjamin was pointing; on the opposite hill-top, beyond the ravine, seven hundred metres away at the very least, the tiny outline of a parapet and a red-and-yellow flag – the Fascist position. I was indescribably disappointed. We were no-where near them! At that range our rifles were completely useless. But at this moment there was a shout of excitement. Two Fascists, greyish figurines in the distance, were scrambling up the naked hill-side opposite. Benjamin grabbed the nearest man's rifle, took aim, and pulled the trigger. Click! A dud cartridge; I thought it a bad omen.

The new sentries were no sooner in the trench than they began firing a terrific fusillade at nothing in particular. I could see the Fascists, tiny as ants, dodging to and fro behind their parapet, and sometimes a black dot which was a head would pause for a moment, impudently exposed. It was obviously no use firing. But presently the sentry on my left, leaving his post in the typical Spanish fashion, sidled up to me and began urging me to fire. I tried to explain that at that range and with these rifles you could not hit a man except by accident. But he was only a child, and he kept motioning with his rifle towards one of the dots, grinning as eagerly as a dog that expects a pebble to be thrown. Finally I put my sights up to seven hundred and let fly. The dot disappeared. I hope it went near enough to make him jump. It was the first time in my life that I had fired a gun at a human being.

Now that I had seen the front I was profoundly disgusted. They called this war! And we were hardly even in touch with the enemy! I made no attempt to keep my head below the level of the trench. A little while later, however, a bullet shot past my ear with a vicious crack and banged into the parados behind. Alas! I ducked. All my life I had sworn that I would not duck the first time a bullet passed over me; but the movement appears to be instinctive, and almost everybody does it at least once.

THE HOUSE OF COMMONS DISCUSSES WAR AND PEACE, LONDON, 2 SEPTEMBER 1939

Mr Ralph Glyn, MP

Diary: September 3

Last night in London was one of the great times in modern history. The half-hour in the Commons – 7.30 to 8 – was perhaps the most decisive half-hour that we have known.

All through the day the House had been in a schoolboyish, almost hysterical mood; they were laughing and shuffling. There was a feeling that something fishy was happening in Downing Street. The Cabinet was still sitting Ministers were telephoning Paris – and the Germans were bombing Poland. *Why* were we not at war?

At half-past seven we met again, this time subdued and tense. Chamberlain we knew would declare war. The Ambassadors were looking down; Count Edward Raczijnsky pale and worn. Chamberlain came in looking grey – a kind of whitish-grey – and glum, dour. Captain Margesson, the Secretary to the Treasury, came behind him, purple with anxiety. Chamberlain's statement! . . . In the house we thought he was only half way through when – he sat down. There was a gasp, first of horror, then anger. His own back-benchers leaned forward to cry, "Munich, Munich!" The House seemed to rise to its feet with Mr Arthur Greenwood, the Labour leader.

Mr L. S. Amery, sitting very small near Anthony Eden, jumped up to shout at Greenwood – "Speak for England." Others took up the cry. Chamberlain white and hunched. Margesson with sweat pouring down his face, Sir John Simon, the Foreign Secretary, punctiliously looking holy.

Greenwood spoke slowly and very simply. He spoke for England and what is more he saved Chamberlain by most skilfully suggesting that it was the French who were delaying. Then one or two back-benchers, Chamberlain's own supporters, got up. It was not a joint Anglo-French pledge to Poland, they said, it was a *British* pledge – why were we not fulfilling it? The House swung against Chamberlain again. Winston Churchill, I saw, was getting whiter and grimmer. He turned round to look at Eden, who nodded as if to say, "You speak, I'll follow." I know that Churchill was about to move a vote of censure on the Government – which would have fallen. But Chamberlain looked across at Churchill: "I'm playing straight," his glance seemed to say, "there really *are* reasons for delay." Churchill sat back, relaxed, uneasy.

Then James Maxton, the pacifist, rose, gaunt, a Horseman from the Apocalypse, doom written across his face: "Don't let's talk of national honour: what do such phrases mean? The plain fact is that war means the slaughter of millions. If the Prime Minister can still maintain the peace he will have saved those lives, he mustn't be rushed." Again the House swung and was poised. We all thought in the curious hush: What if the gaunt figure of doom were right after all? Slaughter – misery – ruin – was he right? But the alternative: Hitler trading on our fears, Germany treading on freedom, Europe under terror. The whole House was swayed in unison with the drama which itself was living.

Another back-bencher spoke. "We must keep our pledge – Hitler must be stopped." Once again we were swinging against Chamberlain, when Margesson, damp and shapeless, rose to move the adjournment. In a kind of daze it was carried.

Britain declared war on Germany at 11 a.m. on the morning of 3 September.

THE *ROYAL OAK* IS TORPEDOED, SCAPA FLOW, 13 OCTOBER 1939

Gunther Prien

The Second World War was barely six weeks old when a German submarine U-47, commanded by Gunther Prien, penetrated the defences of the Royal Navy's base at Scapa Flow and sank the battleship *Royal Oak*.

. . . We are in Scapa Flow.

14.10.39. It is disgustingly light. The whole bay is lit up. To the south of Cava there is nothing. I go farther in. To port, I recognize the Hoxa Sound coastguard, to which in the next few minutes the boat must present itself as a target. In that event all would be lost; at present south of Cava no ships are to be seen, although visibility is extremely good. Hence decisions:

South of Cava there is no shipping, so before staking everything on success, all possible precautions must be taken. Therefore, turn to port is made. We proceed north by the coast. Two battleships are lying there at anchor, and further inshore, destroyers. Cruisers not visible, therefore attack on the big fellows.

Distance apart, 3,000 metres. Estimated depth, seven and a half metres. Impact firing. One torpedo fired on northern ship, two on southern. After a good three and a half minutes, a torpedo detonates on the northern ship; of the other two nothing is to be seen.

About! Torpedo fired from stern; in the bow two tubes are loaded; three torpedoes from the bow. After three tense minutes comes the detonation on the nearer ship. There is a loud explosion, roar, and rumbling. Then come columns of water, followed by columns of fire, and splinters fly through the air. The harbour springs to life. Destroyers are lit up, signalling starts on every side, and on land, 200 metres away from me, cars roar along the roads. A battleship had been sunk, a second damaged, and the other three torpedoes have gone to blazes. All the tubes are empty. I decide to withdraw, because: (1) With my periscopes I cannot conduct night attacks while submerged ... (2) On a bright night I cannot manoeuvre unobserved in a calm sea. (3) I must assume that I was observed by the driver of a car which stopped opposite us, turned around, and drove off towards Scapa at top speed. (4) Nor can I go farther north, for there, well hidden from my sight, lie the destroyers which were previously dimly distinguishable.

At full speed both engines we withdraw. Everything is simple until we reach Skildaenoy Point. Then we have more trouble. It is now low tide. The current is against us. Engines at slow and dead slow; I attempt to get away. I must leave by the south through the narrows, because of the depth of the water. Things are again difficult. Course, 058°, slow – ten knots. I make no progress. At full speed I pass the southern blockship with nothing to spare. The helmsman does magnificently. Full speed ahead both, finally three-quarter speed and full ahead all out. Free of the blockships

– ahead a mole! Hard over and again about, and at 02.15 we are once more outside. A pity that only one was destroyed. The torpedo misses I explain as due to faults of course, speed and drift. In tube 4, a misfire. The crew behaved splendidly throughout the operation.

CHURCHILL TAKES OVER, 13 MAY 1940

Winston Churchill

Speech to the House of Commons.

On Friday evening last I received His Majesty's Commission to form a new Administration. It was the evident wish and will of Parliament and the nation that this should be conceived on the broadest possible basis and that it should include all parties, both those who supported the late Government and also the parties of the Opposition. I have completed the most important part of this task. A War Cabinet has been formed of five Members, representing, with the Opposition Liberals, the unity of the nation. The three party Leaders have agreed to serve, either in the War Cabinet or in high executive office. The three Fighting Services have been filled. It was necessary that this should be done in one single day, on account of the extreme urgency and rigour of events. A number of other positions, key positions, were filled yesterday, and I am submitting a further list to His Majesty to-night. I hope to complete the appointment of the principal Ministers during to-morrow. The appointment of the other Ministers usually takes a little longer, but I trust that, when Parliament meets again, this part of my task will be completed, and that the administration will be complete in all respects.

I considered it in the public interest to suggest that the House should be summoned to meet to-day. Mr. Speaker agreed, and took the necessary steps, in accordance with the powers conferred upon him by the Resolution of the House. At the end of the proceedings to-day, the Adjournment of the House will be proposed until Tuesday, 21st May, with, of course, provision for earlier meeting, if need be. The business to be considered during that week will be notified to Members at the earliest opportunity. I now invite the House, by the Resolution which stands in my name, to record its approval of the steps taken and to declare its confidence in the new Government.

To form an Administration of this scale and complexity is a serious undertaking in itself, but it must be remembered that we are in the preliminary stage of one of the greatest battles in history, that we are in action at many other points in Norway and in Holland, that we have to be prepared in the Mediterranean, that the air battle is continuous and that many preparations, such as have been indicated by my honourable Friend below the Gangway, have to be made here at home. In this crisis I hope I may be pardoned if I do not address the House at any length to-day. I hope that any of my friends and colleagues, or former colleagues, who are affected by the political reconstruction, will make allowance, all allowance, for any lack of ceremony with which it has been necessary to act. I would say to the House, as I said to those who have joined this Government: "I have nothing to offer but blood, toil, tears and sweat."

We have before us an ordeal of the most grievous kind. We have before us many, many long months of struggle and of suffering. You ask, what is our policy? I will say: It is to wage war, by sea, land and air, with all our might and with all the strength that God can give us; to wage war against a monstrous tyranny, never surpassed in the dark, lamentable catalogue of human crime. That is our policy. You ask what is our aim? I can answer in one word: It is victory, victory at all costs, victory in spite of all terror, victory, however long and hard the road may be: for without victory, there is no survival. Let that be realised; no survival for the British Empire, no survival for all that the British Empire has stood for, no survival for the urge and impulse of the ages, that mankind will move forward towards its goal. But I take up my task with buoyancy and hope. I feel sure that our cause will not be suffered to fail among men. At this time I feel entitled to claim the aid of all, and I say, "Come then, let us go forward together with our united strength."

DUNKIRK: THE VIEW FROM THE BEACHES, 30 MAY 1940

Captain Richard Austin

By 21 May the German army had reached the English Channel at Abbeville, encircling the Belgian army and the British Expeditionary Force sent to reinforce the Allied front. On 26 May Lord Gort, commander of the BEF, was authorized to re-embark his army back to Britain, and he began to concentrate the BEF and remnants of the French and Belgian armies – a total of some 400,000 men – at Dunkirk. The evacuation continued for nine days, from 26 May to June 3, all of them under ceaseless attack by the *Wehrmacht* and *Luftwaffe*.

We were now in the region of the dunes, which rose like humps of a deeper darkness. And these in their turn were dotted with the still blacker shapes of abandoned vehicles, half-sunk in the sand, fantastic twisted shapes of burned-out skeletons, and crazy-looking wreckage that had been heaped up in extraordinary piles by the explosions of bombs. All these black shapes were silhouetted against the angry red glare in the sky, which reflected down on us the agony of burning Dunkirk.

Slowly we picked our way between the wreckage, sinking ankle-deep in the loose sand, until we reached the gaunt skeletons of what had once been the houses on the promenade. The whole front was one long continuous line of blazing buildings, a high wall of fire, roaring and darting in tongues of flame, with the smoke pouring upwards and disappearing in the blackness of the sky above the roof-tops. Out seawards the darkness was as thick and smooth as black velvet, except for now and again when the shape of a sunken destroyer or paddle-steamer made a slight thickening on its impenetrable surface. Facing us, the great black wall of the Mole stretched from the beach far out into sea, the end of it almost invisible to us. The Mole had an astounding, terrifying background of giant flames leaping a hundred feet into the air from blazing oil tanks. At the shore end of the Mole stood an obelisk, and the high-explosive shells burst around it with monotonous regularity.

Along the promenade, in parties of fifty, the remnants of practically all the last regiments were wearily trudging along. There was no singing, and very little talk. Everyone was far too exhausted to waste breath. Occasionally out of the darkness came a sudden shout:

"A Company, Green Howards . . ."

"C Company, East Yorks . . ."

These shouts came either from stragglers trying to find lost units, or guides on the look-out for the parties they were to lead on to the Mole for evacuation.

The tide was out. Over the wide stretch of sand could be dimly discerned little oblong masses of soldiers, moving in platoons and orderly groups down towards the edge of the sea. Now and again you would hear a shout:

"Alf, where are you? . . ."

"Let's hear from you, Bill . . ."

"Over this way, George . . ."

It was none too easy to keep contact with one's friends in the darkness, and amid so many little masses of moving men, all looking very much alike. If you stopped for a few seconds to look behind you, the chances were you attached yourself to some entirely different unit.

From the margin of the sea, at fairly wide intervals three long thin black lines protruded into the water, conveying the effect of low wooden breakwaters. These were lines of men, standing in pairs behind one another far out into the water, waiting in queues till boats arrived to transport them, a score or so at a time, to the steamers and warships that were filling up with the last survivors. The queues stood there, fixed and almost as regular as if ruled. No bunching, no pushing, nothing like the mix-up to be seen at the turnstiles when a crowd is going to a football match. Much more orderly, even than a waiting theatre queue.

About this time, afraid that some of our men might be trailing off, I began shouting, "2004th Field Regiment . . . 2004th Field Regiment . . ." A group of dead and dying soldiers on the path in front of us quickened our desire to quit the promenade. Stepping over the bodies we marched down the slope to a dark beach.

We tacked ourselves on to the rear of the smallest of the three queues, the head of which was already standing in water up to the waist. Half an hour passed. Suddenly a small rowing boat appeared. The head of the queue clambered in and was rowed away into the blackness . . .

Along the entire queue not a word was spoken. The men just stood there silently staring into the darkness, praying that a boat would soon appear, and fearing that it would not. Heads and shoulders only showing above the water. Fixed, immovable, as though chained there. It was, in fact, practically impossible to move, even from one foot to another. The dead-weight of water-logged boots and sodden clothes pinned one down. My breeches seemed to be ballooned out with water as heavy as mercury. I was filled with a dread that when the time did come I should be unable to move . . .

Suddenly out of the blackness, rather ghostly, swam a white shape which materialised into a ship's lifeboat, towed by a motor-boat. It moved towards us and came to a stop twenty yards in front of the head of our queue.

"Hi! Hi!" we all hailed, dreading they hadn't seen us.

"Ahoy! Ahoy!" came the lusty response.

"Come in closer," we shouted.

"We can't. It's unsafe. Might upset the boat." But they risked a few more yards . . .

Four sailors in tin-hats began hoisting the soldiers out of the water. It was no simple task. Half the men were so weary and exhausted that they lacked strength to climb into the boat unaided. The sailors, judged the situation perfectly, as being one for rough words, threats, and bullying methods. The only spur sufficient to rouse our worn-out bodies to one last supreme effort.

"Come on you bastards . . ."

"Wake up, blast you . . ."

"Get a move on, Dopey . . ."

The gunwhale of the lifeboat stood three feet above the surface of the water. Reaching up, I could just grasp it with the tips of my fingers. When I tried to haul myself up I couldn't move an inch. The weight of my waterlogged clothes, especially my cherished greatcoat, beat me completely, desperately though I fought. I might have been a sack of lead. A great dread of being left behind seized me.

Two powerful hands reached over the gunwhale and fastened themselves into my arm-pits. Another pair of hands stretched down and hooked-on to the belt at the back of my greatcoat. Before I had time to realise it I was pulled up and pitched head-first into the bottom of the boat.

"Come on, you b—. Get up and help the others in," shouted a sailor, as I hit the planks with a gasp. It was rough medicine. But the right medicine for the moment.

The moment came when the lifeboat could not hold another soul.

"Carry on, Mr Jolly. Carry on," cried the sailor at our helm to someone in the motor-boat. And we got under weigh, leaving the rest of the queue behind to await the next boat,

DUNKIRK: THE VIEW FROM THE BOATS, 1 JUNE 1940

Commander C. H. Lightoller, RNR (Retd)

The evacuation was carried out by an armada of 222 naval units and 665 civilian craft. These vessels succeeded in bringing back to Britain 224,585 British and 112,546 French and Belgian troops. Among the civilian vessels was the yacht *Sundowner* owned by Commander Lightoller. Lightoller had been in history once before: as the senior surviving officer of the *Titanic*.

Half-way across we avoided a floating mine by a narrow margin, but having no firearms of any description – not even a tin hat – we had to leave its destruction to someone better equipped. A few minutes later we had our first introduction to enemy aircraft, three fighters flying high. Before they could be offensive, a British destroyer – *Worcester*, I think – overhauled us and drove them off. At 2.25 p.m. we sighted and closed the twenty-five-foot motor-cruiser *Westerly*; broken down and badly on fire. As the crew of two (plus three naval ratings she had picked up in Dunkirk) wished to abandon ship – and quickly – I went alongside and took them aboard, giving them the additional pleasure of again facing the hell they had only just left.

We made the fairway buoy to the Roads shortly after the sinking of a French transport with severe loss of life. Steaming slowly through the wreckage we entered the Roads. For some time now we had been subject to sporadic bombing and machine-gun fire, but as the *Sundowner* is exceptionally and extremely quick on the helm, by waiting till the last moment and putting the helm hard over – my son at the wheel – we easily avoided every attack, though sometimes near lifted out of the water.

It had been my intention to go right on to the beaches, where my second son, Second-Lieutenant R. T. Lightoller, had been evacuated some forty-eight hours previously; but those of the *Westerly* informed me that the troops were all away, so I headed up for Dunkirk piers. By now divebombers seemed to be eternally dropping out of the cloud of enemy aircraft overhead. Within half a mile of the pierheads a two-funnelled grey-painted transport had over hauled and was just passing us to port when two salvoes were dropped in quick succession right along her port side. For a few moments she was hid in smoke and I certainly thought they had got her. Then she reappeared, still gaily heading for the piers and entered just ahead of us.

The difficulty of taking troops on board from the quay high above us was obvious, so I went alongside a destroyer (*Worcester* again, I think) where they were already embarking. I got hold of her captain and told him I could take about a hundred (though the most I had ever had on board was twenty-one). He, after consultation with the military C.O., told me to carry on and get the troops aboard. I may say here that before leaving Cubitt's Yacht Basin, we had worked all night stripping her down of everything movable, masts included, that would tend to lighten her and make for more room.

My son, as previously arranged, was to pack the men in and use every available inch of space – which I'll say he carried out to some purpose. On deck I detailed a naval rating to tally the troops aboard. At fifty I called below, "How are you getting on?" getting the cheery reply, "Oh, plenty of room yet." At seventy-five my son admitted they were getting pretty tight – all equipment and arms being left on deck.

I now started to pack them on deck, having passed word below for every man to lie down and keep down; the same applied on deck. By the time we had fifty on deck I could feel her getting distinctly tender, so took no more. Actually we had exactly a hundred and thirty on board, including three *Sundowners* and five *Westerlys*.

During the whole embarkation we had quite a lot of attention from enemy planes, but derived an amazing degree of comfort from the fact that the *Worcester's* A.A. guns kept up an everlasting bark overhead.

Casting off and backing out we entered the Roads again; there it was continuous and unmitigated hell. The troops were just splendid and of their own initiative detailed lookouts ahead, astern, and abeam for inquisitive planes, as my attention was pretty wholly occupied watching the steering and giving orders to Roger at the wheel. Any time an aircraft seemed inclined to try its hand on us, one of the look-outs would just call quietly, "Look out for this bloke, skipper", at the same time pointing. One bomber that had been particularly offensive, itself came under the notice of one of our fighters and suddenly plunged vertically into the sea just about fifty yards astern of us. It was the only time any man ever raised his voice above a conversational tone, but as that big black bomber hit the water they raised an echoing cheer.

My youngest son, Pilot Officer H. B. Lightoller (lost at the outbreak of war in the first raid on Wilhelmshaven), flew a Blenheim and had at different times given me a whole lot of useful information about attack, defence and evasive tactics (at which he was apparently particularly good) and I attribute in a great measure our success in getting across without a single casualty to his unwitting help.

On one occasion an enemy machine came up astern at about a hundred feet with the obvious intention of raking our decks. He was coming down in a gliding dive and I knew that he must elevate some ten to fifteen degrees before his guns would bear. Telling my son "Stand by," I waited till, as near as I could judge, he was just on the point of pulling up, and then "Hard a-port." (She turns 180 degrees in exactly her own length.) This threw his aim completely off. He banked and tried again. Then "Hard a-starboard," with the same result. After a third attempt he gave it up in disgust. Had I had a machine-gun of any sort, he was a sitter – in fact, there were at least three that I am confident we could have accounted for during the trip.

Not the least of our difficulties was contending with the wash of fast craft, such as destroyers and transports. In every instance I had to stop completely, take the way off the ship and head the heavy wash. The M.C. being where it was, to have taken one of these seas on either the quarter or beam would have at once put paid to our otherwise successful cruise. The effect of the consequent plunging on the troops below, in a stinking atmosphere with all ports and skylights closed, can well be imagined. They were literally packed like the proverbial sardines, even one in the bath and another on the WC, so that all the poor devils could do was sit and be sick. Added were the remnants of bully beef and biscuits. So that after discharging our cargo in Ramsgate at ten p.m., there lay before the three of us a nice clearing-up job.

THE BATTLE OF BRITAIN, SEPTEMBER 1940

Pilot Officer John Maurice Beard

After the fall of France, Britain stood alone against Germany. Hitler made a peace overture in June, which was dismissed by Winston Churchill, who had taken over from Chamberlain as Prime Minister. The blow came soon after with a full-scale air-attack by Göring's *Luftwaffe*: the Battle of Britain. Beginning in August, it lasted until November, although the peak of the fighting was in September. The RAF was outnumbered in planes and pilots four to one but nevertheless thwarted the Germans' attempt to control the air over the channel. John Beard was one of "The Few", a 21-year-old Hurricane pilot.

I was supposed to be away on a day's leave but dropped back to the aerodrome to see if there was a letter from my wife. When I found out that *all* the squadrons had gone off into action, I decided to stand by, because obviously something big was happening. While I was climbing into my flying kit, our Hurricanes came slipping back out of the sky to refuel, reload ammunition, and take off again. The returning pilots were full of talk about flocks of enemy bombers and fighters which were trying to break through along the Thames Estuary. You couldn't miss hitting them, they said. Off to the east I could hear the steady roll of anti-aircraft fire. It was a brilliant afternoon with a flawless blue sky. I was crazy to be off.

An instant later an aircraftsman rushed up with orders for me to make up a flight with some of the machines then reloading. My own Hurricane was a nice old kite, though it had a habit of flying left wing low at the slightest provocation. But since it had already accounted for fourteen German aircraft before I inherited it, I thought it had some luck, and I was glad when I squeezed myself into the same old seat again and grabbed the "stick".

We took off in two flights (six fighters), and as we started to gain height over the station we were told over the R. T. (radiotelephone) to keep circling for a while until we were made up to a stronger force. That didn't take long, and soon there was a complete squadron including a couple of Spitfires which had wandered in from somewhere.

Then came the big thrilling moment: ACTION ORDERS. Distantly I heard the hum of the generator in my R. T. earphones and then the voice of the ground controller crackling through with the call signs. Then the order "Fifty plus bombers, one hundred plus fighters over Canterbury at 15,000 heading northeast. Your vector (steering course to intercept) nine zero degrees. Over!"

We were flying in four V formations of three. I was flying No. 3 in Red flight, which was the squadron leader's and thus the leading flight. On we went, wing tips to left and right slowly rising and falling, the roar of our twelve Merlins drowning all other sound. We crossed over London, which, at 20,000 feet, seemed just a haze of smoke from its countless chimneys, with nothing visible except the faint glint of the barrage balloons and the wriggly silver line of the Thames.

I had too much to do watching the instruments and keeping formation to do much thinking. But once I caught a reflected glimpse of myself in the windscreen – a goggled, bloated, fat thing with the tube of my oxygen supply protruding gruesomely sideways from the mask which hid my mouth. Suddenly I was back at school again, on a hot afternoon when the Headmaster was taking the Sixth and droning on and on about the later Roman Emperors. The boy on my right was showing me surreptitiously some illustrations which he had pinched out of his father's medical books during the last holidays. I looked like one of those pictures.

It was an amazingly vivid memory, as if school was only yesterday. And half my mind was thinking what wouldn't I then have given to be sitting in a Hurricane belting along at 350 miles an hour and out for a kill. *Me* defending London! I grinned at my old self at the thought.

Minutes went by. Green fields and roads were now beneath us. I scanned the sky and the horizon for the first glimpse of the Germans. A new vector came through on the R. T. and we swung round with the sun behind us. Swift on the heels of this I heard Yellow flight leader call through the earphones. I looked quickly toward Yellow's position, and there they were!

It was really a terrific sight and quite beautiful. First they seemed just a cloud of light as the sun caught the many glistening chromium parts of their engines, their windshields, and the spin of their airscrew discs. Then, as our squadron hurtled nearer, the details stood out. I could see the bright-yellow noses of Messerschmitt fighters sandwiching the bombers, and could even pick out some of the types. The sky seemed full of them, packed in layers thousands of feet deep. They came on steadily, wavering up and down along the horizon. "Oh, golly," I thought, "golly, golly . . ."

And then any tension I had felt on the way suddenly left me. I was elated but very calm. I leaned over and switched on my reflector sight, flicked the catch on the gun button from "Safe" to "Fire", and lowered my seat till the circle and dot on the reflector sight shone darkly red in front of my eyes.

The squadron leader's voice came through the earphones, giving tactical orders. We swung round in a great circle to attack on their beam – into the thick of them. Then, on the order, down we went. I took my hand from the throttle lever so as to get both hands on the stick, and my thumb played neatly across the gun button. You have to steady a fighter just as you have to steady a rifle before you fire it.

My Merlin screamed as I went down in a steeply banked dive on to the tail of a forward line of Heinkels. I knew the air was full of aircraft flinging themselves about in all directions, but, hunched and snuggled down behind my sight I was conscious only of the Heinkel I had picked out. As the angle of my dive increased, the enemy machine loomed larger in the sight field, heaved toward the red dot, and then he was there!

I had an instant's flash of amazement at the Heinkel proceeding so regularly on its way with a fighter on its tail. "Why doesn't the fool *move*?" I thought, and actually caught myself flexing my muscles into the action *I* would have taken had I been he.

When he was square across the sight I pressed the button. There was a smooth trembling of my Hurricane as the eight-gun squirt shot out. I gave him a two-second burst and then another. Cordite fumes blew back into the cockpit making an acrid mixture with the smell of hot oil and the aircompressors.

I saw my first burst go in and, just as I was on top of him and turning away, I noticed a red glow inside the bomber. I turned tightly into position again and now saw several short tongues of flame lick out along the fuselage. Then he went down in a spin, blanketed with smoke and with pieces flying off.

I left him plummeting down and, horsing back on my stick, climbed up again for more. The sky was clearing, but ahead toward London I saw a small, tight formation of bombers completely encircled by a ring of Messerschmitts. They were still heading north. As I raced forward, three flights of Spitfires came zooming up from beneath them in a sort of Prince-of-Wales's-feathers manoeuvre. They burst through upward and outward, their guns going all the time. They must have each got one, for an instant later I saw the most extraordinary sight of eight German bombers and fighters diving earthward together in flames.

I turned away again and streaked after some distant specks ahead. Diving down, I noticed that the running progress of the battle had brought me over London again. I could see the network of streets with the green space of Kensington Gardens, and I had an instant's glimpse of the Round Pond, where I sailed boats when I was a child. In that moment, and as I was rapidly overhauling the Germans ahead, a Dornier 17 sped right across my line of flight, closely pursued by a Hurricane. And behind the Hurricane came two Messerschmitts. He was too intent to have seen them and they had not seen me! They were coming slightly toward me. It was perfect. A kick at the rudder and I swung in toward them, thumbed the gun button, and let them have it. The first burst was placed just the right distance ahead of the leading Messerschmitt. He ran slap into it and he simply came to pieces in the air. His companion, with one of the speediest and most brilliant "get-outs" I have ever seen, went right away in a half Immelmann turn. I missed him completely. He must almost have been hit by the pieces of the leader but he got away. I hand it to him.

At that moment some instinct made me glance up at my rear-view mirror and spot two Messerschmitts closing in on my tail. Instantly I hauled back on the stick and streaked upward. And just in time. For as I flicked into the climb, I saw the tracer streaks pass beneath me. As I turned I had a quick look round the "office" (cockpit). My fuel reserve was running out and I had only about a second's supply of ammunition left. I was certainly in no condition to take on two Messerschmitts. But they seemed no more eager than I was. Perhaps they were in the same position, for they turned away for home. I put my nose down and did likewise.

Only on the way back did I realize how hot I was. I had forgotten to adjust the ventilator apparatus in all the stress of the fighting, and hadn't noticed the thermometer. With the sun on the windows all the time, the inside of the "office" was like an oven. Inside my flying suit I was in a bath of perspiration, and sweat was cascading down my face. I was dead tired and my neck ached from constantly turning my head on the lookout when going in and out of dogfights. Over east the sky was flecked with A. A. puffs, but I did not bother to investigate. Down I went, home.

At the station there was only time for a few minutes' stretch, a hurried report to the Intelligence Officer, and a brief comparing of notes with the other pilots. So far my squadron seemed to be intact, in spite of a terrific two hours in which we had accounted for at least thirty enemy aircraft.

But there was more to come. It was now about four p.m. and I gulped down some tea while the ground crew checked my Hurricane. Then, with about three flights collected, we took off again. We seemed to be rather longer this time circling and gaining height above the station before the orders came through on the R. T. It was to patrol an area along the Thames Estuary at 20,000 feet. But we never got there.

We had no sooner got above the docks than we ran into the first lot of enemy bombers. They were coming up in line about 5,000 feet below us. The line stretched on and on across the horizon. Above, on our level, were assorted groups of enemy fighters. Some were already in action, with our fellows spinning and twirling among them. Again I got that tightening feeling at the throat, for it really was a sight to make you gasp.

But we all knew what to do. We went for the bombers. Kicking her over, I went down after the first of them, a Heinkel 111. He turned away as I approached, chiefly because some of our fellows had already broken into the line and had scattered it. Before I got up he had been joined by two more. They were forming a V and heading south across the river.

I went after them. Closing in on the tail of the left one, I ran into a stream of crossfire from all three. How it missed me I don't know. For a second the whole air in front was thick with tracer trails. It seemed to be coming straight at me, only to curl away by the windows and go lazily past. I felt one slight bank, however, and glancing quickly, saw a small hole at the end of my starboard wing. Then, as the Heinkel drifted across my sights, I pressed the button – once – twice . . . Nothing happened.

I panicked for a moment till I looked down and saw that I had forgotten to turn the safety-catch knob to the "Fire" position. I flicked it over at once and in that instant saw that three bombers, to hasten their getaway, had jettisoned all their bombs. They seemed to peel off in a steady stream. We were over the southern outskirts of London now and I remember hoping that most of them would miss the little houses and plunge into fields.

But dropping the bombs did not help my Heinkel. I let him have a long burst at close range, which got him right in the "office". I saw him turn slowly over and go down, and followed to give him another squirt. Just then there was a terrific crash in front of me. Something flew past my window, and the whole aircraft shook as the engine raced itself to pieces. I had been hit by A.A. fire aimed at the bombers, my airscrew had been blown off, and I was going down in a spin.

The next few seconds were a bit wild and confused. I remember switching off and flinging back the sliding roof almost in one gesture. Then I tried to vault out through the roof. But I had forgotten to release my safety belt. As I fumbled at the pin the falling aircraft gave a twist which shot me through the open cover. Before I was free, the air stream hit me like a solid blow and knocked me sideways. I felt my arm hit something, and then I was falling over and over with fields and streets and sky gyrating madly past my eyes.

I grabbed at the rip cord on my chute. Missed it. Grabbed again. Missed it. That was no fun. Then I remember saying to myself, "This won't do. Take it easy, take it slowly." I tried again and found the rip cord grip and pulled. There was a terrific wrench at my thighs and then I was floating still and peacefully with my "brolly" canopy billowing above my head.

The rest was lovely. I sat at my ease just floating gradually down, breathing deep, and looking around. I was drifting across London again at about 2,000 feet.

THE BLITZ, LONDON, SEPTEMBER–NOVEMBER 1940

Thwarted in its attempt to destroy the RAF, the *Luftwaffe* switched its attention to mass-bombing raids on London. The first of the big raids came on 7 September, when 375 bombers unloaded their bombs on the capital.

Desmond Flower

7 September, London Docks
Suddenly we were gaping upwards. The brilliant sky was criss-crossed from horizon to horizon by innumerable vapour trails. The sight was a completely novel one. We watched, fascinated, and all work stopped. The little silver stars sparkling at the heads of the vapour trails turned east. This display looked so insubstantial and harmless; even beautiful. Then, with a dull roar which made the ground across London shake as one stood upon it, the first sticks of bombs hit the docks. Leisurely, enormous mushrooms of black and brown smoke shot with crimson climbed into the sunlit sky. There they hung and slowly expanded, for there was no wind, and the great fires below fed more smoke into them as the hours passed.

On Friday and Saturday morning the sky grew darker and darker as the oily smoke rose and spread in heavy, immobile columns, shutting out the sun.

At the barracks, drill quickly became monotonous. We had work to do, and we weren't the target. But we couldn't keep our eyes off those sickening, solid columns climbing up like the convolutions of a lazy snake into a torpid sky.

I suppose our masters felt that, although the Battle of Britain had begun, the worst might already be over – I don't know; but they decided to put us recruits in the hat and draw out three for week-end leave. My name came out of the hat first, and I sent a wire to my parents in Sevenoaks to say that I was coming home. My pass was from midday on Saturday, and I got down to the centre of London by Underground. Bombers were coming over at monotonously regular intervals. I walked down to Charing Cross. There was a lot of noise still, and a lot of smoke. As I entered the station the loudspeakers were ordering everyone out because planes were overhead and they were frightened of casualties if the place were hit. I strolled out to the top of that long flight of stone steps down into Villiers Street and sat on the balustrade watching.

Up in the lonely sky there was still one bomber, gleaming silver, and then he dropped a stick just across the Thames from us. Back in the station the loudspeaker announced that the main line was gone and that there wouldn't be any more trains out for hours. Hundreds of people stood around like a flock of sheep which is frightened and can't make up its mind which way to turn. You could see the dead mask of indecision on their faces as they looked about, hoping someone would tell them what to do. I walked out of the station and decided to hitch-hike home. I was lucky; somewhere on the south bank of the river I met a man on a motor-cycle who was going through Blackheath, and he took me on his pillion.

Now we were nearer to the docks. The columns of smoke merged and became a monstrous curtain which blocked the sky; only the billows within it and the sudden shafts of flame which shot up hundreds of feet made one realize that it was a living thing and not just the backdrop of some nightmare opera. There were fire-hoses along the side of the road, climbing over one another like a helping of macaroni, with those sad little fountains spraying out from the leaks, as they always seem to do from all fire-hoses. Every two or three minutes we would pull into the gutter as a fire-bell broke out stridently behind us and an engine in unfamiliar livery tore past at full tilt: chocolate or green or blue, with gold lettering – City of Birmingham Fire Brigade, or Sheffield, or Bournemouth. The feeling was something you had never experienced before – the excitement and dash of fire-engines arriving to help from so far away, and the oily, evil smell of fire and destruction, with its lazy, insolent rhythm.

It looked terrible and hopeless, but there was a kind of *Götter-dämmerung* grandeur about it.

Edward R. Murrow, CBS war correspondent

13 September, London
This is London at 3:30 in the morning. This has been what might be called a "routine night" – air-raid alarm at about 9 o'clock and intermittent bombing ever since. I had the impression that more high explosives and few incendiaries have been used tonight. Only two small fires can be seen on the horizon. Again the Germans have been sending their bombers in singly or in pairs. The anti-aircraft barrage has been fierce but sometimes there have been periods of twenty minutes when London has been silent. Then the big red busses would start up and move on till the guns started working again. That silence is almost harder to bear. One becomes accustomed to rattling windows and the distant sound of bombs and then there comes a silence that can be felt. You know the sound will return – you wait, and then it starts again. That waiting is bad. It gives you a chance to imagine things. I have been walking tonight – there is a full moon, and the dirty-gray buildings appear white. The stars, the empty windows, are hidden. It's a beautiful and lonesome city where men and women and children are trying to snatch a few hours' sleep underground.

In the fashionable residential districts I could read the TO LET signs on the front of big houses in the light of the bright moon. Those houses have big basements underneath – good shelters, but they're not being used. Many people think they should be.

The scale of this air war is so great that the reporting is not easy. Often we spend hours traveling about this sprawling city, viewing damage, talking with people, and occasionally listening to the bombs coming down, and then more hours wondering what you'd like to hear about these people who are citizens of no mean city. We've told you about the bombs, the fires, the smashed houses, and the courage of the people. We've read you the communiques and tried to give you an honest estimate of the wounds inflicted upon this, the best bombing target in the world. But the business of living and working in this city is very personal – the little incidents, the things the mind retains, are in themselves unimportant, but they somehow weld together to form the hard core of memories that will remain when the last "all-clear" has sounded. That's why I want to talk for just three or four minutes about the things we haven't talked about before; for many of these impressions it is necessary to reach back through only one long week. There was a rainbow bending over the battered and smoking East End of London just when the "all-clear" sounded one afternoon. One night I stood in front of a smashed grocery store and heard a dripping inside. It was the only sound in all London. Two cans of peaches had been drilled clean through by flying glass and the juice was dripping down onto the floor.

There was a flower shop in the East End. Nearly every other building in the block had been smashed. There was a funeral wreath in the window of the shop – price: three shillings and sixpence, less than a dollar. In front of Buckingham Palace there's a bed of red and white flowers – untouched – the reddest flowers I've ever seen.

Last night, or rather early this morning, I met a distinguished member of Parliament in a bar. He had been dining with Anthony Eden and had told the Secretary for War that he wouldn't walk through the streets with all that shrapnel falling about, and as a good host Eden should send him home in a tank. Another man came in and reported, on good authority, that the Prime Minister had a siren suit, one of those blue woolen coverall affairs with a zipper. Someone said the Prime Minister must resemble a barrage balloon when attired in his siren suit. Things of that sort can still be said in this country. The fact that the noise – just the sound, not the blast – of bombs and guns can cause one to stagger while walking down the street came as a surprise. When I entered my office today, after bombs had fallen two blocks away, and was asked by my English secretary if I'd care for a cup of tea, that didn't come as much of a surprise.

Talking from a studio with a few bodies lying about on the floor, sleeping on mattresses, still produces a strange feeling but we'll probably get used to that. Today I went to buy a hat – my favorite shop had gone, blown to bits. The windows of my shoe store were blown out. I decided to have a haircut; the windows of the barbershop were gone, but the Italian barber was still doing business. Someday, he said, we smile again, but the food it doesn't taste so good since being bombed. I went on to another shop to buy flashlight batteries. I bought three. The clerk said: "You needn't buy so many. We'll have enough for the whole winter." But I said: "What if you aren't here?" There were buildings down in that street, and he replied: "Of course, we'll be here. We've been in business here for a hundred and fifty years."

But the sundown scene in London can never be forgotten – the time when people pick up their beds and walk to the shelter.

THE HOME FRONT: A CHILD'S VIEW, SHEFFIELD, AUTUMN 1940
George Macbeth

In the morning, I would walk along Clarkehouse Road with my eyes glued to the pavement for shrapnel. It became the fashion to make a collection of this, and there were few days when I came home without a pocketful of jagged, rusting bits, like the unintelligible pieces from a scattered jigsaw of pain and violence.

Of course we didn't see them as this at the time. They were simply free toys from the sky, as available and interesting as the horse chestnuts in the Botanical Gardens, or the nippled acorns in Melbourne Avenue.

It must have been about this time that the British Restaurants were opening, with their austerity jam roll and meat balls; and our own meals were beginning to rely rather more on rissoles and home-made apple sponge. But my mother was always a good manager, and I have no sense of any sudden period of shortage or of going hungry.

Sweets were the great loss. There was no longer an everlasting, teeth-spoiling fountain of sherbet and liquorice, or of Boy Blue cream whirls, or of Cadbury's Caramello. Sweets were hard to come by, and then limited to a fixed ration.

One of the worst casualties was chocolate. The traditional division into milk and plain disappeared, and an awful intervening variety known as Ration Chocolate was born, issued in semi-transparent grease-proof wrappers, and about as appetising as cardboard. In spite of a lifelong sweet tooth, I could never eat it.

THE SINKING OF *REPULSE* AND *PRINCE OF WALES*, 10 DECEMBER 1941

O. D. Gallagher

The principal cause of war in the Far East was Japan's decision to acquire a Pacific empire. She had invaded China in the 1930s but the jewels she truly coveted were the colonial possessions of the British, the French and the Dutch. This imperial desire also led directly to hostilities with the USA, which was zealously protective of her influence in the region. By 7 December 1941 the Pacific was aflame as Japanese units simultaneously attacked Pearl Harbor, Hong Kong, Wake Island, Guam and Midway. To protect the great naval base of Singapore, the British dispatched a surface fleet to intercept Japanese invasion forces while they were still at sea, but in the event the British were spotted first, and attacked by swarms of Japanese fighter-bombers. The British fleet had no fighter protection. The battleships HMS *Repulse* and HMS *Prince of Wales* were sunk within a single hour on 10 December. Two months later Singapore fell to the army of Nippon.

A new wave of planes appeared at twelve-twenty p.m. The end was near, though we did not know it. *Prince of Wales* lay about ten cables astern of our port side. She was helpless. Not only was her steering-gear destroyed, but also her screws by that first torpedo. Unlike the German *Bismarck* caught by the Navy in the Atlantic, which lost only her steering-gear and was able to keep moving in a circle, *Prince of Wales* was a hulk.

All the aircraft made for her. I do not know how many there were in this last attack, but it was afterwards estimated that there were between fifty and eighty Japanese torpedo-bombers in operation during the entire action. *Prince of Wales* fought desperately to beat off the determined killers who attacked her like a pack of dogs on a wounded buck. *Repulse* and the destroyers formed a rough circle around her, to add our fire-power. All ships fired with the intention of protecting *Prince of Wales*, and in doing so each neglected her own defences.

It was difficult to make out her outline through the smoke and flame from all her guns except the 14-inchers. I saw one plane drop a torpedo. It fell nose-heavy into the sea and churned up a thin wake as it drove straight at the immobile *Prince of Wales*. It exploded against her bows. A couple of seconds later another hit her – and another.

I gazed at her turning slowly over on her port side, her stern going under, and dots of men jumping into the sea, and was thrown against the bulkhead by a tremendous shock as *Repulse* was hit by a torpedo on her port side.

The sinking of the two warships was a catastrophe for the British, and spelled the end for Singapore.

THE HOME FRONT: THE GREAT MAN CHASE, DECEMBER 1941

Anon. A member of the British Women's Auxiliary Air Force

The main consequence of a lot of women living together seems to be that since everyone realizes that everyone else's emotions, aims and actions are similar to their own – conventional barriers and restraints are torn down and conversation gets down to bedrock.

The presence of both sexes always imposes restraint in conversation. The soldier's fumbling excuse for hard swearing is always "Oh, well, when a lot of us lads get together . . ." Similarly when women are together in our circumstances, we use words we wouldn't think of bringing out in public.

Not only in choice of words, but also in choice of topic and depth of discussion is this new candour created. Even at women's tea parties . . . women are on their guard against each other and don't admit their basic feelings . . . But here we've got to know each other well: we're all in the same boat and we're all after the same thing. So why kid each other?

And what is this thing we're all after? Obviously, a man. Preferably an officer or a sergeant pilot. I should say that 85 per cent of our conversation is about men, dances (where we meet men), 15 per cent about domestic and shop matters and a negligible proportion on other matters.

But to get a man is not sufficient. It's easy to get a man. In fact it's difficult not to. Competitive factors in the Great Man-Chase are under the following headings:

1. Quality: The desirable qualities are rank, wings, looks, money, youth in that order. Rank is unbelievably important. There's a Wing-Commander here whose only redeeming feature is that he's young. He isn't good-looking, he's owned to be a great bore and he's

extremely "fast" (which is *not* a recommendation) yet he could go out with any woman on the station he cared to ask. No one would refuse . . . The height of sex-rank is commission and wings. Higher commission, the better. Sergeant pilots and ground commissions tie for second place. This includes army officers. Ground stripes come a poor third. For the rest as far as most Ops girls are concerned, there is little hunting-value. In the term "looks" I include charm, personality, etc. This counts only as a narrow comparison viz P/O (Pilot Officer) A is better than P/O B because he is more charming, but we'd rather go out with P/O B who is *not* charming, than with Sergeant C who *is* (and he's good-looking too). Members of the Army without commissions don't get a look in at all . . .

2. Quantity: Naturally the more men one can fasten to one's train the more prestige one gains in the Chase.

3. Intensity – a deliberately vague term embodying length of affair, extent of ardour and its manifestations.

Of course the longer you can keep your man, the higher up you are in the competition. It's better if he's madly in love with you. He shouldn't be seen in public with other women. And telegrams, chocolates, cigarettes and really "classy" evenings out all put you one step higher on the ladder. As far as physical manifestations are concerned, the average Ops girl admittedly likes a man who can kiss well, eyes "wandering" with suspicion and definitely abstains from actual immorality. Technique in kissing is of first importance . . . Further than kissing is not eyed favourably. "I *like* Bill and he *is* a Squadron Leader and all that but I simply can't face the coping I have to do every evening". ("Coping" having become the accepted term for dealing with unwanted passion.) So the eligible men are those who kiss well but "know when to stop" . . .

It seems to me that practically the entire object of the Chase is a matter of vanity and prestige . . .

Becoming of necessity subjective: I allowed myself to drift into this chase for the past few months and have discovered:

a. That I am happiest when I am conducting two or three successful affairs with eligibles as above.

b. That I am second happiest when I am *pretending to other girls* that they are successful affairs as above . . .

A girl in our Control had been trying very hard to get a date with a new officer. She was sitting next to him in the Ops room one day full of concentration in her conversation when suddenly she smiled, looked across at me, and mouthed the words "Got him!"

EL ALAMEIN, OCTOBER–NOVEMBER 1942

The battle of El Alamein was the turning point of the war in North Africa, a decisive victory for General Montgomery's British 8th Army over Erwin Rommel's Afrika Korps.

Erwin Rommel

On the afternoon of the 24th, I was rung up on the Semmering (Germany, where Rommel had been on leave for his health) by Field Marshal Keitel, who told me that the British had been attacking at Alamein with powerful artillery and bomber support since the previous evening. General Stumme was missing. He asked whether I would be well enough to return to Africa and take over command again. I said I would. Keitel then said that he would keep me informed of developments, and would let me know in due course whether I was to return to my command. I spent the next few hours in a state of acute anxiety, until the evening, when I received a telephone call from Hitler himself. He said that Stumme was still missing – either captured or killed – and asked whether I could start for Africa immediately. I was to telephone him again before I actually took off, because he did not want me to interrupt my treatment unless the British attack assumed dangerous proportions. I ordered my aircraft for seven o'clock next morning and drove immediately to Wiener Neustadt. Finally, shortly after midnight, a call came through from the Führer. In view of developments at Alamein he found himself obliged to ask me to fly back to Africa and resume my command. I took off next morning. I knew there were no more laurels to be earned in Africa, for I had been told in the reports I had received from my officers that supplies had fallen far short of my minimum demands. But just how bad the supply situation really was I had yet to learn.

On arriving at Rome at about 11.00 hours (25 October) I was met at the airport by General von Rintelen, Military Attaché and German General attached to the Italian forces. He informed me of the latest events in the African theatre. After heavy artillery preparation, the enemy had taken part of our line south of Hill 31; several battalions of 164th Division and of Italians had been completely wiped out. The British attack was still in progress and General Stumme still missing. General von Rintelen also informed me that only three issues of petrol remained in the African theatre;

it had been impossible to send any more across in the last weeks, partly because the Italian Navy had not provided the shipping and partly because of the British sinkings. This was sheer disaster, for with only 300 kilometres' worth of petrol per vehicle between Tripoli and the front, and that calculated over good driving country, a prolonged resistance could not be expected; we would be completely prevented from taking the correct tactical decisions and would thus suffer a tremendous limitation in our freedom of action. I was bitterly angry, because when I left there had been at least eight issues for the Army in Egypt and Libya, and even this had been absurdly little in comparison with the minimum essential of thirty issues. Experience had shown that one issue of petrol was required for each day of battle; without it, the army was crippled and could not react to the enemy's moves. General von Rintelen regretted the situation, but said that he had unfortunately been on leave and had consequently been unable to give sufficient attention to the supply question.

Feeling that we would fight this battle with but small hope of success, I crossed the Mediterranean in my Storch and reached headquarters at dusk (25 October). Meanwhile, General Stumme's body had been found at midday and taken to Derna. He had apparently been driving to the battlefield along the Alarm track when he had suddenly been fired on in the region of Hill 21 by British infantry using anti-tank and machine-guns. Colonel Buechting had received a mortal wound in the head. The driver, Corporal Wolf, had immediately swung the car round, and General Stumme had leapt out and hung on to the outside of it, while the driver drove at top speed out of the enemy fire. General Stumme must have suddenly had a heart attack and fallen off the car. The driver had noticed nothing. On Sunday morning the General had been found dead beside the Alarm track. General Stumme had been known to suffer from high blood-pressure and had not really been fit for tropical service.

We all deeply regretted the sudden death of Stumme. He had spared no pains to command the army well and had been day and night at the front. Just before setting off on his last journey on 24 October, he had told the acting Chief of Staff that he thought it would be wise to ask for my return, since with his short experience of the African theatre, and in view of the enormous British strength and the disastrous supply situation, he felt far from certain that he would be able to fight the battle to a successful conclusion. I, for my part, did not feel any more optimistic.

General von Thoma and Colonel Westphal reported to me that evening on the course of the battle to date, mentioning particularly that General Stumme had forbidden the bombardment of the enemy assembly positions on the first night of the attack, on account of the ammunition shortage. As a result the enemy had been able to take possession of part of our minefield and to overcome the occupying troops with comparatively small losses to himself. The petrol situation made any major movement impossible and permitted only local counter-attacks by the armour deployed behind the particular sector which was in danger. Units of the 15th Panzer Division had counter-attacked several times on 24 and 25 October, but had suffered frightful losses in the terrible British artillery fire and non-stop RAF bombing attacks. By the evening of the 25th, only 31 of their 119 tanks remained serviceable.

There were now only very small stocks of petrol left in North Africa and a crisis was threatening. I had already – on my way through Rome – demanded the immediate employment of all available Italian submarines and warships for the transport of petrol and ammunition. Our own air force was still unable to prevent the British bombing attacks, or to shoot down any major number of British aircraft. The RAF's new fighter-bombers were particularly in evidence, as is shown by the fact that every one of the captured tanks belonging to the *Kampfstaffel* had been shot up by this new type of aircraft.

Our aim for the next few days was to throw the enemy out of our main defence line at all costs and to reoccupy our old positions, in order to avoid having a westward bulge in our front.

That night our line again came under a heavy artillery barrage, which soon developed into one long roll of fire. I slept only a few hours and was back in my command vehicle again at 05.00 hours (26 October), where I learnt that the British had spent the whole night assaulting our front under cover of their artillery, which in some places had fired as many as 500 rounds for every one of ours. Strong forces of the Panzer divisions were already committed in the front line. British night-bombers had been over our units continuously. Shortly before midnight the enemy had succeeded in taking Hill 28, an important position in the northern sector. (Called by the British "Kidney Ridge") He had then brought up reinforcements to this point ready to continue the attack in the morning with the object of extending his bridge-head west of the minefields.

Attacks were now launched on Hill 28 by elements of the 15th Panzer Division, the Littorio and a Bersaglieri Battalion, supported by the concentrated fire of all the local artillery and A.A. Unfortunately, the attack gained ground very slowly. The British resisted desperately. Rivers of blood were poured out over miserable strips of land which, in normal times, not even the poorest Arab would have bothered his head about. Tremendous British artillery fire pounded the area of the attack. In the evening part of the Bersaglieri Battalion succeeded in occupying the eastern and western edges of the hill. The hill itself remained in British hands and later became the base for many enemy operations.

I myself observed the attack that day from the north. Load after load of bombs cascaded down among my troops. British strength round Hill 28 was increasing steadily. I gave orders to the artillery to break up the British movement north-east of Hill 28 by concentrated fire, but we had too little to do it successfully. During the day I brought up the 90th Light Division and the *Kampfstaffel*, in order to press home the attack on Hill 28. The British were continually feeding fresh forces into their attack from Hill 28 and it was clear that they wanted to win through to the area between El Daba and Sidi Abd el Rahman. I therefore moved the Trieste into the area east of El Daba. Late in the afternoon German and Italian dive-bomber formations made a self-immolating attempt to break up the British lorry columns moving towards the north-west. Some 60 British fighters pounced on these slow machines and forced the Italians to jettison their bombs over their own lines, while the German pilots pressed home their attack with very heavy losses. Never before in Africa had we seen such a density of anti-aircraft fire. Hundreds of British tracer shells criss-crossed the sky and the air became an absolute inferno of fire.

British attacks supported by tanks tried again and again to break out to the west through our line south of Hill 28. Finally, in the afternoon, a thrust by 160 tanks succeeded in wiping out an already severely mauled battalion of the 164th Infantry Division and penetrated into our line towards the south-west. Violent fighting followed in which the remaining German and Italian tanks managed to force the enemy back. Tank casualties so far, counting in that day's, were 61 in the 15th Panzer Division and 56 in the Littorio, all totally destroyed.

Following on their non-stop night attacks, the RAF sent over formations of 18 to 20 bombers at hourly intervals throughout the day, which not only caused considerable casualties, but also began to produce serious signs of fatigue and a sense of inferiority among our troops.

The supply situation was now approaching disaster. The tanker *Proserpina*, which we had hoped would bring some relief in the petrol situation, had been bombed and sunk outside Tobruk. There was only enough petrol left to keep supply traffic going between Tripoli and the front for another two or three days, and that without counting the needs of the motorized forces, which had to be met out of the same stocks. What we should really have done now was to assemble all our motorized units in' the north in order to fling the British back to the main defence line in a concentrated and planned counter-attack. But we had not the petrol to do it. So we were compelled to allow the armoured formations in the northern part of our line to assault the British salient piecemeal.

Since the enemy was operating with astonishing hesitancy and caution, a concentrated attack by the whole of our armour could have been successful, although such an assembly of armour would of course have been met by the heaviest possible British artillery fire and air bombardment. However, we could have made the action more fluid by with-drawing a few miles to the west and could then have attacked the British in an all-out charge and defeated them in open country. The British artillery and air force could not easily have intervened with their usual weight in a tank battle of this kind, for their own forces would have been endangered.

But a decision to take forces from the southern front was unthinkable with the petrol situation so bad. Not only could we not have kept a mobile battle going for more than a day or two, but our armour could never have returned to the south if the British had attacked there. I did, however, decide to bring the whole of the 21st Panzer Division up north, although I fully realized that the petrol shortage would not allow it to return. In addition, since it was now obvious that the enemy would make his main effort in the north during the next few days and try for a decision there, half the Army artillery was drawn off from the southern front. At the same time I reported to the Führer's HQ that we would lose the battle unless there was an immediate improvement in the supply situation. Judging by previous experience, there was very little hope of this happening.

Relays of British bombers continued their attack throughout the night of the 26th. At about 02.00 hours a furious British barrage by guns of every calibre suddenly began in the northern sector. Soon it was impossible to distinguish between gun-fire and exploding shells and the sky grew bright with the glare of muzzle-flashes and shell-bursts. Continuous bombing attacks seriously delayed the approach march of the 21st Panzer Division and a third of the Ariete. By dawn the 90th Light Division and the Trieste had taken up position round the southern side of Sidi Abd el Rahman.

That morning (27 October) I gave orders to all formations to pin down the British assault forces during their approach by all-out fire from every gun they could bring to bear.

The tactics which the British were using followed from their apparently inexhaustible stocks of ammunition. Their new tank, the General Sherman, which came into action for the first time during this battle, showed itself to be far superior to any of ours.

Attacks against our line were preceded by extremely heavy artillery barrages lasting for several hours. The attacking infantry then pushed forward behind a curtain of fire and artificial fog, clearing mines and removing obstacles. Where a difficult patch was struck they frequently switched the direction of their attack under cover of smoke. Once the infantry had cleared lanes in the minefields, heavy tanks moved forward, closely followed by infantry. Particular skill was shown in carrying out this manoeuvre at night and a great deal of hard training must have been done before the offensive.

In contact engagements the heavily gunned British tanks approached to a range of between 2,000 and 2,700 yards and then opened concentrated fire on our anti-tank and antiaircraft guns and tanks, which were unable to penetrate the British armour at that range. The enormous quantities of ammunition which the enemy tanks used – sometimes they fired over 30 rounds at one target – were constantly replenished by armoured ammunition carriers. The British artillery fire was directed by observers who accompanied the attack in tanks.

In the early hours of 27 October, the British attacked again towards the south-west at their old break-in point south of Hill 28. At about 10 a.m. I went off to Telegraph Track. Two enemy bomber formations, each of 18 aircraft, dropped their bombs inside ten minutes into our defence positions. The whole front continued to lie under a devastating British barrage.

Local counter-attacks were due to be launched that afternoon by the 90th Light Division on Hill 28 and by the 15th and 21st Panzer Divisions, the Littorio and a part of the Ariete, against the British positions between minefields L and I.

At 14.30 hours I drove to Telegraph Track again, accompanied by Major Ziegler. Three times within a quarter of an hour units of the 90th Light Division, which had deployed and were standing in the open in preparation for the attack, were bombed by formations of eighteen aircraft. At 15.00 hours our dive-bombers swooped down on the British lines. Every artillery and anti-aircraft gun which we had in the northern sector concentrated a violent fire on the point of the intended attack. Then the armour moved forward. A murderous British fire struck into our ranks and our attack was soon brought to a halt by an immensely powerful anti-tank defence, mainly from dug-in anti-tank guns and a large number of tanks. We suffered considerable losses and were obliged to withdraw. There is, in general, little chance of success in a tank attack over country where the enemy has been able to take up defensive positions; but there was nothing else we could do. The 90th Light Division's attack was also broken up by heavy British artillery fire and a hail of bombs from British aircraft. A report from the division that they had taken Hill 28 unfortunately turned out to be untrue.

That evening further, strong detachments of the Panzer divisions had to be committed in the front to close the gaps. Several of the 90th Light Division's units also went into the line. Only 70 tons of petrol had been flown across by the *Luftwaffe* that day, with the result that the army could only refuel for a short distance, for there was no knowing when petrol would arrive in any quantity and how long the divisions would have to get along with the few tons we could issue to them. The watchword "as little movement as possible" applied more than ever.

In the evening we again sent SOSs to Rome and the Führer's HQ. But there was now no longer any hope of an improvement in the situation. It was obvious that from now on the British would destroy us bit by bit, since we were virtually unable to move on the battlefield. As yet, Montgomery had only thrown half his striking force into the battle.

The end at El Alamein came on 2 November. The leader of the British forces describes how.

General Montgomery

At two a.m. I directed two hard punches at the "hinges" of the final break-out area where the enemy was trying to stop us widening the gap which we had blown. That finished the battle.

The armoured car regiments went through as dawn was breaking and soon the armoured divisions got clean away into the open desert; they were now in country clear of minefields, where they could manoeuvre and operate against the enemy rear areas and retreating columns.

The armoured cars raced away to the west, being directed far afield on the enemy line of retreat.

THE DAMBUSTERS RAID, RUHR VALLEY, 16 MAY 1943

Guy Gibson, RAF

The famous "bouncing bomb" attack on the Ruhr Valley dams by RAF 617 Squadron was intended to disrupt production in Germany's industrial heartland. Nineteen Lancaster bombers led by Wing Commander Guy Gibson took part in the raid, eight of which were lost. Two dams, the Möhne and Eder, were destroyed, bringing widespread flooding; a third dam, the Sorpe, survived the bomb that hit it. Here Guy Gibson describes the attack on the Möhne dam. He was killed in action a year later.

Down below, the Möhne Lake was silent and black and deep, and I spoke to my crew.

"Well boys, I suppose we had better start the ball rolling." This with no enthusiasm whatsoever. "Hello, all Cooler aircraft. I am going to attack. Stand by to come in to attack in your order when I tell you."

Then to Hoppy: "Hello, 'M Mother'. Stand by to take over if anything happens."

Hoppy's clear and casual voice came back. "OK, Leader. Good luck."

Then the boys dispersed to the pre-arranged hiding-spots in the hills, so that they should not be seen either from the ground or from the air, and we began to get into position for our approach. We

circled wide and came around down moon, over the high hills at
the eastern end of the lake. On straightening up we began to dive
towards the flat, ominous water two miles away. Over the front
turret was the dam silhouetted against the haze of the Ruhr
Valley. We could see the towers. We could see the sluices. We
could see everything. Spam, the bomb-aimer, said, "Good show.
This is wizard." He had been a bit worried, as all bomb-aimers
are, in case they cannot see their aiming points, but as we came in
over the tall fir trees his voice came up again rather quickly.
"You're going to hit them. You're going to hit those trees."

"That's all right, Spam. I'm just getting my height."

To Terry: "Check height, Terry."

To Pulford: "Speed control, Flight-Engineer."

To Trevor: "All guns ready, gunners."

To Spam: "Coming up, Spam."

Terry turned on the spotlights and began giving directions –
"Down – down – down. Steady – steady." We were then exactly
sixty feet.

Pulford began working the speed; first he put on a little flap to
slow us down, then he opened the throttles to get the air-speed
indicator exactly against the red mark. Spam began lining up his
sights against the towers. He had turned the fusing switch to the
"ON" position. I began flying.

The gunners had seen us coming. They could see us coming with
our spotlights on for over two miles away. Now they opened up
and the tracers began swirling towards us; some were even bouncing off the smooth surface of the lake. This was a horrible
moment: we were being dragged along at four miles a minute,
almost against our will, towards the things we were going to
destroy. I think at that moment the boys did not want to go. I
know I did not want to go. I thought to myself, "In another minute
we shall all be dead – so what?" I thought again, "This is terrible –
this feeling of fear – if it is fear." By now we were a few hundred
yards away, and I said quickly to Pulford, under my breath,
"Better leave the throttles open now and stand by to pull me out of
the seat if I get hit." As I glanced at him I thought he looked a little
glum on hearing this.

The Lancaster was really moving and I began looking through
the special sight on my windscreen. Spam had his eyes glued to the
bombsight in front, his hand on his button; a special mechanism on
board had already begun to work so that the mine would drop (we

hoped) in the right spot. Terry was still checking the height. Joe and Trev began to raise their guns. The flak could see us quite clearly now. It was not exactly inferno. I have been through far worse flak fire than that; but we were very low. There was something sinister and slightly unnerving about the whole operation. My aircraft was so small and the dam was so large; it was thick and solid, and now it was angry. My aircraft was very small. We skimmed along the surface of the lake, and as we went my gunner was firing into the defences, and the defences were firing back with vigour, their shells whistling past us. For some reason, we were not being hit.

Spam said, "Left – little more left – steady – steady – steady – coming up." Of the next few seconds I remember only a series of kaleidoscopic incidents.

The chatter from Joe's front guns pushing out tracers which bounced off the left-hand flak tower.

Pulford crouching beside me.

The smell of burnt cordite.

The cold sweat underneath my oxygen mask.

The tracers flashing past the windows – they all seemed the same colour now – and the inaccuracy of the gun positions near the power-station; they were firing in the wrong direction.

The closeness of the dam wall.

Spam's exultant, "Mine gone."

Hutch's red Very lights to blind the flak-gunners.

The speed of the whole thing.

Someone was saying over the RT, "Good show, leader. Nice work."

Then it was all over, and at last we were out of range, and there came over us all, I think, an immense feeling of relief and confidence.

Trevor said, "I will get those bastards," and he began to spray the dam with bullets until at last he, too, was out of range. As we circled round we could see a great 1000-feet column of whiteness still hanging in the air where our mine had exploded. We could see with satisfaction that Spam had been good, and it had gone off in the right position. Then, as we came closer, we could see that the explosion of the mine had caused a great disturbance upon the surface of the lake and the water had become broken and furious, as though it were being lashed by a gale.

THE RAILWAY OF DEATH, BURMA, MAY 1943

Jeffrey English

The author was captured by the Japanese at the fall of Singapore. In 1943 he was put to work on the Burma–Siam railway, where conditions caused the death of two out of every three POWs.

The work here was again on a rock cutting, about a mile from the camp and reached through the usual little track of churned-up mud. The shifts changed over down at the cutting, not back at camp, and so the men were paraded at 7 a.m. to be counted, and then had to march down to commence work at 8 a.m. The party coming off duty had to march back to the camp, and did not arrive until some time after 8.30 a.m. But that did not mean ten and a half hours for food and sleep. On five days a week rations had to be collected from the river, which involved going out at 1.30 p.m. and getting back between 5 p.m. and 6 p.m.

At our previous camp the ration parties had been drawn from the semi-sick, but here *all* men not bedded down had to go on the working parties to the cutting, and so the afternoon ration parties had to be found from the now off-duty night shift. A man would work or be going to and from work for the best part of fourteen hours, do a four-hour ration fatigue, and have only six hours out of twenty-four for feeding, cleaning himself up, and sleeping.

For the first week or so, when we still had over 300 "fit" in the combined Anglo-Australian camp, each individual only got two ration fatigues a week. It would have been even less, but of course one half of our 300 were on the day shift, and only the other half were on the unhappy night shift.

On three pints of rice a day, all this, of course, was impossible and flesh and blood could not stand the strain; and in addition to the overwork we had dysentery and other diseases spreading at a frightening pace. As the numbers of "fit" men dwindled, the burden carried by the remainder consequently grew, until after only a few weeks the fitter men were doing all five ration fatigues a week as well as working the night shift in the cutting, and only having two days a week of real rest. As they gradually cracked up, more unfortunates, just past the crisis of their exhaustion or illnesses but in no way fully recovered, would be forced out in their place, lasting in their turn perhaps three or four days before they themselves had to be replaced by yet others not quite so ill.

Just as this gruelling programme put that at our previous camp in the shade, so did the new Nip Engineers make the last lot look like gentlemen. There, they had generally beaten only those whom they caught flagging or had somehow provoked their precariously balanced ill-humour; but here they beat up indiscriminately, beating every man in a gang if they wanted it to go faster, and two of them in particular were simply blood-thirsty sadists.

They were known to us as "Musso" and "The Bull", and they seemed to compete amongst themselves as to who could cause the most hurt. They were both on the night shift, and both would come on duty with a rope's end strapped to the wrist. These they plied liberally, and they also carried a split-ended bamboo apiece, whilst Musso in particular would lash out with anything which came handy, such as a shovel. Every morning two or three men would come back to camp with blood clotted on their faces and shoulders or matted in their hair, whilst others would return with puffy scarlet faces but no eye lashes or eye brows, these having been burnt off where they'd had a naked acetylene flare waved slowly across the eyes – a favourite trick of another Nip known to us as "Snowdrop".

They drove the men on, not just to make them work, but as a cruel master drives a beast of burden to force it on to further efforts greater than it can manage; and one would see half a dozen men staggering along with an 18-foot tree trunk, or rolling an outsize boulder to the edge of the cutting, with the Nip running alongside lashing out at them or kicking their knees and shins and ankles to keep them going.

Frequently men fainted, and to make sure that they weren't shamming, the Nip would kick them in the stomach, ribs or groin. If the man still didn't move, the favourite trick was to roll him over face downwards, and then jump up and down on the backs of his knees, so as to grind the kneecaps themselves into the loose gravel. If he fell on his side, a variation was to stand on the side of his face and then wriggle about, grinding and tearing his undercheek in the gravel: and as a way of telling a faked faint from a real one, both of these methods are, believe me, highly efficacious.

On one occasion a man was beaten up so badly by the Nips that they thought he wouldn't live, and so they got four prisoners and told them to bury him under a heap of rocks. The prisoners observed that he wasn't yet dead, but the Nips indicated that that didn't matter – they could bury him alive. It was only after a great deal of persuasion by a spunky Australian officer (who naturally took a personal bashing for his trouble, but didn't let that deter him) that the Nips eventually changed their minds and let the man be carried back to camp. He was carried on a stretcher, and came round later, but the beating had sent him almost off his head; he disappeared into the jungle and we couldn't find him for two days. On the third day he crept in for food; but he was now quite mental and became a gibbering idiot at the mere sight of a Nip. Had we bedded him down in a hospital tent, he could very well have simply popped off again; and so we found him a job in the cook-house where he would be working with others, and he worked there for a shaky fortnight before he packed it in and died.

CASSINO: THE END, 16–18 MAY 1944

Fred Majdalany

The monastery of Mount Cassino dominated the Liri Valley, and thus the Allied route to Rome.

The guard didn't have to wake us at five. Chilly dawn and a brisk shower of rain proved equal to the task. It was wet and cold and misty when John laid his maps and his notes on the flat bonnet of his jeep, and gave out final orders for the battle. All the familiar phrases. Only the places and the timings different. Two companies forward . . . barrage . . . about four hundred guns . . . tie up with tanks at forming-up place . . . all the details that are so dull in retrospect, so vital at the time. More things to mark on maps beginning to get crumpled and sodden. Officers scribbling details that concern them in every kind of little note-book. Questions. "Do you want me to push something forward to the wood after I've got the farm, sir?" . . . "Am I responsible for the track, sir, or are 'A' Company?" . . . "Are we likely to get a meal up to-night, or does the emergency ration have to last?" . . . "How soon can I expect anti-tank guns in my area?" . . .

The timings again, just to make sure that everyone is certain of them. From here at 07.20 so as to get to the forming-up place by 08.00, which gives us nearly an hour to get together with the tank people. Then from the forming-up place at 08.52, which should just give nice time to cross the start-line at H-hour, 09.00. Remember the barrage is doing four two-hundred-yard lifts, and staying on each one for twelve minutes. Keep close behind the barrage. Close as you can. Everybody clear? A last look through notes. Then away to the companies to pass the orders a stage further.

While the officers are receiving and giving orders the men are shaving and washing. And after they've shaved and washed they go for their breakfast, which has just arrived in containers brought up by the cooks. And while the officers are still giving out their orders, batmen surreptitiously place bowls or tins of water at hand, and the officers' shaving things. And when the officers have at last finished giving out their orders, and are reflectively re-reading their notes and thinking, "Have I forgotten anything?" the batmen produce some breakfast, and with maternal brusqueness order the officers to eat it, as it's almost stone-cold now. The officers eat the breakfast, but the tea is too hot to drink quickly, so they start to shave and while they shave they keep having sips of their tea. And while they are shaving and sipping people keep coming up and asking them questions, and with a shaving-brush in one hand and a mug in the other the officers try to make quick, clear decisions about such varied problems as a man who has lost his nerve and refuses to participate, a vehicle that has burnt out a clutch, probable ammunition requirements that night – while the batmen look on and think, "Can't they bloody well leave him alone for five minutes?"

It is all to the good, really, all this preliminary detail. It keeps your mind off yourself.

07.10 hours. Time to get ready. The shouts of the sergeant-majors. Jokes and curses. The infantry heaving on to their backs and shoulders their complicated equipment, their weapons and the picks and shovels they have to carry, too, so that they can quickly dig in on their objective. The individuals resolving themselves into sections and platoons and companies. Jokes and curses.

"Able ready to move, sir."

"Baker ready to move, sir."

"Charlie ready to move, sir."

"Dog ready to move, sir."

The column moved off along the track we'd taken the previous night. It was Tuesday morning. It was the fifth day of the offensive. In England the headlines were announcing that the Gustav Line was smashed except for Cassino and Monastery Hill. "Except" was the operative word. That was our job now. To break through and cut off Cassino and the Monastery.

On the stroke of nine there was an earth-shaking roar behind us as four hundred guns opened fire almost as one. With a hoarse, exultant scream four hundred shells sped low over our heads to tear into the ground less than five hundred yards in front, bursting with a mighty antiphonal crash that echoed the challenge of the guns. It was Wagnerian.

From then on the din was continuous and simultaneous: the thunder of the guns, the hugely amplified staccato of the shell-bursts close in front, and the vicious overhead scream that linked them with a frenzied counterpoint. And sometimes the scream became a whinny, and sometimes a kind of red-hot sighing, but most of the time it was just a scream – a great, angry baleful scream. The fury of it was elemental, yet precise. It was a controlled cyclone. It was splendid to hear, as the moment of actual combat approached.

The makers of films like to represent this scene with shots of soldiers crouching dramatically in readiness, and close-ups of tense, grim faces. Whereas the striking thing about such moments is the matter-of-factness and casualness of the average soldier. It is true that hearts are apt to be thumping fairly hard, and everyone is thinking, "Oh, Christ!" But you don't in fact look grim and intense. For one thing you would look slightly foolish if you did. For another you have too many things to do.

The two leading companies were due to advance exactly eight minutes after the barrage opened. So those eight minutes were spent doing such ordinary things as tying up boot laces, helping each other with their equipment, urinating, giving weapons a final check, testing wireless sets to make certain they were still netted, eating a bar of chocolate. The officers were giving last-minute instructions, marshalling their men into battle formations, or having a final check-up with the tank commanders with whom they were going to work.

Those who were not in the leading companies were digging like fiends, for they knew that the temporary calm would be quickly shattered as soon as the tanks and the leading infantry were seen emerging from it.

Meanwhile the barrage thundered on, and to its noise was added the roar of the Shermans' engines. A great bank of dust and smoke welled slowly up from the area the shells were pounding, so that you couldn't see the bursts any more. The sputtering of the 25-pounders rippled up and down the breadth of the gun-lines faster than bullets from a machine-gun, so numerous were they.

At eight minutes past nine they moved. Geoff led his company round the right end, Mark led his round the left end of the bank which concealed us from the enemy in front. Then the Shermans clattered forward, with a crescendo of engine-roar that made even shouted conversation impossible. The battle was on.

Geoff and Mark were to reach the start-line in ten minutes, at which time the barrage was due to move forward two hundred yards. Geoff and Mark would edge us as close to it as possible – perhaps within a hundred and fifty yards, and they'd wait until it moved on again, and then, following quickly in its wake, their bayonets and Brens would swiftly mop up any stunned remnants that survived. And while they were doing this the protective Shermans would blast with shells and machine-guns any more distant enemy post that sought to interfere.

Then the barrage would move forward another two hundred yards. The process would be repeated until the first objective had been secured – farm areas in each case. Then Kevin, who would soon be setting off, would pass his company through Geoff's and assault the final objective the code word for which was "Snowdrop". When Kevin wirelessed "Snowdrop" the day's work would be largely done. Highway Six would be only two thousand yards away.

To-day was crucial. To-day would decide whether it was to be a break-through or a stabilized slogging-match here in the flat entrance to the Liri Valley, with our great concentrations of men and material at the mercy of the Monastery O.P.

The Boche reacted quickly. Within a few minutes of our barrage opening up the shells started coming back. The scream of their shells vied with the scream of ours. Salvo after salvo began to rain down on the farms and the groves to our rear, where our supporting echelons were massed ready to follow in the wake of the assault. The sun's rays, growing warmer every minute, cleared the last of the morning mist. The Monastery seemed to shed the haze as a boxer sheds his dressing-gown before stepping into the ring for the last round. Towering in stark majesty above the plain, where the whole of our force was stretched out for it to behold. This was the supreme moment – the final reckoning with the Monastery.

Mortar-bombs began to land on the crest immediately in front. The bits sizzled down on our positions. Ahead the machine-guns were joining in. The long low bursts of the Spandaus: and the Schmeissers, the German tommyguns that have an hysterical screech like a Hitler peroration. There were long answering rattles from the Besas of the Shermans. Then the *Nebelwerfers*, the six-barrelled rocket-mortars, as horrific as their name . . . The barrels discharge their huge rockets one at a time with a sound that is hard to put into words. It is like someone sitting violently on the bass notes of a piano, accompanied by the grating squeak of a diamond on glass. Then the clusters of canisters sail through the air with a fluttering chromatic whine, like jet-propelled Valkyries . . . There were several regiments of them facing us, and the existing cacophony was soon made infinitely more hideous by scores of Valkyries. They were landing well behind. For the time being the Boche were concentrating everything on the farms and the woods, that were crammed with concentrations of trucks and tanks and supplies of all kinds.

"You may as well push off now, Stuart," John said. A minute later the fourth company moved round the right end of the bank and went the way of the others. The first of the prisoners came in. Six paratroops. Able Company's. Four large blond ones and two little dark ones. They were sent straight back.

Smoke-shells were being poured on to Monastery Hill now in a frantic effort to restore the mist. They had some effect, but they couldn't blot it out. The barrage seemed to get a second wind and the guns seemed to be firing faster than ever. The German shells were taking their toll of the rear areas. Four farms were on fire. We could see three ammunition-trucks blazing. Three more prisoners: one wounded, the other two helping him along. A grinning fusilier in charge. Some wounded in from Baker Company. All walking cases. Running commentary from tank liaison officer – "Rear Link". He sits in a Honey tank at our H.Q. and acts as wireless link between the squadron fighting with us in front and the tanks' regimental headquarters. "Both companies moving well. Machine-gun has opened up on Baker Company. Freddie Troop moving round to cope." The sharp crack of the Shermans' seventy-fives, and a burst of Besa that seems to go on for ever. That must be Freddie Troop "coping".

"Okay now," says Rear Link. "On the move again."

The *Nebelwerfers* have quietened down. They're easy to spot. Perhaps the counter-battery boys have got on to them. Our turn now. They're shelling our ridge as well as mortaring it. Some close ones. Rear Link has news. How Troop reports that five men have just come out of a building it has been blasting for five minutes and surrendered. Able Company report all's well. Baker report all's well. Charlie Company, following up, report all seems to be well in front, some wounded on the way back from Able. Three shells just above us. A signaller is hit.

The barrage ends. The effect is like the end of a movement in a symphony when you want to applaud and don't. From now on the guns will confine themselves to steady visitations on the enemy's rear. Unless the infantry want something hit. In which case the whole lot will switch in a very few minutes on to the place the infantry want hit. The infantry want something hit now. The voice on the wireless says, "Two machine-guns bothering me from two hundred yards north of Victor Eighty-two. Can you put something down?" John tells Harry, who is eating a sandwich. Harry gets on the wireless and says, "Mike target – Victor Eighty-two – north two hundred – five rounds gunfire." The shells scream over. Harry says, "We may as well make sure." He orders a repeat. The voice on the wireless says, "Thanks. That seems to have done the trick. They're not firing any more." Harry finishes his sandwich.

Rear Link has been deep in conversation with the left-hand troop commander. Rear Link thinks the companies have reached the first objective. No, not quite. It is all right on the left. But the right company seems to have run into something. Trouble from a farm. Tanks moving round to help. A lot of firing, ours and theirs. Rear Link says the tanks are pouring everything they've got into the farm. Twelve more prisoners – they look more shaken than the others. They had a bad spot in the barrage. Rear Link asks the troop commander how the battle is going on the right. The troop commander says it is a bit confused. A platoon is moving round to a flank. The farm seems to be strongly held. A reserve troop has joined in. A tank has been hit and has "brewed up". Baker on the left report that they are on their first objective. Charlie report they are moving up to pass through Baker. The *Nebelwerfers* again. Not as many as before. Some of them, at any rate, have been discouraged by the counter-battery fire. They seem to be going for the Bailey a mile back on the main track. Our anti-tank guns are in that area waiting to be called forward. Hope they are all right. Get Charles on the wireless and ask him. Charles says two trucks hit. One man killed and ten wounded. It has been all right since the first shelling. Able Company report that they are now firmly on first objective. Some casualties getting the farm. But they've killed a lot of Germans, and got eleven prisoners. They're digging in. The tanks are protecting their right, which seems horribly open. The tanks are in great form. They won't stop firing. They are spraying everything that could possibly conceal a German.

It has become very unhealthy behind our ridge. They are still mainly hitting the top of it. So long as they stay up there it won't be too bad. But there is always a nasty uncertainty about it. If they add a few yards to the range they'll be landing right among us. One or two have already come half-way down the slope.

Rear Link getting excited again. He's been talking to one of the troop commanders. Rear Link says Charlie appear to be on their objective. Can he signal "Snowdrop" to his R.H.Q.? John says, "No, not yet." Rear Link gets another message from the tanks. Rear Link says Charlie have started to dig in. Can he signal "Snowdrop"? John says, "No. They haven't consolidated yet." Kevin reports that he has arrived and is digging in. He says he has sent back more prisoners. More wounded, more prisoners, more *Nebelwerfers*, more shells, and the Monastery horribly clear. Rear Link has another conversation with the tanks. "How about 'Snowdrop', sir?" Rear Link almost pleads. "Not yet," John says. "Not until they have consolidated."

They're shelling us hard now. Not on the crest any more, but just over our heads and to our right. It is a different battery. They seem like 105s. They are coming over in eights. About every thirty seconds. The hard digging earlier in the morning is paying a good dividend. The last three salvoes landed right on our mortars, but they are well dug in and they get away without a single casualty. None of the shells has landed more than thirty yards from the command post. It is very frightening. Kevin on the wireless. Charlie Company are being counter-attacked with tanks. More shells on us. Twelve this time. Two of them within twenty yards. Behind, fortunately. Harry has taken a bearing on the guns and passed it back to the counter-battery people. Kevin on the wireless again. The leading Boche tank has got into a hull-down position fifty yards from his leading platoon. He has had some casualties. Our tanks trying to deal with it but hampered by very close-wooded country and a sunken lane that is an obstacle. Boche infantry are edging forward under cover of the fire from their tanks. More shells on the command post. The same place still. If they switch thirty yards to their left we've had it. That is the frightening thing. Wondering if they'll make a switch before they fire again. The accuracy of the guns is their downfall. John tries to get Kevin on the wireless. The signaller cannot get through. His toneless signaller-voice goes on saying, "Hello Three, hello Three, hello Three, hello Three." But he cannot get an answer. A closer shell blasted me against the bank. It is a queer feeling when you are brought to earth by blast. There is an instant of black-out, then sudden consciousness of what has happened: then an agonized wait for a spasm of pain somewhere on your person. Finally, a dull reactionary shock as you slowly discover you are intact. The signaller's voice again, "Cannot – hear – you – clearly – say – again – say again – that's – better – hear – you – okay." Kevin on the wireless. There is a tank deadlock. The rival tanks are now very close, on opposite sides of the same shallow crest. If either moves the other will get it the second the turret appears above the crest. The German cannot be outflanked. He has chosen his position cunningly. The sunken lane protects him. Kevin has had more casualties. More shells on the command post. Intense machine-gun fire from the direction of Kevin's company. Not a vestige of haze round the Monastery. This is the climax. No word from Kevin. John saying, "Are you through to Charlie Company yet?" The signaller-voice tonelessly persevering: "Hear my signals, hear my signals, hello Three . . . hear you very faintly . . ." Then, after an eternity, "Through now, sir. Message for you, sir." It is Kevin on the wireless. A fusilier has knocked out the tank with a Piat. It has killed the crew. The tank is on fire. The others are withdrawing. The infantry are withdrawing. Charlie Company are getting some of them as they withdraw. The counter-attack is finished. Consolidation may proceed. The tension is broken.

It went from mouth to mouth. "Bloke called Jefferson knocked out the tank with a Piat. Bloody good show! Bloke called Jefferson knocked out the tank with a Piat. Bloody good show! Bloody good show – bloke called Jefferson . . ." It passed from one to another till all the signallers knew, the stretcher-bearers, and the mortar crews, and the pioneers: and the anti-tank gunners waiting some way behind, and some sappers who were searching for mines along the track verges. Till the whole world knew. "A chap called Jefferson . . ."

Kevin on the wireless. "No further attacks. Consolidation completed."

"Get on to Brigade," John said, "and report 'Snowdrop'."

"Snowdrop," the Adjutant told Brigade.

"Snowdrop," Brigade told Division.

"Snowdrop," Division told Corps.

"Snowdrop," Corps told Army.

In all the headquarters all the way back they rubbed out the mark on their operations maps showing our position in the morning and put it in again twelve hundred yards farther forward, on the chalk-line called "Snowdrop". It was ten past two. The battle had been going for six hours.

"Command post prepare to move," John said.

We advanced in extended order through the long corn, as the ground was completely flat and without cover. The smell of the barrage still lingered, and the lacerated ground testified to its thoroughness. Wondering how many of the farms away to the right were still occupied by Boche; wondering how many machine-guns were concealed in the woods and the olive groves which stretched across the front a thousand yards ahead. Wondering if anyone had spotted our wireless aerials, which are impossible to conceal, and which always give away a headquarters.

There wasn't a vestige of cover in the half-mile stretch to where the reserve company had dug in. There was still a lot of firing in front, mainly from the tanks. They were taking no chances with the open right flank. They were dosing all the farms in turn. With nine tell-tale wireless aerials swaying loftily above the heads of the sweating signallers who carried the sets on their backs, we pushed on quickly through the long corn, wishing it was a good deal longer. And the Monastery watched us all the way.

As soon as the command post was established in the area of the reserve company, John went forward to where Kevin's company were, and he took me with him. They had turned the area into a compact little strong-point. It had to be compact, because there were fewer than fifty of them left out of ninety who had set off in the morning. Besides which, the country was so thick with trees that you couldn't see more than fifty yards ahead. They had adapted some of the excellent German trenches to face the other way. Some were reading the highly-coloured magazines left behind by the Boche. These were filled with lurid artists' impressions of the Cassino fighting bearing such captions as "Our paratroop super-men defying the Anglo-American hordes in living Hell of Cassino". They were all on that level. There was one copy of a sumptuous fashion magazine, which seemed slightly incongruous, and suggested that the Rhine-maidens weren't all the drab blue-stockings the Nazis made them out to be. There was one of the famous new steel pill-boxes: an underground three-roomed flatlet, which included a well-stocked larder. Only its small, rounded, steel turret protruded above the ground, and this was skilfully camou-flaged.

A few yards away Jefferson's tank was still burning. They were all talking about Jefferson. They were all saying he saved the company. The tank had wiped out a section at sixty yards' range, and was systematically picking off the rest of the company in ones and twos until fewer than fifty were left. Then Jefferson, on an impulse, and without orders, snatched up a Piat and scrambled round to a position only a few yards from the tank. Unable to get in a shot from behind cover, he had stood up in full view of the enemy and fired his weapon standing up, so that the back-blast of the exploding bomb knocked him flat on his back. Then he had struggled to his feet and aimed a shot at the second tank – but the tank was hurriedly pulling back, and with it the Boche infantry. It was one of those things that aren't in the book. Jefferson was typical of the best Lancashire soldiers – quiet and solid and rather shy, yet able in an emergency to act quickly without seeming to hurry. Such men are nice to have around in battles. It was one of those deeds the full implications of which don't really strike you till some time later, then leave you stunned and humble.

. . . During the night we received orders to continue the ad-vance at 6 a.m. and secure the next objective-line, "Bluebell". This was to synchronize with the Poles, who were to make a final attempt to work round from our old position north-east of Cassino and cut the highway from their side.

It was well after three by the time everyone had been fed, ammunition had been replenished, and orders for the new attack had been given out. Before he went to sleep John said, "I'm going to put Jefferson in for the V.C."

At a quarter to six the earth trembled, and once again the shells started pouring overhead so thickly that at times you fancied you could see them. At the same time another lot of guns began to pound Monastery Hill in support of the Polish attack. In next to no time dust and smoke and yellow flame enveloped the Monastery itself, so that when our Dog and Baker Companies passed through Charlie Company on the stroke of six it was hidden from view. This was the kill. We were going in for the kill. The Poles were sweeping round from the right: we, two and a half miles away in the valley, were on our way to seal it off from the left. It shouldn't be long now. And once we had cut the Highway the very qualities that had made the Monastery an impregnable bastion for so long would turn it into an equally formidable death-trap. For so long the guardian and protector of its garrison, it would round on them in its death-throes and destroy them.

Compared with the previous day, we had a fairly easy advance. There were some snipers and one or two isolated machine-guns, but they didn't seem disposed to resist very strongly, and by ten Baker and Dog, assisted by fresh tanks, were nicely settled on Bluebell, another thousand yards on. We were ordered to push on as fast as possible. So Baker and Dog advanced again to the final objective line, "Tulip", twelve hundred yards farther on. And Able, Charlie and Command Post pushed on to the area just cleared by Dog and Baker. By four o'clock in the afternoon Dog and Baker both signalled that they were established on "Tulip" – both had O.P.s directly overlooking Highway Six. Both asked permission to carry on and cut the road and search beyond it. We were ordered to stay where we were, however, as the exact position of the Poles was not known and mistakes might occur if we both started milling around by the road. We dominated it from where we were. We had done what was required of us. We were to stay where we were until we had further orders. The job was nearly done.

During the night Dog and Baker were told to patrol as far as the road. Not till the following morning were we allowed to send anyone beyond it. By that time it had ceased to be a military feat. It was a formal ceremony. So John sent a special patrol of three corporals, all holders of the M.M. They crossed the Highway and carried out a careful search of the gullies and ruined buildings on the far side of it, but the only Germans they could find were dead ones. Their time was not wasted, however. Each returned with a Schmeisser gun, a camera, a watch and a pair of binoculars of impeccable German manufacture. An hour later the Poles entered the Monastery. As so often happens when great events are awaited with prolonged and excessive anxiety, the announcement of the fall of Monte Cassino was rather an anticlimax. It was Thursday, 18 May. The battle had lasted a week. The job was done.

D-DAY: 6 JUNE 1944

Iain Macleod

The Allied invasion of Normandy, 6 June 1944, was the greatest seaborne invasion in history. Some 160,000 troops – British American, French, Polish and Canadian – embarked in 5,000 craft in southern England to make the journey to "the far shore".

D-Day itself was postponed for twenty-four hours until June 6. Even so, the weather was cold and the sea was rough. General Eisenhower took the greatest gamble in all military history when he launched his armada on such uncertain seas. He was proved right.

The Divisional HQ was split between two ships, and I found myself with men of the 1st Hampshires of 231 Brigade. For the Division this was the second seaborne assault. For 231 Brigade, the third. Moreover, the 50th Division, which had been the last Division to leave the beaches of Dunkirk, was now one of those chosen to be the first to land in Normandy. I had not been with them in 1940, but I had, in fact, been away from France for a few days less. It was about June 10, long after Dunkirk, that I had left St Nazaire in a hospital ship. Four years later, and in the company of the finest fighting Division of the Army, I was going back.

Perhaps I was helped by my early voyages on the Minch, but I slept soundly enough through the rough night, and came on deck somewhere around first light. The waves were still choppy and the landing was going to be a hazardous and in part a haphazard affair. But the day was becoming warm. The coast of Normandy began to take shape through the haze. And then as full light began to come one saw the ships and the planes. It was a sight so paralysing that tears came to my eyes. It was as if every ship that had ever been launched was there, and even as if the sea had yielded up her wrecks. It was as if every plane that had ever been built was there, and, so it seemed in fantasy, as if the dead crews were there too. There had never been since time began such a rendezvous for fighting men: there never will be again. And I remember reciting, not in scorn, but out of sheer delight at being part of that great company in such a place, "And gentlemen in England now abed . . ."

As the fire from the naval guns began to blot out the shore defences, and the endless drone of the planes and the whine of their bombs rose to a crescendo, so came H-hour. 50 Div. were to assault on a front of two brigades, the 69th on the left and the 231st on the right. The Hampshires were to land just east of Le Hamel and to take the village and then the other coastal villages, especially Arromanches which was earmarked as the site of the artificial port called Mulberry. It meant for them a day of heavy fighting and severe casualties. The commanding officer was wounded, and the second-in-command killed. But it was also a day of glory for the regiment that must rank high, perhaps first, among all the Hampshires' battle honours. Watching the LCAs (Landing Craft Assault) carrying the Hampshires pull away and switchback to the shore, and while waiting for our own sea taxi, I thought that as a martial gesture I would load my revolver. When I unbuttoned my ammunition pouch, I found that my batman, who knew more about war than I did, had filled it not with bullets but with boiled sweets. He was quite right. They proved much more useful.

Few things went exactly as planned, and the biggest disappointment was the failure of the secret waterproofed tanks to negotiate the heavy seas. They were supposed to paddle through the last few miles to the beach and provide covering fire for the assaulting companies. In view of the weather, it was then decided to take the craft to the beach, and disembark the tanks. The same dilemma came to the Americans assaulting the strongly-held Omaha beach to our right, but here a different and a tragic decision was taken. In spite of the seas, sixty-four tanks were launched and all were swamped. Nearly all the crews were drowned and, of course, the cover fire was lost.

Presently Bertie and I climbed with elderly dignity down the scrambling nets that were slung over the ship's sides and dropped down into our LCA. We began to cruise in to the beach. Something now went wrong. Perhaps the naval officer in charge decided that too many craft were trying to get ashore at once, perhaps the underwater mines obstructed us. In any event, we began to circle a few hundred yards away from the beach. Quite a long time passed. The sun grew hotter, and I began to doze. Suddenly and equally for no reason that I could see, we stopped turning and ran straight for the beach. The landing ramp smacked down and one stepped or jumped according to taste into the thigh-deep water. Bertie and I stepped, and waded carefully ashore.

The beach was alive with the shambles and the order of war. There were dead men and wounded men and men brewing tea.

There were men reorganising for a battle advance, and men doing absolutely nothing. There were even some German prisoners waiting patiently for heaven knows what. There was a whole graveyard of wrecked ships and craft and tanks of every size. It was like an absurdly magnificent film by Cecil B. de Mille. It was like war.

We wandered over the beaches and climbed the dunes behind them. Everything seemed oddly quiet. The minefields were most carefully marked ("*Achtung Minen*") and wired. The villages to left and right of us were still German-held, although we did not realise it at the time. We must have taken a sand track between them.

We met very few people on the way to the orchard at Meuvaines which was to be our D-Day headquarters. Only a motley collection of vehicles had arrived, but one of them was the intelligence truck and in it a staff officer was busy marking up the reports of the progress of the leading battalions. We were about a mile and a half inland.

The rest of the day is a patchwork of memories. There was a flurry of shots into the orchard from a small nest of Germans we had overlooked. There was a journey back to the beaches to see the build-up. There was a journey on the back of a policeman's motor-cycle to find the forward brigades, and establish contact with their staff captains. I can't remember when I ate, but I remember what I ate. We had been issued with twenty-four-hour packs of concentrated dried food. I expect they had a taste as evil as their appearance. But I don't think many people in 50 Div. tasted them. 50 Div. were used to looking after themselves. From somewhere my batman produced both the great delicacies of 1944 – tinned steak pudding and tinned Christmas pudding. These and whisky were my food.

Night began to fall. Nearly all our objectives had been taken. Patrols were moving into Bayeux, which was to fall next morning. The St Leger feature was in our grasp. The 47th Royal Marine Commando (under our command for the landings) had started its successful battle for Port-en-Bessin. Hideous close fighting in the Bocage lay ahead, but at least on the 50 Div. front the day had gone well.

My batman had secured a corner of the farmer's barn for me, and I was thinking of snatching some sleep when the door opened and Tom Black looked in:

"Is Iain here?" I followed him outside.

"What's up?"

"Nothing. I thought we'd have a drink."

We stood under the trees, drinking from his flask and looking back towards the sea. A few fast German fighter planes were making a tip-and-run raid on the beach, and the red tracer bullets climbed lazily into the sky after them. I looked at my watch. It was exactly midnight. I had lived through D-Day. We had expected anything up to 40 per cent casualties in the landing, and somehow I had been convinced that I would be killed. Now, equally unreasonably, I became convinced that I would live through the war. I would see our second child, who was to be born in October. There would be a life after the war. D-Day was over.

INVASION OF NORMANDY, 6 JUNE–24 JUNE 1944

Sergeant G. E. Hughes

Diary, 6 June 1944
06.00 Get in LCA. Sea very rough. Hit the beach at 7.20 hours. Murderous fire, losses high. I was lucky T[hank] God. Cleared three villages. Terrible fighting and ghastly sights.

June 7. Still going. Dug in at 02:00 hrs. Away again at 05.30. NO FOOD. Writing few notes before we go into another village. CO out of action, adjutant killed. P Sgt lost. I do P Sgt['s job]. More later.

June 8. 07.30, fire coming from village. Village cleared. Prisoners taken. Night quite good but German snipers lurking in wood. Had 2 hrs' sleep. Second rest since the 6th.

June 9. 06.30 hrs went on wood clearing. Germans had flown. Only one killed for our morning's work. We are now about 8 to 10 miles inland. Promoted to Sgt.

June 10. Joan darling, I have not had you out of my thoughts. T[hank] God I have come so far. We have lost some good men. Our brigade was only one to gain objectives on D-Day.

The French people give us a good welcome. Had wine.

June 11. Contact with enemy. Lost three of my platoon. Very lucky T[hank] God. Only had 5 hours sleep in 3 days.

June 12. This day undescrible [sic] mortar fire and wood fighting. Many casualties. T[hank] God I survived another day.

June 13. Just had my first meal since Monday morning. Up all night. Everyone in a terrible state. I keep thinking of u.

June 14. Counter-attack by Jerry from woods. Mortar fire. 13 of my platoon killed or missing. After heavy fighting yesterday CSM also wounded, also Joe. O[fficer] C[ommanding] killed. I am one mass of scratches. Advanced under creeping barrage for 3 miles. Drove Jerry back. It is hell. 3 Tiger tanks came here, up to lines during night.

June 16. [resting] Received letter from home. Wrote to Joan and Mum.

June 17. [resting]

June 18. Day of Hell. Counter-attack.

June 19. Day of Hell. Counter-attack.

June 20. Day of Hell. Advanced. Counter-attacked.

June 21. Quiet day. We have been fighting near Tilley [Tilly]. Bayonet charge. Shelled all day. Letters from home.

June 22. Out on patrol. Got within 35 yards of Tiger before spotting it. Got back safely T[hank] God. Shelled to blazes. Feeling tired out.

June 23. No sleep last night. Exchanged fire, out on patrols all day, went on OP for 4 hours. Stand-to all night. Casualties.
    Just about had enough.

June 24. Had to go back to CCS [Casualty Clearing Station]. Malaria.

Sergeant Hughes was hospitalized with malaria for most of the rest of the Normandy campaign.

"DOODLEBUGS" LAND ON LONDON, JULY 1944

Vere Hodgson

In June 1944, German VI rockets – or "Doodlebugs" – began landing on London and South East England, fired from bases in France and Holland.

Diary:

. . . These Robot Planes go on after daybreak, which the old raids never did. I could hear the wretched thing travelling overhead at 6 a.m. They did not fall on us – but they fell on someone. Our guns barked out and spat and fussed until they had gone. They travel quickly and on Thursday night were low over Kensington. In fact everyone of us was perfectly convinced the thing was exactly three inches above the roof.

Nothing is said on the wireless or in the papers except . . . Southern England! That is us – and we are all fed-up.

Monday was our fire-watch. Mrs Hoare light-heartedly remarked: "I don't think there will be any more air-raids." And in my heart I agreed with her. But not a bit of it! Hitler has still got a sting in his Nasty Tail. At 4 a.m. we were amazed to be roused by a Warning. We all got up. In 20 minutes All Clear. Just as I had bedded down another went. I sat on the steps. It was just getting light. Mr Bendall reported to the Street Leader.

In the morning much discussion, for no one knew about Robot Planes. Cannot remember all the events of Thursday night. We had little sleep. I was in my flat – something trundled across the sky. In the morning nothing on the wireless, and we felt injured – as we needed the sympathy of our friends! On and off all day we had Warnings and gunfire. One Robot fell in Tooley St in the City. One of the women from our Printing Works rang up to say at Eltham they had had a terrible night – all her windows and doors blown out. It all pointed to Kent.

By Saturday we all felt very cheap. I longed to go and see the Invasion pictures, but did not feel equal to cope with queues – so went to a local Cinema and saw a little. All through we had across the screen – Air Raid Warning. Then All Clear. Three times. But the audience was in a light-hearted mood and laughed aloud. We had not learned then to take the Robots seriously . . .

Went to cheer up Auntie. She was not well and had slept little. She had heard something had fallen on St Mary Abbots Hospital. All night long they came. By dawn I could not believe it could

continue. But it did. So got myself a cup of tea. Did jobs. Later felt
sick from lack of sleep, and to the sound of the Brains Trust dozed
off. Later went for a walk. Felt better in the air. Every other person
carrying a tin hat. Went along Marloes Road . . . great piles of
glass marked the route. Heavy Rescue lorries were driving in and
out gathering up the debris. All one roof of the Hospital gone . . .
about 4 a.m. Saturday. One woman said twelve children were
brought out dead. But I don't know, as my informant was too
agitated to be coherent.

They may have to evacuate the Hospital. Many nurses killed.
Heard another had fallen at Marble Arch, and in Putney. As I
walked back through the Park I pondered on these things, and
decided to sleep tonight at the Sanctuary. London is in a chastened
mood after the last three nights.

A VISIT TO BELSEN DEATH CAMP, GERMANY, 19 APRIL 1945

Richard Dimbleby

Alongside the 500,000 Jews from Western Europe who were killed by the
SS, 5.5 million Jews from Eastern Europe were also executed. Some of
these were shot on the spot by special SS squads; most, however, were
transported to the extermination camps, Belsen among them, to be gassed.

I picked my way over corpse after corpse in the gloom, until I
heard one voice raised above the gentle undulating moaning. I
found a girl, she was a living skeleton, impossible to gauge her age
for she had practically no hair left, and her face was only a yellow
parchment sheet with two holes in it for eyes. She was stretching
out her stick of an arm and gasping something, it was "English,
English, medicine, medicine", and she was trying to cry but she
hadn't enough strength. And beyond her down the passage and in
the hut there were the convulsive movements of dying people too
weak to raise themselves from the floor.

In the shade of some trees lay a great collection of bodies. I
walked about them trying to count, there were perhaps 150 of
them flung down on each other, all naked, all so thin that their
yellow skin glistened like stretched rubber on their bones. Some of
the poor starved creatures whose bodies were there looked so
utterly unreal and inhuman that I could have imagined that they
had never lived at all. They were like polished skeletons, the

skeletons that medical students like to play practical jokes with.

At one end of the pile a cluster of men and women were gathered round a fire; they were using rags and old shoes taken from the bodies to keep it alight, and they were heating soup over it. And close by was the enclosure where 500 children between the ages of five and twelve had been kept. They were not so hungry as the rest, for the women had sacrificed themselves to keep them alive. Babies were born at Belsen, some of them shrunken, wizened little things that could not live, because their mothers could not feed them.

One woman, distraught to the point of madness, flung herself at a British soldier who was on guard at the camp on the night that it was reached by the 11th Armoured Division; she begged him to give her some milk for the tiny baby she held in her arms. She laid the mite on the ground and threw herself at the sentry's feet and kissed his boots. And when, in his distress, he asked her to get up, she put the baby in his arms and ran off crying that she would find milk for it because there was no milk in her breast. And when the soldier opened the bundle of rags to look at the child, he found that it had been dead for days.

There was no privacy of any kind. Women stood naked at the side of the track, washing in cupfuls of water taken from British Army trucks. Others squatted while they searched themselves for lice, and examined each other's hair. Sufferers from dysentery leaned against the huts, straining helplessly, and all around and about them was this awful drifting tide of exhausted people, neither caring nor watching. Just a few held out their withered hands to us as we passed by, and blessed the doctor, whom they knew had become the camp commander in place of the brutal Kramer.

I have never seen British soldiers so moved to cold fury as the men who opened the Belsen camp this week.

VICTORY IN EUROPE CELEBRATIONS, LONDON, 8 MAY 1945

Mollie Panter-Downes

When the day finally came, it was like no other day that anyone can remember. It had a flavour of its own, an extemporaneousness which gave it something of the quality of a vast, happy village fete as people wandered about, sat, sang, and slept against a summer

background of trees, grass, flowers, and water. It was not, people
said, like the 1918 Armistice Day, for at no time was the reaction
hysterical. It was not like the Coronation, for the crowds were
larger and their gaiety, which held up all through the night, was
obviously not picked up in a pub. The day also surprised the
prophets who had said that only the young would be resilient
enough to celebrate in a big way. Apparently the desire to assist in
London's celebration combusted spontaneously in the bosom of
every member of every family, from the smallest babies, with their
hair done up in red-white-and-blue ribbons, to beaming elderly
couples who, utterly without self-consciousness, strolled up and
down the streets arm in arm in red-white-and-blue paper hats.
Even the dogs wore immense tricoloured bows: Rosettes sprouted
from the slabs of pork in the butcher shops, which, like other food
stores, were open for a couple of hours in the morning. With their
customary practicality, housewives put bread before circuses.
They waited in the long bakery queues, the string bags of the
common round in one hand and the Union Jack of the glad
occasion in the other. Even queues seemed tolerable that morning.
The bells had begun to peal and, after the night's storm, London
was having that perfect, hot, English summer's day which, one
sometimes feels, is to be found only in the imaginations of the lyric
poets.

The girls in their thin, bright dresses heightened the impression
that the city had been taken over by an enormous family picnic.
The number of extraordinarily pretty young girls, who presumably are hidden on working days inside the factories and government offices, was astonishing. They streamed out into the parks
and streets like flocks of twittering, gaily plumaged cockney birds.
In their freshly curled hair were cornflowers and poppies, and they
wore red-white-and-blue ribbons around their narrow waists.
Some of them even tied ribbons around their bare ankles. Strolling
with their uniformed boys, arms candidly about each other, they
provided a constant, gay, simple marginal decoration to the big,
solemn moments of the day. The crowds milled back and forth
between the Palace, Westminster, Trafalgar Square, and Piccadilly Circus, and when they got tired they simply sat down
wherever they happened to be – on the grass, on doorsteps, or
on the kerb – and watched the other people or spread handkerchiefs over their faces and took a nap. Everybody appeared determined to see the King and Queen and Mr Churchill at least once,

and few could have been disappointed. One small boy, holding on
to his father's hand, wanted to see the trench shelters in Green Park
too. "You don't want to see shelters today," his father said. "You'll
never have to use them again, son." "Never?" the child asked
doubtfully. "Never!" the man cried, almost angrily. "*Never*! Understand?" In the open space before the Palace, one of the places
where the Prime Minister's speech was to be relayed by loudspeaker at three o'clock, the crowds seemed a little intimidated by the
nearness of that symbolic block of grey stone. The people who
chose to open their lunch baskets and munch sandwiches there
among the flower beds of tulips were rather subdued. Piccadilly
Circus attracted the more demonstrative spirits.

By lunchtime, in the Circus, the buses had to slow to a crawl in
order to get through the tightly packed, laughing people. A lad in
the black beret of the Tank Corps was the first to climb the little
pyramidal Angkor Wat of scaffolding and sandbags which was
erected early in the war to protect the pedestal of the Eros statue
after the figure had been removed to safekeeping. The boy
shinnied up to the top and took a tiptoe Eros pose, aiming an
imaginary bow, while the crowd roared. He was followed by a
paratrooper in a maroon beret, who, after getting up to the top,
reached down and hauled up a blonde young woman in a very
tight pair of green slacks. When she got to the top, the Tank Corps
soldier promptly grabbed her in his arms and, encouraged by
ecstatic cheers from the whole Circus, seemed about to enact the
classic role of Eros right on the top of the monument. Nothing
came of it, because a moment later a couple of GIs joined them and
before long the pyramid was covered with boys and girls. They sat
jammed together in an affectionate mass, swinging their legs over
the sides, wearing each other's uniform caps, and calling down
wisecracks to the crowd. "My God," someone said, "think of a
flying bomb coming down on this!" When a firecracker went off, a
hawker with a tray of tin brooches of Monty's head happily yelled
that comforting, sometimes fallacious phrase of the blitz nights,
"All right, mates, it's one of ours!"

All day long, the deadly past was for most people only just under
the surface of the beautiful, safe present, so much so that the
Government decided against sounding the sirens in a triumphant
"all clear" for fear that the noise would revive too many painful
memories. For the same reason, there were no salutes of guns – only
the pealing of the bells, and the whistles of tugs on the Thames

sounding the doot, doot, doot, dooooot of the "V", and the roar of the planes, which swooped back and forth over the city, dropping red and green signals toward the blur of smiling, upturned faces.

It was without any doubt Churchill's day. Thousands of King George's subjects wedged themselves in front of the Palace throughout the day, chanting ceaselessly. "We want the King" and cheering themselves hoarse when he and the Queen and their daughters appeared, but when the crowd saw Churchill there was a deep, full-throated, almost reverent roar. He was at the head of a procession of Members of Parliament, walking back to the House of Commons from the traditional St Margaret's Thanksgiving Service. Instantly, he was surrounded by people – people running, standing on tiptoe, holding up babies so that they could be told later they had seen him, and shouting affectionately the absurd little nurserymaid name, "Winnie, Winnie!" One of two happily sozzled, very old, and incredibly dirty cockneys who had been engaged in a slow, shuffling dance, like a couple of Shakespearean clowns, bellowed, "That's 'im, that's 'is little old lovely bald 'ead!" The crowds saw Churchill again later, when he emerged from the Commons and was driven off in the back of a small open car, rosy, smiling, and looking immensely happy. Ernest Bevin, following in another car, got a cheer too. One of the throng, an excited East Ender, in a dress with a bodice concocted of a Union Jack, shouted, "Gawd, fancy me cheering Bevin, the chap who makes us work!" Herbert Morrison, sitting unobtrusively in a corner of a third car, was hardly recognized, and the other Cabinet Ministers did no better. The crowd had ears, eyes, and throats for no one but Churchill, and for him everyone in it seemed to have the hearing, sight, and lungs of fifty men. His slightly formal official broadcast, which was followed by buglers sounding the "cease firing" call, did not strike the emotional note that had been expected, but he hit it perfectly in his subsequent informal speech ("My dear friends, this is your victory . . .") from a Whitehall balcony.

All day long, little extra celebrations started up. In the Mall, a model of a Gallic cock waltzed on a pole over the heads of the singing people. "It's the Free French," said someone. The Belgians in the crowd tagged along after a Belgian flag that marched by, its bearer invisible. A procession of students raced through Green Park, among exploding squibs, clashing dustbin lids like cymbals and waving an immense Jeyes Disinfectant poster as a banner. American sailors and laughing girls formed a conga line down the middle of Piccadilly and cockneys linked arms in the Lambeth Walk. It was a day and night of no fixed plan and no organized merriment. Each group danced its own dance, sang its own song, and went its own way as the spirit moved it. The most tolerant, self-effacing people in London on V E Day were the police, who simply stood by, smiling benignly, while soldiers swung by one arm from lamp standards and laughing groups tore down hoardings to build the evening's bonfires. Actually, the police were not unduly strained. The extraordinary thing about the crowds was that they were almost all sober. The number of drunks one saw in that whole day and night could have been counted on two hands – possibly because the pubs were sold out so early. The young service men and women who swung arm in arm down the middle of every street, singing and swarming over the few cars rash enough to come out, were simply happy with an immense holiday happiness. They were the liberated people who like their counterparts in every celebrating capital that night, were young enough to outlive the past and to look forward to an unspoilt future. Their gaiety was very moving.

Just before the King's speech, at nine Tuesday night, the big lamps outside the Palace came on and there were cheers and ohs from children who had never seen anything of that kind in their short, blacked-out lives. As the evening wore on most of the public buildings were floodlighted. The night was as warm as midsummer, and London, its shabbiness now hidden and its domes and remaining Wren spires warmed by lights and bonfires, was suddenly magnificent. The handsomest building of all was the National Gallery, standing out honey-coloured near a ghostly, blue-shadowed St Martin's and the Charles I bit of Whitehall. The illuminated and floodlighted face of Big Ben loomed like a kind moon. Red and blue lights strung in the bushes around the lake in St James's Park glimmered on the sleepy, bewildered pelicans that live there.

By midnight the crowds had thinned out some, but those who remained were as merry as ever. They went on calling for the King outside the Palace and watching the searchlights, which for once could be observed with pleasure . . .

"A Correspondent", The Hereford Times
Passing through the village of Stoke Lacy early on Tuesday afternoon one was startled to see an effigy of Hitler in the car

park at the Plough. That evening a crowd began to gather, and word went round that Hitler was to be consumed in flames at 11 p.m. At that hour excitement was intense, when Mr W. R. Symonds called upon Mr S. J. Parker, the Commander of No. 12 Platoon of the Home Guard, to set the effigy alight. In a few minutes the body of Hitler disintegrated as his 1,000-year empire had done. First his arm, poised in the Hitler salute, dropped as smartly as it was ever raised in real life . . . then a leg fell off, and the flames burnt fiercely to the strains of "Rule Britannia", "There'll Always be an England", and "Roll Out the Barrel". The crowd spontaneously linked hands and in a circle 300-strong sang the National Anthem.

THE GRAND NATIONAL, AINTREE, 29 MARCH 1947

John Hislop ("Phantom")

A view from the saddle.

There were fifty-seven of us lined up at the start, like sardines in a tin. Kami's position was about one-third of the way from the inside, between Rearmament and Some Chicken. As usual, there was much restiveness and scrimmaging, with the starter shouting "Keep off the tapes!"

Then the gate went up and we jumped off, most of us as eagerly as if we had only five furlongs to go. Taking into consideration the heavy going after the morning's rain, the initial pace of the field as a whole was such that no horse could hope both to maintain it and complete the course.

Kami was squeezed when the field "broke", but settled into a swinging stride, which was not fast enough to keep anywhere near the solid wall of leaders, and we found ourselves going over the first fence well behind but clear of any interference.

Kami jumped it perfectly, in the style of a real Aintree horse, standing well back and landing without "pitching".

There were two or three other horses lying in the same area as Kami, with a loose horse or two in the vicinity. I went rather a long way round, towards the outside – for two reasons. In the first place the going there was less churned up. Second, I wanted Kami to be completely clear of any bumps or other mishap which would have put a horse of such frail build "on the floor".

He was still jumping perfectly. In fact, Kami never put a foot wrong all the way. His swinging, even gait gave me the greatest confidence and the consistency of his jumping – every fence measured off long before he got to it – made me feel certain that wherever he finished he would complete the course.

As we turned into the country for the last circuit, Kami gradually began to overtake the field. Jumping Becher's for the second time, our hopes of a possible victory became something more than the ambition of every steeplechase rider. There were, I suppose, some six or eight horses – that is, with their riders still on board – in front of me, but most of them were tiring, and as I passed them at least one rider threw me a word of encouragement that means so much in a race of this kind. "Well done, Johnny, keep going," someone said. As we crossed the road with only two more fences to jump I could see Prince Regent in front of me visibly tiring, and, still a good way ahead, the green jacket of Lough Conn and the green and blue of the eventual winner, of whose identity I was as ignorant as, I suppose, were the majority of spectators.

Coming into the last fence but one, there were two loose horses in front of me, and, on the inside, Prince Regent. I realized then that I had no hope of winning, as Kami was tiring; the heavy going had taken toll of his delicate frame and only his courage and innate stamina kept him going. But he jumped the fence perfectly, and went on towards the last with, I think, Prince Regent about level with us, but very tired.

We landed safely with the long stretch to the winning post spread out before us, both tired, but with Prince Regent beaten for sure. I got out my whip and kept swinging it without ever hitting Kami, and he answered nobly, gradually overhauling Mr Rank's gallant horse to take us into third place.

And so the placed jockeys rode back to the three unsaddling enclosures appointed for first, second, and third. Ahead of me went the winner, Caughoo, between two mounted policemen, surrounded by a crowd including owner, trainer, and friends, all running alongside to pat the winning mount and to congratulate his rider.

As for me, my feeling is of three-fold gratitude – to the horse for his courage and the way he carried me; to Tom Mason, the trainer, for Kami's wonderful condition; and to the gods for the luck which followed our journey.

THE KOREAN WAR: LIEUTENANT PHILIP CURTIS WINS THE VICTORIA CROSS, IMJIN RIVER, N. KOREA 22 APRIL 1951

Anthony Farrar-Hockley

The Communist regime of North Korea launched a major offensive in the Korean war on 22 April 1951, breaking through the line held by the United Nations west of Chungpyong Reservoir. The situation for the UN was saved only by the stand of the Gloucestershire Regiment at Imjin River.

The dawn breaks. A pale, April sun is rising in the sky. Take any group of trenches here upon these two main hill positions looking north across the river. See, here, the weapon pits in which the defenders stand: unshaven, wind-burned faces streaked with black powder, filthy with sweat and dust from their exertions, look towards their enemy with eyes red from fatigue and sleeplessness; grim faces, yet not too grim that they refuse to smile when someone cracks a joke about the sunrise. Here, round the weapons smeared with burnt cordite, lie the few pathetic remnants of the wounded, since removed: cap comforters; a boot; some cigarettes half-soaked with blood; a photograph of two small girls; two keys; a broken pencil stub. The men lounge quietly in their positions, waiting for the brief respite to end.

"They're coming back, Ted."

A shot is fired, a scattered burst follows it. The sergeant calls an order to the mortar group. Already they can hear the shouting and see, here and there, the figures moving out from behind cover as their machine-guns pour fire from the newly occupied Castle Site. Bullets fly back and forth; overhead, almost lazily, grenades are being exchanged on either side; man meets man; hand meets hand. This tiny corner of the battle that is raging along the whole front, blazes up and up into extreme heat, reaches a climax and dies away to nothingness – another little lull, another breathing space.

Phil is called to the telephone at this moment; Pat's voice sounds in his ear.

"Phil, at the present rate of casualties we can't hold on unless we get the Castle Site back. Their machine-guns up there completely dominate your platoon and most of Terry's. We shall never stop their advance until we hold that ground again."

Phil looks over the edge of the trench at the Castle Site, two hundred yards away, as Pat continues talking, giving him the instructions for the counter attack. They talk for a minute or so; there is not much more to be said when an instruction is given to assault with a handful of tired men across open ground. Everyone knows it is vital: everyone knows it is appallingly dangerous. The only details to be fixed are the arrangements for supporting fire; and, though A Company's Gunners are dead, Ronnie will support them from D Company's hill. Behind, the machine-gunners will ensure that they are not engaged from the open eastern flank. Phil gathers his tiny assault party together.

It is time, they rise from the ground and move forward up to the barbed wire that once protected the rear of John's platoon. Already two men are hit and Papworth, the Medical Corporal, is attending to them. They are through the wire safely – safely! – when the machine-gun in the bunker begins to fire. Phil is badly wounded: he drops to the ground. They drag him back through the wire somehow and seek what little cover there is as it creeps across their front. The machine-gun stops, content now it has driven them back; waiting for a better target when they move into the open again.

"It's all right, sir," says someone to Phil. "The Medical Corporal's been sent for. He'll be here any minute."

Phil raises himself from the ground, rests on a friendly shoulder, then climbs by a great effort on to one knee.

"We must take the Castle Site," he says; and gets up to take it.

The others beg him to wait until his wounds are tended. One man places a hand on his side.

"Just wait until Papworth has seen you, sir –"

But Phil has gone: gone to the wire, gone through the wire, gone towards the bunker. The others come out behind him, their eyes all on him. And suddenly it seems as if, for a few breathless moments, the whole of the remainder of that field of battle is still and silent, watching amazed, the lone figure that runs so painfully forward to the bunker holding the approach to the Castle Site: one tiny figure, throwing grenades, firing a pistol, set to take Castle Hill.

Perhaps he will make it – in spite of his wounds, in spite of the odds – perhaps this act of supreme gallantry may, by its sheer audacity, succeed. But the machine-gun in the bunker fires directly into him: he staggers, falls, is dead instantly; the grenade he threw a second before his death explodes after it in the mouth of the bunker. The machine-gun does not fire on three of Phil's platoon who run forward to pick him up; it does not fire again through the battle: it is destroyed; the muzzle blown away, the crew dead.

THE GREAT TIDE AT JAYWICK, 31 JANUARY 1953

Janice Farmer

The little town of Jaywick lies smashed and flooded. More than a thousand people are homeless. Some died in their beds as mighty waves swept over the sea wall and down the streets.

By Monday night all the living residents had been rescued. The search for the dead went on. Men in little boats carried on their pathetic door-to-door hunt among the flooded bungalows, breaking in windows and roofs, looking for lost relatives.

Stunned groups of people waited, some for news, some merely from curiosity. One old lady stood silently by a portable receiving set. She spoke to no one. She had been waiting for hours, staring out at the flood.

Bungalows immediately beyond the sea wall were smashed to pieces. Garden walls had been washed away; balconies stood at drunken angles. Windows had shattered.

The streets in some parts were still dry. Here, a few families remained. They were out of danger, and intended to stay.

In one road, a bungalow stood in the centre at an angle. There was an empty plot of ground behind it. But we found the bungalow had been swept from the end of the road – at least sixty yards away. It stood there, undamaged, the furniture still inside, the windows unbroken.

Pets were being cared for at the Morocco Café by the R.S.P.C.A. There were some empty boats nearby. We clambered into one of them.

There was a strong tide running and icy wind. Rowing was hard work. We skirted lamp-posts and bus stops. The tops of garden fences scraped the bottom of the boat.

The bungalows stood five feet deep in water. Cars stood in gardens, almost completely submerged. Dustbins and boxes floated round us.

The disaster had made many heroes. All the rescued praise their rescuers, the men who gathered their small boats like a second "Dunkirk" to help their neighbours.

Mrs A. Cale was rescued from her house at four o'clock on Sunday morning. She and her daughter had realized that floods were likely to come. They tried to rest for a while as waves crashed over the sea wall. They were lucky. Their bungalow stood on high ground.

Mrs Cale said: "We were without gas and electricity but we were all right until the telephone was cut off. Then we realized how bad things were.

"It was dreadful, seeing the waves. All through those hours we heard cries for help and could do nothing. We were rescued in the darkness and taken to Clacton, although our bungalow was still above water. We were very lucky. The men with their boats were wonderful. All day long they were rescuing people."

One of these was a Dutch taxi-driver, who has lived here since the end of the war. "My name? Just call me a Dutchman."

He found one couple in their loft with a dog. They had been there for hours. He helped the man into the boat, and placed the dog on his lap. The woman panicked. She was quite elderly.

She slipped into the water and was swept away in a matter of seconds. There was nothing to be done. "The old man just sat there, holding the dog," said the Dutchman. "He was a bag of nerves. He just could not realize what had happened."

In the many journeys between the waterlogged houses and safety, they passed several floating bodies. But for the moment they were only interested in the living.

At one point, our Dutchman had to be rescued himself. "I saw a woman on the balcony in her underwear. 'All right, I'm coming,' I told her. But just as I got there the boat sank and I was left hanging on to the balcony by my finger-tips. The man in the boat with me, he got wet and was picked up by another boat. I stood on the balcony with the woman and was rescued with her."

Young boys like Charles Patchy were helping, too.

Charles heard a noise coming from a loft. He thought it was a child screaming. He broke in and found a terrified Alsatian bitch. Charles is a great animal lover. The dog would not approach him. It was obviously half crazed with fear. Charlie wrapped it in a wet sheet and lowered the animal into his boat.

Later, he dried it, fed it, and returned it to the owners, where the dog was reunited with its two puppies.

What will happen to Jaywick? Many people think the town is finished. It will be months before it is habitable again.

The floods have occurred in cycles for years. And many people think that the area should be banned as a residential town. The sea seems determined to keep its own.

CONQUERING EVEREST, HIMALAYAS, 29 MAY 1953

Edmund Hillary

Mount Everest, at 29,028 feet the highest mountain in the world, was finally conquered in 1953, by New Zealander Edmund Hillary and Nepalese Sherpa, Tenzing Norgay. Here Hillary describes their assault on the final ridge.

I looked anxiously up at the rocks. Planted squarely across the ridge in a vertical bluff, they looked extremely difficult, and I knew that our strength and ability to climb steep rock at this altitude would be severely limited. I examined the route out to the left. By dropping fifty or a hundred feet over steep slabs, we might be able to get around the bottom of the bluff, but there was no indication that we'd be able to climb back on to the ridge again. And to lose any height now might be fatal. Search as I could, I was unable to see an easy route up to the step or, in fact, any route at all. Finally, in desperation I examined the right-hand end of the bluff. Attached to this and overhanging the precipitous East face was a large cornice. This cornice, in preparation for its inevitable crash down the mountainside, had started to lose its grip on the rock, and a long narrow vertical crack had been formed between the rock and the ice. The crack was large enough to take the human frame, and though it offered little security, it was at least a route. I quickly made up my mind – Tenzing had an excellent belay and we must be near the top – it was worth a try.

Before attempting the pitch, I produced my camera once again. I had no confidence that I would be able to climb this crack, and with a surge of competitive pride which unfortunately afflicts even mountaineers, I determined to have proof that at least we had reached a good deal higher than the South Summit. I took a few photographs and then made another rapid check of the oxygen – 2,550 lb. pressure. (2,550 from 3,300 leaves 750. 750 over 3,300 is about two-ninths. Two ninths off 800 litres leaves about 600 litres. 600 divided by 180 is nearly 3½.) Three and a half hours to go. I examined Tenzing's belay to make sure it was a good one and then slowly crawled inside the crack.

In front of me was the rock wall, vertical but with a few promising holds. Behind me was the ice-wall of the cornice, glittering and hard but cracked here and there. I took a hold on the rock in front and then jammed one of my crampons hard into the ice behind. Leaning back with my oxygen set on the ice, I slowly levered myself upwards. Searching feverishly with my spare boot, I found a tiny ledge on the rock and took some of the weight off my other leg. Leaning back on the cornice, I fought to regain my breath. Constantly at the back of my mind was the fear that the cornice might break off, and my nerves were taut with suspense. But slowly I forced my way up – wriggling and jambing and using every little hold. In one place I managed to force my ice-axe into a crack in the ice, and this gave me the necessary purchase to get over a holdless stretch. And then I found a solid foothold in a hollow in the ice, and next moment I was reaching over the top of the rock and pulling myself to safety. The rope came tight – its forty feet had been barely enough.

I lay on the little rock ledge panting furiously. Gradually it dawned on me that I was up the step, and I felt a glow of pride and determination that completely subdued my temporary feelings of weakness. For the first time on the whole expedition I really knew I was going to get to the top. 'It will have to be pretty tough to stop us now' was my thought. But I couldn't entirely ignore the feeling of astonishment and wonder that I'd been able to get up such a difficulty at 29,000 feet even with oxygen.

When I was breathing more evenly I stood up and leaning over the edge, waved to Tenzing to come up. He moved into the crack and I gathered in the rope and took some of his weight. Then he, in turn, commenced to struggle and jam and force his way up until I was able to pull him to safety – gasping for breath. We rested for a moment. Above us the ridge continued on as before – enormous overhanging cornices on the right and steep snow slopes on the left running down to the rock bluffs. But the angle of the snow slopes was easing off. I went on chipping a line of steps, but thought it safe enough for us to move together in order to save time. The ridge rose up in a great series of snakelike undulations which bore away to the right, each one concealing the next. I had no idea where the top was. I'd cut a line of steps around the side of one undulation and another would come into view. We were getting desperately tired now and Tenzing was going very slowly. I'd been cutting steps for almost two hours, and my back and arms were starting to tire. I tried cramponing along the slope without cutting steps, but my feet slipped uncomfortably down the slope. I went on cutting. We seemed to have been going for a very long time and my confidence was fast evaporating. Bump followed bump with maddening regularity. A patch of shingle barred our way, and I climbed dully up it and started cutting steps around another bump. And then I realized that this was the last bump, for ahead of me the ridge dropped steeply away in a great corniced curve, and out in the distance. I could see the pastel shades and fleecy clouds of the highlands of Tibet.

To my right a slender snow ridge climbed up to a snowy dome about forty feet above our heads. But all the way along the ridge the thought had haunted me that the summit might be the crest of a cornice. It was too late to take risks now. I asked Tenzing to belay me strongly, and I started cutting a cautious line of steps up the ridge. Peering from side to side and thrusting with my ice-axe, I tried to discover a possible cornice, but everything seemed solid and firm. I waved Tenzing up to me. A few more whacks of the ice-axe, a few very weary steps, and we were on the summit of Everest.

It was 11.30 a.m. My first sensation was one of relief – relief that the long grind was over; that the summit had been reached before our oxygen supplies had dropped to a critical level; and relief that in the end the mountain had been kind to us in having a pleasantly rounded cone for its summit instead of a fearsome and unapproachable cornice. But mixed with the relief was a vague sense of astonishment that I should have been the lucky one to attain the ambition of so many brave and determined climbers. It seemed difficult at first to grasp that we'd got there. I was too tired and too conscious of the long way down to safety really to feel any great elation. But as the fact of our success thrust itself more clearly into my mind, I felt a quiet glow of satisfaction spread through my body – a satisfaction less vociferous but more powerful than I had ever felt on a mountain top before. I turned and looked at Tenzing. Even beneath his oxygen mask and the icicles hanging from his hair, I could see his infectious grin of sheer delight.

BANNISTER BREAKS THE FOUR-MINUTE MILE, OXFORD, 6 MAY 1954

Athletics Correspondent, **The Times**

R. G. Bannister accomplished at Oxford yesterday what a whole world of milers had recently been bracing themselves to achieve first – the four-minute mile. He did so in conditions which were far from promising, and he did better than even time, for he finished weary but triumphant and mobbed by an encircling crowd, in 3 min. 59.4 sec. – three-fifths of a second less than the magic four minutes. On the way, at 1500 metres he had equalled another world record, shared by Gundhar Haegg, the previous holder of the world record of 4 min. 1.4 sec. over the mile, Lennart Strand, another Swede and Walther Lueg, of Germany.

The occasion was the annual match between the University (Oxford) and the Amateur Athletics Association which one fears was rather forgotten in the general excitement. For the record, the A.A.A. won by 64 points to 34 in the 16 events. The crowd might have been larger but at least it did all it could to make up for the lack of numbers by an intelligent enthusiasm which enabled many among them to realize when the last lap was being run and Bannister raced well ahead that something big was about to be recorded by the time-keeper – almost certainly a world record – perhaps even the four-minute mile itself.

The conditions have been described as unpromising because a strong gusty wind was bound to handicap the runners part of the time as they ran round the Iffley Road track and one or two early showers threatened worse things still. Actually, the weather was fine for the race. The match itself was not started until five o'clock in the evening and an uneasy hour passed with little success for Oxford. C.E.F Higham's excellent time of 14.8 sec. In the high hurdles only inches behind P.H. Hildreth, the A.A.A. champion, in spite of a slow start, was the best thing seen so far. H. H. Boyd's victory in the half-mile to a great extent made up for his failures through unfitness in the university sports.

But all this was quickly forgotten when the mile was announced and the six runners lined up. Bannister, C. J. Chataway, W. T. Hulatt, and C. W. Brasher represented the A.A.A and G. F. Dole and A. D. Gordon ran for Oxford. Bannister's great time of 4 min, 3.6 sec last year was well in mind and Chataway started as a university record holder, but nothing dramatic enough happened during the first two laps to excite more than the actual time keepers.

Brasher, always a gallant and willing runner – or steeplechaser – set the pace and the first quarter was completed with Brasher a stride or two in front of Bannister and Chataway about the same distance away, third.

Chataway went ahead about half-way down the back-stretch during the third lap and Bannister went after him. Brasher dropped back and, one fears, became forgotten though he had deserved well of all concerned. At the bell, Chataway was still a little in front of Bannister and one had to wait again for the back-stretch to see a new and decisive phase in the race unfold itself. Bannister now lengthened his magnificent stride and, obviously going very fast, passed Chataway and raced farther and farther ahead.

Spectators now really sensed a triumph of above the average and as Bannister broke the tape some 50 yards ahead of Chataway there was a general swoop on the centre of the field. Bannister was encircled and disappeared from view, but somehow the news leaked out. There was a scene of the wildest excitement and what miserable spectators they would have been if they had not waved their programmes, shouted, even jumped in the air a little. It is hard not to believe that Bannister's time will not be accepted by the world authorities, for whatever else could be said the wind was at least as much a handicap as occasionally it was a help. Chataway's time of 4 min 7.2 sec. was his own personal best.

The following are Bannister's times for each quarter mile: 57.7 sec., 60.6 sec., 62.4 sec., and 58.7 sec.

THE SUEZ INVASION, EGYPT, 5–6 NOVEMBER 1956

Donald Edgar, London Daily Express

The nationalization of the Suez canal led to military intervention in Egypt by Britain and France, with airborne troops landing at Port Said on 5 November. Donald Edgar accompanied the seaborne troops, who landed at Port Said on the following day.

It was a sunny morning with a blue sky and our ship was in the centre of a great array of warships and transports which covered a great arc of sea from Port Fuad to the left of the Canal to Port Said in the centre and Gamil airfield on the right. Our ship was nearly stationary about three miles off shore, distant enough to reduce the scene to the size of a coloured picture postcard and the warships to toys on the Round Pond in Kensington Gardens.

It was only with an effort of will I could grasp that it was all for real, not a sequence from a film. It was really happening.

To the left of the Canal entrance a great cloud of black smoke from burning oil tanks was drifting over the city forming a sinister cloud. Along the sea-front puffs of white smoke were rising from shell-fire and red flames were taking hold on the right where the shanty town lay. Just off shore a line of elegant destroyers were moving along the beach firing into the city. As they had guns of only small calibre the reports at this distance were no more disturbing than the muffled woofs of a sleeping dog.

But to the extreme left, off Port Fuad, the French sector, lay a great battleship, the *Jean Bart*, and from time to time it fired a heavy shell from its great guns which made the air tremble a little where I stood.

Around us and further out to sea were cruisers and an aircraft carrier or two, waiting in ominous silence. Helicopters were ferrying back and forth from the beach. I learned later they had carried the 45 Royal Marine Commando in to support 40 and 42 Commandos which had earlier landed in their Buffalos together with C Sqdn of the 6 Royal Tank Regiment. I watched one helicopter fall into the sea and a ship nearby suddenly leaped forward to the rescue with the speed of a greyhound. I learned it was HMS *Manxman*, the fastest ship in the Royal Navy at the time.

I took in everything I could and asked questions of the Captain, who tried to be helpful within his limits. He told us with a wry smile that there had been trouble with the American Sixth Fleet which was in the area, escorting a shipload of American refugees from Alexandria. In fact, I gathered the Anglo-French convoy was being closely shadowed by the Americans and the air had been filled with tough, rude radio exchanges. Hanson Baldwin smiled – but in somewhat wintry fashion. I did not really believe that Eisenhower would give orders to the Sixth Fleet to blow us out of the water, but I knew the political situation was so tense that even the impossible might happen.

I was busy making notes, drawing rough sketch-maps and then began to feel somewhat dispirited as the first excitement wore off.

I kept telling myself how lucky I was – standing on the bridge watching the most impressive military operation the British had put on for many a year, with parachutists, Marine Commandos, tanks, aircraft and a naval bombardment. What is more I was looking at it all in safety. In the cussed way of the English I think this last factor was beginning to have its effect on me. I was beginning to feel sorry for the people of Port Said who were on the receiving end.

I remembered only too well what it felt like. In 1940 in France it was the Germans who had the tanks, the aircraft and the overwhelming force and I was at the receiving end, taking shelter in ditches and cellars.

However, I fought these feelings back. A few miles away British troops were fighting their way through a city, perhaps against heavy opposition, suffering casualties. What is more in a few hours I could well be in danger myself.

The captain went to the radio room and came back to say that as it was taking longer than expected to clear the area round the jetties of the Canal we should not be landing until the afternoon. He suggested we had lunch.

It was a lunch to remember. A steward served us imperturbably with a drink while we studied the menu. Another took our order with the same solicitude as a head-waiter in the Savoy Grill. A wine-waiter suggested an excellent Burgundy. Outside, not far away, the marine Commandos with the Centurion tanks were fighting their way through the wrecked buildings of Port Said. No doubt men, women and children were dying in fear and anguish. Yet here was I sitting down to an excellent lunch as if I was a first-class passenger on a luxury Mediterranean cruise.

But I ate the lunch and drank the wine with enjoyment. All my instincts as an old soldier came to my aid – eat and drink whilst you can, you never know where the next meal is coming from. Whilst we were finishing our coffee and brandy the ship started to move gently towards the Canal.

We went up again to the bridge. The ship was easing its way towards the jetty on the right-hand of the entrance to the Canal and the scene of destruction along the water-front cleared through the smoke. Crumbled masonry, blackened walls still standing with nothing behind, burnt-out vehicles, debris scattered over the road. A few soldiers hurried to and fro, but the firing – rifle and machine-gun and mortar – seemed to be concentrated a few hundred yards down the Canal. The captain had a radio set on the bridge tuned to the BBC and we heard a bland voice announcing that all resistance had ceased in Port Said. It was just then when with a great scream that froze me in terror, a section of naval fighter-bombers dived down over us dropping their rockets and firing their cannon just ahead of us. Almost quicker than sight they wheeled away into the sky while clouds of grey smoke rose into the air. We were all silent on the bridge for a minute or two. This was the attack by Sea Furies on Navy House where 40 Commando had encountered tough resistance from a hundred-odd Egyptians who had barricaded themselves in. Even the tanks, firing at point-blank range had been unable to dislodge them so the Navy was called in to help with an air-strike. The Navy complied, but with some regret for the building had become over the years part of the Royal Navy's heritage. Even after this devastating attack, however, the Egyptians fought on and a Marine officer told me they had to clear them out room by room. "They didn't know how to fight professionally," he said to me. "But by God they fought to the end."

It was not until the next day that twenty survivors gave themselves up. Their bravery was another proof that the Egyptians, often abandoned by their officers, can fight magnificently.

By now it was late afternoon. In front of us a transport was unloading more tanks and paratroops who moved off down the Canal road. There were two barges from the *Jean Bart* filled with French paratroops lying down philosophically in the open holds. I noticed with a certain surprise, some female contours among the camouflage uniforms. I had not known till then that the French paratroops had women in their ranks among whose duties were cooking and first-aid. It was an imaginative re-creation of the traditional *vivandières*!

As I was looking at the quayside I saw a group of senior officers who seemed to be waiting for transport while snipers' bullets seemed to me to be getting uncomfortably close. Campbell recognized the leader – Lt General Sir Hugh Stockwell, the Allied Commander, who cheerily waved his swagger-stick at the passing troops. He had been spending a few hours looking at the situation and was trying to get back to the headquarters ship, HMS *Tyne*. I was not to know then

I went out to the road. Night had fallen and the fires had dimmed. Sentries had been posted. Out at sea there was not a light to give a hint of the great convoy and its accompanying warships. A few shots sounded in the distance, but silence was enveloping the stricken city.

The Anglo-French Suez expedition was called off after joint pressure from Washington and Moscow. It marked a humiliating climb-down for the British, and many date 6 November 1956 as the day when Britain ceased to be a world power.

SUBURBAN LIFE, 1959

P. Willmott and M. Young

From a survey of Woodford, London.

. . . Home and work place are certainly separated by distance. Of the 572 people in the general sample who were in paid work, 76 per cent worked outside the borough. Taking London as a whole the *average* time taken from door to door in the journey to work was 42 minutes, in Woodford many people have much longer to go than that.

> "I have to walk to the station first of all. It takes me altogether an hour and a half to get to work and more to get home at night. They push them into the trains like sardines. I can't even read my evening paper till Leytonstone, there's such a crush."

What the wife does in Essex and the husband in London are quite different. Here are some extracts taken every three-quarters of an hour or so from the diaries written by a teacher and his wife for a particular Thursday morning in October 1959.

MR MATTHEWS

7.15 a.m.

Got up reluctantly when the alarm rang. Went downstairs, put the dog out and made a pot of tea, taking a cup to Doris. Took my own cup of tea into the bathroom, while I washed and shaved. Finished dressing and then downstairs to breakfast.

8 a.m.

Left the house. A brisk walk to the station as usual – otherwise I would miss the train that goes through Snaresbrook at about 8.10. Bought my *Times* at the

MRS MATTHEWS

Frank brought me my usual cup of tea in bed. Got up and went down in my dressing-gown to get his breakfast. Said good morning to our little Sealyham, Dennis – he rolls on his back and waits for me to tickle him.

Frank left for work and Dennis and I walked to the gate to see him off. Waited until Frank had disappeared round the bend in the road, then went indoors and station bookstall, where I have one ordered. Read *The Times* on the train and was irritated by being turned out at Leytonstone to wait for another.

8.45 a.m.
Arrived at school. Collected the classroom key and went to unlock door. Eastwood and Good, who are monitors, were waiting outside the door as usual. Took my coat to the staff room, and when I got back found that most of the other boys had arrived. Took the register and went up to Assembly with the class. The Head announced the times of the Record and Chess clubs, but as usual no one could hear him.

called the children and prepared their breakfast.

Got Susan ready for school and took her round there. Then went on to the shops. On the way back saw Mrs. Rayburn, who has been ill with flu – I stopped to ask her how she was feeling.

9.15 a.m.
Returned to classroom for first period. Awaited arrival of 4C, which takes ten minutes longer than anyone else. We made a start on the trial scene from *The Merchant of Venice*; they seemed to get the general feeling of it well, but will they understand most of the detail when we come to examine it more carefully next week?

Arrived home. Combed Dennis, then did the bed-making, then started on the dishes. I like to see the bright cheerful colours of the plates emerge from the soapy water. "House-wives' Choice" on the radio also cheers me up.

10 a.m.
Second Period. I took the Second-year 6th A-level group. Harrington announced that he did not intend to go on to

My friend Joyce called. She wanted to know if I would go over to her house for tea that afternoon, instead of the next do S-level after all, because his parents couldn't afford any more years at school. I tried to dissuade him and the period developed into quite a discussion.

10.45 a.m.

Morning break. I went to the staff room for tea. Talked with Anderson about two boys in my class. He says he caught them fighting quite violently yesterday. This might not matter so much if they were younger, but they are 16. Anderson and I discussed tactics – which made a change from the interminable political discussions we've had lately in the staff room.

day, as previously arranged. I agreed. We started a discussion about washing machines.

Joyce having gone, I took Dennis out for his morning walk in the Forest. We have made a lot of friends on these walks – dog-owners seem to find it very easy to get talking to each other. Saw my friend Shirly out with her Dachshund, Oscar. We stopped for a chat about the party we both were at last Saturday.

Obviously it is not easy for Mr. and Mrs. Matthews to share their interests in the way they would if they ran a farm together. Mrs. Matthews likes to hear about the people her husband works with; she is not thrilled to hear about S-level candidates, and even if she were once, the excitement would not last long.

PROFUMO MEETS KEELER, CLIVEDEN, JULY 1961

Lord Alfred Denning

The relationship between Tory War Minister John Profumo and prostitute Christine Keeler was the great scandal of the Sixties. Not only did Profumo mislead parliament about his liason with Keeler, it also transpired that she was involved with a Russian spy, Captain Ivanov. The affair helped bring down the Macmillan government. The extract below is from Lord Denning's official inquiry into the scandal.

The week-end of Saturday, 8th July, 1961, to Sunday, 9th July, 1961, is of critical importance. Lord and Lady Astor had a large party of distinguished visitors to their great house at Cliveden.

They included Mr. Profumo, the Secretary of State for War, and his wife, Mrs. Profumo, who stayed the week-end. Other visitors came to meals but did not stay the night. Stephen Ward entertained some young girls at his cottage. One of these was Christine Keeler, who was then living with him. Captain Ivanov came down on the Sunday. There is a fine swimming pool in the grounds at Cliveden near the main house, and Lord Astor, on occasions, allowed Stephen Ward to use it with his friends so long as it did not clash with his own use of it.

On the Saturday, after nightfall, Stephen Ward and some of the girls were bathing in the swimming pool when one of them, Christine Keeler, whilst she was in the water, took off her bathing costume, threw it on the bank, and bathed naked. Soon afterwards Lord Astor and a party of his visitors walked down after dinner to the swimming pool to watch the bathing. Lord Astor and Mr. Profumo walked ahead of Lady Astor, Mrs. Profumo and the others. Christine Keeler rushed to get her swimming costume. Stephen Ward threw it on one side so that she could not get it at once and Christine seized a towel to hide herself. Lord Astor and Mr. Profumo arrived at this moment, and it was all treated as a piece of fun – it was over in a few minutes, for the ladies saw nothing indecent at all. Stephen Ward and the girls afterwards got dressed and went up to the house and joined the party for a little while.

On the Sunday, after lunch, Stephen Ward and the girls and Captain Ivanov went to the swimming pool. Later Lord Astor and others of his party came down to swim too. There was a light-hearted, frolicsome bathing party, where everyone was in bathing costumes and nothing indecent took place at all. Photographs were taken by Mr. Profumo and others. They showed, of course, that Mr. Profumo was there with some of the girls but nothing improper whatever.

Captain Ivanov left Cliveden in the early evening and took Christine Keeler back with him to town. They went to Stephen Ward's house and there drank a good deal and there were perhaps some kind of sexual relations. Captain Ivanov left the house before Stephen Ward himself got back at midnight. But Captain Ivanov never became the lover of Christine.

It is apparent that during this week-end Mr. Profumo was much attracted by Christine Keeler and determined to see her again, if he could. This was, of course, easy, through Stephen Ward. In the next few days and weeks Mr. Profumo made assignations with Christine Keeler. He visited her at Stephen Ward's house and had sexual intercourse with her there. Sometimes he called at a time when Stephen Ward or someone else was there, he would then take her for a drive until the coast was clear. On one occasion he did not use his own car because his wife had it in the country. He used a car belonging to a Minister which had a mascot on it. He drove her to see Whitehall and Downing Street, also Regent's Park. Mr. Profumo wrote two or three notes to Christine Keeler and gave her one or two presents such as perfume and a cigarette lighter. She said her parents were badly off and he gave her £20 for them, realising that this was a polite way on her part of asking for money for her services. In August, 1961, whilst his wife was in the Isle of Wight, he took Christine Keeler to his own house in Regent's Park. Altogether I am satisfied that his object in visiting her was simply because he was attracted by her and desired sexual intercourse with her. It has been suggested that Captain Ivanov was her lover also. I do not think he was. The night of Sunday, 9th July, 1961, was an isolated occasion. I think that Captain Ivanov went to Stephen Ward's house for social entertainment and conversation, and not for sexual intercourse. I do not believe that Captain Ivanov and Mr. Profumo ever met in Stephen Ward's house or in the doorway. They did no doubt narrowly miss one another on occasions: and this afforded Stephen Ward and Christine Keeler much amusement. (Later on a great deal has been made of this episode. It has been suggested that Captain Ivanov and Mr. Profumo were sharing her services. I do not accept this suggestion.)

About this time, probably during the Cliveden week-end, Captain Ivanov told Stephen Ward that the Russians knew as a fact that the American Government had taken a decision to arm Western Germany with atomic weapons, and he asked Ward to find out through his influential friends when this decision was to be implemented. Without saying so in so many words, Captain Ivanov with some subtlety implied that if Stephen Ward supplied the answer his trip to Moscow would be facilitated.

One of the most critical points in my inquiry is this: Did Stephen Ward ask Christine Keeler to obtain from Mr. Profumo information as to the time when the Americans were going to supply the atomic bomb to Germany? If he did ask her, it was probably at this time in July, 1961: for it was the very thing that Captain Ivanov had asked Stephen Ward to find out from his influential friends. I am very dubious about her recollection about this. She has given several different versions of it and put it at different dates. (She once said it was at the time of the Cuban crisis in October, 1962.) The truth about it is, I think, this: There was a good deal of talk in her presence, between Stephen Ward and Captain Ivanov, about getting this information. And Stephen Ward may well have turned to her and said, "You ought to ask Jack (Profumo) about it". But I do not think it was said as seriously as it has since been reported. Stephen Ward said to me (and here I believed him).

"Quite honestly, nobody in their right senses would have asked somebody like Christine Keeler to obtain any information of that sort from Mr. Profumo – he would have jumped out of his skin".

If said at all by Stephen Ward, it was, I believe, not said seriously expecting her to act on it. I am quite satisfied that she never acted on it. She told me, and I believed her, that she never asked Mr. Profumo for the information. Mr. Profumo was also clear that she never asked him, and I am quite sure that he would not have told her if she had asked him. (Later on a great deal has been made of this episode. I think the importance of it has been greatly exaggerated.)

On the 31st July, 1961, the Head of the Security Service suggested to Sir Norman Brook (the then Secretary of the Cabinet, now Lord Normanbrook) that it might be useful for him to have a word with Mr. Profumo about Stephen Ward and Captain Ivanov. (I will deal with the reasons for this later when I deal with the operation of the Security Service.) In accordance with this request on 9th August, 1961, Sir Norman Brook suggested to Mr. Profumo that he should be careful in his dealings with Stephen Ward. He said there were indications that Stephen Ward might be interested in picking up scraps of information and passing them on to Captain Ivanov. Mr. Profumo was grateful for the warning. He told Sir Norman that he met Captain Ivanov at the Cliveden week-end and then, after the encounter at Cliveden, he saw Captain Ivanov at a reception at the Soviet Embassy. On that occasion Captain Ivanov seemed to make a special point of being civil to him. These were the only two occasions on which Mr. Profumo had come across Captain Ivanov. On the other hand he was better acquainted with Stephen Ward. Mr. Profumo went on to say that many people knew Stephen Ward and it might be helpful if warning were given to others too. He mentioned the name of another Cabinet Minister whom Sir Norman afterwards did warn. Sir Norman Brook referred rather delicately to another matter which had been suggested by the Head of the Security Service. Was it possible to do anything to persuade Ivanov to help us? But Mr. Profumo thought he ought to keep well away from it.

It has been suggested that Sir Norman Brook went beyond his province at this point: and that he ought to have reported to the Prime Minister, and not taken it upon himself to speak to Mr. Profumo. I think this criticism is based on a misapprehension. Neither the Security Service nor Sir Norman Brook had any doubts of Mr. Profumo. They did not know that he was having an affair with Christine Keeler and had no reason to suspect it. I have seen a note made by Sir Norman Brook at the time of all that he was told by the Head of the Security Service. The main point being made by them was that Stephen Ward might be indiscreet and pass on bits of information to Captain Ivanov. It was therefore desirable to warn Mr. Profumo of this possibility. Furthermore there was a thought that Captain Ivanov might be persuaded to defect. These seem to me to be matters which were very suitable for the Secretary of the Cabinet to mention to him, but hardly such as to need the intervention of the Prime Minister.

It was on Wednesday, 9th August, 1961, that Sir Norman Brook spoke to Mr. Profumo. It made a considerable impression on him. Mr. Profumo thought that that the Security Service must have got knowledge of his affair with Christine Keeler: and that the real object of Sir Norman's call on him (though not expressed) was politely to indicate that his assignations with Christine Keeler should cease. It so happened that Mr. Profumo had already arranged to see her the next night (Thursday, 10th August) but, as soon as Sir Norman left, he took steps to cancel the arrangement.

On the very same day as Sir Norman Brook spoke to him, Mr. Profumo wrote this letter to Christine Keeler:

9/8/61

"Darling,

In great haste and because I can get no reply from your phone –

Alas something's blown up tomorrow night and I can't therefore make it. I'm terribly sorry especially as I leave the next day for various trips and then a holiday so won't be able to see you again until some time in September. Blast it. Please take great care of yourself and don't run away.

Love J.

PS: I'm writing this 'cos I know you're off for the day tomorrow and I want you to know before you go if I still can't reach you by phone."

I am satisfied that that letter, if not the end, was the beginning of the end of the association between Mr. Profumo and Christine Keeler. He may have seen her a few times more but that was all.

CASSIUS CLAY BEATS HENRY COOPER IN THE FIFTH, LONDON, 19 JUNE 1963

Donald Saunders, London Daily Telegraph

Cassius Clay, the Louisville Lip, added another accurate prediction to his long list at Wembley Stadium last night, when he stopped Henry Cooper, the British heavyweight champion, in the fifth round, just as he said he would.

But victory did not come in quite the fashion the young American had expected. Tommy Little, the referee, was forced to intervene midway through the round, because blood was streaming from cuts over Cooper's so-often-injured left eye.

And a few minutes earlier, Clay had looked anything but "the greatest" as he landed in an untidy heap on the canvas after taking a left hook flush in the jaw.

The cocksure American, taking one chance too many, had walked into that punch in the dying seconds of the fourth round.

He slumped to the boards and came to a rest with his head against the bottom rope. The roar of the crowd prevented even those of us at the ringside hearing the bell. At all events, Mr Little continued the count under the new rule, until Clay heaved himself up at five; and walked poker-faced to his corner.

What might have happened had the round not ended then no one can say. Clay looked more surprised than hurt, but who knows what might have been the outcome had he been obliged to meet the full fury of Cooper instead of being able to walk to the safety of his stool?

In my view, Clay could have finished this fight in the third or fourth round, but instead kept things going so that he could stupidly hold up his five fingers triumphantly for the cameramen later.

As it happened, he got away with it, but perhaps when tempted henceforth he will remember the end of that fourth round against Cooper, and wonder whether the bell will always toll in his favour.

But let us now turn away from the future and go back over those five memorable rounds.

No one on this blustery, chilly night could accuse Cooper of being worried. The British champion has not for years made so aggressive a start.

He charged forward repeatedly trying to nail the poker-faced Clay with his left hook. Sometimes he got through, sometimes he missed badly, but never could he persuade his opponent that he was a potential menace.

Then, as Cooper walked back to his corner at the end of the round blood began to trickle from a cut over his left eye. Despite urgent attention during the interval, that trickle changed into a stream early in the third.

Clay, more and more confident with every second, just punched when and where he chose.

I thought it might end in the fourth when Clay once or twice cut loose with both hands. But then the "Louisville Lip" remembered that he was supposed to be the greatest and pranced contemptuously in front of the half-blinded Cooper.

Desperately Cooper let go a left hook and a split second later Clay, now looking like a spanked child, was sitting wide-eyed against the ropes.

But any hopes we had that Clay might have overstepped the mark ended when he walked off to his stool. A minute later he came storming out of his corner, tore into his opponent with both hands, and as blood spurted from perhaps the worst eye injury Cooper has ever suffered, Mr Little had no alternative but to step between them.

THE BEATLES TAKE NEW YORK, 7 FEBRUARY 1964

Tom Wolfe

John, Paul, Ringo and George arrive in New York on their first US tour.

By six-thirty a.m. yesterday (7 February), half the kids from South Orange, NJ to Seaford LI, were already up with their transistors

plugged in their skulls. It was like a civil defence network or something. You could turn anywhere on the dial, WMCA, WCBS,
WINS, almost any place, and get the bulletins: "It's B-Day! Six-
thirty a.m.! The Beatles left London thirty minutes ago! They're
thirty minutes out over the Atlantic Ocean! Heading for New York!"

By one p.m. about 4,000 kids had finished school and come
skipping and screaming into the international terminal at Kennedy Airport. It took 110 police to herd them. At one-twenty p.m.,
the Beatles' jet arrived from London.

The Beatles left the plane and headed for customs inspection and
everybody got their first live look at the Beatles' hair style, which is
a mop effect that covers the forehead, some of the ears and most of
the back of the neck. To get a better look, the kids came plunging
down the observation deck, and some of them already had their
combs out, raking their hair down over their foreheads as they ran.

Then they were crowding around the plate-glass windows overlooking the customs section, stomping on the floor in unison, some
of them beating time by bouncing off the windows.

The Beatles – George Harrison, 20; John Lennon, 23; Ringo
Starr, 23; and Paul McCartney, 21 – are all short, slight kids from
Liverpool who wear four-button coats, stovepipe pants, ankle-high
black boots with Cuban heels. And droll looks on their faces. Their
name is a play on the word "beat".

They went into a small room for a press conference, while some
of the girls tried to throw themselves over a retaining wall.

Somebody motioned to the screaming crowds outside. "Aren't
you embarrassed by all this lunacy?"

"No," said John Lennon. "It's crazy."

"What do you think of Beethoven?"

"He's crazy," said Lennon. "Especially the poems. Lovely
writer."

In the two years in which they have risen from a Liverpool rock-
and-roll dive group to the hottest performers in the record business, they had seen much of this wildness before. What really got
them were the American teenage car sorties.

The Beatles left the airport in four Cadillac limousines, one
Beatle to a limousine, heading for the Plaza Hotel in Manhattan.
The first sortie came almost immediately. Five kids in a powder
blue Ford overtook the caravan on the expressway, and as they
passed each Beatle, one guy hung out the back window and waved
a red blanket.

A white convertible came up second, with the word BEETLES scratched on both sides in the dust. A police car was close behind that one with the siren going and the alarm light rolling, but the kids, a girl at the wheel and two guys in the back seat, waved at each Beatle before pulling over to the exit with the cops gesturing at them.

In the second limousine, Brian Sommerville, the Beatle's press agent, said to one of the Beatles, George Harrison: "Did you see that, George?"

Harrison looked at the convertible with its emblem in the dust and said, "They misspelled Beatles."

But the third sortie succeeded all the way. A good-looking brunette, who said her name was Caroline Reynolds, of New Canaan, Conn., and Wellesley College, had paid a cab driver $10 to follow the caravan all the way into town. She cruised by each Beatle, smiling faintly, and finally caught up with George Harrison's limousine at a light at Third Avenue and 63rd St.

"How does one go about meeting a Beatle?" she said out of the window.

"One says hello," said Harrison out of the window.

"Hello!" she said. "Eight more will be down from Wellesley." Then the light changed and the caravan was off again.

At the Plaza Hotel, there were police everywhere. The Plaza, on Central Park South just off Fifth Avenue, is one of the most sedate hotels in New York. The Plaza was petrified. The Plaza accepted the Beatles' reservations months ago, before knowing it was a rock-and-roll group that attracts teenage riots.

About 500 teenagers, most of them girls, had shown up at the Plaza. The police herded most of them behind barricades in the square between the hotel and the avenue. Every entrance to the hotel was guarded. The screams started as soon as the first limousine came into view.

The Beatles jumped out fast at the Fifth Avenue entrance. The teenagers had all been kept at bay. Old ladies ran up and touched the Beatles on their arms and backs as they ran up the stairs.

After they got to the Plaza the Beatles rested up for a round of television appearances (the Ed Sullivan Show Sunday), recordings (Capitol Records), concerts (Carnegie Hall, Wednesday) and a tour (Washington, Miami). The kids were still hanging around the Plaza hours after they went inside.

One group of girls asked everybody who came out, "Did you see the Beatles? Did you touch them?"

A policeman came up, and one of them yelled, "He touched a Beatle! I saw him!"

The girls jumped on the cop's arms and back, but it wasn't a mob assault. There were goony smiles all over their faces.

THE KILLING OF GEORGE CORNELL AT THE BLIND BEGGAR PUBLIC HOUSE, LONDON, 9 MARCH 1966

Ronald Kray

The Kray twins, Ronnie and Reggie, ran a Mafia-type gang or "firm" in the East End of London in the 1960s. George Cornell was a member of the rival Richardson firm, and had been implicated in the shooting of a Kray associate, Richard Hart.

Richard Hart had to be avenged. No one could kill a member of the Kray gang and expect to get away with it. The problem was, both of the Richardsons and Mad Frankie Fraser were in custody and likely to remain so. That left Cornell. He would have to be the one to pay the price. And, let's face it, who better? All I had to do was find him. The next night, 9 March, I got the answer. He was drinking in the Blind Beggar.

Typical of the yobbo mentality of the man. Less than twenty-four hours after the Catford killing and here he was, drinking in a pub that was officially on our patch. It was as though he wanted to be killed.

I unpacked my 9mm Mauser automatic. I also got out a shoulder holster. I called Scotch Jack Dickson and told him to bring the car round to my flat and to contact Ian Barrie, the big Scot, and to collect him on the way. As we drove towards the Blind Beggar, I checked that Barrie was carrying a weapon, just in case.

At eight-thirty p.m. precisely we arrived at the pub and quickly looked around to make sure that this was not an ambush. I told Dickson to wait in the car with the engine running, then Ian Barrie and I walked into the Blind Beggar. I could not have felt calmer, and having Ian Barrie alongside me was great. No general ever had a better right-hand man.

It was very quiet and gloomy inside the pub. There was an old bloke sitting by himself in the public bar and three people in the saloon bar: two blokes at a table and George Cornell sitting alone on a stool at the far end of the bar. As we walked in the barmaid was putting on a record. It was the Walker Brothers and it was called "The Sun Ain't Gonna Shine Any More". For George Cornell that was certainly true.

As we walked towards him he turned round and a sort of sneer came over his face. "Well, look who's here," he said.

I never said anything. I just felt hatred for this sneering man. I took out my gun and held it towards his face. Nothing was said, but his eyes told me that he thought the whole thing was a bluff. I shot him in the forehead. He fell forward on to the bar. There was some blood on the counter. That's all that happened. Nothing more. Despite any other account you may have read of this incident, that was what happened.

It was over very quickly. There was silence. Everyone had disappeared – the barmaid, the old man in the public and the blokes in the saloon bar. It was like a ghost pub. Ian Barrie stood next to me. He had said nothing.

I felt fucking marvellous. I have never felt so good, so bloody alive, before or since. Twenty years on and I can recall every second of the killing of George Cornell. I have replayed it in my mind millions of times.

After a couple of minutes we walked out, got into the car and set off for a pub in the East End run by a friend called Madge. On the way there we could hear the screaming of the police car sirens. When we got to the pub I told a few of my friends what had happened. I also told Reg, who seemed a bit alarmed.

Then we went to a pub at Stoke Newington called the Coach and Horses. There I gave my gun to a trusted friend we used to call the Cat and told him to get rid of it. I suddenly noticed my hands were covered in gunpowder burns, so I scrubbed them in the washroom. I showered and put on fresh clothing – underwear, a suit, a shirt and tie. (We had spare sets of "emergency" clothes at several places.) All my old clothing was taken away to be burned. Upstairs in a private room I had a few drinks with some of the top members of the firm – Reg, Dickson, Barrie, Ronnie Hart and others. We listened to the radio and heard that a man had been shot dead in the East End. As the news was announced I could feel everyone in the room, including Reg, looking at me with new respect. I had killed a man. I had got my button, as the Yanks say. I was a man to be feared. I was now the Colonel.

ENGLAND WIN THE WORLD CUP, LONDON, 30 JULY 1966

David Miller

They had fetched him, three and a half years ago, from quiet Ipswich, a taciturn, shy, deeply reserved man, and calmly leading with his chin, as they say, he had promised to win them the World Cup. There were those who laughed, and some were still laughing when the tournament began. Yet by the finish, with a relentless inflexibility of will, with sterling courage, with efficiency that brought unbounded admiration, his team, England's team, helped to keep that promise.

They did it, Alf Ramsey and England, after just about the worst psychological reverse possible on an unforgettable afternoon. With victory dashed from their grasp, cruelly, only seconds from the final whistle, they came again in extra time, driving weary limbs across the patterned turf beyond the point of exhaustion, and crowned the ultimate achievement with a memorable goal with the last kick of all by Hurst, making him the first player to score a hat-trick in the World Cup Final.

We had all often talked of the thoroughness of preparation of the deposed champions, Brazil, but England's glory this day, to be engraved on that glinting, golden trophy, was the result of the most patient, logical, painstaking, almost scientific assault on the trophy there had perhaps ever been – and primarily the work and imagination of one man.

For those close to him through the past three exciting seasons, Ramsey's management had been something for unending admiration, and the unison cry of the 93,000 crowd, "Ram-sey, Ram-sey" as his side mounted the steps to collect Jules Rimet's statuette from the Queen was the final rewarding vindication for one who had unwaveringly pursued his own, often lonely, convictions.

As the crowd stood in ovation, Greaves looked on wistfully. Injury had cost him his place, and though he recovered, Ramsey had resisted the almost overpowering temptation to change a winning side. This, too, was vindication, his whole aim since 1963 having been to prepare not a team but a squad, so that at any moment he might replace an out of form or injured man without noticeable deterioration in the side. When the time came, the luckless Greaves's omission caused hardly a stir of pessimism.

At the start of the tournament, I had written that if England were to win, it would be with the resolution, physical fitness and cohesion of West Germany in 1954, rather than with the flair of Brazil in the two succeeding competitions. And so it proved, with the added coincidence that it was the Germans themselves, as usual bristling with all these same characteristics in profusion, who were the unlucky and brave victims of England's methodical rather than brilliant football. Before the semi-finals I said that the deciding factor of this World Cup, when all others had cancelled out in the modern proficiency of defensive systems, would be character, and now the character of every England player burned with a flame that warmed all those who saw it. The slightest weakening, mentally or physically, in any position, could have lost this match a hundred times over, but the way in which Ball, undoubtedly the man of the afternoon, Wilson, Stiles, Peters, Bobby Charlton and above all Moore, impelled themselves on, was something one would remember long after the tumult of excitement and the profusion of incidents had faded. Justifiably, Moore was voted the outstanding player of the competition; his sudden, surging return to form on tour beforehand had helped cement the castle at the critical hour.

All assessments of great events should be measured by absolute standards along with the quality of contemporaries, and therefore one had to say that England were not a great team, probably not even at that moment the best team in the world, depending on what you mean by best.

What matters is that they were the best there at Wembley in July, on that sunny, showery afternoon, best when the chips were down in open combat, and that, after all, is what counts – the result, rather than its manner, goes into the record books. Besides, Ramsey had not set about producing the most entertaining but the most successful team. Could he afford to be the one romantic in a world of hard-headed, win-at-all-costs efficiency? Could he favour conventional wingers who promised much and produced little? A manager is ultimately only as good as the players at his disposal; handicapped by a shortage of world class, instinctive players of the calibre of the South Americans, Italians, Hungarians, or his own Bobby Charlton, and by an over-abundance of average competence, Ramsey had slowly eliminated all those who lacked what he needed for cohesion. What greater demonstration of unity of purpose could there have been than the insistence of the winners, for all the emotion of the moment, that the eleven reserves join them on the lap of honour, and after share equally the £22,000 bonus.

Some complained England were helped by playing all their matches at Wembley, yet certainly in that mood and form they could and would have won anywhere in the country. Besides, under Ramsey, England had had more success abroad than ever before. If nothing else, this World Cup, penetrating almost every home in the land, should have persuaded the doubters, the detractors and the cynics that this is the greatest spectator sport there is, and the Final was a fitting climax.

At the start England asserted themselves – Bobby Charlton exerting a telling influence in midfield, even though closely watched by Beckenbauer sent Peters streaming through with fine anticipation, into spaces behind the German midfield trio. Suddenly, however, in the thirteenth minute, England found themselves a goal down for the first time in the competition. It was not an error under pressure, it was unforced. As a centre from the left came over, Wilson stood alone, eyes riveted on the dropping ball. He made to head it down to Moore, but his judgement betrayed him, sending it instead straight to Haller, who whipped in a low skidding shot past an unsighted, helpless Banks.

The strapping Germans and their flag-waving supporters bounced with joy, but within six minutes England were level. Midway inside the German half, on the left, Overath tripped Moore, and even before the referee had finished wagging his finger at Overath, Moore had spotted a gaping hole in the German rearguard. He placed the ball and took the kick almost in one move, a dipping floater that carried thirty-five yards and was met by Hurst, streaking in from the right, with another graceful, expertly-timed header like that which beat Argentina.

The pattern swung once more in the ten minutes before half-time. The three German strikers, nosing in and out like carnivorous fish, began to create havoc that was only averted after extreme anxiety. In between, Hunt, from a glorious pass by Bobby Charlton, hammered a thundering shot, a difficult one running away to his left, straight at Tilkowski. On the stroke of half-time, it was England who were desperately lucky, when a fast dipper by Seeler was tipped over by Banks, arched in mid-air like a stalling buzzard.

Little happened for nearly twenty-five minutes after half-time, the lull punctuated only by "Oh, oh, what a referee," as Mr Dienst went fussily about his business. Then, with twenty minutes to go, England's rhythm began to build up again, Bobby Charlton, Ball and Peters stretching the Germans to the extreme of their physical endurance with passes that again and again almost saw Hurst and Hunt clear. With eleven minutes to go, Ball won a corner, put it across, the ball was headed out, and hit back first-time by Hurst. It struck a defender, fell free, and Peters swooped to lash it home.

England, sensing victory, played it slow, slow, but Hunt wasted a priceless chance when it was three red England shirts to one white German on the edge of the penalty area, by misjudging his pass. With a minute left, all was disaster as Jack Charlton was most harshly penalized for "climbing" over the top of Held. Emmerich blasted the free kick. A German in the penalty area unquestionably pulled the ball down with his hand, and after a tremendous scramble, Weber squeezed the ball home to level the match.

You could see England's spirits sink as the teams changed over for extra time but, quickly calmed and reassured by the emotionless Ramsey, they rallied themselves instantly. Ball, still unbelievably dynamic, going like the wind right to the finish, had a shot tipped over, Bobby Charlton hit a post and with twelve minutes gone, England were once more in front as Stiles slipped the ball up the wing to Ball, whose cross was thumped hard by Hurst. The ball hit the bar, bounced down and came out, and after consultation with the Russian linesman, Bakhramov, a goal was given. I had my doubts, doubled after later seeing television, but that surely had to be the winner, for now, socks rolled down, both teams were physically in distress. Again England sought economy with gentle passes, keeping precious possession, wearing the Germans down yet further. Poor Wilson hardly knew where he was after a blow on the head. Slowly the minutes ticked away, agonisingly, until with the referee looking at his watch, Hurst staggered on alone from yet one more of Moore's perceptive passes, to hit the ball into the roof of the net with what little strength he had left, and make England's victory, like their football, solid and respectable. Whether Ramsey, as silent in victory as defeat, could achieve the impossible and adapt these same characteristics to win in Mexico in 1970 was a chapter that would unfold over the next four years.

ENGLAND: – Banks (*Leicester*); Cohen (*Fulham*), Charlton J. (*Leeds*), Moore (*W. Ham*), Wilson (*Everton*); Stiles (*Manchester*

United), Charlton R. (*Manchester United*), Peters (*W. Ham*); Ball (*Blackpool*), Hunt (*Liverpool*), Hurst (*W. Ham*).

WEST GERMANY: – Tilkowski: Hoettges, Schulz, Weber, Schnellinger; Beckenbauer, Haller, Overath; Seeler, Held, Emmerich.

Referee: – G. Dienst (Switzerland).

Linesmen: – K. Galba (Czechoslovakia), T. Bakhramov (USSR).

"BLOODY SUNDAY" IN LONDONDERRY, NORTHERN IRELAND, 30 JANUARY 1972

Sean Collins

Soldiers from the British Paratroop Regiment opened fire on a civil rights protest by Irish Catholics, killing thirteen.

Oh at the time of Bloody Sunday I was only a wain, a child of nine. There were seven in our family: my mother, my father, and five of us kids. We all lived in a two-bedroomed flat on the eighth floor of one of the blocks in Rossville Street. We didn't know then of course, but that was going to be right overlooking where the shootings were. The flats had been built to be occupied by Catholic families: there was a strict policy of segregation of areas on a religious basis in Derry, and the one we were in was called Bogside. Everybody more or less knew everyone else there, and everyone was poor.

The police used to patrol the Bogside a lot. I remember the police from the beginning, they were part of the everyday scenery. I don't recall much animosity towards them though. As a kid you knew there were occasions when there was trouble, protests and riots and all that, but you'd no idea what it was really about.

Sometimes the police'd appear in armoured cars which were called "pigs": you'd see them firing gas or rubber bullets at people if there was a crowd. But it was something which had nothing to do with you: that was the adults' world, and what happened in it was what happened, that's all. I remember one of our favourite games we played was to imitate it: we didn't play "cowboys and indians", we played "cops and rioters". Today it was your turn to be one, then the next day you were the other.

We'd never any understanding at all what it was about. My family wasn't Republican: all they cared for was we should keep out of trouble and not get hurt. They always told us if we saw something going on anywhere, we were to come straight home and stop inside. 'Course we never did though: we used to try and find good places to watch from, then afterwards we'd run round all the streets to see if we could find rubber bullets as souvenirs. An empty gas canister, well that'd be a great prize.

I remember it clearly when the soldiers came: our parents told us they were there to protect us and they were our friends. The first ones I ever saw were standing around in the street, and women were going up to them and talking to them and giving them cups of tea. To us wains they soon became sort of like hero figures: they gave us sweets, and asked our names, talked to us about different places in the world they'd been. The biggest thrill of all would be if one specially liked you and would let you touch his rifle, and hold it while you had a look along its sights. To me the soldiers were fascinating. I thought they were wonderful. None of us feared them at all in any way: grown-ups as well, we were all pleased and glad they were there.

The day of Bloody Sunday itself, all kids were told that after morning Mass we had to be home by 12 o'clock latest, and afterwards there'd be no going out playing for the rest of the day. Our parents said there was going to be a big march, it was going to come down from the Creggan and go to the Guildhall. If we were good we could go out on the balcony of the flat to watch it in the distance, but that was all. No one knew beforehand it was going to be diverted down Rossville Street and come right towards us. So there was great excitement then when it was, when it started to come right in our direction.

At first it looked peaceful enough. There was some shouting but only a little: but then after a while we began to hear some shooting from somewhere towards the back. I thought it was going to be an ordinary riot, and the police'd try to contain it as they usually did, by shooting off some rubber bullets and perhaps sending in some gas. But then suddenly I realized there was something different about the sound. It wasn't like one I'd ever heard before. When rubber bullets are fired, you hear "Bang, bang, bang" like that. This wasn't that noise: it was much sharper, going "Crack, Crack, Crack". Then somebody on the balcony said, it was one of the adults I think, "Jesus, that's rifle fire, they're using real bullets they are!" And we saw the marching column start to break up, people beginning to run away from it as hard as they could.

What I saw next after that I couldn't believe, not really at first at all. An army troop carrier appeared, and it started coming slowly towards us down the street. A man was running away from it and they were chasing him and trying to pin him against the wall. He escaped somehow, I think he dodged off somehow to the side. So then the troop carrier stopped, and out of it, or from out of another one that'd come along by its side, half a dozen soldiers jumped out. They stood by the vehicle a minute: and then slowly and deliberately each one of them went down on one knee and started to fire steadily into the crowd. It was like as if they were doing a sort of training demonstration, that's the only way I can describe it.

People were falling hit, and there was complete pandemonium. Some were stopping to try and help those who'd been hurt to get up, and others had for their only thought to get away. I saw a priest crouching down at the end of a wall: and when I looked at him I knew him, he was our own priest, Father Daly. He crawled from behind the wall to go to a man who was lying in the open a few yards away from him. I looked back where the soldiers were, and I saw one of them look up and he saw us watching from the balcony. He brought his gun up and took aim, but I didn't wait to see if he was really going to shoot or not; like everyone else there I ducked down. So whether that soldier fired or not, I don't know. Afterwards though nine bullet holes were found in the brickwork of the front of the flats, some of them as high up as the floor above ours.

Most of all what comes clearly back to me was my feeling of surprise. It was surprise that these men, the soldiers who I'd liked so much and admired – suddenly they weren't good people or heroes like I'd thought. They were cruel and heartless causing death and panic, putting terror into the hearts of the ordinary people of the community I lived in. It's difficult to judge the effect of it afterwards, but I'd say for me it was like the smashing up of a dream: sort of the end to my innocence somehow, the innocence of a child who till then had thought there was something noble and romantic about soldiers. I didn't think that afterwards, not ever again.

THE SEX PISTOLS PLAY THEIR FIRST CONCERT, LONDON, 6 NOVEMBER 1975

Adam Ant

The harbingers of punk rock played for the first time in public at St Martins School of Art, London. The band was formed by entrepreneur

Malcom McLaren initially as a means of publicizing a clothes shop he ran with designer Vivienne Westwood.

For their first ever gig . . . the Sex Pistols were support group to the band I was in, Bazooka Joe. I'll never forget it. They came in as a gang: they looked like they couldn't give a fuck about anybody. John had baggy pinstripe trousers with braces and a ripped-up T-shirt saying "Pink Floyd" with "I Hate" over it. Jonesy was tiny, he looked like a young Pete Townshend. Matlock had paint-spattered trousers and a woman's pink leather top. Paul Cook looked like Rod Stewart, like a little Mod really.

I watched them play: Malcolm was at the front, orchestrating them, telling them where to stand. Viv was there. There weren't many there: maybe a dozen of their people – Jordan, Michael Collins, Andy Czezowski. They did "Substitute", and "Whatcha Gonna Do About It" with the lyrics changed: "I want you to know that I *hate* you baby." Then John lost interest. He'd eat sweets, pull them out and suck them and just spit them out: he just looked at the audience, glazed.

There were no guitar solos, it was just simple songs. They did five and that was it: goodnight. The rest of my band hated them because they thought they couldn't play: in fact somebody said as much to Glen and he said: "So what?" But I thought they were very tight. It was only John who hadn't learned how to make the voice last, but over a fifteen-minute burst, he was very clear. At the end Rotten slagged off Bazooka Joe as being a bunch of fucking cunts and our guitarist Danny Kleinman leapt from the front row and pinned John against the back wall: he made him apologize.

The impression they left on me was total . . . They had a certain attitude I'd never seen: they had bollocks and they had very expensive equipment and it didn't look like it belonged to them. They had the look in their eyes that said: "We're going to be massive." I stood there transfixed. When Danny jumped John, I didn't jump in to help him. I left Bazooka Joe the next day: I came out of that gig thinking, "I'm tired of Teddy Boys" and it seemed to me that the Sex Pistols were playing simple songs that I could play. I just wanted to go away and form my own band.

THE SAS RELIEVE THE SIEGE AT PRINCE'S GATE, LONDON, 5 MAY 1980

Anon. SAS Trooper

The Iranian embassy in London had been taken over on 30 April 1980 by six Arab gunmen, who had held the staff hostage as a means of forcing Iran to concede to their demand for the liberation of Khuzestan. When Iran had failed to make any concessions, the gunmen had shot one of the male hostages. At that point, 5 May, the British government ordered a waiting unit of Special Air Service soldiers to storm the embassy building.

We took up a position behind a low wall as the demolition call sign ran forward and placed the explosive charge on the Embassy french windows. It was then that we saw the abseiler swinging in the flames on the first floor. It was all noise, confusion, bursts of submachine-gun fire. I could hear women screaming. Christ! It's all going wrong, I thought. There's no way we can blow that charge without injuring the abseiler. Instant change of plans. The sledge-man ran forward and lifted the sledge-hammer. One blow, just above the lock, was sufficient to open the door. They say luck shines on the brave. We were certainly lucky. If that door had been bolted or barricaded, we would have had big problems.

"Go. Go. Go. Get in at the rear." The voice was screaming in my ear. The eight call signs rose to their feet as one and then we were sweeping in through the splintered door. All feelings of doubt and fear had now disappeared. I was blasted. The adrenalin was bursting through my bloodstream. Fearsome! I got a fearsome rush, the best one of my life. I had the heavy body armour on, with high-velocity plates front and back. During training it weighs a ton. Now it felt like a T-shirt. Search and destroy! We were in the library. There were thousands of books. As I adjusted my eyes to the half-light – made worse by the condensation on my respirator eyepieces – the thought occurred to me that if we had blown that explosive charge we might have set fire to the books. Then we would really have had big problems: the whole Embassy would have been ablaze in seconds.

The adrenalin was making me feel confident, elated. My mind was crystal clear as we swept on through the library and headed for our first objective. I reached the head of the cellar stairs first, and was quickly joined by Sek and two of the call signs. The entry to the stairs was blocked by two sets of step-ladders. I searched desperately with my eyes for any signs of booby-traps. There wasn't time for a thorough check. We had to risk it. We braced ourselves and wrenched the ladders out of the way.

Mercifully there was no explosion. The stairs were now cleared and we disappeared into the gloom of the basement. I fished a stun grenade out of my waistcoat and pulled the pin. Audio Armageddon, I thought as I tossed the grenade down into the darkness. We descended the stairs, squinting into the blinding flashes for any unexpected movement, any sign of the enemy, and then we were into the corridor at the bottom. We had no sledge, no Remington with us, so we had to drill the locks with 9-milly, booting the doors in, clearing the rooms methodically as we went along. Minutes turned into seconds; it was the fastest room clearance I'd ever done.

It was when I entered the last room that I saw the dark shape crouched in the corner. Christ! This is it, I thought. We've hit the jackpot. We've found a terrorist. I jabbed my MP 5 into the fire position and let off a burst of twenty rounds. There was a clang as the crouched figure crumpled and rolled over. It was a dustbin!

Nothing, not a thing. The cellars were clear. I was now conscious of the sweat. It was stinging my eyes, and the rubber on the inside of the respirator was slimy. My mouth was dry and I could feel the blood pulsing through my temples. And then we were off again, no time to stop now, up the cellar stairs and into the Embassy reception area. As we advanced across the hallway, there was smoke, confusion, a tremendous clamour of noise coming from above us. The rest of the lads, having stormed over the balcony at the front and blasted their way into the first floor of the building with a well-placed explosive charge, were now systematically cleaving the upper rooms, assisted by a winning combination of the stunning effect of the initial explosion, the choking fumes of CS gas, the chilling execution of well-practised manoeuvres and the sheer terror induced by their sinister, black-hooded appearance. We were intoxicated by the situation. Nothing could stop us now.

Through the gloom I could see the masked figures of the other team members forming into a line on the main staircase. My radio earpiece crackled into life. "The hostages are coming. Feed them out through the back. I repeat, out through the back."

I joined a line with Sek. We were six or seven steps up from the hallway. There were more explosions. The hysterical voices of the women swept over us. Then the first hostages were passed down the line. I had my MP 5 on a sling around my neck. My pistol was in its holster. My hands were free to help the hostages, to steady them, to reassure them, to point them in the right direction. They looked shocked and disorientated. Their eyes were streaming with CS gas. They stumbled down the stairs looking frightened and dishevelled. One woman had her blouse ripped and her breasts exposed. I lost count at fifteen and still they were coming, stumbling, confused, heading towards the library and freedom.

"This one's a terrorist!" The high-pitched yell cut through the atmosphere on the stairs like a screaming jet, adding to the confusion of the moment. A dark face ringed by an Afro-style haircut came into view; then the body, clothed in a green combat jacket, bent double, crouched in an unnatural pose, running the gauntlet of black-hooded figures. He was punched and kicked as he made his descent of the stairs. He was running afraid. He knew he was close to death.

He drew level with me. Then I saw it – a Russian fragmentation grenade. I could see the detonator cap protruding from his hand. I moved my hands to the MP 5 and slipped the safety-catch to "automatic". Through the smoke and gloom I could see call signs at the bottom of the stairs in the hallway. Shit! I can't fire. They are in my line of sight, the bullets will go straight through the terrorist and into my mates. I've got to immobilize the bastard. I've got to do something. Instinctively, I raised the MP 5 above my head and in one swift, sharp movement brought the stock of the weapon down on the back of his neck. I hit him as hard as I could. His head snapped backwards and for one fleeting second I caught sight of his tortured, hate-filled face. He collapsed forward and rolled down the remaining few stairs, hitting the carpet in the hallway, a sagging, crumpled heap. The sound of two magazines being emptied into him was deafening. As he twitched and vomited his life away, his hand opened and the grenade rolled out. In that split second my mind was so crystal clear with adrenalin it zoomed straight in on the grenade pin and lever. I stared at the mechanism for what seemed like an eternity, and what I saw flooded the very core of me with relief and elation. The pin was still located in the lever. It was all over, everything was going to be okay.

But this was no time to rest, this was one of the most vulnerable periods of the operation, the closing stages. This is where inexperienced troops would drop their guard. The radio crackled into life.

"You must abandon the building. The other floors are ablaze. Make your way out through the library entrance at the rear. The Embassy is clear. I repeat, the Embassy is clear."

I joined Sek and we filed out through the library, through the smoke and the debris. We turned left and headed back for number 14, past the hostages, who were laid out and trussed up on the lawn ready for documentation, past the unexploded explosive charge, past the discarded sledgehammer and other pieces of assault equipment – all the trappings of battle in the middle of South Kensington. It was 8.07 p.m.

As we made our way through the french windows of number 14, the Gonze, ex-Para, a new boy in the regiment from one of the other call signs, removed his respirator and asked the Irish police sergeant on duty at the door what the Embassy World snooker score was. A look of total disbelief spread across the policeman's face and he just stood there shaking his head from side to side.

I crossed the room to my holdall and as I began pulling off my assault equipment I could feel the tiredness spreading through my limbs. It wasn't just the energy expended on the assault, it was the accumulation of six days of tension and high drama, of snatched sleep in a noisy room, of anxiety and worry over the outcome of the operation. I looked to my left. The Toad had just returned. He looked tired, his face was flushed and he was out of breath. He looked at me and shook his head. "I'm getting too old for this sort of thing."

"So am I," I replied.

Within fifteen minutes most of the team members had stripped off their assault kit, packed it into their holdalls and parcelled their MP 5s into plastic bags to be taken away for forensic examination. Before moving out through the front door of number 14 to the waiting Avis hire van, we had a dramatic visit from Home Secretary William Whitelaw, old Oyster Eyes himself. He stood before us, tears of joy unashamedly running down his cheeks, wringing his hands in relief. He thanked the assembled team members for what they had done for the country that day. "This operation will show that we in Britain will not tolerate terrorists. The world must learn this." It was a fine personal gesture and rounded the operation off perfectly.

THE FALKLANDS WAR: THE FIRST MAN INTO PORT STANLEY, 14 JUNE 1982

Max Hastings

The war between Britain and Argentina for the South Atlantic Falkland Islands (Malvinas) came to an end on 14 June 1982, with the surrender of the Argentine forces led by General Menendez. The first Briton into Port Stanley, the Falkland's capital, was the war correspondent, Max Hastings.

British forces are in Port Stanley. At 2.45 p.m. British time today, men of the 2nd Parachute Regiment halted on the outskirts at the end of their magnificent drive on the capital pending negotiations.

There, we sat on the racecourse until, after about twenty minutes I was looking at the road ahead and there seemed to be no movement. I thought, well I'm a civilian so why shouldn't I go and see what's going on because there didn't seem to be much resistance.

So I stripped off all my combat clothes and walked into Stanley in a blue civilian anorak with my hands in the air and my handkerchief in my hand.

The Argentinians made no hostile movement as I went by the apparently undamaged but heavily bunkered Government House.

I sort of grinned at them in the hope that if there were any Argentinian soldiers manning the position they wouldn't shoot at me.

Nobody took any notice so I walked on and after a few minutes I saw a group of people all looking like civilians a hundred yards ahead and I shouted at them.

I shouted: "Are you British?" and they shouted back: "Yes, are you?" I said "Yes."

They were a group of civilians who had just come out of the civil administration building where they had been told that it looked as if there was going to be a ceasefire.

We chatted for a few moments and then I walked up to the building and I talked to the senior Argentinian colonel who was standing on the steps. He didn't show any evident hostility.

They were obviously pretty depressed. They looked like men who had just lost a war but I talked to them for a few moments and I said: "Are you prepared to surrender West Falkland as well as East?"

The colonel said: "Well, maybe, but you must wait until four o'clock when General Menendez meets your general."

I said: "May I go into the town and talk to civilians?" He said: "Yes," so I started to walk down the main street past Falklanders who were all standing outside their houses.

They all shouted and cheered and the first person I ran into was the Catholic priest, Monsignor Daniel Spraggon, who said: "My God, it's marvellous to see you."

That wasn't directed at me personally but it was the first communication he had had with the British forces.

I walked on and there were hundreds, maybe thousands, of Argentinian troops milling around, marching in columns through the streets, some of them clutching very badly wounded men and looking completely like an army in defeat with blankets wrapped around themselves.

There were bits of weapons and equipment all over the place and they were all moving to central collection points before the surrender or ceasefire.

Eventually I reached the famous Falklands hotel, the Upland Goose. We had been dreaming for about three months about walking into the Upland Goose and having a drink, and I walked in and again it was marvellous that they all clapped and cheered.

They offered me gin on the assumption that this is the traditional drink of British journalists, but I asked if they could make it whisky instead and I gratefully raised my glass to them all.

Owner of the Upland Goose, Desmond King said: "We never doubted for a moment that the British would turn up. We have just been waiting for the moment for everybody to come."

The last few days had been the worst, he said, because Argentinian guns had been operating from among the houses of Stanley and they had heard this terrific, continuous battle going on in the hills.

They were afraid that it was going to end up with a house-to-house fight in Stanley itself. The previous night when I had been with the Paras we were getting a lot of shell fire coming in on us and eventually we sorted out the coordinates from which it was firing. Our observation officer tried to call down to fire on the enemy batteries and the word came back that you could not fire on them because they are in the middle of Stanley.

So the battalion simply had to take it and suffer some casualties.

Anyway, there we were in the middle of the Upland Goose with about twenty or thirty delighted civilians who said that the Argentinians hadn't done anything appalling. It depends what one means by appalling, but they hadn't shot anybody or hung anybody up by their thumbs or whatever.

They had looted a lot of houses that they had taken over. At times they got very nervous and started pushing people around with submachine guns in their backs and the atmosphere had been pretty unpleasant.

Robin Pitaleyn described how he had been under house arrest in the hotel for six weeks, since he made contact by radio with the *Hermes*. He dismissed criticism of the Falkland Island Company representatives who had sold goods to the occupiers.

"We were all selling stuff," he said. "You had a simple choice – either you sold it or they took it. I rented my house to their air force people. They said – either you take rent or we take the house. What would you have done?"

Adrian Monk described how he had been compulsorily evicted from his own house to make way for Argentinian soldiers who had then totally looted it. There appears to have been widespread looting in all the houses of Stanley to which the Argentinians had access.

The houses on the outskirts of the town in which the Argentinians had been living were an appalling mess full of everything from human excrement all over the place to just property lying all over the place where soldiers had ransacked through it. But they were all alive and they all had plenty of food and plenty to drink and they were all in tremendous spirits.

It wasn't in the least like being abroad. One talks about the Falklanders and yet it was as if one had liberated a hotel in the middle of Surrey or Kent or somewhere.

It was an extraordinary feeling just sitting there with all these girls and cheerful middle-age men and everybody chatting in the way they might chat at a suburban golf club after something like this had happened.

I think everybody did feel a tremendous sense of exhilaration and achievement. I think the Paras through all their tiredness knew they had won a tremendous battle.

It was the Paras' hour and, after their heavy losses and Goose Green and some of the fierce battles they had fought, they had made it all the way to Stanely and they were enjoying every moment of their triumph.

A question that has to be answered is how the Argentinian troops managed to maintain their supplies of food and ammunition.

I think it's one of the most remarkable things. I think intelligence hasn't been one of our strong points throughout the campaign.

Even our commanders and people in London agree that we have misjudged the Argentinians at several critical points in the campaign.

Our soldiers have been saying in the last couple of days how astonished they were when they overran enemy positions. We have been hearing a great deal about how short of food and ammunition they were supposed to be but whatever else they lacked it certainly was not either of those.

They had hundreds of rounds of ammunition, masses of weapons and plenty of food.

The civilians told me they had been running Hercules on to the runway at Port Stanley despite all our efforts with Naval gunnery, with Vulcans, with Harriers up to and including last night and, above all, at the beginning of May they ran a very big container ship called the *Formosa* through the blockade and got her back to Buenos Aires again afterwards. She delivered an enormous consignment of ammunition which really relieved the Argentinians' serious problems on that front for the rest of the campaign.

I think in that sense we have been incredibly lucky. The British forces have been incredibly lucky.

Considering the amount of stuff the Argentinians got in, we have done incredibly well in being able to smash them when they certainly had the ammunition and equipment left to keep fighting for a long time.

So why did they surrender? I think their soldiers had simply decided that they had had enough. Nobody likes being shelled and even well-trained troops find it an ordeal.

Even the Paras freely admit that it's very, very unpleasant being heavily shelled.

The last two nights, the Argentinian positions had been enormously heavily shelled by our guns. They gave them a tremendous pounding and when an Army starts to crumble and collapse it's very, very difficult to stop it.

I think that the Argentinian generals simply had to recognize that their men no longer had the will to carry on the fight.

This story of the fall of Port Stanley begins last night, when men of the Guards and the Gurkhas and the Parachute Regiment launched a major attack supported by an overwhelming British bombardment on the last line of enemy positions on the high ground above the capital.

Three civilians died in British counter-battery fire the night before last, as far as we know the only civilian casualties of the war. Mrs Doreen Burns, Mrs Sue Whitney and 82-year-old Mrs Mary Godwin were all sheltering together in a house hit by a single shell. Altogether only four or five houses in Stanley have been seriously damaged in the battle.

At first light the Paras were preparing to renew their attack in a few hours after seizing all their objectives on Wireless Ridge under fierce shell and mortar fire. Suddenly, word came that enemy troops could be seen fleeing for their lives in all directions around Port Stanley. They had evidently had enough. The decision was taken to press on immediately to complete their collapse.

Spearheaded by a company of the Parachute Regiment commanded by Major Dare Farrar-Hockley, son of the regiment's colonel, British forces began a headlong dash down the rocky hills for the honour of being first into Stanley.

I marched at breakneck speed with Major Farrar-Hockley through the ruins of the former Royal Marine base at Moody Brook, then past the smoking remains of buildings and strongpoints destroyed by our shelling and bombing.

Our route was littered with the debris of the enemy's utter defeat.

We were already past the first houses of the town, indeed up to the War Memorial beside the sea, when the order came through to halt pending negotiations and to fire only in self-defence.

The men, desperately tired after three nights without sleep, exulted like schoolboys in this great moment of victory.

The Parachute Regiment officer with whom I was walking had been delighted with the prospect that his men who had fought so hard all through this campaign were going to be the first British troops into Stanley. But they were heart-broken when, just as we reached the racecourse the order came to halt.

Major Farrar-Hockley ordered off helmets, on red berets. Some men showed their sadness for those who hadn't made it all the way, who had died even during the last night of bitter fighting.

The Regiment moved on to the racecourse and they tore down the Argentinian flag flying from the flagpole. Afterwards they posed for a group photograph . . . exhausted, unshaven but exhilarated at being alive and having survived a very, very bitter struggle.

After half an hour with the civilians I began to walk back to the British lines. Scores of enemy were still moving through the town, many assisting badly wounded comrades, all looking at the end of their tether.

Damaged enemy helicopters were parked everywhere among the houses and on the racecourse. Argentine officers still looked clean and soldierly, but they made no pretence of having any interest in continuing the struggle.

Each one spoke only of "four o'clock", the magic moment at which General Moore was scheduled to meet General Menendez and the war presumably come to a halt.

Back in the British lines, Union Jacks had been hoisted and Brigadier Julian Thompson and many of his senior officers had hastened to the scene to be on hand for the entry into the capital.

Men asked eagerly about the centre of Stanley as if it was on the other side of the moon.

By tomorrow, I imagine, when everyone has seen what little there is of this little provincial town to be seen, we shall all be asking ourselves why so many brave men had to die because a whimsical dictator, in a land of which we knew so little, determined that his nation had at all costs to possess it.

"WE HAVE ONLY TO BE LUCKY ONCE": THE BRIGHTON BOMBING, 12 OCTOBER 1984

Provisional IRA

The official communique of the IRA on the occasion of the bombing of the Grand Hotel, Brighton, site of the 1984 Conservative Party Conference.

The IRA claim responsibility for the detonation of 100 pounds of gelignite in Brighton, against the British cabinet and the Tory warmongers. Thatcher will now realise that Britain cannot occupy our country, torture our prisoners and shoot our people on their own streets and get away with it.

Today we were unlucky, but remember, we have only to be lucky once. You will have to be lucky always. Give Ireland peace and there will be no war.

RAMPAGE, HUNGERFORD, 19 AUGUST 1987

David Rose

In a grove of trees headed by an ancient standing stone, near the cricket pitch used by the school in Hungerford where gunman Michael Ryan holed up, a body last night lay covered by a blanket and guarded by a single policeman in the gathering dusk.

Nearby, on the corner of Priory Avenue and Hillside Road on the 1930s residential estate where mayhem had broken loose, a red Datsun, its lights still on and its windscreen smashed, stood parked. Inside was another body, its stained shroud failing to conceal the human form within. That victim, according to one of the local residents standing in bewildered groups along the street, was the father of the estate's beat policeman. He had come to visit his son.

Further back along Priory Avenue, the neat privet hedge by Alan Lepetit's coal yard presented a gaping, earthy gash where a Ford Transit van had ploughed into it after its driver had been shot through the neck.

Next door, Mr Roy Fox stood by his mini-market, where Mr Lepetit had run across the road, bleeding copiously from a shoulder wound, after seeing the gunman casually approach his children waving his weapons as if they were toys. The doorway of the shop was still spattered with blood, and inside Mr Fox showed the dark stain where his friend had lain in a pool of blood for half an hour until an ambulance arrived. "I thought he was going to go, he's lost so much blood," Mr Fox said.

Earlier, at about 4pm. Chief Inspector Laurie Fray told reporters: "Every time officers from the police or the ambulance have approached the area where the incidents have taken place they've been shot at. There are people lying there and we just can't get to them."

It was not until 7pm that fire engines were at last able to move into Southview. By that time Ryan's house and three adjoining dwellings were gutted. All afternoon, smoke from the blaze had hung over the estate – eerily silent, with the only traffic armoured police vehicles – in a thick pall. Late in the day, the panic of lunchtime still sometimes broke through. "I've been at work since 6am and I'm bloody well not going to let you stop me getting home," a teenage girl shouted at a policeman who blocked her way.

Elsewhere on the estate there was a stunned calm. Residents leaned anxiously from their windows, asking whether it was safe to go out now. Others worried about elderly neighbours left alone. Telephone lines had been cut off by police, but the news about the dead and wounded spread across the estate. People compared notes across hedges and garden gates, conferring in shocked tones about those from their community – the taxi driver they had all known, and Mr Khan, the elderly Pakistani whom everyone knew – who had died in the shootings. Many residents had been unable to get back home from work, and there were relieved and tearful scenes as the cordon relaxed a little after 7pm and those who were simply delayed returned to their families.

THE GULF WAR: THE BOMBING OF BAGHDAD, 17 JANUARY 1991

John Simpson

John Simpson, Foreign Affairs Editor of the BBC was in the Iraqi capital when Operation Desert Storm, the Allied operation against Saddam Hussein and his occupation of Kuwait, began.

It had taken us much too long to get our gear together. I was angry with myself as we ran across the marble floor of the hotel lobby, scattering the security men and Ministry of Information minders.

A voice wailed after us in the darkness: "But where are you going?" "There's a driver here somewhere," said Anthony Wood, the freelance cameraman we had just hired. When I saw which driver it was, I swore. He was the most cowardly of them all. The calmer, more rational voice of Eamonn Matthews, our producer, cut in: "We'll have to use him. There's no one else." It was true. The other drivers knew there was going to be an attack, and had vanished.

We had no idea where we wanted to go. There was no high ground, to give us a good shot of the city. We argued as the car screeched out of the hotel gate and down into the underpass. "No bridges," I said. "He's heading for 14 July Bridge. If they bomb that we'll never get back."

The driver swerved alarmingly, tyres squealing. At that moment, all round us, the anti-aircraft guns started up. Brilliant red and white tracers arched into the sky, then died and fell away. There was the ugly rumble of bombs. I looked at my watch: 2.37

a.m. The bombing of Baghdad had begun twenty-three minutes earlier than we had been told to expect. For us, those minutes would have made all the difference.

The sweat shone on the driver's face in the light of the flashes. "Where's he going now?" He did a wild U-turn, just as the sirens started their belated wailing. Anthony wrestled with the unaccustomed camera. "I'm getting this," he grunted. The lens was pointing at a ludicrous angle into the sky as another immense burst of fireworks went off beside us. It was hard not to flinch at the noise.

"The bloody idiot – he's heading straight back to the hotel." The driver had had enough. He shot in through the gates and stopped. We had failed ignominiously in our effort to escape the control of the authorities and now we were back.

I had become obsessed with getting out of the Al Rasheed Hotel. It smelled of decay, and it lay between five major targets: the presidential palace, the television station, an airfield, several Ministries. I had no desire to be trapped with 300 people in the underground shelters there, and I wanted to get away from the government watchers. Television requires freedom of action, and yet we were trapped again.

In the darkness of the lobby angry hands grabbed us and pushed us downstairs into the shelter. The smell of frightened people in a confined space was already starting to take over. Anthony held the camera over his head to get past the sobbing women who ran against us in the corridor. Children cried. Then the lights went out, and there was more screaming until the emergency power took over. Most of the Western journalists were hanging round the big shelter. I was surprised to see one of the cameramen there: he had a reputation for courage and independence, but now he was just looking at the waves of frightened people with empty red eyes. Anthony, by contrast was neither worried nor elated. He was mostly worried about getting his equipment together.

Not that it *was* his equipment. Anthony had stepped in to help us because our own cameramen had to leave. It had been a difficult evening. As more and more warnings came in from New York, Paris and London, about the likelihood of an attack, almost every news organization with people in Baghdad was instructing them to leave. The personal warnings President Bush had given to American editors suggested that the coming onslaught would be the worst since the Second World War.

I remembered my grandfather's stories of men going mad under the bombardment at the Somme and Passchendaele. This would be the first high-tech war in history and most newspapers and television companies were reluctant to expose their employees to it. The BBC, too, had ordered us out. Some wanted to; others didn't. In the end it came to a four-three split: Bob Simpson, the radio correspondent and a good friend of mine for years, decided to stay; so did Eamonn Matthews. I was the third. In our cases the BBC, that most civilized of British institutions, came up with a sensible formula: it was instructing us to leave, but promised to take no action against us if we refused.

We still needed a cameraman. But by now there were several people whose colleagues had decided to move out, but who were determined to stay themselves. We found two who were prepared to work with us: Nick Della Casa and Anthony Wood.

There seemed to be no getting out of the shelter. Guards, some of them armed with Kalashnikovs, stood at each of the exits from the basement. They had orders to stop anyone leaving. The main shelter was now almost too full to sit or lie down. Some people seemed cheerful enough, and clapped and sang or watched Iraqi television. Children were crying, and guests and hotel staff were still arriving all the time from the upper floors.

In the general panic, the normal patterns of behaviour were forgotten. A woman in her thirties arrived in a coat and bath towel, and slowly undressed and put on more clothes in front of everyone. Nobody paid her the slightest attention. The heavy metal doors with their rubber linings and the wheel for opening and closing them, as in a submarine, stayed open.

Even so, I felt pretty bad. From time to time it seemed to me that the structure of the hotel swayed a little as if bombs were landing around us. Perhaps it was my imagination. To be stuck here, unable to film anything except a group of anxious people, was the worst thing I could imagine. Anthony and I got through the submarine door and tried to work our way up the staircase that led to the outside world. A guard tried to stop us, but I waited till the next latecomer arrived and forced my way through. Anthony followed.

The upper floors were in darkness. We laboured along the corridor, trying to work out by feel which was our office. Listening at one door, I heard the murmur of voices and we were let in. The sky was lit up by red, yellow and white flashes, and there was no need for us to light torches or candles. Every explosion had us cowering and ducking. I wandered round a little and asked a friendly cameraman to film what's called in the trade "a piece to camera" for me.

Despite the crash and the whine of bombs and artillery outside we whispered to each other. By now, though, I was acclimatizing to the conditions, and sorted out the words in my head before I started. You are not popular with cameramen if you need too many takes under such circumstances.

Back in the corridor there was a flash from a torch, and an Iraqi called out my name. A security man had followed me up from the shelter. In order to protect the others I walked down towards him in the yellow torchlight. I had no idea what I was going to do, but I saw a partly open door to my left and slipped inside. I was lucky. The vivid flashes through the window showed I was in a suite of rooms which someone was using as an office.

I worked my way past the furniture and locked myself in the bedroom at the end. Lying on the floor, I could see the handle turning slowly in the light from the battle outside. When the security man found the door was locked he started banging on it and calling out my name, but these doors were built to withstand rocket attacks; a mere security man had no chance.

Close by, a 2,000-pound penetration bomb landed, but contrary to the gossip in the hotel neither my eyeballs nor the fillings in my teeth came out. I switched on the radio I found by the bed and listened to President Bush explaining what was going on. It was 5.45, and I was soon asleep.

At nine o'clock there was more banging on the door, and more calling of my name. It was Eamonn, who had tracked me down to tell me he had got our satellite telephone to work. Smuggling the equipment through the airport two weeks before had been a smart piece of work, and in a city without power and without communications we now had both a generator and the means to broadcast to the outside world.

Eamonn moved the delicate white parasol of the dish around until it locked on to the satellite. It was hard to think that something so complex could be achieved so easily. We dialled up the BBC and spoke to the pleasant, cool voice of the traffic manager. It was just as if we were somewhere sensible, and not sheltering against a brick wall from the air raids. I gave a brief account to the interviewer at the other end about the damage that the raids had caused in the night: the telecommunications tower damaged, power stations destroyed. I had less idea what was happening on the streets. Directly the broadcast was over, I headed out with Anthony for a drive around. "Not good take picture now, Mr John," said the driver. He was an elderly crook but I had an affection for him all the same. "Got to work, I'm afraid, Ali." He groaned.

It was extraordinary: the city was in the process of being deprived of power and communications, and yet the only sign of damage I could see was a broken window at the Ministry of Trade. The streets were almost empty, except for soldiers trying to hitch a lift. "Going Kuwait, Basra," said Ali. Some were slightly wounded, and their faces seemed completely empty.

Iraqis are normally animated and sociable, but there was no talking now, even in the bigger groups. A woman dragged her child along by its arm. A few old men squatted with a pile of oranges or a few boxes of cigarettes in front of them. An occasional food shop or a tea-house was open; that was all.

"Allah." A white car was following us. "He see you take picture." I told Ali to take a sudden right turn, but he lacked the courage. The security policeman waved us down. "Just looking round," I said, as disarmingly as I could. "He say you come with him." "Maybe," said Anthony.

We got back into the car, and followed the white car for a little. The Al Rasheed Hotel was in the distance. "Go there," I said loudly, and Ali for once obeyed. The policeman waved and shouted, but by now the sirens were wailing again and the Ministry of Defence, on the left bank of the river, went up in a column of brown and grey smoke.

Ali put his foot down, and made it to the hotel. The policeman in his white car arrived thirty seconds after us, but obediently searched for a place in the public car park while the three of us ran into the hotel and lost ourselves in the crowd which filled the lobby.

In a windowless side office, where our minders sat for safety, I spotted a face I knew: Jana Schneider, an American war photographer, completely fearless. Throughout the night she had wandered through Baghdad filming the falling missiles. Near the Sheraton she had watched a "smart" bomb take out a Security Ministry building while leaving the houses on either side of it undamaged.

I found it hard to believe, and yet it tied in with my own

observation. This extraordinary precision was something new in warfare. As the day wore on, Baghdad seemed to me to be suffering from an arteriosclerosis – it appeared unchanged, and yet its vital functions were atrophying with each new air raid. It was without water, power and communication.

I was putting together an edited report for our departing colleagues to smuggle out when someone shouted that a cruise missile had just passed the window. Following the line of the main road beside the hotel and travelling from south-west to north-east, it flashed across at 500 miles an hour, making little noise and leaving no exhaust. It was twenty feet long, and was a good hundred yards from our window. It undulated a little as it went, following the contours of the road. It was like the sighting of a UFO.

Another air raid began, and I ran down the darkened corridor to report over our satellite phone. Lacking the navigational sophistication of the cruise missile, I slammed into a heavy mahogany desk where the hotel security staff sometimes stationed themselves. I took the corner in the lower ribs and lay there for a little.

When I reported soon after that I was the only known casualty of the day's attacks among the Al Rasheed's population and explained that I had cracked a couple of ribs, this was taken in London to be a coded message that I had been beaten up.

I was deeply embarrassed. Having long disliked the journalist-as-hero school of reporting, I found myself a mild celebrity for something which emphatically hadn't taken place. An entire country's economic and military power was being dismantled, its people were dying, and I was broadcasting about cracked ribs. Each time they hurt I felt it was a punishment for breaking the basic rule: don't talk about yourself.

In the coffee shop, a neat but exhausted figure was reading from a thick sheaf of papers. Naji Al-Hadithi was a figure of power for the foreign journalists in Baghdad, since he was Director-General of the Information Ministry. Some found him sinister: a *New York Times* reporter took refuge in the US embassy for four nights after talking to him. I thought he was splendid company, a considerable Anglophile, and possessed of an excellent sense of humour. Once I took a colleague of mine to see him, and he asked where we'd been. "We went to Babylon, to see what the whole country will look like in a fortnight's time," I said. For a moment I thought I'd gone much too far, then I saw Al-Hadithi was rocking with silent laughter.

Now he looked close to exhaustion, and his clothes were rumpled. He read out some communiques and a long, scarcely coherent letter from Saddam Hussein to President Bush. Afterwards we talked about the censorship the Ministry planned to impose. In the darkened lobby of the hotel, with the candlelight glinting on glasses and rings and the buttons of jackets, we argued amicably about the new rules. It seemed to me that it was the Security Ministry, not his own, that was insisting on them.

That evening Brent Sadler, the ITN correspondent, rang me. CNN had warned him that our hotel was to be a target that evening. I told the others. No one wanted to go down to the shelter. We decided instead to do what Jana Schneider had done the previous night, and roam the streets.

I cleared out my safety deposit box, and gathered the necessities of my new life: identification in case of arrest, money for bribes, a hairbrush in case I had to appear on television, a notebook and pen. No razor, since without water shaving was impossible. But we were unlucky again. The sirens wailed early, at eight o'clock, and the automatic doors of the hotel were jammed shut. Once again, we were taken down into the shelter.

The whole cast of characters who inhabited our strange new world was there: Sadoun Jenabi, Al-Hadithi's deputy, a large, easy-going man who had spent years in Britain and stayed in the shelter most of the time now; and English peace campaigner, Edward Poore, who was a genuine eccentric, carried a cricket bat everywhere and had knotted a Romanian flag round his neck to remind himself of the time he spent there in the revolution; most of our minders and security men; just about all the journalists; and a large number of the hotel staff and their families, settling down nervously for the night. It was cold. I put a flak-jacket over me for warmth and used my bag as a pillow.

THE BODY OF DIANA, PRINCESS OF WALES, IS FLOWN HOME, RAF NORTHOLT, ENGLAND, 31 AUGUST 1997

Jonathan Freedland, Guardian

The icon of the latter half of the twentieth century, Diana Spencer, ex-wife of the Prince of Wales, was killed in a car crash in Paris, 30 August 1997.

In the end, they let her go quietly. No drum, no funeral note – only a dumb silence as the body of Diana, Princess of Wales, returned to the land she might have ruled as queen.

There was no crowd to meet her, none of the hordes of flagwavers she so delighted in life. Instead the flat, grey tarmac of RAF Northolt, windy as a prairie, a line-up of dignitaries – and a hearse.

She had made the journey from Paris by plane, on an RAF BAe 126. They kept the coffin in the passenger cabin, within sight of her two sisters, Lady Jane Fellowes and Lady Sarah McCorquodale, and her former husband, the Prince of Wales.

The skies themselves seemed to make way for her arrival, the clouds parting like an honour guard. Once the plane had landed, it nudged toward the welcoming party hesitantly, as if weighted down by its tragic cargo. Waiting there was the kind of receiving line Diana met every day. In the middle, arms by his sides, fists clenched tight, the Prime Minister. A cleric stood close by, bright in scarlet cassock. None of them said a word.

Eventually the plane door opened, and the Prince appeared head down, hands clasped behind his back. He was guided by the Lord Chamberlain, the Earl of Airlie. In another context it might have been a standard royal visit: Charles shown round a new factory or hospital wing. But he had come on a more baleful duty. He took his place in line – as he has done so often.

By now, the team of coffin bearers, each one in the crisp uniform of the Queen's Colour Squadron, had completed its precise march toward the other side of the aircraft. At the stroke of seven o'clock, the hatch opened revealing a glimpse of colour, the Royal Standard clinging to the hard, square outline of the coffin. It seemed an unforgiving shape: just a box, with none of the curve or sparkle of the woman whose body lay within.

The silence of the air was cut, and not just by the sound of distant traffic – which rumbled on, as if to prove that the clocks never stop, even for the death of a princess.

The air was filled with the *chickageev, chickageev* of the thousand camera lenses pointed at the scene ahead. Even now the world's telephoto eye was still staring at her, more focused than ever. Despite everything, everyone still wanted a piece of Diana. The cameras kept up their din, but there was an eerie silence from the men who held them. Once they would cry out, "Diana! Diana!" – urging her to look their way or to flash just one more of those million-dollar smiles. But there was no shouting yesterday. And no smiles either.

The bearers of the body inched their way to the hearse. They stood, swivelled on their heels, and clasping tight with their white gloved hands, lowered the coffin as smoothly as a hydraulic pump. They were about to turn away, but a bit of the flag was still spilling out; it had to be tucked in, just like the train of one of Diana's more lavish ball gowns.

The sisters stepped forward, each one turning to curtsy for the man whom Diana had once loved. Charles kissed each one before they stepped into the royal Daimler. The next car was filled with bouquets.

The Prince himself did his duty, talking to each one of the VIPs who had stood beside him. Tony Blair clasped both royal hands in a double handshake, nodding intently. Charles made a gesture with upturned palms, as if to say What Can I Do? He thanked the RAF guard and disappeared back inside the plane, heading for Balmoral and his newly bereaved young sons. "He's going back to the boys," said his spokesman.

And then, on the final day of August, the sky darkened, and the wind whipped harder. It felt like the last day of summer, and the beginning of a long winter.

766.609 MPH: BRITISH JET-CAR SETS LAND SPEED RECORD, BLACK ROCK DESERT, NEVADA, USA, 15 OCTOBER 1997

Associated Press

Gerlach, Nev. – Trailing a huge plume of dust across the desert, a British jet-powered car blasted through the sound barrier twice yesterday, shattering the world land-speed record.

"It's been a magic morning," said a beaming Richard Noble, the car's owner.

The Thrust SSC took advantage of cool, clear weather for back-to-back runs that pushed the land-speed record above Mach 1, the speed of sound.

The car, with Royal Air Force pilot Andy Green at the controls, went 759.333 mph on its first run and 766.609 mph on the second. Under a formula used by the United States Automobile Club, which times the records, the record was set at 763.035.

The speed of sound, which varies according to weather and altitude, was calculated yesterday at 748.111 mph. The average of the two runs was provisionally set at Mach 1.02.

The new mark broke the old record, set by Green just three weeks ago, by nearly 49 mph.

The two runs had to be made within an hour of each other for the record to be official. Green made his second dash with about five minutes to spare.

When he throttled up for the return trip, dust from his first run still hung over the desert on the crisp, sparkling morning.

The sleek, black car broke the sound barrier twice on Monday but missed the record books because a problem with a drag parachute delayed the team and it took 61 minutes to start the second run.

Five-time land-speed record holder Craig Breedlove, an American who had hoped to be the first to break the sound barrier on land, watched yesterday's sprints.

"It was a beautiful run," he said. "You could see the shock waves."

TOTAL ECLIPSE, ENGLAND, 11 AUGUST 1999

Nicci Gerrard, Observer

The last total solar eclipse of the second millennium was watched by an estimated two billion people as it made its three-hour journey along a 75-mile-wide band from east of Cape Cod, USA, to the Indian Ocean.

Milton called it the disastrous twilight. For two minutes last Wednesday, when the moon blotted out the last glowing rind of the sun, it was possible to imagine a sunless, dying world: cold rocks and a stony wind and no birds singing.

For a while, it looked as though the eclipse was going to be diminished into a very English event: organized so badly that no-one would turn up; hyped . . . until it lost its power to enchant and terrify us; built up as an unsuitable risk until some experts were telling us not to look at it at all, not even through a welder's mask, a Marmite jar, not even when it was obscured by thick clouds. Turn your back and look at it on television, government officials said – as if all reality can now be transferred to the screen, and relived through endless replays. As if the moon and the sun were just two more stars that would turn up for the cameras. Experiencing "totality" even sounds like American movie jargon for stunning sexual satisfaction, or some chemically induced high. Yet the Babylonians predicted the exact time.

Driving into Cornwall just before the eclipse was a pretty wretched experience – past the vast car parks empty of cars, the huge camping sites piled high with crates of bottled water but empty of tents, the hopeful signs to rock concerts that had to be cancelled at the last minute due to lack of interest. Cornwall was never going to be the prime place for the eclipse; it only ever had a 45 per cent chance of a clear sky. That statistic dwindled: by Monday it was 25 per cent; by Tuesday evening it was 10 per cent. By Wednesday morning it was just a pitiful 5 per cent – but by then you just needed to step outside and look up at the banked dark clouds to know that the show in the skies was going to be largely invisible. On TV, reporters in cagoules, with cold noses and strained smiles, stared into the drizzle. Patrick Moore said that a cloudy eclipse was like going to the opera and standing in the foyer.

I read in an eclipse guide that if you imagine a football pitch, then the sun, placed on one goal line, is a three-foot beach ball, and the earth, on the opposite goal line, is a golf ball. The moon, one foot away from the earth, is a peppercorn.

We sat in the garden, heads tipped back, as the peppercorn moon nibbled away at the sun. Through breaks in the cloud we could see the sun disappearing. When it was about 95 per cent gone – just a gleaming crescent sailing through the clearing skies, looking just like the invisible moon – the light became drab; the wind cooled.

Count down. A flock of birds flew over our heads, home to roost. In the garden next to us a baffled cockerel crowed twice.

Ninety-eight per cent. An eerie twilight. Suddenly, it was very cold, very still in the garden. No one spoke. Bats flickered round the garden on silent wings. A child whimpered; an adult swore under their breath. Then all the lights went out. I don't believe in God, but it was as if His stern hand had been laid over the rim of the world. And in absolute silence, startled and cold and aghast, we sat and waited. One hundred per cent. For a few seconds, day turned into night, and night was like the end of the world. We all sat pressed back in our chairs, holding hands. It really was like the end. Like death blowing over us in the darkness.

The sun returned, new dawn flooding back from all sides at

once. The wind changed direction, softened. The bats disappeared, like ash settling on the ground. The birds flew back. We heard them sing in the green trees. The ghastly chill lifted and it was warm in the garden again. Champagne and laughter and golden light, and did you feel like that too? What was it like for you? Did you feel vertiginously small and frail and random, staring up at the sun that had gone? Was it as strange, as unnerving, as beautiful and scary and sad? Were you also dazzled by the dark?

SOURCES AND ACKNOWLEDGMENTS

The editor has made every effort to locate all persons having any rights in the selections appearing in this anthology and to secure permission from the holders of these rights. Any queries regarding the use of material should be addressed to the editor c/o the publishers.

Part One: Ancient & Dark Age Britain, 55BC–AD,

Alfred the Great, "The Dooms of Alfred" quoted in *English Historical Documents*, Vol I, ed Dorothy Whitelocke, 1968

Anglo-Saxon Chronicle, "The Vikings Raid Britain", "The Vikings Martyr Archbishop Aelfheah" from *The Anglo-Saxon Chronicle*, trans GN Garmonsway, 1953. Copyright © JM Dent 1994

Anon, "Graffiti", from *The Romans in Britain*, AR Burn, 1932 and *The Archaeology of Roman Britain*, RG Collingwood, 1930

Anon, "Charm for Stomach-ache", from *Anglo-Saxon Magic*, G. Storms, 1948

Asser, "Alfred Saves England", "The First Candle Clock", from *De Rebus Gestis AElfredi Magni*, trans JA Giles, 1848

Bede, "The Conversion of King Edwin" from *Historia Ecclestiastica Gentis Anglorum*, trans JA Giles, 1847

Ceasar, Julius, "Julius Caesar Invades Britain", "A Chariot Fight", "The Britons", from *Commentaries on the Gallic War*, trans W. McDevitte and W. Bohn, 1872

Gildas, "The Ruin of Britain" from *The Works of Gildas*, trans JA Giles in *Six Old English Chronicles*, 1885

Gregory I, "Instructions on Converting the Pagans" *from English Historical Documents*, Vol I, ed Dorothy Whitelocke, 1968

Henry of Huntingdon, "Canute and the Waves", quoted in *They Saw It Happen 55BC–AD 1485*, ed WO Hassall, 1957

Stephanus, Eddius, "Synod of Whitby", from *The Life of Bishop Wilfrid by Eddius Stephanus*, trans B Colgrave, 1927

Tacitus, Cornelius, "The Romans Massacre the Druids" "Boudicca Revolts", from *Annals, XIV*, trans Arthur Murphy, 1794

William of Malmesbury, "Devils Take the Witch of Berkeley's Soul", from *Chronicle of the Kings of England*, trans JA Giles, 1847

Part Two: The Middle Ages, 1066–1485

Adam of Usk, "The Capture and Imprisonment of Richard II", from *Chronicles of the Revolution 1397–1400*, trans and ed Chris Given-Wilson, 1993

Anglo-Saxon Chonicle, "The Sack of Peterborough", *The Anglo-Saxon Chronicle*, trans JA Giles, 1881

Anglo-Saxon Chronicle, "A Reckoning of William the Conqueror", "The Anarchy of the Barons" from *The Anglo-Saxon Chronicle*, trans GN Garmonsway, 1953. Copyright © JM Dent 1994

Anon, "The Coronation of Richard I", from *Itinery of Richard I* in *Chronicles of the Crusades*, 1865

Anon, "Recipes", quoted in *English Historical Documents*, Vol IV, ed AR Myers, 1970

Anon, "A Baker's Tricks", from *Memorials of London*, ed HT Riley, 1868

Anon, "The Domesday Inquisition", quoted in *English Historical Documents*, Vol IV, ed AR Myers, 1970

Anon, "The Coronation Feast of Henry VI", from *English Historical Documents*, Vol IV, ed AR Myers, 1970

Anon, "The Assessment of the Canons of Herefordshire", from *The Domesday Book: Herefordshire*, 1983

Barton, Friar, "The Battle of Bannockburn", quoted in *They Saw It Happen 55BC–AD 1485*, ed WO Hassall, 1957

Beha-ed-Din, "The Third Crusade: Richard I Massacres Mussulman Prisoners", quoted in *The Faber Book of Reportage*, ed John Carey, 1987

Bishop of London, "Excommunication of Boys for Playing ball in St Paul's Cathedral", quoted in *Chaucer's World*, comp. Edith Rickert, 1948

Brews, Margery, "A Valentine", from *Illustrated Letters of the Paston Family*, ed Roger Virgoe, 1989

Calendar of the Coroner's Rolls, quoted in *Chaucer's World*, comp. Edith Rickert, 1948

Calendar of Inquisitions, "Violent Deaths", quoted in *English Historical Documents*, Vol IV, ed AR Myers, 1970

Chastellain, George, "Margaret D'Anjou Flees the Yorkists", quoted in *The Wars of York and Lancaster*, trans Edith Thompson, 1892

Customal of the Manor of Islip, "The Duties of a Villein", from *How They Lived*, Vol I, ed WO Hassall, 1969

Fitz-Stephen, William, "A Picture of London", quoted in *Survey of London*, ed Henry Morley, 1890

Froissart, Sir John, "The Battle of Crecy", "The Peasants Revolt" from *Chronicles of England, France & Spain*, trans Lord Berners, 1523–5

Grim, Edward, "The Murder of Becket", from *St Thomas by Contemporary Biographers*, ed D. Nutt, 1889

Gerald of Wales, " 'The Character & Customs of the Welsh", from *Gerald the Welshman, Descriptions of Wales*, trans RC Hoare, 1806

Gerald of Wales, "Beaver on the River Teifi", from *The Journey Through Wales*, trans Lewis Thorpe, 1978

Hentzner, Paul, "A Traveller's View of the Bear-Garden", from *Journey into England*, Paul Hentzner, 1598

Joan of Arc, "The Hundred Years War", quoted in *The Medieval Source Book* website Jocelin of Brakelond, "A Boxing Day Affray" from *Chronicle f the Abbey of Bury St Edmunds*, trans and ed Diana Greenway & Jane Sayers, 1989

John of Arderne, "The Surgeon's Code", from *Treatise of Fistula in Ano*, ed D'Arcy Power, 1910

John of Salisbury, "The Duty of a Knight", quoted in *The Portable Medieval Reader*, ed JB Ross and MM Mclaughlin, 1981

Knighton, Henry, "The Black Death", from *Chronici Henry Knighton*, ed JR Lumby, 1900

Langland, William, "The Peasant's Life", quoted in *The Portable Medieval Reader*, ed JB Ross and MM Mclaughlin, 1981

London. Bishop of, "Excommunication of Boys", from *English Historical Documents*, Vol IV, ed AR Myers, 1970

Matthew of Westminster, "The Execution of William Wallace", quoted in *They Saw It Happen 55BC–AD 1485*, ed WO Hassall, 1957

Paris, Matthew, "The Weather, 1236", from *Matthew Paris's English History*, trans JA Giles, 1852–4

Paris, Matthew, "Castration of a Knight", from *The Illustrated Chronicles of Matthew Paris*, trans & ed Richard Vaughan, 1993

Peter of Blois, "A Portrait of Henry II", from *Epistolae*, ed JA Giles, trans AB Hawes, 1847

Polydore Vergil, "The Battle of Bosworth", from *English History*, Camden Society, 1844

Roger of Hovedon, "Laws of Richard I Concerning Crusaders Who Were to Go By Sea", from *Select Historical Documents of the Middle Ages*, ed Ernest F Henderson, 1896

Robert of Avesbury, "Flagellants", from *British Latin Selections AD500–1400*, ed RA Browne, 1954

Roger of Wendover, "Londoners Riot Against the Talliage Tax", from *Flowers of History*, Mathew Paris's addition, trans JA Giles, 1849

Roger of Wendover, "The Winning of the Magna Carta" from *Chronica Majora*, trans JA Giles, 1849

Russell, John, "How to Prepare the Master's Bath", quoted in *The Babee's Book*, Edith Rickert, 1908

Simeon of Durham, "Famine in England", from *The Church Historians of England*, Vol 3, trans Rev. J. Stevenson, 1855

Tetzel, Gabriel, "A German at the Court of Edward IV", quoted in *English Historical Documents*, Vol IV, ed AR Myers, 1970

Vergil, Poydore, "Richard III Murders the Princes in the Tower", from *Three Books of Polydore Vergil's English History*, ed H Ellis, 1844

Vergil, Poydore, "The Battle of Bosworth", ibid

Wavrin, Jehan de, "The English Longbow Wins the Battle of Agincourt", from *Collection of Chronicles*, Jehan de Wavrin, trans William Hardy and ELCP Hardy, 1864–91

William of Malmesbury, "The Death of William Rufus", "The Cistercians' from *Chronicle of the Kings of England*, trans JA Giles, 1847

William of Newburgh, "Heretics Beaten", from *History of England* in *English Historical Documents* 1042–1189, ed DC Douglas & GW Greenaway, 1953

William of Newburgh, "The Green Children", from *Church Historians of England*, ed J. Stevenson, 1856

Part Three: The Tudors & The Stuarts, 1486–1687

Anon, "The Restoration: Charles II Returns to England", from *England's Joy*, Anon, 1660

Anon, "The Burning of Archbishop Cranmer", from *Memorials of Archbishop Cranmer*, 1854

Anon, "The Arrest of the Catholic Priest Edmund Campion", from *English Garner*, 1877

Anon, "Unconsummated Child Marriage", quoted in *The Penguin Book of Childhood*, ed Michael Rosen, 1994

Anon, "The Glorious Revolution: William of Orange Invades England", quoted in *They Saw It Happen 1485–1688*, ed CRN Routh, 1956

Aubrey, John, "Bess Broughton Sets Up For Herself", from *Brief Lives*, John Aubrey, ed John Buchanan-Brown, 2000

Carey, Sir Robert, "The Death of Queen Elizabeth", from *English Historical Documents* Vol VI, ed Douglas Price, 1959

Carleton, Sir Dudley, "The Murder of the Duke of Buckingham", quoted in *Original Letters Illustrative of English History*, ed H Ellis 1824–46

Cavendish, George, "The Magnificence of Cardinal Wolsey", quoted in *They Saw It Happen 1485–1688*, ed CRN Routh, 1956

"CH", "The English Civil War: Edgehill", quoted in *Original Letters Illustrative of English History*, 1824–46

Cranmer, Archbishop Thomas, "The Coronation of Anne Boleyn", from *Original Letters Illustrative of English History*, ed H Ellis 1824–46

Cromwell, Oliver, "The English Civil War: The Death of a Nephew at

Marston Moor", from *Cromwell's Letters and Speeches*, ed Thomas Carlye, 1845

Crotchett, Robert, "The English Civil War: The Execution of Charles I", from *Derbyshire in the Civil War*, Brian Stone, 1992

De Cuellar, Francisco, "The Armada: The San Pedro Flounders", quoted in *Millennium Eyewitness*, ed Brian Stone, 1997

De Soncino, Raimondo, "The Pretense of Perkin Warbeck" quoted in *They Saw It Happen 1485–1688*, ed CRN Routh, 1956

Elder, John, "The Marriage of Mary and Philip II of Spain", from *The Copie of a letter sent in to Scotland*, 1555

Elizabeth I, "Elizabeth I Rejects a Suitor", quoted in *The Word of a Prince: A Life of Elizabeth I*, Maria Perry, 1990

Ellis, John, and Charles II, "Lost: The King's Dog", quoted in *Source Book of English History*, ed EK Kendall, 1908

Evelyn, John, "The Glorious Revolution: James II Falls", "A Journal of the Plague year", quoted in *English Diaries of XVI, XVII and XVIII Centuries*, ed James Aitken, 1945

Evelyn, John, "Whale", quoted in *The Macmillan Anthology of English Prose*, ed Edward Leeson, 1994

Fawkes, Guy, "The Gunpowder Plot", quoted in *They Saw It Happen 1485–1688*, ed CRN Routh, 1956

Foxe, John, "The Martyrdom of Dr Rowland Taylor", from *Foxe's Book of Martyrs*, ed Rev T Pratt, 1858

Gerard, John, "The Torturing of a Jesuit Priest", from *The Autobiography of an Elizabethan*, John Gerard, trans Philip Caraman, 1951

Giustinian, Sebastian, "Henry VIII", quoted in *Source-Book of English History*, ed EK Kendall, 1908

Hentzer, Paul, "A Traveller's View of the Bear-Garden", quoted in *Life in Shakespeare's England*, ed John Dover Wilson, 1911

Heriot, Thomas, "The Virtues of Tobacco", quoted in *Voyages*, R. Hakluyt, 1589

Henry VIII, "Mine Own Sweetheart", from *Intimate Letters of England's Kings*, 1959

Highfield, John, "The Fall of Calais", quoted in *They Saw It Happen* 1485–1688, ed CRN Routh, 1956

Howard, Edmund, "Incontinent with Piss", from *The Lisle Letters*, ed Muriel St Clare Byrne, 1985

Howard, Lord, "The Spanish Armada: The English Engage", from *State Papers relating to the Defeat of the Spanish Armada*, ed JK Laughton, 1894

Hurault, Andre, "An Audience with Queen Elizabeth I", *Journal of an Embassy from Henry IV to Queen Elizabeth*, 1597, trans GB Harrison and RA Jones, 1931

London, John, et al, "The Reformation in England: A Visitation to the Monasteries of Buckinghamshire, Kent and Suffolk", from *Letters to Cromwell*, ed GH Cook, 1965

London, Lord Mayor of, "A Petition", quoted in *Life in Shakespeare's England*, ed John Dover Wilson, 1911

Markham, Gervase, "Treatment for the Plague", from *The English Hus-Wife*, Gervase Markham, 1615

Mildmay, Lady, "Housekeeping List for Christmas Week, "1594", from "An Elizabethan Gentlewoman: The Journal of (Grace) Lady Mildmay", *Quarterly Review*, vol 215, 1911

Moryson, Fynes, "The Land and People of England", from *Itinerary*, Fynes Moryson, 1617

Newton, Sir Isaac, "Sir Isaac Newton Experiments on Light", quoted in *The Ascent of Man*, J Bronowski, 1973

Pepys, Samuel, "The Great Fire of London", from *Diary*, Samuel Pepys, ed Robert Latham and William Matthews, 1970–83

Phillips, Miles, "A Prisoner of the Inquisition", quoted in *Voyages*, R. Hakluyt, 1589

Raleigh, Sir Walter, "Raleigh Sacks Cadiz", quoted in *The Life of Sir Walter Raleigh*, Edward Edwards, 1868

Rushworth, John, "The Attempted Arrest of the Five Members", from *Historical Collections*, John Rushworth, 1691

Ruthven, Lord, "The Murder of Rizzio", quoted in *They Saw It Happen 1485–1688*, ed CRN Routh, 1956

Smith, John, "The Discovery of Virginia", from *The Generall Historie of Virginia*, John Smith, 1624

Stubbes, Philip, "A Bloody and Murdering Practice", quoted in *Life in Shakespeare's England*, ed John Dover Wilson, 1911

Stukely, Doctor, "The Prodigious Boyhood of Sir Isaac Newton", from *Collections for the History of the Town . . . of Grantham*, ed Edmund Turnor, 1806

Teonge, Henry, "A Naval Cuckold Spared", quoted in *English Diaries of XVI, XVII and XVIII Centuries*, ed James Aitken, 1945

Tomson, Richard, "The Armada: Attack on a Spanish Galleas", from *State Papers relating to the Defeat of the Spanish Armada*, ed JK Laughton, 1894

Warwick, Sir Philip, "A Portrait of Oliver Cromwell", quoted in *They Saw It Happen 1485–1688*, ed CRN Routh, 1956

Weston, William, "Friar William Weston Dashes for the Priest-Hole", quoted in *Every One a Witness – The Tudor Age*, comp AF Scott, 1975

Weldon, Sir Anthony, "A Sketch of King James", quoted in *James I*, SJ Houston, 1973

Wharton, Nehemiah, "The English Civil War: Nehemiah Wharton Skirmishes . . .", quoted in *Echoes of War*, ed Robert Giddings, 1992

Willis, E, "A Cockfight", quoted in *Life in Shakespeare's England*, ed John Dover Wilson, 1911

Wynkfielde, Robert, "The Execution of Mary, Queen of Scots", from *Original Letters Illustrative of English History*, ed H Ellis, 1827

Part Four: The Age of Empire, 1689–1899

Anon, "The Massacre of Glencoe", from *A Letter from a Gentleman in Scotland to his friend at London, who desir'd a particular Account of the Bussiness at Glenco*, 1885

Anon, "Drawing the Boundaries: The Laws of Cricket", quoted in *The Sunday Times: Pages from History*, 2000

Anon, "Women Convicts", quoted in *English Historical Documents*, XI, ed A. Aspinall & E. Anthony Smith, 1969

Bamford, Samuel, "Peterloo", from *Passages in the Life of a Radical*, 1840–5

Barter, Richard, "Indian Mutiny: Cawnpore After the Massacre", from *The Siege of Delhi – Mutiny Memories of an Old Officer*, Richard Barter, 1869

Beatty, Dr William, "Trafalgar: The Death of Nelson", from *Despatches and Letters of Nelson*, 1845

Beaver, Lt Philip, "Naval Mutiny at Spithead", from *Letters of the English Seamen*, ed EH Moorhouse, 1910

Berry, Captain Sir Edward, "The French Revolutionary War: The Battle of the Nile", quoted in *They Saw It Happen*, ed T. Charles-Edwards & B. Richardson, 1958

Blackburn Times, "The 1882 Cup Final", quoted in *They Saw It Happen*, ed T. Charles-Edwards & B. Richardson, 1958

Boswell, James, "A Rake's Progress", from *Boswell's London Journal 1762–63*, ed Frederick A Pottle, 1951

Bronte, Charlotte, "The Great Exhibition", from *The Brontes' Life and Letters*, ed Clement Shorter, 1907

Burney, Fanny, "A Meeting with Mad King George", from *English Diaries of XVI, XVII and XVIII Centuries*, ed James Aitken, 1945

Byrom, Elizabeth, "Bonnie Prince Charlie Invades Manchester", from *English Diaries of XVI, XVII and XVIII Centuries*, ed James Aitken, 1945

Cartwright, Edmund, "Invention of the Power Loom", quoted in *History of the Cotton Manufacture of Great Britain*, E. Baines, 1835

Clarke, William, "A Day at the Seaside", quoted in *The Albatross Book of English Letters*, 1936

Cooper, J.S., "The War of 1812: A Reluctant Fusilier at New Orleans", from *Rough Notes of Seven Campaigns*, JS Cooper, 1869

Cooper, Thomas, "A Chartist Speaks", quoted in T*he Chatto Book of Dissent*, ed Michael Rosen & David Widgery, 1991

Cullwick, Hannah, "Below Stairs" quoted in *Life and Diaries*, Arthur J Munby, 1972

Darwin, Charles, "Darwin in the Galapagos", from *Journal of Researches into the Natural History and Geology of the Countries visited during the Voyage of HMS Beagle*, Charles Darwin, 1846

Davies, Rowland, "The Battle of the Boyne", from *Journals*, Vol LXVIII, Rowland Davies, 1857

Defoe, Daniel, "The Cloth Market at Leeds", from *Tour through Great Britain*, 1735

De Quincey, Thomas, "London on Saturday Night", from *Confessions of an English Opium Eater*, 1822

De Saussure, C., "Public Executions at Tyburn", from *A Foreign View of England in the Reigns of George I and George II*, 1902

Engels, Friedrich, "The Industrial Revolution: Working Class Manchester", from *The Condition of the Working Class in England*, 1962

Forster, William, "The Irish Potato Famine", quoted in *Source Book of English History*, ed EK Kimball, 1908

Goldsmith, Oliver, "Bath Under the Code of Beau Nash", from *Life of Richard Nash, Esquire*, 1762

Grattan, William, "Storming Badajoz", *Adventures with the Connaught Rangers*, William Grattan, 1902

Harris, Rifleman, "Plundering a Dead French Soldier", from *The Recollections of Rifleman Harris*, ed H. Curling, 1848

Hazlitt, William, "Bull Neate v The Gas-Man", quoted in *The Macmillan Anthology of English Prose*, ed Edward Leeson, 1994

Holland, Vyvyan, "Wilde Romps with His Children" from *Son of Oscar Wilde*, Vyvyan Holland, 1954. Copyright © Vyvyan Holland, 1954

Holwell, JZ, "The Black Hole of Calcutta", from *The Annual Register*, 1758

Hook VC, Henry, "Rorke's Drift" quoted in *Imperial Echoes*, ed Robert Giddings, 1996

Hootton, Ellen, "The Industrial Revolution: Child Labour", quoted in *The Penguin Book of Childhood*, ed Michael Rosen, 1994

Kemble, Fanny, " 'First Excursion on the London–Manchester Railway" from *Record of a Girlhood*, Fanny Kemble, 1878

Kilvert, Francis, "Easter Sunday in the Country", from *Kilvert's Diary 1870–8*, ed William Plomer, 1939

Knox, John, "The Death of General Wolfe", quoted in *They Saw It Happen 1689–1897*, ed T. Charles-Edwards & B. Richardson, 1958

Livingstone, Dr David, "Discovering the Victoria Falls", *Missionary Travels and Researches*, David Livingstone, 1857

Lock, John, "Initiation into the Toll Puddle Union", quoted in *They Saw It Happen 1689–1897*, ed T. Charles-Edwards & B. Richardson, 1958

Lunardi, Vincent, "The First Aerial Voyage in England", from *The First Aerial Voyage in England*, Vincent Lunardi, 1784

Mayhew, Henry, and John Binny, "An Aerial View of London", quoted in *Pandaemonium*, ed Humphrey Jennings, 1985

Nasmyth, James, "The Industrial Revolution: The Black Country", quoted in *Pandaemonium*, ed Humphrey Jennings, 1985

Naval Chronicle, "Fatal Duel", *Naval Chronicle*, Vol XVI, 1806. Cited on the *Maritime History* website

Parker, Midshipman William, "The French Revolutionary War: "The

Glorious First of June", quoted in *The Life of Admiral of the Fleet Sir William Parker*, Augustus Philimore, 1876

Peel, Sir Robert, "The Qualities of a Policeman", quoted in *English Letters of the XIX Century*, ed James Aitken, 1946

Priestley, Joseph, "The Industrial Revolution: A Scientist Against the Mob", quoted in *The Albatross Book of English Letters*, 1936

Russell, William Howard, "The Battle of Balaclava", from *The Times* 14 November 1854

Sala, George Augustus, "Explosion Aboard the SS Great Eastern", *Daily Telegraph*, 12 September 1859

Sam, "Trafalgar: the View From the Lower-Deck", from *Letters of the English Seamen*, ed EH Moorhouse, 1910

The Times, French Revolutionary War: Rules on Eating for the Rich and Poor", *The Times*, 23 July 1795

Stanley, Sir Henry Morton, "Meeting Livingstone", from *New York Herald*, 10 August 1872

Steevens, George Warrington, "Omdurman", from *With Kitchener to Khartum*, 1898

Steevens, George Warrington, "After the Manner of His Race", from *With Kitchener to Khartum*, 1898

Tristan, Flora, "Prostitutes, Pimps and Peers; Scenes from London's Demi-Monde", "Women Prisoners in Newgate" from *The London Journal of Flora Tristan*, trans Jean Hawkes, 1982

Trelawney, Edward, "The Cremation of Shelley", *The Last Days of Shelley & Byron*, Edward Trelawney, 1858

Troubridge, T., "French Revolutionary War: Attack on Tenerife", from *Letters of the English Seamen*, ed EH Moorhouse, 1910

Victoria, "Princess Victoria becomes Queen", from *Letters of Queen Victoria*, ed AC Benson and Viscount Esher, 1908

Victoria, "The Coronation of Queen Victoria", from *Letters of Queen Victoria*, ed AC Benson and Viscount Esher, 1908

Victoria, "The Diamond Jubilee", from *Letters of Queen Victoria*, ed AC Benson and Viscount Esher, 1908

Walpole, Horace, "The Effects of an Earthquake", from *English Diaries of XVI, XVII and XVIII Centuries*, ed James Aitken, 1945

Walpole, Horace, "George II Interred", from *Correspondence*, ed WS Lewis, 1937–83

Wellesley, Arthur, "Wellington Meets Nelson" quoted in *The Correspondence and Diaries: John Wilson Croker*, Vol II, ed Louis J. Jennings, 1884

Wheatley, Edmund, "Waterloo", from *The Wheatley Diary*, ed C. Hibbert, 1961

Wordsworth, Dorothy, "Beggars", quoted in *The Macmillan Anthology of English Prose*, ed Edward Leeson, 1994

Part Five: Modern Times, 1900–2000

Adam Ant, "The Sex Pistols Play Their First Concert", quoted in *England's Dreaming*, John Savage, 1991. Copyright © Jon Savage 1991

Anon, "The Great Man Chase", from *Speak For Yourself*, ed Angus Calder and Dorothy Sheridan, 1984. Copyright © The Tom Harrisson-Mass-Observation-Archive 1984

Anon, "Tutankhamen's Tomb is Opened", from *The Times*, 17 February 1923. Copyright © *The Times* 1923.

Anon, "The SAS Relieve the Siege at Prince's Gate", from *Soldier "I" SAS* by Michael Paul Kennedy, 1989. Copyright © Michael Paul Kennedy 1989

Austin, Captain Richard, "Dunkirk: The View from the Beaches", from *Return Via Dunkirk*, 1940

Beard, John, "The Battle of Britain", from *Their Finest Hour*, Allan Machie and Walter Graebner, 1941. Copyright © Harcourt Inc

Bleriot, Louis, "Bleriot Flies the Channel", from *Scrapbook 1900–1914*, ed Leslie Bailey, 1957

Bride, Harold, "Titanic Sinks", from *The New York Times*, April 1912

Buttlar Brandenfels, Treusch von, "Zeppelin Raid on London; quoted in *Anthology of Armageddon*, ed B Newman and IO Evans, 1989

Chadwick, Roy, "The Jarrow March", from *Manchester Guardian*, 13 October 1936. Copyright © Guardian Media 1936

Churchill, Sir Winston, "Churchill Takes Over", quoted in *The World's Great Speeches*, ed Lewis Copeland et al, 1999

Collins, Sean (interviewed by Tony Parker), Bloody Sunday", quoted in *New Statesman & Society*, 1992

Connolly, James, "The Easter Rising", quoted in *They Saw It Happen 18970–1940*, ed Asa Briggs, 1960

Crozier, Brig-Gen FP, "A Firing Squad at Dawn", from *A Brass Hat in No-Man's Land*, 1930

Denbigh, Countess of, "Victoria's Funeral Procession", quoted in *The Faber Book of Reportage*, ed John Carey, 1987

Dimbleby, Richard, "A Visit to Belsen Death Camp", from *Richard Dimbleby: Broadcaster*, ed Leonard Miall. Copyright © The BBC 1966

Edgar, Donald, "Suez Invasion", from *Express 56*, Donald Edgar, 1957

English, Jeffrey, "The Railway of Death", from *One for Every Sleeper*, Jeffrey English, 1989

Farmer, Janice, "The Great Tide at Jaywick", *Essex Chronicle*, 6 February 1953

Farrar-Hockley, Anthony, "The Korean War: Lieutenant Curtis Wins the Victoria Cross", from *The Edge of the Sword*, A. Farrar-Hockley, 1956. Copyright © A. Farrar-Hockley, 1956

Flower, Desmond, "The Blitz", from *The War 1939–1945*, ed Desmond Flower and James Reeves, 1960. Copyright © Desmond Flower 1960

Freedland, Jonathan, "The Body of Princess Diana is flown home", *The*

Guardian, 1 September 1999. Copyright © *The Guardian* 1999. Reprinted by permission of Guardian Media

Gallagher, OD, "The Sinking of the *Repulse* and *Prince of Wales*", *Daily Express* 11 December 1941. Copyright © Express Newspapers 1941. Reprinted by permission of Express Newspapers

Gaitskell, Hugh, "The General Strike", from "At Oxford in the Twenties", quoted in *Essays in Labour History*, ed A Briggs and J Saville, 1960

George I, "Britain Declares War" quoted in *Voices 1870–1914*, ed Peter Vansittart, 1984

Gibson, Guy, "The Dambusters Raid" from *Enemy Coast Ahead*, Guy Gibson, 1956. Copyright © 1956 the Estate of Guy Gibson

Graves, Robert, "Joining Up" from *Goodbye to All That*, Robert Graves, 1929. Copyright © Rovert Graves 1929, 1957, Reprinted by permission of AP Watt Ltd

Hastings, Max, "The First Man Into Port Stanley", *Evening Standard* 15 June 1982. Reprinted by permission of Atlantic Syndication

Hillary, Edmund, "Conquering Everest" from *High Adventure*, Edmund Hillary, 1955. Copyright © 1955 Edmund Hillary

Hislop, John, "The Grand National", *The Observer*, 30 March 1947

Hodgson, Vere, "The Blitz", *Few Eggs and No Oranges*, 1999

Hughes, GE, "Invasion of Normandy", unpublished diary, Imperial war Museum, London. Kendall, Captain HG, "The Arrest of Dr H Crippen", quoted in *Scrapbook 1900–14*, ed Leslie Bailey. 1957

Kipling, Rudyard, "Skirmish at Kari Siding", from *Something of Myself*, Rudyard Kipling, 1937

Kray, R&R, "The Killing of George Cornell" from *Our Story*, R& R Kray (with Fred Dineage), 1988 Copyright © 1988 Bejubob Ltd

Lawrence, TE, "Entry into Damascus", from *Seven Pillars of Wisdom*, TE Lawrence, 1926. Copyright © 1926, 1935 Doubleday & Co

Lightoller, Commander CH, "Dunkirk: The View from the Boats", quoted in *Dunkirk*, AD Devine, 1945

Lytton, Lady Constance, "Force Feeding a Suffragette", *Prisons and Prisoners*, Constance Lytton, 1914

Macbeth, George, "The Home Front: A Child's View", from *A Child of War*, George Macbeth, 1978

Macleod, Ian, "D-Day", from *Articles of War*, edited by Fiona Glass and Philip Marsden-Smedley, 1989. Copyright © *The Spectator* 1989

Majdalany, Fred, "Cassino", from *The Monastery*, Fred Majdalany, 1945. Copyright © the estate of Fred Majdalany 1945

Marconi, Guglielmo, "The First Radio Signal Across The Atlantic" quoted in *Scrapbook 1900–1914*, ed Leslie Bailey, 1957

Mosley, Sydney, "I Watch Television", *The Private Letters and Diaries of Sydney Mosley*, 1960

Murrow, Edward R, "The Blitz", a CBS broadcast, 13 September 1939. Copyright © CBS Inc 1940

Nicolson, Harold, "The Signing of the Treaty of Versailles" *Peacemaking 1919*, 1933

Orwell, George, "A British Socialist in the Spanish Civil War", from *Homage to Catalonia*, George Orwell, 1938. Copyright © The Estate of Eric Blair 1938, 1953. Reprinted by permission of AM Heath & Company

Panter-Downes, Mollie, "VE Day", *The New Yorker*, May 1945. Copyright © Mollie Panter-Downes 1945

Phillpott, HRS, "The Gresford Colliery Disaster", from *Daily Herald*, 24 September 1934

Piratin, Phil, "The Battle of Cable Street", from *Our Flag Stays Red*, Phil Piratin, 1948. Copyright © Lawrence & Wishart 1948

Prien, Gunther, "The Royal Oak is Torpedoed", from *Hitler and His Admirals*, Anthony Martienssen, 1948

Profumo, John, "The Profumo Affair" from *John Profumo and Christine Keeler, 1963*, Lord Alfred Denning. Copyright © The Stationery Office 1999

Radcliffe, JV, "Tonypandy Riot" from *The Guardian*, November 1910

Richards, Frank, "Christmas in the Trenches 1914", from *Old Soldiers Never Die*, 1933

Rommel, Erwin, "El Alamein" from *The Rommel Papers*, ed BH Liddell-Hart, 1953. Copyright © BH Liddell-Hart, renewed 1981 Lady Liddell-Hart, Fritz Bayerlain-Dittmar and Manfred Rommel

Rose, David, "Rampage", from *The Guardian*, 20 August 1987. Copyright © Guardian Media 1987

Scott, RF, "Antarctic Expedition", from *Scott's Last Expedition*, RF Scott, 1913

Steward, Bert, "The Taking of High Wood", *The Guardian*, September 1990

Willmott, P. and M. Young, "Suburban Life", *Family and Class in a London Suburb*, 1960. Copyright © P. Willmott and M. Young 1960. Reprinted by permission of ITPS Ltd

Wolfe, Tom, "The Beatles Take New York, from *The New York Herald*, February 1964. Copyright © *The New York Herald*.

APPENDIX II:

Prime Ministers of Britain 1721–2001

Sir Robert Walpole	Apr. 1721	Sir Robert Peel	Dec. 1834
Earl of Wilmington	Feb. 1741	Viscount Melbourne	Apr. 1835
Henry Pelham	Aug. 1743	Sir Robert Peel	Aug. 1841
Duke of Newcastle	Mar. 1754	Lord John Russell	June 1846
Duke of Devonshire	Nov. 1756	Earl of Derby	Feb. 1852
Duke of Newcastle	July 1757	Earl of Aberdeen	Dec. 1852
Earl of Bute	May 1762	Viscount Palmerston	Feb. 1855
George Grenville	Apr. 1763	Earl of Derby	Feb. 1858
Marquess of Rockingham	July 1765	Viscount Palmerston	June 1859
Earl of Chatham	July 1766	Earl Russell	Oct. 1865
Duke of Grafton	Oct. 1768	Earl of Derby	June 1866
Lord North	Jan. 1770	Benjamin Disraeli	Feb. 1868
Marquess of Rockingham	Mar. 1782	William Ewart Gladstone	Dec. 1868
Earl of Shelburne	July 1782	Benjamin Disraeli	Feb. 1874
Duke of Portland	Apr. 1783	William Ewart Gladstone	Apr. 1880
William Pitt	Dec. 1783	Marquess of Salisbury	June 1885
Henry Addington	Mar. 1801	William Ewart Gladstone	Feb. 1886
William Pitt	May 1804	Marquess of Salisbury	July 1886
William Wyndham		William Ewart Gladstone	Aug. 1892
Grenville	Feb. 1806	Earl of Rosebery	Mar. 1894
Duke of Portland	Mar. 1807	Marquess of Salisbury	June 1895
Spencer Perceval	Oct. 1809	Arthur James Balfour	July 1902
Earl of Liverpool	June 1812	Sir Henry Campbell-	
George Canning	Apr. 1827	Bannerman	Dec. 1905
Viscount Goderich	Aug. 1827	Herbert Henry Asquith	Apr. 1908
Duke of Wellington	Jan. 1828	David Lloyd George	Dec. 1916
Earl Grey	Nov. 1830	Andrew Bonar Law	Oct. 1922
Viscount Melbourne	July 1834	Stanley Baldwin	May 1923
Duke of Wellington	Nov. 1834	James Ramsay MacDonald	Jan. 1924

Stanley Baldwin	Nov. 1924	Sir Alec Douglas-Home	Oct. 1963
James Ramsay MacDonald	June 1929	Harold Wilson	Oct. 1964
Stanley Baldwin	June 1935	Edward Heath	June 1970
Neville Chamberlain	May 1937	Harold Wilson	Mar. 1974
Winston Churchill	May 1940	James Callaghan	Apr. 1976
Clement Attlee	July 1945	Margaret Thatcher	May 1979
Winston Churchill	Oct. 1951	John Major	Nov. 1990
Sir Anthony Eden	Apr. 1955	Tony Blair	May 1997
Harold Macmillan	Jan. 1957		